SCHOOLCRAFT COLLEGE LIBRARY

S0-AEG-131

SEX AND POWER

ALSO BY DONALD MEYER

The Positive Thinkers
The Protestant Search for Political Realism

Donald Meyer

SEX AND POWER

The Rise of Women in America,
Russia, Sweden, and Italy

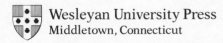

Wesleyan University Press
Middletown, Connecticut

HQ
1426
.m49
1987

Copyright © 1987 by Donald Meyer

All rights reserved.

LIBRARY OF CONGRESS CATALOGING-IN-PUBLICATION DATA
Meyer, Donald B.
  Sex and power.
  Bibliography: p.
  Includes index.
  1. Feminism—United States—History. 2. Feminism—
Soviet Union—History. 3. Feminism—Sweden—History.
4. Feminism—Italy—History. 5. Power (Social sciences)
6. Industrialization. I. Title.
HQ1426.M49 1987   305.4'2   87-6080
ISBN 0-8195-5153-8

All inquiries and permissions requests should be addressed to the
Publisher, Wesleyan University Press, 110 Mt. Vernon Street,
Middletown, Connecticut 06457.

Distributed by Harper & Row Publishers, Keystone Industrial
Park, Scranton, Pennsylvania 18512.

Manufactured in the United States of America

First Edition

This book is dedicated to Jean
tuo sempre sempre sempre

Contents

Preface

At no time have I felt as fully a member of the cosmopolitan fellowship of historians as during the work on this book. It could not have been written without the wealth of recent modern American scholarship on Russian women. I have read as widely into Italian and Swedish scholarship on Italian and Swedish women as seemed helpful. American scholarship on women has been transformed in the last twenty-five years. No debts could have been incurred more gladly. I have indicated at least some of my particular debts in the footnotes.

I owe special thanks to the trustees of the Josiah Meigs Foundation: Meigs grants provided critical support for time to do research. I owe thanks also to the John Simon Guggenheim Foundation and the American Philosophical Society for grants. My thanks are abundant to the librarians at Olin Library, Wesleyan University, and to its Interlibrary Loan Department in particular, as well as to librarians at the University of California, Los Angeles, and at the Vatican Library, the Istituto Gramsci, the Centro Studii Americani, and the Biblioteca di Storia Moderna Contemporanea, all in Rome. Rebecca Berwick and Candy Ruck provided endless clean copy for rewriting.

Jeannette Hopkins at Wesleyan University Press, William Leach of the New York Institute for the Humanities, and the late Warren Susman offered insistent and acute judgments on the manuscript, in both structure and detail. My gratitude to them is deep. This book has roots in the classrooms and corridors of UCLA: I am fortunate to have known Kenneth Pratt, Robert Winter, Linda Mehr, Frances Tanikawa Makreel, Keith Winsell, Murray Kranz, Robert McGlone, Jane Mulligan, Ronald Hoaglund, Martin Van Buren, Roxanne Dunbar, Jeanette Gadt, Gene Lesner, and the late Mary Lou Diamond. A long friendship with the late Flora May Fearing began in Los Angeles. The friendship and scholarship of Lawrence Friedman, Larry May, Lewis Erenberg, Elaine Silverman and Sheldon Silverman, as well as T. J. Jackson Lears has uplifted, stimulated, and enlightened me. To my colleagues at Wesleyan, Philip Pomper for tireless collegiality, and Jeanine Basinger and Sheila Tobias for team-teaching experiences in the history of women at once inimitable and indescribable, many thanks. I am lucky to have known Jane Mathews, Linda Kerber, Dorothy Ross, and Mary Berry on the American Historical Association's Committee on the Status of

Women. I have learned much, for years, from Christopher Lasch. I owe thanks to Elizabeth McMurray Johnson, Robert Brentano and H. Stuart Hughes for special courtesies. I am lucky to have been able to enjoy for more than twenty years the friendship, innovative scholarship, and vigorous discourse of G. J. Barker-Benfield. To Page Smith, friend and colleague of forty years, my debts have long ago etherialized into grace. This book has its deepest historical root in the teaching of my first teacher of history, the late Emma Beekman Gavras, friend and colleague of nearly half a century. Sheila Gilmore and the late Myron Gilmore helped distill incomparable moments along the way. Rebecca, Sarah, Jeffrey, Rachel, and William have seen me through, sometimes seen through me. She to whom this book is dedicated has lived with its making as well as with me as though both were worth it.

DONALD MEYER
East Haddam, Connecticut
March 17, 1987

Introduction

This book tells four stories of the rise of women in the United States, Russia, Sweden, and Italy, from the mid nineteenth century to 1987. The great transformations in women's lives did not take place according to some preordained schedule. They followed no inevitable route. On the other hand, they did not occur as a consequence of "accidents" or sheer will on the part of anyone. The main "material" basis for revolutionary transformation in the lives of women has been no mystery. Those societies in which these transformations most forcefully emerged were industrializing societies. This was not a rigid law. Where a small, mostly nonindustrial nation evolved next door to major industrial centers—Denmark, say, or Norway—there too women's lives were transformed. The linkages of necessity between one thing and another in history are best kept loose, flexible. But not too much so: industrial England's pastoral neighbor, Ireland, still exhibits quasi-medieval aspects in the lives of both sexes. Peripheral exceptions aside, the correlation with an industrial economy cannot be ignored in any stories of women's changed lives.

Yet, the ways in which Italy, Sweden, Russia, and the United States industrialized differed widely. In this book, I have begun, not with stories of material change, but with political economics. Politics did not shape industrialization the same way in these four countries, but in every case politics played such a compelling part that it shaped economic history into what I have presented as dramas. Specific men struggled with problems that were unique to their nations. No Joseph Stalin promoted Sweden's rapid industrialization, but Stalin is inextricable from Soviet Russia's story. The script written for American industrialization by Alexander Hamilton gathered dust in the archives of paths not taken, but so did that of Henry Carey, author of an exact counter-vision: America as a collection of decentralized self-sufficient harmonic neighborhoods. The great mass market of capitalist America emerged as though by a kind of improvisation, yet compelled all the while by the uniquely American politics of federal democracy. Meanwhile, the fits and starts of Italian industrial growth proceeded inseparably from a cramped, hectic, and finally polarized political life. All these dramas of political economy carried compelling significance for women. In Part I, I have presented these dramas of national transformation in Italy, Sweden, and Russia in anticipation of the dramas of consciousness and self-consciousness, among and about women, that accompanied them.

Since the last century, women in growing multitudes have begun thinking about themselves in new ways. Mostly, they, like men, have come to recognize themselves as historical agents. They have extricated themselves from the idea that their lives are properly prescribed for them, from outside themselves, whether by nature, historical necessity, divine order, or the good of society. Like men, they have come to realize that "nature," "necessity," "divine edict," and "society" are all ideas generated by minds. They want to generate ideas too. They too want to make themselves, make their own history. But these ideas and these wishes did not arrive in women's minds—and in the minds of the men who agreed with them—simply from material reality, let alone on angels' wings. Although without the ores of reality, the human mind can only burn itself out, the reality that most richly fed women's minds was that of their own nation's transformation, not of social transformation in general. In Part II I have followed the opportunities and obstacles, the conflicts and dilemmas impelling and shaping consciousness among and about women in each national drama.

The most revolutionary potential in the awakening of widespread thought among and about women was that it would drive to the very roots of human identity. That awakening could quickly impinge upon politics, labor markets, and legal codes shaping relationships between the sexes in public institutions and marketplaces. In feminism as a political movement, the new ideas often pressed hard for rearrangements in such public realms, as though these contained the sum of important change. Yet this only began to express the inwardness waiting for expression. Unlike revolutions potential in relationships of ideology, class, race, religion, culture, science, tribe, folk, or nation, revolutions potential in sex could cut into the most private mores, the most secret wishes, into family, child-rearing, marriage, love, sexual intercourse—realms commonly left in older societies to magic, incantation, prayer, unconsciousness. The awakening of consciousness and political thought among and about women had the potential of bringing all these realms of private, sub-political life onto public political agendas. In effect, the politicalization of the private would make all relationships between the sexes themes of history, not of nature. It was to invite ideas about how these relationships could be "made," made different, made by choice and politics. None of this potential, however, was decreed for fulfillment by material reality. Nor was it guaranteed by political drama. In Part II, I have tried to stress, in the stories of consciousness in Italy,

Sweden, and Soviet Russia, the degree to which this potential of awakening among and about women was encouraged and discouraged by the circumstances of the dramas of political economy. I have not told these as stories of determinism, but it is not necessary to impute some random unboundedness to a historical drama in order to identify its relative, comparative possibilities. I have sought out individuals in these stories: Anna Maria Mozzoni in Italy, frustrated for lack of the peers she needed, and a Mussolini as inclined to realism as to ideology about gender but finally forced by his own political necessity to invent myths of gender; in Sweden, early theorists of sexual harmony, followed by a Strindberg enraged at the response of the guardians of good order to his realism; utopian Alexandra Kollontai confronted by the revolutionary puritanism of Lenin, then swamped and silenced by Stalin's heroic totalitarianism. Again, I suggest that the most powerful force playing upon women's awakening to self-consciousness was the national drama itself. The men about whom women were being stimulated to think were not men-in-general, but Italian men, Swedish men, Russian men. The impulse in feminism to fulfill itself in universal generalizations about the reason for women's condition would often obscure this fact of national difference and difference among men, sometimes to its harm, sometimes to its relief from hard questions.

Feminism itself was—and remains today—a political movement, not an intellectual movement. While feminist ideas about women—and, most of all, about men, masculinity, mankind—and all those institutions with meaning for women, from love to war, exfoliated for over a century in a kind of prodigy of intellectual innovation, feminism itself was from its origins a quest for power. This meant that at every step along the way its thought, its very consciousness, was inflected by considerations of tactics and strategy. In an ultimate case, such as the Soviet Union, feminist thinking would confront outright coercive suppression; feminism would be forced underground, into social, probably also personal, unconsciousness, leaving historians hard-pressed to devise techniques for discovering whether any feminism still existed in the Soviet Union at all. At what might look like a simple polar extreme, in the United States, where feminists had ready access to public forums as well as rich resources of personality and organization, and money, by no means did such relative freedom spell freedom from tactical, political calculation. In the United States feminists had what Russian women certainly did not have, a whole precinct of culture all their own, a sphere of their own, a whole world of "love and ritual," in Carroll Smith-Rosenberg's telling phrase, within which to shelter themselves, explore themselves, devise new modes and means for expressing themselves.[1] Yet, far from constituting a simple net addition to women's consciousness, this precinct posed an anguishing dilemma, not just for expedient tactics, but for consciousness itself. What did women want—more resources for their own womanly lives in woman's sphere, or escape from that sphere altogether? One peculiarity of the drama of American women was their greater opportunity to be torn between conflicting wishes. In the history of feminism, the heart of the drama has not been women's straightforward pursuit of their goals and wishes, sometimes successful, sometimes not, but their struggle to figure out what they wished in the first place, what they really wanted. Far from wishing to find features in each separate story that can be abstracted to tell one big story, I have preferred to stress the differences.

It follows that this study contains an implicit critique of certain other ways of telling the story of the rise of women. One that emerges from the political heart of feminism is perhaps the most familiar: women's lives through most of history have been those of victims. In a narration of her own conversion to feminism, a modern American feminist testified to the kind of historical imagination that underwrote such a view: "I couldn't believe—still can't—how angry I could become, from deep down and way back, something like a five-thousand-year-buried anger."[2] Since the epiphany here constituted a kind of anthropological extrapolation from personal experience, it was not surprising that the temporal depth of 5,000 years should metamorphose into spatial universality: from *Sisterhood Is Powerful* to *Sisterhood Is Global.*[3] Rage at 5,000 years of history was unlikely to generate much history. A search for shorter-term mechanisms mediating oppression worth historical analysis sometimes led to concepts of "patriarchy," which, in turn, often induced (dialectically?) a search for conviction on the question of a prepatriarchal age of "matriarchy." Although prehistorical matriarchy had little immediate salience for contemporary feminism, it did offer one solid lever, at least: if patriarchy had not in fact existed from the beginning of humankind, then it was not founded in "nature," but in history and politics, and might one day be brought to its historical end politically. Of course it also entailed the bitter question: Why then had women fallen? A further shortening of the implicit eternity of 5,000 years could be realized in modifying patriarchy to its presumably latest, and possibly most lethal, yet most vulnerable, form: capitalist patriarchy. The criticism of such perspectives contained in this book is not that they lack merit, but that, when imposed upon such local dramas as those told here, they leach from their vitality as stories, not of victims,

---

[1] Notes are on p. 639.

but of fully active persons confronting the concrete hazards and dilemmas of particular lives. At its most diffuse and simply polemical, the "universalizing" perspective is to be seen in the evocation of sexism as a principle explaining every otherwise problematic handicap or inequality confronting women, and it is the quite deliberate assumption of this book that that label has not yet offered much light to the historian.

Still, so far as American historians are concerned, the present exploration of feminist history owes at least some of its charge to failed alternatives in the recent past. In 1922, in the euphoria after the long-sought triumph of the woman suffrage amendment, the pioneer of American social history, Arthur Schlesinger, Sr., announced that, in "the new era of historical writing" impending, it would be "unthinkable" for historians' prior neglect of women to continue. Although he did not spell it out, presumably he reasoned that, with suffrage, women themselves would insist somehow upon their inclusion in historians' stories. We can hardly be sure why his call went unheeded. His idea was that women had in fact played "their full part" in American development, hence historians had simply to show that fact. Women had been "heart and soul" in the Revolution, an indispensable balance in the westward movement, "a part of the war machine quite as fully as men" during the Civil War, and again an "indispensable part" of American involvement in the World War. It would be too much to say there was a hidden agenda in all this. Schlesinger quite openly declared that his reading of American women was as contributors to "this the greatest democracy in the world."[4] Accordingly, it would have been difficult for those picking up his call to have given a clear reading to Tory women who had despised the Revolution, pioneering women who despaired at the prospect of Ohio or Oregon, Confederate women with hate in their hearts for Abraham Lincoln, Irish women outraged at finding their men forced to fight for Orange and Tan Great Britain. But we have no way of arguing that it was the triumphalism in Schlesinger's agenda that spelled its failure. Perhaps had an active feminism survived the suffrage triumph it might have generated interesting history in criticizing his. At the very least, it can be said that, whatever it was that feminists had meant to achieve with their votes, it evidently did not include a supplement to American history.

The work of the most prominent woman historian who did flourish in the interwar years, Mary Ritter Beard, only further illuminated the central issue for the history of women. Beard's most explicit presentation of her outlook came with the last of her books, in 1945, *Woman as Force in History*.[5] Earlier, she had exemplified this outlook in practice, in several books, beginning with *Woman's Work in Municipalities* (1915) and in *On Understanding Woman* (1931), both of them avalanches of data on women in vigorous action. The formidable array of famous, anonymous, forgotten women she assembled in 1931, engaged in everything from running countries to bloodiest battle, from philosophy to courtesanship, seemed to Beard amply to have proved the point she argued in 1945: women had been "force," not passivity in history. She mocked the suffragists' monumental *The History of Woman Suffrage* for its relapses into the pathos of victimology, when their own data showed strong effective women. She taunted Bryn Mawr's Mary Carey Thomas, a successful college president, for bemoaning women's "twi-light life, a half-life apart" in "a man's world." For a lugubrious lament of Charlotte Perkins Gilman, she felt scorn:

> Close, close /man/ bound her, that /woman/ should leave
>   him never.
> Weak still he kept her, lest she be strong to flee;
> And the fainting flame of passion he kept alive forever
> With all the arts and forces of earth and sky and sea.

Mary Beard had not the slightest interest in debating the significance of "passion" on either side, but she found laughable the use by such palpably strong women as Elizabeth Cady Stanton, Susan B. Anthony, M. Carey Thomas, and Charlotte Perkins Gilman of the victim-martyr model. Yet Beard never made her own point. By demonstrating simply that women had been present far more often than historians had recognized in all sorts of important places and vital activities, she was not demonstrating that "woman"—or even "women"—had been a "force." They had simply shared in various histories with men, like men. The critical omission in Beard's histories was indeed exactly here: her work lacked men. In Schlesinger's agenda, as women were inducted into history, men would still continue very much to be present, winning the Revolution, the West, the Civil War, the World War, only, now, with their woman helping. Men had had their compelling purposes; women had agreed with them. In Beard's histories, men's purposes faded simply into a spectacle of flux, though now some women were part of the flux.

Refinements of Schlesinger's and Beard's approaches would not fail to appear in contemporary feminism. A Swedish feminist, Birgitta Wistrand, has asked, "What, after all, is more worhty of historical analysis," the "doings of male politicians or of female servants?"[6] In this, we can hear the note of animus, for the answer Wistrand wanted was not that both were worthy: we should ask ourselves, she said, "whether what men think to be politically important really is, compared to what women think important." But the animus, preferring the history of female servants to the history of male politicians, could be extracted without blurring her essential point: from the standpoint of justice, no one ought be neglected in historical narratives. Everyone deserves a part in the stories historians tell. Wistrand herself made the point in terms of Swedish feminist politics by dismissing all schemes for improving women's representation in various quarters according to one formula or another: there was only one justifiable formula, fifty-fifty everywhere. This approach was useless to the historian faced with having to choose somehow, someday, on some reasoned ground, whom he was going to include, and whom he was not, in his stories but it underwrote feminism's own irreducible necessity, that its stories, about women, and for the sake of women's further liberation, had to include men. Were American men sexist capitalist patriarchs? Or were they heroes of democratic revolution, pioneers in new land, fighters against evils foreign and domestic? The same issue inhabited feminism in Italy, Sweden, and Russia. Were Italian men the heroes of Risorgimento national liberation, or Catholic-Masonic-positivist sexists? If they were both, then Italian feminists would realize that the men they confronted were not "males" or mankind, but Italian men, some of whose peculiarly Italian aspirations might invite collaboration from Italian women. Should Swedish women find the Social Democratic Party's apparently unconscious habit of looking to paternal life-term leaders a sign of the ubiquity of patriarchalism, or an assuring sign of Swedish stability? Should Russian feminists oppose Bolshevik manhood for being notably tough, aggressive, and masculine? Nor was it as though simply refraining from the imposition of universal, transnational perspectives on particular national stories guaranteed clear narratives. Feminist history had to grasp the terms, not of the general conflict between man and woman, 5,000 years deep, but of conflict specific to each particular national story.

Nevertheless, after all this is said and understood, it remains true that each particular story cannot be told simply for its own sake, free of any reference to some single point of comparison. The argument in this book accords with the basic thesis propounded by Simone de Beauvoir in *Le deuxieme sexe*, in 1947. Indifferent to such evidence as Mary Beard's, that there had in fact been many women through history who had not been "second," and Schlesinger's, that women had been helpmeets in all good things, de Beauvoir set herself to explain secondness, women's longtime and widespread subordination, their dependency. Her method was to write a general history of men. In this history, men, through much struggle and with many defeats, had extricated themselves from being victims, changed themselves into actors. They had challenged animals, the weather, wildernesses, nature, had levered themselves free of nature. They had generated material tools—

stones, clubs, arrows—by which the weakness and inferiority of their own bodies compared with mountains and rivers and other animals had been transcended. In the process, first without realizing it, then, more and more systematically, they had invented immaterial tools: hunting groups, work teams, tribes, eventually society itself—above all, the idea of society. It grew plain that the greatest power to be won from tools was not over nature but over other human beings. One tribe struggled with another tribe. One race sought to kill, then expel, then enslave another. The fact that this process quickly, perhaps almost from the start, induced conflict between men did not undermine its basic thrust: men were creating themselves as no longer unconscious but conscious, no longer reactive but active and purposive, no longer immanent but transcendent. The process might be fitful, selective, accidental. Some men progressed toward transcendence in one direction, others in another. Some men categorized other men as, still, parts of nature, to be dominated not accommodated.

Obviously heavily indebted to her partner's, Jean Paul Sartre's, existentialist modernization of German idealist philosophy of history, de Beauvoir expounded it unflinchingly in her analysis of women's state. Women had become secondary because men had become purposive, primary. De Beauvoir made clear that women's subordination derived from the positive, not the negative, aspects of the historic enterprise of men. Men had not generated great myths of women as "immanent" as a consequence of anxieties provoked by their own freedom, or identified them with "nature" and the cyclical because their own transcending activities had induced guilt or run into "contradictions." De Beauvoir approved of activity, transcendence, purposive identities. She wished these for women. She was not going to blame men for them. But there was no easy guarantee that men would easily think about women in a new way, as comparable to themselves. Men's purposive myths about woman had value. And this was true "everywhere," "universally." The physicality of women's reproductive lives was not a historical variable; it was the same everywhere, always, in all societies, tribes, races. It was as though all men in all societies continually could reexperience, through their relations with women, their first step into manhood in history.

The elaboration of cultural myths about women could be, in principle, unlimited, as variable as the variations in mankind. In this book, the proliferation of such myths will not be at issue. The application of de Beauvoir's thesis that this book proposes inheres in its basic division into four stories. Perhaps the most compelling creation of purposeful manhood to date has been that of nation-states, of nations. Philosophers have extrapolated salvationary futures into some ultimate polity coterminous with mankind. As the motivations for such a transcendence of nations shift from the positive, in hopes for the fulfillment of humanity, to the negative, in fear of the destruction of humanity, in some final conflict of nations, the prospects for such a future more certainly partake of prophecy than of probability. Until quite recently, philosophers projected another creation of man too as a basis for transnational bonding, far stronger than mere hopes and fears, that is, science. But today, at least, and without evident imminent reversal in the near future, science itself has been seized by nations. Transnational aspirations of religion still bubble up from time to time and place to place, but the ability of nations to co-opt religions to their purposes remains conspicuous. Among the newly awakened women of the past century, many, usually feminists, have reached out for both science and religion as tools of their own to gain leverage on forces they find blocking their way. But rare indeed have been women, feminists or otherwise, who, in their turn to science against myths of women's passivity, or to the criticism of patriarchal religion in the name of a new, or renewed, religion of Mother-Father, have followed their pioneering into confrontations with the national interest. Quite simply, the most compelling part of that man-made world with which modern women have had to reckon has been nations, for all women one particular nation, for every woman her own men's nation. And one powerful condensation of this national purpose has followed: national character. National character has been masculine character. The men with whom Anna Maria Mozzoni and her Risorgimento friends sought equality were not men-in-general but Italian men; the men with whom Alexandra Kollontai sought revolutionary fraternity were not men but Russian Communist men.

Rather than tell the stories of political economy and consciousness in the United States, along with those of Italy, Sweden, and Russia, I have saved them for a separate section, Part III. As a historian of the United States, my first question was whether the American story could be told without identifying what might be special, peculiar, and characteristic about it. Thus, my purpose in investigating other stories was, in the final reckoning, to earn more light on the story closest to my professional identity. I cannot deny that, in the course of inquiry, my interest in Italy, Sweden, and Soviet Russia flourished. I could not at all times resist fascination with their stories quite apart from their usefulness as light adjusted to beam on the American scene. I cannot promise that all signs of such enchantment have been purged, but by isolating the American story I have meant to stress its characteristics in contrast with all others and emphasize comparisons between the others far less.

I have also divided the American story in a different way. No particular historical logic decrees dividing the drama of its political economy at 1920, but I have done so in accord with what may well be the most significant feature peculiar to American feminism: its climax after long labors in a notable political triumph, the Nineteenth Amendment to the Constitution of the United States. There followed its almost eerie subsidence for more than forty years, through the great political dramas of the Jazz Age, the Depression decade, and World War II and its aftermath. I am not acquainted with any hypothesis about international feminism-in-general that could integrate this chapter into its story.

By organizing the American story in this way, I trust it will be more understandable why I have chosen Italy, Sweden, and Soviet Russia as my counter-dramas, rather than, say, England, France, and Germany. At the start of a reconnaissance like this, one would like to know ahead of time everything one will eventually learn. Some comparative enterprises come near to preordination. When Crane Brinton set out to see if "revolution" had an "anatomy," he could hardly have considered ignoring the French and Russian revolutions; popular labeling made it difficult to leave out the English and American, even though suspicion might rise that perhaps not all was revolution that carried the label.[7] For the theme of this book, popular labels offered neither help nor hazard. The rise of women can be studied on a dozen stages; industrialization has been examined in a score of major nations. Obviously, trying to cope with all, or many, aside from its practical difficulties, would be to build in from the start a drift toward morphologies, structures, anthropology. A search for "anatomy" would be nearly irresistible. Choices had to be made. I have not wholly dissolved regret at foreswearing the opportunity to think my way further into the minds of Stendhal and George Sand, as well as of de Beauvoir, or, on the other side of the Channel, of Jane Austen and George Eliot. Sticking to my intention, not simply to indulge personal interests but to win illuminating perspectives on American history, I decided that one case, at least, of a nation whose industrial fortune had, in contrast to America's, been notably troubled and frustrating would serve the purpose: Italy. I then wanted a case where general humane values, commonly linked to the rise of women, had, at least in common repute, been given deliberate political expression, in contrast to the far more special-interest-oriented politics of the United States: Sweden. Although I had wanted to include the Soviet Union from the start, as a case of linkage between politics and economics in extreme contrast with the United States, I for some time doubted that, lacking any knowledge of Russian, I could learn enough about Soviet women to justify an effort. Before it was too late, I found myself beneficiary of the first waves of research into Russian women coming out of American universities, in English. Thus, a certain amount of the arbitrary inheres in these choices, but no choices could eliminate that.

Upon proceeding, these choices seemed to hold promise on a secondary ground: religion. Catholicism and the Vatican in Italy; Sweden's state church Lutheranism and hard-pressed popular evangelicals; and the Soviet Union's coercive antireligiousness imposed on an ancient orthodoxy—all invited comparison. Actually, I have come to be impressed more by the religiousness manifest in the United States, and evident among American women, in contrast with the lesser popular evangelicalism of the other nations, rather than by contrasts between "church" traditions. Indeed, as various pages will suggest, much food for thought is contained in the question whether in all three other nations, popular religiousness is not rooted far more in a sense of place and its special past than in the formal apparatuses of churchly Christendom. At all events, while I have no doubt that my essential themes could have been told also through the stories of other nations—Canada, say, and, possibly most promising of all, for anyone competent to penetrate it, Japan—I leave it to what follows to justify my choices. If they have illuminated American history, well and good.

If this enterprise reawakens familiar old arguments about American "exceptionalism," also well and good. While I have no particular interest in rehearsing familiar arguments, I have not discounted the testimony of two of the exponents of perhaps the most influential model of transnational history, history that focuses particularly on industrialization, as key to modern times. In 1852, Karl Marx, writing to Joseph Weydemeyer, commented on America's failure to live up to theory. The empty land, the religious pluralism, the ethnic heterogeneity, constituted obstacles in the way of those "basic" forces making for the predicted dialectic of history. But, Marx added, this was but a temporary resistance. In time, America, too, would obey the universal laws. Thirty-four years later, however, Friedrich Engels, writing to Florence Kelley Wischnewetsky, repeated the same theme. America was still resistant, "lawless." Engels too insisted that the United States must eventually—and, in the lurid afterglow of the Haymarket riot, probably much sooner than later—take its place in accord with true philosophy.[8] Dialectical materialism's hopes rose once again after 1929: at last, the illusionary wonderland was ending; and again during the troubled 1970s. One might wonder how many chances prophecy has to prove itself.

Following his visit to the United States in 1909, Sigmund Freud commented to the same effect, declaring that, although American civilization was a remarkable experiment in optimism, it would not finally succeed. Repression had its rights.[9] The United States too must suffer civilization's discontents. Though Marx's and Freud's particular judgments need not discourage us from helping ourselves to all their ideas that seem helpful, it must be at least intriguing that the genius of European philosophy has found it hard, if not impossible, to give the United States a historical reading. Years before, Alexis de Tocqueville tried to show Europeans that America was real, but many would never believe it.

In Part IV I return to Italy, Sweden, and Russia, with the United States, for a reckoning that, still inflected by national identities, breaks the boundaries of nations. The inquiry proceeds to various writers: Gabriele D'Annunzio and Sibilla Aleramo in Italy, for instance; Carl Almqvist, Fredrika Bremer, August Strindberg, and Elin Wägner, among others, in Sweden; Boris Pilnyak, Alexandra Kollontai, Yuri Trifonov, and others in Soviet Russia; and a range of Americans, from Harriet Beecher Stowe through Kate Chopin, and Stephen Crane to John Berryman. Although I restrict myself mostly to novelists, plus a few moviemakers and a poet or two, I do not mean to imply privilege for this medium. My point is general. Politics, whatever its goal—feminism, industrialization, social security,—focused on debate, entangled with tactics, preoccupied with gaining public power, necessarily conspires with compromise, mediation, evasion. Politicized cultures sag by inertia toward conventionality. In contrast, literature, generating itself out of the appetite for fresh perception, has no alternative to freshness in language and must win its audiences despite, and at best through, defying them, puzzling them, unsettling and arousing and shocking them. It cannot avoid freedom. Contemplating the difficulties of writing the history of democratic nations, where major deeds were not centered on a few notable officials, Tocqueville worried that historians, out of fatigue from tracing a multitudinous collection of persons, would tire, and come to prefer "to link facts together to make a system." They would flinch from trying to search out "the genius, vices, or virtues of individuals."[10] It is perhaps forgivable, then, that historians of democracy seeking to escape "system" look for heroic ways to do so. Evidences of the reality of individual autonomy can be sought everywhere, even in politics, but literature offers obvious advantages. Not all those individual furnaces of fresh language I have discussed fueled themselves exclusively, or even primarily, on the dilemmas of sex and power, but all registered a heat to melt down roles, scorch through the walls of social order, break free of cool compromise.

I cannot claim to have chosen only the best examples. Some I would argue are fated, inevitable, essential: D'Annunzio in Italy, say, and Pasolini; certainly Kollontai, since even though her purely literary

achievements were slight, they exactly registered where her more theoretical and politically limited writings were impelling her; and, above
all, Strindberg. I would not disagree with those urging that no modern
rendering of the anguishes of sex surpasses those of Ingmar Bergman,
but I have chosen, in respect to my own limits as an interpreter of films,
to draw upon a far less powerful, but possibly more symptomatic—for
my purposes—film, Vilgot Sjoman's *I Am Curious, Yellow*. But could
not Alberto Moravia have been included for Italy? Elsa Morante? Leon-
ardo Sciascia? Dacia Maraini? And any reader of American literature
might wonder at the absence of Edith Wharton and Ellen Glasgow,
Theodore Dreiser and Frank Norris. Why ought not Norman Mailer's
offer of himself as philosopher of sex be preferred to his refraction in
the glass of Kate Millett's criticism? And should not Philip Roth's
definitive comedy of sex be appreciated, and John Updike's WASP pen-
itentials arranged for observance? Having no intention of discerning
myth or revealing discourse, I have had no urge to be inclusive or
identify the representative. To escape system, the historian must seek
the universal in the individual. De Beauvoir's own tract makes the
point. Written out of personal intellectual resources tangential to established French intellection, and received on its first appearance mostly
with indifference in both Paris and in translation, *The Second Sex* for
some time loomed as a kind of monument to individual enterprise
affiliated with no movement, taken up in no schools, submitted to no
debate. Yet a historian cannot possibly be intimidated in his judgment
of its importance by its reception by others; he or she must go it alone.

In my view, Strindberg offers the most compelling rendition of this
argument. In examining his literary career, I have tried to do maximum
justice to what is Swedish in his story, but at the same time read him
finally for a universal theme. Strindberg's life—from boyhood to death—
was a continuous struggle to sustain imaginative energy. As he said, he
was practically constitutionally determined to defy conventionality in
feelings, thought, relationship, language. What he gained was the power,
through his language, to live multiple lives. His significance for this
book inheres in his extreme sensitivity to the links between imaginative
freedom and the experiences of childhood, marriage, and sex. It was
not that he psychoanalyzed himself, though he did. It was that his self-
psychoanalysis strengthened him to persist in resistance to engulfment
in any role or relationship. He was the modern man par excellence—
alienated, fragmented, narcissistic, inexhaustible, free. I have hazarded a guess, derived more from his work than any other's: no modern
(liberatory) literature without the battle, not so much of the sexes, as
of sexuality, a battle within each individual as well as between individuals.

Understandably, men have resisted submitting their most basic relationships with women—as mother, wife, saint, whore—to any critical
analysis that threatens to undercut their power. Since they have used
their power, not just to defend themselves, but to change things—invent
and destroy tools; establish and transcend nations; build industry,
then break out of industry's iron cage; imagine gods, then escape them—
this disinclination has posed the most formidable challenge to feminism. In their wish to escape the roles prescribed by men for women,
women have had to ask whether they want the same powers men have
had. If so, equality, as an ideal, has not sufficed. Equality can be shared
by the powerless. The politicalization and historicization of the "eternal" roles of women gain power from the wish of individuals to be
powerful, to be furnaces eager to refine meaning for themselves. In his
attack on what many Swedes of his time—men and women—cherished,
a vision of a harmony at the heart, of Sweden as a hearth, a little home
in which the Swedish folk might shelter, Strindberg was psychologically correct. Home is not the locus for heat and daring. His protest
offered the abiding theme for feminist history, the history of feminism,
and the history of women, and, accordingly, for liberal democratic
history of all men and all women. Like all women, all men too deserve
to be free.

Part I Industrialization as National Drama

In the three dramas of political economy that follow, the stakes for women were high. Italy, Sweden, and Russia each went through profound transformations. These national transformations held the potential, or, rather, the certainty of profound transformations in the lives of women. But each national transformation had its unique aspects, and I have argued that these unique aspects were of critical importance. All these transformations proceeded on the dynamic of industrialization. Yet the word "industrialization" does not begin to summarize them or even explain them. In each case, I have stressed how each nation's own particular past, its preindustrial past, strongly inflected and directed industrialization. Women's stake in industrialization was quite different in each nation, precisely because of the difference in the historical heritages brought into industrialization and because of the dramatically different politics each heritage prompted. All of this is presented in anticipation of the story of consciousness itself in Part II, consciousness of women and feminist consciousness about women's stake. The priority in Part I, thus, is to power, the powers generated in the politics of industrialization in the form of parties, unions, and so on. This means that the dominant figures in these stories are men. Women had their future at stake in what these men were doing.

1 Italy. An Epic of Pathos

The Slow Painful Emergence of Independent Italy: From Heroics to Economics

On February 9, 1849, for the first time in 502 years a republic was proclaimed in Rome. Later that same month, Giuseppe Garibaldi arrived with his legions to defend and protect it. On March 5, Giuseppe Mazzini arrived, to be quickly elected head of an executive triumvirate. The millennial dreams of Young Italy seemed about to take form. For considerably more than 300 years, Italians had been divided and degraded under the rule of foreigners—French, Austrians, Spaniards, even Germans. Now, rebirth had occurred, a reassertion of Italian identity and Italian manhood.[1]

Numerous intelligent liberal-minded women of many nations admired and supported Mazzini. Many came to join him in the battles of the new republic. Princess Cristina di Belgiojoso Trivulzio had already organized a force of 200 men for fighting against Austrians in Milan. Now she came to Rome to take charge of the hospitals. Mazzini's leading American admirer saw him in an aura of radiance: "He looks more divine than ever. . . . The crisis is tremendous . . . all will come on him . . . if anyone can save Italy . . . it will be he. . . . But he is very doubtful. . . . Freely would I give my life to help him.[2]

Mazzini's fervent nationalism differed dramatically from those exponents of national power who engaged in Europe's jostling power-politics. In Mazzini's vision, Italy was to be reborn hardly in terms of power at all, but in terms of spirit.[3] Indeed, Europe itself must be reborn as a kind of family of nations, all peoples freed from external domination—Poles liberated from Russian Tsardom, Hungarians from Austria, Greeks from Turks, just as Italians were to be released from Spanish and German clutches. Each was to fulfill itself in its proper ancestral homeland. Italy's own contribution to the family of nations would be, presumably, to resume its old role as teacher of all the arts and crafts and graces of civilization. No one would need fear it. All could once again love as well as respect it.

Although the elections held in Rome early in 1849 to elect a constituent assembly had been held on the basis of male suffrage only, Mazzini himself had nothing to do with that exclusion. Had the republic survived, had it proved to be the heart of a new unified Italy under Mazzinian influence, it most likely would have embodied the sentiments Mazzini expressed in later years, in exile again, after French troops arrived to dispel the republic's defenders. "Cancel from your minds every idea of superiority over woman," he counseled. "You have none whatsoever." This had practical meaning: "Consider her your Equal in your civil and political life." Only historic circumstances, not inherent traits, could explain the fact of inequality: "Long prejudice, an inferior education, and a perennial legal inequality and injustice, have created that *apparent* intellectual inferiority which has been converted into an argument for continued oppression."[4]

Of course by the time French troops had broken into Rome early in July, the hopes for a new Italy had already been dispelled, with Austria's defeat of Piedmont's army in March; blockaded Venetians were the last to hold out. Mazzini fled to England, never to return. The new Italy of 1860 did not please him. He was a republican; he had no use for a king. Most tellingly, Mazzini had no practical economic policies for Italy. Once Camillo Cavour and his colleagues had negotiated their way through the rapids of European diplomacy to the united Italy of 1870, they could not avoid facing the fact that Italy was not, as Mazzini had believed, vital and strong, but, rather, backward, poor, and weak. Their measures were, therefore, economic. Cavour's first post in Piedmont's government, back in 1850, had been to head the ministry of agriculture, commerce, and marine. He had gone in for roads and railroads. If it was to rival Marseille, Genoa needed wharves, docks, basins, warehouses, brokers, bankers, shipping companies. Much of this drew Italy directly into international capital markets. For rails, rolling stock, locomotives, Piedmont had to import. One exception: for railroad ties, Italians clear-stripped their hillsides, thus inducing the erosion of a landscape that had been kept unspoiled by poverty.

By 1850 industry had appeared in some concentration. Several hundred small silk-throwing mills were in operation in Piedmont and Lombardy, mostly manned by women. Until competition arose from China and Japan, they made money. Yet Italians produced few finished goods in silk, for a simple reason: few Italians had the money to buy them. By mid-century, too, women were weaving fabrics from the output of small new cotton and flax mills, and some of these operations made money. For all this, however, it was hardly obvious that seeds were being planted for irresistible economic growth. The nation's economic situation was fragile in 1860, still so in 1870. Whatever the policy chosen, the way would be precarious. If Italy strove to grow from within, cultivating native roots, its progress would be certain to be slow. If it sought stimulation from infusions of capital from abroad, it risked unbalanced growth and losing control of its own economic destiny. By 1900 it was plain that Italy's economic progress had been both slow and unbalanced.[5] Per-capita income in 1890 barely surpassed that of 1860. The industrial sector remained what it had been in 1860, about 20 percent of the whole. The industrial work force remained that of a nation still in the earliest stages of industrialization. Nearly 50 percent of the work force were women; only 28 percent men; the rest, children. Three-quarters of all industrial workers were still in textiles, where only 15 percent of the workers were adult males.[6]

Far from beginning to catch up with the major nations in whose league Italian politicians hoped to compete, Italy in 1885 about matched Belgium in industrial output. With ten times Sweden's population, it did outproduce Sweden but not by much, and soon, in the first lift of its surge to industrial modernity, between 1888 and 1896, Sweden was leaving Italy behind. After its own modest spurt in the 1880s, Italy sagged back into near-stagnation in the Nineties.

Some years later, writing in a Fascist prison, the Communist intellectual Antonio Gramsci argued that Italy's sad retardation was the fault of her first political leaders.[7] They had failed to promote a social revolution to accompany their political revolution. In France, he pointed out, the Jacobins who had led the political revolution had taken care to win the peasants to their side by giving them land taken from the nobility. As a consequence, in France effective national unity had been established on the basis of a powerful bourgeoisie. The Italian Risorgimento, by contrast, he said, had been only a "passive" revolution. The Italian bourgeoisie had not undertaken to reduce the landowners and had recoiled from confronting the pope, who, with his international, "cosmopolitan" interests, remained hostile to the new Italy and its state. While the fruit of the French Revolution, then, had been the unification of France as a modern state, stable, compact, capable of major policies, the fruit of Italy's had been a state that remained weak, incapable of energizing an economy that also remained weak. Gramsci did not have to warn that, in the absence of genuine unity, a delusory one would be supplied, for he was its victim as he composed his revisionist history, telling not of heroes and their illustrious mothers, but of ordinary politicians who lacked the will of true revolutionaries.

Had the policy commended by Gramsci been chosen, presumably Italian women would have enjoyed an option that the Italian economy was not in fact generating for them, namely, life as middle-class housewives and as daughters of middle-class households, in numbers and with resources comparable to the more advanced nations Italy strove to emulate.

Not all future historians would agree with Gramsci. In 1956 Rosario Romeo argued that exactly because land had remained concentrated in the hands of the landlords rather than being diffused among millions of peasant families, not only had agricultural output risen between 1860 and 1880, but capital had been generated for investment in industry. This was hard-headed realism, indeed, for it was in the Eighties that the largest single mass action ever undertaken by Italians got, underway—the abandonment of Italy for Marseille, for the Plate, Brazil, New York, by hundreds of thousands of southern Italian peasants. By the twentieth century, emigration had become an annual outpouring, right up till 1914. In an immediate and narrow sense, this exodus proved a benefit, because multitudes of the emigrants, in heavy majority men, sent back remittances to their families in a thousand villages. But in a longer and larger view, the exodus showed that Italy had not yet become a nation capable of sustaining anything near its population. Romeo's analysis suggested an Italy industrialized for the few rather than the many.[8]

Mazzinians did not disappear in the new Italy, despite Mazzini's own self-exile and sense of alienation. Many schoolteachers in the new Italy were at once Mazzinian and feminist, pressing for more and better schools for girls as well as boys. Because the pope and his church boycotted the new nation, such teachers directly expressed Mazzini's idea of a new kind of religiousness, a religion of culture. They were working at odds with the policy of Cavour.[9] Cavour had proclaimed a "free Church in a free State" and "separation of Church and State," both meant to woo the pope from his sullen withdrawal, but both antithetical to Mazzini's vision of a state suffused with the motives of a religion of humanity. In such a state, Catholicism's ancient exclusion of women from sacred offices would simply cease to matter. In a community of idealists in service to the whole, women would figure not only as schoolteachers but also as ministers of education, as superintendents of community works, doctors, hospital supervisors, and diplomats, all perfectly in harmony with Mazzinian hopes.

Cavour's Italy had less to offer women. As myths of heroic origins began to evolve, they did not ignore, but exalted women; yet the exaltation took a direction quite different from that which Mazzini had seemed to intend. A story of *maternità illustri* began to be told, of "illustrious motherhood," and ironically enough Mazzini's own mother figured as the most illustrious.[10] The honor was just. Maria Drago Mazzini had been a splendid mother to her son. The young Giuseppe had suffered some sort of infirmity, affecting his ability to walk, and his mother had devoted herself to seeing it overcome. The myth underemphasized other qualities in Maria Drago Mazzini. Maria Drago had been a city girl, brought up in a highly political city, Genoa, in a highly political household. The kinds of young men who would later conspire with her son had been familiar in her own girlhood and youth. As a young woman she had lived through Genoa's own revolutionary transformation into the Ligurian Republic in 1797. The man she married, a doctor, many years older, who fathered Giuseppe, kept a comparable household, vibrant with liberal political idealism and conspiracy. For Giuseppe Mazzini, then, from his experience, motherhood was fused with politics. Mothers could be political people too. One did not define one sphere separate from the other. The myth of *maternità illustri* leached out such egalitarian elements. Just as Mazzini himself was dispatched out of politics into a pantheon of reverent memory, so, too, were the women who had joined him in battle, Belgiojoso and Ossoli, Jessie White Mario, Georgina Crawford Saffi, Giulia Calame Modena.

As it was, Cavour's successors appeared almost to conspire in proving parliamentary government weak, prompting a turn in the second-generation leadership that was brutal, harsh, and active with a new heedlessness. Twice premier, Francesco Crispi turned to action with a vengeance. By the end of his terms in office, early in 1896, he had managed to shatter whatever Mazzinian assumptions he may once have shared. He was impatient with his predecessors' habit of trying to deflect opposition by means of patronage, bribes, suasions, and co-optation, generally, and although once a man of the extreme parliamentary Left himself, he called in police to deal with the newly organized Socialists. Impatient with waiting for the natural processes of the market to bring economic health, he pressed the government directly into the midst of finance and industry. Impatient with lurking on the peripheries of big-power diplomacy, he lunged for colonies, first in Eritrea, successfully, then disastrously at Adowa in Ethiopia. He did remain anticlerical to the end, certain that the Vatican meant no good to Italy. Gramsci once characterized Crispi was *vero uomo della nuovo borghesia,* a true man of the new bourgeoisie, but the Socialists whom Crispi tried to suppress knew better. Representing no coherent interests of any coherent class, Crispi registered in himself the fact of Italy's own incoherence, its lack of any class with hegemony, its reliance upon the improvisations of one man.[11]

With Crispi, Italy's fate seemed sealed: to go on trying to become a real modern nation. Its own history had offered it an alternative. Italy's historic Renaissance apogee had been reached not as a nation but as city-states, and the identity of these city-states had persisted through all the long years of humiliation under foreign rule. Nothing decreed that the new Italy had to be a unitary state on the French model. A federal Italy, over which the Piedmont king might preside, or even the pope, might have drawn on the old local vitalities while avoiding the new dilemmas. Perhaps no policy could have stanched the flow of emigrants, but an economy drawing less on models of other nations' industrialization and more on Italy's climatic advantages agriculturally and its various traditions of craft production might have stimulated a larger home market and begun the process of probing for niches in international trade. But, as Machiavelli had said, it had been division and fragmentation that had brought down on Italians their woes, and the dream of a national Italy had both humiliation and ambition behind it. The warnings of a Carlo Cattaneo, that true freedom, individual freedom, had much to fear from a new state with a new prince and would be served better by local freedoms, were ignored even by Mazzini. No one can say whether some Italian women might have benefited from a decentralized Italy. In the United States, Henry Carey urged decentralization as a policy favorable to prosperous homes. If Naples and Calabria and Sicily had remained poor, perhaps Piedmont and Lombardy and the Veneto might have enjoyed their advantages free of such governments as Crispi's. Perhaps the logic that was to lead to Mussolini might have been cut off at its start.

Ironically enough, a second expansion in industrial output got started during Crispi's tenure; it lasted until 1908, averaging a bit less than 7 percent per year, well below the rate at which Sweden and Imperial Russia and Japan all surged during their epochs of industrial "breakout" or "takeoff." Thus, while the economic historian Alexander Gershenkron identified this period as the birth of modern Italian industry, he agreed that it was an unimpressive birth.[12] Worse, during the last years before the war, Italy fell back to rates of under 2.5 percent per year. The great outflow of hard-working emigrants continued. If possible, politics after Crispi grew harsher. His successors, uncelebrated men named Rudini and Pelloux, the first in a brutal repression in Milan in 1898, the second in an illegal adjournment of parliament in 1900, seemed to demonstrate that the state itself was on the edge of disintegration in favor of sheer force.

If Mazzini's utopian Italy had held promise for women, the reality of Cavour's Italy shriveled it. The subordination Catholic ideology prescribed for women had been underwritten by the national economic backwardness. So it continued. New jobs opening in the silk mills offered little more than one form of exploitation for another. Italian women were not being offered the chance to elaborate a woman's sphere on their own time and in their own terms, supported by the wages and salaries of men who had escaped the old rural poverty for new jobs and professions in an expanding economy. Certainly they were not being invited into an economic mainstream. Ideological limits hardened with the economy's torpor. The Vatican's deepening involvement in banking, heavily funded by the Catholic Veneto and the northeast, resonated with its boycott of the state to render a kind of Catholic capitalism into a most special special-interest group. So far as women were concerned, the state could not afford to indulge whatever egalitarian impulses might still remain from its Mazzinian heritage, for fear of sharpening the quarrel with the church.

Reinventing Italy: Women's Stake in Social Science, Social Catholicism, Socialism

If politicians had become frustrated by Italy's delay in modernizing itself, men of thought had become far more so. Alberto Asor Rosa has told how disappointing the Italian intellectuals found the Italy of 1870–90. The poet Giosue Carducci wrote a friend in 1877: "I have no interest in public life. . . . I wish I were back in the days when no one knew me but a few friends. . . . Does this new Italy seem a beautiful thing to you? I don't find it so. But in order not to depress others I keep quiet about it." For a person whose calling was words, silence was hard. But, as another asked, "Are we supposed to sing praises to . . . the budget, extol the virtues of the ministry, laud the parliament, cheer the triumphs of our diplomats?" Under any such compulsion, "silence is patriotism."[13]

Asor Rosa has argued that this *deprecato temporum* derived not so much from the failures of post-Risorgimento Italy as from a certain displacement experienced by the traditional Italian intellectual.[14] This familiar figure thought of Italy less in terms of society or politics, let alone of economics, than in terms of a culture that was essentially literary rather than, as with Mazzini, religious. Such a figure appeared more and more irrelevant as Italy struggled with its practical tasks. Carducci himself withdrew into a deliberately hermetic life. By the 1880s younger men were emerging, no less hostile to the increasingly crude, materialistic, and often corrupt Italy of parliament, Masonry, and nascent capitalism, but far more emphatic in expressing themselves. In the United States the men who found roaring post-Civil War America dismaying came to be known as a "genteel" generation, but there was nothing genteel about Gabriele D'Annunzio or Benedetto Croce, or a little later, Luigi Pirandello. Run for parliament? asked one of Pirandello's characters as late as 1913—better run for the sewer.[15] If it was an essentially unpolitical, antieconomic humanism that recoiled from the Italy of Crispi, Rudini, and Pelloux, it was not going to go into its good night only ironizing, as did Charles Eliot Norton and Henry Adams. D'Annunzio, Croce, and Pirandello would all three have difficulty taking the measure of Fascism.

The commanding myth of the old generation of Italian humanists had been that of a mostly pastoral and organic, not so much feudal as simply premodern culture, an embowering in which each soul had its place. None was to exploit another for anything as brutal as capital accumulation. Italy was to be unified into a personal, humane family-nation-folk. The single greatest text for this myth had been Alessandro Manzoni's *I promessi sposi* of 1825, the definitive evocation of *Italia umile*, the humble Italy that would continue to echo in the minds of alienated Italian intellectuals till the 1970s and Pier Paolo Pasolini. But there had always been something wrong with this literature of humble Italy. As Gramsci pointed out, Manzoni, after writing his masterpiece in a demotic, popular Italian true to its true-to-life characters, had been unable to resist rewriting it in the elegant and elite Tuscan by which it came to be known. Manzoni had converted his masterpiece into condescension, not revelation. In this it only perpetuated the Vatican's historic practice of teaching and controlling its children rather than eliciting their own voice. What the Italian intellectual had found special about Italy was himself.[16]

One escape from this self-enclosure was to repudiate the idea that Italy was special. In a famous book devoted to forcing public attention to the appalling social and economic conditions of Italy's south, Pasquale Villari spelled out this option:

The first step is to admit our wounds, and put aside our national illusions and prejudices. If you take all the branches of human culture one by one, you can see where we stand, behind all other civilized nations. No one can doubt that in science, letters, industry, commerce, education, public order, work habits, we lag France, Germany, England, Switzerland, Belgium, Holland, America. But when one comes to try to sum this up, there is always someone to say that nevertheless we have a *certain something* that makes us still superior. Well, if this *certain something* really exists, we must show what it is if we want anyone to believe it is real and if we are to get any benefit from it. But if this certain something exists only to excuse us from the infinite toil and trouble and effort by which other nations earn their civilizations, then far better not to have the possession of this mysterious lamentable gift at all.[17]

Villari was quite a different kind of man from the poet Carducci or a philosopher such as Croce. Along with Giuseppe Ferraro, Vilfredo Pareto, Roberto Ardiga, Gaetano Trezza, and others, he found orientation not in Italy's literary past but in Comte, Taine, David Strauss, Spencer, and Darwin, in science and social science. As Asor Rosa has pointed out, as early as 1864 Villari declared that Italy too had its own glorious heritage in science, in Macchiavelli, Galileo, Vico. But Italy had lost that thread and would not recover it by pretending that it still possessed a "certain something" that excused it from learning from others and from pursuing its course with toil and trouble.

Another of these new men, Cesare Lombroso, destined for fame as inventor of a new social science called "criminology," surpassed Villari in blunt scorn for the fantasy of Italian superiority:

One would have to be blind, ten times blind, not to see . . . for all our absurd need always to be Number One, that we are in fact last . . . last as to morality, as to wealth, as to education, industrial and agricultural vitality, last in equity and justice, above all last in the well-being of our poor, those from whom a people's real happiness derives as it does from the poor in Switzerland or Norway. And in what are we first? Lands lying waste and malarial, endemic sicknesses, crime, the burden of debt. I don't for a minute imagine these evils can be dispelled in one fell swoop, but let us not, dear Lord, in our vanity, let them swell, let us not, with still more medieval violence, deepen the natural differences between our classes that misery has already rendered so sharp and dolorous.[18]

Of course the need to believe in a saving "certain something" in Italy would not disappear simply from the criticisms of social science. Indeed, as an essentially dialectical product of Italy's frustrating history, the need to believe would be reaffirmed with heartfelt insistence by the most implacable critic of the traditional literary intellectual, Antonio Gramsci himself, and in a far darker hour than Villari or Lombroso ever knew. Meanwhile, though, neither the disaffection of the traditional intellectuals nor the harsh realism of the new positivists consolidated into a movement for effective reform. In the United States, faith in social science after the Civil War flourished for fifty years, infusing a score of great research universities, guiding a score of major politicians and, not incidentally, offering place and promise to dozens of notable women. Social science, social reform, and social housekeeping collaborated, each affirming the others. None of this happened in Italy. The new Italian social scientists had no broad institutional base. Rising in antagonism to, rather than in collaboration with, its host society, Italian social science could hardly expect to receive what little support might have been wrung from a straitened economy.

Hopes for a new beginning, then, had to be vested in resources already available in Italy, resources in the common life. Ironically, and tragically, it would be just those who sought this grounding in democratic life who would find themselves unable to collaborate at the time of Italy's maximum peril, for these were the social Catholics and the Socialists, who saw each other as antagonists.

The quarrel of Pius IX with the new Italian state had been over political authority. Pius would not concede that the Papacy ought to abstain from temporal, worldly power. On matters of economic and social substance, however, no conflicts had occurred. The church's new social fortress was now the emergent group of small farmer-industrialists in the northeast, linked to banks and other financial institutions, particularly in the Veneto. Politicians had no intention of affronting this element. Out of economic self-interest, the Vatican fully agreed with high tariffs to protect this fortress against American grain. Church and state agreed on one crucial item in politics, too. Neither had any impulse to broaden the suffrage, the politicians, ironically enough, partly out of fear of clerical influence on voters, the church out of ideological suspicion of democracy.

By the 1890s the church's interests appeared to be threatened by a movement rising outside the government. An Italian Socialist Party was organized in 1892. Socialism appeared to be attracting the slowly growing industrial working class and the farm laborers as well. The church had set up its Opera, a program of work among laity, and also a program to counter rising new "red" labor unions with Catholic-sponsored "white" ones, which quickly made headway among the women textile workers.[19] The largest official move came in an encyclical, *Rerum novarum*, from a new pope, Leo XIII. Promulgated in 1891, with its praise for "corporatism," emphasis upon an "organic" model of society, defense of a tutelary hegemony for the church, and of course hostility to an independent labor movement, *Rerum novarum* announced the return of the church to Italian politics.[20] It also signaled a program for Catholic activism elsewhere, especially in France and Germany.

All this repeated the standard Vatican approach of proceeding from high to low, of claiming paternal authority for the hierarchy over the people. A younger generation of Catholics, mostly university-trained and usually of bourgeois or otherwise middle-class rather than aristocratic or peasant background, found the Vatican's approach too defensive. To them the faith ought be expressed in a positive quest for social justice and the common good. Traditional Catholic leadership, one of them said, seemed "almost afraid of the people."[21] Socialism must indeed be resisted since, with its doctrine of class struggle, it divides the people, but Catholicism must identify itself with the people. Certainly this movement among educated middle-class Catholics did not begin to grant that social renewal might come from below. It did not seek its guidance from the popular piety that had shown itself in millenarians such as Davide Lazzaretti and the Benevento Band earlier in the century, let alone popular ideas about "Jesu socialistà." Yet some of the new "democratic Christians" began to feel that powerful elements within the official church wished only to coopt the new currents of social Catholicism for the sake of the old Church Triumphant. Father

Romolo Murri, well aware of how many ordinary Italians thought of themselves as both Catholic and socialist, felt a new strategy essential. This double loyalty was nicely shown in the declaration of a farm worker printed in March 1899, by the democratic Christian weekly *Il Popolo italiano*:

I believe, from the Holy Spirit and Holy Scripture, that socialism is simply a means by which God carries Catholicism to its goal, defined by Jesus Christ our Savior. . . . God founded humanity on the family, therefore made property social, that is, one, a symbol of divinity. But Satan . . . divided property . . . Socialism is the sign of the coming of Jesus Christ for which all Christians pray every day.[22]

Murri wanted to tap the feelings of such people rather than combat them.

Had a Catholic socialist movement flourished, its significance for women most probably would have soared. Perhaps the most sensitive lines of battle for democratic Catholicism were drawn among women. As the "white labor" unions that were intended to keep women workers uncontaminated by socialism grew, some of them took on autonomy, inducing the church to send in waves of nuns to try to return the working girls to docility. "In response to revolutionary songs the Catholic working girls found nothing more galvanizing than the Te Deum; to the somewhat childish and exhibitionist cool of the socialist girls—cigarettes, a flask or two, some cuss words—the Catholic girls responded with 'for shame,' anathemas, ostentatious devotions." A process of indefinite potential for women's sense of identity had begun. In some democratic Christian circles, women of unmistakable feminist inclinations emerged, though still Catholic—Adelaide Coari, Adele Colombo, Angiolina Dotti, Pierina Corbetta, and others.

Father Murri's fall and the collapse of the Catholic democratic movement followed from the higher politics of the Vatican under Pius X.[23] In his encyclical of 1907, directed against "modernism" and "Americanism," Pius registered a sharp refusal to tolerate any further growth in popular lay influence within the church. At the same time he was setting a new course in Italy. By 1913 a kind of treaty of reconciliation between state and church, the Gentiloni Pact, was ratified, following which Catholic men were encouraged to vote in state elections.[24] The purpose was not to advance Father Murri's hopes, but those hopes had been picked up by another dissident young priest, Don Luigi Sturzo, who by 1905 had urged not only that Catholics participate in politics, but that they organize their own political party.[25] This was to be a laymen's party, free of manipulation by the hierarchy, a party acting independently of priests. Sturzo called for a Catholic People's Party;

the party would one day be known as the Partito Popolare Italiano. When the PPI reached its high point in 1919, with the second highest vote cast for any of the competing parties, it would endorse woman suffrage. But in this it would not have the blessing of the Vatican. The Vatican had signaled how it meant to participate in Italian politics in the pact of 1913, from which the last thing it wanted was a movement of Catholic democratic socialism.

Other young men of educated, middle-class, bourgeois background headed in a quite different direction, toward Marxist Socialism. Like Carducci and the young literary men, Filippo Turati felt himself affected by a general national malaise. At twenty-three he wrote a friend of his "restless irresolution" and "desperate fatigue," of his "disorganized brain."[26] In the Italy of 1881 he, like his fellows, seemed to find little to live for. Turati went on, however, to find purpose in socialism and in the party to which he devoted the rest of his life.

In a generous passage, Benedetto Croce once credited this new socialism with restoring Italy itself to life:

The ferment caused by the reception of Marxian socialism . . . could not give back to Italy the spirit of romanticism, idealism, and the Risorgimento, because there is no going back to the past . . . but it did raise her from the depths into which she had sunk when the spiritual force of her heroic age had spent itself. . . . With the Marxians, Macchiavelli returned to Italy. In the opinion of foreigners, Italians had always had him on their minds; but in fact he had been forsaken and forgotten since the middle of the seventeenth century.[27]

According to Croce, Marxism offered Italy a reason for hope. Evils that the new realism and scientific analysis could expose but not prescribe for came to be seen as the fruit of determinant causes open to politics. The ideas and will of men acting on a long-range outlook would matter. The determinisms of Spencer and Darwin and "nature" evaporated. The socialism expounded by Turati and the journal he founded, *Critica Sociale*, was, Croce agreed, "heretical," but since this heresy served Italian republicanism, democracy, and liberalism, that was "to its honor." Croce did not neglect to point out that one man had set about these revisions with systematic theoretical as well as practical political intent—namely, himself.

The young Turati of the 1880s doubtless engaged in wishful flights on the virtues of a "working class," with which he was not acquainted and which in any case barely existed yet in Italy. Far more important, he did not engage in the equal and opposite denigration of all things "bourgeois" that constituted the essential motive power of many young radicals in the nineteenth century. The lifelong leader of the "reformist" wing of the Socialist Party in its perennial debate with the "revolutionaries," Turati held steadily to his sense that democratic socialism in

Italy would not emerge as a consequence of some breakdown of capitalism but as an evolution of the heritage of republican democratic liberalism, an evolution impelled by the growing class of industrial workers. When Antonio Gramsci came to brood upon a "national people," he remained linked with this early reformist socialism.

None of this meant that Marxism in Italy would be free of its own dilemmas. The Socialist Party (PSI), founded in 1892, set out to win industrial workers and form industrial unions. So long as Italian industry itself remained paltry, however, the base for the party remained narrow. Turati and his colleagues were ideologically committed to democracy.[28] Yet expansion of the franchise could well mean a surge in antisocialist votes from the Catholic workers in the white unions and the illiterate peasants in the south, both presumably obedient to priestly instruction. The PSI could hardly oppose votes for its own key constituency, male blue-collar workers in the new factories, but woman suffrage was another matter. Marxist ideology affirmed gender equality; and Turati's closest woman associate in the PSI, Anna Kuliscioff— Russian by birth, Italian by choice—persistently pressed him to come out for woman suffrage. Turati favored it in private, but he could never free himself from political calculations that held him back through all the years before World War I.[29] One problem was the specter of the priests. More subtle but probably more powerful was another factor internal to the party. Turati had no reason to imagine that blue-collar industrial workers favored woman suffrage. As heavy industry began to appear between 1900 and 1914, the workers in steel, metallurgy, autos, and so on knew well enough what they wanted. They wanted full-time wages adequate to support a family. Well aware of the conditions in the textile mills, the last thing they wanted was for their wives and daughters to have to work there. As a reformist party, the PSI had no quarrel with any of this. Nor, Turati believed, was his task to ponder endlessly a strategy for the day of capitalist collapse, but rather to improve conditions for workers here and now. Of course the PSI hoped to attract women working in the textile mills, too, as well as the *braccianti*—laborers, both men and women—in the Po countryside, but because of the positive response of the early industrial workers to PSI efforts, they were the prime constituency, and their family-oriented goals shaped his political calculation.

The deepest conundrum for the PSI was economic. Clearly, the textile mills and sugar factories of early Italian industry could not have survived without low wages. As heavier industry began to appear, even paying the low wages it did, it could make no headway in international markets. The temptation of reform Marxism, eager to win higher wages, shorter hours, and better working conditions for workers as soon as possible, was to agree to a policy of protection for Italy, closing it off from international capitalism and foreign competition. Yet nothing at all indicated that Italy could draw itself up into industrial modernity by its own bootstraps. For the still inchoate revolutionaries, the question was irrelevant. The time for Italy to seal herself off under Socialist leadership was after, not before, the breakdown of capitalism. This outlook remained profoundly repugnant to Turati and his colleagues, for the whole point of socialism had been its restoration of hope in Italy's own resources, not its prediction of Italy's failure. Ironically, when the PSI did finally split, in 1920, into two wings, it was not over what to do about a breakdown, but whether or not a breakdown had occurred.

Neither the new social scientists nor the social Catholics nor the Socialists of the PSI made an effective entry into politics. The social Catholics were dragged down by a past they could not shake; the PSI could base its actions only on a future that was refusing to hasten; while the social scientists, in effect, had only themselves to offer as experts. The undertow dragging politics toward rule by police was dangerous; Rudini and Pelloux might be followed by a tyrant who knew his business. It remains a question whether it was out of some inner logic of Italian politics or sheer luck that prewar Italy was saved from this fate by a man of consummate parliamentary talents, Giovanni Giolotti.

Democratization: Men Only

Italy's Franklin D. Roosevelt: so has at least one historian characterized Giovanni Giolitti.[30] Dominant during the years 1901–14, Giolitti practiced a pragmatism—called *trasformismo*—free of anxiety over ideological and tactical consistency. Offering high tariffs to the new northern industrialists, he then offered high wages to their workers, expecting both to see their mutual self-interest. While encouraging unions in the north, where they fit into a scheme for economic progress, he harassed them in the south, where they did not. After pursuing a policy of "opening to the left," appealing to the Socialists, Giolitti later turned around, faced right, and made his deals with the Catholics. Presumably respectful of normal political bargaining, nonetheless, when his northern support proved inadequate to sustain solid parliamentary majorities, he exploited the pathetic vulnerabilities of politics in the south by offering bribes and gross patronage that could only further corrupt a world of *clientelismo* and *mafia*. All of this might seem both more and less than Rooseveltian. If both Giolitti and Roosevelt could be said to have found no truly effective economic policy, both could be said to have postponed, through political agility, the problem of the economy for a later day. So far as their economies were concerned, both were rescued by war. Giolitti, however, never won, or tried to win, the charismatic personal stature through which Roosevelt's revivification of politics was achieved. Yet Giolitti, too, impelled a dramatic democratization of Italian politics.

Italian suffrage had remained extremely narrow right into the twentieth century. Seventy-five percent of Italians were still illiterate in the 1890s, and illiteracy remained the barrier to a widened suffrage in the minds of liberals who might otherwise have combined to expand it. Illiteracy remained widespread, especially in the south, to 1912. But Giolitti pushed through new rules that swelled the eligible voters from around 3,300,000 in 1912 to 8,670,000 in 1913, one of the most abrupt democratizations in western European history.[31] Giolitti realized that the new voters would not constitute a bloc. They would be divided by region, class, religious outlook, special interest. Moreover, expanding the suffrage would help solve the Catholic question. Although still a man of the Risorgimento, convinced that Italy must never be hostage to the Vatican, Giolitti also understood that the Catholic boycott of the state must be ended one day. Both his opening to the right and his suffrage bill were intended to draw Catholics into the parliamentary system and to his "party," and to head off any Vatican temptations to form a new, separate, hard Catholic party. In effect, in a way neither the social Catholics nor the Socialists nor the social scientists could do, Giolitti had acted to vastly enhance the political unity of the nation.

As the franchise was broadened, women had been left out.[32] Giolitti had no ideological convictions on the matter one way or the other. Had granting women the vote served his political ends, he would have pushed for woman's suffrage. But votes for women would have spelled trouble, not strength. While those who remained social Catholics still welcomed women as voters, and would do so nine years later in Luigi Sturzo's PPI, those Vatican Catholics with whom Giolitti had negotiated his pact of reconciliation were ideologically hostile to woman suffrage, and Giolitti had no reason for taking on conflict with those with whom he was seeking concord. To his left, meanwhile, the Socialists whom he had at first courted, then spurned, still harbored their own reservations about women as voters, particularly once the suffrage had been so dramatically expanded. Most new women voters would not be predominantly bourgeois women or even the wives of good socialist blue-color workers, but the presumably priest-ridden women of the great peasant masses of the south. Both the potential for active conflict, then, and the absence of active support stranded the small vanguard of liberals and feminists who favored woman suffrage.

Nonetheless, Giolitti's embrace of near-universal manhood suffrage held great potential for Italian women. Once the bar of illiteracy excluding the vast majority of both men and women from the polls had been struck down, it could not be used against women alone. In addition, once Giolitti had drawn Catholics back into the normal political process, objections to women on the basis of their religiousness would have to be much more modulated and subtle to satisfy standards of political decorum. Exploiting this potential might prove possible quickly, as 1919 was to show. Resistance to exploiting it might, on the other hand, prove enduring, as Palmiro Togliatti was to learn as late as 1948. At the minimum, though, by 1913 the ground had been cleared for a straightforward confrontation with gender in Italian politics.

Giolitti's economic policy held steady. Despite a slowdown after 1908, lasting until the war, he persisted in trying to encourage heavy industry, shipyards, durable goods manufacturing, and mechanization of production. Cost accounting alone decreed that this meant further concentration of the industrial sector in the northwest Turin corner of the nation. An Italy tautly stretched between modernization and backwardness grew ever more evident. Giolitti's politics, drawing on an ever broadening spectrum from industrial unionists on the left to Vatican Catholics on the right, served to contain this tension, presumably on the thesis that if breakdown could be held off indefinitely, sooner or later an economic tide would rise to lift the nation from its premodern "Mediterranean" reefs and float it onto the high seas of affluence and major nationhood. In the final reckoning, Giolitti's politics had bought time. Unfortunately for Italy, the time he bought would not stay bought.

The Surge of a People's Italy: Men and Women Together

For Italy, war might mean stimulus to a lagging economy. Women might be called on for war work and, should all go well, might go on working in an enhanced postwar economy. Naturally, it would be important to emerge from the war as a winner. Giolitti himself did not want Italy to go to war. He sensed that, win or lose, Italy was more likely to be tossed about by the unpredictable storms released in any conflict between the major powers. Taking Libya in 1911 was one thing; engaging in a vast and indeterminate conflict was another. He had already begun to disentangle Italy from its agreements with Germany and Austria. Then, in the very month of Sarajevo—July 1914—the country underwent another of those popular outbreaks that had marked it for a century, this time not in the dim, hopeless south but in Emilia and Romagna in the north.[33] Peasant leagues boycotting middlemen erupted in violence, then strikes broke out among urban workers. Spontaneous "republics" popped up everywhere. The old specter of disintegration into that parochialism which, in Macchiavelli's mind at least, had been the very definition of Italy's woe, stalked the land again. The most notable new leader in this "Red Week" was a new recruit to the gospel of class struggle, Benito Mussolini.

With plenty of domestic reasons for pursuing neutrality, the government (headed by Antonio Salandra from March 1914, Giolitti having had to resign owing to a defection within his cabinet) negotiated a shift in its alliances. By May 1915 it was ready to join the war, but against only Austria, not Germany. Even so, a parliamentary majority resisted. When asked after the war why he had gone to war, Salandra explained that it had been "to raise Italy to the status of a Great Power."[34] Yet neither before nor after May 1915 did he try to shape a national government that might have tapped broader and deeper emotional resources. Until the devastating retreat of the army at Caporetto, the Italian soldier was still being treated as he always had been, as a peasant-object rather than a patriot-person. After that defeat, leaders hastened to provide entertainments for him on leave and improve his basic comforts. Promises were made: after the war peasants would have land, and artisans and factory workers better pay and jobs. World War I was really the first time that an Italian government had to respond to the masses directly. The wartime army itself put ordinary Italians from the whole country in touch with one another, and the condition of the army seemed to register the condition of the country. Great antiwar food riots broke out in Turin in August 1917. Women working in the wartime factories there were conspicuous in these riots.

The seeds of mass organization and mass action had been planted before the war, with Giolitti's blessing, in the form of the unions among textile, metal, and auto workers. Most arresting, a National Federation of Workers on the Land—Federterra—had enrolled 125,000 members by 1914. While the wartime governments did not try to suppress such organizations, wartime exigencies inevitably checked their expansion; but the war only kept popular feeling pent up. Seven thousand strong in 1914, the metal and auto workers union, part of the Socialists' General Confederation of Labor (CGL), soared to 104,000 in 1919, to 160,000 in 1920. CGL textile workers doubled in membership between 1918 and 1920, from 71,000 to 145,000. These were of course the "red" textile unions, by contrast with the "white." Membership in all CGL unions passed two million by 1920. Catholic labor unions swelled, too, many of them linked to Don Luigi Sturzo's new social movement. Most sensational of all, Federterra, based in the valley of the Po in Romagna, tripled its 1914 membership to 760,000 by 1920. It was the single largest autonomous mass organization of Italians in history.[35]

The translation of this populistic energy into effective politics was another matter. The postwar government of Francesco Nitti responded to the new atmosphere with plans for ameliorating the labor market through modest old-age pension plans, some insurance for the unemployed, even a start on health insurance. But in the elections of November 1919 these efforts were not rewarded. Instead, Sturzo's new PPI got the second largest number of votes and seats in parliament, and the Socialists the most. The Socialists, however, had just fallen victim to the millenarianism in their own ideology. Up until then, Turati and his reformists had succeeded in checking the "maximalists" with their fixation on the fantasy of a revolutionary transformation, but events far away proved irresistible. In October 1919 the party went through one of its periodic debates.

Turati went on explaining: "We must prepare our hearts and minds for the advent of socialism. But at the same time we must work for the gradual transformation of society." A voice interrupted him: "That's too long." Turati answered: "If you know a quicker way, tell me." And many voices came back: "Russia! Russia! Lenin!"[36]

The maximalists took control, and the party that won the most votes next month was, in the grip of its ideological certitude, unprepared to participate in any government. Soon it would split openly, a new Italian Communist Party (PCI) taking its place to the left of the PSI. Support for woman suffrage, which at last had been explicitly affirmed by the party in the November 1919 elections, thereby led to nothing.

Following the elections of November 1919, parliamentary government became difficult. The largest single bloc, PSI, was unavailable for any coalition. The second largest, PPI, was a house very possibly built on sand. The remaining elements, a congeries of liberal leftists, liberal centrists, democrats, nationalists, and rightists, while in sum a majority, were hardly a coherent one. Postwar inflation raised the temperature of all. Popular discontent, mediated through the unions, seemed to suggest the possibility of extraparliamentary confrontations threatening landholders and even industry itself. The climactic moment arrived in September 1920. Four hundred thousand metal workers peaceably occupied their factories, mostly in Turin but also in Milan and a few other northern cities. Now seventy-eight years old, Giolitti was once again prime minister. He turned to his old tactic of letting workers and industrialists test each other's strength, then come to a realization of their common interests. To industrialists who protested this hands-off policy, he sardonically offered to recover their factories for them by means of the army's artillery. The leader of the new *Fasci di Combattimento*, Benito Mussolini, met with one of the top labor leaders, Bruno Buozzi. According to Buozzi, Mussolini too was neutral. It mattered little to him, Buozzi related later, "if the factories were in the hands of the workers rather than the industrialists." If the occupation developed into a constructive revolutionary movement, he would be on the side of the "revolutionaries."[37]

For labor union leaders and the leaders of the Socialist Party, the occupation of the factories posed a mighty question: had a revolutionary moment arrived or not? In Turin the workers began to work the factories. They scheduled shifts, coordinated supplies, controlled inventory. Railroad workers began to deliver coal, iron, and other raw materials. Workers' committees began to arrange for sales, including deliveries to the Soviet Union. Antonio Gramsci had observed Turin's workers for years as they created shop councils to manage their work. He thought they were transforming "a primitive and mechanical human aggregate into an organic brotherhood, a living creation." Gramsci hoped for a constructive result: "[The] workers themselves must build the first historic cell of the proletarian revolution which thrusts through the general crisis with all the irresistible power of a force of nature."[38] In Genoa too, also dominated by a few large operations, some movement toward actual worker operation appeared.

The party and union leaders could not follow a politics based on a "force of nature." They had choices to make. Meeting in Turin, the CGL union leaders asked the leaders of the party if they were ready to take revolutionary action. In reply, Palmiro Togliatti warned that only simultaneous action on a national scale could possibly prevail. Turin could not act alone. The next day, however, after intense debate, the party leaders proposed to take command and carry the movement to the nation in hopes of finding widespread support. Meeting separately, the union leaders now resolved that their goal was not in fact revolution, but simply union control over working conditions. That evening, union and party leaders met together again. Some union leaders, saying they were unwilling to take responsibility "for throwing the proletariat to suicide," offered to resign, evidently so that the party leaders could lead the proletariat to that fate. Party leaders at last realized that, without solid and public union support, revolutionary action would indeed be suicidal. In the impasse, a motion was proposed to empower the party to take over the workers' movement and proceed to revolution. By a vote of 590,000 to 410,000 (based on each union's membership), the motion lost.

Historians of the Left have since debated whether any of this constituted a failure of nerve on the part of Socialist or union leaders or both, or if, instead, it was sheer realism on the part of those who prevailed. No historians have ever argued that the model pulsating in many minds—"Russia! Russia! Lenin!"—was relevant. Lenin seized power in the shambles of all other powers. No one claimed in 1920 that Italy was in a state of collapse. Some simply hoped that revolution would prove the wish of an effective democratic mass. Yet the very vote of the union leaders showed the lack of anything like a consensus even on the populistic left. Had the factory union leaders voted alone, they would have sanctioned the party leaders' revolutionary effort. The decisive majority against it had come from Federterra, the farm workers' union. In Russia no democratic vote had been taken by Lenin. In Italy, on the other hand, the democratic vote was split.

Ironically, the first broad violence committed by the growing fascist forces was visited not on the revolutionary industrial workers but on Federterra and the farm workers. Federterra looked to the expropriation and socialization of the land, and therefore constituted a mortal peril to small landholding farmers in the north. These farmers found it easy to act as *squadristi*, as the fascist strike forces liked to call themselves, whereas the farm workers in their local meeting places were particularly vulnerable. Fascist beatings, fire bombings, and shootings proliferated nowhere more than in the country towns and crossroads of the lower Po. With no capacity to defend itself, Federterra melted from more than 760,000 members to less than 300,000 in a year. Many urban Italians had no idea of what was going on. As for the industrial centers, split even prior to the events of September 1920, the PSI had no effective leadership to offer. The metalworkers fell from 160,000 to 129,000, the textile workers from 145,000 to 88,000 in a year.[39] Luigi Sturzo's PPI, unable to collaborate with the PSI or Federterra, and soon undercut by a Vatican that had never watched its victories with anything less than suspicion, dwindled in a dying dance of its own. The aged Giolitti, returning to the prime ministry one last time, again tried his trick of "transforming" adversaries into supporters: he would draw Mussolini and the Fascists into the cabinets and so constitutionalize them. Since Mussolini, in less than ten years of political life, had declared himself for and against socialism, for and against nationalism, for and against war, industrialists, labor, and religion, the Fascist leader looked like another exponent of pragmatism. The failure of the forces opposed to Mussolini to find a younger, fresher, harder man than Giolitti, itself testified to the impasse into which Italian politics had got itself.

No one could possibly say whether the collapse of the workers' movement in September 1920 spelled good or ill for Italian women. Certainly the women of Turin who rushed with their children to ring the factories their men were occupying felt short-term relief from the fear that their men might be consumed in a social conflagration. On the other hand, under Fascism these same workers were stripped of their unions, and their families underwent a squeeze on wages. Presumably, had the workers' movement prevailed, women of the bourgeois and middle classes would have suffered with their men. As for the vast majority of peasant and farm women, Italian revolutionaries had as little clarity on agricultural policy as Lenin and his Bolsheviks were showing. Only pure ideology could presume to know that revolution would have liberated Italian women, as August Bebel and the Marxists had promised that it would all women.

There was an alternative to Italian stagnation more available than "Russia! Russia!" It was spelled out in a Fascist prison,but Antonio Gramsci had formulated the essence of it before. Having observed the workers of Turin during and after the war, he had visualized a "humanism of work."

Work alone produces moral impulses. Work is the crucible in which are volatized these spiritual powers that can give shape to life. . . . Country, family, humanity, goodness, justice—all these, in order to become real, have to be given form every day in all those slightest acts requiring effort and sacrifice, acts that also bring satisfaction and joy. They must be transformed, these words, into tools, into machines for action. Morality consists of suiting the smallest actions to the largest goals, and thus a life of such activity, life as an unending rosary of daily deeds, is necessary.[40]

Explicitly formulated as early as 1920, this humanism of work drew Gramsci into a lyric celebration of basic Italian character. As Joseph Femia has shown, Gramsci sought escape from Leninist models of revolution. In his concept of "hegemony," he offered ideas for popular participation before revolution, and he tried persistently to imagine means for such participation after revolution. But all this supposedly "universal" reflection was heavily influenced by his feelings for Italian history, the Italian folk, an Italian nation:

Must the political movement of national unification . . . necessarily issue in nationalism and militaristic imperialism? One could argue that this result is anachronistic, anti-historical, that is, artificial and of no long life, really against all the traditions of Italy, Roman and Catholic. Italian traditions are cosmopolitan. . . . Mazzini and Gioberti both sought to fuse the national movement with the cosmopolitan tradition, to create the myth of a mission of Italy reborn in a new European and world Cosmopolis. But their myth was verbal, rhetorical . . . without roots in the present. . . . Modern day expansion is powered by finance-capitalism. In present-day Italy "man" is either the man-of-capital or the man-of-work. Italy's expansion can only be that of the man-of-work, and the intellectual who speaks for this man-at-work will not be the intellectual of tradition, swollen up with rhetoric and memories of the past. Traditional Italian cosmopolitanism must become a modern cosmopolitanism, assuring the conditions for the development of the Italian man-at-work in whatever part of the world he finds himself. He will not be a citizen of the world in the old Roman sense or the old Catholic sense but rather as a producer of civility and civilization. The Italian tradition will be perpetuated, not in the old relation of traditional citizen and traditional intellectual but in a new dialectic between working people and their intellectuals. The Italian people is that people who, as a "nation," is most interested in a modern cosmopolitanism. Not only the workers but the peasants, and especially the southern peasants, make up this people. National collaboration in a reconstruction of the whole economy is in the tradition of Italy and the Italian people, not to win hegemony or to expropriate the fruit of the labors of others, but to live and grow precisely as the Italian people. . . . Nationalism of the French sort is an excrescence on Italian history, the product of people whose heads face backwards as among the damned in Dante. The "mission" of the Italian people lies in resuming Roman and medieval cosmopolitanism, but in its advanced and modern form. This is a proletarian nation . . . proletarian because it has constituted a reserve army for foreign capital, because, along with the Slavic people, it has given workmen to all the world. Precisely as such it must lead in reorganizing not only the Italian but the whole world of work, a whole world it has helped create with its own hands.[41]

At every appropriate polemical moment Gramsci continued to affirm his debt to Marxism as an "international" movement. "[Our] party is a single section of a greater party, of a world-wide party." "An international character is essential for a workers' party; without that, ideological and practical degeneration among both leaders and rank and file is inevitable."[42] Yet this affirmation remained empty and abstract, when compared to the emotional, indeed mystical faith in Italian experience that he carried to prison and that sustained him there.

The ordinary Italian people in whom Gramsci vested his populistic love were the peasants. Though as a Sardinian by birth and upbringing he knew very well the ugliness, deformities, and brutalities in Italian peasant life, he nevertheless saw the humanism of work emerging as a consequence, not of the discipline of industrialization, but of the persistence into the industrial era of the old Italian. "The new type of worker will be a repetition, in different form, of peasants in the village." Mystical insight revealed that Italian workers possessed a special readiness for modern industrial culture:

In reality skilled workers in Italy have never, as individuals or through union organizations, actively or passively opposed innovations leading toward lowering of costs, rationalization of work . . . or more perfect forms of automation. . . . [It] was precisely the workers who brought into being newer and more modern industrial requirements . . . and upheld these strenuously.[43]

Italy, then, despite Pasquale Villari, did possess a "certain something" that fitted it above all others—except possibly the "Slavic peoples"—

for welcoming industry and technology, since that certain something meant that industrial technology, rather than imposing itself on man, would be converted by humanistic work into a "living creation."

In Gramsci's vision Italy's certain something included women, not because of Marxist mandates but because of Italian culture. Certainly *man-at-work* included *woman-at-work*. Still more important, though, was the fact that humanist work provided the foundation for equanimity in the deepest relationship of the sexes, as Italian peasants showed in their history:

The peasant who returns home after a long and hard day's work wants the "veneram facilem parabilemque" of Horace. . . . He loves his own woman, sure and unfailing, who is free from affectation and doesn't play little games about being seduced or raped in order to be possessed. It might seem that in this way the sexual function has been mechanised, but in reality we are dealing with the growth of a new form of sexual union shorn of the bright and dazzling colour of the romantic tinsel of the petit bourgeois and the Bohemian layabout.[44]

The honest, healthy, home-loving, monogamous union of the countryside was ideally suited for the factory-based cities of the industrial future. Protected against the tinsel and chaff, the decadences and artificialities of the bourgeois marketplace, it would underwrite indefinite progress by means of humanized technological innovation. For modern as for premodern Italians, life would continue to be a "rosary of daily deeds," unending, eternal.

Gramsci's Italian populism pointed the way to a Via Italiana for Italian Communism. Palmiro Togliatti proclaimed it after 1945. Although Gramsci himself continued to insist on the primacy of workers—rural and urban—in a revolutionary movement, Togliatti would herald the Italian Communist Party (PCI) as a "mass" party, that could include shopkeepers, small landowners, everyone but the magnates. Although Gramsci continued to regard parliaments as tools for the ruling classes, the PCI explicitly presented itself as a parliamentary party. Whereas Gramsci continued to insist that revolution must inevitably involve some "rupture" in history, some violence, the PCI would explicitly promise a peaceful, parliamentary, democratic route to revolution. Ideological critics of these postwar policies would one day criticize Gramsci himself for opening the door. They would miss a deeper point. Gramsci never ceased being an *Italian* revolutionary.

Fascist Italy: Women First? Last? Always?

Having themselves intensified the disorder of Italy during 1920–22, Mussolini's Fascists took power with the mandate to restore order.[45] At first Mussolini governed within the bounds of the parliamentary system, devising mixed cabinets and responding to opposition. By 1925 the time seemed ripe for liquidating parliamentary democratic government in favor of Fascism's unopposed rule. Fascists were a mass party, Mussolini declared, and it followed that no organizations independent of the party could be tolerated. The labor unions were dissolved. Autonomous social organizations were prohibited. Fascist organizations were set up for the professions, schools, youth groups, and recreation.

Had unity alone been Italian Fascism's purpose, Mussolini could simply have withdrawn Italy as far as possible from the world, in resistance to any further modernization and industrialization. As Antonio Salazar's Portugal would show, nothing inherent in a modern right-wing dictatorship impelled it to engage in expansion rather than isolation. For Italy, the question remained open whether its best course was to try still to become a Mediterranean Germany or even just a France, equipped with metallurgy, durable-goods plants, and the mills, yards, and foundries of a standard big-power nation. As the prospect of electric power emerged, to make up for Italy's lack of coal and oil, a new strategy more directly adapted to Italy's primary need could be considered. Italians needed jobs. Capital-intensive heavy industry might increase wealth on a national accounting, but labor-intensive industries were needed to put the surplus peasant population to work. Light manufacturing, producing finished silk goods, finished textiles, gloves, shoes, light utensils, objects for decoration and furnishing, disposable conveniences, and crafted luxuries might hold competitive promise. None of this would have been likely to revive Carlo Cattaneo's vision of a decentralized harmonious Italy. In Spain, Francisco Franco persecuted decentralizing regional autonomists implacably. Yet Mussolini himself sought Italian self-sufficiency in wheat and might well have calculated the benefits of multiplying jobs rather than industrial output. But it was almost certainly too late for him, or for any leader, to turn deliberately back to some policy of a "little Italy." That would have been to ask the industrialists of Turin, the shipbuilders of Genoa, and the bankers of Milan to forgo their own ambitions. Fascism without FIAT, Ansaldo, and Pirelli would have been an empty shell. Italy had gone too far to turn around. Yet Mussolini rightfully regarded his policy less as a response to these powerful constituents than as an act of heroic realism. "We live in a barren century," he told parliament, "even a sad one if you like. But we accept it. Why? Because we can't change it. This is the century of capitalism." He carried his realism to the most emphatic point possible: he confronted a kind of generalized fear that Italy's very identity might be lost.

Maybe you believe that all this is destroying the poetry of life? No! It is only inspiring another kind. Every century has its own poetry. . . . The new poetry puts life on another plane. Where there is still mind, soul, spirit, poetry will shape things; things will never create poetry. Some may say, "But we, we are Italians! . . . We are, we want to be a brilliant exception!" But we must recognize the facts. The folklore of nations is in retreat. Why? Capitalism is standardizing life everywhere. National differences are disappearing. Up and down, we are all living to the same rhythms.[46]

The decisive point in Mussolini's development as a politician had been his turn from the international traditions of socialism to nationalism, a turn that had helped fracture the PSI after 1912. Presumably he had gone on to become an Italian nationalist devoted to Italy as a nation with its own past and traditions, its own nature, its own certain something. But now, in this speech of May 15, 1925, the nation of which Mussolini was becoming *il Duce*, the leader, was not distinguished by its *Italianità*, by what had burned in the minds of Mazzini and the Risorgimento leaders, but rather, as he would reiterate in speech after speech, by its need to catch up with other nations, to compete with other nations on the same terms, to become like other nations. A nationalist, he was no longer an Italian nationalist. His relationship with the industrialists would be one of no narrow expediency, but of broad mutual dependency.

The context in which Mussolini had delivered himself of this harsh realism was a debate over votes for women. Fascism did not come to power vaunting some return to ancient gender verities, some scorn for modern ideas as to women's proper role. During the electoral campaign of 1919, the small band calling themselves Fascists had announced that woman's suffrage suited Fascist principles completely.[47] Between November 1919 and the march on Rome in October 1922—years of Fascist *squadristi* in the villages and streets, and of Fascist parliamentarians' obstructionism—Mussolini had many women followers, both passive enthusiasts and fervent activists. Fascism's heroes included women. Mussolini had no need to forsake any of the components of the populistic surge of exasperation with growing parliamentary confusion. He had no need to cater to traditional Catholic gender ideology.

There were, of course, many fascisms, not just one. Some fascists were complaining about women workers as early as 1919. The "clerical fascists" who would see their concerns gratified in the Concordat of 1929 expounded traditional views of women's proper place. As time would show, some fascist ideologues revealed such feelings toward modern women as to qualify them, not so much as traditionalists but as active misogynists. But one fascism was Mussolini's, however that too might vary over time, and what he expounded up to 1925 was what he prided himself on as realism, frank, courageous, free of Italian sentimentalities. Plans for full woman's suffrage had been derailed in parliament since 1919, but plans to grant women the vote in "administrative"—meaning local—elections had been discussed for several years. Mussolini came before parliament in May 1925 to support a bill granting such a vote. By then parliament was controlled by the Fascists, but a majority had proved unwilling to support the bill. Mussolini meant to change their minds by demanding that they give up their old-fashioned illusions. He linked this demand with Fascism's own specific history:

I have here a stack of telegrams from fascist women's leagues—fascist women, I say—who ask for this modest right. The first carries a signature that should make us think; "Mrs. Pepe, the mother of Hugo Pepe, assassinated in Milan." The telegram says, "Strong group of fascist women and families of fallen fascists ask me to convey support for woman's vote."

But his larger argument drew from his insistence that the past be put behind them. "Gentlemen," he asked, "what century are we living in?" Inviting his Fascist colleagues to join him in clearheaded, man-to-man thinking, he proceeded to dispel the miasma that had persistently accompanied women even in liberal Italy, the miasma of gallantry. "Are we maybe still in the Middle Ages when ladies, locked up in their castles, waited on balconies for their lords to return from the crusades?" With gallantry, at once sentimental and selfish, dismissed, he went on to describe the real new world:

This is the century of capitalism. Capitalism is a definite system of social life that has drawn women in their millions from hearth and home and thrust them into factories, into offices, has immersed them violently in society. While you are frightened at the thought that every four years a woman will be dropping her ballot in the ballot box, you aren't afraid when you see women teachers, professors, lawyers, doctors methodically invading all fields of human activity. And not from whim or caprice. From necessity. This necessity is becoming ever more impelling. Times are hard, families, in order to live, require the work of two. In the morning, the man leaves the house for the factory, the woman for the office.[48]

If we assume that, in some meaningful sense, Mussolini meant what he said on May 15, 1925, what could that have been, since during the rest of the year, local elections were abolished so as to reduce local government to an arm of the Fascist state, thus abolishing not only women's but men's votes as well? As a mass democracy, Fascism dispensed with all except occasional elections. Yet Mussolini's message had not concerned woman's suffrage alone. He had expounded upon the necessity for women to work outside the home, in offices, schools, factories, hospitals, and shops of a modern capitalistic society. Whether a Fascist government had much directly to do with the rise in economic activity during the 1920s would be as hard for historians to clarify as the connection between Crispi's government and the economic surge of 1896–1908, or that between Giolitti's governments and the stagnation of 1908–14. But whatever the wishes of clerical and other traditionalists may have been, driving women out of the labor force (as distinguished from certain privileged sectors) did not serve the interests of the government. One of the principal policies of the Fascist state was to emasculate the labor unions, and women's cheap labor meshed with this effort perfectly. What Mussolini had expounded as inevitable necessity—support of the family by not one but two workers—revealed Fascism's determination to undermine a blue-collar male elite that was demanding a family wage.

Gender realism could not be sustained as policy, however. The industrial sector, flourishing through the mid-1920s, ran into trouble after 1926. Light export industries stumbled, and unemployment rose. Most of all, the great mass of Italians remained in the countryside. As a party of unity, Fascism had to confront agriculture. Despite its underlying economic irrationality, Mussolini embarked on his quest to make Italy self-sufficient in grains—the "battle for wheat." He drained the malarial Pontine swamps south of Rome—within easy distance for admiring visitors. He dug irrigation ditches and planted trees. He offered the *ruralizzazione* of Italy as his new realism. "When you hear me speak of [it], do you think I am speaking just for love of those beautiful words that I detest?"[49] No Italian leader since independence had seemed to base himself so firmly on the vast majority.

The rural idyll fitted perfectly with Mussolini's policy on religion. An Italian leader proclaiming his base in the masses could not maintain a quarrel with the Catholic church. Claims to unity would be hollow with such tension. Despite the voting pact arranged by Giolitti, the pope still sulked in his "captivity" in the Vatican. Mussolini's treaty of 1929 resolved the problem by conceding to the church territoriality in the Vatican, as well as religious teaching in the schools and autonomy for various church organizations under Catholic Action. Within church Catholicism, the central social myth had been and remained that of simple rural faith. In no way had the church allowed concessions to the "necessities" that Mussolini said had been decreed by capitalism. In church mythology, woman's place remained strictly that of helpmeet to her husband on the farmstead. Church workers were not following young Catholic women into the cities with sympathy for their problems. Catholic leaders continued to counsel Catholic women working in factories to patience and resignation. Based on mutual self-interest, the collaboration of Fascism and the Vatican cast a veil over the reality that Mussolini had earlier felt impelled to reveal.[50]

The policy of gender realism also lost out to the stress Mussolini soon began placing on another reality, that of population. During a speech on Ascension Day, 1927, he confronted those who still said Italy was overpopulated. Without quite denying that it was, he turned to present trends. From 39 per 1,000 in 1886, the birth rate had declined to 27 per 1,000 in 1926. Inference told him—correctly—that a sharper decline impended. His prime emphasis was upon reproductive geography. In urbanized Piedmont, Liguria, Tuscany, and Lombardy, where women had been marrying at a later age, marital fertility had begun its "modern" decline before 1900. Mussolini assigned these tendencies to a moral *vigliaccheria*—cowardice, ugliness, dastardliness—on the part of the "so-called superior classes," who had forsaken their village roots. In announcing next year that Fascism's task would be to determine whether Italy really had lost its soul to *edonismo, borgesimo, filisteismo*, Mussolini plainly relocated Italy's soul among the still morally intact child-producing peasants of the eternal countryside. He concluded on a ringing note of masculine identity: "Fascists of Italy! Hegel, the philosopher of the State, has said: 'He is not a man who is not a father!' "[51]

What was the point of this anxiety about population? Historians have debated—and will continue to debate—the roots of what was to become Mussolini's aggressive and expansionist foreign policy of the 1930s. On Ascension Day he simply presented a picture of an Italy outnumbered:

What are forty million Italians compared to ninety million Germans, two-hundred million Slavs? And to forty million French with their colonies with ninety million, and with forty-six million English plus four-hundred-fifty million in their empire?

By 1950, Mussolini said, Italians must number not forty but sixty million. The next year, in a preface for a book by a young German prophet of race suicide, Richard Korherr, Mussolini let nightmares run. What awaited Europe facing a Russia already 140 million strong and growing fast? And the West, facing 400 million Chinese? (But he did deny that "blacks" were at the gates of Sicily.)[52]

Certainly Mussolini understood that nothing he said or did in 1927 could change effective manpower by, say, October 1935, when he invaded Ethiopia. Moreover, the laws passed in subsequent years hardly constituted a determined effort to achieve a boom in babies. Bans against means of and information about contraception introduced in 1926 were strengthened in 1931, but patterns of evasion had already been perfected. Tax breaks for larger families enacted in 1931 and 1932 were minor. Direct bonuses for babies were raised beyond a paltry figure only in 1935, the first year in which more than trivial awards were offered to young people to marry. Although a mild bachelor tax of 1926 was renewed in 1932 and made stiffer in 1934, the real issue was delay in marriage and the taxes hardly spoke to that. The notorious prizes to superprolific mothers, awarded by Mussolini in person, were a feature of the middle to late 1930s. No data showed any of these measures to be effective. Even if they had been, only an irrational leader could have failed to realize that boy babies born between, say, 1930 and 1940 would not be available as soldiers before 1950 to 1960.[53]

Despite his warnings of a demographic crisis, for many years Mussolini hardly ever addressed Italian women directly. Then, between 1935 and 1937, he issued forth in what a modern feminist later called a "verbal landslide." In speeches from his balcony over the Piazza Venezia to more than 100,000 women in May 1936, to more than 70,000 in September, and to "oceanic" multitudes of women elsewhere, he hailed Italian women as the heart of the nation-cult itself. Having invaded Ethiopia, Italy found itself embattled at the League of Nations, threatened with economic sanctions, its strength and resolve called into question. Greeting women as mothers from whose loins the soldiers of contemporary Italy had sprung back in 1905, 1910, 1915, Mussolini aimed to stabilize mass feelings, centering them on the most unshakable base. Reciprocally, he now presented himself also as a focus for mass certitude, the wholly virile embodiment of national identity— "Mussolini, Maschio, Marito," Mussolini, He-man, Husband.[54]

The basic challenge that confronted Italian women in Fascism lay not in its economic policy or in some inherent misogyny, but in its mystifications. The blending of Mussolini's with Catholicism's celebration of country virtue hid the realities of factory, city, office. The battle of demography and exaltation of motherhood concealed the nation's inability to achieve industrial takeoff. Through the 1930s, as the regime struggled to hold off the world depression, the Fascist state intervened in the economy directly. In 1933 the Istituto per Ricostruzione Industriale (IRI) was created; it brought the state deep into banking and, in consequence, into industry itself, so that by the eve of World War II a state sector of significant dimensions had emerged in Italian capitalism. Most of these new state corporations would be carried into the postwar economy. All this was veiled by the continued mobilization of mass feelings around the cults of countryside and motherhood, and by the cult of Mussolini himself as an eminently virile, masculine leader.

The shift from the gender realism of 1925 did open the way for unrestrained ideologues such as Paolo Ardali, who in 1929, vilified modern women:

Not only Italian women but also young girls have learned from exotic romances the apology for sterile love affairs, have learned the aphrodisiac temptations of subtle, refined artificial sensual and sentimental complications. The traditional sense of home and family, rooted and firm in the hearts of Italian women, seems at times about to be blown away, like some great oak apparently good for a century but all of a sudden uprooted by a turbid flood . . . when necessity holds her the livelong day within the sacred walls of house and home, her heart remains pure. . . . Social and economic conditions have contributed to alienating the woman from the domestic life. . . . The power of fashion to enslave her seems almost like the diabolic power of evil itself.[55]

When Ardali went on to complain that a woman dressed in the new fashions did not think of the effect she had on the men she met in the streets, especially "men already close to the grave," men not prepared for *turpi pensieri* (vile thoughts), he seemed to project an image of the Fascist male as a kind of unstable combination of lust and innocence, senility and puberty, D'Annunzio and St. Francis. Drawing on the obvious implications of Ardali's lament, Ferdinando Loffredo, a true extremist in Fascist misogyny, later recommended a kind of Moslemization for Italian women:

The abolition of women's jobs must follow from two converging factors. There must be laws, but there should also be public disapproval. The woman who leaves the domestic enclosure to go to work, the woman who shows herself on the sidewalks, on the streetcars, the buses, who lives in factories and offices, must become, far more than the object of laws, the object of public reproach.[56]

Had men like Ardali and Loffredo occupied places of influence in the Fascist state, evictions of women from the workplace might have been pursued as systematic policy. The Catholic agencies to which Fascism surrendered some jurisdiction over women might have been prelude to an effort at harsh seclusion. But Fascist leaders had enough trouble trying to steer the economy toward better performance without sacrificing women's cheap labor for ideological gratification. Women did not disappear from the marketplace under Fascism; their numbers grew. But none of this was given open recognition. The facts were not accepted as reason for realistic debate. Italy's basic problem, of establishing national unity on an economic basis that offered promise to some large fraction of its people for a better life, never had yielded to realistic treatment anyway. Mussolini's own early inclination to candor and tough-minded rejection of the illusions of the past might not have worked any better. In any case, the promise of stabilization of mass feelings through the manipulation of myth proved irresistible. Most Italians, men and women alike, either supported or reconciled themselves to Mussolini's leadership. For thirteen years, from 1925 to 1938, he provided unity, security, and a modicum of economic promise.

The Phoenix: Italy from 1944 to 1948

World War I had heightened all the potentials in Italy—for industrialization, for democracy, for social conflict. World War II brought collapse. The historian Ernesto Ragionieri has described it:

The disintegration of the country went far beyond its mere division between two warring armies. Particularly in the South, the social and political collapse . . . reduced life to levels hardly anyone remembered, dissolving the economy into black markets, pre-capitalist expedients of barter and simple subsistence. The connective tissues of society dissolved, the life of the people broke up into an infinitude . . . of personal and family efforts at sheer survival.[57]

Multitudes of Italians would carry into the postwar years of recovery a searing lesson: No matter how seductive modern ideologies might be, no matter how plausible the promises of modern economy, one forsook reliance on the most elementary means of survival only at one's peril. American social scientists, blithely unacquainted with any but their own fortunate history, would one day study and indict what they called "amoral familism" widespead among Ialians as well as third-world countries, a refusal to concede claims of society and nation.[58] But family alone had offered society to those multitudes of Italians who had seen nation, community, and economy crumble in 1943–44. As an economic "miracle" emerged in the 1950s, Italians would welcome it, but they would not be persuaded that the social, economic, and even political, as well as psychological, need for the family was obsolete.

In June 1944 a kind of coalition anti-Fascist government was arranged in liberated Rome, comprising the six major party groups, from Liberals through Christian Democrats to Communists, which had actively resisted the Fascist regime during the war. Not all the triumphant Allies were eager to help all the resistants. Preoccupied—apparently sincerely—with fears of an Italy lost to Communism, Winston Churchill harassed the new government. Two of the moderate groups withdrew in protest, leaving the prime minister, Ivanoe Bonomi, trying to ride astride a monarchist horse to his far right and a Communist horse to his far left. Coalition government persisted, however, for there was no basis for any other. Bonomi soon gave way to one of the great leaders of the Italian anti-Fascist resistance, Ferruccio Parri. Parri represented the Action Party, derived from the anti-Fascist exile group Justice and Liberty, led by Carlo Rosselli in Paris in the early 1930s. With his "liberal socialism," Rosselli had been the direct heir of Giuseppi Mazzini. He too called on Italy to embody political democracy, social justice, and spiritual freedom. On Mussolini's orders, French Fascists murdered him in Paris in 1937. Leading the Action Party thereafter, Parri for a time during the war had become supreme chief of all Italian resistance forces. His elevation to the prime ministership in June 1945 evoked enthusiasm from a whole spectrum of anti-Fascist political life. His cabinet included no fewer than three heads of party, the Socialists' Pietro Nenni, the Communists' Palmiro Togliatti, and the Christian Democrats' Alcide De Gasperi. In Parri and the Parri government, a new Risorgimento for a democratic Italy could be anticipated.[59] So also was victory for the wartime ideals proclaimed by the Western allies.

Parri's Action Party's own idea was to define and hold a center: to purge both government and the public/private economic monopolies of the most prominent Fascists; to encourage more democratic partic- ipation at all levels of public life; to encourage the revival of small and middle-sized enterprises by controlling and allocating scarce raw ma- terials; to pay for emergency short-term welfare by high taxes on the Fascist monopolies. But this was to cater to a class that hardly yet existed. It was a policy of fending off the mobilization of Right and Left while striving to nurture what Italy had never had: a broad-based middle-class public. Meanwhile, huge numbers of uprooted people wandered over a desolate landscape, many of them ex-soldiers who had fought both for and against the Axis and Germany, many of them ex- prisoners of war, some from German and some from Allied camps, along with ex-partisans of various backgrounds. Full of impatience and bit- terness, they alarmed those many other Italians whose primary im- pulse was to try to defend what little in the way of shops, lands, and mills was left to them from the war. Even had Churchill avoided med- dling—and even had Ferruccio Parri himself been a more experienced and adept politician—the Parri coalition could hardly have withstood the centrifugal forces that were to give shape to postwar Italian politics.

The vote came to Italian women with neither fanfare nor protest.[60] De Gasperi for the Christian Democrats and Togliatti for the Commu- nists proposed a suffrage decree, all parties supported it, and it was issued on February 1, 1945, as fighting still continued in the north. No debate, no anxieties over women's proper place, at women's subservi- ence to priests, over women's special nature were to be heard. Women's participation, 100,000 strong, in the resistance had forestalled any such hesitations. Women voted in the local elections of March 1946, and in the elections for a constituent assembly in June, with a heavy majority for abolishing the monarchy, and then climactically in the national election of April 1948. Had the Parri government taken root, or had the postwar parties of a broad middle class begun quickly to flourish, women's role in postwar Italian politics might have been quite other than it proved to be. But the breakdown of 1943–45 offered no social base for the growth of a multiparty system, or for a party system focused on a broad constituency between extremes. Instead, as early as November 1945 postwar politics was moving into the polarization displayed ever since.

The Parri coalition's fall came with the withdrawal of support by the Christian Democrats. The small Liberal Party had preceded it, but it was the loss of the DC that doomed the government. Parri promptly denounced the DC as a revival of "those political and social forces that had formed the basis of the Fascist regime."[61] This was unfair. De Gasperi had earned his credentials as a postwar leader with a term in a Fascist prison. He and his closest colleagues favored free labor unions, social insurance, land reform, separation of church and state, economic growth—in short, the liberal democratic capitalism sought by the pre-Fascist politicians. Certainly, at the same time, as an heir of Romolo Murri and Luigi Sturzo, De Gasperi saw his program as not only a good in itself but as the best means for holding off socialism. In itself, however, this was far from constituting Fascism. Yet the DC, precisely in aiming at broad popular support, could not avoid heavy reliance on the Vatican and the church. It could not possibly hold off popular radicalism on the one hand while holding off organized Catholicism on the other. Moreover, as the DC moved toward economic recovery by working with, rather than breaking up, the great industrial, financial, and commercial complexes left over from Fascist corporatism, its contact with the mass discontent generated by the war grew more tenuous, rendering its reliance on the church's instruments of social control all the greater. For women, hence, one of the two great postwar parties would carry a special burden: whatever its policies might or might not offer women by way of security for families, jobs, or education, that party would not be friendly to feminism.[62]

Behind the scenes, the Communist Party too had moved to undermine the Parri government. Having returned to Italy from Russia, Palmiro Togliatti from the start expounded an Italian way to Communism. Proclaiming his vision of a mass party, he foresaw Communism coming to power by democratic means within the terms of the new constitution, working through institutions, especially those of local government. Meanwhile, pending that victory, the party would become more than a party. A Communist would be able to read a Communist paper, take Communist-sponsored vacations, share in Communist study groups, work as a Communist union member. Communists were indeed destined to win election after election for decades in a large number of provinces, cities, and towns. There Communism would subsist as a near-autonomous local culture in an entirely orderly, molecular, democratic way. For women who were themselves Communists, or the wives, daughters, and mothers of Communists, the party would provide a home, just as the DC might for their Catholic counterparts. But to women discontent with standard gender roles, impatient with traditional subordinations, and potentially feminist in their aspirations, the PCI would not be responsive. Not only did Marxist ideology traditionally date women's liberation after the revolution; the very hopes of the PCI of becoming a "mass" party depended upon its discretion in respecting the culture of the masses, and this, as Gramsci had seen, remained traditional in Italy in all that concerned gender.[63]

In short, a party as geared to economic growth as the DC but without its burden of Vatican ideology, and/or a party as dedicated to social equality as the PCI but without its anti-individualism, might have promised more to women, feminists included. But such a party, secular, middle-class, democratic, liberal, failed to flourish. It was not that the center had failed to hold; there had been no center in the first place.

Still in the name of Resistance unity, Christian Democrats and Communists governed together in coalition, under De Gasperi, until April 1947. Then the DC, for reasons of both economic and foreign policy, denounced the Communists and their Socialist Party allies. Ironically, just previously the Communists had joined the Christian Democrats in an act that incited outrage in all the small parties of secular and liberal outlook. They had ratified inclusion of the Lateran Pacts, signed by Pius XI and Mussolini back in 1930, in the new constitution, perpetuating the privileges of the Catholic church. The Communist daily, *L'Unità*, in justifying the Communist vote, "defined it as 'the highest example of national responsibility for religious peace and the unity of the workers.' "[64] An act of self-interest, intended to keep the way open for the party to become a "mass" party, it did not prevent a break that was to remain permanent.

Modern Italy: A People Polarized—Together

In May 1947 the Christian Democrats undertook to govern alone, bringing to an end the epoch of governments based on the wartime unity of the Resistance. Through the rest of 1947 tense confrontations inside and outside parliament took place. The ultimate test of De Gasperi's new strategy of discarding the Left, the first postwar election, came in April 1948. Prognostications were heard of stalemate, of an electorate so divided among three or four or five parties that no one could prevail. Since the referendum of June 1946, Communists had won many local elections, seating mayors not just in "Red Bologna" but in Florence, Venice, Turin, and Genoa. Milan had a joint Socialist-Communist city administration. Many took these results as prophetic. Yet in April 1948 the Communists suffered a devastating defeat. In the

Popular Front combining Socialist with Communist tickets in many places, the Socialists actually outpolled their supposedly dominant partner, with the two together winning only 31 percent of the total popular vote. The DC won 48 percent on its own, for a sweeping absolute parliamentary majority. There could be no doubt that the Italian people had spoken: no less than 92 percent of eligible voters had voted.[65]

The result constituted a minicrisis for Communist Party leaders:

Togliatti, who had himself presented the resolution for women's suffrage [in 1945] . . . had to undertake a tour . . . in order to calm down the comrades, arguing far into the night on one topic alone: "Were we wrong to give votes to women?" ("Yeeeees," muttered the comrades.) As late as 1953 meetings were still being held on the topic, "Was it correct to give the vote to women?" ("Noooooo," the comrades mumbled.)[66]

The hostility of the comrades was misplaced. Even a broad differential between men and women would not have won the election for the PCI. But many Communists never forgot.

The basic shape of the 1948 election would be confirmed at every Italian national election thereafter. Never would the DC get an absolute popular majority, but never would it fail to come in number one. Soon the Socialists would fade back well behind the Communists, and the PCI would slowly but surely increase its popular vote, into the 25 percent range, then 30 percent, inching toward 35, as the DC slowly sagged below 40 percent; but the lines never crossed. Even as PCI hopes grew that eventually the party would outpoll the DC and at last be able to demand entrance into a government again, its returns began to sag. The Italian people repeated their original decision, not so much to sustain the Christian Democratic Party as to restrain the Communist Party in permanent exile from government. Christian Democracy operated less and less as a unified body, more and more as a kind of consociation of wings, tendencies, factions, fractions, and fusions, while the Socialists, caught between the DC and the PCI, suffered splits and schisms. Only the Communists in their ostracism maintained reasonably compact coherence. As in Lenin's party, fierce debate went on among the leaders—but behind the scenes, never democratically, always resolved by the public proclamation of unity.

Much helped by American aid, the economy returned to prewar levels of output by 1949–50.[67] A decade of strong expansion followed. For the first time the Italian iron and steel industry, heavily underwritten by state participation, began to achieve competitive status in international markets, assisted by the low wage levels of its workers. In the 1950s the Italian auto industry began to stabilize as an effective mass producer. State and private interests collaborated in setting up ENI, a public/

private corporation to deal with the problem of oil. The chemical industry expanded. Industrial workers grew from 29 percent just after the war to 37 percent of all workers by 1961. Industrial production swelled by 8.3 percent and net investment by 9.9 percent per annum. Yet while a minority of workers in Turin and elsewhere in the northwest began to gain in real wages, real wages for most workers did not rise during the decade of the economic miracle. Consumption grew only half as fast as the net national income. In 1960, Italian per capita income was about half that of Great Britain, France, and West Germany, and about one-fifth that of the United States.

In effect, Italy was still building its capital plant, toward the day when it would begin to generate a higher standard of living for more and more consumers. How distant this day still was could be seen even as the miracle continued. More workers still worked in agriculture than in industry at the end of the decade. The DC governments addressed themselves to the perennial problem of the south with loan schemes, direct industrial subsidies, distribution of land. None of it worked, if only because all these measures were too limited; the industrial surge was not strong enough to afford the taxes necessary to transform Sicily, Catania, Sardinia, and Apulia. Nor was the industrial surge strong enough to provide jobs for all Italians; a high unemployment rate persisted, still 7.3 percent in 1961 compared to 7.8 percent in 1950; many began to emigrate again, increasingly to north of the Alps. Women workers grew to 26 percent of the nonagricultural work force by 1960, and while this was low compared to most industrialized countries, presumably the direction of change was established. Only about a quarter of Italian women worked in the marketplace—again a rate that was low, but since the proportion of women in agriculture remained high, presumably it was the direction of change rather than the rate itself that mattered most.

The economic miracle sufficed to generate the basis for the emergence of a kind of woman's sphere within the social whole, picking up from a middle class feminine culture taking form from the late 1920s under fascism and cut off by the war. New national magazines for women, running up to 500,000 in circulation, sought and found a variety of audiences. Some—*Confidenze, Brava, Intimità*—simply ignored feminist issues. Others—*Grazia* and in particular *Gioia* with its specifically Catholic inflection—explicitly deprecated organized feminism. *Amica* and *Annabella* supported freedom of divorce; *Annabella* welcomed career women as a cutting edge. *Arianna*, upon effecting its partnership with *Cosmopolitan*, took up that American magazine's preoccupation with sexuality.[68] Continued economic growth was necessary, if such media were to facilitate a culture among Italian women increasingly free of the constraints of the past—a past characterized by rural poverty and subordination to the church.

Whatever its limitations, the economic miracle incited DC leaders to political flexibility. Eager to forestall parliamentary instability, the DC overreached itself in 1953 by proposing, in an unfortunate echo of a similar Fascist scheme, that any prearranged party coalition that won at least 50 percent or more of the votes be guaranteed 65 percent of the seats in parliament. The DC's coalition was rebuffed in the next elections. In 1955 a prominent DC leader, Giovanni Gronchi, began to urge an "opening to the left" aimed at the "inclusion of the masses into the state"—a plain confession that the DC electorate constituted a collection of special interests rather than some broad popular constituency identifiable as the nation or the masses. By 1962 such an opening appeared possible and desirable to the majority of DC leaders. Along with an internal evolution, two things had happened outside the party to render the move to the left attractive. First, the accession of John XXIII to the papacy in 1958 had boxed off right-wing clerics in the Vatican. Second, Pietro Nenni's Socialist Party found itself being destroyed by its de facto alliance with the Communists. Whereas the PCI continued steadily to construct its own separate realm, the Socialists, behaving as a traditional party, lost followers to the PCI while winning none to its right. With new DC leaders insisting that some of the gains of the economic miracle be applied to such problems as welfare, health, old-age pensions, and education, a reformist majority within the PSI, willing to give the DC a chance to cut its links to political corruption, clerical reaction, and economic injustice, sealed the bargain. Once again prospects brightened for a real center in Italian politics and life. With its new allies to the left, the DC would be free to spurn residual Fascists to its right, while undertaking to win the mass back from Communism.[69]

As though economics and politics could never run in tandem, however, the economic miracle expired even as the DC and the PSI entered their collaboration.[70] An export boom became an import boom; inflation reignited; interest rates went up; production began to fall. Right-wing opponents blamed the recession on the opening to the left, while Communists blamed it on the Socialist betrayal. On the assumption, possibly reasonable, that the recession would prove but a cyclical dip in a long-term upward course, the new DC/PSI governments persisted in their course, however, and committed the economy to an expensive list of social charges as well as to higher wages negotiated by newly strengthened unions. Inflation-adjusted escalator clauses were built into the operations not only of sensibly lean enterprises but also of the vastly overstaffed public/private corporations bequeathed by Fascism. Thus the first OPEC oil shock of 1973 hit an economy not only heavily oil-dependent but with large rigidities built into its response to revived inflation.

A remarkable story began to emerge. Evidently, the 6,500,000 women at work in 1959 declined to 5,110,000 by 1972—a unique development in Western nations, where the numbers of women in the work force had been mounting. In the tertiary white-collar service sectors, women's numbers did continue to grow by about 11 percent between 1959 and 1972, but this was not nearly enough to compensate for the decline in the industrial sector. A pattern of hiring single women and married men had appeared:

In substance, the strategy of the managers has been to raise labor productivity by reducing absenteeism and union pressures; women have been harmed by this because they are considered less productive than men. . . . The tendency of the market to prefer men, and younger women, is easily explained. Because they are responsible for the support of a family, men are held at blackmail, so to speak, while young unmarried women, without family responsibilities, and less likely to incur social charges for pregnancy and sickness, are at once less given to absenteeism and come cheap.[71]

Since the working force that appeared to be missing in Italy was that of married women, this analysis of employer discrimination had merit. But another explanation had even more plausibility. The women who had apparently vanished from the labor rolls had not vanished from the work place. They were still at work, but untabulated, often working for longer hours and lower pay at harder tasks, in an underground "black economy," sewing shoe tops in garrets, stitching gloves in dark corners, carving cameos in bone for tourist shops, repairing lace. The underlying economics of the black economy were clear: black labor escaped the tax officers, the health inspectors, the insurance monitors. It was the cheapest labor. For those who worked, it was better than no job at all.[72]

At the same time, thousands of modernized women began to appear by the late 1960s and particularly through the 1970s. The economic miracle itself had not generated large numbers of careers for university-educated Italians, men or women, but as a sense of democratization spread, more young women began training for such careers. When the center-left governments responded to student protest in 1968–69 by a broad democratizing of university education, the universities began to turn out more graduates than ever, women increasingly numerous among them—indeed, far more graduates than there were opportunities. Some Italian observers wondered whether Italy, while hoping to become a prosperous and equable Sweden, was not in fact fast drifting toward becoming a hectic and decrepit Argentina.

As the gradual disintegration of the Christian Democrats continued, the opening to the left finally saw governments for the first time since 1946 headed by other than a DC prime minister—first the Republicans' Giovanni Spadolini, then the new head of the PSI, Bettino Craxi, despite the fact that the PSI remained far smaller than its Communist rival, let alone its DC partner. There was economic as well as political adaptation.[73] As though to confirm Gramsci's notion that Italian workers welcomed technological progress, workers at Turin's FIAT auto plant repudiated their leaders and agreed to the introduction of robots on the assembly floor: better some jobs than no jobs. By 1983, FIAT was exporting more cars to the rest of Europe than any French, German, or British carmaker. With brilliant new designs, office-machine maker Olivetti reconquered old markets. Benefiting from the lira's evidently irresistible decline, Italian wine producers found themselves not only selling more wine to the United States than French vineyards did, but selling to the French, too. Italian fashion designers exported licenses. The underground economy poured shoes, gloves, "antique" furniture, and Jesus jeans onto world markets. An ancient craftsmanship and an innovative vitality confirmed Gramsci's sense of the Italian as *uomo lavoro* and *donna lavora*.

Whether all this was advancing Italy's stability as a productive modern nation, or simply keeping it one step ahead of crisis, remained debatable. The political evolution of the Christian Democrats from right to left had not yet changed one basic fact: the Communist Party had "succeeded in creating a state within a state and in freezing almost 35 percent of the Italian electorate in an attitude of systematic and intransigent opposition."[74] Yet this opposition had never taken the form of an economic plan for Italy's prosperity. The Communists had always been hazy about what they would do, were they to come to power, whether by democratic vote or out of revolutionary breakdown. Essentially, they proposed to remove Italy from the pressures of international capitalism, and, behind protective walls, pursue an economy of justice. No Communist had ever explained how this could also be a prosperous economy. Of course the barrier faced by the Communists in Italy concerned more than economics; it concerned international politics. In an attempt to overcome this barrier, Palmiro Togliatti's successor, Enrico Berlinguer, announced a new policy of "Eurocommunism," according to which Western Communist parties rejected Moscow's direction. Maybe a Communist Italy could remain in NATO! Already anticipated in Togliatti's "Italian way," Eurocommunism was to be understood as an evolution within Western culture rather than as a revolutionary disruption of it. Resonating in Eurocommunism was Gramsci's faith that, within Western culture, the Italian branch was already peculiarly fitted for a humanism of technology and work.

While this ideological shift was being propounded, however, another major shift was going on within the party, by no means in consistency with party intentions.[75] First, the party's basic working-class constituency began to shrink. As a new, younger generation of factory workers confronted the problems of the 1970s, standard Communist views began to appear irrelevant, particularly the intransigent opposition to efforts at improving productivity. Second, losses among elite industrial workers were being made up by gains among other kinds of people—white-collar workers, teachers, underemployed and unemployed professionals and subprofessionals, artisan craft workers, even small merchants. As the party slipped in some familiar old red strongholds, it gained strength in traditionally anti-Communist old Catholic centers like Verona, Padua, Trieste, Venice, and Brescia, as well as in the south. As it became less a working-class party, the PCI became a party reflecting a multiplicity of layers, quarters, and sectors of Italian society. Just what these new members expected of their new party was by no means clear. They were registering bitterness at the failure of the economy to fulfill their hopes. The PCI did not grow in size. The long Craxi government suggested the potential for a new stabilization of Italian politics and economy, reducing the danger of a crisis. Yet as the focus for revolutionary inertia, the Communist Party gained appeal precisely as it ceased to threaten the interests of all but one class and, instead, offered itself as the vent for protest from many quarters. The prospect for a Communist government in Italy had not changed, for international interests would guarantee that Italy not withdraw from its ties with either the European Economic Community or the North Atlantic Treaty Organization. Yet as long as the PCI remained a "state within a state," the option of mediating protest through a new Leader had not been foreclosed.

For women, a party that attracted support from a variety of sectors rather than from only one, from professional, service-oriented, and white-collar circles rather than from blue-collar workers only, would obviously be more attractive. But the new coalition governments were also better placed to appeal to modern women, and by the 1980s the PCI's opportunity seemed to have been closed. Some feminists, determined to remain revolutionary, moved to its left.

Italy's Future as Past: What Place for Women?

The basic hope for women in Italy lay in a flourishing economy and a democratic political movement. A flourishing economy could have dissolved black labor, eased the pressure on families and multiplied women's options. Political democracy would begin the process of prying loose the hold of church and feudal landholders on ordinary life. The hope of Mazzini, Garibaldi, and the democrats around them had been for political democracy. The hope of Cavour and the "liberals" around him had been for a flourishing economy. The failure of both did not follow from their failure to collaborate, for Italy's economic problems were too vast for any reasonably expedient solution, but the disintegration of Risorgimento hopes for a secular democracy can hardly be distinguished from the perpetuation of impoverishment as the ordinary style of Italian life. Italian feminists would find no natural, obvious allies, once unification had proved an inadequate stimulus to an Italy revitalized in economy and in social relations.

Still, the failure of one generation need not decree that of the next. Giovanni Giolitti's method of political manipulation might well have led Italy out of the shadows of its post-Risorgimento stagnation. Had universal manhood suffrage had a chance to take root, the context for women's consciousness might have taken on a nineteenth-century American shape, with women's exclusion from politics not so much the measure of their weakness as the stimulus to their sense of difference. Nothing in Giolitti's practice decreed that it could not prove the dawn of a new day. But Italy did not, perhaps could not, escape testing in the war, and the rapid passage from popular mass emotion to Fascism registered the fact that Giolitti had not had time to infuse the nation's prewar political economy with strength and vitality.

Mussolini's own reliance on the Catholic church and Catholic ideologies of rural virtue registered the shortage of resources available to Fascism itself for a true mobilization of the nation. Ironically, had Fascism been more thoroughgoing, capable of a totalitarian mobilization comparable to that of Stalin's Russia, Italian women would have experienced more material transformation in their lives than they did in fact. So long as that material transformation faced totalitarian politics, of course, it could not be registered in consciousness. Yet once a real material transformation did begin, with the economic boom after World War II, and did so in the ambience of democratic politics, women were not offered simple freedom but a hard choice. Each of the two dominant postwar parties bore a powerful ideology as to women, the ideology of Catholicism on the one hand and the ideology of Marxism on the other, both deeply inflected by attachment to the traditional Italian gender relations of the countryside. Italian feminists themselves might well choose neither, favoring a kind of unaffiliated enterprise, but if they did, they would be isolated.

2 Sweden. Family Tale

A Premature Modern Folk

Mid-nineteenth-century Sweden was sunk in backwardness, its government archaic, its economy rural. Yet Swedes themselves were not a backward people. Attached to their ancient villages, they had never been oppressed. Serfdom had never overcome them. Neither were they the sheep of shepherds. Catholicism had never sunk into the heart in Sweden. Villagers' economic lives, rather than subsisting in those almost vegetal routines that nurtured myths of nature, instead prompted consciousness, especially between the sexes. Countrymen customarily spent long stretches away from home, working iron and timber. In some regions back home women worked the fields, in others they did not, but in all places they pursued the crafts of household subsistence, in the context of a rough equality. Young women might spend whole summers in the mountains, alone, with their cows.[1]

Among country Swedes, manners and morals were their own. While Lutheranism had made them literate, it had not made them puritanical. A certain long-practiced permissiveness suited village psychology, and alarmed no one, because it was, inevitably, "premarital," a passage toward marriage, babies, family.[2] Entrance into adulthood followed for both young men and young women as affirmation of self. No "society" bore in against individuals, no church, no state, no "values," no system.

The underlying individualism of this popular culture had long been reenforced from outside, by brutal politics. In the seventeenth century Gustavus Adolphus had gambled Sweden's security on intervention in Europe's bloody religious wars. For a brief unreal moment, little Sweden bestrode European power politics. For ordinary Swedes the foreign campaigns had deepened patterns of separation of husband and wife. National benefits followed, however: the best artillery of the age, wrought by Swedish steelmasters; Dutch and English capital, flowing in. Gustav polished his machinery of government and had the country surveyed. Sweden was moving into the age of science, technology, reason.

Gustavian preeminence could not last. The throne fell, irrationally, to a teen-ager. Gifted no doubt, but headstrong, deluded, and misogynist, Charles XII, from 1697, sucked Swedes behind him into whirlpools of military fantasy. Sweden's fields, villages, timber, mines, milling, and foundries remained intact, but Charles had shaken the people. As Vilhelm Moberg has suggested, once again the nation's continuity flowed through its hard-working women. Swedes needed freedom from power politics. They needed a little Sweden.

Over the next fifty years, while country folk enjoyed the luck of decades of good harvests, gentry and townspeople, plus the court bureaucrats, evolved two-party politics embracing the whole of a slowly emerging middle class. Issues dividing "caps" from "hats" were those of profit, not principle. Newspapers were appearing by the 1750s. Parliament passed a Freedom of the Press Act in 1766. Even before England or France, or Benjamin Franklin's Philadelphia, population data were being systematically collected. For the wives and daughters of this embryonic center, a future was opening, of wider private space, richer in social detail, more compelling in hopes for love, husbands, children, self. This psychosocial promise did not lack material plausibility. Ironmasters and the state collaborated in maintaining high prices for the high-quality iron exported from hundreds of mills scattered through the forests. Banking devices were innovated; fresh manufactories were imagined and capitalized. Swedes were beginning to practice every sort of modernity.[3]

Isolation could invite overestimation of the nation's strength, however. Ten years before Adam Smith, as Swedish historian Eli Heckscher has pointed out, Anders Chydenius, a clergyman-economist, criticizing his government's preference for monopoly, articulated a "clear and simple exposition of the fundamentals of economic liberalism."[4] Whether or not Sweden was ready for foreign competition as early as 1766, the question was soon smothered. Once again engorged and impetuous youth arrived to undo long evolution.

Gustav III would prove one of eighteenth-century Europe's enlightened monarchs. He admired performance. Ability attracted him more than birth. He liked building useful things—canals, roads, hospitals, prisons. He stabilized a wobbly currency. He fancied himself a man of reason, an intellectual. But Gustav missed the point. Swedes were ready for democracy. He cut away at the new press freedoms. Parties withered. His addiction to French manners, French theater, the French tongue blighted Swedish self-respect. A genuinely Swedish poet, Anna Maria Lenngren, wife of one of the embattled newspapermen, visited contempt on what she saw as a foreign court. Though Gustav was assassinated while still in his prime, the wars he had entered proved another swamp, and by 1810, the whole country neared collapse. The new king— Napoleon's Marshal Bernadotte—imported by desperate gentry (and suitably Lutheranized and rebaptized as Karl Johan) served his country well: he extricated it from its fatal alliances. Swedes were never to fight another war. They found themselves returned to poverty, but once again withdrawn into themselves.

As the old villages soon began to disintegrate under the pressure of new methods, new men, new science, ordinary Swedes would face a crisis. But they would not face it as a people unawakened to history. Their greatest resource for coping with modernity would be their own identity, awakened to its very depths of gender. They would not regard industrialization as a kind of affliction or storm to be borne. They would know what they wanted of it.

Uprooted Together: Ordinary Country Men and Women in Crisis

When Thomas Malthus, the English clergyman and social philosopher, visited Scandinavia in 1800 in search of data to support the gloomy theory he had already devised—"Population will always tend to outrun production"—he found Sweden in sorry shape. Farmers' boys in Norway, he found, "were fatter, larger, [with] better calves to their legs," whereas "their neighbors the Swedes were absolutely starving." Norwegians had a sensible appreciation for the limits of their rugged land, whereas Swedish politicians and political economists were— "strange to say"—constantly calling for more and more babies. In fact, Sweden was "peopled up."[6] Its overpopulation symbolized a general heedlessness in the country. Sweden did not recognize its problems; it had no policy.

By 1810 a cohort of young Swedes had come to believe that something had indeed gone badly wrong. At the university at Uppsala a group of young men founded a "Gothic Society." Whatever terrors the name "Goth" might hold for more southern Europeans, among Swedes it roused thoughts of ancient honor, glory, strength, fortitude. The Gothic Society was an exercise in conservative nationalism; its leading figure, Eric Gustav Geijer, then twenty-eight, was already recognized as a hero of his generation.[7] The son of one of the country's numerous small ironmasters, Geijer had grown up at a foundry deep in the countryside, where he came to know as by instinct the interweaving of land, mines, mills, and rivers as an age-old whole. A talented poet, he now began writing about Vikings, sturdy yeomen, hardy soldiers. History became his genre. Were there not, after all, powerful resources in legend and mythology for facing down the awful present in Swedish history? Let old Sweden be reawakened. Let all notions of reform, modernization, liberalization be rejected, lest they cut the link to basic vitality. Sweden should be nurtured by strong Swedish men like the Vikings, the old kings, and the yeoman farmers, men such as Geijer, presiding in increasingly patriarchal honor in his post at unreconstructed old Uppsala, proceeded to be. By 1832 his masterpiece, *The History of the Swedes*, had been completed.

But all this proved to be false, not only to the real life of nineteenth-century Sweden but to Geijer's own mind. He had no real bent for the myths and mystifications that were the stock-in-trade of post-Napoleonic conservatism elsewhere. Nor had he ever really thought of poetry as incantatory music for evoking tribalism rather than politics. Like all great lyric poetry, Geijer's poetry was an exercise in the honing of consciousness, not of unconsciousness. In his boyhood experience he had learned the source for a quite un-Gothic, post-Gothic transformation of Sweden—the foundries and lumber mills. It occurred to him that, while old Sweden had always been poor, poverty was no necessary virtue in a Sweden revived. In a calculated act, in 1838 Geijer at fifty-five announced his conversion from conservatism to liberalism. It was national drama. New friends rejoiced; old friends despaired; some reviled him. Whether Geijer's new liberalism reached to include economic as well as political and social liberalism was debated then and has been debated since.[8] Part of Geijer's conservatism had been his fear of the rule of "money." Presumably, money would rule if liberal free trade were installed. But the question was minor. What Geijer had done, as no one else could have, was to bring to a focus that kind of "folk rationality" that had been imminent in the eighteenth century's age of freedom. The way forward for Sweden would not be through affirming ancient myths but through fulfilling Swedish democracy. Let the absurd old parliament be abandoned, for instance; let suffrage be broadened. Let the energies of the people be truly freed.

The life of the people was, however, in the process of disruption. To the occasional tourist, Sweden's countryside of the 1830s and the 1840s could seem puzzling, at once old and new. Swedish villages incarnated the rural ways of centuries past. But elsewhere new farmsteads seemed fenced in, thought out, cinched up in a new spirit. Since the previous century, modern-minded gentry had been introducing new methods that promised greater efficiency and production.[9] A parliamentary act of 1827 strongly encouraged the consolidation of the strips and scraps of land surrounding the villages into compact blocs. Village-centered ways, shaped by tradition, gave way to farmer-centered ways, the villages themselves beginning to empty, crumble, vanish. One day economic historians would argue that it was the progress here, in agriculture, that contributed most to the industrial takeoff of the late nineteenth century. Certainly, in generating a body of new prosperous farmer-owners, it contributed to a new shape of politics as these farmers, recognizing their separate self-interest, organized to protect it. But these new farmers were no longer the old Swedish folk.

One ... [sees] the degradation in which the vast mass of the agricultural population is held ... [those] who are not owners of land or houses, must have a patron, or sort of master, who is responsible to the government for the conduct of his client! When we first heard of this ... we absolutely could not believe it. ... All such men ... the overwhelming mass of the country people ... must have ... a written document ... from some proprietor. ... [This] ... renders the poor man an humble, cringing dependent. ... If a poor man cannot find a patron ... he is liable to be thrown into prison as a vagabond.[10]

Sweden's efficient census did not confirm that the "vast mass" of the country people had been reduced to dependency, but the direction and rate of such change was unmistakable.[11] In 1770 some 200,000 farmers owned land, whether in large plots or small. Another 65,000 or so farmed as crofters—tenants with more or less stable claims to farming rights—or as cottagers and live-in laborers. By 1850 the landowning farmers, whether large or small, had grown to around 220,000, while the crofters, cottagers, and other landless farmers had quadrupled to around 250,000. Fewer crofters, cottagers, and live-in workers had wives and families than the landed. In addition, an amorphous category of sons living at home and of servants had doubled to more than 350,000; while some of these were putative heirs of farmers, the vast majority were not. Sweden was rapidly generating a rural proletariat. Some figures grew particularly ominous. Marriage in the countryside was customarily contracted when the young couple had a farm to move onto, or at least a croft or a cottage to rent. In 1850 some 17,000 married farm workers contracted for work only on an annual basis and were housed in barracks and tenements. By 1880 there were triple that number, more than 50,000. Marriage itself came under pressure, as Horace Marryat saw in 1860:

Next day was Sunday. The annual "Pigmarkned" (girl-market) [was] held for three successive Sabbaths in July, on the square of Västeras. ... Hundreds of girls stand marshalled in rows to be hired out by the month or year, each with book in hand containing certificates of her former masters as to her honesty and sobriety—morality not alluded to.[12]

Bitterness grew among the dispossessed at the new farmer-magnates—herrarna—who were untroubled by any memories of shared poverty in the villages of the past.

Some visitors thought they saw an answer. Charles Loring Brace visited some farmer-manufacturers in the 1850s. One ran a putting-out system:

He directed us to some of his manufacturing hands, who lived at a little distance. The houses were pretty little log-cottages, among flower-beds and potato-patches . . . everything clean and white-washed. . . . Four women, with ruddy, cheerful faces, were at work on the handlooms. . . . There were curtains . . . perfectly white . . . the youngest, a mere girl, [earned] only twelve cents—not poor wages . . . where a carpenter . . . gets thirty cents a day.

Others had built factories. One employed two hundred hands. "Most . . . were women, though many children." Brace, intrigued to "meet a class of people . . . peculiar to Sweden—the ancient peasantry of Bonders, changing into rich manufacturers," had the impression he was witness to the country's future. "Here dwell the rich, aristocratic peasant manufacturers of Sweden—a class not yet raised out of its ancient position, but, with wealth and enterprise, certain soon to be thoroughly modernized."

But however well adapted these early manufactories might have been at absorbing the growing surplus of population in the countryside, they were economically irrational. Brace himself, traveling on one of the still miserable roads, came upon "a long train of little one-horse carts, each with his bale . . . of cotton, driving laboriously on to the spinners and factories. . . . The freight from the sea is several dollars on each bale."[13] With no state to force it by one means or another, industrialization for Sweden lay decades in the future. But the nation faced a population crisis now, and the population faced demoralization.

In Sweden as elsewhere, the stresses of modernity inspired internal remobilizations. From the mid-eighteenth century on, ordinary country Swedes were engaged in religious rituals independent of the state church. Basically populistic and democratic, this movement led people sometimes to criticize official church ways, and sometimes to abandon the official church, even when that was to their legal peril. In its most molecular form, private lay groups engaged in "reading"; the readers (*Läsare*) might well be women reading Luther, English Methodist tracts, and the Bible to their groups. Here and there appeared organized mission societies, local charismatic leaders, seasons of evangelical passion. Yet in contrast to America, the evangelical impulse never reached flood nor did it emerge as a basic order of culture for modernizing Swedes. For one thing, it was not a "revival," for as the Scottish rationalist free trader, Samuel Laing, thought, "no spirit truly religious has ever been generally kindled in [Sweden]." The Reformation, he said, "had merely substituted one ceremonial church for another."[14]

Thus, whereas in the United States popular, lay-generated religious life offered old identities in a time of change to women in particular, in Sweden this recourse proved of far less avail. Moreover, Swedish evangelicalism, mild and localized as it was, was carried off to America, leaving Sweden's religious culture as cool as it had been before.

In Sweden, as elsewhere, internal remobilization was sought through temperance also. Under Gustav III the state had tried to establish a liquor monopoly for itself, but for various reasons this had failed, so that liquor production was left to tens of thousands of farm distilleries especially adept at producing a potato brandy. In the early nineteenth century Swedes were among the heaviest drinkers in the world. The new French king himself had been shocked on his arrival: "Brandy will be the ruin of the Swedish people."[15] An early wave of popular reform, prompted partly by American visitors invited by Swedish clergy, crested in the 1860s, with a second wave rising in the 1880s, again influenced by America. Yet the Swedish temperance movement had no strong clientele or clear focus. No such mobilization of women as created the Women's Christian Temperance Union in America was possible in a country where 80 percent of the people in 1850, and 75 percent as late as 1900, still lived by the habits of the countryside. Although both popular evangelical faith and temperance made their way into the democratizing Swedish political parties and parliaments by the early twentieth century, that very cooptation reduced their significance as alternative means for self-expression, particularly to women. Finally, temperance too, along with religion, found much of its future in leaving Sweden for America.

The first great outpouring of emigrants occurred in 1868–69. This first flood quickly subsided, as though, with the largest pain eased, many waited for some reaction. Hemorrhaging began again in 1880 and continued to 1893.

The great majority of [the emigrants] were young men and women without any landed property or enterprise of fixed employment. . . . At an early stage, there was a shift from family and group emigration to individual departures. . . . A very numerous group among the emigrants were housemaids, whose wages, housing conditions, and social status were constantly bad.

To many thoughtful Swedes this hegira appeared less alarming than relieving. The overpopulation observed by Malthus had only seemed to get worse over the decades; now it was being lanced. Yet when a third surge of departures seemed to be beginning in the early 1900s, widespread anxiety and dismay followed. One cause for alarm had become apparent. Industrialization had begun to take hold; continued emigration would amount to a drain on the potential industrial work force, thus to a limitation on industrialization itself. In short, a solution to Swedish overpopulation had emerged at last, and a new danger followed, that of underpopulation. The government appointed a commission—the usual Swedish response to any perceived social issue—to inquire into the reason.[16]

Young Swedes, the Emigration Commission found, had not left Sweden in a mood of melancholy or fond regret. They had left in active anger and bitterness. Driven to hopelessness by the closing of the countryside and to hostility by the "conceited," "pompous," and crudely exploitative new *herrarna*, and deeply frightened at the prospect of falling into subservience, they chose to abandon the ancient homeland, however painful the severance.

Their brothers and sisters who stayed went to the cities and towns, into the multiplying mills, shops, and factories, but they too felt a pervasive sense of anxiety and anger at the loss of the stability and equality of the old countryside. Industrialization was providing jobs to Swedes who had far outpopulated the countryside, but within one generation those Swedes had committed themselves to a new institution that promised the old stability, security, and equality: they committed themselves to labor unions. No more than their old lives would their new lives be hazarded to the mercies of unmediated competitive individualism.

Lucky Sweden: A Home Industrialized

Not much could be done for economic progress in Sweden until transportation was improved. The Swedes had recognized this in the visionary state-sponsored cross-country Göta canal project. By mid-century it was obvious that railroads were needed, too. The Swedish state presided over railroad development. For all the cogency of Anders Chydenius's arguments for free trade back in 1765, most Swedish leaders agreed that the risk of opening Sweden up to unrestrained outside investment was too great. The Swedish economy might be engulfed by larger economies, and Sweden lose control over its own destiny. Hence, with the Swedish state managing the business of loans, Swedish railroads were built as Swedish governors decided. Swedish banking too commenced in intimate collaboration between banker and government. The great Swedish banking family of the Wallenbergs was notably "nationalistic" from the start, remaining so to the present day. The dismantling of tariffs and other restraints on international trade, urged by Chydenius a century earlier, and now again by those agreeing with Samuel Laing that Sweden needed stimulus and competition, proceeded cautiously during the 1850s and 1860s. Then nervous alarm, from both farmer and hopeful industrialist, led to a return to protection by the 1880s. Sweden remained vigilant: no economic colonization.[17]

Foreign visitors might imagine that Sweden was about to take off into a standard transformation. Traveling in 1860, the Englishman Horace Marryat found a Liverpool in Göteborg and a Sheffield in Eskilstuna, while Jonköping seemed "a little Swedish Manchester."[18] But Swedes were not heading toward a little England. It was not that they had taken note of England's transformation from green and pastoral land to the soots and smokes of modernity. Quite literally, Sweden was saved from much of the torment of industrial transformation by its lack of coal. But most of all, even Swedish liberals were cautious about throwing the country open, while leaders of the old guard were determined that Sweden must keep control of her own destiny. The leading churchman of the epoch, Bishop C. A. Agardh, insisted that "the basic subject matter of economics is not the wealth of the nation but its power to preserve its independence."[19]

Without good luck, this cautious policy might have delayed industrial development and brought on Sweden a truly severe population-based social crisis. But Sweden had luck.[20] Old Sweden had been, besides a countryside, a land of iron and wood, and a land based on iron and wood the new Sweden much remained.

Iron was exploited in Sweden long before the Middle Ages. . . . This early stage was highly individualistic. . . . Rudimentary blast furnaces were scattered over the countryside, near the deposits . . . the woods . . . [and] the waterways. . . . [once] the conversion of pig iron into bar iron [became practical in the mid-sixteenth century] . . . the industry developed from its earlier individualistic basis into a more highly organized, capitalistic form. Many of the famous rural iron works were founded at this time . . . some . . . have kept their typical character . . . up to the present [1940].[21]

With its fortunate propinquity of ore and charcoal, the eighteenth-century Swedish iron industry had enjoyed considerable success in exports. Swedish ironmasters had not sought to maximize these advantages but rather to nurse them along, limiting rather than expanding output to keep up prices. New technologies and trade relations had spelled danger in the early nineteenth century, and Swedish exports declined. But the Swedes learned new English methods and, besides, added a new form of export, iron ore itself. Sweden entered the twentieth century with a more productive and profitable iron industry than ever. Thus evolution, rather than convulsion marked its progress, so that twentieth-century ironworks could be traced back in unbroken continuity to the eighteenth, the sixteenth, even the thirteenth century.

These works were part of still larger complexes. "Not only did they

have their blast furnaces and forges but . . . their own mines . . . fuel
. . . metal manufactories. They employed an appreciable permanent
force of labor, and to provide for [themselves] cultivated their own
farms and established their own trading centers." The line between
these and neighboring rural lives was not sharp: "Charcoal burning
and wood cutting were still subsidiary occupations of considerable
importance for the surrounding farming population; and independent
miners continued to produce."[22] The extinction of this old iron industry
was neither so early nor so sweeping nor so complete as in, say, the
United States. More than two hundred works still produced pig in 1876;
there were still 86 in 1912. The 327 works still producing Sweden's old
export specialty, "Lancashire" iron bars, in 1876, were more severely
reduced to 47 by 1912, but some 200 works of all kinds in 1900 still
numbered 75 in 1930. The one great new enterprise was devoted to
mining, not manufacturing, in a great emptiness—Kiruna on its iron
mountain in the far north. Altogether, Swedish iron would indeed
display that concentration and rationalization characteristic of modernized industry everywhere, but with a notable continuity with the
past. Horace Marryat notwithstanding, no great iron cities emerged,
no Manchester, no Magnitogorsk, no Pittsburgh.

Sweden's old forest-based industry went through something of the
same cycle of early nineteenth-century decline from a long-fortunate
eighteenth-century complacency, followed by a revival of energy. The
surge in timber production after 1850 represented ad hoc response to
external changes in the world market, not any coherent policy. Serious
issues of overcutting, taxes, and wages emerged. An American-style
exploitation of the forests had begun to appear, complete with itinerant
lumber-camp labor conducive to radical unions. The potential for class
conflict got savage confirmation in the famous timber industry strike
in Sundsvall in 1879. Vicissitudes were probably more responsible than
policy for keeping this situation from sinking into long-term bitterness,
as pulp and paper exports emerged to compensate for new difficulties
in timber and lumber.

In all this, Sweden was simply lucky. It might easily have settled into
a kind of third-world dependency, its basic raw material resources
hostage to world markets, its consumers dependent upon the prices of
imports from the centers of mass production. Instead, Sweden took a
chance on protection and won. Sweden continued to enjoy profit from
its raw materials into the twentieth century. At the same time its farms
began to show the fruits of consolidation and science, gradually relieving the country of its periodic dependence on outside succor during
recurrent famine. The base was laid for a more complex growth.

The stimulation of Swedish lumbering, which meant Swedish sawmills, stimulated Swedish engineering. It was a matter of further luck that foreign capital-goods producers were not yet in a position to undercut Swedish capital for Swedish projects. This germinal capital-goods industry then reached out into furniture. Engineering drew stimulus from the "reindustrialized" Swedish iron industry as well, and could soon transfer methods into provision of machinery for a nascent dairy industry, itself drawing on the progress of agriculture. Swedish shops provided the machinery for a new sugar industry, based on beets, and if cotton had once induced delusion, wool proved to be a real foundation for textiles. All these new industries, feeding off the two great export traditions, laid the basis for Sweden's becoming something unique, a kind of replica in miniature of the multiform, balanced, "self-sufficient" industrial systems of the giants of the world, Britain and the United States. Within a single generation, the base had been laid in Sweden for a high-cost, high-technology, high-priced steel manufacturing industry, and for industries specializing in the export of high-finish, high-priced vanguard goods: "Swedish modern" in glass, based directly on traditions of local crafts centuries old; Swedish styles in textiles and clothes, picking up directly from that old-country Sweden famous for its snowy linens made by thousands of female hands in thousands of farmhouses; and styles in furniture, drawing directly on traditions of ax, saw, and plane as old as the Swedish forest. Swedish industry in the twentieth century, as no other did, generated a style in which "folk" and "modern" were identical.

It took some time to secure the base. Sweden fell into serious difficulty immediately after World War I. Labor strife punctuated the 1920s as unemployment refused to decline. Sweden had capital to export, and instead of lending it to foreign companies, the Swedes invented "multinationals" of their own. The most famous of these, Ivar Kreuger's match combine, collapsed in 1932. By then, Sweden too had been sucked into the world depression. But Sweden made an early recovery, and a pattern was set for the indefinite future.[23] The Social Democratic government elected in 1932 practiced Keynesian economics: the assumption was established that in free private Swedish capitalism, government would be a strong presence. But again, Sweden was lucky: its recovery depended heavily upon reviving trade, especially with Germany and England. The Swedes were on their way to affluence. Astonishingly, they would even be able to afford an automobile industry of their own.

But industrial success did not necessarily mean the disappearance of old Sweden. The number of people living in cities over 25,000 grew from about 180,000 in 1865 to 1,285,000 by 1930, but this meant that, by 1930, only a bit over one-fifth of all Swedes lived in towns of 25,000 and more. There was only one "great" city, and that was not great by world standards, old Stockholm with over 500,000 by 1930, still very much an administrative, governmental, transport, communication, and commercial center, rather than an industrial center. There were only two other cities of more than 100,000 by 1930, both of historic, commercial, preindustrial roots, Göteborg and Malmö. By the census reckoning, more than 4,000,000 Swedes still lived in "rural places, fewer than 2,000,000 in urban places, even allowing "urban" to run as small as 5,000. Yet by 1930 more Swedes (54 percent) worked in industry and commerce than in agriculture (39 percent); the others were in professions and government. The explanation for the apparent anomaly was soon picked up by the census and social topographers. Only a little over one-half of the 455,000 industrial workers (including crafts workers) in Sweden lived in urban centers. About one-third of these lived in Stockholm, Göteborg, amd Malmö. About one quarter lived in more or less purely industrial towns, the largest of these a town of only 43,000, Norrköping. The rest, two-fifths, lived in several dozen small to middle-size towns of heterogeneous nature, ranging from fishing ports to cathedral towns, from resorts to administrative seats. Thus even in its urban half, the industrial population of Sweden in 1930 remained unconcentrated, diffused, dispersed.[24]

The other half was still to be found under the heading "rural." Since such a heading was more disguise than illumination, the demographer Dorothy Swaine Thomas and her associates in 1940 refined this category into "agricultural," "rural mixed," and "rural industrial." As distinguished from "rural mixed," where "agriculture was predominant . . . but industry slightly developed," the "rural industrial" category applied where, "along with considerable agriculture, industry and trade were carried on extensively." Of the 203,000 craft workers in Sweden in 1930, far more than half lived in these various rural circumstances, but so did nearly half—49 percent—of the industrial workers. History helped show why. The old mining and basic iron industry remained rural; only the new engineering and metal-manufacturing enterprises grew in towns, with 72 percent of their workers urban. The old sawmill and timber enterprises too remained in the rural areas, while the new clothing and chemical industries were urbanized.

Within one generation Swedish workers committed themselves to labor unions, the first mass organization to which Swedes ever had committed themselves.[25] They had never embraced a church. No political party had mobilized them. In modern Sweden more than 70 percent of four million workers would belong to the unions. The unions were less a response to the shock of industrialization than a reflection of the commitment of Swedes to recover what they had lost in the countryside—the egalitarian security they had known as a people living over the centuries in the same place as the same stock. The unions of course did serve direct economic ends, but they also helped frame and impel a scheme for a society and its culture. The relationship capitalism would bear to labor and to the nation was given formal expression in the famous Saltsjöbaden Agreement of 1938, between the Swedish Employers' Association and the Swedish Labor Organization, at the initiative of the government. Agreeing to bargain with each other regularly under the government's benign watch, capital and labor in effect conceded that each would calculate its self-interest by reference to the interest of the economy as a whole. Sweden would remain as "protected" as it had been in the nineteenth century.

However evolutionary Swedish industrialization proved to be, it nevertheless entailed local gender imbalances, with the towns and cities drawing young women from the countryside, while men stayed where the classic industrial jobs in mining and iron were to be found. The ratio of unmarried men rose in the countryside, while that of unmarried young women rose in the cities.[26] The new job market manifested gender segmentation as markedly as in any other nation, and women's segments would be less well paid than men's. Women workers in Sweden, therefore, had the usual immediate interests that unions might serve, and Swedish women, unlike women elsewhere, joined unions in great numbers. Though women were only one-seventh of the membership of the federation of basic blue-collar unions—the LO—in 1935, they represented a much higher proportion of white-collar union membership, and in Sweden white-collar workers would continue to be more highly organized than anywhere else. The proportions of women in all unions continued to climb decade after decade. Beneficiaries of narrow bread-and-butter union work, Swedish women workers identified even more than men with the broader goal of the union movement as a whole, pursued in league with its political partner, the Social Democratic Party. That goal was to restore Sweden as a *folkshem*, a people's home, a nation for everyone.

Democratizating: Women's Share

The eighteenth-century promise of Swedish politics did not revive in the nineteenth.[27] Government remained essentially the king plus his bureaucrats recruited from a cadre of old noble country families. A strange old four-house parliament that had survived Gustav III remained functionally incapable of either impeding or forwarding important business. The use of standing committees gradually become the chief reliance of Swedish government, eventually supplemented by ad hoc committees assigned special tasks. Drawing on the same rationality that had inspired Gustavus Adolphus's maps and the national census, such committees developed formidable habits of investigation and broad consultation. Such committees were to exercise formidable influence upon twentieth-century parties and parliaments. Thus the emergence of modern politics in Sweden would not be so much an escape from simple backwardness as perpetuation of a habit of looking at every issue for Sweden's interest as a whole. Each committee constituted a king-surrogate, paternal, patient, responsible.

Whether conservative or liberal in spirit, or, like Erik Geijer, first one and then the other, reformers—newspaper editors, bishops, poets, entrepreneurs, enlightened gentry—agreed that reform was needed. A new constitution was indeed ratified in 1866, but given all the restrictions on suffrage, even then only about one Swedish adult male in ten could vote for the more democratic new Second Chamber, let alone for the far more narrowly based First. Men like Adolph Hedin understood that the need was not so much for new constitutional structures as for fresh political life, political debate, political parties.

Hedin founded his Liberal Party in 1868. He had a full vision for Sweden's future. At one point he prophesied that not Sweden alone but all Europe had a choice: either to succumb to its inertias, eventually surrendering to "Asiatic barbarism"—by which he meant, with a Swede's special disgust, Russia—or to become "Americanized." Hedin welcomed Sweden's—and Europe's—Americanization. He believed that the United States was already the most civilized nation in the world. This was so for the simplest reason: civilization was measured by the degree of active participation in the affairs of a nation by its people, by democracy; the United States was the world's great democracy, in contrast with Russia, the world's great autocracy. Hedin's early Liberal Party thus stood for the democratization and Americanization of Sweden.

Such democratization and Americanization would include, specifically, the induction of women, at once and without limit, into political life: the Liberal Party called for universal, including woman, suffrage. Hedin spent no time puzzling over the limitations still imposed on women in the great North American democracy; probably he was not thoroughly aware of them. His larger perception, that in the democratic life of the United States not only the common man but his wife and daughters too enjoyed far greater freedom and opportunity than in any European nation, sustained his certainty about the basic direction for reform.

But the Liberal Party quickly disintegrated. No doubt there were many kinds of people who found its principles attractive, its attacks on inherited power and privilege welcome, and who saw as cogent its call for new, open, modern methods, its invitation to Sweden to come out from behind its walls to experience the bracing airs of free trade in ideas as in commerce, in manners as in arts and skills. Newspapermen, important merchants, doctors, scientists, manufacturers, writers, and women of advanced views might all be Liberals. But quite apart from whether this was too heterogeneous a set of interests for coherent politics, such a grouping was still too small. The same 88 to 90 percent of Swedes living by agriculture in 1768 were still living so in 1868. The elements for Sweden's industrial revolution were in place, some of them already synthesizing, but no preponderant modern middle class had begun to appear.

The only stable party to emerge after 1866 belonged to the beneficiaries of the consolidation of the old village strips—the new farmers, employers of the growing numbers of homeless rural youth. The hope of such a man as Emil Key—a man typical of the old-fashioned "enlightened" gentry, educated in Rousseau, and father of the feminist-to-be, Ellen Key—that the Farmers' Party might someday be the agency of Sweden's rebirth, never approached realization. The Farmers' Party soon showed itself as what it would remain, a party attached to immediate money issues. The Farmers' Party never had any interest in actually taking the reins of government; it sought only to defend its members against government. The party resisted spending public money on schools. It even found it hard to agree to spend money for national defense. The potential of the Farmers' Party as a vehicle for women thus was nil. Not only did it perpetuate old patriarchal solidarities, but it also fed on the vulnerability of the growing landless to be trapped in neofeudal service.

After the early collapse of Hedin's Liberal Party, not only government but politics remained for another generation in more or less the same heads as before—those of the men of the old historic bureaucracies, intimate with the king, and of nobility long identified with the law courts as well as the royal court, with the regional administrators, the tax officers, the regulators, overseers, surveyors, and investigators. These were not only not a new middle class but not even the seeds of one. Insofar as Swedish feminism was to have a political existence in the 1870s and 1880s, it would have to live with, or against, this traditional establishment.

Consequently, once again hunger for national renewal bubbled up among young men at the universities. Again at Uppsala, in 1882, students formed the club Verdandi, to work for Sweden's future, its name referring to one of the ancient, pre-Christian Swedish nature gods, invoking distant roots. One of the students, Karl Staaff, soon entered parliament and in due course helped organize another Liberal Party, actually the Liberal Coalition Party, in 1900; he became prime minister in 1906.

The cause of universal suffrage pulsed at the heart of late nineteenth-century Swedish liberalism and this new Liberal Party.[28] The first real exercise of mass politics in Sweden had been in circulating suffrage petitions and holding mock "folk parliaments" based on popular voting in the 1890s. A Universal Suffrage Association had been formed in 1896. Always, Liberal leaders had affirmed woman suffrage as inherent in true universal suffrage. Staaff's first government set out to expand the franchise. Owing to political fortuities it failed, but the impetus it had lent the issue could not be denied. Reaction to the Liberals' formation had precipitated the old factions and groups clustered around the king and in the bureaucracies into a new party, too, the Conservatives, and for a time it seemed that the basic debate in Swedish politics would be between these two, with the Farmers an opportunistic satellite. The Social Democratic Party founded by a handful of Socialists back in 1892 appeared for some years but a sect. Obviously aware it must compete on new democratic terms, the Conservative government following Staaff doubled the number of eligible voters.

With the new broader suffrage in place, Staaff and the Liberals won an impressive victory in 1911 over the Conservatives, as well as over the now-growing Social Democrats. Once again prime minister, Staaff called for woman suffrage, but again, with the collapse of a complicated deal whereby the Conservatives would drop their resistance to woman suffrage in return for various desiderata, he failed, and it remained, ironically, for woman suffrage to be installed in Sweden during the tenure of one of its erstwhile enemies, the Conservatives, at a moment of postwar panic in 1919, provoked by the specter of social revolution. But by then the Liberal Party itself had passed from its brief glory into invincible minorityhood.

No one thing explained the failure of Staaff's Liberal Party to become the dominant party in Swedish politics. For a start, it had no single solid center of gravity. Reaching out to farmers disaffected by the Farmers' Party's increasingly reactionary tendencies, and reaching out also to the growing numbers of professional people impatient with old restraints, to businessmen still favoring free trade, to intellectuals eager for reform in everything, it had constituencies that did not necessarily cohere. Staaff himself, moreover, in his nearly populistic hostility to the ancient nobility and the new farmer *herrarna*, felt great sympathy for the hard-working artisans and others in the small towns, as well as the classic working men in the old ironworks and lumber mills. His outlook thus was shaped more by the past than by a future defined by industrialization and a growing industrial labor force. And, though personally secular-minded, Staaff felt sympathy for the evangelical and even the prohibition movements as genuine expressions of democratic dignity and of grievance against the old class order. Growing numbers of public schoolteachers, in heavy majority women, were also an important constituency of Staaff's party, and in them too the prospect of a Sweden transformed by technology and modern organization aroused ambivalence, not enthusiasm. Staaff, in short, was the champion of a "little Sweden" which, while attractive to most Swedes, was not necessarily adapted to save them.

Nevertheless, Staaff's party might not have failed, if another had not succeeded. Had the Liberals had only the Conservatives to face, plus the Farmers' Party, they might well have won dominance, given time and an evolution in leadership. The Swedish Conservatives were not likely to strike an alliance with industrial working men in the fashion of Disraeli's Tories or Mark Hanna's Republicans. The Liberals would have been free to evolve an industrial strategy more in tune with the times than Staaff's. Politically minded women might have found the party to their interests. Indeed, Liberal women did make their move in the 1920s. But the party's decline spelled theirs.[29]

From Liberals to Social Democrats: Women's Stake

In the United States the labor pool for industry filled up increasingly with men and women from outside the ethnic, religious, and racial mainstream of preindustrial America. In Sweden industrial labor came directly from the heart of Swedish manhood and womanhood. It came swiftly. It saw its interests quickly in the unions and quickly found its political champion. In America, it would take southern and eastern Europeans and Southern blacks decades to find strength in unions and parties; meanwhile, the two great parties could proceed on their way indifferent to the wants of those groups.

In its earliest days after 1892, the Swedish Socialist Party still showed its international and Marxist roots. In fact, its roots had been less Marxist than German. Spending some time in Germany as a young man, August Palm had been much impressed by the German Social Democrats and had brought his enthusiasms back with him to Sweden, where he helped found the Swedish party in 1892. But in Germany, Social Democracy had been forced back upon itself by Bismarck's harsh repressions. Tending the flame of pure intentions, German Socialist debate circled round the day of revolution. Albeit against their will,

German Socialists drifted toward becoming a sect in their own country. But in Sweden, as Herbert Tingsten has shown in his classic study, the Socialists, after brief early loyalty to the abstractions of international Marxism, quickly became Swedish nationalists.[30] Palm's leadership quickly gave way to that of Hjalmar Branting, a friend of Staaff's at Uppsala and a fellow Verdandi member, who was likewise sure that an ancient Swedish culture was worth preserving. The first Social Democrat to be elected to parliament, in 1897, Branting was for several years the only Social Democrat there, where he soon won a reputation as a serious politician and statesman. Square, solid, instantly recognizable as a pure type of benignant Swedish patriarch, Branting was the perfect leader for a party with a simple message: no Swede would be abandoned, none would be run over by the juggernaut of industrial progress. Liberated from aristocratic encrustations, the Swedes' own traditions as a unitary folk offered concrete substance to socialism.

Perhaps the decisive moment in the history of the Swedish Social Democrats was the Great Strike of 1909. Led, or at least strongly urged on, by still ideological leaders, the Swedish workers defeated in the Great Strike presumably came to realize that the route for labor was through, not against, the government and through, not outside, politics. Rejecting the ideological Socialists, they welcomed Hjalmar Branting back as the obvious leader of a Swedish working-class party and, with him, proceeded to power.

Even this story suffers somewhat for its emphasis on conflict. The defeat of the unions in 1909 had been prepared well before in a sharp decline in union membership, from around 200,000 in 1906–7 to perhaps half that by 1909. It would make sense, then, to guess that the mistake of their ideological leaders had already been perceived by Swedish workers before their defeat in the Great Strike.

From this point, the way was open for the Social Democrats to build toward their majority. Industrial workers were not then, nor would they ever be, anything approaching a majority of the work force. The majority of Swedes were workers nonetheless, farm workers and artisan and craft workers, as well as industrial workers, and to the fact that they all felt alarm at the prospect of being rendered placeless in a new rationalized Sweden, the Social Democrats owed their rise. It would be years yet before the party found its basic formula: high taxes on highly protected private industrial enterprise to pay for broad welfare. Meanwhile it profited from the failure of Conservatives and Farmers to speak to the anxieties of the people already gathering themselves into their unions, and from the failure of the Liberals to find coherence and deliver on their promises. As Douglas Verney and others have noted, it was Karl Staaff and the Liberals who, back before World War I, had installed the first Swedish welfare measures, copied from Bismarck's Germany—accident insurance, health insurance, old age insurance. But it was the Social Democrats who made these seeds grow. The Liberals distrusted a powerful new state, and their ideas of welfare lacked the context of powerful economic expansion.

Branting headed a brief Social Democratic government after the war. He died in early 1925. By now easily the largest parliamentary group, though not quite a majority, the party left office in June 1926. A man somewhat in Branting's mold, Per Albin Hansson, calm, patient, practical, with some of Branting's skill in political maneuvering, took over as party head in time for the elections of 1928. By then a number of highly skilled party experts in the tradition of efficient Swedish bureaucracy had emerged, notably an economist, Ernst Wigforss, and a sociologist, Gustav Möller. Out of power, the Social Democrats in parliament had sharpened their differences with Conservatives and Liberals. In 1928 Hansson, backed by the experts, offered his famous vision of Sweden as a "good home," *folkshemmet*, the people's home, a Sweden that belonged to the Swedish people. "In the good home there are no privileged or deprived members, no pets and no step children. . . . In the good home there is equality, solicitude, cooperation and helpfulness."[31] Certainly, Hansson said, Sweden was "not yet the good home of the citizen," but it soon could be, and the Social Democrats in 1928 appeared bent upon doing more about it than they yet had been able to do. For one thing, they proposed an increased inheritance tax. Since Hansson had said that the basis of the people's home is "community and solidarity," Wigforss, the author of the tax bill, explained that, "to tell the truth," the tax proposal was "quite simply" "a final attempt to stretch out a hand to the old bourgeois left." Would not the Liberals at least—it was too much to ask of Conservatives or Farmers—admit that economic inequality in Sweden offended their own principles and required melioration? Surely a stiffened inheritance tax was not too much to ask of them to prove their sincerity.

But the Social Democrats had not yet fully understood their route to dominance. They aroused suspicion with a final whiff of ideology. Wigforss himself seemed to carry a club in his other hand: what if the Liberals rejected the offer made to them? Another Social Democratic leader explained that "we need the money for social revolution." Most damaging was one little sentence in a party motion: "Poverty can be endured with equanimity when it is shared by all."[32] That this raised the prospect of expropriation was plain, and those fearful of being expropriated could vote. But far more hurtful was the priority implicitly given to equality over growth. As the Emigration Commission had

discovered, hundreds of thousands of Swedes had left Sweden in resentment at Swedish inequalities, and there had always been those,
travelers included, to comment on Swedish "jealousy," the ready envy
at any show of superiority among peers. But old ideas, expressed by
such famous writers as Carl Jonas Love Almqvist and August Strindberg, that Swedish virtues were linked with Swedish poverty, had begun
to fade at the prospect of growth, abundance, and prosperity. Presumably this new prosperity was to be shared, but severing equality from
prosperity led the Social Democrats to their first great defeat. Not the
abstractions of "socialism" but the concrete values of a real history,
Sweden's history, would prevail. Swedes had always been at home in
their own land; feudalism had not enslaved them. Now, as the land
could no longer support them, what they wanted was the same sense
of possession they had once enjoyed. Talk of virtuous poverty did not
attract them. Ideologists such as Wigforss drew back. Again led by
Hansson, who soon settled in as the party's lifetime patriarch, the
Social Democrats began winning elections again in 1932, and for the
next forty-four years, until 1976, controlled the government and shaped
industrial Sweden into its people's welfare society. At its heart was the
Saltsjöbaden Agreement of 1938, drawing big business and labor unions
into a kind of tripartite working relation with government, to negotiate
all issues in the context of national parameters.

For women, the Swedish Social Democrats would offer at once security and temptation: the security of various social insurance schemes,
the temptation to settle for that.[33] In modern Sweden mothers were
not to be left to struggle on unaided, or aided only at the price of
humiliation; no children were to be left to the mercies of feminized
poverty and single parenthood. On the other hand, the clear thrust of
the union-centered Social Democratic Party was to protect labor at its
heart—those full-time male workers determined to earn a decent family wage. Neither economic nor political motives impelled the party to
press for full-time employment for women also to be paid a family
wage. The clear focus of the Social Democratic welfare policy for a
"national home" was upon women as mothers. For women whose lives
were not necessarily complete within the role of mother, this focus
could seem like constraint.

The chance for women to express wishes as women within Social
Democratic institutions had not been improved. While the proportion
of union members who were women rose over the years, this was not
reflected in leadership. A Women's National Trade Union, started in
1902, was dissolved in 1909, not so much from "Socialist" mandates
putting class above gender as from the rising "national" mandate

putting Swedishness above class and gender. The effective meaning of all this for women within labor unions was spelled out by a militant feminist writer-journalist, Eva Moberg, at the time of a great sex-role debate in 1962.

Moberg laid out a pattern of data.[34] Three hundred and twenty-five thousand women belonged to the LO, the national labor organization—22 percent of the total membership. And how many women were on the LO board of directors? Not one. Further, 20,000 women and 6,000 men belonged to the clothing workers union; of the 17-person board, 13 were men; of the 25 union officers, 20 were men. Women made up about half the membership of the TCO, the white-color union, by 1960; 9 men and 2 women constituted its board. Leadership and even office jobs in its separate constituent unions repeated the model at the top. The segregation of women into separate sections supplied rationalization for these proportions, but only that. The reasons were obviously deeper.

So too did the parties belong to the men. Here, what might hopefully have been a clear lead for the Social Democrats did not prove out. With but 30 percent of its membership women, the Social Democrats in fact surpassed only the tiny Communist party with its 20 percent. The Liberals numbered 40 percent women, the Conservatives over 40 percent, and the Center (the farmers and their allies) no less than 50 percent! In parliamentary representation the Social Democrats did a bit better, their one-sixth of seats occupied by women surpassing the Conservatives' one-eighth and the Liberals' one-twelfth. (Only one of fifty-four of the rural Center Party's seats was held by a woman—clear existential refutation of any significance in that party's high ratio of women members.) In county and local councils, the Social Democrats were little different from Conservatives and Liberals, with about the same one-ninth of seats held by women. But in a comparison of the crucial central committees, where significant party power really lay, the Social Democrats were embarrassed, having only one woman out of twenty-one members, compared to the Liberals' four out of twenty-eight, while the Conservatives, who had a party rule mandating one-third of its central committee seats for women, had six out of twenty. An occasional outstanding woman intellectual such as Alva Myrdal might play an important part in Social Democratic councils from time to time, but for all the party's steady development of security for mothers and children, it showed no obvious tropism toward women as leaders. Its first postwar leader, another in the line of plain, four-square types, Tage Erlander, prime minister for twenty-three years (1946–69), spoke for the jobless, the sick, and the poor, but in no special way for women.

Perfecting the New Home

The genius of the Social Democratic Party and its economists was its refusal, despite its policy of assuring social security for all in Sweden, to withdraw Sweden from competitive world capitalism. If that had been its deepest temptation back in 1928, it had since learned that for a policy of general welfare to prevail, a policy of economy vitality had to be nurtured.[35]

Neutral during World War II, the Swedes plunged back into the world market afterward. No illusions about Swedish self-sufficiency were indulged. To prosper, Sweden had to trade. Though the effort failed, the Swedes first pursued the idea of a kind of Nordic common market: with six other countries they then organized the European Free Trade Association in 1959, a parallel to the European Economic Community of the major nations. When the EFTA disintegrated, Sweden, for diplomatic reasons, refused to enter the EEC directly, but negotiated many agreements to keep its trade with Great Britain, Germany, and a growing list of other nations healthy. In effect, Sweden submitted itself to the tests of international competition. No attempts were made to save old craft methods of production. No attempts were made to save privileged centers of local enterprise. The rationalization of agriculture proceeded apace: soon just 6 percent of the total national work force was producing more in agriculture than ever before. Swedish business went in for bigness and centralization. Becoming an economy of giant corporations, Sweden, on a per-capita basis, soon led the world in multinationals. In terms of ownership, the Swedish economy remained, perhaps paradoxically, one of the most undemocratic in the Western world. Not only did the clear majority of Swedes own nothing but personal property, but a mere handful of Swedes owned most of the private productive sector, with one family, the Wallenbergs, with roots deep in the Swedish past, controlling a larger proportion of Swedish enterprise than any other family in any other nation in the West. But the Wallenbergs had worked closely with king and state in the past; they worked now under the Saltsjöbaden Agreement. They paid their taxes. They did not rail against government, welfare, or labor.

None of this powerful evolution was imagined to be the work of abstract market forces. While 90 percent of Swedish business still remained in private hands, Swedish business continued to arrange affairs with labor according to the 1938 agreement. This collusion in a national capitalism had its fiscal dimensions. Tax laws favoring the growth of investment reserves in the Riksbank provided a kind of gyroscopic mechanism steadying the economy's overall growth. Business, labor, parties, parliament, and government collaborated in an "active labor market policy." No myths of technological progress were allowed to disguise its costs, and the costs were paid. Tax funds subsidized retraining and personal mobility for workers displaced by new machines, so that the opposition to technological innovation among working people common in other nations was averted.

Thus the most important political competitors of the Social Democrats, the Liberals, were outflanked. Exponents of more private initiative, of lower taxes, of less government surveillance over affairs large and small, the Liberals, as critics of public bureaucracies, had principles that made alliance with Conservatives and with the farmers in the Center Party difficult. Most of all, they found themselves deprived of what otherwise would probably have been their strongest card. They could not plausibly criticize the system the Social Democrats had devised, as Trotsky had criticized Stalinism in Russia and Ronald Reagan would criticize "government" in America. For the economy flourished under the Social Democrats: their bureaucracies worked.

But social security was achieved not simply through social insurance paid for by high taxes on efficient large-scale business enterprises. It was also achieved through a lush network of voluntary associations. Alexis de Tocqueville had praised Americans back in 1830 for their propensity to organize, and Americans were to display that propensity for the next century and a half. But while Swedes were later than Americans to organize, they carried their impulse more deeply into the basic structures of the political economy. Both the evangelical and temperance movements that had flourished in the nineteenth century continued to win adherents in the modern epoch, despite their losses to America. In addition, organizations for sports, gymnastics, adult education, and so on proliferated, usually with some national entity holding local branches together. But the essential heart of the voluntary movement was made up of the cooperatives. The Kooperativa förbundet (KF) was founded in 1899, and its growth proved vast. Soon finding its basic mission as a wholesale agency supplying retail outlets especially in food but also in other commodities, it enlisted over one-third of all Swedish families after World War II. After 1917, tenants' associations evolved into housing co-ops. The co-ops developed significant bargaining power in the economy. There were no antitrust laws in Sweden; trusts and cartels were common. The "powerful consumer-cooperative movement . . . frequently . . . served as a check against . . . cartel abuses."[36] The KF found itself getting into the manufacture of electric lights, pottery, rubber goods, and other light articles as well as into food processing and packaging. The KF originated a Cooperative Women's Guild and a Swedish Housewives Alliance. Questions of marketing, household economics, recreational travel for children, and home furnishing induced still more organizations with their own umbrella, the Housewives Joint Committee (HFI). The HFI sponsored a Home Research Institute investigating almost every imaginable matter of concern to homemakers. The KF published *Vi* (We), the most widely read family magazine in Sweden.

While one American scholar has described Swedish society as *genomorganiserat*—saturated with voluntary associations—the impulse was not so much to "complement individualism" as to perpetuate what Swedes feared they were losing with the destruction of the villages and the onset of industry. In the United States, women of the rising industry-based middle classes would find opportunity to generate a sphere of their own, a woman's sphere. The realm of voluntary and cooperative association in Sweden was not such a woman's sphere, but rather a sphere where women had the chance to engage themselves in far more than domestic isolation without necessarily identifying themselves with a job or career. The co-ops were a world of men and women, yet a world especially adapted to women. So was the world of local and municipal government, which, while not voluntary in the fashion of the co-ops, nevertheless, in its susceptibility to local initiatives, its vague organizational structures, and its reliance upon volunteers, also constituted a realm attractive to women who had no desire for career or job, but likewise no desire to stay home all day in a four-room apartment. Through the 1930s, 1940s, and 1950s it was national policy to encourage local communal autonomy, if only on the budgetary ground that local government did many jobs cheaply. In sum, as the basic Swedish structure of big business, big labor, and strong government settled into place, its potential for inducing indifference and withdrawal into private alienation on the part of the mass of citizens was counteracted by the grass-roots proliferation of community associations. If the Social Democrats were building the frame of the national home, the Swedes themselves were furnishing it as the national village they wanted. In this, women played a far greater share than in the framing.

The new national home did not check a precipitous decline in the birthrate. From a nation that still showed almost the highest birthrate in Europe in the 1880s, Sweden found itself within forty years with the lowest. The reproduction rate crossed below the replacement line in 1925. In 1934, two of Sweden's own traditional sort of expert, the social scientist in public service, published a report to which they deliberately gave an urgent title, *The Population Crisis*.[37] Soon, Gunnar and Alva Myrdal said, Sweden would be entering upon actual population decline, if the birthrate did not recover. Neither the Myrdals nor the Social Democrats generally ever proposed anything remotely coercive.

Indeed, an anticontraception law passed in 1910 and still in force was repealed. The Myrdals and the parties agreed on a principle: every baby should be wanted.

Nevertheless, as Gunnar Myrdal explained in lectures at Harvard in 1938, the population crisis that he and his wife had proclaimed had led to propaganda efforts not wholly compatible with the principle of free choice.

Pictures of children are being used more and more in advertising . . . political elections. . . . have [used] an advertising apparatus which utilizes home, mother, and child. . . . The beautiful young mother with healthy, lively children was for a time used as the conventional sign and symbol for everything . . . progressive.

More responsible than anyone else for this campaign, even if only indirectly, at Harvard Myrdal could not quite bring himself to express regret and guilt for it, but he knew he should. Such advertising was an insult to rational people, to Swedes. He did observe, in a kind of reverse expiation, that the advertising had probably had no effect. "Swedish culture has, on the whole, a strongly rationalistic and technical slant. . . . The general public reads books and is apt to pursue quite complicated arguments." Such manipulations were unworthy not just of Swedes, however, but of everyone:

I . . . [assume] that . . . it is not possible, or in any case not desirable, to make people less rationally deliberate. . . . there can never be talk of appealing to the citizen's feeling of "duty" to have a family. . . . Having children is an especially private matter. . . . there is no country in which individuals will marry and have children out of a sense of duty. A people which would reproduce itself out of a sense of duty is a people of robots, a mentally impoverished race. . . . Families ought to have children not in obedience to the good of the State but for their own private happiness.[38]

The correct policy had been initiated in 1937–38 by what came to be called the "parliament of mothers and children." A start was made on various tax-funded programs that, in principle, would guarantee that no woman would suffer poverty for having a child, and that no child would suffer from having an impoverished mother. No bonuses would be offered, as Stalin and Mussolini were offering, to tempt women to have babies they might not otherwise have, but all women would be sure that their motherhood would enjoy direct support in the national home.

Sweden would never really know whether this new policy worked or not. The first significant mother subsidies awaited the end of the war, after 1945.[39] Yet the birthrate in Sweden, which had already been rising slowly since 1934, jumped dramatically between 1942 and 1946, before settling into another modest postwar baby boom lasting into the early

1960s.[40] As Swedes had left the land, the proportion of women at work in jobs outside the home, most of them young and unmarried, had risen steadily to over 30 percent by 1930. Then, with sex ratios returning toward a balance, and women marrying younger and more often, the proportion lagged through the war. But during the 1950s, and 1960s it began to rise once again, to over 50 percent by 1968, and then, swiftly in the 1970s to 75 percent by 1980, when, of slightly more than 4,000,000 workers, over 1,800,000 were women. Practically all the expansion of the Swedish labor force in the 1970s was from women. Most of the new jobs were part-time; women took 80 percent of them. Most of the new jobs were in public service, not manufacturing sectors.[41] In effect, Sweden was entering a postindustrial epoch. Industrial growth depended not on more labor power but upon continuing technological and managerial innovation. Clinics, local government, supervision of children, the co-ops, not factories, offered the new jobs. Typically flexible and part-time, these were obviously adapted to mothers.

The Social Democrats themselves had provided the single sharpest lure to women to go to the job market in their tax reform of 1970. Until then the income of husbands and wives had been lumped and taxed as a single income. With Sweden's extremely high and progressive taxes, there had been little incentive for a wife to work. With incomes taxed separately, a married couple after 1970 had such an incentive.[42] Whether the response testified to a long-simmering resentment of high taxes or a newly awakened appetite cannot be determined. The motive behind the Social Democrats' new law was the party's continuing push toward equalization everywhere. By 1971 wildcat strikes had broken out among various organized professional people—and even some government administrators—against new wage-equalization schemes. Certainly some of these protesters were women. The reform presumably also reflected a shift from the old national political consensus about women's work. Through the 1960s all four major parties had agreed that women should have a free choice between working or not. But this consensus could mean different things for different groups. For some it meant enhancing the appeal of jobs, through such means as day-care centers, more equal pay, and, in 1970, the new tax incentives. The issue of part-time work remained a point of contention. For some, part-time work made it more attractive for women. For others, it kept women locked in low-paid gender ghettos. Meanwhile, the government could pursue other policies without concern for their impact. Sweden saw a boom in apartment-house construction in the 1960s. Many of these new complexes were located far from town centers, however, in their own kind of suburban isolation, rendering efforts to combine job and family harder, not easier.[43] New schedules of rights and subsidies introduced into the family codes in 1972 clearly expressed a new presumption— that every adult Swede, woman as well as man, should be self-supporting. Of course, the ideal for the Social Democrats was to upgrade the jobs commonly done by women, but a gap between ideal and reality remained. Swedish women in full-time blue-collar jobs already made nearly what their male counterparts did, but few women held such jobs. The Social Democrats were betting on continued economic growth and affluence. Such growth would allow the new postindustrial public-service jobs to be upgraded.

Entirely on their own, Swedes had already been devising new modes of family life before the tax and family code revisions of 1970 and 1972. In 1966 Swedes contracted 61,000 marriages, an all-time high. By 1972 a larger total population contracted only 38,000 marriages. Thereafter, the number of marriages never rose above this figure. In 1965, 43 percent of young women, twenty to twenty-five years of age, were married; in 1975, 22 percent were. The rest were not necessarily lingering in pre-marital loneliness: 29 percent were "cohabiting." The generation of Swedes born during and after World War II was giving up marriage in favor of "consensual unions." Swedish sociologists speculated that these were in fact a revival of an old institution, itself a reflection of Swedes' relatively shallow Christianization: in the ancient villages of the countryside, engagement had commonly been followed by "betrothal," a relationship short of marriage during which sexual intercourse and even living together were permitted. Then, upon pregnancy, marriage followed.[44] The tax code may have been of more relevance than history. But cohabitation did not decline after the tax reform of 1970; on the contrary. Moreover, as cohabitation proved attractive to the baby boom generation in the United States too (and in still other Western nations), explanations transcending Sweden's particular case would emerge. But the strength of the new mores became undeniable. In 1965, 14 percent of Swedish babies were born out of wedlock. By 1970, 18 percent were, and by 1977 over one-third, 35 percent, of babies were born to nonmarried mothers.[45] Not that these babies were going to be raised by a single parent necessarily: many were born to a couple living in a consensual union who might very well persist in as permanent a relationship as many marriages. Swedish law took care to qualify these new citizens as fully "legitimate" as their peers born to married parents, although inevitably, reformers would find endless hidden pockets of inequality to be flushed out.

For Sweden's long-range future the new mores were less important in themselves than for what they signified. Once again, it appeared,

Sweden faced a population crisis. In 1977, almost in echo of the Myrdals forty-five years before, two government experts spelled out various implications of the decline in fertility that had overtaken the country from the mid-1960s. Cohabiting couples had fewer children than married couples. Moreover, abortion had risen to become a standard means of birth control. The 3,000 abortions of 1960 had quintupled to 16,000 in 1970, then doubled to the 32,000 of 1975. In that year the abortion laws were revised, in the name of equality, to make abortion free and on demand, but the transformation in the mores had already been achieved: abortions stabilized at slightly more than 30,000 per year thereafter.[46]

Again Sweden faced zero population growth; indeed, on some assumptions, eventual slow decline. By 1977, however, national consensus had been wrought in rejecting any further use of one possible solution. Like other countries in northern and western Europe, Sweden had opened its doors during the 1960s to immigrants. While many of these had been from other Scandinavian countries—from long historic affiliation, Finns enjoyed a "right" to unlimited immigration into Sweden—many others had been from the underdeveloped European southeastern fringes, notably Turkey. Swedes had come to realize that their ancient homogeneity was being threatened. Highly sensitive to memories of having had to stifle moral indignation at Nazi Germany in the interests of neutrality during World War II, and fancying themselves as having, precisely as a long-time neutral, a special relationship with third world countries, Swedes took pains to insist that closing their doors to further non-Scandinavian immigrants expressed, not racial, let alone racist, promptings but a legitimate concern to perpetuate an ancient cultural identity. In any case, the decision to reserve the people's home for Swedes only rendered the population question still more poignant. Carl Aberg and Allan Nordin, the authors of the 1977 report, pointed out that it would entail some severe economic strains too. Within half a century, they said, Swedes over sixty-five would require half the national product. Assuming that the social policies in place for children and youth were continued, half the rest would be going to these age groups. One-quarter of the national product would go to the working-age population. Not all agreed with the two pessimists. Some said significant reserves of untapped female labor still existed in various pockets of the nation to be tapped by "mopping-up operations."[47] Others still held faith in further gains from technology. None of the major parties was ready to embrace policies aimed directly at stimulating fertility. Not only had Gunnar Myrdal himself agreed, back in the 1930s, that anything less than utter freedom on the matter of procreation was unworthy of a free people. Social Democrats were unwilling to jeopardize any of the egalitarian goals to which they remained committed, in the name, say, of encouraging more, earlier, and more procreative marriages. Conservatives still smarted from having once helped sponsor the anticontraception law of 1910 out of military anxieties. The population debate remained muted, muffled, fragmentary. Sweden's economic success seemed sufficient to dull its edge, as had not been true in the early 1930s.

Ironically, the population question had returned just as Sweden's economy itself began giving new signals. After some little delay, Sweden, too, began experienceing the shriveling winds of inflation, worldwide recession, and the rising competition for markets of the late 1970s. For the first time in more than forty years, in 1976 the opposition parties won election as a coalition and took over from the Social Democrats.[48] The election of 1976 hardly turned on recession; complaints at high taxes had been endemic for years and now peaked. But the opposition coalition had no intention of repudiating the social-security system; that had become untouchable. Instead, the coalition sought to strengthen it by various means, most of all, by checking incipient inflation. The Social Democrats lost in another close election in 1979, remaining by far the strongest single party but unable to hold off the combination of the other three. But the coalition and minority governments of 1976–82 proved unable to head off swelling deficits, or a negative balance of trade, or more high prices. They lacked a great communicator to assure the public that deficits, trade imbalances, and disintegrating industries did not matter. One result was that, instead of finding itself in need of more workers, modern Sweden faced the prospect, for the first time, of serious unemployment. The heart of the economic problem lay in the classic export industries. Sweden contemplated a future wherein men's jobs deteriorated as women's grew.

When the Social Democrats, led by Olaf Palme, returned to office in October 1982, they immediately devalued the kronor, imposed wage reductions and embraced austerity. The age of affluence seemed to be ending. Essentially, the SSD determined to press forward with its social plans as though no hard choices had to be made. Palme himself, perhaps out of repressed ideological urges now reawakened, revived an old scheme for investing "wage-earners' funds" in industry. Offered on the one hand as a means to stimulate the faltering export industries, the plan also pleased socialists in the party's left. Since the funds were controlled by unions, the already large—and recently growing—power of union leaders in the economy would be further enhanced. Industrial managers themselves protested, seeing in the plan the inevitable growth of political intervention in the economy in contravention of the basic spirit of Saltsjöbaden.[49]

The Home Under Constant Care: Women's Place

The wage-earners'-fund plan nicely illuminated the effective meaning of the equalization of women in the marketplace. Swedish women had come to hold jobs far more commonly than before, and more commonly than women in any other Western democracy, but their status as workers—and professionals—had had little political translation. While all four of the major parties had their separate women's federation, the very need for such separation testified that nothing like even partial integration of women into the parties' normal operations had been achieved. With their rule, which they lived up to, that at least 40 percent of the places on every party organ, from top to bottom, be held for women, the Liberals proved most intent on pursuing equality, and the chairman, Karin Ahland, of the parliamentary committee on Equality between Men and Women during the coalition was a Liberal. There had been little change in the proportion of women found in parliament and in local—municipal and district—governments in the fifty years to 1970. Then this standard 15 percent doubled in local bodies during the next decade, with a lesser rise in Stockholm. But these changes occurred exactly as analysts were noting that effective power was being drained from elected government, especially local councils, in favor of the unions and the boards of business corporations. With the Social Democrats pressing more and more union leaders onto corporation boards, the unions were becoming perhaps the central institutions in Sweden, and in them women's subordination remained striking. In the most important union organization, the blue-collar Landsorganisation (LO), while women were over one-third the membership, they still provided none of the executive directorate, fewer than 10 percent of the general council. Their near 50 percent of the membership of white-collar unions (TCO), still supplied less than a fifth of the directorate, and in the unions of the professionals (SACO) their one-third membership yielded again less than a fifth of the leadership.[50] The ultimate focuses of power in Sweden perhaps remained those commissions and committees, standing and ad hoc, that had been the chosen instruments of investigation and law-making as far back as the archaic days before parliamentary reform in 1866. However democratic the parties might, or might not, have become, they understood that the commissions provided precious things to Swedish life. They were media for the maximum of consultation before action. They were media for the maximum development of rational consideration, free of emotional politicking. They protected against haste. Basically, they generated consensus. Here, ultimately, was the focus of the peculiarity of Swedish politics.

Though eminently democratic in its suffrage and in its encouragement of wide public debate, Swedish politics never finally grew open to direct populistic feeling. It remained heavily under the control of highly trained experts, an elite of professional social managers. Few women ever appeared among these managers. But precisely as a consequence of the system's consensus-generating dynamics, few women could feel their exclusion harmful in any direct way. Highly skilled professional women enrolled in the Liberal Party might feel impatient with the Social Democrats' high taxes, as in 1971, but their feelings had nothing to do with their status as women, but, rather, with their status as members of a class. Similarly, there were no obvious new policies that would be installed in the social insurance system were women to dominate, for the policies already installed plainly reflected the divisions among women themselves, between women who might well have liked to earn higher full-time salaries, women who might well have liked to stay at home raising more children, and women interested in various combinations in between. Women had not really penetrated further into politics since Eva Moberg's complaints in the 1960s, but what had that cost them? Something of the frustration came through in the effort of a political-minded woman in 1981 to show what difference women might make were they to have more power than they did. A referendum on nuclear power was held in Sweden in 1980. The campaign against nuclear power, Birgitta Wistrand said, was above all one "by women on behalf of female values." But never before had female values been attached to questions of energy. Wistrand's implication, that women were united against nuclear power, presumably because of female values, nicely illustrated how the logic of equality by no means automatically gratified feminist impulses. Equality was simply irrelevant to the question of nuclear power. Exactly what the female values were that impelled women to oppose nuclear power, Wistrand did not say. Implicitly, of course, she was invoking the unearned luck of Sweden's own peculiar freedom from the far more environmentally blighting source of energy in coal in favor of water-generated electricity. Similarly, she declared that, when it came to debating day care versus military defense, "women have another view than men,"[51] as though Swedish women had believed their nation's good luck as a neutral had derived from pacifism rather than politics. In both these cases, she showed that she understood where the political frustration for Swedish women lay, in the very social-welfare politics that the Social Democrats had been pursuing for fifty years, and to which, by the 1970s, all parties subscribed. As tightly linked as their family and even sexual lives had become to economics and politics, Swedish women would find it practically impossible to mobilize for any basic change in the system without finding some way to stress their differences from men rather than simply pursuing equalities with men further. Paradox seemed to have overtaken them: they found themselves far more important and integrated into the economy than ever before, but hardly more self-directed.

3 Soviet Russia. Morality Play

The Last of the Old Russia: Women's Lives in Change

Count Sergei Witte, Russia's Alexander Hamilton, insisted that the industrialization of the Russian Empire required vigorous action by the state. Trained in railroad administration, he pushed railroad building hard; the Trans-Siberian was begun in 1891. The state's purchases of iron and steel for the railroads, and also for the army, became the major stimulus to the coal, iron, and steel industries. Witte reorganized the State Bank to make capital more readily available. A textile industry surged in central Russia, drawing on central Asian cotton. Oil inspired a hectic development in Baku. At 8 percent, Russia's economic growth rate in the 1890s, during Witte's term as minister of finance, was the highest in the world.[1]

This priority given industrial development went hand in hand with a deliberate neglect of agriculture. Agricultural experts agreed that farm production would increase if the peasant communes were broken up in favor of individual ownership. On the other hand, such a transformation required easing the peasants' land payments to the government for the loans by which ex-serfs were enabled to get land in the first place, and required reducing their taxes as well. Besides, much of the wheat exported from Russia was grown on large estates in the southeast, where peasant labor was hired. Finally, land available on the frontier to the east, in Siberia, was already being taken up by hundreds of thousands of peasants who gave promise of becoming a class of independent farmers. For Witte, the best policy was to let agriculture evolve as it might, taxing it to the maximum for the sake of "industrialization from above."

Witte's economic policy was consciously geopolitical. He found capitalists in Europe—Britain, Germany, France, Belgium—eager to invest for the high profits he promised. At the same time he saw the industrialization of Russia not as a contribution to an emerging world market, but as a necessary response to industrialization in the West. "For me it is evident that, in giving us capital, foreign countries commit a political error, and my one desire is that their blindness continue for as long as possible." Russia was to be a capitalist country, but not a democratic capitalist country. Witte actively obstructed liberal efforts toward parliamentary government, because democracy in Russia would mean the predominance of agriculture. The Russia of the future, strong and secure, required collaboration between enlightened, modern-minded public officials like himself and the new industrial leaders he and his colleagues encouraged. Under Count Witte and his high tariffs, favorable loans, and profitable purchasing, industrialists became a new source of support for an autocratic centralized state, making up for the disaffection of the old landowners. The peasants, left to their own devices, would inevitably be drawn off their miserable plots for work in the new mines, mills, and factories.[2]

Probably the best friend the Czar ever had, Witte led a regime that exposed the basic vulnerability of the system. A weak, passive, and unimaginative man, Nicholas II dismissed Witte in 1903 essentially for being strong, energetic, and farseeing. The time was not yet ripe for the collapse of a system that depended to such an extreme upon the qualities of one man chosen for power by the accident of birth, but in the dismissal of Witte imperial Russia showed its basic inability to guarantee its future.

Yet the possibility of evolution remained. Staggered by defeat at the hands of Japan in 1904, nearly brought to its knees by the revolutionary ferment of 1905, czardom persisted for nearly another decade under another imaginative leader, Peter Stolypin, premier from 1906 to 1911.[3] Under Stolypin, the fast pace of industrialization resumed, ever more clearly in the form of vast concentrations fed from above. Witte, in a last few months of service in 1906, succeeded in getting funds transfused into the nation's desperate financial bloodstream from the West. Labor surpluses from the countryside allowed huge operations to be run profitably. The textile mill at Yaroslavl was the largest in the world. Its labor force reflected the dislocations overtaking the peasant population. One visitor was told "that the majority of the machine operatives in these factories were girls who came into the mills at about fifteen to seventeen years of age. . . . [These] girls lost their capacity to make good operatives when they reached thirty." In these utterly new, raw, giant enterprises, everything had to be supplied. Housing took the form of "huge barracks in which almost military discipline was observed."[4] Such workers were poor and disorganized. In the Ukrainian steel mills and Donbas coal mines, too, where labor from the countryside was abundant, the government's prohibitions on trade unions and political activity worked. Only in St. Petersburg, where prior urban life and a relative paucity of hands obtained, were seeds of working-class consciousness beginning to sprout.

Stolypin reversed Witte's nonpolicy toward peasants. Since peasants on the communes had shown themselves no more loyal to the government in 1905 than the independent peasant landholders were, there was no more political reason to tolerate their inefficiencies. Stolypin proposed a straightforward bargain based on mutual self-interest. Let the commune no longer be protected. Let the maximum number of peasants be encouraged to farm individually. Let the government encourage mechanization. Let the new farmers be brought into a rationalized, updated system of marketing. Let peasants too become capitalists. Let us, Stolypin proposed, "wager not on the drunken and the weak"—now assumed to flourish in the noncompetitive security of the communes—"but on the sober and the strong—on the sturdy individual proprietor."[5] Stolypin's obvious assumption was that a greater mutually stimulative interaction than the one envisioned by Witte's policy could be set up between the two sectors.

Here was the greatest revolution yet foreseen in Russian history, a revolution in the basic character of the Russian peasant, the overwhelming majority of the nation. In effect, the peasant would become—at last—farmer. Stolypin's further assumption, that such a new farmer class could provide greater political stability to the nation, was not destined to be tested. Some six million small landholders had emerged by the eve of World War I. Russia's annual export of cereals and other foodstuffs swelled to 15 million tons in the last five years before the war. The heavy majority of Russians on the land remained peasants, most of them tied to communal landholding, most of them still in poverty, backwardness, and ignorance. Yet a direction had been established at last.[6] Would that new class of farmers help stimulate further industrial growth, or would they resent it? Bolsheviks would debate that question. Would such new farmers develop a political consciousness of their own, averse perhaps to direction from above? Lenin and Lenin's heirs would debate that, too. They would have far more power than the Czar's ministers to make their decisions stick.

For every new farmer there was a farmer's wife. As family farms emerged in Russia, the working unit would become man and wife. In the old communes with their extended families, women often worked together. They could easily lose their sororal sharing under Stolypin's policy. At the same time, the old communes encouraged gender polarities. Sunk in an ethos of poverty and the uselessness of effort, the commune's men indulged in the compensations of drink. Drink led to brutalities toward women. Would a woman be safer alone with a husband on a family farm? Such issues were in ferment in Russia before the war, beneath the notice of government and policy makers. Women had much at stake, with few chances to discuss it or debate it or even think about it. Their lives were being transformed without their will. If a new kind of woman was being generated by Stolypin's new policy, a farmer's wife, her future might depend on whether she would ever be able to make herself heard.

One Year Too Many: Old Russia's Last Charge

World War I stimulated Russia's industrial growth. The government's subsidies between 1914 and 1917 surpassed those of the whole nineteenth century. The Russian machine-tool industry boomed. Chemical production boomed. Textiles grew. Russian production of shells, artillery, and rifles soared. What Germany had feared in 1914 was coming to pass: a modern industrialized Russian state, potentially far more powerful than Germany or any other Western European state. The collapse of Czarism then, early in 1917, did not follow from economic collapse. Nor did it follow from military catastrophe or collapse. The Russian army had had significant successes in 1916. In the spring of 1917 it remained large and undefeated. No strategy promised victory to the Germans. At the same time, the incompetence of the Russian General Staff had become evident. It did not know what to do with General Brusilov's victories of 1916. Certainly the Czar did not. It was by a kind of grass-roots popular consensus that the default of leadership was taken by the troops as definitive. But the new Provisional Government had no intention of quitting the war, nor did the troops. If all idea of new offensives was abandoned, the continued defense of Russia remained unquestioned, and, as it happened, from March to November 1917 the eastern front remained relatively inactive. The destruction of the Czar, in short, had been a consequence of Russia's vitality, not of its deliquesence. The destruction of the Provisional Government, too, followed, not from Russia's backwardness, but from its headlong career into modernity, too fast, too soon.[7]

The expansion of industry during the war had expanded the ranks of industrial workers, many of them drawn from the peasantry. Increasingly aware of the breakdown in management, these workers organized themselves into "councils"—soviets—which began to try to conduct factory affairs themselves. Similar councils appeared among peasants and among the soldiers, most of whom were themselves young peasant boys. The seeds of these soviets were in the communal sociology of the peasant countryside itself. But however populistic and quasi-revolutionary these councils may have seemed, they offered no policies for Russia. They looked to the Provisional Government for leadership. Only the Provisional Government could carry on the war and defend Russia. But the Provisional Government found itself caught in the contradictions the rapid industrial expansion had already generated. War production had taken the form, perhaps inevitably, of collaboration between the government and the large-scale monopolistic enterprises typical of Russian capitalism under the autocracy. In the process, millions of peasants who had supported themselves, not by farming at all, but by household crafts—cottage industry—were wiped out, leaving widespread unemployment. And the industrial expansion had been paid for by inflation. Aware of the fragility of its support, the autocracy had not dared impose taxes to pay for the war. By early 1917 prices had multiplied by seven over the prewar levels of 1914. The Provisional Government could not keep them from doubling again. Real wages did not begin to keep pace; even workers with jobs had begun to go hungry by the late summer of 1917. Paradoxically, the high prices of food in the cities did not benefit farmers. As agricultural machinery broke down and fertilizer production fell, the production of the export-growing estates of the landed gentry fell, as did that of Stolypin's new efficient ambitious farmers on their family farms. Production held up and often increased on the classic peasant communes, with their primitive methods. But the peasants could not get their crops to market. Military mismanagement of the railroads was one reason. Another was the breakdown of the complicated chain of middlemen between commune and market. One consequence was the growth in numbers of farm animals. Cattle, sheep, pigs multiplied as factory workers grew thin. A heritage of anger and suspicion was stored up: not the vast impersonal processes of imperfect systems were held to blame, but peasant greed, the avarice of bankers, speculators, capitalists. Peasants themselves, meanwhile, were stimulated to covet more land, more animals, more hope. With one of its most important parties, the Kadets, heavily made up of gentry landholders, the Provisional Government was in no position to satisfy such appetites. As the eagerness for land spread among soldier-peasants, the question took on military implications. When strikes spread among factory workers protesting their condition, industrial production began to fall, undermining the provisioning of the army with its very weapons. Women of course shared in all these contradictions with their men. No arts of domesticity equipped gentry women to repel the implacable undermining of their husbands' estates, no household skills impeded the blighting of hope among the aspirant farmers. Women often found themselves on their own in the factories; some of these made up the ranks of those women marching in the streets of Petrograd on the eve of the second revolution.[8]

Although the exponent of a philosophy, practically a metaphysics of historical determinism, V. I. Lenin could not throughout his life resist repeated affirmations of personal grit and determination and will. "Give us an organization of revolutionaries," he had promised, "and we will overturn Russia."[9] But Lenin and his Bolsheviks did not over- turn Russia. Russia was overturned from within itself. Lenin found it extremely hard to wait. Early on, he proposed open opposition to the Provisional Government. Many of his own followers rejected his call. Then, in July 1917, when mobs in Petrograd did respond eagerly to his call for revolutionary overthrow, he himself drew back, as though aware of the contrast between mob and "organization." The time seemed riper late in the summer and early fall. Workers began taking over factories directly and peasants the land, in the Ukraine, Finland, and the Caucasus the voice of ethnic independence groups was to be heard, and in the army desertion itself appeared to be spreading. Again, Lenin's Bolshevik colleagues in Petrograd disagreed with his insistence that the time had come to seize power at last. Instead they took part in a Democratic Conference called by the government. They had both rea- son and politics on their side. As late as March 1917, on the Czar's abdication, the Bolsheviks had constituted little more than a dispersed, divided, and conspiratorial sect. But by the autumn the party itself numbered at least 200,000 and, far more significant, was winning elections in local workers' soviets all over the country. Even better, with a new slogan, "Peace, Land and Bread," the party had begun to win some peasants. Elections were scheduled for November to a new Con- stituent Assembly which would draw up the new national constitution. While it was clear that the peasants' Socialist Revolutionary Party would win a majority to the assembly, it was also clear that its growing left wing was sympathetic to Lenin's ideas for a worker-peasant pro- letarian alliance. Moreover, in a Bolshevik-Left Socialist Revolutionary coalition, the Bolsheviks' far greater organizational and political ex- perience would give them crucial leverage. Certainly the Left SR leader, Maria Spiridonova, would be no match for Lenin. In short, Lenin was offered an entirely democratic route to power.

Exactly why he did not accept it remains a question open to historians and biographers. As usual, Lenin had supplied himself with theory to justify his choice. In *The State and Revolution*, written while he was hiding in Finland in August under ban of the Provisional Government, he had announced that parliamentary government—the kind of gov- ernment the Constituent Assembly would presumably install—could serve only capitalism, not socialism. Since capitalism could not be democratic, neither could parliamentary government. Only the direct participation of workers and peasants—and, in the desperate circumstances of late 1917, soldiers—in their councils, the soviets, spelled democracy. Just why all this was so, Lenin never really explained. If some parliamentary systems excluded workers and peasants, why must all do so? But Lenin was not really writing political theory, only immediate tactics. Soon, it became clear Lenin did not intend that the democratic workers and peasants should rule either. The soviets were scheduled for their own Second All-Russian Congress on November 7. Thus, when Lenin pressed his Red Guards into action on November 7, he not only overthrew the Provisional Government, he also preempted the congress of the "democratic" soviets. To argue that Lenin acted as he did because what he wanted—perhaps had wanted all along—was unchallenged power for himself is of course to awaken the spirits of psychology in biography. The defense against these has been simple: while Lenin may have been heroic, his heroism was in perceiving what simply had to be done. He had the courage to accept inevitability. Here the problem of Russian history still has its focus, and necessarily the focus of a history that includes women. Lenin's greatest decision after seizing power was to take Russia out of the war. In effect, he surrendered vast precious limbs of the motherland to the hated enemy. Was he manifesting "will" and "determination" in this act? And did this will evince a psychological masculinity that was soon to appear vividly symptomatic of the triumphant Bolsheviks generally? Peace was often—then and, in Russia, as often today—thought a goal peculiarly linked to women. Yet in Russia in 1917 most women political leaders were for more war, more defense of the motherland. As inclusion of gender history deepens its stories, the question will have to be further explored, whether Lenin simply rose above any such gender categorizations in his coup d'état of 1917 and his peace with the enemy. Of course many further hypotheses can be—must be—kept alive. Might a reasonable man in November 1917, considering the military and economic disintegration, have feared some reactionary counterrevolution, if not in the name of the Czar, then under brute military auspices? Might not such a man have concluded that the chances for democracy had been wholly extinguished for any immediate future and that its chances for some middle-range future depended on action by those who at least honored its ideal in name? On the other hand, coldly calculating reasonable men might also have totted up the odds on Russia's going down to heroic military defeat at the hands of the Germans in 1917 and being rescued and revived by the West in 1918. The inevitability, the necessity, of Lenin's decisions of 1917 cannot be demonstrated by the facts of 1917. Justifying them by facts since 1917 has lent Soviet history its eerie air of overdeterminism.

Women in the Maelstrom: 1917

Between March, when the Czar abdicated, and November, when Lenin seized power, many important gains had been registered for women, especially for politically active women.[10] This in itself was no startling revolution. By no means had the autocracy pursued some ideology consigning women to backwardness. Numerous Russian women enjoyed opportunities closed to their Western sisters. From 1872 the government opened the doors of higher education to young women. Though its motives were conservative and expedient, no gender ideology had held it back. Hundreds of young Russian women had been going to Zurich to study medicine as well as other courses; many were being radicalized. The government saw that its self-interest lay in allowing such training at home. Soon entry into every university was offered to women, and from that standpoint, Russian women enjoyed greater opportunities than their Western sisters did. Nonetheless, only a few could qualify, and the educational reforms did not remotely affect the overwhelming majority in either the cities or the countryside. No self-supporting middle class was growing in Russia. Under the Czars, landowning women had long enjoyed various legal rights unknown in the West; they did not suffer from the Napoleonic Code, the English common law, and Blackstone. But again, these constituted a tiny, privileged minority. Politically, women had shared in the emergence of that special category known as the "intelligentsia" in Russia, those for whom more or less persistent attention to questions of social reform became the center of life. Often the children of priests but just as often of landlords and even nobility, these were not a party or a sect, let alone a class, but a kind of yeast within what seemed to be the vast inertia of imperial Russia. Such people were testimony to the fact that, while autocratic, Russia was not yet totalitarian. Leading lives sometimes open, sometimes underground, at once puzzling to and harassed by the police and the bureaucracies, the intelligentsia formed a kind of moral fraternity open to all active imaginations. Nothing in Russian history impeded women from sharing. Every story, every novel, every treatise on "what was to be done" about Russia showed young men and young women together, and sometimes the most vivid focus of their ethos bore upon new relations between the sexes, upon love and marriage.

Insofar as revolutionary politics emerged out of this ethical life, revolutionary politics too was open to women. When young educated idealists went "out to the people" in the 1870s, young women were among them. One, Ekaterina Breshkovskaya, a daughter of the nobility, later became a Socialist Revolutionary and remained active in 1917, famed as "the little grandmother of the Russian Revolution." Another,

Vera Zasulich, went on from this "populism" to an attack on the life of the governor of St. Petersburg. When the government staged political trials of fifty revolutionary radicals in 1878, sixteen were women. In another "great trial," thirty-seven of 193 accused were women. In the terrorist People's Will group, devoted to assassinating Alexander II and his officials, ten of the twenty-eight-member Executive Committee were women. One, Sophia Perovskaya, was hanged, along with four men, for the assassination of the Czar in 1881. Another, Vera Figner, was sent to prison in 1883 for terrorist activities, but emerged in time to be on the scene in 1917. Richard Stites has calculated that, in the 1870s, the more radical the activities, the higher the proportion of women involved.

Following Alexander's assassination, repression and depression set in among the intelligentsia. By the time hope and activity resumed, a problem had been generated for women within the increasingly Marxist Left itself. The leading Marxist text on women had been published in Germany in 1879—August Bebel's *Woman and Socialism*. Bebel was clear about many things—the degradation of women under capitalism, the equality to be enjoyed by women under socialism. But Bebel was not clear about feminism. At times he evinced warm sympathy for feminist efforts in Germany and elsewhere, particularly as to woman suffrage. At times he appeared to believe that women had a sisterly unity in oppression that undercut—or transcended—class. Yet he by no means rejected the standard Marxist idea that class took priority over gender. But the leading woman Marxist in Germany, Clara Zetkin, dispelled the blurring of lines that Bebel had bequeathed.[11] She attacked feminism as a "ladies' rights" movement, dismissed the sisterhood of women as a myth, and insisted upon "class war" as against the "battle of the sexes." She rejected feminists' invitations to working women to collaborate in demanding women's civil rights. Not only did she repel the feminists; she induced splits within the German socialist movement itself. Eventually the most intellectually creative of German socialist women, Lily Braun, left the German Social Democratic party.[12] In Russia, where the Marxist Social Democrats had split into Mensheviks and Bolsheviks over questions of party organization and leadership, both branches adopted Zetkin's position on feminism. Feminism was a bourgeois movement: there could be no alliance of socialists and feminists.

Lenin always affirmed the full equality of women as a socialist ideal.[13] He always thought of it literally. Women could not be men's equals if they stayed at home. They too must be active in the world. He established his sincerity well enough, in taking women as some of his closest collaborators. Indeed, he ran prewar Bolshevism as a bit of a family enterprise. Collaborating with his wife, Nadezhda Krupskaya, on her book, *The Woman Worker* (1900), a brief but grim portrait of both peasant and urban working-class women in Russia. In 1913 he made her editor of *The Working Woman*, a paper he started in response to his wife's insistence that Russian Marxists were missing a bet in ignoring the political education of working women. As his Paris editor of the paper he appointed his closest woman friend (not a mistress), Inessa Armand. As his St. Petersburg editor he appointed his sister, Maria Ulyanova.

But the most conspicuous and compelling Marxist woman was no relative but the independent Alexandra Kollontai.[14] Born in 1870 in St. Petersburg, Kollontai had received a good education encouraged by her father, an enlightened soldier. In her mother, the owner and manager of a money-making estate in Finland, she had a model of intelligent, independent womanhood. Her husband, Vladimir Kollontai, offered no objection when his wife, at twenty-six, announced that she meant to lead a new life. Nor did her parents. She left her young son behind at first, then retrieved him and kept him with her. She was attracted to Germany by the intellectual vitality of the socialist women's movement there. She returned to Russia intent upon persuading the Mensheviks in St. Petersburg of the importance of political work among women. She had also been persuaded by Clara Zetkin's views on feminism. In 1908 Kollontai made herself felt by arranging for the disruption of an "all-women's" conference scheduled in St. Petersburg, declaring it feminist, class-bound, individualistic, non- and antisocialistic. In "The Social Basis of the Woman's Question," Kollontai offered her formal discourse on the theme. But she found herself embattled on the opposite front, too. Her male Marxist Menshevik colleagues failed to respond to her urging of political work among women. By then the most famous of all European Marxist women, Rosa Luxemburg, was carrying Zetkin's views still further: women's questions were irrelevant to the revolution; first the revolution, then the liberation of women. Kollontai could not agree. She had reasons for socialism that were special to women. Whether Kollontai might have been able to persuade Russian Marxists to undertake a direct political work among women, had she been able to shake off all hints of feminism in herself, one can hardly say. Kollontai herself began to suspect that the "Russian" component of Russian Social Democracy might be responsible for the indifference.

Kollontai's eventual turn to Lenin and the Bolsheviks did not stem from approval of Lenin's own belated sponsorship of a women's paper. She had much preferred the Mensheviks' idea of the party as a collaboration with the workers to Lenin's view that the party must be made up of tightly disciplined professional revolutionaries who would lead and direct the workers. Had the Mensheviks offered warm response to her own plans for women, Lenin might never have won her. He did so only when the German Socialists, forgetting class in favor of country, voted war credits; Lenin's declaration that true Marxists could not support either side in an imperialist war struck her as not only correct but brave. It was then that she became a Bolshevik. So ended any chance that Kollontai might in the end lend her remarkable talents to a Russian feminist movement.

Marxists hardly prevented the eight months of revolution before they seized power late in 1917 from being fruitful for women.[15] Only a week into the revolution, on March 20, after the new premier, Prince Georgi Lvov, appeared to wobble on woman suffrage, feminist organizations mobilized the first great street demonstration. Universal suffrage for all over twenty was guaranteed by July 20. Thus Russian women had the vote before French, German, British, American, Swedish, or Italian women. Women had already been granted the right to sit on juries, and women lawyers the right to practice before the bar. Soon all women in the civil service were granted equality of pay, fringe benefits, titles, and eligibility: of these, schoolteachers were the largest group. Plans were set afoot for fully equal university education, fulfilling hopes that had been frustrated since 1881. Feminists in the Equality League, the Women's Progressive Party, and the Mutual Philanthropic Society, all founded in 1905, geared up to lobby for an eight-hour day in industry, protective legislation for women workers, mother-and-child programs, professional equality in medicine and engineering, and humane rehabilitation of prostitutes. None of these came from the Bolsheviks. Alexandra Kollontai was still busy assailing such feminists.

Continuity with the revolutionary past emerged in this pre-Bolshevik period of the revolution. The aged Vera Figner rode at the head of a feminists' procession in March. The aged ex-terrorist Vera Zasulich went out to counter the Bolsheviks' antiwar propaganda. The aged Catherine Breshkovskaya also joined the feminists. The failure of Lenin and the Bolsheviks to attract such women followed plainly from Lenin's broadest logic: the revolution must be captured by one party, one philosophy, one head. The appeal of feminism to such women, on the other hand, could be seen in the figure of a new leader, the head of the Women's Progressive Party, a doctor, Maria Pokrovskaya. In her work Pokrovskaya had treated working women, soldiers' wives, and prostitutes. She had grasped the link between ill-paid labor and prostitution. She had seen the inadequacy of the diets of the children of soldiers and workers. She despised the capitalism she saw. She also despised Marxist theories, whether Menshevik or Bolshevik. Women's suffering, she believed, was due to men. No men's utopias impressed her. Fundamentally, Lenin and the Bolsheviks were telling working women, let us radical men save you. Pokrovskaya said, we must save ourselves.

The old revolutionaries all showed that in the depths of their revolutionary hearts they had always harbored a vision of Russia reborn, not of a world reborn. So did the feminists. Vera Figner wanted Russia to go on fighting, stop the Germans, and avoid a brutal defeat. So did Zasulich. So did Breshkovskaya. And so did Pokrovskaya. Pokrovskaya enthusiastically supported the Women's Battalion that was reported on with exaggerated glamour in newspapers in the West. None could accept the reality that Russia had already been defeated and that its brutalization could not be averted. Like Alexander Kerensky and the Provisional Government, they could not welcome a maelstrom.

Bolshevism as Masculinity

"We shall now proceed to build socialism," declared Lenin on November 8, 1917. First, however, he had to secure power. A decree abolishing private ownership of land confirmed the peasants' seizure of it. "We, a democratic government, cannot ignore the will of the people, even if we do not agree with it." But here was a step toward the loss, not the consolidation, of power. Soon the Bolsheviks—who relabeled themselves "Communists" in March 1918—had to forcibly "requisition" farm production.[16] A duel between the new leaders and the peasants had begun. For rural women much was at stake. Standard portraits of the Russian peasant woman by the intelligentsia correctly stressed her heavy burdens, her privations, her long suffering. Yet new women had begun to appear in the countryside, young wives newly protected by some of the reforms of the 1880s. Long oppressed by the rule of mothers-in-law, young peasant wives found it easier to refuse the old arrangements. Often young farm wives were as interested as their young husbands, if not more so, in opportunities for individual farming. When Communist ideologues, justifying their expropriations of the farmers' crops, labeled them "kulaks," "capitalists," and "farmers," often as not these new farmers—Stolypin's "sober and strong"—were wives prodding their men forward into modern productivity. Had Lenin not had to grant them land in order to win his political gamble, he would not have chosen to do so.

Granting control of the factories to workers was easier. In 1918 the workers had been won to Bolshevism; they were presumably ready to follow the lead of the Communists. Soon, however, by 1921, a Workers' Opposition would emerge, protesting that the workers were not enjoying any real power, but by then the Communists had survived the worst of their trials.

The worst of those trials were only beginning as Lenin took power. First there were the Germans, who had to be bought off by a humiliating peace. Then there came anti-Bolshevik Russians, assisted by Allied interventions in hopes of bringing Russia back into the war. Various right-wing SR leaders proved sympathetic to these Whites. But the SR Right disappeared from politics. Only the Mensheviks remained, and they were liquidated as a party by 1920. Lenin and the Communists ruled alone.[17]

It has sometimes been argued that the Leninist party of iron discipline, "democratic centralism," rigid hierarchical authority, and secret police was as much a function of these desperate years of civil war as of Lenin's own philosophy. Since the philosophy had been clearly enunciated long before, it seems reasonable to conclude that the civil war, however much it may have required iron leadership, provided justification rather than reason. Nevertheless, the civil war generated its own legitimation. Lenin himself was mesmerized by it. Russia came near utter collapse in 1918–20. The invading armies pressed on the heartland from Siberia, from the Cossack and Ukrainian plains, from the west, even from the Arctic. Bands of disaffected peasants marauded in the countryside. Famine swept away millions. Riots broke out in towns and cities. Streaks of rust marked railroads, jumbles of iron what had once been factories. Peasants who had been drafted into the Red Army deserted in droves. Farmers in Siberia welcomed the counterrevolutionary armies of General Kolchak. Yet somehow the new regime survived. It almost seemed a miracle. Said Lenin: "If anyone were to gauge exactly how thin is that strain of advanced workers and Communists who with the support of the worker and peasant masses have administered Russia in these last twenty months, it would seem truly incredible."[18] Did the dialectic of historical materialism depend on a few heroes after all?

In fact, the Communists had been saved in considerable part by their enemies.[19] As the various armies tried to penetrate to Moscow, they followed no master strategy; uncoordinated, they could be halted and defeated one by one. The Western governments that had intervened in 1918 lacked the will to press on in 1919, once Germany had been defeated. Most of all, none of the invading forces understood what had happened inside Russia. Wherever they appeared, White armies stripped peasants of their new-won land, flogged them, sometimes killed them, as though Czarist feudalism were to be restored. Such peasants rallied to the Communists in profound self-interest. Without them, heroics alone would not have availed.

Nonetheless, the Bolsheviks had shown themselves to be a remarkable breed. Lenin's own immediate circle, forever given to the most intense debate and division, constituted a core of seasoned political men. Nothing like them had ever been seen in the revolutionary groups of the old intelligentsia. There were no women among them and never would be. The terms of debate and personal testing were such that a woman would have had to be stripped of all femininities almost before she grew up. Moreover, as a new, less politically sophisticated, younger breed began to swarm into the party, it too had an unmistakably gender-linked quality:

In the morning in the *Execcom* . . . there gathered, sign of the times, leather men in leather tunics, (bolsheviks!) everyone a standard leather man, each of them hefty, and hair in curly ringlets sticking out of his neck from under a forage cap—but what more than anything else made them was the purpose in the tight-drawn muscles of the cheek, in the folds at the lips, in their rigid movements—the purpose and the insolent courage. . . . As for Karl Marx, probably not one of them had read him.[20]

The Communist Party was open to women; women made up more than one-fifth of its membership by the early 1920s. Yet mere membership in the party was only the first step toward power. Power came from implacability, from methods of self-management and self-assertion learned only at high risk. A woman who might have such qualities would find herself defeated if only because of her implausibility. The Communist Party's ladder offered no route to equality for women.

Mesmerized by the "incredible" heroics of the civil war, once the war was over, Lenin let Leon Trotsky assign his uniformed soldiers to "building Communism," just as though the same methods used for fighting the war could be used for building a society. Such soldiers were peasants who wanted to go home, however, and soon they were doing so, contributing to great new peasant riots in 1921, directed precisely at the heroic Communists who were trying to continue their requisitions with wartime fervor. Lenin later confessed his mistake, the mistake of "deciding upon an immediate transition to communist production and distribution: Life has shown us our mistake."[21] By March 1921 he began to introduce a New Economic Policy (NEP), presumably in a concession to "life." Peasants would be allowed access to real markets. Some small private commercial enterprises would be allowed, some small-scale trading, various small industries. "Capitalism" would be readmitted. All large-scale enterprises were held firmly by the state, however, no matter how rusted and decrepit they might be.

Above all, many in the party wanted it to tighten its own internal life.[22] Not all agreed. While favoring the one-party dictatorship, many Communists, especially of the old persuasion, were proud of the party's tradition of internal debate. After all, as a party devoted to a "science" of leadership, teaching, and control, where else should the most thoroughgoing debates be held? Such debates were resuming in 1920 and 1921, openly, with party groups taking such labels as "Workers' Opposition" and "Democratic Centralists." At the Tenth Party Congress of March 1921, Lenin pushed through a resolution banning "platform factions," groups organized to support specific policies. The Workers' Opposition had urged that control over factories be returned to the workers themselves, as it supposedly had been back in November 1917. Under the new rule, the Workers' Opposition was dissolved. Its spokesmen were forbidden contact with the workers' trade unions. Debate within the party would go on, but ever less equipped with regular forms, ever more muffled, "Aesopian," further hidden from outside publics that would find it hard to know even that debate was occurring. The role of monitors, bureaucrats, controllers, and police expanded. The ranks of the party had swollen, from 200,000 or so in 1917 toward half a million. Periodic purgations of the party lists became a new method of control. If the New Economic Policy ever began to generate new possibilities, new publics, and new ideas in Russian life, it would still find an unchanged politics to confront it.

Last Chance for a Liberal Russia: Women's Stake

The New Economic Policy was resisted by many Communists as an abandonment of socialism, a surrender to "bourgeois" psychology, a revival of capitalism.[23] But to Lenin and those he persuaded, the single most urgent task seemed obvious. The nation was in ruins. Revolts in the countryside had shown that the coercive, military methods of "war communism" would not work. A turn in policy need not be surrender. It could be thought of as mere retreat, one step backward now in order to take two steps forward later. Still, this was not a wholly satisfying formulation then, nor has it satisfied all historians since, for it implies that the Communists, Lenin included, knew exactly what they were doing. In fact, they did not. They were debating it.

The immediate economic effects of the NEP were evident within five years. By 1926–27 Russia was back in production. Agriculture overall was about back to the levels of 1913, and so was industrial production. Exports, nearly extinguished in 1920, reviving to 80 million rubles by 1922, surged to over 300 million by 1924. The bartering, payments in kind, and makeshift commodity cards that had replaced money after the incendiary inflation of 1920–21, had been replaced not only by good paper money but by solid silver coins and even gold. Russia was back in the international market as a reliable participant. The Soviet Union stood at the beginning of a boom.

In the autumn of 1924, the results . . . were visible on all sides. The *kulaks* in the villages had quickly taken advantage of the situation to enrich themselves; and the peasants as a whole were enjoying . . . a comparative prosperity. The middlemen and the private traders in the towns and cities had been enabled to make large profits. Many small manufacturers had been quick to re-establish themselves, and reaped a rich harvest in supplying the shortage of commodities. The boarded-up shop windows of Moscow and Leningrad were rapidly giving place to more or less prosperous-looking retail establishments. Restaurants in the cities were reopening, and night after night the newly enriched "Nepmen" could be found there spending their easily acquired gains.[24]

Some members of the governing cabinet—the Politburo—warmly supported continuation of the NEP. Nicolai Bukharin had been spelling out theories for a permanent NEP for some time. Against Trotsky and the Left, who believed the peasants basically to be an obstacle to industrialization, Bukharin argued that industry and agriculture must proceed together. Communists should work "genetically," collaborating with the active forces of the country as they were, rather than trying to impose, "teleologically," ideal models they might hold in their own heads.[25] This meant industrializing on the basis of rising consumption among the peasants, for the obvious reason that they were the overwhelming majority of potential consumers, but also on the basis of rising consumption among urban workers, shopkeepers, professionals, and so on. This meant growth of light industry first, and only afterward that of heavy industry. Another Politburo member, Alexei Rykov, a man of peasant background, brought deep conviction to the populistic and even democratic qualities in this outlook, sharing Bukharin's profound fears that Communism could relapse into Czarism and end up grinding its "iron heel"—Jack London's novel had burned itself into Bukharin's imagination—into the body of the people. Politburo member Mikhail Tomsky, the leading trade-union leader since the revolution, saw in Bukharin's view of the NEP the preservation of new powers of working class self-determination. Joined by Joseph Stalin, these three men made up the effective majority of the Politburo during the four years after Lenin's death early in 1924.

Quite apart from debates over theory, however, it was reasonably clear that the NEP was not being given a good-faith opportunity from the start. Scorned by true Bolsheviks as parasites, the Nepmen in fact challenged Bolshevism at its heart. They took away total control. Capitalism sucked authority away from the state.

Hence it was that in 1924 a slow policy of retrenchment began. Acting on general instructions from the political chiefs . . . the tax collector commenced to de-

mand extortionate taxes from private traders, industrialists, and kulaks. . . .
Long before 1927, this policy had become general, and a large percentage of
private traders had been forced to abandon the unequal fight. . . . In Leningrad
. . . three old employees of the great provisioning firm of Elyseev opened a small
shop for selling hams, dried fish, caviare, and other *sakuska* (*hors-d'oeuvres*)
products. The business prospered until a tax collector called and demanded a
turnover tax on an imaginary figure amounting to several times their actual
turnover. Payment was obviously impossible, and the ultimate result was that
the members of this enterprising little group . . . were called upon by the
O.G.P.U. late one night, and [soon] found themselves members of a labour gang
going northwards.[26]

By 1926–27 larger problems with the NEP were becoming clear.
While idled factories in light industry had been successfully reacti-
vated, not enough new ones were being built. Concomitantly, new investment in basic heavy industry, as well as in new transport facilities
and new energy sources, could not be deferred much longer without
choking off further recovery in light industry as well as agriculture.
According to a new labor registration system, unemployment was growing, 1.5 million out of work in 1926 growing to more than 2 million in
1927. At the same time shortages of skilled workers—machinists, weld-
ers, engineers—appeared. The situation had a gender inflection.[27] Owing to the killing times of 1914–20, in 1926 5 million more of the Soviet
Union's 147 million were women than men. In the labor market the
skewing was greater. Among those over 30 years of age, for every 100
women there were 88 men; among those between 25 and 29, there were
only 83 men for every 100 women. So severe was unemployment that
some trade-union leaders dismissed women workers in favor of men
and discouraged women job applicants. In general, the improvement
of agriculture had impelled multitudes of surplus landless people into
the cities, but so far the NEP had generated too few jobs for them.
Among the most desperate were the hundreds of thousands of women
without men.

But it was in agriculture that difficulties became crisis.[28] Late in
1927, despite good harvests, grain deliveries to the market were running
sharply lower. What many Communists unsympathetic to the NEP had
long suspected appeared to be happening: peasants were withholding
their harvest in hopes of a better price. Bukharin himself had never
been a friend of the successful individual farmers, the kulaks. He had
nursed the old notion that the life and practices of the communal
farmers constituted a germ of socialism, and through state loans and
tutelage, had hoped to encourage these "middle" and poor peasants to
improve their operations. Collective farming would emerge as by a kind
of evolutionary persuasion. Still, Bukharin did not find the crisis of
1927 reason for heroic measures. A Five-Year Plan aiming at balanced

collaboration among all the productive forces of the nation seemed sufficient. The party could preside over the process as a kind of regulator.

Economic facts did not decree the end of the NEP. Its demise coincided with the emergence of Joseph Stalin as sole leader of the party. Late in 1927 Leon Trotsky, implacable foe of the NEP from the start, was expelled from the party, on his way to exile. Then, early in 1928, tens of thousands of new young Communist militants from the cities were sent into the countryside to begin seizing stores and arresting peasants. Local party officials were ordered to cooperate. By December 1929 a new mission had been announced: to "liquidate the *kulaks* as a class." Having evicted Trotsky, his most dangerous rival, Stalin had then assumed Trotsky's policy and driven Bukharin and his colleagues from the field. The result followed not just from Stalin's personal maneuvering, but from the loyalty that all his rivals maintained to Lenin's party. Those who favored pressing on with the NEP were supported by broad democratic publics: the flourishing peasants, the workers in their still quasi-independent trade unions, artists of every sort still enjoying professional freedom, shopkeepers certainly, the many small manufacturers, many engineers, and many of the intelligentsia. Yet, trapped inside the mystique of the party, neither Tomsky, Rykov, nor Bukharin would carry their debate, first with Trotsky, then with Stalin, outside the secret councils of the party.[29] Good Communists, they shrank from carrying their case to the public. Good Communists, they accepted defeat in silence. Presumably Bukharin at least, and probably others, expected discussion within the party to continue. They may have hoped to prevail again, after another cycle, later. They did not understand Stalin. They did not sense the momentum that Stalin's policies would generate.

The NEP of 1922–27 was Russia's last chance at becoming a Western nation. For peasant women anxious to shake free of the old oppressions, the NEP held an ambiguous promise. One of the leading Communist economists, Evgeny Preobrazhensky, proponent of rapid industrialization and thus an opponent of Bukharin, thought that the young wives unwilling any longer "to submit to the rule of their husbands' parents"[30] were the main factor in the breakup of the old communes and extended families. Preobrazhensky found this gratifying, insofar as it suggested a growing number of peasants accessible to the methods of a more productive agriculture. But insofar as such methods were expanding the numbers of kulaks, young wives might find themselves under a new tutelage, no longer that of their in-laws but that of their enterprising husbands. Still, as a new force in Russia, independent, hard-working, successful farm families could well have been the promise of new freedoms for both husband and wife. In the urban world stimulated by the NEP, some women at least were becoming the full-time housewives so scorned and reviled by Lenin.

Lenin's famous contempt for the stultifications of housewifery was based on practically no knowledge.[31] Nineteenth-century Russia had had no middle class in any Western sense. The "bourgeoisie" Lenin enjoyed traducing were simply parts of the imperial apparatus, lacking any of the autonomies standard in the middle classes of Western nations, overwhelmingly so in the United States. Lenin really had known no middle-class housewives. The NEP was on its way to providing Russia with such women. At the same time, the gender egalitarianism of both the Communists and Russian intellectual culture generally held open practically every kind of job and profession for women. So long as the crisis of unemployment persisted, women particularly would suffer. Their demographic excess meant little hope for marriage for millions; practically all the hundreds of thousands of single women in the cities had to support themselves. Some of the anti-NEP Communists pointed out fringes of corruption and prostitution as evidence of the return of "capitalism." What some Western observers saw as a period of great moral experimentation during the 1920s was often desperation. Yet nothing decreed that the crisis of unemployment could not be eased, if not solved, under the NEP. The demographic distortion wrought by the wars would not go away, whatever the policy.

Ultimately, what Bukharin and his allies agreed on with Joseph Stalin was the danger entailed in letting life in Russia escape direction by the party. Soon, not only peasants and workers were taken in hand, but also artists, writers, lawyers, trade unionists, and movie makers. A plan was presented to everyone, in everything. The party had to remain free.

Politics Triumphant: Stalin and the Creation of a Female Labor Force

Why did Joseph Stalin embark upon crash industrialization in 1928, crash collectivization of the countryside in 1929? By 1928 Stalin was identifying himself with Peter the Great, who, "competing with the more developed Western countries, feverishly constructed industrial works and factories to provide supplies for the army and to strengthen the country's defense, . . . to liquidate her backwardness."[32] How far this was straightforward, how far a rationalization for what he meant to do anyway, can only be debated. The leaders of the NEP had strongly favored, not withdrawal from the rest of the world, but collaboration with the Socialist parties and trade unions in Western nations. Soviet diplomats had been exploring collaboration with the Kuomintang in China. Trade relations had been opened in 1921 with Great Britain, and a treaty made with Weimar Germany in 1922. Diplomatic recognition was granted by Britain in 1924, with most other Western nations except the United States soon following. But in 1927 Chiang Kai-shek repudiated the Soviet connection. Relations with trade-union groups in Britain foundered. Russia seemed to be pushed back into isolation. Soon, Stalin sharpened his explanation:

To slacken the tempo would mean falling behind. And those who fall behind get beaten. But we do not want to get beaten. . . . One feature of the history of old Russia was the continual beatings she suffered. . . . She was beaten by the Mongol Khans. She was beaten by the Turkish beys. She was beaten by the Swedish feudal lords. She was beaten by Polish and Lithuanian gentry. She was beaten by the British and French capitalists. She was beaten by the Japanese barons. All beat her—for her backwardness: for military backwardness, for cultural backwardness, for political backwardness, for agricultural backwardness.[33]

While this might have justified Stalin's rejection of Bukharin and the NEP in 1928, it hardly explained his purge of Trotsky, for Trotsky had been the prime exponent of the policy of crash industrialization upon which Stalin was to embark. After World War II, on February 9, 1946, Stalin recurred to the same theme of his visionary farsightedness: "The Party knew that a war was looming, that the country could not be defended without heavy industry . . . that to be behind with this would mean to lose out. . . . Accordingly the Communist Party of our country . . . began the work of industrializing the country by developing heavy industry."[34] Yet neither Stalin nor economic historians showed—or could show—why Stalin's particular route to industrialization was necessary.[35] There were those in the West, such as John Maynard Keynes, who foresaw another world war as a consequence of the disastrous peace arranged after World War I, but Stalin's ex post facto prevision rationalized his own power so neatly as to suggest a need for such rationalization.

The destruction of peasant agriculture in favor of collective agriculture took five years. By 1933, 25 million peasant families had been organized into 250,000 collective farms. Stalin himself told Winston Churchill the process cost 10 million lives. Some resisters in the countryside were killed by the young Communist militants on the spot. Others were transported to various virgin lands in the east, where many died. Still others were sent to work for the secret police on vast construction and mining projects; many of these died. Women and children, of course, shared the fate of their men. Since this revolution had nothing to do with technology and modern methods, but rather with politics, productivity and production plunged. Cattle herds, painfully rebuilt under the NEP, fell in five years from 68 million head to 38 million. Famine swept the southeastern grain lands in 1932; Stalin sealed the area, kept it a secret, and let the peasants starve. In 1933 M. I. Kalinin, formal head of state, observed: "[The] collective farm people this year have passed through a good school—for some this school is quite ruthless."[36] The Soviet Union had embarked upon its career of chronic agricultural deficiency.

Stalin had reversed Stolypin's policy. Instead of encouraging "the sober and the strong," he set about to destroy them. The writer Boris Pilnyak imagined his way into the minds of the peasants involved. They faced an "incomprehensible" dilemma:

The problem's incomprehensibility lay in the fact that the peasants were divided about fifty-fifty. Fifty percent of them got up at three o'clock in the morning and went to bed at eleven, and in their families everyone, young and old, worked day in and day out . . . their huts were kept in good repair, as were their carts; their cattle were well fed and well cared for . . . taxes in kind and other state dues they paid promptly.

These peasants "feared the authorities," and with good reason: "they were considered enemies of the Revolution."

The other 50 percent of the peasants each had a hut open to the winds, a scraggy cow and a mangy sheep . . . in spring they went to town to collect a state seed loan; half the seed loan they ate . . . the other half they scattered—shouting distance from seed to seed—and there was no harvest in the fall; they explained the poor crop to the authorities by the lack of manure from the scraggy cows and the mangy sheep; . . . the state relieves them of tax . . . and they were considered friends of the Revolution.[37]

To the "enemies" of the revolution, it appeared that a good 35 percent of the "friends" were drunkards and most of the rest "idlers, gabbers, philosophers, loafers, bunglers."

At the height of the chaos of collectivization, Stalin himself appeared to realize that utter collapse might be impending. Of course the long-range "teleological" visions included typically Bolshevik schemes for huge "tractor stations" servicing vast *sovkhozes*, industrial farms based on supermechanization. Stalin, however, seemed to sense that people might matter, too, that if he dared not let a capitalist spirit modernize the peasants, he might have to appeal to another spirit. In a speech to farm "shock workers" in 1933, he singled out one category of the new collective workers for special comment, a category perhaps less given to gab, drink, and immemorial resistance to change.

Now a few words about the *women*, and *women collective* farmers. . . . I know that many of you under-rate the women and even laugh at them. That is a mistake, comrades, a serious mistake. . . . The women on the collective farms are a great force. . . . Of course, not long ago, the Soviet government had a slight misunderstanding with the women collective farmers. That was over the cow. But now this business about the cow has been settled. . . . We have reached the position where the majority of the collective farm households have a cow each. Another year or two will pass and there will not be a single collective farmer who will not have his own cow. We Bolsheviks will see to it that every one of our collective farmers has a cow.[38]

If still somewhat in embryo, the basic form of the new Soviet agriculture was here being accepted. Cereals and other basic crops might be grown by collective methods on the kolkhozes, but the real energy, the care, persistence, and devotion would be spent on the garden plots, the private huts, a cow, other animals, and poultry for private tending. Women were already a strong majority on the collective farms; during World War II they would effectively be the rural work force. Stalin consciously and deliberately invited women to identify their interests with the collective system. Hailing the "remarkable and capable women" who were being trained for "leading positions" on the new farms, he then reminded peasant women of what he had saved them from, inequality:

As for the women collective farmers themselves, they must remember the power and significance of the collective farms for women; they must remember that only in the collective farms do they have the opportunity of becoming equal with men. Without collective farms—inequality; in collective farms—equal rights."[39]

History would show otherwise. As heavy industrialization was pursued, the collective farms were left to chiefly human labor. These were mostly women. As late as 1959, 36 percent of all Soviet workers still worked in agriculture; of these, 54 percent were women. Eighty-two percent of all male agricultural workers were classified as "physical," and 97 percent of women. Some physical workers were nonetheless classified as "administrative and supervisory" and "skilled and junior supervisory"; 85 percent of these were men. By far the largest single category on the whole elaborate roster of Soviet occupations and specialties in 1959 was that of "nonspecialized agricultural worker." There were 22 million of these; about two-thirds were women. Nikita Khrushchev in 1961 was franker than Stalin: "It turns out that it is the men who do the administering and the women who do the work."[40]

With the collectivization of agriculture, the individual peasant joined the landlords, industrialists, private bankers, and big and small businessmen in the ranks of the liquidated. With the First Five-Year Plan for heavy industry gearing up, Communist planners found that even industrial workers were disappearing. Numbering about 2.5 million adult men on the eve of World War I, this class too had lost heavily during the war and civil war. More important, Communist ideology had drawn large numbers of ex-industrial workers into administrative work, party work, and trade-union work. These posts were far more desirable than factory jobs, and the workers had preference. Although unemployment had begun to swell on the job registration rolls, this did not represent a pool of surplus industrial workers, but rather the surplus of peasants come to the cities. "The new Russian working class constituted essentially a part of the peasantry transported to the cities."[41] In the ten years between 1905 and World War I the old industrial workers—often enough peasant-born themselves—had had some chance to build up organizations of their own, the Soviets. That was why they could play a real not merely symbolic, role in the Bolshevik revolution. The new workers had no such traditions. The trade unions over which Mikhail Tomsky had watched with pride were stripped of all autonomy and integrated into the state. Strikes became as impossible in Soviet Russia as under the Czar and Witte.

During the First Five-Year Plan the numbers of industrial workers about doubled, with men and women showing approximately the same rate of growth. Then in the second plan, from 1932 to 1937, the vast majority of all new workers were women. About four times as many women were at work—not all in industry—by 1939 as in 1929, when the plans began. From about 27 percent of the whole work force in 1914, women grew to 42 percent by 1940. Adult men over 23 made up 62 percent of the work force in 1914; adult men made up about 38 percent of the 7.8 million persons working in heavy industry in 1937. The new Soviet working class "consisted for the most part of women and youths."[42]

The success of the policy of crash industrialization was hardly undone by the insistence of its Communist managers in exaggerating it. Soviet claims of industrial growth at the rate of 12.5 percent per annum for the whole period 1928–40 could not bear scrutiny, but even the gains guessed at by less partial outsiders of up to 8.9 percent per annum were unprecedented.[43] That it could not have been achieved without the new labor force, with its heavy proportion of women and girls, was not so interesting as why such a labor force could be assembled. For the most part the new women workers were young, unskilled, at first unmarried. They came cheap. Real wages attached to industrial jobs plunged in the First Five-Year Plan, but for the real people taking them, the jobs often constituted escape from rural poverty, urban unemployment, and futurelessness. Presumably in loyalty to socialist ideology, wage scales had been equalized in 1918 and 1919, then abandoned during the NEP system of individual initiative, then reinstituted as the NEP was abandoned. In 1932, differential wages were introduced again, and from then on Soviet workers were gradually presented with a complex of grades, ladders, steps, echelons, bridges, and so on, by far the most elaborate in the world–effectively a new piece-work system, such as had been resisted by every trade-union movement before. For women workers, however, this system offered the first chance women had ever had on such a scale to seek improvement in their lives by meeting prescribed standards.

Many young women responded with enthusiasm to industrial opportunities. A higher percentage than male workers participated in the organized "socialist competitions" and "shock brigades" of the First Five-Year Plan. Women outdid men in the compulsory examinations given to industrial workers in 1935–36. Novels describing young women workers, often recruited directly from the *komsomolski*—members of the Communist youth organization—as working "on tiptoes" were not utterly without a basis in reality.[44] A peasant girl born in 1912 in a poor village northwest of Moscow nicely exemplified a common sense of liberation.[45] Masha finished village school in the harsh days of war communism. Then, walking five miles each way daily, she attended one of the new secondary schools set up by the Communists, from which she graduated after several years. Then, as her older siblings had already done, she went to Moscow. Just possibly, she might have chosen a more political course than she did and entered the ranks of the truly privileged new class of bureaucrats, managers, and administrators.

[The] state apparatus . . . which . . . had lost a substantial portion of its old former revolutionary energy . . . was replaced by cadres of new apparatus. These were the youth trained in the Communist Youth League (Komsomol), elevated by it from the lowest strata of the workers, peasants, and petty-bourgeoisie, and provided with an access to education and to professions that previously had been altogether inaccessible. Growing up into the Soviet regime . . . the youthful Soviet generation acquired not only its political ideas but its political psychology . . . the fruit and result of the whole long history of Bolshevism and the Soviet regime. The boundless devotion . . . and an extreme heroism . . . were combined in this youth with an unwavering austerity, indifferent to "sentimentality." . . . It self-sacrificingly burnt out its energies in the fire of "industrialization," which without it would have been impossible.[46]

This, however, was a route far more common to young men. Instead, Masha Scott studied math and physics, then again followed a sister to the new Five-Year-Plan city of Magnitogorsk. Interviewed by the American writer Pearl Buck after World War II, she recalled her feelings:

I wish I could tell you what it was to me when I saw the new city on the bare steppe. . . . Hundreds of miles we had come with no big city anywhere. There was only the bare grassy land of the steppe rising against the brightly blue skies. And then on the horizon suddenly I saw the shapes of great buildings, houses, factories, and even the flames of the blast furnace—our blast furnace, which we had made ourselves. . . . I cannot tell you how beautiful Magnitogorsk was to me.[47]

It was true that few peasant girls enjoyed such good fortune as did Masha Scott, who soon earned the considerable sum of 500 rubles a month teaching math. But for many of the millions of women who found jobs of a humbler and more onerous sort, the trend of their historical experience too promised much. Comparison mattered most. Masha Scott had still been a village girl when the leading local farmer, a kulak who had become the community's leading business entrepreneur during the NEP, found out what being liquidated "as a class" meant. One day he simply disappeared, his house and all his properties being appropriated. Pearl Buck asked Masha what she felt about this episode. She explained that the kulak had only got his deserts. He had become "a dictator in our village . . . because he was rich."[48]

In addition to the new industrial working class, a new industrial subclass was generated. With their new criminal code of 1922, Communists had installed what they proclaimed to be the most humane prison system in the world, rehabilitative, planned on the assumption that crime would gradually disappear with the construction of socialism. By 1926 the prisons were congested; between 1922 and 1929 the prison population quadrupled; and "administrative" punishments—those without trial—sextupled. Few prisons had workshops; there was relatively little forced labor. A labor camp for political prisoners had been started in 1923, with about 6,000 prisoners by 1927 and then, with the purge of Trotskyites, 30,000 by 1930. The expansion of labor camps began with the collectivization of agriculture. The camps were put under the secret police. In 1934 the whole system was organized into a Chief Administration of Corrective Labor Camps and Labor Settlements. The GULAG Archipelago had been born.[49]

Perhaps 650,000 in 1930, forced laborers numbered about 6 million by 1935. Forced labor under the secret police was used to build highways in the north, to dig gold mines in Siberia, to lumber, to build railroads, to open coal mines and iron mines. The biggest single project was digging the White Sea-Baltic Canal between late 1931 and 1934. One hundred and forty miles long, provided with docks, locks, and dams, and completed on schedule, the canal was a major contribution to upgrading the Soviet transport system. Communist spokesmen spoke of the beneficent effect on the criminals of having been allowed to do worthwhile work. Of the 300,000 utilized, perhaps a quarter died. By definition, statistical reckonings of the contribution of forced labor to the Soviet economic miracle have been difficult. The practice resembled the use of serf and forced labor by Peter the Great. Whether the numbers of those in the Gulag in the late 1930s approached 8 or 12 or 20 million could be determined by no one.

Women were to be found in the Gulag. It is unlikely they numbered as many as 10 percent. Sometimes women's servitude took on other forms than those of the camps. Under the new inequality of the Five-Year Plans, Masha Scott was able to afford a maid in Magnitogorsk, another young woman who had left the countryside. This was Vera, paid a tenth of what Masha made. Sadly, in 1938 Vera, along with "several thousand other disfranchised minors," was herded onto a freight car on twenty-four hours' notice, and shipped from Magnitogorsk to her next post in an armaments factory in Chelyabinsk. Vera was the daughter of a kulak.[50]

With the forced labor camps growing, the death rate among Russian men once again surpassed that of Russian women. In European Russia itself, from which most of the men were shipped to the wastes of Siberia and the Far East, women may have outnumbered men by 9 million. The war for which Stalin had been planning presumably would entail another demographic catastrophe. Russia was becoming a land of women workers run by male bureaucrats.

Everybody at Work: the Soviet Economy's Women Since 1945

World War II did not bring the Soviet economy to the near collapse of 1918. The feminization of the rural work force allowed wartime agriculture to come through. Though enemy conquest entailed vast losses of industrial capacity, the government's emergency programs of transporting whole factories lock, stock, and barrel to the east, preserved major capacities throughout the war. Heroic efforts by the British and Americans got far more supplies through to Stalin than to the Czar in World War I. Reconstruction got under way as early as 1943. A new Five-Year Plan was set afoot in 1946. Concentrating again on heavy industry and military production. Russia had reaffirmed its industrial power by 1949 with its first A-bomb, and with its hydrogen bomb in 1953.

Nevertheless, a disaster had been inflicted upon the labor force. The war had cost perhaps 20 million lives. Since many of these were women who would have borne children, only a sharp baby boom could have compensated, but no such boom occurred.[51] But men had been the heavy majority of casualties. By 1945, in the age group of 16 to 34, only 70 to 75 men were left for every 100 men. In 1960, by some reckonings the population of the Soviet Union was 25 to 30 million lower than it would have been, had the war not occurred. Women made up 60 percent of the Soviet population over sixteen at the end of the war, and 56 percent of all workers. With the return of the soldiers to the work force, women's proportion of all workers declined for a few years, then rose again to over 50 percent by 1970, where it remained in the 1970s. About 90 percent of all women were either working or in school, a figure so high that some Soviet sociologists began to suggest that it posed serious demographic issues.

The vast majority of Soviet women continued to work in gender ghettos and earned, on average, 65 percent of what men earned. The greatest gender ghetto continued to be the "physical" work on the collective farms, and "earnings" here were not straightforward. The countryside continued to supply workers to the factories, with the rural work force only 30 percent of the whole by the 1970s, compared to over 50 percent as late as 1950, and a steady process of diversification was going on among women workers. Just before the war, in 1939, only 13 percent of women at work were in professional or semiprofessional posts; by 1970, 35 percent were so employed. Rates in extreme contrast to the West began to appear. Women had been conspicuous in medicine in Russia from Czarist times; their dominance reached 77 percent of doctors by 1950; then, as Soviet medicine began to upgrade its methods along Western lines, the percent of women medical students declined; the percent of women doctors had fallen to 70 percent by 1977. Women grew from 32 to 40 percent of the engineers in Russia over the 1960s; 60 percent of the chemical engineers were women, and even more in food technology. Women made up 63 percent of hydrologists and meteorologists, rates quite unknown in the West. Women were on the executive level of research institutes, schools, universities. Women judges were common in local courts.[52]

Traditions of triumphalism were available to interpret such conditions. Summarizing with pride the findings of a seminar held in Moscow in 1956 for nearly one hundred women invited from thirty-nine countries, Anna Pankratova, chair of the Soviet Union's association for liaison with the United Nations and chair of the seminar said: "Our guests . . . saw for themselves that in our country true equality for women has been not merely proclaimed, but actually accomplished."[53] Outsiders echoed such sentiments decades later:

.... if we are to accept the assumption that the right and the opportunity to work and earn one's own money is at the heart of women's liberation, it is clear . . . that few societies have done as much in this direction as has Soviet society. . . . The structure of female liberation, having survived[Stalin], has become a permanent feature of the system, and no further whim of administrative fashion is likely to alter its basic form that is as much a part of Soviet life as is the absence of capitalism.[54]

Another approach was simply to emphathize with the existential reality:

Reflect back for just a moment to the 1940's and early 1950's when much of the country's adult male population was enlisted in one of four armies: [the army] . . . of the dead . . . of the imprisoned . . . [of] the [soldiers] . . . and . . . [of] . . . the bureaucrats. It was women's energy that flowed in to fill the huge gaps in the economy and family. . . . The women of that time became accustomed to doing everything themselves; they had no one to depend on; they really were independent, by necessity rather than choice.[55]

The demographic imbalance did not lead to change within the Communist Party itself, however. As the party recovered from Stalinism, women were destined to number no more than a quarter of party membership. Having embarked on crash industrialization and collectivization, Stalin had proceded in the mid-1930s to extinguish his own generation of old Bolsheviks, leaving himself unchallenged. (In the process, he gutted the old army leadership as well, just in case.) After the war, fought under the banners not of class or Communism but of Motherland/Fatherland/Holy Russia, Stalin returned to purges, first, of rising new leaders in the party, and second, of hopeful postwar intellectuals and artists. Stalin's politics had generated a new privileged class of bureaucrats in an ever more complex system of management and control radiating out from the center. It seems likely that his purges were intended to assure that no portion of this new class, including the mass of the party itself, should ever generate autonomous energies of its own. How he envisioned a succession to his own increasingly unrationalized one-man rule, he never explained. While his successor, Nikita Khrushchev, attacked Stalin for his crimes (in his secret but soon famous speech to the party congress in 1956), he himself was eventually forced out as a consequence of excessively personal—and too often unsuccessful—interventions in party as well as economic and diplomatic affairs. The logic of Lenin's party restored itself as a kind of collective leadership to which any party secretary had to refer for sanction in policy changes. Thus the party was restored as the key ladder to power in the Soviet Union. The crucial arena in which the ambitious competed for success in the matured Soviet system had become, as Boris N. Volgin described it, the "business conference," the daily hours-long consultation among the bosses in the steel combines, the press combines, the scientific institutes, and the party's own high councils.[56] The Soviet system had, in effect, become ruled by insiders.

Endlessly reaffirming their solidarity even as they jockeyed among themselves for place, these insiders were in near unanimity men.

For all the rise of women in professions, practically no women rose in higher politics. One investigator, Joel C. Moses, attempted to locate women's place within the party, which he construed as a pyramid. At each higher level he found fewer women, running from their 25 percent or so of membership to 4 percent of district party secretaries, and less than 3 percent of the Central Committee. In the Politburo, the unbroken male tradition persisted: not one woman appeared among its two dozen or so members until 1986. No ideology of Soviet womanhood ever explained how a woman might one day win out over the likes of a Nikita Khrushchev, a Yuri Andropov, a Mikhail Gorbachev. Moses found gender-linked specialization within the party. Of 119 party women in regional political offices in 1970, more than half were concentrated in one political specialization known as "indoctrination." Effectively, they were party housekeepers.

Soviet women who have accepted [the] "housekeeping" function of indoctrination appear conditioned to a role not unlike that characteristic of Western female political activists. . . . That is, like the wife, a female political activist tends to specialize in the "expressive functions" of those concerned with the *affairs of the system, the maintenance of integrative relations between its members.*[57]

This "housekeeping" function within the party was not likely to claim high prestige from men in "business conferences," dedicated to "getting the job done."

. . . . indoctrination officials have traditionally held a rather low status within the Party elite . . . their training . . . and their humanistic backgrounds proved incompatible with the . . . production-oriented concerns of many regional Party leaders . . . a functional conflict . . . has been transformed into a struggle between . . . pragmatic "men of deeds" and . . . impractical "women of words."[58]

Ironically, then, party women, manifesting "rigid political orthodoxy," were better Communists than party men, whose expedient, self-interested, bargain-making, power-oriented negotiations were carried on in the business conferences behind the screen of true faith.

Stalin carried his sense of a Russia encircled into the postwar years, the United States now substituting for Germany and Japan as a threat. Priority in the economic recovery was given to heavy industry and armaments. The countryside was left to stumble on; when another great famine swept the south, Stalin again kept it secret. If in some sectors production at his death had recovered to 1940 levels, in many other sectors it had not recovered to the levels of 1928 under the NEP. The political destruction of the peasants had not led to agricultural success; by 1963 the country had to make large purchases of foreign grain. Khrushchev's major investments in chemical fertilizer, large-scale mechanization, and the opening up of new lands drew resistance from leaders of industry and the military, who helped pave the way for his fall. In addition to more investment, his successors offered higher prices, directly threatening the highly subsidized low prices for bread and other basics long enjoyed by the urban population. Farm production grew marginally, but by the mid-1970s serious failures resumed. Not the least of the problems were the rising expectations among Russian consumers, partly prompted by the leaders themselves. After a quarter century of bread and potatoes, Russians were coming to expect more meat, more vegetables, milk, some fruit, a little sugar. Under pressure, the regime had to allow private plots to be enlarged. But by the late 1970s it was clear that the investments, running up to 20 percent of total national investment—a rate three times that in the United States—were still not paying off in a newly fruitful agriculture. Dismantling the apparatus of collective management in favor of a return to market efficiencies threatened even larger dangers, however. Where inefficient collectives had been protected for political reasons, unemployment would reemerge and, at the same time once again, the seeds of a coherent rural interest group.[59]

Both Khrushchev and his successors under Leonid Brezhnev revived the old pre-Stalin promise that socialism would someday be validated by abundance, offering every citizen a standard of living far above that of the poor in capitalist economies, even above that of the average. Perhaps the most persistent and oppressive failure of the Stalinist regime had been in housing. As workers flocked into the old cities and built the new ones, crowding on a scale unknown in the West increased. Moscow was by all reckonings far and away the most crowded major city on several continents. The situation persisted deep into the postwar years. In 1963 the Italian ambassador to Russia, Luca Pietromarchi, who published his impressions of Soviet life and found much to admire, could find only reasons for compassion in the conditions of housing:

[The] overcrowding is an intolerable martyrdom for the Russians. . . . not to have a place in which to withdraw, in which to live his family life away from the prying eyes of his neighbor. Never can the Soviet citizen have a moment's freedom; never has he the right to be alone. It is like condemning a whole people to supervised imprisonment. Perhaps it is this lack of a domestic hearth that is the reason for the deep melancholy that one sees in so many Soviet people, and especially the people of Moscow.[60]

Gradually, steadily, the regime began to build up the housing stock, in the form of large high-rise apartment complexes ringing the old cities and forming the axes of new ones. Gradually, steadily, through the 1960s and into the 1970s, the new apartment dwellers got a refrigerator, a stove of their own, vacuum cleaners, and basic mass-produced furniture.

These developments seemed to proceed in parallel with another. By the 1960s the standard Soviet urban couple, both partners at work, was having but one child, certainly no more than two. Once Soviet health services recovered from the war, the death rate continued its steep decline, thus masking the long-term potential in the decline of the fertility rate. By the 1960s, however, the death rate was nearing its standard modern low, and by the 1970s, as investments in agriculture that promised to release still more workers for urban service went flat, something like a labor shortage appeared to loom. In 1975 Brezhnev called on the Twenty-fifth Party Congress for an "effective demographic policy."[61]

Just what this policy might be was not clear. Soviet women could not be sent home to have babies; they were essential in the labor force. Indeed, two signals suddenly appearing in the late 1970s implied problems deeper even than that of declining fertility. The first, an apparent sudden rise in Soviet infant mortality rates, hitherto unheard of in any industrial nation, subsequently seemed, upon careful analysis, perhaps more artifact than reality.[62] Soviet collection of statistics had not been as good as assumed in the earlier postwar decades; improvement in collecting statistics rather than a decline in infant care was a likely explanation. But a mortality rate suddenly on the rise among men between the ages of twenty and forty-four was another matter. Men in these age groups were dying three times more often than women. Two-thirds of the deaths were from coronary heart disease, linked to abuse of alcohol. Vodka was not cheap in the Soviet Union. Whereas beer cost only twice the work time it took to buy it in the United States, vodka cost between seven and eight times as much, but in the "second" economy, the black market, it could often be bought adulterated, raw, lethal. In 1976 there were 400 deaths from alcohol poisoning in the United States, as against 40,000 in the Soviet Union. One Soviet author, writing in *The Economic Newspaper* in 1981, said: "[In] some regions of the country, infant mortality has risen, cardiovascular and other diseases are becoming 'younger,' the gap in life expectancy of men and women is not lessening, drunkenness among the population is not declining."[63] A group of Soviet economists in one of the great new academic institutes in Novosibirsk drew up a severe judgment on the work force that amounted at the same time to an existential explanation for death by vodka:

The type of worker that . . . [the] system cultivates not only falls short of the needs of developed socialism but fails to match the requirements of modern production. His common traits are low labor and productive discipline, an indifferent attitude toward work, a shoddy quality of work, social inactivity, a well-pronounced consumer mentality and a low code of ethics.[64]

More women were being left as single heads of family by their husbands' premature deaths than by divorce. If the steadily multiplying new small nuclear families in the apartment complexes were not reversing the decline in fertility, what would? Investment sufficient to underwrite a more abundant, less cramped, more individualized, less socialized style of life for the new families would have to be taken from further investment in heavy industry and armaments. Such a development might entice women to leave the labor force, even while offending against the ideology identified with Lenin that bequeathed to socialism the liberation of women from the slavery of domesticity. The peculiar circumstances in which the Soviet Union found itself were nicely summarized by an observer who applied modernization theory:

In Soviet Russia conditions required to support a middle-class style of living and value system were to emerge far later than in Western Europe. Only in recent decades have the severe economic conditions and the shortage of males finally abated. . . . The spread of middle-class values may be a product of increased prosperity that has reduced the need for women to work or at least to work full-time. . . . [If] Soviet women had withdrawn from the workforce at some previous period, their participation in the labor force might have had a different meaning. . . . This suggests that the meaning and significance of women's labor participation may be very different in the United States than in the Soviet Union. A women judge or steel-worker . . . may constitute very much more of a discontinuity in a nation in which middle-class values and family living are already prevalent.[65]

In effect, then, far from constituting a vanguard in some transnational story of women's liberation, the Soviet Union was still catching up with Western economies. What the regime could not afford to do, however, was to underwrite the growth of a middle class sufficiently enriched and autonomous as to constitute a threat to the gender-equal labor market. Its attempt to meet the demographic problem by investing in more day-care centers and canteens—cultural icons standard from the heroic days of "building socialism" in the 1920s—was relevant primarily for the factory workers, who were not part of the incipient new middle class, but distasteful to that new class, whose position of privilege as the administrative, managerial, and technocratic elite transcended old socialist austerities.

By the 1970s the regime had no more surpluses to draw on—no reserves of rural labor, none of female labor. The margins of maneuver in reallocating resources between armaments, further heavy industry, light industry, and agriculture had been much narrowed. Any return to the cheap costs of the forced-labor camps, dismantled after Stalin's death, was out of the question on both political and economic grounds. As the leaders after Brezhnev's period of prolonged inertial compromise sought new ways to stimulate the economy, they faced a still further deterioration. Political and economic inertia appeared to be infecting technology. One of old socialism's proudest claims was that it, not capitalism, would bring the blessings of modern science and technology to the masses. Socialism alone could penetrate to the objective heart of science, and free it from the subjective restraints of class, of tradition, of the fear of change. But as early as 1968 those able to see, such as physicist Andrei Sakharov and others, were warning that the Soviet Union was not keeping up. In its old Stalinist push for coal and iron and steel it continued to swell, but in automation, computers, petrochemicals, and especially industrial research and development it was falling behind.[66] Soviet realization of the long-term implications of these trends could be postponed for a few more years. After the deepening split with China, from 1959 on, and Khrushchev's humiliation in Cuba in 1962, the regime committed itself to building toward military nuclear parity with the United States, particularly in the form of powerful intercontinental ballistic missiles. As in the case of the A-bomb and the H-bomb, once again, presumably, the Soviet Union had shown that it could match Western technology, step for step. But by the mid-1970s and early 1980s, those familiar with the facts realized that a new cycle of worldwide technological evolution was well underway and the Soviet Union was not keeping step. By 1973 Sakharov's point was repeated in official organs such as the *Journal of World Economics and International Relations*.[67] Sakharov himself believed that it was the very system of Soviet political control over economy, science, culture, and life itself that was at fault. The party was of course determined to control debate over what to do. As late as 1980 no Soviet economist could yet safely criticize the old controls. The regime tried new ways of arranging the work of its most creative scientists. Purchases of Western technology ten and twenty times greater than decades ago were underway in the 1980s, while industrial espionage was sharply accelerated. The old parasitism on the West that Count Witte had hoped to exploit had appeared again. Russia had not won what Stalin had wanted, security through self-sufficiency.

As the fully employed partners of their men in the Soviet system of the 1960s, 1970s, and 1980s, Soviet women presumably had some of the same interests as their men. Any political, organized "feminism" of course continued to be suppressed. Had feminists been allowed a voice, they might or might not have asked for other than what Russian men wanted, perhaps some escape from the hard choices that pressed upon them in combining work and family. Ironically, one of the deeper structural reasons why the Soviet Union found itself falling behind in the evolution of technology was precisely its long reliance upon cheap labor. Cheap labor had excused Soviet leaders from pressing hard for up-to-date labor-saving methods in everything. It had been partly just because they did work for less that women had been so welcome as workers. Their presence in the labor force in such high ratios thus had made women part of the problem as well as part of the solution in Soviet politics. A drive for complete economic equality for women might well sharpen the spur to technological modernization. Yet, while this might then allow some women to stop working and have babies, it seemed unlikely that the Soviet planners could accept such a change readily. The focus of labor demoralization was among men, not women. Not only were women workers cheaper than men, but they were better workers. Soviet managers were not likely to let such a resource slip away.

The New Class: Women's Share in Modern Soviet Inequality

The problems of Russia were political. By 1985 the task of transforming the peasantry for urban industrial society had long been completed. Following upon the party's efforts at mobilization in the 1920s, Soviet schools had trained multitudes for the technical tasks of a machine-based economy during the 1930s, 1950s, and 1960s. Higher proportions of Russian women, in particular, moved into a wider variety of tasks than anywhere else in the world. Counting both men and women, the Soviet work force may have been the best prepared for modern production of any anywhere. Yet this work force was not allowed to invest its best energies in the system. As Soviet leaders watched their system slow down, they were inhibited from conceding the source of their troubles. It was in themselves. The Leninist system of a command economy, taken to apotheosis by Stalin, was not suited to a modernized people. Yet were the commanders to give up the system, they would be giving up their own positions of power, prestige, and privilege.

The Soviet Union had become a class society. That was the single overwhelming point to emerge in modern Western scholarship on Soviet life. The French Marxist Charles Bettleheim's massive study represented a conclusion that had been emerging for years. David J. Dallin informed American readers of the "new Soviet social structure" with its "new upper classes" in 1944, during the war years of alliance between East and West. The Italian Bruno Rizzi, onetime member of the Italian Communist Party, had written *The USSR: Bureaucratic Collectivism* by 1939.[68] Many of the themes of Rizzi, Dallin, Bettleheim, and their peers had been anticipated as early as 1925 by Yevgeny Zamyatin in his modernist novel, *We*, a prophetic vision of Russian life in "the Single State" over which the Benefactor presided. Deep forces may have been preparing this destiny from long before 1917. As Alfred G. Meyer has noted, Friedrich Engels himself foreboded disaster as early as 1853: "In a backward country . . . which possesses an advanced party . . . at the first serious conflict and as soon as real danger sets in, the advanced party will come to power, and that is certainly *before* its normal time."[69]

The reason that the Communist ruling elite in the Soviet Union could not relax its control was not simply greed for its perquisites. This mistaken view weakened Leon Trotsky's sense of what was going on as he excoriated Stalin and his managers for their failures in the 1930s. Relaxation of control promised not simply to jeopardize class privilege, but to bring the return of chaos. Having had as their first task the restoration of some kind of order out of the chaos of 1917–20, the early Bolsheviks brought with them no memory of having successfully overthrown a society, but of having barely forestalled the total collapse of one. Building socialism was never remotely within their reach. Handing the nation over to the peasants, to the people, seemed a formula for final disaster. The people, one of Boris Pilnyak's prophets said in 1919, did not want Peter the Great, machine Europe, a state. They did not even want the church: "orthodox Christianity came with the Tsars, with the government of foreigners." The people's revolution would be "like a forest path—a thousand years, pillage and reconstruction, fields, reploughings—a thousand years of it." The new religion would be the people's own, the old religion; "instead of Easter, popular festivals and the capture of brides, on wooded hills and in glades. Praying to Egory the God of Cattle."[70] The Bolsheviks feared this creative populistic energy, so disintegrative of all machines, integrated systems, organization. The revolution could have reduced Russia to wood demons and witches and water sprites, invaded periodically by new waves of armored foreign automatons. Destroying this antimodern revolutionary folk hardly freed the Bolsheviks from fear, however. On the one hand, no amount of mobilization could ever bring assurance that freedom would not prove the mobilization only skin-deep, revealing powerful impulses to overflow and undermine authority altogether. On the other hand, as control from above gradually induced stagnation and immobility, further mobilization was obviously no longer of any use. Effort and energy from within the workers themselves had to be elicited somehow, without loosening control.

Historians have apparently not yet asked themselves whether the Soviet class system was facilitated by the high employment of women. Most discussions of the surge in the numbers of the industrial work force in the 1930s, for instance, proceed as though gender differentials are not worth notice. Some Western feminist historians—but by no means all—describe the labor market of post-Stalin Russia simply as a remarkable progress toward equality for women. Yet at no point was the mobilization of women into the Soviet labor market anything other than a response to imperatives from above. That fact alone strongly suggests the worth of a hypothesis that women contributed a vital component to Stalinism and to the class system that has followed it. Certainly at no point could Soviet industrial development have given a family wage to its factory workers, let alone a family salary to its office workers. Moreover, as malaise overtook the labor force in the epoch of Leonid Brezhnev's politics of immobility, that malaise clearly infected men far more than women. While women were at work in the marketplace, they continued to take major responsibility for family. While their two roles meant they spent far more time at one kind of work or another than their men, the meaning of their work remained clear and within their control. They could be counted on to work more faithfully and effectively than their men. The equality Russian women had been given had been part of a bargain from the start. At least one Western visitor, the American newspaperwoman Dorothy Thompson, summed it up in 1928: "Russia claims to have 'emancipated' women, to have done more for women than any other country. It has, indeed, done everything to make women independent of men and dependent on the state."[71] So far as it went, this was true. But whatever the plans of some Bolsheviks might still have been for the family in 1928, in 1985 it was clear that the managing elite had left babies and the family to women themselves. Whether they would be able to make some freedom out of this, we shall try to see in Chapter 6, looking into feminism and consciousness among Soviet women.

Conclusion

In Italy, Sweden, and Soviet Russia economic history generated different dramas, sometimes binding and bonding, sometimes dividing, men and women. In Italy the confinement of the young nation's first industrial efforts to Piedmont opened the question whether Italian industry ever would break out from the upper Po and shape the nation. But if it could not shape, it shook the nation. The hemorrhage of Italians from the southern countryside was the clearest possible comment on the need for greater economic energy. Emigration often divided men from women, but the family motive remained foremost. Italians would reconstitute their preindustrial villages and families in America. In Italy, however, economic growth continued to induce more stress than relief, stress issuing finally in the political polarizations that followed World War I. If Fascism constituted a more stable resolution of Italy's economic problems than any previous approaches, it was at the cost of political rationality. Had Fascism not collapsed in World War II, it might have prevailed for another generation, but Mussolini's adventurist foreign policy was probably inherent in his politics. The marriage of the state with private capital behind the façade of "corporatism" did not generate vital new economic energy. It depended upon the destruction of Italian labor unions and the wage structure. Women were pushed out of professions and white-collar jobs, down the occupational ladder, but not off it, for they continued to be what Fascism needed, cheap labor. Under Fascism most Italian men and women more nearly approached equality, as underpaid and overworked. Such "middle classes" as had begun to emerge grew more completely attached to government and bureaucracies, as well as to the state's ideological ally, the Catholic church. Middle-class Italian women were held firmly under tutelage; their separate sphere was not one inviting autonomous action. Not only were they confined by the ideologies of both church and regime, but they were poor. The Italians who most resembled them were their own men.

In Sweden the crisis of the countryside undermined security and identity for both men and women. Many abandoned Sweden in bitterness for America, they too with the goal of reconstituting family. The conviction of some modern-minded Swedes, in the tradition of Anders Chydenius, that what Sweden needed most was open doors, free trade, Americanization, could not prevail against the sense of dislocation, humiliation, uncertainty. The very continuity of the early industrial surge in iron and timber with the past meshed with perpetuation of the paternalistic outlook of the government. Had Swedes in transformation from peasants to workers not remobilized themselves in unions, Swedish economic history might have followed the more chaotic pattern anticipated at Sundsvall in 1879, and Swedish society been more strongly divided by class. Swedish politics might have followed the lead offered by the Liberal Party. As union members, however, Swedes collaborated in shaping Swedish industry into highly innovative large-scale enterprises, privately owned and managed, but subject to the discipline of broad national bargaining with labor. Men and women shared in this process. The underlying motivation that brought the Social Democrats to forty-four years of power was social security. The motive was shared by men and women. The 1937–38 parliament of mothers and children anticipated the eventual formula—high taxes placed upon a powerful economy to pay for a welfare system leaving no one forgotten. The common welfare reached to both sexes just as had the common distress from which it derived.

Common economic experience in Russia partook of the epic. In the surge of industrialization under the Five-Year Plans, men and women shared alike, flooding in their millions into the labor market through the 1930s, until the Soviet industrial labor force was the most gender-integrated of any in the world on the eve of World War II. This industrial labor force—this proletariat—was also probably the most impoverished in the Western world, the worst-housed, worst-clothed, most poorly fed. As economic historians know, real wages declined precipitously from 1928 through the 1930s. Yet, for many, probably most, of the new workers, what they experienced was not decline and impoverishment but escape from worse, from the chaos of the countryside, from unemployment, from social nowhereness. Women had not been "essential" in Swedish industrialization; its takeoff from its origins in iron and timber had perpetuated male labor. Nor were women essential in Italian industry insofar as there were too many of them, just as there were of men; Italian women's cheap labor suited the Italian economy's fitfulness but also helped prevent its takeoff. But Stalinist industrialization could not have taken place without women—without all the women available. Stalinist industrialization required all the men possible too: the destruction of craft labor and craft unions fed the labor pool just as did the destruction of the successful peasantry. Since craft labor had been a monopoly of men, its destruction and women's induction into the industrial economy constituted an advance toward equality. Similarly, since peasant women had been subject to a harsh dominion of peasant men, the destruction of the peasantry in favor of collectivized agriculture constituted an advance toward equality. None of this was a product of economic determinism. Stalin himself justified his Five-Year Plans on purely political grounds: let Russia be prepared for her enemies. Had politics not ended the New Economic Policy, a more complex economy and society might have emerged in Russia, with the appearance of a middle class, wherein growing numbers of Russian women might have been afforded a separate sphere. Given the revolution's extinction of the privileges of the ancient church, such women might have found far more freedom than their Italian counterparts. (And Russian leaders might have been freer to pursue a more flexible diplomacy in sorting out who was friend and who was enemy.) As it was, the massacre of Russian manhood in World War I came to be repeated in World War II, and the need for women in the fields, the factories, the mines, as well as in the shops, the offices, the schools, the clinics, the institutions and bureaus and agencies proved even more acute after 1945. As sharp upgrading of the labor force through training and education began, women shared in it. A higher proportion of Russian women more nearly led the same kind of lives as did their men, than did women in Italy or Sweden, or, for that matter, in any other industrialized nation. By no means were their lives more prosperous. The Russian economy continued to lag far behind Sweden's, let alone Italy's, in production for consumption. But the sexes shared in this backwardness more equally.

The economic drama in all three nations, while different in each, differed even more from that of the United States. The core population of preindustrial northern white Americans never underwent any such debilitating experience of overpopulation as overtook Swedes and Italians. It never underwent the catastrophe of depopulation undergone by Russia. The shape of American industrial culture would not be influenced by people made anxious by uprooting, eager to recover a security they had lost. Women contributed richly toward American economic takeoff, in work in a hundred small mills, thousands of shops, a million home industries, even in backwoods forges and foundries. Yet it was precisely in the flourishing of these enterprises that a middle class began to emerge and grow, and it was in this middle class that men and women more and more led different, often separate lives. American industrialization generated growing opportunities for women not to have to work, to quit directly productive work for reproductive work, not just in home and household but in all that rose and spread as "woman's sphere," including its obvious potential for expansion. The ultimate logic of industrialization was to extract more production from less manpower, by means of greater machine power. In the United States women benefited directly from this gain, in a way quite different from men. This separation of the spheres had roots in preindustrial sources; American industry confirmed it. So powerful was it that it ultimately was to underwrite a family wage for unionized immigrant-based industrial workers, able then to embrace middle-class outlooks themselves. At all times, through the nineteenth century, into the twentieth, it was clear to everyone—to industrial workers themselves, to the middle classes, to reformers, to feminists—that by far the best thing for women was not to have to do industrial work at all. By far the better rule was for industrial workers to be men earning a family wage so that their women and children would not have to work. Certainly millions of industrial workers and their wives and children suffered for lack of such a wage. But a clear model had been underwritten with powerful economic substance.

The ways in which economic modernization brought different lives to men and to women became clearer after Italy and Russia, and Sweden, too, passed beyond their most serious times of troubles. In Italy, economic recovery after wartime breakdown did not bring a return to multi-party democratic debate, but a new polarization. Women linked, on the one hand, to the Christian Democrats and, on the other, to the Communists could hardly have known a greater ideological opposition. At the same time, women in both camps experienced a growing differentiation between themselves and their men. Christian Democracy encouraged an American-style separation of spheres, but with the special emphasis of the Catholic church's traditional gender doctrines, while the heart of Communism's politics was to hold blue-collar union workers, among whom women at work were more competition than ideal. Incipient feminist impulses toward women's self-consciousness as a separate interest group would meet opposition in the party of both the pope and Marx. In a nation replete with ironies, the revival of "sameness" and equality among Italian men and women would be seen most clearly when—and where—the postwar economic miracle sputtered to a halt and Italian women joined their men in the most underpaid and overworked of black labor. The renewed strength of Italy's giant industrial corporations in the mid-1980s did not at the same time inspire a breakthrough into a postindustrial epoch of growth in which better jobs for women would proliferate and in which young women trained at universities would find professions welcoming them to practice and careers to pursue. There were still too many Italians. Just as the family had brought Italians through the collapse of 1943–44, so the family offered social security to the unemployed, sheltering the young, especially, from drift. Here was the focus of demand for the continuing hegemony of woman as mother.

In Soviet Russia, by contrast, by the late 1960s, if not before, the economic managers faced a labor shortage. Women were needed as much as ever, and women found their way into broader sectors of the economy, and onto more ladders of management, than in the West. The reason was political. By the late 1960s Russia was paying the price for having availed itself for so long of cheap labor. Its basic need was for dramatic technological progress. But the monopoly of command by the Communist Party interfered. Thus, if, through all the crash industrialization of the 1930s, the postwar reconstruction of the 1950s and the gathering post-postwar slowdown of the 1970s and 1980s, Russian men and women had shared work with near equality, that was an equality now linked with structural contradictions. The contradictions showed up most clearly precisely where the gender equality least prevailed. The gender equality most Russians experienced was of course that of the politically powerless. Among those who enjoyed the monopoly of power, gender equality did not prevail. Women played a minor role in the Communist Party, and an even slighter role in its key centers of authority. The women who belonged to the elite of Russia were wives and daughters, mothers and sisters, mistresses and protégés, not themselves managers, directors, district leaders. Communism had generated an old-fashioned ruling class, completely gender-segregated. Under such circumstances, any relaxation of political superintendence might invite criticism of the equalities of powerlessness and shortages, comparable to Trotsky's fifty years before. Some women might complain about their equal lives. Not only were they still responsible for home life. Since the economy was being run not for the sake of the workers who staffed it, potential consumers one and all, but for the political purposes of the managerial elite, women workers might feel a special grievance against the managers' resistance to transferring resources to production for consumption. In this, they could hardly be accused of disloyalty to basic Marxist and Leninist precepts, for both Marx and, especially, Lenin had consistently heralded socialism's promise of an abundant material life for all. Land of full employment for men and women alike, Soviet Russia was not living up to its other promises.

By comparison, post-World War II Sweden was a success story. Steadily, the Social Democrats raised taxes to expand the general social-security system, of particular importance to women with children. The Social Democrats assumed that Sweden was underpopulated rather than overpopulated. They thus encouraged technological efficiency. This meant encouragement not just of engineers and inventors, but of labor. Workers need not fear technological unemployment, since the social-security system would provide for job retraining and relocation along with other cushions. The individual was not to be sacrificed to the general welfare. The system worked. For Swedish women, this meant that there was no compelling appetite in the marketplace for their labor, as in Russia, or on the level of family survival, as in Italy. High taxes meant that few Swedes could aspire to a level of material abundance that might inspire both man and wife to full-time work; the long tenure of the Social Democrats attested to modern Swedes' persisting allegiance to the rough egalitarianism of the ancient villages. Better a high standard of living for all than hopes of riches for any. Outsiders called it envy; Swedes, equality. With an economic spur to gender equality lacking, gender equality in Sweden tended to come to focus in the need of the Social Democrats for some kind of ideological legitimation. The search by government commissions for wage inequalities, the devising of curricula to teach girls so they could have the same prospects as boys, the offer of parental leave to fathers as well as mothers, all proceeded from the central logic of the Social Democratic Party: that Swedes were one great family, living in a *folkshem*, and in the good family all were equal. In these circumstances it would be difficult for Swedish women to find a focus of self-consciousness around which to mobilize. They had not had a century of experience of homosociality in a sphere of their own. They were not confronted by economic privation. No totalitarian politics dominated them. What was there to be criticized, after all, in a modern nation generated by a man of whom there was nothing but good to say, by a Hjalmar Branting?

In the United States a quite different story would continue to unfold. Still larger numbers of women enjoyed the choice of not working, and the young among them collaborated with their male analogues in generating new notions of life together that undermined the old woman's sphere. At the same time even larger numbers, of recent immigrant background, hard at work in the marketplace, saw their work as temporary, their goal being reconstitution of the family left broken in Sicily or County Cork or Värmland or Posen. While depression and World War II would deflect the new relations emerging between men and women in the 1920s, the strength of the economy would allow a kind of resumption of the new mores in the 1950s. Both political parties ratified it. Both were dependent on it. Both continued to live by the logic of the long boom, now fully launched into the epoch of production for consumption in a way unknown in the Soviet Union, only yearned for in Italy, and heavily contained by politics in Sweden. In the United States the very survival of feminism would depend on its ability to confront these powerful forces. Indeed, the peculiar shape of American feminist history would be defined by that relationship. It would be in America, where economics and politics appeared to offer women the most freedom and the most choices, that feminism shriveled and died, and had to be born again, in a way unknown in Italy, Sweden, or Russia.

Part II Consciousness and Feminism

Dramas of economics and politics do not in themselves generate growing consciousness and self-consciousness. Indeed, as we have seen in both Italy and Soviet Russia, one major effort in some modern politics has been to control, dominate, and discourage consciousness. Consciousness among modern women has had a history of deliberate, purposeful cultivation. To that I turn next. However, my purpose is not to condense some histories of feminism in Italy, Sweden, and Russia. Although often incited and inspired by politics and economic change, feminism has also had to struggle with both, sometimes resist and oppose. It has not always prevailed or survived. My basic thread therefore has been with the opportunities and threats, the incentives and disincentives to greater consciousness and self-consciousness among women. Often the greatest resource for any broad social movement is a single individual consciousness. I have therefore not hesitated to highlight individuals. While I do not believe individuals have arbitrary freedom, I am convinced that by far the most rewarding focus for study of consciousness is in certain individual brains. By no means are all those I highlight feminists, but all, I think, cast strong light on the issues of feminism. I do not believe any general formula serves to measure the significance of individuals in any particular story. The history of feminist self-consciousness in Soviet Russia could not be extricated from the story of Alexandra Kollontai. On the other hand, in Italy feminists such as Anna Maria Mozzoni and Anna Kuliscioff, while richly rewarding to any inquiry, do not begin to dominate their stages as did Kollontai. August Strindberg was enough in himself to lend Sweden's story a unique dimension, against whom feminists themselves—Fredrika Bremer, Ellen Key, Ellen Wägner—often seemed to define themselves.

119

4 Italy. Frustration

Feminism as Eighteenth-Century Individualism:
Anna Maria Mozzoni

The heroines of the Risorgimento—Maria Mazzini Drago, Anita Garibaldi, Filippina Cavour de Sales, Adele Cavour De Sellon, Adelaide Cairoli Bono, Giuditta Sidoli, Teresa Confalonieri—won no place for women in the new Italian state. By a law of 1861 the new parliament explicitly excluded women from the franchise. Six years later a southern deputy, Salvatore Morelli, introduced a bill for woman suffrage that got nowhere. Morelli had published *La donna e la scienza*, the first clearly feminist work in Italian history, but the book had generated no political following. A small political group calling themselves "Democrats" went on record favoring woman suffrage in 1881, but the Democrats were but a vestige of the movement that had sustained Mazzini in the years of hope.[1] Mazzini himself held all such efforts useless. Hoping to get the emancipation of women from a parliament dominated by the monarchy, Mazzini said, was "as though the first Christians had hoped to get paganism to accept monotheism and abolish slavery."[2] Mazzini and the Mazzinians held to their line: "Prima la repubblica. Subito dopo viene per noi la questione della donna."[3] First, the republic—then we'll get to you women immediately.

Some saw in the early parliaments not only the influence of the monarchy but also of Catholicism. Though the Pope had become united Italy's enemy and, after 1870, had shut himself up like a prisoner in the Vatican, Catholicism still loomed large as mental outlook, special interest, and political dilemma. In addition, while Masons and anticlericals were numerous in the early governments, by no means were they always friends of women's political equality.[4] The heroines of the Risorgimento had been mothers above all, and anticlericals such as Francesco Crispi could be as emphatic about women's proper place as the most ideological Jesuit writing in *Civiltà Cattolica*.

Men like Morelli belonged in the tradition of Italian utopianism, brimming with certitude about the powers of reason, certain that no classes of persons were debarred from autonomy by nature, only by ignorance and injustice. His was the tradition of liberal democratic individualism, in short. Years later, in 1923, as Italy entered upon a new kind of unity, another, different sort of feminist, a "nationalist" feminist, Teresa Labriola, offered sweeping summation of the fate of liberal feminism in Italy in a commentary on the life of Italy's first career feminist, Anna Maria Mozzoni, dead at eighty-three in 1920: "An imperial society will not tolerate individualistic feminism," she said. "It will not tolerate the proclamation of abstract innate rights."[5]

Anna Maria Mozzoni registered the frustrations of Italian feminism to the very eve of the Fascist blackout.[6] Born in 1837, Mozzoni had been too young to share in the heroic days of 'forty-eight herself, but she had known Austrian horses stabled in her own homestead in Lombardy and had witnessed the Austrian defeat in 1859. Until the age of fourteen she had been educated at a school for poor girls of high birth that lent her a lifelong certainty about what education for girls should not be. Back home, reading widely in the family library, she discovered modern philosophy and science. Her father, though not quite able to distinguish the science of experiment and logic from science as the "key" to "mysteries," was a typical anticlerical of his time and class, sure that one way or the other science was on its way to evict the superstitions of religion. Mozzoni's reputation as a personality notable for composure and fact-mindedness undoubtedly drew on her father's influence.

In a brief book, *La donna e suoi rapporti sociale* (Woman and her social relationships), published when she was twenty-seven, Mozzoni addressed herself first simply to "young women," then more pointedly to *gentili signore* (gentle ladies) and *donne ricche e colte* (rich and cultured women).[7] She spoke of indolent and vacuous lives, useless existences, parasitic beings. Nothing in her book was addressed to the conditions of life for the vast majority of Italian women on the land. Her references to "industry" were positive, it being a sphere that women should enter; she had nothing to say of the conditions under which the girls in the early silk mills were laboring. It was a book by a middle-class young woman addressed to other middle-class young women. Its message was clear: young middle-class Italian women must awaken to a wider life than Italian tradition offered them. In this, Mozzoni was rejecting, not so much the tradition of Catholic ideology, for that was obviously insupportable, but that of her own hero, Giuseppe Mazzini, who persisted in seeing woman's highest development—and fullest freedom—in her practice of those eternally feminine virtues most neatly embodied in her status as *angelo del focolare*, angel of the hearth. This was part of Mazzini's sense of Italy as different. Mazzini drew his visions for Italy's future from his vision of Italy's past. For Mozzoni, however, Italian women's future was prefigured in the feminism already at work outside Italy—in France, in England, especially in the United States. Mozzoni translated John Stuart Mill's *The Subjection of Women* in 1869.

She knew of the American women abolitionists, of Harriet Beecher Stowe. She regarded Wyoming as living refutation of Italians' fear of woman suffrage. As the first governments of united Italy pursued their conservative way, then, in the 1860s Mozzoni grew impatient:

While America, England, Switzerland, even Prussia and Austria, hasten to dismantle their antique institutions, cannot Italy, if not lead the way, at least follow them? Will she always be . . . buried under the debris of centuries past? Will the future never inspire her? Will she never take the initiative?[8]

In 1868, with the first issue of *La Donna*, a fortnightly published in Venice, Mozzoni and other Italian feminists had their first reliable public outlet. Its adept editor, Gualberta Beccari, the daughter of a Risorgimento patriot, a Mazzinian, a republican, carried the journal to Bologna in 1878, then to Turin in 1892, where it remained to her death in 1906. *La Donna* published an array of poets and correspondents from all over northern Italy. Its main writer was Mozzoni. It developed a particularly interested readership among schoolteachers. But above all it published news of women abroad, and especially of American women and feminists. So marked was this cosmopolitan quality that the most popular woman writer of the day, Mathilde Serao, attacked *La Donna* in 1888 for its "foreign" model of the woman citizen, and that at a time—Italy was at war in Libya—when she said Italian women ought to adjure *egoismo* for the sake of their nation.[9]

In effect, Mozzoni—and *La Donna*—hoped that Italy would grow to resemble France, Britain, and America, where there were women's clubs, women's journals, women's associations, where there seemed to be much writing by women about women for women. Women seemed to be active in charity, reforms, education. Women appeared to be entering civic life. Without ever quite formulating the situation for themselves in so many words, Mozzoni and her peers argued for a middle class in Italy. Her hope lay in education, and indeed, if a single group of younger women of substantial weight for Italian feminism emerged over the entire period from 1860 to 1900, it was the school-teachers. Nothing seemed more shamefully backward in the new Italy than its vast illiteracy, and illiteracy was used repeatedly as justification for keeping women off the voting lists (just as it was for keeping men off, too). Certainly in Mazzini's vision schools would become a glory of Italy reborn.[10]

Yet the schoolmistresses of united Italy more nearly recorded the crumbling than the embrace of Risorgimento ideals. The new state could not doubt its educational task but utterly lacked the resources for it. The bill to pay for anything like an adequate system would have been immense. The solution? Proceed with a cheap system, poor, crowded normal schools, risible budgets for schoolhouses, schoolbooks, school equipment, and budgets of tragic want for schoolteachers' salaries. Finally, leave schools and teachers to the mercies of local government. In the United States teachers going south to teach ex-slaves at least had the Freedmen's Bureau and even the army behind them; those going west to Illinois, Kansas, and Oregon had the ambition of pioneer communities behind them. In large regions of Italy schoolteachers often had trouble finding a room, let alone friends, let alone respect. Unlike other local state functionaries, they did not arrive by means of politicking, or wear a uniform or exercise powers to which other adults were vulnerable. Often enough the parents whose children they taught preferred to have their children at work in the streets, shops, or fields. Often the teacher was in conflict, whether she chose it or not, with local nuns and priests.

Here, then, in a most crucial sector, the sheer economic basis for the emergence of a flourishing middle-class culture was not being built. Following the advent of the parliamentary Left to government in 1876, Mozzoni got together a petition for woman suffrage in 1877; went to Paris as Italy's representative to a congress on women's rights and education in 1878; and joined with various other republicans, radicals, and socialists in an assembly of Democrats in 1881, calling for universal, including woman, suffrage. But the connection between all this and Italy's struggles for economic takeoff remained obscure. In the United States feminists could work for suffrage in the context of a long and powerful economic expansion, and in Sweden universal suffrage could be pursued while the nation's economic transformation proved itself securely under way. In Italy, Mozzoni and her friends could take nothing for granted. During the early 1880s Mozzoni collaborated most closely with Italian Freemasonry along with the republicans, liberals, and others who made up a kind of independent Left, but these too offered no particular choices germane to the question, not so much whether middle-class Italian women would bestir themselves from parasitic domesticity, but whether there would be jobs and careers for those who might want them in the first place—in teaching, journalism, science, commerce, government, welfare, health, law, and so on. The republican, anticlerical, liberal Left proved at once economically inept and increasingly indifferent to democracy. Mozzoni's twenty-odd years as a Western-style feminist had come to naught.

By the 1880s Mozzoni began calling herself a "socialist." Her disillusionment with liberal governments grew. The efforts of *La Donna* and her own work had not stirred a growing feminism. Education was not rearing a new generation of ambitious younger women. Neither then nor later did she embrace the Marxist faith that capitalism would spawn a saving proletariat. Certainly in the young female factory workers of the Italian textile industry, feminists saw the single largest group of women directly exploited by the new economy, yet Mozzoni was never to be at one with Socialist Party policy toward these workers. The party's most prominent woman, Anna Kuliscioff, the Italianized exile from Russian reform circles, propounded the need of the textile workers for protective laws. Seeing in such laws not-so-subtle barriers to women entering the work place, Mozzoni objected.[11] Over the years, this division reflected the deeper issue of the party's basic constituency. The new blue-collar male industrial workers did not favor women working. Mozzoni's turn to socialism hence appeared more a kind of last recourse than a positive adhesion. On one issue she and Kuliscioff stood together, first to last—the vote for women. But here Kuliscioff herself stood toward one side of her party. Many Socialist Party leaders, including the most eminent, Filippo Turati, while professing personal wishes for woman suffrage, professed also to find the party's support for suffrage inexpedient. The party was split sectionally as well. One of its young leaders, Gaetano Salvemini, an intellectual from the south, attacked the party's "northern" policy bitterly, declaring that a Socialist Italy would be impossible without an alliance between northern workers and southern peasants. Ordinarily a straightforward supporter of votes for women, Salvemini at one point drew back out of fear of the influence of priests over southern peasant women.[12]

The Socialist Party hardly offered itself to feminists as a vehicle they could trust, and Mozzoni did not in fact ever enter the party. Instead, she persisted in autonomous feminism, partly through a League for the Promotion of the Interests of Women that she had founded in 1881, partly through *La Donna*, partly in various further political manifestations for the vote. Essentially, Mozzoni did not give up her original outlook, that of an educated middle-class young woman impatient with the prospect of life as wife and mother. Once at least, in 1899, she declared that, for the "transformation of domestic economy," industrial progress was necessary, if not sufficient.[13] It was the lack of such industrial progress that haunted Mozzoni's whole feminist career. Socialism had no program for breaking the country's economic impasse, except on the basis of some supposition that a nation more united in justice might generate new economic energies. For many, this was the route to a new nationalism, with its bitter aftermath. Mozzoni, however, did not take the next step. As skeptical of myths of a united popular Italy as she was of clerical Italy, she continued to take aim at her basic target, the ideology that equated women's nature with a proper place for women. She continued to hold to the eighteenth-century ideology of the essential equality of all individuals, women included. And she continued to sense that in Italy the resistance to this idea persisted among the most advanced as well as among the most retrograde of traditional intellectual leaders. In 1911 Benedetto Croce, for example, the self-conscious exponent of new ways of thinking for a renewed Italy, replied to an inquiry on feminism sent out by an intellectual journal: "Feminism is a movement that seems to me self-condemned in its very name. It is a 'feminine' idea in the bad sense of that word. Men too have their particular problems but they haven't invented 'masculinism.' "[14]

Two Kinds of Feminism: Catholics versus the Church

Was there any ground anywhere for an Italian feminism of woman's sphere? Italy had not yet generated a flourishing middle class with the objective economic and social resources that could offer women time and space of their own, a chance for communion, discourse, and rituals that were not simply the sum of prescribed roles and duties but a register of their own energy. Yet a woman's sphere had been invented in Italy. Pious works had been set afoot—philanthropic, medical, didactic—and educational activities supported. High-born ladies from families long linked to papal courts were often chosen to head such agencies, while aspiring women of the new bourgeoisie might seek to aid them.[15] This was Catholicism in its Vatican extrusions, and of course the Vatican's ideology regarding women was antifeminist. But the lay Catholicism stimulated by such priests as Romolo Murri, often with French precedents in mind, that arose in the 1890s found women heavily involved. Face the facts, Paolo Arcari urged upon Catholic leaders: Italian women were no longer living according to standard Catholic ideology. Hundreds were already attending secondary schools; thousands were at work in the spreading industrial economy. If the church did not watch out, it would see an entire new generation of Italian workers lost to the faith—socialism, the Socialist Party, anti-Christian culture would inherit them.[16]

Here of course was a purely expedient, opportunistic rationale, hardly feminist at all. But within the circles of the Murrian movement, of "democratic Christianity," of "Christian feminism," debate began over votes for women. Murri himself was reluctant. Some pointed in warning to the experience of those states in the United States where women already voted. But the prominent Luigi Stirati, declaring the American experience positive, urged the vote. With the small, secular Radical Party trying to take over the issue to its own advantage, more and more of the Christian feminists found tactical reasons for embracing the cause. Murri himself by 1906 was supporting the vote for various categories of women. Always, the cause of suffrage was tied to the cause of the family, of protective laws for women who worked, of allowing working women to return home, of a "family wage" for male workers so that their women need not work. Always, as Luigi Stirati said, criticizing the Socialists' August Bebel, the family remained "absolute" and "indestructible." But Christian feminism saw every reason to draw women more and more deeply into open political nurturing of this "eternal" complex.[17]

Important new women's voices were heard from within these circles: Elisa Salerno, Adelaide Coari, Dora Melegari, Elena da Persico. Da Persico involved herself with the new Catholic "white" labor unions. Sketching a minimum feminist program, Coari advanced a frame that, beginning with traditional Catholicism's exclusive emphasis upon "woman for the family," ended, after passing through "woman for society," with "woman for herself." After noting that, of all European women, Italian women were probably least known and most stereotyped, Melegari went on to discuss why feminism in Italy had been so weak but now was starting to rise.[18]

Throughout, of course, this Christian, Catholic feminism was explicitly competitive with the feminism of women's rights, of the anticlerical liberals, of Mozzoni. Of course, it was intransigent against socialism. "There are two feminisms, which, while not always opposed on particular issues, remain in profound antagonism as to their essence." The one—secular, individualistic, bourgeois—spoke of "rights," while the other—pious, community-based, organic—spoke of "service." The one demanded equality with men, the other drew on the equality of supernatural vocations between men and women. In 1899, Fascio Femminile Democratico Cristiano got organized in Milan, with its journal. It was hard not to wonder whether, had the secular feminists and socialists not seemed about to steal a march on Catholicism, the religious movement would have started up at all, but there were differences among the Catholic groups. Elena da Persico's journal, *L'Azione Muliebre*, took a "prudent and conservative" line, while Adelaide Coari's *Pensiero e Azione* expressed the outlook of young workers and other young women. The more openly the latter explored the needs of its constituents, the more it found itself agreeing with secular feminists, above all on the vote. "For one brief moment," in the "illusion of a possible convergence" with secular feminists, the Christian feminists around Coari and her *Pensiero e Azione* were tempted to make themselves into the avantgarde of the whole Italian women's movement. In 1906 Pius X repeated his opposition to the vote. *Pensiero e Azione* was not discouraged: "Our readers will notice that, as to votes for women, our view differs apparently from that of his holiness. I say apparently, because the Pontiff has not made it a question of law but of opinion. His judgment can only spur us on to work." The energies of lay Catholics had been released, in short, and most notably the energies of young lay women. Should the hierarchy and the Vatican allow the movement to expand indefinitely, a major reform in Italian life would occur.[19]

By 1908 the feminist scene in Italy had been enriched with a few more local groups, such as the Associazione Nazionale per le Donne, founded in Rome in 1897, and the Unione Femminile Nazionale, founded in Milan in 1899. When a Consiglio Nazionale delle Donne Italiane was organized in 1903, it rapidly became the leading national feminist group, drawing members from both north and south, avoiding "confessional" dimensions, whether Catholic or Socialist, and aiming to provide maximum room for the greatest variety of women ready to think of themselves as feminists. Some were Socialists, some were Catholics. Though most Consiglio members were bourgeois, others were of old aristocratic background, and a few had working experience, though these were not peasant women. In 1908 the Consiglio held a national congress, its first and the first such in Italy. It was intended to be open, ecumenical, pluralistic. Several countesses were in attendance. At the inaugural session, the Queen herself attended, as well as the minister of education and the mayor of the city, an eminent Mason. By all intentions and all evident auguries, it was Italian feminism's coming of age, its access to the stage of public and political respectability.

In the positivistic style of such congresses, various topics were scheduled for discussion at separate meetings. Remarkably, one topic had been forgotten—woman suffrage—and had to be hastily added. Most of the discussions went off without heat: the moral and legal status of women; public assistance; health; women's arts and letters; emigration. Two did not. One dealt with divorce, the other with religious education. The differences between Catholics and others on divorce were papered over in an agreement to support further and deeper study of the issue. The debate over religious education in the schools, however, had repercussions that would echo for decades. A Socialist delegate, Linda Malnati, introduced a resolution urging that, in the name of religious equality, religion not be part of elementary schools' curricula at all, while in secondary schools religion be the subject of "objective" teaching. A Catholic delegate offered an opposing motion. Debate, including protests against any consideration at all, moved implacably to a vote. Malnati's resolution won more than 1,100 votes, the Catholic resolution a few more than 100. Further debate broke out within the circles of Catholic feminism. Coari and her colleagues argued that it was better to seek an "organic penetration" of the women's movement than to withdraw in "segregation and opposition." They wanted to find ways to continue the convergence. Da Persico and her colleagues, in contrast, condemned the majority as "composed of persons of only a thin religiosity, ignorant of the questions of religion." The anger here was directed far more at the rationalistic laicism that had accompanied Risorgimento Italy from its birth than at the Socialists, for the Socialists at least made clear where they stood on religion. Da Persico's charge that the congress's majority manifested a "theosophical" outlook testified in effect to the failure of Italian liberalism to generate its own convincing center of loyalty. Challenged on its left by the rising new gospel of socialism, it now found itself challenged by the ancient force on its right that it had succeeded in neither dissolving nor finessing.

Within weeks the Pope was listening to proposals brought to him by Princess Cristina Giustiani Bandini for a new Catholic women's organization bound tightly to the Vatican. Advising that the charter of the organization should specify the "exclusion of politics and of claims for rights that are in direct contradiction with the providential mission of women," Pius X approved. The Unione fra le Donne Cattoliche came into official being in April 1909. The convergence of Catholic with lay and even Socialist feminism was over. The last issue of Coari's *Pensiero e Azione* had appeared the year before. Catholic feminism was over.[20]

Italy as Balancing Act: Giolitti and the Failure of Woman Suffrage

When parliament took up Giovanni Giolitti's proposal of 1913 to expand the suffrage to all men, including illiterates, Giolitti responded to an amendment including women, saying that woman suffrage would be a "leap in the dark." "We're already expanding the electorate by eight million. Adding women would mean another eight million, sixteen million in one fell swoop. The increase in the illiterate voters would be in proportion. Let's take one step at a time. Let's take a moment to catch our breaths."[21]

It was arguable that the civic condition of women in Italy had declined between 1860 and 1913. To be sure, the numbers of women with schooling had risen; the numbers of women in professional and poorly paid quasi-professional posts had risen slowly; the numbers of women at work in textile mills, rice fields, shops, and offices had risen; and certain reforms in women's property rights in marriage had been passed. Yet even so, women remained as far outside civic life as ever. A good many women had found ways to participate in the Socialist Party, but even there their presence was precarious and shadowy. Once it might have been hoped—had been hoped—that as the franchise was expanded to include larger classes of men, whether defined by taxes, education, or property, comparable classes of women might be included, too. But they had not been. Now, in 1913, all men could vote, but no women could. Once it had been imagined that women might, in a kind of step-by-step initiation, be granted the right to vote in administrative (local) elections. But they had not been. Now, all men could vote in all elections, but no women in any.

By any reckoning, Giolitti's franchise reform of 1911–13 was sweeping. It was entirely consistent with his own ideological past, as a man of liberal governments over forty years. It was a democratic act. It challenged that tradition of condescension in intellectual circles that had long demanded schooling, in a nation with as much backwardness as Italy's, as a necessary preliminary to suffrage. Of course, had he pressed for woman suffrage as well, Giolitti could have claimed even broader sanction from the liberal past. He could have found words of Mazzini and Garibaldi to strengthen his case, and his act would have been even more democratic. And, gratifying Mozzoni's hope that for once Italy should lead rather than lag behind, he could legitimately have offered Italy's example for imitation by all those envied nations to the north and west with which Italy had been striving to catch up.

Giolitti had not acted in order to be liberal, though, or to be democratic, let alone to win honor for Italy on an international stage. Expanding the franchise to all men was part of his perennial effort to improve the stability of Italian politics and thus head off the social instabilities that Italy had inherited from its unhappy past. These remained as evident in 1913 as they had been in 1860: the contrast between north and south, the tension between church and state, the split between antimodern Catholicism and modern secular culture. To these old divisions had been added a new one: the rise of a small but potent industrial sector, containing its own poles of owners and workers. Giolitti's policy was to try to give all these elements a stake in the political system. Each had power and its legitimate self-interests. None was to be left to simmer in reactionary or revolutionary resentment.

From Giolitti's standpoint, then, woman suffrage had nothing in its favor. While the decade or so preceding the suffrage expansion of 1913 had seen more feminist activity than at any time in the forty years before, this by no means added up to the creation of a new interest group. The one party to give any significant support to woman suffrage, the Socialist, was itself still divided on the issue, while being also divided from other suffragists, regarding them as bourgeois and therefore basically anti-working class (and consequently against working-class women). The middle-class suffrage circles, heirs of Anna Maria Mozzoni, had no effective political weight. They propounded no views on Italian economic policy. They carried within themselves the polarization that took open form at Rome in 1908. Ironically, their most visible impact seemed to confirm that Italy's traditional gender sociology remained valid. From 1899, with its founding by Ersilia Majno, a new Unione Femminile Nazionale busied itself for a decade with Casse di Maternità (Maternity Funds), Aiuti Materni (Mothers' Aid), and other agencies of welfare and assistance for women.[22] The Unione, a genuine feminist organization, also pressed for suffrage, but its activities—to be taken up by the Fascist regime—appeared to define women's basic interests in traditional ways. If what women wanted was what the Unione Femminile was doing, an electoral revolution was hardly needed.

Only one of the three arguments for women's votes—and women's civic equality—was compatible with Giolitti's politics of perpetual adjustment. Mozzoni's standard eighteenth-century rationalist argument for women's rights, respecting the equality of all individuals, remained simply a luxury inherited from the Risorgimento, and neither Giolitti nor Italy had been able to afford luxuries. The Socialists' partial adhesion to women's equality simply as a dimension of socialism obviously linked woman suffrage with an interest, that of industrial labor, which the large majority saw as threatening. Only the Catholic feminists' view of woman suffrage as a means to women's service to an organic community melded with the politics of accommodation and adjustment. The Catholic feminists, however, remained a small and suppressed minority within their own faith. As Giolitti moved to draw Catholics into his coalitions, he had no reason whatever to bring an intra-Catholic dispute in, too.

The move to universal manhood suffrage had followed upon no broad popular movement demanding it. There was no such current as that in late-nineteenth-century Sweden for feminists to launch themselves upon. This isolation discouraged feminism from imaginative expansion. Nineteenth-century Italian feminists avoided the marriage question and the sexual question. Mozzoni, free enough personally to lead an unconventional private life, raising her daughter by herself, kept private life private. Kuliscioff too, autonomous in her own private life, did not press an argument that the "private was political." Hence some of the deepest roots of traditional Italian views on women went unexamined.

On September 9, 1919, the lower house of parliament voted in favor of woman suffrage by a vote of 174 to 55, in a near exact reversal of the 209 to 48 vote by which that suffrage had been refused just seven years before. Not only had the war intervened, with its stimulus to mass organizations in which many women shared, but a new political universe had been created. In the November elections the Socialists would show that they could attract the largest number of voters, and the Socialists had at last agreed on women's votes. Don Luigi Sturzo's new party of Catholic laity came in second, and it too supported women's votes. But one of the purposes of the Catholics' party was precisely to head off socialism, and the meaning of women's votes was diametrically opposite in each. The small group of Fascists favored woman suffrage, too. Almost every organized political group did, and it was precisely in such heterogeneity that the weakness of the parliamentary support lay. When the Senate, as always dominated by the monarchy, refused to join the House, only concerted political support could have sustained the issue. But no concert could be elicited with schisms on the left, aggressions on the right, and cabinets crumbling under the pressure of nationalists embittered at Italy's failure to reap rewards from the war. Woman suffrage got lost just as it reached its high point. By then feminism itself was crumbling, as some feminists followed the Communists out of the Socialist Party, others defended their middle-class Consiglio against increasingly illiberal nationalists, while still others embraced that nationalism as the bearer of feminism. Neither the vote against suffrage nor the vote for suffrage had followed broad and sustained debate. When circumstance made suffrage seem possible, circumstance also rendered it impossible.[23]

Fascism's Women

The extinction of Italian feminism by Fascism was a process not of straightforward political conflict but of organic cooptation. The war had split feminists. The middle-class Consiglio found itself confronted on one front by a new group, Patria, Famiglia, Humanità, which subordinated feminism to uncritical nationalism, and on another front by peace activists. When the suffrage organization Pro Suffragio announced its adherence to the war effort in 1915, such Socialist feminists as Ada Dobelli resigned. Dobelli later, in December 1918, presided over a postwar convention that affirmed a familiar prewar trinity of socialism/feminism/pacifism.

Wartime divisions were not healed after the war. To the contrary. As nationalist voices grew, with a new Unione Nazionale Politica fra le Donne Italiane being formed, harshly antiunion, antisocialist, and anti-Soviet Union, the Consiglio, still led by Countess Spalletti Rasponi, bourgeois to its core and still linked to American, English, and other feminists on the international circuit, repelled the attempted embrace.[24] Many well-known Catholic feminists likewise scorned the rising Fascist call. Elisa Salerno, a baker's daughter of forty-four, perhaps ideally representative of all that *terra incognita*, a popular Catholicism at once authentic in its piety and suspicious of the authoritarian church, had already replied to her critics in *Per la riabilitazione della donna* in 1917. In this work she had gone so far as to assail the church's shiny new Thomistic apologetics as but old triumphalism writ new. The rehabilitated Thomism no less than the old, she said, simply assigned everyone, and most certainly women, to a fixed place, ahistorical, unappealable. During Fascism, consequently, Salerno was in disfavor with both church and state. She lived to write *Il neoantifemminismo* in 1948, still as a Catholic in her own, that is, in populist Italy's sense.[25] After the failure of her *Pensiero e Azione* in 1908, Adelaide Coari had gone on working for collaboration between Catholic bourgeois secular and Socialist feminists, finding in Sturzo's Popular Party a promise of a more open religious feminism. During Fascism Coari worked in the schools of the church's Catholic Action, not in submission to the regime but rather from lifelong religious impulses: Fascism had driven such imaginations into tight corners.[26] Maria Guidi, the young wife of a Popular Party deputy, worked in Catholic labor unions. As Fascism took over all the unions, she also retired within the precincts of Catholic Action, again in withdrawal from a politics that had destroyed the chance for religious expression. After the war Guidi helped start the Italian chapter of the Federation of Business and Professional Women.[27]

It was perhaps women like these who posed for Mussolini the problem he took some little time to solve. Certainly from 1919 to 1922 Mussolini did not want to be outflanked by some surge of populism that included women.[28] His was to be a politics that transcended class divisions, thus quenching them, a politics that bound all the elements of the nation into a single bundle. If not only his own women enthusiasts and activists but the women of a responsive Catholic Italy might add to his strength, it was not unthinkable to enfranchise them. After all, why might not women vote, not only for Fascism, but for motherhood, family, and the organic roots of Italy?

Early Fascism's women had not been antifeminists. Teresa Labriola, for instance, had spoken for both feminism and socialism for years before the war. Certainly both her feminism and her socialism had been of a special sort. A student of anthropology, she had criticized the excessive "logicality" and utopianism of the individualistic middle-class feminists, and she had criticized the Socialists in 1902 for supporting divorce, an "individualistic" reform. Labriola had early spoken of the need for European women to constitute a counterbalance to the rise of the *negri*. It was hardly surprising, then, that Labriola became a fervent nationalist during the war. From nationalism to Fascism was not a big step, but in taking it Labriola did not forsake her own kind of feminism and socialism.[29]

Another example was Regina Terruzzi. The director of a girls' secondary school in the 1890s, Terruzzi had belonged to the Lega Femminile in Milan. She became secretary of the Gruppo Femminile Socialista there in 1897 and helped lead the drive within the Socialist Party for protective laws. She became a member of the party's national women's section. Then, in 1919, she shared in founding the Fasci di Combattimento. Even more than Labriola, Terruzzi saw in Fascism a defense against the modernizing disintegrations in Italian life. She was appalled at the possibility of imitations in the Italian countryside of Bolshevik models of collective agriculture. For her, as for Emilia Mariani and other Socialist feminists, socialism meant the sheltering, nurturing, and perpetuation of the Italian peasantry and its culture, including its family life.[30]

Another kind of woman also joined Mussolini. One of the reasons for giving women the vote, Mussolini said, was that they had been the mothers of heroes—heroes of the war, but now Fascist heroes, too. Not all the women who helped him were simply heroes' mothers; some were themselves heroes. After Red Cross service during the war, Elisa Majer Rizzioli supported Gabrieli D'Annunzio in his capture of Fiume and then joined the Fascists in 1920, eventually becoming an important figure of Fascism's "earliest hours." Young women like her and Ines Donati wanted more than home and motherhood. Donati saw in Fascism an opportunity for young girls too to be involved in politics, in struggle, in heroics, and was photographed heroically helping male Fascist *squadristi* keep the streets of Rome clean during a streetsweepers' strike[31]

Even women who were drawn primarily to Mussolini's personal leadership might have something other than a conventional, conventionally subaltern background. The well-known Margherita Grassini Sarfatti, who wrote the first biography of Mussolini widely read in English translation, *Dux*, had been active in cultivated literary circles before the war, and also in feminist circles that included Anna Kuliscioff and other Socialist feminist women. Close to the Duce, she continued to write on art, painting, and culture in the Fascist years, before she was compelled to leave Italy because of her Jewish ancestry.[32]

As late as May 1925, when Mussolini no longer had any opposition to fear, but nonetheless came to parliament to support votes for women in local elections, he came with a fund of experience with political women for which he could be grateful. Certainly, when ideologues such as Paōlo Ardali and Ferdinando Loffreddo were left free by 1929 or so to vent their more or less openly misogynistic and quasi-pornographic fantasies, the early heroines of Fascism could hardly have been pleased.

Terruzzi went on working on rural projects into the 1930s, being described in her files as someone still living in the past of "twenty years ago." Mussolini might indeed have been happy, had it been feasible to include such women in important posts in his regime. By no means would they have been incompatible with his vision of a heroic Italy forsaking its old divisions. One Fascist union leader, Renato del Giudice, actually renewed the old call for equal pay. A Fascist feminist historian, Maria Castellani, pointed out, in 1937, in criticism, that women had been herded into the most monotonous, tiring, menial, and ill-paid work.[33] But Mussolini had compromised his freedom to pursue visions of a new order. His pact with the industrialists of the north committed him to cheap labor; Giolitti's old hope that high profits and high wages might go hand in hand had faded. Further, Mussolini's pact with Pius XI and the Vatican committed him to standard Catholic ideology about women. Thus the hopes of the social, lay Catholics had been smothered; the "heroics" of Fascism would be severely limited to half the nation.

Meanwhile, choosing for some of its leadership to remain underground in Italy rather than to retreat abroad, the new Communist Party had defined its own attitude toward efforts in the here and now. "Our party is simply not concerned over the question of votes for women in the coming elections," Amadeo Bordiga announced in 1921; "let the other parties chatter on about that." Communists, he said, know that true equality for women will come as they share in the construction of a new Communist society. Sharing in the work of the party itself could begin forthwith. As the Fascist regime gradually imprisoned or exiled the party leadership, a woman, Camilla Ravera, took over for a few years, until prison reached out for her too.[34]

Class versus Mass: Feminism in Divided Italy, 1945–1968

Italian resistance to the Germans began in September 1943, as American and British armies struggled south of Rome to cope with an enemy whose strength they had not expected. Postwar Italy would be shaped by the division between a north where resistance heroes were made, and a south under an Allied military government skeptical of all Italians. A number of women already politically active in the north, mostly in Lombardy and Piedmont, formed Gruppi di Difesa della Donna e per l'Assistenza ai Combattenti per la Libertà" (Women's Defense Groups for Aid to the Fighters for Liberty). Their manifest purpose hardly concealed a latent one: "They wanted, for once, to live like men." This latent purpose was made more manifest eight months later, in June

1944, when the groups' national committee explained itself to the over-all direction of the resistance, the Committee for National Liberation. It aimed, it said, "to organize women for the conquest of their rights as women and as Italians in the context of the battle of all the people for national liberation."[35]

Once again a season for heroines as well as heroes was at hand, but this time, unlike in the Risorgimento, the heroines were not going simply to serve as "mothers illustrious" and martyr wives. This time they, like Ada Gobetti, wife of the well-known leader of the anti-Fascist Justice and Liberty movement, would take the field, too. Yet mystification and mythification awaited, ready to wrap these as well as all the Resistance in haze and glamour. Historians were not going to find it easy to explain such groups, and parties would fight over their claims to Resistance glory. Gobetti herself radiated a highly particular kind of consciousness. She was glad that the Gruppi had worked in collaboration, not in contention, with men. She could see that the Resistance made such collaboration easy. Without suppressing such traditionally divisive issues as equal pay and the vote, it offered great and noble goals that men and women could pursue shoulder to shoulder—liberty, justice, peace—at least for a while, for in the Italy of 1943 and 1944 these were not mere abstractions. But what Gobetti enjoyed most was the opportunity offered by the Resistance for women to prove that they were indeed equals of men, just as enduring, strong, brave, resourceful, and implacable, just as virile. In the Resistance, gender-typing of roles could fade away.[36]

The formation of a Unione delle Donne Italiane (Union of Italian Women, UDI) in the areas liberated by Allied armies late in 1944 displayed a will to perpetuate the values in this Resistance experience.[37] UDI was open to all women of anti-Fascist commitment. Not only Communist and Socialist women joined, but also women of anarchist and syndicalist origins and persuasions. Liberal, old radical, and republican women—that is, non-Catholic middle-class women, joined. So did Catholic women. Maria Guidi, the onetime Popular Party deputy's wife, after weathering the Fascist years, entered the UDI. There were even a few women, such as Flavio Steno, who had worked in Fascist organizations, who were awakened by the collapse of Italy and joined the UDI, brands from the burning.[38]

But this ecumenicity in itself did not solve, but indeed sharpened, the basic challenge to the UDI in its postwar environment. In the Resistance, women's *gruppi* had collaborated with men's groups, often consciously in the name of unity against the common enemy. With what men, then, with what groups, organizations, and parties would the UDI collaborate after the war? Would Catholic women follow the lead of

Communist women? Would Communist women heed women of old liberal and republican, often Masonic, roots?

In its first months, the UDI found itself able to reach out easily to other organizations as these too, newly born after the period of Fascist monopoly, moved forward, free of bureaucratic weight, to consider any causes and any allies. At a convention of reborn labor unions, UDI representatives called on the unions to support equal pay, nurseries for the children of working mothers, and women on union boards. Late in 1944 the UDI called on the seven or eight new political parties to support votes for women. In August 1944 the UDI set up its own journal, *Noi Donne*, open to all contributors.

Again, circumstances helped soften certain hard issues. Should the UDI consider pressing the familiar idea of getting women out of the home for the sake of their minds, hearts, and souls? Or should it stress the need for help and subsidies for mothers and children? In 1944 this was not a difficult choice: hundreds of thousands of mothers and children were in desperate need. Certainly no resources were remotely in sight for some acceptable new theory of "social" child-rearing. The Italian family required patching up as it was, in the quickest way. The abstractions of Engels and Bebel—and Lenin—could wait, and did. At its first national congress, in Florence in October 1945, the UDI, while reaffirming its welcome to all women, including professional women, also affirmed its commitment to the "renewal of the institution of the family that is for us the fundamental and irreplaceable basis of society." Still, this restorative policy could include radical demands. In May 1945, with the war in Europe hardly over, UDI women went into the ministry of justice to urge repeal of all the old laws spelling out fathers' and husbands' rights over daughters and wives. And of course the UDI itself, along with all the new parties, endorsed the new suffrage for women.

Who really led the UDI? What was its first priority? In the fall of 1944 UDI directors had explicitly invited Catholic women to join the organization. Catholic women had continued to be the concern of the Unione Donne di Azione Cattolica, constituted in Rome in 1908 in reaction to the anticlerical currents in the Consiglio Nazionale. Given official sanction by the Concordat of 1929, Catholic Action had defended its position during the last decade of Fascism. Naturally, it had its own interests to calculate in 1944.

One new organization created for the modern circumstances was Il Movimento Femminile, a kind of auxiliary of the new Christian Democratic Party. One of the MF's early leaders was a member of the Resistance, Bianca Maria Chiri; another was Maria Guidi Cingolani, elected to parliament and, as undersecretary for industry and commerce, the first woman to hold a post in the government. Soon enough, the MF showed itself to be almost completely an agency of the Christian Democratic Party. The party itself proved more or less consistently deaf to MF initiatives, and those initiatives soon faded away. But a later cooptation cannot be read backward, into 1944, to explain the organization of still another Catholic women's group, the Centro Italiano Femminile. The CIF was the more direct Catholic response to the UDI's invitation. Guidi Cingolani had evidently found it possible, for a few weeks, to belong to both the UDI and the MF, presumably on the assumption that the UDI was truly an ecumenical organization. But with the formation of the CIF she left the UDI. Clearly church leaders, including Pius XII, felt the importance of a Catholic presence directly among active women, uncomplicated by entanglement with the Christian Democrats. To what extent the CIF's essentially defensive origins continued to control its work could be determined only by assuming that its religious commitment was itself defensive. The CIF pressed for reforms respecting working mothers, adoption laws, health care, and nurseries. That women would hold jobs it took for granted, and it worked for equal treatment. In its journal, *Cronache e Opinioni*, it reported on the work of local chapters and offered analyses of how the new mass media promoted false values both within and outside the family. The CIF was, in short, a postwar middle-class organization, its Catholic dimension a testimony to the more or less final fading of that old anticlerical, positivistic, secular, and science-minded tradition that had once, after the Risorgimento, seemed to be Italy's middle class in the making. At the same time, this was no longer either the church's own women's department, dominated by the hierarchy, or that "social Christianity" that had sought its freedom from the hierarchy and had persistently displayed hostility to capitalist Italy. Though pressing reforms earnestly, the CIF took basic economic structures for granted. It did not, however, despite Guidi Cingolani's example, press for more opportunity for its own members in professions, careers, business, and politics, so much as seek justice for others.[39]

Together, the Movimento Femminile and the CIF defined one boundary to the UDI's reach for unity. Others were less distinct or else more limited. The reborn Radical Party revived its old commitments to the rights of the individual, including divorce and abortion, but also its old detachment from social issues. The Socialist Party, which with Turati and Kuliscioff had long ago been the leading political force for women's issues, now, so long as it pursued its policy of alliance with the Communists, refrained from forming a woman's organization of its own, leaving its voice to Socialist women in the UDI. But the potential for a renewal of the break between the two remained.

The UDI, then, faced open competition from Catholic centers, implicit opposition from such individualistic and middle-class quarters as the Radicals, and potential schism among the Socialists. But this left open a mighty field. The man who defined the UDI's strategy no later than early 1945, if not before, was the leader of the postwar Communist Party, Palmiro Togliatti. It would be possible for historians, looking back, to refer to a "dialectical" relationship between the UDI and the PCI. "At certain periods the PCI line prevailed . . . and at others the contrary."[40] But even in this formulation of the relationship, the historian might note that when the party's line did prevail, the Communist members of UDI attempted to carry it out in the UDI, whereas when the UDI generated positions of its own, these were simply "reported" to the party, "enriching" it, without obligating the party to act. It was possible also that, whereas the UDI may have had some meaningful independence in its early years, any such independence was lost later and the organization became wholly "instrumentalized" to the PCI, just as the Movimento Femminile had been to the Christian Democrats all along. But even some such periods of relative UDI autonomy—up to 1964, say, or even 1969—could only have been a function of Togliatti's and the PCI directorate's policy. The UDI can best be read as part of the record of the Communist Party's vision of Italy.

In its first incarnation, after its split from the Socialist Party in 1921 until its suppression by Mussolini, the PCI had pursued a different approach to the question of women.[41] Organized into 1200 sections on a territorial basis, the party had included 96 sections of women. But these were not territorial in the same sense. Most of the women's sections were in the north, and they were organized side by side, so to speak, with the regular sections. What did a woman do who lived where there was no women's section? She joined the regular section in her area. In fact a woman in, say, Turin, who could join a women's section if she wished, might not do so, on the grounds that the women's sections were in fact only auxiliaries, ghettos segregated from basic decision-making and basic action. A Communist woman eager to work for the general ends of the revolution might find a women's section demeaning. This first solution to the women's question, then, contained basic "contradictions" that only Mussolini's suppression prevented from working themselves out.

When feminist historian Franca Pieroni Bortolotti came to write of the political parties' involvements with feminism during those hectic years in *Femminismo e partiti politici in Italia 1919–1926* (1978), she included a chapter on Alexandra Kollontai and the Bolsheviks in Russia.[42] As Antonio Gramsci's own thinking began to evolve ideas about popular participation in tension with and soon at odds with Lenin's insistence upon a closed and exclusive party, sympathy for some of Kollontai's own hopes remained possible within the Italian party, even if Gramsci's own feelings ran more toward contempt for the little sexual games he saw—or thought he saw—among the decadent Turin bourgeoisie and affection for what he saw—or imagined he saw—as the stable, solid, monogamous sexual ethic Horace, too, had once extolled as the spirit of the countryside.[43] But as the party entered upon its years of persecution and underground twilight, such possibilities for further thought were starved. A woman, Camilla Ravera, did head the party until she was imprisoned in 1930, but she knew her job was to serve survival, not debate. Invited by Gramsci to head the party's paper, *Ordine Nuovo*, in 1921, Ravera had been no more an orthodox Leninist than Gramsci himself, but, if only in the exigencies of the times, she found it easier to think of the scene before her in standard Marxist terms than in Gramsci's more exploratory ones. In the postwar book she wrote, in 1951, *La donna italiana dal primo al secondo Risorgimento*,[44] in which she rehearsed a standard indictment of capitalism for women's exploitation, Ravera not only abstained completely from any revelation of personal feeling, but she evinced no interest in that "national popular" culture Gramsci had tried to imagine. She thus remained wholly unalert to the feelings that led Togliatti to his "Italian Way."[45] Nor was Ravera unique. For another party woman, too, Teresa Noce, the long persecution, then the war, promoted attachment to the party as a fixed point of security through brutal times, the focus of a cult.[46] Noce became, quite simply, a Stalinist, along with many of her colleagues (including her sometime husband, Luigi Longo) in that important wing of the party that found Togliatti's Via Italiana basically heretical, if not indeed a betrayal of revolutionary rigor. In short, whatever chance there may or may not have been of the Italian Communist Party picking up on themes advanced by Kollontai, Fascism and war had shriveled them. Gramsci's vision of a national route to revolution would not die, but Gramsci himself had already made plain his own disdain for sexual revolution.

Togliatti's idea of a unified woman's movement was consistent with his general strategy of an Italian way to socialism. He himself shared in government, as minister of justice, during the unity governments of 1944–46, and clearly expounded, as head of his party, but also as a member of the governing coalition, his idea of what women should do.

If women want to help Italy in its new rebirth, they should claim all their rights, struggle for the complete recognition of these rights, above all for complete equality with men in politics, the economy and society. Just to the extent that they break the chains that have held them back from becoming a great progressive force and from maturing their own personalities, they will serve Italy.

As Aida Tiso has observed, this was the first time a major Italian politician did not repeat the familiar old call upon women for self-sacrifice, silent suffering, resignation for the sake of God and country. Togliatti was explicit in affirming the all-class, or non-class, or trans-class nature of women's interests:

The emancipation of women is not and cannot be the task of only one party or one class. . . . Italian women must be understood as a single body with a common interest in their own emancipation, in a profound transformation of their own conditions of life, and therefore in the renewal of the whole country which alone will make that transformation possible.[47]

But affirmation was one thing, reality another. In June 1946 the first postwar nationwide elections proved a disappointment. The Communists received only 19 percent of the vote, compared to the Socialists' 21 percent and the Christian Democrats' 35 percent. In September Togliatti had to repel suggestions that UDI be liquidated. He stigmatized the attitudes of various labor leaders and working men as "backward." But there were women who had complained, too, party women averse to UDI's implicit message that the business of Communist women was to work with women, that is, to do "women's work." "It seems," Togliatti said, "that, ideologically speaking, they have put pants on."[48]

Later in the year, in October, Pius XII entered the lists with a discourse on women:

Every woman is destined to be a mother. . . . For true women, all life's problems are understood in terms of the family. . . . Equality with men, outside the home where she is queen, subjects the woman to the same burdens the man has. The woman who goes to work outside the home . . . dazzled by the tinsel of a counterfeit luxury, becomes greedy for unworthy pleasures.[49]

Part of a general new anti-Communist crusade, the Pope's position offered opportunity to the UDI. What if the economy should, as the church itself had to hope, enter on a real recovery? Would that not invite women into better jobs and careers? Pius's traditional rhetoric would be undercut. Yet was not the "Italian way to socialism" going to involve some kind of reconciliation with Catholicism? Togliatti had already recognized this problem and formulated a clear position: "I do not believe that the religiousness of Italian women is the cause of their backwardness, just as I do not believe that religiousness must be an obstacle in their struggle for emancipation and democracy."[50] The UDI must not engage in anti-Catholic religious polemics. The Catholic Centro Italiano Femminile might resist the UDI's ecumenicity, but the UDI was to make it possible for as many Catholic women as feasible, as individuals, to join in the UDI's Italian way. Thus in the UDI the Marxist identification of the struggle for socialism with class struggle was rejected; also rejected was the Marxist identification of religion as an opiate of the people. In Italy the way to socialism was to be the people's way, a democratic way, and in Italy the people were, in large part, particularly in its female part, a Catholic people. Why not a Marxist-Catholic people?

But the Italian way to socialism would suffer more shocks than the election of 1946. The postwar all-party government broke up in that year. Then, in the first postwar elections to parliament, in April 1948, came the disaster: the Christian Democrats won a clear majority, the Communists suffered a painful defeat. Had they been defeated on a surge of women's votes turned out by a church campaign underwritten by the United States? Togliatti had to go out on his tour of mollification among the disaffected comrades. No, it had not been wrong to give votes to women. Yes, the party would go on supporting rights for women.

But even as the relationship between Christian Democrats and Communists took on further animus introduced from outside by the Cold War, the party in Italy had reasons to preserve its policy of following an Italian way. Although they lost the vote of June 1946, Communists had gone on in the autumn to win local victories all over the north. "Red Bologna" and also Florence, Venice, Turin, and Genoa chose Communist mayors, and Milan got a joint Communist-Socialist administration. Maybe there really was a democratic wish for socialism; to reject it in favor of ideological rigor would be to give up the party's mass character for mere sectarian purity. Few Italian Communist leaders were inclined to put the Kremlin's international politics first in Italy anyway, and Palmiro Togliatti was not one of them. The UDI thus would continue to pursue a line as something more than a mere party agency; it would offer a forum where women of various backgrounds could discuss women's issues and seek consensus—consensus consistent with the party's other commitments, hopefully, but an "autonomous" consensus nonetheless.

Yet it was from its own logic that the UDI drew down the fate eventually laid upon it, that of being attacked as timid, too calculating, too opportunistic, too political. Precisely as the church voiced more and more traditional views—"the woman must be subordinate to man, his intelligent and affectionate companion. And this subordination of the woman in home and church must be extended into civil life"[51]—UDI was drawn into tactical traps. It was Teresa Noce, resistance heroine and Communist deputy, who introduced the law of 1950 putting Italy in the van in Europe on the rights of working mothers. (The Christian Democrats, catching up, insisted they must at least be married mothers.) By 1956 this eagerness to prove itself and the party the only real protectors of mothers and families left the UDI in a dilemma. When the discussion of rights turned toward divorce, abortion, and birth control, it was embarrassed. Already the very word "emancipation" had been allowed to disappear from the pages of UDI's journal *Noi Donne*, in obvious concession to the fact that, for the masses of Italian women, emancipation had never been a demand but, more often, an alien and disturbing challenge, since they were still good Catholic mothers.[52] From 1956 on some younger members of UDI began questioning whether the organization had real autonomy after all and demanding that it have it. As these demands were brought forward, the specific issues had to do with the relationships not of classes and nations but of the sexes as individuals. The crucial institution no longer seemed the bourgeois state of capitalism, but marriage. Were these new demands to be rejected as "bourgeois"? Were they to be rejected because not yet validated by workers, by peasants, by working-class unions, by working-class culture? Were the women raising these issues to be categorized as feminist and heretical?

As if these internal contradictions were not enough, the church chose, as successor to Pius XII, Cardinal Roncalli, John XXIII. In 1960 John XXIII simply ignored Pius's declamations of only fifteen years before. Speaking to a congress of "white" unions, he declared that women's lives pivoted on "two centers, two nuclei; those of the family and of work."[53] Here was a notable break with Pius XII's old Catholic insistence upon women's identification with the fireside. In their effort to command as much territory as possible to their right, up to the very sanctuary of Catholicism, the Communists and the UDI had let themselves be outflanked to their left, and by a Pope at that.

By 1960 younger women were beginning to wonder whether the UDI was necessary. Was not women's struggle identical with class struggle after all? Should not women's problems be integrated into the general strategy of the party? By 1960 the postwar economy appeared to be securely on its way, and Italian women were beginning to take jobs again, catching up with women in other Western nations. Should not the problems these women workers faced—unequal pay, lower-paid types of work, and so on—be confronted along with the problems of workers in general? A UDI director, Marisa Rodano, responded.[54] Yes, there was an organic connection between an autonomous women's movement and the workers' movement, but the goal was not mechanical equality. Rodano had already, in 1959, argued that what impeded women was less mere inequality as such than the fact that they confronted a masculine society. Winning equality in a society built by and for women would not fulfill women's goals. It was the bourgeoisie who aimed at abstract equality, she said. In place of a masculine society there must be a society that recognized diversity. Communism must mean a society accommodating the differences between women and men. Specifically, agreeing with John XXIII, Rodano said that in a postmasculine society women would be able to harmonize family and work. Neither would be sacrificed to the other. A "double militancy" was required, on the front of the family as well as that of the labor market.

In 1972, rejecting the thesis that women's issues could be subsumed wholly under class issues, Enrico Berlinguer, the future party leader, reaffirmed the original Togliatti line.[55] But he commented on the continuing "backwardness" within the party on these matters. Yet what was the "specificity" distinguishing women's problems from class problems? Within the UDI the answer came repeatedly from its youth centers: birth control, sexual education, divorce, abortion. The pressures from the youth groups met resistance from the party UDI directors. Did these issues have any real political significance? Were they perhaps not private matters, to be excluded from politics? This approach did at least leave one obvious political route open: let the UDI and the party insist upon freedom in private matters. Let them insist upon repeal of prohibitions on contraceptions, abortion, sexual education, and divorce. As private matters, these might safely be closed to intervention by the state. This was of course the political line of the old, now minuscule, lay parties, the Republicans and the Liberals, the still anticlerical bourgeois parties. Could the UDI, could the Communist Party, identify itself with such bourgeois "reforms"?

The UDI and the party continued on Togliatti's—soon Berlinguer's—line. As though Marx, Marxists, and Marxism had never spoken, neither the UDI nor the party would take clear positions on sexual issues. Berlinguer, in his "autocritical" reproof to the party for having neglected women, had spoken of the specifically Italian aspects of the situation. And as the young Communist women pressed their demands, the leadership took refuge in references to a popular morality that, in Italy, had its own firm sexual culture. In effect, the Communist oligarchs said, the rebellious young Communist women were behaving, not so much like bourgeois women, as like non-Italian, perhaps English or American, women. Italian Communism had the traditions of the Italian people to rely on; these radical young were behaving like individuals and individualists.

Whatever resources the UDI ever had for autonomy were steadily sapped. With the breakdown of the postwar alliance between Togliatti's

Communists and Pietro Nenni's Socialists, Socialist women withdrew from the UDI in favor of their own new Anna Kuliscioff circles. Though neither the Centro Italiano Femminile nor the Christian Democrats' Movimento Femminile ever approached becoming a mass organization as the UDI always aspired to be, John XXIII's *Pacem in terris*, with its chapter on women, "Signs of the Times," changed the orientation of ideological Catholicism from defensive to positive. By no means were the Christian Democrats succeeding in Don Sturzo's old ambition of claiming Italy for a progressive Catholicism. And by no means was the church's own old mass organization, L'Unione Donne di Azione Cattolica, setting out to fulfill the mandates of *Pacem in terris*. But the UDI's old hope of speaking for all women was becoming less plausible, even as it became more difficult for it to return to an old-fashioned, orthodox "class" position. It was this competitive situation, practically requiring the UDI to remain in touch with Socialists and with liberal Catholics, too, that shaped Togliatti's last statements in 1964. The family "always has been and always will be," he insisted, as though the family lived outside history on purely natural foundations. The family will be "a center and a force in the free development of the human person," as though it had a kind of essential autonomy. New juridical norms as to divorce, illegitimacy and *parità* that might jeopardize the family were, Togliatti said, for "us," that is, for Italian Communists, "inconceivable."[56]

Italian Marxists were close to the most fundamental heresy of all. After all, if Karl Marx had been anything, he had been a Hegelian, aware that all things historical must change, and that whatever does not change cannot be historical. It was Catholicism, with its resistance to history, its determination to pluck things out of history and grant them absolution as absolutes—itself, its dogma, its ethic—that spoke of the family as beyond the reach of history. If history itself ultimately was simply the power to conceive of how things could be different, then the "inconceivable" existed only in a domain apart, in an inconceivable domain. But of course it was not the Roman Catholicism of John XXIII, let alone of Pius XII, that had exerted this sway on Togliatti. It was Italy.

Woman to Woman in Humblest Italy: A Communist in Naples

In one odyssey of particularly revelatory force, a noted Communist feminist journalist, Maria Antonietta Macciocchi, had already glimpsed the heart of humble Italy's unshakable foundation. In 1968, while serving as Paris correspondent of the party newspaper, *Unità*, Macciocchi was summoned by the party directorate to run for parliament in Naples. She had been part of the anti-Nazi Communist underground in Rome, then had done party work in Salerno and Naples before becoming director of *Noi Donne*, UDI's journal, in 1950, then of *Vie nuove* in 1956. Thus she was part of the old, not the new, generation. She had been in Paris since 1962. Not expecting election, Macciocchi decided to use her candidacy to revive and deepen her acquaintance with the women of the Naples area, compiling a kind of journal while doing so. The result, published as a book, was a mordant analysis of the party's failure to serve or even comprehend the impoverished people of Naples. Although the Communist slate won an impressive victory, and Macciocchi was elected, the results did not soften the sting of her critique.

Here is the general setting: a dirty courtyard in the Borgo section, behind Piazzetta San Fernandino, where the famous. . . . Repertory Theatre is located. It is a quarter of cigarette vendors, black-marketeers, street pedlars. . . . The women, unkempt and uncombed, with one baby inside and one just out, at the breast, come to watch from their balconies. . . . I call them out. . . . The first . . . to speak is Giuseppina Parente, twenty-eight . . . six children and one on the way, with a husband who is a *piattaro*, selling crockery from a barrow. She tells how . . . at home there isn't any food. . . . As the women speak, I find out . . . these women . . . are not housewives at all—which is the way they are officially registered . . . but *underpaid labourers*. They are labourers and they do not even know it . . . no insurance, no social security, no pension. [They] sew shoe uppers, gloves, umbrellas, trousers . . . the bosses have no faces. . . . Naples has never changed its basic structure, which is that of a "pile of houses," as a German 19th-century poet described it. The *bassi* are a tangle of structures made up each of a single room, or cave. . . . Since there are no windows, the doors . . . serve for ventilation. . . . In the *bassi*—which are house, workroom, and shop all in one—space is so restricted that people are born and die there side by side; the toilet . . . is right next to the stove and pans. . . . There is only one light in them at night. . . . In order to make living conditions hygienic, the women work incessantly . . . continuously [washing] the paving stones and [they] never stop laundering. This . . . is the . . . explanation for all those mysterious lines of washing strung out across the alleys.[57]

Macciocchi discovered class hostility in Naples, but it was not that of workers for bourgeoisie, of middle for lower classes, but, for Communists, a far more crucial one. Among the Naples subproletarians it was the working class, with its secure wages and unions, that was considered to be privileged: "the sub-proletariat dismisses the workers as capitalists, the workers have nothing but scorn for the sub-proletariat.[58] In this vast subproletariat, which in Naples was larger than the working class—as it was in all the swollen proletarian suburbs around the bay, and in a thousand Italian villages, towns, and cities—it was the women who supported the men. While the men could not find regular jobs, the women slaved over their "black work." It was these women with whom the party was out of touch.

The reasons for the Communist Party's failure to reach the women of the *bassi* were assignable to more than sexism. Macciocchi did find prejudice against herself as a woman candidate within the party, in the general misogyny of the south. "The comrades seem to suffer from many complexes, and to feel humiliated by a woman who is involved in politics." And in seeing in the party elite a body of intellectuals perpetuating a traditional "pride (inherited from Croce) in being members of a 'superior' class—with its special meeting places, in which it can mingle and 'discourse' among equals," she no doubt sensed the same condescension to women that Croce himself had manifested. But it was also true that the women of Naples posed a daunting challenge. "They almost never come to speeches. . . . I know that . . . if you want to find women, you have to go to their homes." Even in their homes, however, talking about one central question, children, remained painful.

Birth control, in my opinion, can become a political propaganda theme for these women, who give birth to sickly offspring here in the stench of the back streets. Naples boasts the highest birth-rate in Italy. . . . At the same time, the infant mortality rate . . . is also the highest in Italy.

But Macciocchi found no help in the party.

To myself I think: is it possible to raise the issue of "The Pill"? Are they interested? But the comrade from the section interrupts . . . before I can open my mouth, and . . . lets me know I have committed a *gaffe*. "Babies are so beautiful," he says, all effusive, and the next thing you know, he is kissing all the little kids. . . . "I would like ten of them. . . . Maybe my wife could have some more; after all, she is only forty." And the women chime in: "Of course she could!" . . . It is clear . . . that the comrades have discarded, *a priori*, any question of the Pill. They think that . . . it is a bad idea to talk about it.

But the women themselves had antipill motives: "Family allowances and other subsidies . . . to larger families; child labour . . . one of the pillars of support for the family; and, finally, the myth of a man's 'virility.' " Macciocchi located Naples's teeming fertility in a simple and pathetic ultimate existential fact:

[The] proletariat has nothing, it is dirt-poor. No one drinks . . . or gambles . . . the only really happy pasttime is the conjugal bed. "We don't have anything"— that is what the father of twelve . . . [said], "the only thing I can do is go to bed with my wife." Around here, what they say of someone with ten children is "poor guy," but in an affectionate, almost envious way, the way you would talk about an unrepentant womanizer in Paris.

The final result of this situation came to Macciocchi perhaps more clearly because she was a woman:

I learned that you never ask a woman, unless you want a suspicious or hostile answer, "But why do you have so many children?" It would be like saying, "But why do you make yourself so loved?" or "Why does your husband find you so attractive?"[59]

Macciocchi had discovered a people among whom there was no sexual question, no marriage question, no subordination of women on account of sex. Was a woman of the Naples subproletariat a *donna vaginale* or a *donna clitoridea*? It made no difference. Wife abuse, child abuse, incest, desertion, all the usual pathologies were to be found in the slums of Naples. But the basic sexual ethic from which these were deviations was founded on an equality that was in turn inextricable from poverty. The slums of Naples did not show, as did American ghettos, women leaving for work while their men lingered useless on the streets, or the corrosion of men by alcohol, as in the communes of Russia and the farmsteads of Sweden. If the ultimate cause of the subordination of women was, as Simone de Beauvoir said, in the psychic mechanism of men using women as means of support for every high enterprise, then where it had been understood for generations, as in Naples's "pile of houses," that high enterprises had no chance, such a psychic mechanism was absent. It had been Antonio Gramsci's plain implication that, for the sober and honest sexual ethic of the country-side, the hard work that sustained it was inextricable from poverty. So, too, in Naples. It might be dangerous for Italy to become Sweden or America.

Man versus Woman: *Separatezza*, 1968–1976

In a kind of fury of exasperation at the timidities of leftist politics, young feminists began forming organizations of their own. From the late 1960s Lotta Continua, Gruppo Demistificazione Autoritarianismo (DEMAU), Rivolta Femminile, Fronte Italiano di Liberazione Femminile, Movimento di Liberazione della Donna (MLD), and others abruptly wrenched Italian feminism into a new, more heated, far more outspoken epoch.[60] Sometimes these initiatives led on to new economic viewpoints. Thus in 1972 Lotta Continua, a group including men and women, spawned the Comitato per il Salario al Lavoro Domestico (Committee for Household Salaries, or SLD). It seized on the fading economy for a dramatic new demand.[61] The SLD accused labor unions of collaborating in pushing women out of the marketplace, but instead of trying to reverse the process, the SLD said women must be paid for what they did do. If more and more were going to be driven back to housework only, let them be paid for that. The SLD had not given up radicalism, but it was coming to terms with Italian realities. Far more often, however, the new groups undertook an analysis not of the economy but of sex. Broad popular feelings among women were waiting to be tapped. As early as 1957–60, Gabriella Parca had received for her newspaper column "Piccola posta," hundreds of letters sent from all parts of the country and many stations in life, detailing private anguish over intimate matters—early sex, pregnancy, abortion, adultery, violence, divorce, abandonment.[62] Collectively, these letters conveyed a sense of women caught claustrophobically in a world of silence. Not only were they at a severe disadvantage in their relations with men, but they apparently could hardly talk among themselves about their woes.

During the 1960s an awareness of Italian backwardness on the most elementary matters grew until, by 1970, action became possible. Late in that year parliament passed a law introduced by the Socialists and the three small lay parties, with the Communists carefully refraining from open sponsorship but in support, legalizing divorce. Opposing Christian Democrats led by Amintore Fanfani arranged a popular referendum and there were many who assumed that, as in 1948, a wave of women would help restore the old order and repeal divorce. The victory of the prodivorce voters in the 1974 referendum registered, for the first time in the history of united Italy, the voice of a people no longer under tutelage.[63] The defeat of the church and its DC ally was overwhelming. The Communists, who had maneuvered in fear of an antidivorce tidal wave, were caught out at their most opportunistic. Women had unquestionably determined the result and had listened only to themselves. By 1971 the courts, dismissing the laws against birth control as the product of Fascist demographic politics, already had opened the door to general liberalization in both education and practice. A new family code, debated since 1967, was installed in 1975, abolishing the legal supremacy of husband and father and substituting equality. Most remarkably, in 1976 abortion was legalized and, with its provision that an Italian woman had the right to state funding for her abortion (in the first trimester), Italy moved at last to lead Europe.[64] Another referendum was scheduled, with both DC and PCI politicians maneuvering to win credit whichever way the vote came out. Again, a popular outpouring in 1978 saved the new freedoms. No more could Italian women be thought of as a kind of immobile "south" locked in silence. In the referenda they, not the Left, had become progressive Italy, devoted to the welfare of individuals above state, race, and sect.[65]

The young radicals turning to questions of sex after 1968 did not

limit themselves to these matters. Many demanded not the reform but
the abolition of marriage. Many demanded not just the reform of the
family but its abolition. At the cutting edge of radical feminism some
went even further, to the very physical ground of sexuality. After all, as
social, legal, and historical categories, marriage and family could be
abolished without any effect on sexual relations. "The oppression of
women dates from millennia," Carla Lonzi of Rivolta Femminile wrote;
"capitalism, rather than its cause is its inheritor. . . . Historical materialism has missed the emotional key that led to private property. . . .
The archetype of property, the first object conceived by man is the
sexual object."[66] In its motto, "We spit on Hegel," Rivolta Femminile
summed up the universal failure of past politics to help women. Analyzing history as a dialectic between masters and slaves, Hegel had
shown how masters were destined to be eliminated and slaves to come
to freedom. But no such dialectic would ever eliminate the master sex
and bring the subordinate sex to freedom. The Marxists' materialization of Hegel made no difference; the dialectical liberation of the proletariat was paralleled by no such liberation of women. In a world made
up only of liberated proletarians and slaves, half would still be men,
half women. In rejecting the old Marxist Left and the PCI, the new
radical feminists were in no way offering comfort to capitalism and
Catholicism. Instead, they argued that the standard materialist criticism of both capitalism and family had fallen far short of what was
needed:

The family is the keystone of the patriarchal order, and it is founded not on
economic interests alone but on the psychic mechanisms of men who in every
epoch have seen women as objects for dominion and as the means of support
for every high enterprise.[67]

The practical result of this failure was the social disaster to be seen in
the Soviet Union and other practicing communisms:

In Communist countries socialization of the means of production has not touched
the traditional family. It has re-enforced it, instead, by re-enforcing the prestige
and role of the patriarchal figure. . . . The liberation of women has not been
resumed in the socialist countries. There, the social structure has taken on
medieval rigor by means of the authoritarian imposition of patriarchal myths
reborn in the revolution.[68]

Understanding the roots of the subjugation of women required a far
more basic analysis. It required investigation into men's need for a
sexual object.

    One solution to women's sexual subjugation proposed among the new
young radical feminists followed as by a kind of necessary logic: let
men be deprived of women. In *La donna clitoridea e la donna vaginale,*

Carla Lonzi spelled out the most literal basis for such a policy. Clearly, a system of subordination worked best when those who were subordinated agreed that their subordination was necessary and even desirable. Women, Lonzi argued, drawing on the research of American sexologists Alfred Kinsey, William Masters, and Virginia Johnson, had been persuaded that they could achieve true fulfillment as women, as sexual human beings, only in response to intercourse with men. This conviction took the specific form of a belief in vaginal orgasm. Women who failed to experience vaginal orgasm in intercourse were frigid. Here was the sexual ideology at its most sophisticated, keeping even sophisticated modern women in thrall. Freudianism in particular, with its insistence that a woman's failure to transfer her cathexis from clitoris to vagina was a sign of delayed maturity, had gained intimidating influence in advanced circles. In Lonzi's reading of the physiological sexologists, the Freudian view was itself absurd: it defied a physical fact, that "a woman has her place, privileged and precious, perfect and infallible, from which all the ecstasy anyone can experience flows, quite independent of the penis."

One possible, though not necessary, implication in this was lesbianism, and lesbianism constituted one node of feminist debate and practice in the early 1970s. Feminist collectives in Milan and elsewhere tried practicing the maximum possible separation from the masculine world.[69] This led to "theorizing the necessity of homosexuality among women, intended as a practical politics for reappropriating their own bodies and their own sexuality from captivity in the masculine world."[70] From theory a few moved on to action. In a few years it was clear that they would not be a flourishing community, in practice or in theory. At a national convention in Paestum in December 1976 a kind of accounting was drawn up. From the Milan groups, Grazia Francescato, editor of one of the new feminist journals, *Effe*, reported: "Homosexuality is accepted among us, but must not be a norm. Everyone must choose her sexuality, but for most of us, we meet the enemy in bed and often we love him. He is our man." Biancamaria Frabotta, editor of a collection entitled *La politica del femminismo*, declared: "Relations with men are unsatisfying and precarious, but I see no valid alternative. Sexual relations between women are dolorous and often artificial."[71] Others complained of lesbianism having itself become an ideology, intimidating heterosexual feminists as themselves being "deviant" and still obedient to traditional norms. Some homosexual couples were said to simply replicate the standard roles of man and wife. By no means did the thousand or so participants at Paestum arrive at a consensus. Instead, they took away a chastened feeling that the new feminism had found no new unity. Some, accused of having come to Paestum looking for mystic rites among moonlit temples, a Bacchic orgy, contemplation of the depths, no doubt returned home still determined to live as though they were already liberated.[72] Most had concluded that feminists must return to politics, seeking reforms in the real Italy surrounding them, including Italian men. Carla Lonzi had spelled out what relations between the sexes could be like once women realized their own sexual autonomy:

The "donna clitoridea" has nothing basic to offer a man and she expects nothing basic from him. She does not suffer from any duality and is not seeking to be made whole. She doesn't aspire to a patriarchy. . . . She wants caresses, not heroics; she wishes to give caresses, not absolution and adoration. A woman is a sexualized human being. Life between the sexes begins beyond the elemental union. There will be no more heterosexuality at any price but heterosexuality that does not exact any price.[73]

Return to Eternal Italy

As the powerful impulse toward separation crested and broke, radical Italian feminists felt the appeal of Italy itself once again. Some tried to do justice to the new demands from within the PCI. Adriana Seroni, a party member since 1944, a parliamentary deputy in 1972, agreed that, yes, the old Communists had been puritanical and expedient as to women and sex, for good historical reasons perhaps, but reasons no longer valid. The cry that "the personal is political" had truly enriched politics and must not be abandoned. Yet, asked to account for "anti-Communist feminists," Seroni could only reply:

[To] be anti-Communist . . . is historically to be the enemy of the greatest force of the Italian left, of the great party of the worker and the people. . . . I don't know how many "anti-communist" girls there may be, but certainly when I hear that such-and-such are feminists and anti-communists, it seems to me to be a contradiction in terms: how can one fight the battle of liberation for women and at the same time fight against the political force and social classes that have been and are the engines of progress for all Italian society?[74]

This was really no longer adequate. It was no longer adequate to criticize, as Seroni did, "the younger generation" for thinking "only of the individual" and for ignoring "reality, the really objectively real." It was Seroni and her generation of Communist feminists who were being outflanked by reality. With the PCI's loss among industrial blue-collar workers being compensated by its gains among white-collar workers, teachers, professionals, small merchants, and craft workers, a constituency far more individualistic in outlook had begun to emerge, with women far more notable within it, bringing with them their concerns over marriage, family, sexuality.[75] For such women a far more personal, even confessional, mode of politics than that still practiced by Seroni seemed needed.

One of the new dissenters, Rossana Rossanda, active in a small party to the left of the PCI, the Partito di Unità Proletaria (PDUP), reflected on the differences between a party loyalist such as Camilla Ravera and a literary, confessional independent such as Sibilla Aleremo, author of a famous novel, *Una donna*. Aleremo above all revealed herself, while the party veteran never did. "She has no time to look at herself. The eyes of Camilla Ravera look outside herself. Maybe the young feminist comrades who hear her interpret the world through the party and its history feel there is no place there for a feminine dimension. They are right."[76] The new feminists did not want to hear what the party thought. They wanted to hear what Seroni thought, what Ravera thought, what Berlinguer thought. When the Unione delle Donne Italiane finally cut all its ties with the PCI, relinquishing its last financial subsidies in 1982, even then it could not explain clearly whether this too still proceeded from tactics, maneuver, expediency, or at last from the heart. New feminists such as Rossanda "disbelieved" in party as much as in church. Lidia Menapace, fired from the Catholic University in Milan for radical ideas, then ousted from the Communist Party for the same, declared that Italy no longer needed institutions such as party and church. It had achieved a "historical maturity" in which it needed tutelage by no one; its socialism would be simply Italy fulfilled. In Assisi, Franciscan Catholics professing a liberation theology hostile to the Vatican and the church welcomed feminists to their conferences, and left-wing Catholic journals lavish with feminist themes began circulating widely in schools and universities.[77] Still another wave of faith had risen, that in Italy what was needed was not revolution but a chance for the people themselves. However educated, individualistic, and middle-class the new radical feminists might be, their deepest impulse ran toward embrace in the arms of a common popular culture. Surely Italy itself, the Italy of neither capitalism nor bureaucratic Communism, did not constitute an alienated partriarchy, to be rejected and consigned to a dustbin of history.

The Italy in Italian Feminism

In a society deeply divided, as was modern Italy at its birth in 1860, between north and south, church and state, intellectual elite and traditional folk, the hope for a liberal future depended heavily on economic growth providing means to lubricate all frictions. Early Italian feminism as embodied in Mozzoni clearly identified with liberal values. It asked for better education, more political rights, and fuller economic opportunities for women exactly as it understood all these were needed too for the masses of Italian men. The fate of Italian liberal feminism was that it could never find a proper, that is, successful, bearer of liberalism itself in which it could then demand partnership. The Italian economy refused to expand in a way that eased inherited social conflict; on the contrary, its weakness and shape tended to sustain those conflicts. In that situation, feminism itself appeared to be simply a new cause of conflict, and the major liberal politician of the first sixty years, Giolitti, rejected it as a luxury Italy could not afford.

With the inadequacies of liberal politics patent, feminists naturally looked for alternatives. Some found one in the new Socialist Party founded by Turati and others in 1892. But with the Socialists, Italian feminists found themselves essentially engaged in utopia-waiting. Never did the Socialists come close to propounding a policy for Italy as it was. For years deliberately refusing to hear of any role in government, they provided feminists, not a chance to debate concrete issues confronting Italian women in a hundred situations, but preoccupation with party tactics, consistently to the feminists' loss.

The effort of some women, in conjunction with some priests and other men, to propound a Catholic foundation for feminism, was addressed to a very real, hugely concrete issue, namely the posture of the Vatican and the hierarchy of the church. The view of Mozzoni and the liberals was simply that the church must be outwaited; modernity, science, industrialization would be a kind of erosive process eventually reducing the church to a mere remnant, should it persist in the line drawn by Pius IX of defying modernity and liberalism outright. This was to underestimate the value the church still offered to those for whom modernity and liberalism were not in fact yet providing those goods and services that might lead them not to need those the church supplied. Attempting to forge a feminism within the church was a confrontation with reality. But the struggle, unequal from the start, grew even more unequal as politicians themselves came to find that collaboration rather than confrontation with the church was the best policy even for liberalism.

That some feminists should find promise in early Fascism was logical. Like socialism, Fascism appeared to realize that the liberal politics of trying to balance interest groups while stimulating economic growth was not working. Unlike socialism, Fascism offered a unity and stability that drew directly on deep reservoirs of the Italian past; once sealed with the Concordat between state and church, Fascism's unity could seem organic. At that point, of course, anything like coherent liberalism disintegrated, for demands for rights, freedoms, and individuals had come to seem unaffordable.

Once post-World War II politics settled into its long-term shape, the pathos of Italian feminism returned with redoubled intensity. It was clear that the major forces in postwar Italy—including American foreign policy—would exert every resource to keep the Christian Democrats as a permanent governing party. But the Christian Democrats were effectively sterilized against feminism by one of those forces, the church. Whatever Alcide de Gasperi's personal links with Don Luigi Sturzo and the Popular Party of 1919–20, his Christian Democrats had far less freedom to entertain broadly liberal social reforms in which feminists might have shared than the Popular Party, in its brief life, had had. Precisely in becoming far more politicized, the postwar church constituted a far more pervasive obstacle to feminist action and even feminist imagination.

The consequence was to leave feminists—women who wanted political life and could not surrender feminist goals—trapped with a party doomed to permanent minorityhood. The postwar Italian Communist Party's basic strategy of seeking to become a mass party was brilliant. In effect, it offered those Italians alienated both from the postwar capitalist economy and from the church an alternative church. For millions of party members, Communism became an alternative Italy within Italy. For feminists, however, the party offered nothing but the standard abstract utopian hope that, one day, all Italy would be Communist and thus all women equal; meanwhile they faced the problem that there was no equality available to women within Communism except, here and there, to a few activists. Once again, Italian feminists were drawn away from Italian reality into dreams.

That a feminist energy nevertheless remained, deep and widespread, untapped by the Communist Party, only erratically tapped by quasi-feminist groups themselves, and against the indifference of the Christian Democrats and the wishes of the church, was demonstrated by the referenda on divorce and abortion of the 1970s. These were not so much expressions of a program or a movement as a kind of collective spasm, repelling retrograde efforts to take back modern freedoms far too long postponed. They hardly spoke to the issues of the Italian economy, of social and economic justice, of political impaction, but they clearly registered a determination no longer to allow traditional Italian culture to deny elementary personal freedoms.

In the turn of post-1968 feminist protest groups toward separation from men, a deep frustration with all mainstream politics and economic programs found its plainest vent. But this impulse was bound to be short-lived. It did not register the emergence of some postindustrial affluence offering a widening choice of life-styles. Its rapid transformation into still another version of an Italy unified in a kind of mysticism of the whole, mingling grass-roots Catholicism and hardworking craftsmanship, recalled Gramsci's own faith that Italy already had all it needed for its salvation, if it would only trust it. In his, as in Manzoni's own pious imagination, men and women were not at odds in the real, the people's own, Italy.

5 Sweden. Co-optation

Female Poets of the Heart and of the Nation

Probing for early feminism in Sweden in literary rather than organizational, intellectual, political, or academic guise makes sense. As
elsewhere, women of the upper strata in eighteenth-century Sweden
tended to second their men, whether in the political competitions of
the constitutional period or among the courtiers of Gustav III. In contrast, the overwhelming mass of women were simply hard at work in
the countryside. Here and there, though, daughters of the lesser gentry
or of an occasional emergent professional, learning that life could lie
in letters as well as in society or work, might find a little personal space
for self-creation. Nothing political or organized need be supplied them
in order that they might begin to write. They need not even have an
audience in mind at first.

Hedwig Charlotta Nordenflycht, who was born in 1718 and died at
forty-five in 1763, wrote of an entity neglected in both the courts and
the fields, the individual human heart.[1] Accident prompted her. She
married a clergyman, Jacob Fabricius, and was happy, but Fabricius
died when she was still young. She drew on impersonal and intellectual
language for the poetry she composed following the love and sorrow of
this marriage. Then, in her early forties, she fell in love again and began
to write in a more immediate, expressive, emotional way. Her lover,
Johan Fischerstrom, in his early twenties, admired but did not love
her. Her poetry revealed little about him, just as earlier it had revealed
little about her husband, but unmistakably she had learned to reveal
more of her own self. Whether poetry "of the heart" was in and of itself
feminist it would be up to later critics, defining a new canon, to debate.
Perhaps most crucial for the Swedish case, Nordenflycht had no successors. She would not be figured as a harbinger, an omen, a pioneer.

Anna Maria Lenngren, who was nine years old when Nordenflycht
died, was not a poet of the heart.[2] Happily married to an editor in
Stockholm, cultivated not only in literary but in social values, she had
a distinct political outlook. She despised the old Swedish nobility. She
especially despised its influence on women, manners, and marriage.
She had seen the nobility weakened by Gustav III and, as Gustav's court
took on French characteristics, soften into, as she thought, immorality.

She saw it as helpless after Gustav's assassination. Two years later, at forty, she started to write. Rather than expressions of self, Lenngren wrote poetic "sketches of everyday life." Sociology rather than psychology was her science. In her mind the Sweden of the real Swedish people remained healthy and uncomplicated. Some of her best poetry, full of detail, such as "Den gladen festen," reporting a birthday party at a country parsonage, celebrated this common life. To her own daughter, poetically—and thus to all daughters—Lenngren commended the life of a good wife and mother; she counseled against aspirations to blue-stocking status and fascination with politics. The good life, the happy life, the fulfilled life lay at hand, beyond vanities.

Since Lenngren at once portrayed and commended old ways, she could be thought a conservative, or even worse, a nostalgiac, even a reactionary, but since she was also a critic of the high and mighty, the court and nobility, she obviously belonged with that generation coming after her, including Erik Gustav Geijer, who, appalled at the evidence of Swedish deliquescence and decline, looked to a better future reformed according to the virtues of the Swedish past. Why Lenngren stopped publishing—and presumably writing—after only five years we do not know. Perhaps she had found too few readers for satisfaction; perhaps she had had her say. In any case, by contrast with Nordenflycht, Lenngren had anticipated the whole movement of reform in nineteenth-century Sweden, soon to come to a kind of climax in the utopianism of the 1840s, while Nordenflycht's poetry of the heart more nearly anticipated that Swedish individualism in which all questions of culture were questions of heart, destined for apotheosis in August Strindberg. For Swedish feminism the contrast would prove difficult.

Vision Unlimited: C. J. L. Almqvist and Utopian Sweden

Quite another kind of explorer of an ideal Sweden was Carl Jonas Love Almqvist.[3] Born in Stockholm in 1793 in humble circumstances, Almqvist had to scratch for a living. After some minor government jobs and a stay at a commune in the country, he returned to Stockholm to head one of the new intermediate schools that were springing up to tend the teen-age children of the capital's reviving cadre of professional men. There, for a few years his writing poured forth—stories elaborating fantasy, offering scenes set in exotic times and places, conveyed in language rich in figure and invention, all with a certain personal abandon. He worked in many forms—plays, novels, poetry, sketches, tales, "pieces," essays—sometimes mystical, sometimes ironic, sometimes foolish, sometimes epic. He was a typical provincial writer, self-conscious, artificial, exaggerated. As though aware of this, as if realizing he was undergoing a prolonged apprenticeship, he withheld much of this early writing from publication for years. He did not make a living at his desk. Until well past forty, Almqvist continued to write in his idiosyncratic ways, faithful to a whole generation of Swedes imitating their metropolitan betters.

Yet Almqvist was far from a facile imitator. The hard heart of modern Romanticism beat strongly in most of this early writing. In other minds, Romanticism's quarrel with the Enlightenment's sobriety and cool impersonalities might have curdled into ominous backward-looking tribalisms and future-located collectivities, but Almqvist remained a radical individualist. His writing itself was practically a laboratory demonstration of the central Romantic tenet that the beginning and end of all truth and beauty, the very locus of creative energy, lay in the individual, in the individual heart. Societies had tyrannized over the individual. The restoration of goodness required remaking society to the measure of the heart.

Often, indeed, Almqvist fleshed out this bare argument in terms of a heroine. Early on, he had echoed Rousseau's anxious disdain for girls with pretensions, the educated woman, the blue-stocking. Rousseau was afraid of losing mother. But as early as 1821 Almqvist began to get beyond this simplistic paranoia in favor of a more complex notion. Anthropological data on the religions and cultures of India, purporting to show the high status of women there, had begun to filter into Sweden, and Almqvist picked them up. Perhaps more important had been his grandfather, from whom Almqvist learned of the Moravians and their assignment of high status to women in religious life. Almqvist got to know personally a young woman of unusual intellectual gifts who had been raised among Stockholm's Moravians. No doubt such sensitizing experiences as these left him ready to be angered at the harsh attacks of the Swedish state church clergymen on the rising evangelical movement, in which many women served as readers and even preachers. In one play he presented a woman priest. In a novel his heroine Aurora shared the love of science with her lover. Woman as Rousseau's merely domestic comforter gave way to woman as vitality and wisdom. The climax to this theme was no doubt Almqvist's utterly bald presumption of presenting the ultimate woman, God's own mother, in his 1837 play, entitled with God's own mother's Hebrew-Aramaic name, *Marjam*.[4]

In *Marjam*, Almqvist pressed his arguments to a point of specificity that, had Sweden still been Catholic, would have brought down on him more than mere obloquy. Exalting mother-love, Almqvist emphasized with irony and some anger that, contrary to the Vatican's propaganda campaign for a new dogma of the Immaculate Conception, mothers were not in fact virgins. Saying that they were virgins, Almqvist argued, was to shrink and undercut—as Christianity, notably through Paul, had indeed shrunk and undercut—the ancient religion of Magna Mater, the Great Mother of the ancient East, source of all mankind's religions; furthermore, it was to shrink the significance of the "ordinary" motherhood of all men. The play, revealing Almqvist's most concerted use of anthropological ideas, was of course indebted to more systematic writers elsewhere, especially German, and in particular to David Strauss's *Life of Jesus*. But Almqvist's drama was no mere academic display. By 1837 he was eager to become more contemporary, realistic, explicit, as though to test the meaning of basic wishes themselves.

Whatever scene he drew, whether of the countryside or the Queen's glittering court, of Spain or Italy, of ancient Hinduism or modern Christianity, and finally of human history itself, Almqvist could not help indicating that behind the immediate surface reality lay a deeper reality, a paradise lost that could be regained, a paradise best manifest in undistorted, natural womanhood, the paradise of an earth presided over by God herself, an earth in the arms of a mother. It is irresistible to tie biography into this vision. Almqvist's mother died when he was twelve. He thought of her as having been sensitive, intuitive "heart," as distinguished from his father's aggressive, practical, performance-oriented "head." But this contrast—conventional enough—was overlaid by the more suggestive fact that, after his mother's death, Almqvist enjoyed as mother surrogate his mother's father, the Moravian grandfather who served his own religious community, as well as Almqvist, as a kind of Marjam until his death at eighty, when Almqvist was eighteen.

In *Sara Videbeck*, his most famous novel, set, in contrast to all his earlier exotic scenes, in rural Sweden, and written, in contrast to his previously mannered style, in lucid, limpid, simple prose, Almqvist condensed all his previous romanticizings into a simple story of two young people falling in love. He made plain that what mattered most in sexual relations and marriage was not the reproduction of the race or service to society or perpetuation of a family line, but the two individuals involved. The word for what mattered was itself simple: happiness. This was the irreducible heritage of the Romantic imagination. In Rousseau it had issued in such sensational selfishness as Rousseau's repudiation of his role as father, by placing his children in an orphanage, as well as Rousseau's demand that wives be perfect servants. Almqvist's rejection of this Rousseauian model was presented in his hero's awakening to the fact that his lover's independence, individualism, and equality actually stimulated his love and sexual feelings and made him happier than conventional women did. In effect, Rousseau had not known how happy he might have been. Nothing could justify any compromise of this happiness. For a young man and a young woman to marry for children was the same sort of mistake as to marry for property.

But of course children were a potential issue from love. Almqvist found no occasion for concerted discussion of the means to have children always by choice, but everything in his logic indicated that the procreation of the race should be as completely in the hearts of individuals to control, as biology, science, and true morality made possible. The premise, that is, for dealing with the problems of raising children was that these children be wanted. After publishing *Sara Videbeck*, Almqvist went on to write essays spelling out his deepest utopian vision of Sweden.

In order not to become routine to each other, husbands and wives would not live together, neither would mothers and fathers. Children should grow up with their mothers. Fathers would visit their children but not live with them. Children would take their mothers' name, and to the extent that inheritance mattered, would inherit from her. They would not depend on their fathers' support, nor indeed on their mothers'. Instead, all families, made up of mothers and their children, would be supported by society, by means of taxes administered through a "child insurance fund." Thus fathers would support all children indirectly, through the taxes laid upon all men's estates at their death. By this scheme, Almqvist felt that several purposes would be served. One was the amelioration of certain pressing social tragedies, notably, the plight not just of unmarried mothers but of their helpless children, which Stockholm's Foundling Hospital met only at terrible costs. Another was the equal treatment of women. By supporting children through taxes, for instance, mothers too would continue to be free to work at jobs they wanted, free of the necessity of working to pay for the children. Still another goal, much more basic, was the liquidation of the structural domination of men over women that went far beyond a matter of laws and economics. Removing men from the family as fathers would end male authority in its most powerful form. The most fundamental purpose of all, however, to be served by these new arrangements, was the encouragement of the individualization of everyone, men and women alike.

Almqvist felt that children got messages from mothers different from those they got from fathers. From mothers they derived an ineradicable conviction that happiness was possible. From fathers they derived a sense of power, authority, and outside forces. While these were not in themselves either good or bad, they could limit, compromise, and defeat happiness. The abandonment of the traditional family thus meant that children would not have to grow up with their will to happiness fatally crippled. They would be free to experience the deep happiness of union with another, equally free and individual, as life's one sure boon.

Almqvist's program cannot be said to have stopped short of any such programs in the roster of nineteenth-century Romantic utopias, including those of the French utopians of the 1830s and 1840s. His differed from most of the others crucially in his refusal to propose collective child-rearing, whether superintended by women only or by women and men. He feared such methods would produce all-too-socialized people, unequipped with the psychological strengths necessary for real individualization. His problem was not how to chasten hostility, competition, aggression, and "excessive" individualism with "communal," "cooperative" upbringing. Nor was his program a criticism of masculinity in favor of a more collaborative, socialistic, nurturant femininity. As a personality, his heroine Sara Videbeck had been as much like an energetic, cheerful, nonhostile young man as like an incipient mother. Nor did the slightest impulses toward "sisterhood" escape her. The methods proposed by Almqvist aimed to strengthen neither masculinity nor femininity, manhood nor womanhood in particular, but rather to strengthen, for both, the resources for growing up to be individuals, rather than socialized clones incapable of personal happiness. In a certain purely formal way, his "realism" proved nowhere more evident, then, than in this exercise in logical utopian fantasy, as he sought to ground his central Romantic impulse in specific social institutions.

Almqvist's impression, received through the anthropology of the day, that the systems he proposed for Sweden and Europe—"matrilineal" and "matrilocal"—had already been practiced in the ancient East and still practiced there by a few distant people, probably counted for him more as a symbol for history than as an argument about it. Once J. J. Bachofen's *Das Mutterrecht* (Motherright) broke upon the European intellectual scene in 1861, many philosophers would try to devise historical sequences according to which a movement from matriarchy to patriarchy would count either as progress or, in the eyes of some feminists, as regress. But for Almqvist the "lesson of the East" had less to do with historical progress or regress than with the possibility and, in fact, necessity of recognizing in every historical chapter—in modern Sweden as well as the Sweden of the Sagas, in modern Europe as well as the mysterious ancient East—the pulse of utopian energy. The pressures of the wish for happiness beat against privilege and power always; the acids of individualism ate constantly at the foundations of great, gray, stony institutions. The appeal of the idea that, in moving forward with the works of progressive social reform, one was in fact working back to a freedom that had once existed, of course matched the feeling that a growing up out of dependency into adulthood, one brought into one's own command the perfect happiness once enjoyed with one's mother.

In this going back to the East, Almqvist was also asserting something about the Swedes as a people. They had not been irredeemably corrupted by Christianity. Catholicism's Virgin Mother had been discarded; now, in the nineteenth century, Swedes might reawaken as what they really were—a folk that in its straightforward poverty was still umbilically attached to its own origins, its own "East," its life two, three, or four thousand years old, ever in one single place, among the Swedish lakes and forests, where they had always tried to pursue happiness in simple domesticity. Ultimately, Almqvist's myth fed no Viking fantasies but rather that of little Sweden, asking nothing but its right to good mothers.

Great Mother: Fredrika Bremer

Perhaps for fear of certain reactionary tribalisms, Almqvist never recurred to Sweden's own real-life historical Marjam, that Magna Mater of the race, St. Birgitta herself. After thirty-three years of marriage, after raising eight children, after counseling kings, at forty-six Fru Birgitta Gudmarsson had felt free to embrace her spiritual calling at last, and just as Queen Christina would later, left Sweden for Rome, where she died after twenty-four years, in 1373, never having come back. But during all her years in Rome, Birgitta never forgot Sweden. She wrote—or rather spoke—constantly about Sweden. She received hundreds of direct revelations about conditions in Sweden. She suffered from fears for Sweden, of Sweden ruled by the devils of drunkenness, lasciviousness, and homosexuality. In Rome she developed—still through her revelations—the plans for what eventually became the monastery at Vadstena, on Lake Vättern, mother house for the worldwide Order of St. Birgitta. There the sick, the poor, and the needy would be tended. "Sweden has produced other geniuses—Swedenborg, Linnaeus, Strindberg. But their fame dwindles beside that of St. Birgitta."[5] After her death, her bones, their scourged flesh boiled away, were sent from Rome back to Vadstena. Investigations into her credentials for sainthood commenced promptly. Less than twenty years after her death, the Swedes heard of her elevation.

When Sweden turned Protestant, Lutheran, "Swedish" Lutheran, St. Birgitta proved an embarrassment. Her bones were taken from the monastery at Vadstena and hidden. Her revelations became embarrassing: were they not hallucinations rather than communications from God? Swedish historians like Geijer began insisting on Sweden's kings as the heads of the Swedish folk, offering unbroken continuity to those foggy, terrible Vikings who had proved masters everywhere. Though neither sectarian nor royalist, Almqvist may not have felt enough mythic power in St. Birgitta in the nineteenth century to warrant her resurrection. But it is hard not to see in Fredrika Bremer's *Hertha* more than just old bones.

Like Lenngren, Bremer launched her career with "sketches," *Teckningar utur hvarddagslivet* (Sketches from Everyday Life), in 1828.[6] In contrast with those—at this time still including Almqvist—who cast scenes in distant times and exotic places, she seemed to present the real Sweden for the first time in fresh, direct language, unaffected by Parisian ideas of style, a Lenngren in prose. Real Swedes, real Swedish home life, Swedish joys and Swedish sorrows, as distinguished from heroic knights, sturdy yeomen, and musty Goths, were now about to be captured in literature. During the next several years, Bremer turned out several longer works—"novels," for want of a more precise label, all of them "family novels." The notion that "Fredrika Bremer is . . . the Miss Austen of Sweden,"[7] absurd as it was, may have had significance for a growing new audience. Austen's apparent basic material, a home circle including several unmarried young girls plus a father, a dim mother, and assorted others including suitors, presumably spoke directly to the concerns of a readership that Bremer herself often identified in addressing them as "my sweet female reader" and "thou, my young sixteen-year-old reader." One explanation for Lenngren's early retirement might be that this readership had not yet been ready in 1795 or 1800. By 1835 it was, if not on the same scale as in England and America. (Actually, Bremer's four novels were all promptly translated into English and read widely in England and America in the mid-1840s. In America her nominal themes were soon taken up by Louisa May Alcott and others, while her own books faded into obscurity.)

After her fourth novel, *Hemmet* (The Home, or Family Cares and Family Joys), in 1839, Bremer went into a long dry spell. She broke it with a utopian book, *Syskonlif* (Brothers and Sisters), laid in the United States, in 1848. She visited the United States on a long tour two years later, which provided the materials for *Hemmen i den Nya Världen* (The Homes of the New World), still a book of great interest to students of American history. After her early success in writing popular sentimentality, with these two volumes of reportage Bremer seemed launched on a new stage in her career, practicing a more serious journalism, general in its interests yet liberal and reform-minded, offering her opportunity perhaps to lay out her thoughts on what might be done in Sweden, and indeed in the United States, to improve home, marriage, child-rearing, and women. She might have begun laying out ideas for feminism. Instead, as though realizing she had not exhausted or even understood what she had really been dealing with in her first novels, she returned to the fictional form and, in 1856, brought out *Hertha*, the novel that won her status as Sweden's first feminist.

Although sometimes described as a "social pamphlet in fictional form," *Hertha*'s strength was its testimony to an implacable inner need. In her heroine, Hertha Falk, Bremer at last embodied her own remorseless need to escape dependency and be free. Its expositions of explicit ideology, never clever, were often dull. The largest single event in the book, a whole town's destruction by fire—despite the credibility it drew from the going up in flames of numerous real-life nineteenth-century Scandinavian wooden cities—lost all believability by being moralized into abstraction. Nevertheless, *Hertha* was, and remains today, by far the most readable of Bremer's novels, and for a single reason. The book clarified none of the roots of its heroine's determination to be free. She experienced no crucial moments of recognition or revelation; she was her own indomitable self at the start as at the end. But as a register of authorial smoldering, *Hertha* had power and lived.

The reform movement with which Bremer's novel is always linked is of course feminism.[8] More specifically, *Hertha* is linked to the abolition of the laws of guardianship that kept unmarried women, regardless of age, subordinate to their fathers. In a preface for the English translation, Bremer avowed her reform intention explicitly: "The patriarchal bonds which keep back the growth of woman's mind and social life in Sweden, and which sometimes amounts to the most crushing tyranny, I have shadowed forth in these pages, often with a heavy heart."[9] Here was a rather different emphasis from that found not infrequently in her earlier stories:

Will you see [the arts], see Italy, see France; will you see the consecrated earth of home, of families, see Sweden! See everywhere among the rocks and the forests those quiet dwellings, where man enjoys an ennobled natural life; where, in the bosom of holy and precious relationship, are developed piety and bravery, the national virtues of Sweden.[10]

Bremer's own childhood, in a home of substantial country comfort, is commonly said to have been one of personal unhappiness, with a father reportedly distant and arbitrary. Evidently now, in *Hertha*, she was going to tell the truth.

One of Hertha's sisters, Alma, twenty-nine, is already sunk in and dying of grief at the opening of the book, as a consequence of her father's refusal some years before to let her marry a penniless suitor. Hertha's indignation at this blighting of her older sister's life was focused on property. Had Alma had her property, presumably, she could have married her propertyless lover, whatever her father felt. But her father, by law Alma's custodian, had refused to let her have it. Bremer's evident failure to realize that, in this complaint over paternal tyranny, she was conceding that love was not enough, nicely illustrated how emotion took precedence over exact reformist motives in the book's origin. Comparably, Hertha's later accusation that her father's tyranny had likewise ruined the lives of her two younger sisters did not square with facts narrated elsewhere, namely, that one sister was taken in by an eminently loving couple as surrogate parents, and that the other enjoyed the best possible fate, adoption as child surrogate by the noblest of all mother surrogates, Hertha herself. From time to time the question was raised whether Hertha should appeal to the court of justice in Stockholm, as was her right, or "go to King Oscar," to be granted her majority directly and be assigned control over her own share of the property left by her mother. Bremer had in fact taken this step in real life in 1840. In the novel, Hertha did not. One reason would seem plain enough in the resolution of Hertha's relationship with her father.

At first, Director Falk was shown displaying himself in childish autocracy, berating his twenty-six-year-old daughter for returning home from a town meeting twenty-two minutes late. His legal patriarchal authority had rendered him a parody of petty selfishness and greed. His greed showed madness in his response to the fire, that, along with his city, consumed his house. Rushing to his cash box, with his fingers practically fused to his money, he was trapped by the holocaust, only to be delivered by, logically, Hertha: "Faithful as a mother who holds her child clasped to her breast, held she her father." From then on, a shell of himself, Director Falk was not a father to fear at all. "[She], from the hour in which she saw in this despotic father, a weak, ailing child, felt once more that she could love him." Her love alone then, became a reason for not going to King Oscar, for this would be to humiliate him, and from that, in his decline and quasi-senility, what satisfaction could there be? In other words, there was absolutely nothing in the story of Hertha Falk and her father to indicate that either he or Sweden's patriarchal laws of 1734 had blighted in the slightest the emergence of Hertha's own powerful, dominating personality. Hertha's conflict with her father was not due to bad laws at all.

On the other hand, Hertha's role in rebuilding her home town, Kungsköping (King's Market), after its fire, was real. There was nothing very wrong with Kungsköping. For antidote to the boredom and sheer weariness of provincial life, its citizens had recourse to the usual coffee parties, novel reading, card playing, and punch drinking. This was nothing evil. Prompted by the local clergyman, a Ladies Society was in process of forming, while the town's protocol secretary took the role of its leading, slightly foolish antifeminist. But the great fire offered the opportunity for Hertha's spirit to preside over rebirth anyway, as the town became a myth place, "our town," emblematiac of Swedishness, now revealed in its potential for Mother-headed unity. The fire set the terms for the one political act by Hertha in the book. Kungsköping's fire was a criminal act. It had been set by Hertha's own cousin Rudolph, a youth both physically and morally weak. Guilty of furtive longings for his cousin Hertha, he meant his fire to consume Hertha's father's house and therewith Hertha's father, thus removing, as he imagined, the essential barrier between himself and the object of his desire. But the fire spread. On discovering his responsibility, Hertha took it upon herself to dismiss this incestuous youth not only from Kungsköping but from Sweden, thus purging town and country of an element alien to true, pure Swedishness.

The means by which Hertha then emerged from private life to communal headship was the "educational institute" she opened. Realizing she lacked "the necessary gifts" to be a writer, she chose this less ultimate but finally more powerful medium. With her father continuing to deny her her own property, she drew on the support of townspeople. Although originally intended for the improvement of girls only, the institute soon admitted boys, too. "The youths were uncertain and bashful . . . but they are beginning now to exhibit themselves in a beautiful light."

With the power of her personality, Hertha was able to wreak transformation in other people's status. One unfortunate young woman in Kungsköping, Amalia by name, had been seduced, abandoned, and left to raise her child in shame. Of course Hertha did not spurn her, and toward the end of the book Amalia found herself elected to the board of Kungsköping's Infant School. She did not lack opposition. "She has," one town moralist observed, "an illegitimate child, no right, no claim, . . . [no] name." Hertha knew better. "Call her Mother!" And as "Mother Amalia" the unmarried mother joined the ranks of the town's emergent ruling sisterhood. By this time the antifeminist protocol secretary not only had failed to complete his antifeminist book but was married to one of Hertha's sisterhood.

Hertha's status as headmistress of this school swelled into that of headmistress to the town. As her inner powers emerged, she appeared "a model for a Sibyl, or for the prophetess Vala," or still better, "the type of the Maccabean woman, 'the mother of the Martyrs.' " Religious effulgences surrounded her, not merely classical and Christian, but those of Freya. Hertha became a St. Birgitta who stayed in Sweden, a Christina who did not go to Rome. The end of the book registered worship. A young woman, Eva, with whose wedding ball the book had begun, and who had been rescued by Hertha from her marriage, a loveless trade of young flesh for old property, was observed to be living "Egeria-like, concealed in a sacred grove. . . . She will never marry; her only passion in this world was Hertha."[11] Bremer's concluding assemblage of "views," praises and poems inspired by Hertha, as well as Hertha's own diary entries "discovered" after her death, constituted the documentation for an elevation.

The Woman's Question

Fredrika Bremer died in 1865. In 1865 also the last of the old four-house parliaments commenced debate on a motion by two members that teachers colleges for women be started. Debate soon spread to include such issues as women taking the college-entrance exams and entering medical and law schools. Stockholm's newspapers joined in; the "woman question" had come to Sweden for good.[12]

Feminist women too soon had their own paper, *Tidskrift för Hemmet* (The Home Journal). One of its editors was the daughter of an old gentry family, Sophie Leijonhufvud, who upon marrying a high government official became Sophie Leijonhufvud-Adlersparre. Under the *nom de plume* Esselde, Adlersparre was herself an author. The other editor was Rosalie Olivecrona, the daughter of one upper-class man and wife of another. Adlersparre and Olivecrona differed in 1866 on the extent to which the new educational opportunities being debated should be allowed to draw women away from their primary roles of wife and mother. During debate on whether the priesthood (in the Swedish state church, of course) was or was not a proper "womanly" calling, again the two divided, Olivecrona feeling it was not. When debate took up woman suffrage, following the publication of John Stuart Mill's *On the Subjection of Women*, the *Home Journal* held back, Adlersparre in uncertainty, Olivecrona in vigorous opposition. The *Home Journal* itself had not taken note of Mill's book in the first place, although it was available in Sweden the year of its publication in England. Another young woman of old family, Ellen Anckarsvärd, urged discussion of suffrage and criticized the *Home Journal* for its timidity. Anckarsvärd did observe, though, that for the sake of cooling off the debate, it might be better not to use the word *emancipationen*, a foreign import, but rather *qvinnofrågan*, the "woman question." Between 1868 and 1870, the *Home Journal*, through Adlersparre, urged women to seek political influence by instilling patriotism, and ran articles discussing Swedish national defense as Bismarck's Prussia expanded. While publishing Ellen Anckarsvärd's articles urging reform of the married women's property laws, the *Home Journal*'s editor carefully distinguished their own views from hers. But the harshness, even malice, in some of the attacks hurled at the property law reform in 1877 took even the *Home Journal* editors aback, although they had not been among those pressing it.

With whom might these feminists strike alliances? On whom could they rely as friends? Midcentury male friends of women in Sweden could be found among both conservatives and liberals. The conservative bishop-economist, Carl Agardh strongly urged the King to abolish the many guild restrictions that barred women from various work. Agardh said that denying young women reasonable chances to support themselves directly fed the deplorable moral situation in Stockholm. Leading educational reformers, such as Johan Olaf Wallin, calling for more and better schools for girls and young women, were sometimes conservatives. A leading conservative gentry landowner, Hugo Tamm, called for changing the laws that denied women property rights. By the 1840s many conservative men could see practical and economic reasons for abolishing the old scheme.

But on the whole it was liberals who most often urged new things for women, men like the editors Lars Hierta and F. T. Borg, the government official Hans Hildebrand, the politician Adolf Hedin, even the farmer-parliamentarian C. J. Svensen—liberals all. Men like these prodded through some of the early reforms. The restrictive guild laws began to be lifted piecemeal from midcentury on. After first simplifying the means for young unmarried women of twenty-five to make their application for adulthood, the parliament in 1863 made it automatic at twenty-five, and at the same time freed young women of the need for consent from their nearest male relative to marry. It was no paradox that the minimum age for marriage was raised from fifteen to seventeen: women were being thought of more in terms of self-possession.[13]

Had Adolf Hedin's Liberal Party of 1866 taken root and flourished, perhaps these early reforms would have been gathered up as the harbingers of a movement. Though Hedin was an Americanizer, an advocate of individual freedoms, his liberalism included due care for the injuries free enterprise could wreak, as shown by his intervention in the 1880s to propose a commission to study old-age pensions, accident insurance, and even unemployment insurance. This Swedish liberalism, pressed by a Liberal Party, might have been an ideal culture in which feminism could grow. The twin tendencies within feminism, toward individual freedom and categorical concerns—tendencies that in Sweden led to division—might both have found nourishment and a kind of partnership. Certain tendencies toward more liberations did persist anyway. Teacher-training institutes were founded in 1859, and expanded the next year to include preparation for high school teaching. By 1900, 60 percent of the nation's rapidly growing public school teachers were women. Schools themselves thus became a significant new means for women's self-support. But a successful political entity sympathetic to women's hopes might have made much more of such teachers.

As it was, early debate over women's issues tended to serve the appetites of the newly ambitious press, which quickly raised specific issues to general, and more passionate, levels. In November 1869 the *Nya Dagligt Allehanda* ran a series, "Woman's Place in Society." Making much of *hemmets stilla verld* (the quiet world of home), the paper took an old-fashioned line on education, property, and women at work. *Aftonbladet* ran a series on how the United States was going about the education of women, and Mill was discussed. In 1870 the parliament approved further professional opportunities for women, to the dismay of *Nya Dagligt Allehanda* but to the measured approval of most other papers. In the same year the doors of the universities were opened, but since secondary school training for girls remained paltry, it would be years before young women could enter in telling numbers. The debate was by no means clearly polarized. From a conservative point of view, one of August Strindberg's boyhood teachers warmly approved of higher education for younger women precisely to fit them better for the quiet world of the home.[14] Catherine Beecher would have approved. Nor were the debaters always careful to hide certain brute assumptions. During the debates in the last of the old parliaments, in 1865–66, it was a Liberal, W. F. Dalman, who declared that so far as equality between the sexes was concerned, it was one thing for the working classes, quite another for the better. If not already a fact, equality amounted to a necessity for the former, and seemed to work out well. If, however, women of the higher orders wanted more than house and home, they might write stories or teach school, but become doctors, lawyers, civil servants, politicians? Never! They would be competing with men. Presumably, when *Nya Dagligt Allehanda* warned later that women forsaking their own sphere risked becoming "hermaphroditic beings, half-men," these were assumed to be upper-class women.

Also, the more the debate on education moved forward, the clearer it was that this spoke only to unmarried women of whatever class. Again prompted by thought of England and America, politicians and newspapers took up the rights and wrongs of married women, much energized by *Aftonbladet's* now veteran editor, Lars Johan Hierta, joined by his daughter, Anna. A Society for Married Women's Property Rights was formed in 1873 (the year of Hierta's death), with newspaper editors the most important of its some three hundred members. By 1874 Swedish married women, the first to follow the lead of England and most American states, had control over their own earnings, though much more remained to be gained. But the society itself provoked debate into a storm in 1877. Proposing the outright abolition of a married couple's community of property, which had always amounted to the husband's assumption of control over the property brought to the marriage by his wife, the society insisted that the husband must nevertheless remain fully responsible for the support of his wife. This seeming new reverse inequity drew fire. Reform was held up, and remained so for many more years, in fact, until after World War I.

Popular debate in Sweden had meanwhile reached out for new excitement next door. The Norwegian novelist Camilla Collett, who had been a powerful voice dispelling women's "speechlessness" for twenty years, wrote a series on "Women in the Novel" for *Aftonbladet* in 1876, focusing on the theme of marriage.[15] Sophie Adlersparre had followed Collett's critical writing since the 1860s; she was fascinated by Collett's insistent attack on the passive *tala-bara-tiga-lida* (patient, silent, and suffering) ideal of womanhood. But when Collett's outlook received its first fully realized voice in 1879 with Henrik Ibsen's *A Doll's House*, Swedish debate threatened to get out of hand. True enough, just as Sweden's own Carl Almqvist's novel of free love, *Sara Videbeck* back in 1839, had been answered by Sophie von Knorrings's *The Peasant and His Landlord* (1843), purporting to show that duty must prevail even at the expense of love, so answers to Ibsen were provided in criticism and literature, showing that Nora was not right to leave husband, child, and home. But this time the climactic argument only stimulated still more urgent statements.

In Sweden, as novels of significance by women began to appear again after twenty years, Anne Charlotte Edgren and Alfhild Agrell portrayed wives whose justification for rebellion cast Nora's into triviality. The most extreme portrayal came again from a Norwegian, Björnstierne Björnson, who had been writing of marriage since 1875. In his play *The Glove*, in 1883, the heroine rose to the supreme pinnacle of a new morality in applying that object to her fiancé's cheek, repudiating him for having failed to preserve his virginity until marriage. Adlersparre and those around the *Home Journal* were deeply drawn to Ibsen's—and Björnson's—basic argument. But that argument could be carried to a troubling precipice. As two of Adlersparre's friends, Urban von Feilitzen and Lawrence Heap Aberg, developed it in the *Home Journal*, the idea began to emerge that, if Ibsen's play was right, then a marriage that lacked love was no true marriage at all. Divorce was already simple enough in Sweden for those with time and money enough for the courts. Could not an assault on cold, loveless, "false" marriages lead too easily to divorce? Might not the ideas of a new "higher" morality lead to an old immorality?

It was in this context that the elite feminists of the *Home Journal* began to take up questions of sexual morality. In 1878 a Swedish branch of Josephine Butler's English—and "international"—organization, which she had started in 1875 to combat legalized prostitution, was begun in Sweden, with its own journal, *Sedlighets-Vännen* (The Friends of Morality).[16] Although evangelical pietism distinguished certain of the founders of the Morality Federation, and a religious, Christian cast suffused the organization from first to last, many others of its early members had been active in the married women's property rights and school campaigns on plain secular grounds.

Sweden's—or rather Stockholm's—supposed sexual depravity had fascinated tourists for decades. Whereas in Paris, always conceded mid-nineteenth-century primacy as the very sink of modern sexual laxity, one in five births was out of wedlock, Stockholm's 30 percent surpassed that. "In no other Christian community is there a state of female morals approaching to this," concluded the English free-trader, Samuel Laing. Laing blamed this condition on the ruling class, many personally dissolute, with their example inducing idleness and immorality among the people. Of course it was this ruling class that refused to open Sweden to the bracing winds of free trade as Laing wished. The American Robert Baird, sure that a good dose of evangelical religion was what Sweden needed, had a rather different explanation for the immorality, but in addition he penetrated closer to the institutional center of Sweden's sexual statistics, the capital's Foundling Hospital, where babies were accepted with neither question nor charge. Thomas Malthus had spent much thought on the foundling hospital, as he found it in both Stockholm and Moscow, pondering its impact on population. Foundling hospitals might save some lives in the short run, he concluded, but in the long run, they encouraged licentiousness, which in turn discouraged marriage; therefore, since in the long run it was in marriage that fertility most flourished, foundling hospitals did not favor population. But while Malthus was in favor of population control, he could not favor licentiousness, so his discussion led into an impasse. The Swedes, in any case, had kept their foundling hospital. Baird's analysis too, like Laing's, implicated the upper classes, if not specifically their licentiousness. Stockholm's "ladies of rank," he said, appeared unwilling to nurse their own babies, and thus offered a steady market for wet nurses from among the girls who abandoned their own babies. The two, hospital and market, meshed. "Is it wonderful," then, he asked, "that illegitimacy should prevail?"[17]

For the statistically minded, Sweden's census did offer food for thought. An out-of-wedlock birthrate of around 25 per 1,000 unmarried women who were between twenty and forty-five years of age had remained a kind of norm from the mid-eighteenth century to around 1810. Then came a gradual rise to a rate of 35 around 1835. This rate then remained fairly steady, rising only after 1900 to 40–45. The first rise, from around 25 to around 35, had taken place during the first serious disruptions of the old villages by the agricultural revolution, while the second came as the cities grew, filling up especially with young women. While the national rate remained steady, the rate in the countryside may have been declining, to around 31 in 1860–70, with the rate in the towns no less than 59. From this widest point of difference between urban and rural rates, the two rates then began to converge, meeting at around 38–40 in 1910–20. By the 1920s the urban out-of-wedlock birthrate had fallen to below 25, while the rate in the countryside remained around 35.[18]

Figures like these were never cited in popular debates, where everyone much preferred Stockholm's titillating figure, but they constituted a kind of unconsciously intuited basis for a startling idea. What if none of these rates meant "immorality" at all, let alone "prostitution"? This idea was put forcibly to Charles Loring Brace in 1856 by an army officer he met in the provinces: "You cannot judge from Stockholm, sir. It is true there are very many illegitimate children there, but *there are no prostitutes*. We hear of fifty thousand women in London who are damned for this world utterly. There is hardly one in Sweden."[19] Brace was not quite ready to concede that the Swedes were no worse than anybody else. Did not even the Swedish Prayerbook include a petition for "Mothers, who have been deceived by promise of marriage"? But Brace began reasoning that out-of-wedlock births may have had an economic root, and besides, he was informed, very many of these babies were legitimated legally by a later marriage anyway. Brace finally came to a handsomely generous summation. "The *grisettes* of Stockholm," he wrote, "preserve some decency and have a chance at least of a better life. They are occupied as seamstresses, or servants, or shopwomen, and frequently after many years of unlawful companionship, are married. The cause of these numerous *liaisons* is probably here as with us, the difficulty of women's earning an honorable support."[20]

But whatever the sophistication of travelers or the naïveté of local patriots, in 1847 the civic authorities in Stockholm decided to draw up regulations, obviously on the assumption, whatever Brace's informants may have come to think, that prostitutes, not only mistresses, did exist. The rules, true to bureaucratic inwardness, soon became intricate. Prostitutes were to lead life quietly. They must abjure conspicuous clothing and stay away from certain restaurants, inns, and coffeehouses. At the theater, they must sit in the darker corners. Showing themselves in lighted windows behind venetian blinds or shutters would be a violation.

Exactly why the Friends of Morality set out to attack this system thirty-one years after it was installed is not certain. Most likely they were drawn into it by the needs of feminism itself for issues. No evidence was offered that prostitution in Stockholm had been made worse—or less, for that matter. As for a general rationale, no more than its counterparts elsewhere did the Swedish reform group make progress in escaping the dilemmas that haunted all attempts to cope with prostitution. Essentially, the Swedish federation found offense more in the tacit legality than in the sheer fact of prostitution. This could be asserted as a question of public morality, and in morality feminism might find its high ground.

But it was this moralistic approach, rather than some more sociological analysis that searched for causes and cures, that drew the Friends of Morality to fiasco. Choosing to bring scandalous facts to the attention of a broad public, the columns of the *Friends of Morality* offered vivid word pictures of venereal infection and moral degradation. A strong tendency toward highlighting specifically masculine iniquities showed itself. After a certain pause, counterattack began. The Friends of Morality were themselves accused of offense against public decency in spreading lurid charges that decency understood were best kept for the eyes of responsible men and from the eyes of everyone else, including respectable women. By 1880 there were probably about a thousand members of the federation, many more than belonged to the Married Women's Property Rights group, with the heavy majority of them women. Sophie Adlersparre was one, and she had opened the *Home Journal* to the Morality Federation's interests. But by mid-1881, following *Aftonbladet's* devastating countercharge that the federation gave off the "unhealthy odor" of prurience, membership fell sharply to below 450, and by 1882 to below 300. These remaining few held fast; they circulated another petition against regulation in 1883, gaining 2,500 signatures, but regulation remained in force in Sweden.

Meanwhile, public discussion of contraception began. In February 1880 a young instructor at Uppsala, Knut Wicksell, addressed the local temperance society on the causes of student drunkenness.[21] Wicksell was a young man of unmistakable promise for the next generation of Swedish intellectual leadership. He possessed a wholly secular mind. Student drunkenness, he said, derived from student problems and discontents generally. And what were these? In expounding them, Wicksell was really expounding changes that had overtaken life for more and more young Swedes in a changing Sweden. More and more men were going to university to prepare for the professions and tasks of a successfully modernizing society in law, medicine, government, and education. Such preparation was taking longer than it had before. Years of poverty and hard work, therefore, were the expectation for this new educated class. Postponement of marriage until thirty and even later was steadily becoming the norm. The discontent of this Swedish youth was, in a phrase, sexual starvation. Wicksell did not believe that all unmarried young men practiced abstinence, but their only recourse was to prostitution in some version or another, which carried its own special dangers. Those who did practice abstinence often drank.

Wicksell explicitly dismissed sexual abstinence as a moral option. It was deleterious not only to body but to soul. He therefore called upon the university and doctors to provide students with means for birth control. With such means students could get married, confident that their studies would not be compromised or canceled by producing a child to support.

Wicksell's talk drew fire from several directions. Doctors attacked quickly. Hostage to their rising professional respectability no less in Sweden than in the United States, unready to risk either status or fees, doctors preferred their new prestige to old ideals. A "Christian" point of view also mobilized, to highlight Wicksell's not only obviously secular but coolly disdainful rationalism. But exactly what the Christian point of view was to be fell short of utter clarity, for the clergymen of the established state church, never notable in Swedish history for shining chastity themselves, tended toward silence, leaving the Christian point of view to be elucidated by self-appointed evangelicals and lay leaders. But of all interested parties, the feminist Friends of Morality were least well positioned to cope with Wicksell. First, by composing his argument entirely in terms of the problems of university students, who happened still to be overwhelmingly male, he rendered slightly absurd the notion implicit in even such powerful voices as Collett's and Ibsen's, that the primary interest in the marriage question and even the woman question was women's. Then too, Wicksell deplored promiscuous bachelorhood and supported a single standard in place of the old double standard. But Wicksell's single standard was based on more rather than less sexual expression, on sexual abundance rather than sexual scarcity. The attack on Wicksell, in which the Friends of Morality shared, thus seemed to connote a hostility to sex itself.

In the summer of 1884 Sophie Adlersparre, with an old friend, Fredrika Limnell, vice-chair of the Married Women's Property Rights group since its start in 1873, and an activist in the Morality Federation, proposed the creation of a truly feminist organization, an organization devoted to the interests of women as such. Reaching out, they invited friendly critics of the new *Home Journal* such as Ellen Anckarsvard to participate. Rosalie Olivecrona was to have a part. The organizers had no notion of a purely female group; the government's Keeper of the Monuments, Hans Hildebrand, a longtime supporter of reforms for women, helped in planning, as did eminent academics such as Gustav Sjöberg. By December the Fredrika Bremer Society was formally constituted. Of its twenty-four members of the board, ten were men, including both the chairman, Hildebrand, and the vice-chairman, the Steward of the Royal Court, Adolph Bortzell. But of course the effective leader was Adlersparre, together with Olivecrona and the manager of the society headquarters, Gertrud Adelborg, daughter of a high naval officer. Later the *Home Journal* gave way to *Dagny*, a "journal of social and literary interests," still edited by Adlersparre. In 1913 *Dagny* became *Hertha*.

With the formation of the Fredrika Bremer Society, Swedish feminism presumably was to come into its own.[22] Without repudiating its affiliations with feminism everywhere, in its very name it affirmed the relevance to Swedish women of a specifically Swedish past. With the change in its journal's name, it affirmed that women's interests included more than home. Tacitly superseding previous organizations, it implied that not only married or only unmarried women, not only young women hungry for education, not only women condemned to sin and prison, but all women together constituted some kind of identity and interest group. At the same time, with its board composed of both men and women, it signaled a readiness to collaborate and cooperate with some men, at least, rather than standing apart from all. What kinds of men, the Bremer Society's first board seemed to show.

Feminist Antifeminism: August Strindberg

During the summer of 1884, while Adlersparre and her friends were busy about their plans for the new organization, the well-known young writer August Strindberg was readying the proofs of his new book for publication in September. The book, to be called *Giftas* (Married), would consist of several short stories about courtship and marriage, and would include a preface in which the author explained his own views on the woman question. Strindberg very much hoped his book would be a success.

In his Preface to *Married*, Strindberg insisted that he too was a feminist. Women had the same right to education as men, he wrote, and should have the same education. Furthermore, boys and girls should be educated together, not separately, not simply to guarantee equality but to head off what Strindberg had long felt to be one of the strongest, if subtlest, forces against sexual equality—gallantry. Two years before, in a chapter he had devoted to women in an anti-Geijer history of "ordinary" people, he had discussed how women—obviously upper-class women—had been turned into dolls by the gallantry of the eighteenth century. He had unambiguously condemned this conversion of women from useful, self-respecting beings into ornaments. Gallantry was nothing less than condescension and as such ought to be purged, and coeducation would help purge it. Women should have the vote, too, Strindberg agreed. Women should also be eligible for all occupations. Though such views were hardly startling in Sweden by 1884, they placed Strindberg among the enlightened minority. And he went on to more vivid, less *pro forma* affirmations: "The girl shall have the same freedom to 'run wild' and choose what company she pleases [as the boy]." Those who marry should draw up a contract on the terms they want, for the term they want, state and church having nothing to do with it. As he would explain in *A Madman's Defense*, he and his wife Siri had done just this themselves, when they married in 1877. "Separate bedrooms shall be the rule from the beginning." So they had been for him and Siri. He went on to further contingencies: mothers with full-time responsibilities should receive guaranteed allowances from the state. Widows should be protected from poverty by state insurance. He ended with a flourish: "[The] freedom [woman] is now demanding is the same freedom that all we men demand too. We must get it together, as friends, not as enemies." For most practical purposes, Strindberg had affirmed the very program that the Swedish Social Democrats would begin carrying into law fifty and more years later in the name of justice and equality. How then could Strindberg, holding these views, come to be found offensive to feminists and women?[23]

This feminist program occupied only the last several pages of his twenty-page preface. Much the bulk of the preface he devoted to a polemic against Henrik Ibsen, and to an attack on marriage and the family. By the time the reader arrived at Strindberg's feminist program, he—or she—had been escorted over ground quite unreminiscent of ordinary approaches to feminist ideals. Strindberg's antagonism to Ibsen no doubt had several roots. Jealousy was one. Not only had Ibsen occupied ground that Strindberg felt must be his, that of the woman question itself, but he posed a threat to Strindberg's own ambition to become Sweden's leading writer. Obviously, Sweden would have no leading writer, if a Norwegian were conceded to be Scandinavia's greatest writer. But just as Gustav àf Geijerstam would later appear to be an extreme case of the writer as panderer to popular audiences, so too did Ibsen seem, in Strindberg's acute intuition, to be an example of the writer in dalliance with his audience, an audience of women, of feminists—the same, implicitly, that Geijerstam would please with his lesser art later. Finally—though we cannot be sure—in Ibsen Strindberg appears to have seen a threat not just to his own status, not just to the truth about marriage, but to art itself. Ibsen was writing propaganda art; propaganda could not long remain art, any more than prostitution could long remain moral. Yet his hostility to Ibsen would always remain suspect for its personal edge of jealousy.

The attack on Ibsen, as a writer catering to the feminists' view of women as martyrs, fed into an attack on marriage in general. Strindberg offered purely "political" analyses of marriage that were virtually calculated to give offense. Taking the familiar idea that the man's freedom in courtship to propose and the woman's restriction to replying only "yes" or "no" was a manifest inequality, he drew another inference:

A man chooses his wife, and is usually in love with her. . . . It is by no means certain that she returns his love, for she was not the one who chose. This gives her the upper hand. . . . For the sake of domestic peace the man consents to anything and everything, for domestic peace was one of his boldest hopes of matrimonial bliss.[24]

Thus Strindberg succeeded in at once rejecting a familiar feminist view while in no way defending established manners. When he then proceeded to declare that only some "interests in common," not real affinities, kept many marriages together, he arrived at his most radical point: "[Now] comes the great, unfathomable question: is it the duty of the individual to surrender his individuality from the moment he reproduces himself, and live only for his children?"[25] Among the "other" mammals that live as long as man, Strindberg noted, "motherhood lasts for one or two years only." Then the female is free until the next offspring arrives. But as "a result of civilization," the female of the human species is essentially tied for life. Strindberg drew the large, political inference:

There is consequently something natural about the dissatisfaction of the cultured woman with her prolonged motherhood, and her apparent opposition to nature is really an opposition to culture, just as her opposition to the tyranny of her husband is quite simply a revolt against their common enemy, against whom he too revolts, namely our topsy-turvy society, though she sees the constraints of this society personified in her husband.[26]

All this prepared for Strindberg's assault on the home, by which he meant home in one of its specific manifestations:

The home here in the North is much praised in song. The homes in the South are less stifling. It is a question of climate. The Scandinavian home with its double windows that ruin the air, with its porcelain stoves (the domestic hearth!), with the long winters and autumns and springs that torment people by forcing them together. . . . One moral code inside the home, another outside it. . . . The child . . . will silently criticize its parents. . . . It is one long chain of hypocrisy. . . . When the child gets out into the world it feels so inordinately happy, that at best it only goes home to dinner on Sundays.[27]

In this indictment of the standard Swedish family, Strindberg did not single out women or the mother. He did, however, leave his own thinking on child-rearing unevolved. In some essays in lightly fiction-alized dialogue form, written at the same time he was writing his stories in *Married*, he sketched out some fantasies of a better way. Intrigued by what he had heard of a *familistère* in northern France, he described a community of several hundred families that conducted all life in common, with children raised in common. As Martin Lamm points out, a trip to observe the French reality disillusioned Strindberg and he pursued the subject no further.[28]

In the end, Strindberg's feelings in 1884 came to rest in a kind of obscurantism that followed, not from some hidden allegiance to old ways, but from the sheer unchartedness of the ground onto which he had tried to break. In the end he recommended love, "a natural force that survives the individual's reasoned arguments . . . defies all imaginable storms . . . all imaginable whims." It was this nonrational love, he said, that gave the "greatest guarantee of happiness" in marriage. Strindberg found no allies here among those debating the woman question: not the feminists of the Bremer Society and the Friends of Morality, not the defenders of the old patriarchal order, such as it was, not the new rationalists like Knut Wicksell. Even his suggestion as to a rational policy for encouraging this nonrational love would find no takers: "[Love] . . . would be free to function more often if the sexes were allowed to function more freely." By this he meant that girls should be freer to express their sexual feelings and freer to take the initiative with boys. Neither feminists nor traditionalists nor rationalists were attuned to this.

Ultimately, Strindberg charged feminism with being a malady of Sweden's weaker self, the malady of a Sweden that hung back from modernity, from sophistication, from testing itself in the great world:

The whole Swedish literature of feminism is ultra-Norwegian; it contains the same immodest demands on the man and petting of the spoilt woman. . . . Let us welcome foreign influence which is cosmopolitan; but not Norwegian, for that is provincial, and we have plenty of the same kind ourselves.[29]

He carried his criticism of Ibsen's Nora into myth:

Nora is related to the Icelandic women who wished to set up a matriarchate; she belongs to the weird imperious women . . . who . . . are pure Norse. In them the emotions have become frozen or distorted by centuries of cognate marriages.[30]

His ultimate criticism of Swedish women, then, was that they were cold. This was not their fault, but the fault of their history. But theirs was a faulty history, and feminism's way of wanting to change it would compound the fault.

The stories themselves in *Married* were not pitched against wives or indeed any category of person. More sketches than stories, written in swift, short strokes, some told of life's ups, some of its downs. In "Love and the Price of Grain" the prodigal newlyweds, after feasting on quail and strawberries, find her father's dour warning of "hard times ahead" all too true; they have to part. But the story is not really cautionary, for with no more prudence another couple ends up happy. In one story, a baby brings depression and apathy to a young mother, but in another, radiance and pride; Strindberg judges neither. The language in all the stories is innocent of all that is suggestive. At the same time the tone is crisp, if ironic yet light, if satiric yet quick, eminently readable.[31]

Within days after his stories were published, Strindberg found himself indicted and scheduled for trial. Nothing in *Married* was vulnerable to charges of obscenity. None of the stories trafficked in salacity. As would always be true, Strindberg's language sustained a scrupulous cleanliness. In the midst of the frankest exposition of sexual reality, he disdained the least appeal to prurience. Destined to become one of the world's most famous spokesmen on sexual themes, Strindberg remained the least pornographic of writers, surpassing even Tolstoy and Flaubert in clinical restraint. Nor had Strindberg, in his preface, made shocking recommendations such as those made by Knut Wicksell four years before. So the conspirators were forced into a pretext, isolating an incidental passage in his first story, "Theodore," for their charge, a quintessentially Strindbergian passage in its combination of corrosive sarcasm with arresting detail:

In the spring [Theodore] was confirmed. This agitating performance, at which the upper classes force the lower classes to swear by the body and word of Christ that they will never concern themselves with what the [former] do, haunted him for a long time. He did not devote any thought to the impudent deception practiced with Högstedt's Piccadon at 65 öre the half gallon, and

Lettström's wafers at 1 crown a pound, which the parson passed off as the body and blood of Jesus of Nazareth, the agitator who had been executed over 1800 years earlier, for this was not a time for thought, for you were there to receive "grace."[32]

Turning to an archaic law, the authorities indicted him on the basis of this passage for blasphemy.

Strindberg was in Switzerland, living there with his family, and therefore safe, but he returned to Stockholm, if only to save his publisher, the distinguished house of Bonnier, from having to stand in his place. He trembled, for it seemed to him that only a kind of cabal in high places could have been responsible, and therefore that he could be in real danger. With a suspicious speed, remarkable even for that simpler day, Strindberg was tried late in October. But the court was not as spineless as his enemies hoped. He was acquitted in November. The cabal, if such there had been, had overreached itself.

Among all those who had long felt Sweden in urgent need of the cleansing winds of intellectual honesty, realism, and social reform, Strindberg's acquittal was hailed. Strindberg had been recognized as a scouring force for some years. In previous books he had already portrayed Swedish university life, Swedish journalism, churches, business, and culture as at once decrepit and stiff, elaborate forms empty of life. In Svenska folket ("The Swedish People"), in 1882, he had shown how Swedish history ought to be written, not as the story of the usual Vikings and kings and great warriors but of the people at large over the centuries of their ordinary life.

But in the tight little society of Stockholm's establishment, The Swedish People caused much irritation, as had his earlier sketches. When, then, with prodigious energy, Strindberg went on to produce another collection of stories by the end of 1882, Nya riket ("The New Nation"), excoriating his critics and once again mocking, satirizing, and ridiculing Swedish pomp, Swedish hypocrisy, Swedish vainglory, his reputation was fixed. Still more stories the following year added to the conviction: here was a formidable troublemaker. He meant to "unmask the entire Swedish nation," he had written a friend in 1881, and then, this done, go into exile and "become a real writer." And in 1883 he did, taking his wife and babies with him, first to France, then to Geneva. What he meant by being a "real" writer was "[not] the kind who works with belles-lettres, but one who writes the things he cannot speak. Ruthlessly!"[33]

Swedish scholarship appears not to have found in the archives proof of just who set on foot the prosecution for Married. Only high-placed persons could have done so. By 1884 the secretary of the Swedish academy, Carl David àf Wirsen, had finally resolved that Strindberg was an incorrigible enemy of the establishment. Wirsen was destined to remain implacable and certainly influential. He held his office long enough to help see to it that Strindberg never got the Nobel Prize. But the Queen too, Sophia of Holland, was most probably a factor in the decision to prosecute. A pietist, a close friend of Sophie Adlersparre, the Queen adhered to the ideas of the Friends of Morality. She was an admirer of Ibsen's *A Doll's House*. Strindberg had attacked both the Friends and Ibsen. The Queen could agree: Strindberg was a threat to social order.

In fact, it was not so much blasphemy that Strindberg had committed in "Theodore" as lèse-majesté, and this was undoubtedly his deepest offense. The marriage portrayed in "Theodore" came the closest to being absurd. Basically, the story followed a young man's growing up. He was a confused young man, overmothered, intimidated by a bluff, soldierly older brother, full of fears intellectual and social as well as sexual. Eventually, though, he met a "virtuous maiden" whom he married. This virtuous maiden was thirty-five, practically old enough to be his mother. Her name was Sophia Leidshütz, that is, roughly, "Sophia Bleeding-Heart." In one of the chapters of his earlier book of Stockholm sketches, *Röda rummet* (The Red Room), Strindberg had already satirized Swedish lady-do-gooders, but in "Theodore" the satirical portrait had an extra bite, for Sophia Leidshütz was irresistibly identifiable with that most famous Sophia, the Queen, famed for her Dutch piety and pious works, the founder of Queen Sophia's Protection Society.[34] A Sophie too could be remembered by those of a mind to— Sophie Adlersparre, leader of the feminists and one of the Queen's intimates. In his preface to *Married*, moreover, Strindberg had already offered provocation to various feminist writers on the grounds of their spinsterhood. Readers could then recall the unmarried status of the feminists' self-chosen heroine, Fredrika Bremer herself, and of Hertha, her heroine.

However adolescent or projective or even slightly paranoid Strindberg's performance in "Theodore" and in his preface to *Married* may— or may not—have been, the links between these first organized feminists and his enemies were fateful. Enraged by his trial, Strindberg turned immediately to another set of stories, published under the title *Married II*, and in his preface to this collection, among all the targets he might have chosen for his sarcastic lash, he singled out the feminists as the most overt of all aggressive women. A new figure appeared in some of these stories, a kind of vampire woman. Soon, in his 1887 play *The Father*, the most monstrous of all his vampire women would reduce the hero, her husband, to a straitjacket and literal insanity.

After his trial Strindberg left Sweden again, and returned there to live only after more than fifteen years. Narrowly, he feared the ability of the high-placed clique that had had him prosecuted to continue to do him damage. At least here he was right, for it did. Wirsen and his tame critics pursued Strindberg's literary appearances with venomous scorn. Production of his plays was made difficult. Though one of the most copious and innovative writers of the nineteenth century, Strindberg made almost no money from his work. In a widely distributed pamphlet of 1887, he was pilloried as a bad influence on Swedish youth. Hostile machinations would not have mattererd, had Sweden had an abounding middle class occupying significant space between the overwhelming rural majority and the disintegrating old establishment. Those who understood him had cheered his acquittal. But they were few and often without the money to attend plays and read books. In that sense, Strindberg was trapped whether he had enemies in high places or not. But Strindberg's larger motive for living outside Sweden followed from his sense that in Sweden not only the old order but the new reformers also were oppressive. If the new Sweden was to be the work of the Friends of Morality, Queen Sophia's Protection Society, and the Fredrika Bremer Society, a real writer could only get out.

Motherhood as Feminist Antifeminism: Ellen Key

Remarkable women such as the novelist Victoria Benedictsson and the teacher-reformer Ellen Key would prove quite capable of entering the ruthless world in which Strindberg tested himself. The activities of feminists of the Fredrika Bremer Society, however, did suggest that Sweden was a place to be pure and safe.[35] One of its early projects was an exhibition of books for children and young people suitable for Christmas gifts. Another was an employment exchange. A third was an office to encourage health insurance for teachers and other women wage earners. It also set up a plan for county scholarships for worthy young women, and the training of nurses drew its attention. In 1896 a society circular to every public girls' school in the country provided information about job opportunities. In 1890 it sponsored an investigation into the reasons why Swedish girls emigrated to Denmark to jobs as servants and maids. Its attempt to pursue the problem of regulated prostitution led to a modest schism in 1887, but the society persisted and sent delegates to the 1899 London congress on the international traffic in prostitution.

The society's position on the marriage and morality questions drew it toward a conflict with one of the nation's most notable women, Ellen Key, who found the traditional single-standard notions of sexual abstinence unacceptable. As a new generation arose, the obvious question for the Fredrika Bremer Society was its ability to attract that generation. Cautiously, in 1899, it began reaching out to the suffrage question. But the society was lagging behind the times. Its first chairman, Hans Hildebrand, served until 1903, and his successor, Agda Monelius, was the wife of Hildebrand's successor as Keeper of the Monuments in the government. A new, younger suffrage leader, Kata Dalström, found some of the Bremer Society's projects suspiciously like catering to those interested in a reliable supply of cheap servants, nurses, and teachers. Dalström disdained the group as an upper-class club. She herself joined the new Social Democrats.

Perhaps it was this class inflection that explains early Swedish feminism's indifference to the two popular movements in which women had an interest, temperance and evangelical religion. All mid-nineteenth-century travelers commented on Swedish drinking. This class inhibition might be temporarily and superficially eased by Queen Sophia with her copy of Dwight Moody on her bedtable, but the deeper sociology of both temperance and evangelicalism made fusion with elite feminism impossible. (Typically, as temperance failed to triumph as a popular movement in Sweden, its triumph through bureaucratic and professional channels imposed a system at once undemocratic and unfeminist. After 1914, Swedes who wanted a bottle of liquor had to present a *motbok*, or passbook, in which their wealth, income, occupation, size of family, and so on, as well as record of sobriety or otherwise, would be entered. While no formal bar operated against women also getting this certificate of good character, inevitably the implicit invidiousness of the system made it unattractive to them. Certainly, of about 1.25 million *motboks* outstanding in 1930, women held but 125,000, or 10 percent.[36] After forty years or so, Swedes threw out the *motbok* system and began mulling over their statistics on alcohol still again.) The real issue was whether feminism itself would find, not so much movements of popular dissidence, as new numbers of young women leading new lives.

As new kinds of newspapermen, such as Ernst Beckman, and new political figures, such as R. E. L. Svensen, began to discuss the "woman question" in newly enlarged terms, the Bremer Society itself became simply one voice among many. Svensen's tract of 1888, *Kvinnofrågan* (The Woman Question), as conspicuous a piece of feminist writing as any of the time, simply took for granted that all political interests would have some interest in the question, one way or another.

In 1892 the well-known girls' school teacher, Ellen Key, prompted by a young woman active in the labor movement named Anna Soderberg, started what came to be known as the "dozens," women meeting in groups of twelve to share personal experiences, discuss issues, and exchange views. In these groups the middle-class young women of the "radical" 1880s, liberal and individualistic, and not attracted by the Bremer Society, met working-class women at a time when the Social Democratic Party had not yet resolved on its ideological path. Effectively, Key's "dozens" raised the question whether there could be a women's version of the nationalism earlier expressed by Geijer and the Gothic Society and, in their own day, by the Verdandi Society, a women's vision of Sweden transcending class.

The richest version of this vision came from Ellen Key herself.[37] Born the same year as Strindberg, in 1849, Key is commonly said to have grown up, like Fredrika Bremer and Victoria Benedictsson, unhappy. Key's father, Emil Key, combined two traditions, both of them among those outside stimuli upon which Sweden had so often drawn. The name "Key" came from a Highland Scot who joined Gustavus Adolphus's armies and stayed on to take Swedish land and found a Swedish family. The name "Emil" reflected the enthusiasm of a Key grandfather for Jean-Jacques Rousseau. Emil Key gained prominence in Swedish politics as a liberal warmly in favor of reform, and helped sustain the change to a new parliament in 1866 when his daughter was seventeen. Yet apparently it was Ellen Key's mother rather than her father who guided her to books, music, culture. The daughter of an old, truly Swedish noble family, Fru Key sustained the tradition in such families that well-born girls were born for far more than domesticity. During her twenties Ellen served not only as her father's aide and helper in politics but as his companion during tours to several parts of Europe. Thus she became a cosmopolitan not only through books but through travel. Like Nordenflycht, Lenngren, and Bremer before her, and like her contemporary Benedictsson and like Selma Lagerlöf after her, Key turned in her first flights as a writer to those sketches of Swedish country life that seemed to have more than mere pictorial significance for Swedish women writers. But in Key's case stories were not to prove her métier, nor did she ever write a novel.

When Key was thirty, her father's affairs collapsed. Like any Jacksonian American, and like hundreds of Swedish and European land-owners everywhere, he had speculated in land and new businesses and had lost. The comfortable family life vanished. Key had to go to work. She did, and for the next twenty years evolved gradually into a well-known figure in Stockholm and the whole country, a teacher at the progressive girls' school headed by Anna Whitlock. By the 1890s she was the guiding spirit in a circle of liberals. Perhaps Key's chief interest as a writer was in bringing women writers from all Western Europe to the attention of Swedish women. She wrote about the Norwegian feminist Camilla Collett. She wrote about George Eliot. She wrote a long appreciation of the tragic Benedictsson for the Bremer Society's new journal, *Dagny*. In her writing and teaching, but above all in her very person, independent of any institution, she was a kind of Hertha come to life, a human anticipation of the organizational welfare world soon to take shape with the National Association for Social Work. Years before she wrote the books that won her an international reputation, she was the inspiration for the younger women in the "dozens" who would carry her sense of things into the Sweden of the 1920s and 1930s, in clear anticipation of the social democracy of the 1940s and 1950s. In her will, Key left her country home, Strand, not far from Vadstena, the monastery founded by St. Birgitta, to the use of working women and these "dozens."

Yet it was by no means obvious that Key was a feminist. In 1896 Key began publishing books of her own. During the next fifteen years she produced a shelf of them that left her famous in Germany, England, and America as well as in all Scandinavia. The first were *Missbrukad kvinnokraft* (Woman's Power Mis-used), 1896, and *Kvinnopsykologi och kvinnlig logik* (Woman's Psychology and Womanly Logic), also 1896. Here, as later, Key criticized feminism that aimed for equality, that demanded equal rights for females to pursue goals as men did, a feminism she clearly linked with upper-middle-class ambitions, including the ambitions of the Fredrika Bremer Society. Such feminism, she said, neglected that which women had to offer to the world as women. There really was a womanly psychology, a womanly logic, and both were to be respected and cherished. Since Key had gone so far as to question the wisdom of votes for women, these views could easily be viewed as retrograde, and were. At the same time, since they were not expounded with an animus against men, they might have been welcome to someone like Strindberg; indeed, in the Key of 1896 there was probably nothing to provoke the kind of caricature that Strindberg wrote of her later and published in 1907 in *Black Banners*. Like Strindberg, Key found hostility to sex as such among the organized feminists. In their preoccupation with prostitution she sensed a distorted notion of their own natures. In their demand that a new single standard be that of the old type of good woman, she intuited failure of imagination.

Soon, Key was expounding fuller views with sweep and vigor. Her celebration of motherhood was not really conservative, for the motherhood she celebrated lay not in the past but in the future. Key's criticism of the old order equaled at least that of the feminists. Their attack upon patriarchy left the question of child-rearing in limbo, whereas Key insisted upon a child-rearing agenda explicitly aimed at freedom. The motherhood she praised was a means. Its service to child-rearing lay in nurturing autonomous individuals. As she grew bolder, she did not hesitate to draw lines she felt necessary. She changed her mind to support woman suffrage, but strove to distinguish herself not just from bourgeois Swedish feminists but from the American feminist scene, which in Sweden was widely believed to be the most advanced in the world. Summarizing Charlotte Perkins Gilman's ideas on child-rearing by experts, she carefully presented her counterviews. At their heart was her feeling that communal child-rearing would cause "torment to individual spirits." Of course Key's position had most salience in Sweden with respect to the Socialists. She had taken care to attack Socialist feminists. Whether she was aware that Gilman liked to say on occasion that she was a Socialist is not clear. Plainly, it was the self-interested motive in Gilman's communal schemes that she was criticizing when she called Gilman "amaternal." The "professional" child-rearing hailed by Gilman, Key felt, had as its real purpose not children's welfare but that of ambitious women. If only rhetorically, Key did not flinch from hard choices: "If the destruction of . . . homes were the price the race must pay for woman's attainment of full human dignity and citizenship, then the price would be too high."[38]

Key was advancing onto radical, not just regressing back to traditional, ground. That was clear from her expositions on marriage and love. Children and child-rearing demanded their own separate honesty, but so too did the relationship between man and woman. Again, the heart of Key's analysis was the claim of the individual. Love and only love justified marriage. Love itself was an individualizing force: "personal characteristics have tended more and more to inspire love, and love has more and more developed personal characteristics." As few of the classic Romantics had done, she noted explicitly that such individualization might "in a sense" become "antisocial." But she went on to observe that a richer notion of what served the race might show that such antisocial love was in fact ennobling and socially beneficial.

Key had contempt for the new moralists who preached a single standard of abstinence:

The book world is now full of works on purity, written by men as well as women. . . . Now it is the story of a woman who breaks with the man she loves when he confesses his past; now that of a woman who forces her lover to marry another because the latter has borne him a child. . . . Literature . . . announces the approach of . . . that army of strong women who are to educate men to chastity by denying them their love.

She approved one of the more shocking new ideas turned against this musty chastity: "We seldom hear it asked nowadays of a woman: *Why has she not married?* But it is all the more frequently inquired:

What has her love-story been, *since she has never married*"[39] The disentanglement of a woman's sexual life from marriage Key now saw as essential to, and perfectly compatible with, celebration of motherhood.

But perhaps most impressive were Key's justifications for the erotic freedom not just of women but of men. Liberated women had been justifying their free lives for a century, but hardly any had troubled to approve masculine sexuality. Feminists' demands for virgin bridegrooms seemed to Key sterile. What "stained" a man was not the fact of having had sexual experience but rather the quality—or lack thereof—of the experience:

If no baseness is connected with these earlier experiences, if he has not degraded himself . . . —and bought love is always such a degradation— . . . if he has not treated any woman as a means . . . then he does not enter "impure" into his marriage, even if he has not evidence of abstinence.

Though this explicit countenancing of premarital sexual intercourse was not yet a recommendation of it, to Key it was clear that the way to deal with Don Juan was not to attack sex:

. . . when sensuousness—in alliance with the mission of the race—regains its ancient dignity, then the power of giving erotic rapture will not be the monopoly of him who is unhuman in his love. . . . the force of primitive animality [is] still erotically attractive even to the spiritually sensitive. Men and women with the power of elementary passion, intoxicate because they are themselves intoxicated.

Key thus felt scorn for the hostility to men she found in some celebrations of womanhood:

At a Scandinavian meeting on the woman's question, a cantata was sung which proclaimed that the human race under the supremacy of man had stumbled in darkness and crime. But the race was now to be newly born from the soul of woman, the sunrise would scatter the darkness of night. . . . That men during the period of their ascendancy had nevertheless produced a few trifles—for example, religions and laws, sciences and arts, discoveries and inventions—all this her majesty woman was pleased to forget.

Strindberg could hardly have said it better.

Certainly, Key's rejection of a new virginal single standard did not mean embrace of a new qualitative single standard, for Key found no meaning in equality where erotic fulfillment was concerned.

The modern woman's great distress has been the discovery of the dissimilarity between her own erotic nature and that of man; or rather, she has refused and still refuses to make this discovery and thinks that only the custom of society

. . . has brought about the difference which exists and which she would abolish.[40]

How had Key made this discovery? What did she have for evidence? How did she "know"? There was little doubt: the "data base" for her position was personal. But the important point was that she had defined the position. If the haunted ground of female sexuality was ever going to be honestly explored, no automatic acceptance of the compass of "equality" would do.

At times, Key seemed to think her ideas about a new sexual morality were already being practiced by the modern-day people of the late nineteenth century. "Free love" was "their idea of love's chastity," she wrote approvingly. On the other hand, this could seem simply an old Swedish—and European—toleration of sexual intercourse for the betrothed, a kind of freedom which "our working classes" had long enjoyed, now at last being "taken up by the young men and girls of the upper classes." But these rather bland notions could give way to darker views, that only "stubbornly waged class war" could rescue single women from their privation and bring sexual freedom within reach of all women.

But the center of gravity of Key's public views remained focused in motherhood, where, ultimately, woman's own erotic fulfillment was to be found, and here she remained an independent, if not a liberal, uneasy about class tactics, uneasy about the rising Social Democrats. Key's defense of motherhood remained linked to her defense of individualism. When she attacked the "soul murder" wrought upon children by the schools, she was attacking what Strindberg attacked. She offered sociological extension of his pyschological criticism: "It is even now a serious loss to culture that school-life makes children uniform." But the psychological issue framed all others, for even diversity was imaginable without necessarily allowing freedom. In effect, Key postulated that in motherhood there inhered a logic that would nourish children's egos. The service of motherhood was not to "socialization," then, not to society, morality, goodness, or peace, but to freedom. Mother love truly did love, for what it wanted for its love object was that it be strong. A child reared by mother love would always trust inner abundance. Key's feminism came to balance here, in boys and girls raised by ideal mothers to be strong. It was in this inwardness, not in sociological outwardnesses, that Key located women's, as well as men's liberation.

Thus, only once the Swedish Social Democrats themselves had identified with a Swedish "people's home," could they hope to absorb Key in their "mothers and children" welfare policies. But how much of Key's individualism might dissolve away in their embrace was another question.

Feminism and Class: Dilemmas of the Social Democrats

Meanwhile, the sharpest new voices in pre-World War I feminism were affirming class. Younger women like Dalström, Anna Sterky, and Elma Sundqvist—well-educated, well-bred, coming to adulthood in the radical 1880s, contemptuous of the Bremer Society's ties to court and bureaucracies—took up socialism in a hard, ideological form and questioned feminism altogether.[41] At the Swedish Social Democrat party congress of 1897, Dalström insisted that women did not have their own interests; she questioned separate women's sections and unions, declaring that there was no woman question within the labor movement. She even expressed doubts about woman suffrage: who would benefit but the bourgeoisie, for who but bourgeois women would vote? One of the party's finest speakers, Dalström insisted that her job was to speak not just to women but to men, and not just on women's issues either. At the Malmö Workers' League in 1889, Elma Sundqvist declared that the poverty suffered by women workers would be overcome only by common ownership of the means of production, and another speaker, one Fru Vestdahl, asking "What Do We Want?," answered that she wanted society transformed so that the capitalists could no longer take the lion's share. These were as much men's as women's issues.

None of this, however, meant an easy relationship between such orthodox Socialist women and their party, or even their unions. At the SSD party congress of 1905, Agda Ostlund warned the leaders that women workers' ignorance of socialism was the labor movement's main handicap. This was not simply to say that women were the problem. Socialist men had problems. To the Malmö group (the first working women's group in Sweden founded in 1888), Axel Danielsson, a Socialist (and husband-to-be of Elma Sundqvist), warned that if women got the same rights as men, the institution of marriage would vanish. The following year, at the party congress, Danielsson said that separate women's political organizations would be not only inconsistent with socialist theory but "unnatural." Some of the deeper roots of this were dug into at the 1905 congress. Erika Lindqvist, agreeing on the urgent necessity for propaganda work among women workers, went on to point out how difficult it was to find instructors. Lindqvist named one man who would do, because he at least "was one of the few men who do not

see in a woman a sex-object rather than a comrade." When Frans
Binnkvist of Stockholm announced at the same congress that women
were no good in organizational work since, after a spurt of enthusiasm,
they soon put organizational duties second to home duties, Ruth Pet-
tersson responded by ascribing his views to "unmotivated hate of
women."

Such potentials for friction seemed strewn everywhere. The Social
Democrats' youth group had pursued a campaign against dirty books.
A women workers' club in Göteborg sent a statement of support to the
party paper, including a call to all women: "Find out what is being
offered in the book stalls! See what gets into the hands of children. . . .
It is shameful for this to be offered for sale in the marketplace." Although he published the statement, the newspaper's editor added his
comment: "We have not refused to print the above, which is a beautiful
example of women's club mentality. . . . Censorship of legal literature—
that's what socialism means to the women. Father, forgive them."
Thereupon the editor of *Morgonbris*, a Women's National Trade Union
paper, replied:

No doubt working-class women have to learn what's what, but one could wish
that within our party they might be allowed to express an honest opinion
without provoking sneers. . . . Our manly party-friends should learn something
too: we are taking our rights to speak our minds not only on party matters but
on any other questions that are close to us, whether as workers or as mothers.[42]

No doubt the top level of party leaders, and certainly Hjalmar Branting, were most sensitive to the hurts and cross-purposes generated by
trying to combine class and sex. But the union leaders were surely not
as sensitive. In all sectors of the labor market, even where women were
the heavy majority of workers, as in textiles, men were more highly
organized than women. Nothing in Swedish labor leadership, or in
Swedish Social Democratic leadership, overcame the tendencies that
produced patterns in Sweden similar to those everywhere else.[43] Yet
even in this earliest period the meaning of this pattern had a special
Swedish inflection. Even though Swedish working women, like working
women elsewhere, joined unions less often than did men; even though
Swedish women, like their sisters elsewhere, worked in pink-collar
ghettos for less pay than men; even though Swedish union women failed
to win a proportional influence in their unions and their party, still, the
deepest problem for women in the unions and their party was located
less in whatever outside forces explained these things than in the heads
of such women as Dalström, Sterky, Sundqvist, and Ostlund. Rejecting
both the elite feminism of the Bremer Society and Key's individualistic
suspicions of socialism, they supposedly stood for solving women's

problems through solving the problems of the working class. Justice and equality for women would follow from justice and equality for all workers. Yet it was reasonably apparent that what the unions and party provided of keenest interest to these women was careers. Indeed Dalström, even as a member of the Social Democrats, also served on the board of directors of Stockholm's General Women's Club in 1896, where professional and working women shared concerns. In effect, Dalström too was a professional woman. But were careers really the goal of socialism for working women at large? Essentially, Dalström, Sterky, and their colleagues were working in the interests of women who did not share their own personal ambitions. While the basic commitment of the unions and party to a family wage for full-time work did not necessarily imply that women workers should be content with less, neither unions nor party ever urged that all women should become like all men, full-time workers.

Paradoxically, it was outside the unions and their party that Swedish feminism's resolution of the tension between individualism and, if not socialism, then at least a concern for the whole, was clearest. The greatest spokeswoman for woman suffrage, who toured the country for years, had been neither a "Fredrikorna"—a Bremer Society member— nor a socialist, but a professor of what would one day be called "social work" and a Liberal, Ann Margaret Holmgren. The organization of the Landsföreningen för kvinnans politiska röstratt (National Woman Suffrage Association) in 1903 came from her, along with another social worker and teacher, Emilia Broome, and a school principal, Anna Whitlock, both Liberals, as well as a Fredrikorna, Gertrud Adelborg. From 25 chapters and about 4,000 members in 1904, the LKPR grew to over 17,000 members in 200 chapters by 1913. These women were in touch with activists in other countries and brought an international suffrage congress to Stockholm in 1911.[44]

In these groups support was strong for fundamental revisions, at last, in the marriage laws. Wives received powers over property equal to those of their husbands. Wives got the right to take jobs without their husband's permission. In the Liberal Party itself, an organized women's section had been accustomed to simply support the party's program, but in 1923 the Liberal Women announced a program of their own, an act presumably more significant for having been taken at all than for any specific demands. But one of the Liberal women's concerns had a special reverberation. School reformers of the nineteenth century had insisted upon the importance of abolishing class distinctions in the schools, and the feminists among them had stressed the importance of abolishing sexual inequality. Now, in the spirit of Ellen Key, the Liberal women attacked the new school system as detrimental to individuality.

The schools were becoming like factories, "milling" students into standardized products. Here was a concern consistent with all that free-trade tradition of both liberalism and Liberalism in Sweden, a tradition that had always insisted that what Sweden needed most was freedom. But the Liberal women's criticism of the equalizing schools had a special twist, again in Key's manner: the processing of Swedish children followed a standard developed for boys. In effect, Swedish girls were being processed into men. The schools must recognize sexual differences.[45]

Yet, that these crosscurrents within middle-class liberal feminism might issue after all in some kind of powerful new emphasis upon opening careers, professions, new roles, and new lives for growing numbers of individual young women seemed less likely in the 1920s than before World War I. By then, the "social work" side of Ann Margaret Holmgren's evangel had begun to mature. The Centralförbundet för Socialt Arbete (The National Association for Social Work, or C.S.A.), had been started in 1903 on the initiative of an investigator into women's occupations and conditions of work, Gerda Meyerson. It became a gathering place for a variety of organizations with special concerns, such as the Federation of Charities and the Cooperative Union. Here, in the C.S.A., the Fredrika Bremer Society met the Social Democrats' Stockholm Women's Club. Out of the C.S.A. emerged groups occupied with poor relief, criminology, housing. A program for training people in social and communal work began in 1909. A kind of shadow policy for eventual state consolidation had been generated, waiting only for powers to tax to be fully confirmed. In 1920 the impulse of the C.S.A. led to the Institute of Social Politics in Stockholm, which later spawned branches in Lund and Göteborg. This rich scheme for a welfare society found important reinforcement in practical areas. The schoolteachers formed their union in 1906 and Swedish nurses theirs in 1910; they did not necessarily have the widest social purposes in view, but even in their pursuit of narrow economic dignity they guaranteed crucial staff to the rising communal welfare system.[46]

There was ambiguity in this emerging welfare culture. For welfare professionals themselves, welfare culture meant careers, just as socialism meant careers for Dalström and her colleagues. But did the welfare leaders' careers offer a model for women in general? Welfare leaders hoped to rescue poor women from want, prostitutes from degradation, the vulnerable from crime. Yet this was perfectly compatible with wishing to see them safely back in snug Swedish homes and families. Even the aim of improving education had no inevitable feminist cut. Did welfare leaders hope or not hope that more women, perhaps many, possibly most, would aspire to jobs, careers, professions?

Moreover, since they were not part of labor unions or Social Democratic politics, they could not fancy themselves to be reforming the work that thousands of Swedish women were in fact already doing in factories, shops, stores, banks, and co-ops, by trying to make it less routine, less underpaid, less unfulfilling, less alienating. The welfare complex could very well contribute to keeping traditional Sweden traditional.

By no means was the labor-based politics of Swedish Social Democracy the saving alternative. As the Social Democrats in 1928 pridefully called for equality in poverty, they revealed some incomprehension not just of the meaning of economic abundance but of individualism. Yet when the Farmers' Party gained four seats, and the Conservatives eight, while the Liberals gained none, no one else appeared to be defending liberal individualism successfully either.[47] Ellen Key's motherhood had not been intended to offer security but strength, just as Strindberg's socialism had not meant to offer safety but joy—"brutal" joy, if necessary. What if the equalities of the *folkshem* slaked feelings of envy and jealousy rather than thirsts for freedom and opportunity?

The Anxiety of Motherhood: Elin Wägner

One of the new, younger feminist writers, Elin Wägner (1882–1949), caught some of the ambiguities and ambivalences in this scene.[48] Wägner had been a young friend of Key's, a visitor at Key's country home, a follower of sorts. In *Pennskaft* (The Penholder), 1910, she had resumed the kind of liberal tradition that had been opened up by earlier women writers, such as Benedictsson in the 1880s, but not carried forward, the tradition of the individual determined to find her way alone in a world designed, not for women, but by men and for men. But by the 1930s Wägner had embarked upon a more literally autobiographical work, intended to be emblematic of the Swedish woman's experience generally since the turn of the century. In one volume, *Genomskada* (Unmasked), 1937, she presented a lightly fictionalized sketch of Key in a spirit of teasing admiration. Showing "the good aunt" preaching motherhood to a younger generation, some of them uncomprehending, others moved to reverence and tears, Wägner went on to write an openly political book entitled *Väckarklocka* (The Alarm Clock), published in 1941, in which she reached for a fully feminist analysis of the catastrophe that had overtaken Europe.

Looking back to the beginning of postwar reform in Sweden, she recalled with some pride the spirit of the Liberal women in 1923, who had hoped to redeem institutions. She did not doubt the greater justice in the new laws respecting marriage. She of course welcomed the end of the old degradation of regulated prostitution. But Wägner wondered why the reforms seemed to observe certain limits—why, for instance, sexual expression outside marriage remained under police regulations. Further, Wägner noted that when the Myrdals raised the cry of a population crisis in the early 1930s, the Population Commission had severed the question from the question of peace, in effect aiming to depoliticize it, to sterilize it of political meaning. She suggested that the peace movement and the decline in fertility had been linked phenomena, both essentially a women's protest against a society increasingly lethal to human growth. Her heroine was the pacifist Jane Addams. She noted that birth-control propaganda as such was strongly class-linked. She judged that for the peace movement to survive, a strong spirit of motherliness was essential, as among the Sardinian or Balkan mothers demonstrating during World War I. Searching for a larger reading of the times, she reached back to Johan Jakob Bachofen and his theory of an age of matriarchy. She understood the scholarly criticism that Bachofen had incurred, but noted that without Bachofen she—and others—might still labor under the delusion that prior to the Greeks, prior to Western civilization, there had been only primitivism, tyranny, chaos. She recalled how Robert Briffault, author of *The Mothers*, had found meaning and order where traditional anthropologists had seen only curiosities in those early times. She noted several brilliant studies by women scholars in Germany developing cultural history from the perspective of women. And in Fanina Halle's *Frauen des Ostens* she noted the story of women of Moslem Central Asia in the Soviet Union who, awakened by Lenin's ukase and the Women's Department, had dropped their veils and learned to read, write, and chair the village Soviets.[49]

Clearly, Wägner wanted women to lead a movement of profound social change. Nothing less would speak to the times, measured best by the war and the declining birthrate. Quoting an early historian of Swedish feminism, Lydia Wahlström, she noted that feminist politics before 1890 had been a man's affair, the work of Swedish Liberals primarily concerned for women's legal equality. Ellen Key, she said, had inaugurated the real women's feminist movement with her ethic of love. But love must not serve the (male) institutions that had brought Europe to disaster.

In effect, Wägner called for a completely new feminist politics. Women's gains had mattered little because they had not been won by women. Women had not won the vote; men had won it for them. Women had not shaped and shared in the debates over contraception. Even "radical" Social Democratic women had thought of themselves as dependent on their men. Wägner noted how, in the early 1930s, economic depression had led to new attacks on working women, often joined by working men's wives. Proposals for subsidizing motherhood, guaranteeing prenatal care, and guaranteeing child support, stimulated by the population crisis, implicitly invited women back to passivity at home. The specific cry, that some women at least must once again undertake to bear four children, invidiously commented upon those who would choose to have none. "Our population debate has been a male monologue."[50] Underneath lurked the obvious horror, that babies were needed because war could not be stopped. So it seemed evident that new departures were called for. Wägner recommended that women work outside the parties as well as within, with the obvious implication that the parties were inadequate and that women must become an independent force on their own, as women.

In all of this, Wägner asserted, the single greatest obstacle was women themselves. Women suffered from a form of unawareness. They were unaware of how organized modern society had damaged them. They had lost their own history. In thus reviving the old idea of a kind of maternal prehistory before history, Wägner was raising for herself the problem implicit in old Swedish idylls of equality. If the modern world of abstraction, of centralization, of declining birthrates, of war, was hostile to essential womanhood, then was Sweden itself, still neutral, less centralized, at least potentially more social-democratic, perhaps slightly less hostile? Was Swedish feminist criticism of the world implicitly at least a retreat into little Sweden? Wägner made no concessions on this account. She asserted plainly that the route for Swedish women was not that of simply demanding equality in jobs in the Swedish marketplace. That would only perpetuate women's alienation in a world they never made. The world was to be remade. In the world women had once made they had always worked, just as they had borne and raised children. A world constantly forcing choices between home and marketplace, between work and sociability, between love and politics, sex and security, was not worth saving. A complete rethinking of the relationship between home and industry was indicated. The question of whether work required the large-scale organizations supposedly mandated by modern industry needed reopening.

How this perpetuated Ellen Key's ultimate evangel of love, Wägner did not say. Had loving motherhood prevailed in those long ages hidden behind history, in "prehistory"? Wägner had not quite revived Bremer's *Hertha*, for she took Key's sexual teaching for granted, but by doing so she had dulled whatever radical edge it might have had, letting it seem that sex too—Key's "free love"—like the vote, like contraception, like protective welfare laws, had mattered little in changing the world.

No such women's movement as Wägner hoped for ever even began to emerge in Sweden. The motherhood subsidies of the Social Democratic governments would undercut any potential that motherhood might serve as the basis for dramatic social change such as Wägner, and Key before her, had imagined. Challenging the Social Democrats would be far harder than challenging a free market that abandoned motherhood to private care. For women impatient at confinement to domesticity and motherhood and with resources for breaking beyond them, women who in America were the inspiritors and constituents of individualistic feminism, a vision like Wägner's could only seem retrograde. Without necessarily agreeing that their hope was to make it in a man's world, such women might find the call back to mother right more coercive than fulfilling. They might be prepared to try to juggle divided lives. Paradoxically, of course, they too would not find modern Sweden comfortable and encouraging. Those who sought to make it on their own still had to pay the high taxes for the social insurance system.

Equality—for What?

In 1956 Alva Myrdal, collaborating with the English psychoanalyst Viola Klein, published *Women's Two Roles*. The book picked up a theme generated out of the Population Commission's lengthy reports back in the 1930s and distilled by Myrdal in her book of 1940, *Nation and Family*. In both books Myrdal assumed that most women wanted jobs and careers, and undertook to show that affording them such jobs and careers would also benefit society. The book of 1956 somewhat sharpened that theme, declaring that it was the "need of society" that all "available labor resources, male and female," be utilized. It speculated that in the future "it will be . . . impossible to exempt" women from work. Just why this was so Myrdal and Klein did not explain. In the Soviet Union the need of society for women's work would be clearly proclaimed by the central committee of the ruling party. Who had spelled out such a need in Sweden? (Or in England, for that matter?) In the same year in which Myrdal had published *Nation and Family*, Wägner had deeply questioned whether more jobs and careers in society as it was, and specifically in Sweden as it was, would benefit women. The kind of work women wanted, women who were conscious of women's nature, was not, she said, automatically provided by the job market. Myrdal and Klein tried to preempt this ground, too, implicitly:

. . . .The futility of existence in the upper middle class was the very mainspring which motivated the social revolution usually called the emancipation of women. . . .

Those who oppose the extension of married women's work outside their homes in the name of tradition, have fixed their eyes . . . on the nineteenth century. Such traditionalists would be well advised to look a bit further back.
. . .

Revolutionary as . . . outside work for married women may appear . . . it is a readjustment, under changed conditions, to a more equitable division of labour between the sexes such as existed before . . . industrialization . . . if women are today leaving their homes to set out on a new road to work, this is a road which will take them "back home" to their proper place in the community.[51]

But however well this might have fitted English history, it had little purchase on Sweden. The woes of upper-middle-class futility had never defined a cutting edge of Swedish feminism. And in neither Sweden nor England were data cited to suggest that women's work in the 1950s and 1960s might resemble that in, say, the 1750s, let alone in those prehistorical epochs recalled by Wägner.

Women's Two Roles anticipated what was to become the dominant theme in Swedish feminism in the 1960s and on into the 1970s. As long as women had two roles and men only one, women would still suffer from inequality. The answer was plain: men must share roles with women, men too must have two roles. Myrdal and Klein explicitly formulated this position:

Making husbands, and fathers, full partners in the affairs of their families, instead of mere *"visiteurs du soir,"* seems to us so much to be desired that, with a general shortening of working time in mind, we think the full-time employment of married women preferable to their doing part-time work.[52]

Obviously, here Myrdal and Klein gave no thought not just to Wägner but to such writers on marriage and family as Strindberg. Their indifference to Key's perspective was obvious. In Bremer, Key, and Wägner, Swedish feminism had flowed from positive wishes, hopes, desires. It had expressed what some women wanted both for themselves and for all women sharing their feelings. In Myrdal-Klein's *Women's Two Roles* feminism took on abstract and universalistic dimensions. Myrdal and Klein told women they were not to be exempted from work; not their needs but the needs of society were imperative. In a spirit of perfect equality, Myrdal and Klein extended the same logic to men. Swedish men had not evinced a dissatisfaction with their roles in their families. But Myrdal and Klein were able to discern from the perspective of their abstract egalitarianism the desirability of some new scheme of sharing in the family, just as they were able to discern that the preference of many Swedish women for part-time work was not to be rejected in favor of full-time employment. Neither Bremer nor Key nor Wägner had thought in these terms. They had thought from the perspective of

womanhood, of what was womanly, of a world remade on the foundations of womanliness if only because the world that had ignored it was
crumbling. Which would finally prove to be most "Swedish," this tradition of womanhood or the outlook of abstract, internationally minded
reformers, was at issue in Swedish politics.

In 1962 the sex-role debate in Sweden was brought to a hard focus
by writer-journalist Eva Moberg in her long essay *Kvinnor och människor* (Women and Men).[53] Moberg rehearsed the data that showed
women underrepresented in the councils of the unions and the central
committees of the parties. She noted the special backwardness of the
party most committed to welfare and equality, the Social Democrats.
But the roots of all this went deep. In "organization Sweden" even
students' organizations mattered, and they too showed the same bent.
As Moberg noted, the Swedish Student Union constituted a kind of
training ground in the universities for later leadership in political,
social, and welfare institutions. The student electorate at Lund, she
noted, though 40 percent women, chose hardly any women at all for
leadership posts. In Stockholm, where 47 percent of the student electorate was female, only two of the seventeen members of the steering
committee were women. Uppsala's students, a third of them women,
elected one woman to a board of twelve. Moberg refused to consider
whether such data registered deliberation, consciousness, self-consciousness, or choice. For her, they registered wrongness, inertia, the
unredeemed past.

After 1962, discussion spread beyond the intellectuals. All the labor
organizations now spoke out on the sex-role question. So did the Swedish Employer's Association. A political program, *Kvinnans jämlikhet*
(The Equality of Women), was published in 1964 with contributions
from members of the government. In a radio debate late in 1967 sponsored by the Fredrika Bremer Association, all five major political parties
were asked to explain their views on sex roles. Naturally, Swedish social
scientists were hard at work devising research on the matter. The
Swedish government reported to the United Nations in 1968: "There
are probably few countries in which the roles of men and women in the
family and in society have been so thoroughly analysed and discussed
as in Sweden during the 1960's."[54] While conceding that "practical
equality" between men and women would not appear "for a long time
to come," the report radiated certitude that equality was what mattered, and that the nature of equality was known. A certain peremptory
note again crept in:

Today there are 700,000 Swedish women under the age of 65 not gainfully employed, who are not looking after children, not ill and do not study, but who somehow or another are getting a living. No men enjoy such an existence.[55]

Moberg's tears for men were crocodile: she had no new evidence that men were eager to get these women to work. Moberg did concede that 200,000 of these women would work, could they but find work, but that left 500,000 unexplained. It again appeared that women had not just the right but the duty to work.

In 1968 the Social Democrat soon to be prime minister, Olaf Palme, speaking to American Democratic women in Washington, D.C., declared that his government had recognized that women could not have true equality in the marketplace unless they had it at home as well. Therefore, he said, the Swedish government had propounded a demand for "male emancipation."[56] Since what he had just discussed had been the conditions for "female emancipation," it was not clear why what he had in mind was an "emancipation" for men at all. Typically, like the authors of Sweden's *Report to the United Nations* on the status of Swedish women, Palme carefully blurred the question not only of where the demands for "male emancipation" were coming from, but also regarding the kinds of indices of women's progress utilized in the report.[57] Like the *Report*, Palme systematically wove back and forth between "rights" and "duties" without explaining any differences. In 1974 "paternity leave" was in fact written into the Swedish law alongside maternity leave. The Social Democrats were not yet ready for coercion, however. The law was permissive, not mandatory, though it did offer extra rewards to couples both of whom availed themselves of their opportunity. Soon, egalitarians were debating a thirty-hour week for parents. Hardly any disagreed that the option should be available for both father and mother. But should thirty hours of work be paid the same as forty hours? If not, would not many parents feel unable to avail themselves of the right? And would not most couples decide to leave the husband on full-time work while his wife went onto part-time?

As the imaginative energy of Swedish lawmakers explored ever more distant frontiers of equality, Swedish feminism itself grew less, not more, energetic. The Fredrika Bremer Society ticked on, but hardly as a large or militant force. A number of Socialist women calling themselves Group 8 had appeared, but far more out of irritation with the Social Democrats' Women's Federation than from some upwelling of new energy. This muting and even muffling of the voice of feminism by no means followed from some sense of complacency, some certitude that, in Sweden, the task was done, feminism no longer needed. One visitor found quite a different inhibition:

Talking with Swedish women, one gets the impression that they are less concerned with job satisfaction than they are disturbed at being forced to work. Swedish women, particularly professional women, seem to be much less achievement oriented than their American counterparts. They are more reluctant to engage in outright competition with men . . . nowhere does this reluctance to compete with men show up more strongly than in the radical feminist organizations themselves. Feminism seems almost to have been an afterthought in Sweden—voicing ideological principles rather than pushing in any practical way to revolutionize social relationships.[58]

Such a judgment may have been speculative, even fanciful, but much suggested that the further Sweden moved toward equalizing men and women, especially husbands and wives, the murkier issues seemed to become. One feminist who was outspoken, Birgitta Wistrand, noted how a conceptual shift had been occuring in the 1970s. Whereas once the familiar old word "jämlikhet" had served, now another word, "quite new to the Swedish language," had emerged, "jämställdhet." As Wistrand explained, the old word, "equality," had meant treating men and women as though they were the same. The new word recognized that they were different. Both were still "entitled to the same practical opportunities in family life, working life, and society." But that did not mean men and women were not different. Ironically enough, according to Wistrand, it was Sweden's own relative success at achieving equality that had lent the matter its importance:

Sweden, despite all that remains to be done, is a more integrated country than most in the sense that women are involved in one way or another in virtually every aspect of national life. This can make it difficult for women as a group to stake out their own domain and develop their own ideas.[59]

From this standpoint, then, it seemed that Swedish Social Democracy had been all too successful.

Yet neither Wistrand nor any Swedish feminist group proceeded to clarify just what differences might follow from pursuit of *jämställdhet*—equality of opportunity—rather than plain equality. Was it possible, for instance, that pursuing equality of opportunity rather than equality of condition meant accepting the situation Eva Moberg had deplored: women's absence from positions of influence and power as a choice of women themselves? If Swedish women were in fact already well integrated in the nation, what reason was there any longer to assume they were not capable of deciding what they wanted? Wistrand was not ready for any such concession. In speculating on the question "Why do women not vote for women?" she identified with a grievance about politics itself.

Sometimes one can wonder just how seriously politicians grapple with the really difficult political issues. It seems that those issues that do become politically important are not necessarily the real or important questions for the individual person in our society. When women are asked why they are not more politically active, they often point to the fact that the political debate is so uninteresting. Politics deal with the wrong issues, they complain—not with those issues that concern them most.[60]

But Wistrand knew better. In Sweden politics had dealt with the issues that presumably concerned women most—child support, day care, parental leave, a wife's equality as wage earner, and so on. Much might remain to be done, but feminists could not fault politics as irrelevant. The real problem for Swedish feminists was to explain how Swedish Social Democracy could have prevailed without women in places of power. It was this puzzle that drew Wistrand on to claim nuclear energy and peace as women's issues. But questions of energy and national security were not issues of equality at all, whether jämlikhet or jäm-ställdhet. Men had as much at stake in them as women. Evidently, what was needed was not better or different issues but a transformation in the very culture of politics.

Today politics is often conducted on terms dictated by "unliberated" men. Those men who take their full share of family responsibility have no time for politics. They are helping to care for the home and children. Evening and weekend meetings keep many parents of small children from becoming actively involved in politics.[61]

But just what was the reform this correlation between unliberated men and politics implied? When Wistrand declared that "a fair representation—50 percent women—would . . . make possible a change in the way political work is carried out," it was as logical to conclude that some sufficient number of women should be liberated from child-rearing in order to be free for politics as that unliberated men should not be eligible for politics.

For Wistrand and the egalitarian Social Democratic feminists of Sweden, the sex that really needed help, the sex that really needed a chance to "develop its own ideas" and realize its own best interests, was men, not women. Men should be helped to see that housework and child-rearing were "to the benefit of [their] own personal growth and maturity." Women must " 'allow' men to try out other ways of living. . . ." What Wistrand hoped for she saw already coming to pass:

More and more men have begun to discover new sides of themselves, new needs and desires. As a result, some have chosen to "drop out" and turn their backs on a career. In the past few years several politicians have made emphatic exits from public life, explaining that they wanted more time for themselves and their families.[62]

Since the feminist meaning in such anecdotes could only have been that each male dropout opened a place for a woman, the appeal to men's sense of "personal growth and maturity" was disingenuous. In the United States, the National Organization of Women had already gone so far as to hire men to spread the same evangel among their fellows.[63]

In the final reckoning, the Swedish Social Democratic feminists were not interested in reviving Fredrika Bremer and the idea of women's special point of view. They continued to stand for equality, not just equality of opportunity. "There is the basic question of justice. Women comprise 51 percent of the electorate and ought therefore to hold half the elective places." But since women, who could at any time have elected more women, did not, Wistrand found herself in the end demanding that women be like men after all.

We must urge women to go into production, to take the initiative, to be enterprising, to accomplish more. Up to now it has nearly been taboo for women to work with money or to earn a lot of money. . . . Why should it be "uglier" for a woman to have a high income than for a man? . . . Why should women refrain from or be barred from taking the most desirable and highest-paid jobs?

Obviously this could carry all the way to undermining the very politics that had impelled women's equality in the first place:

Is it possible to talk about women wanting and needing careers in private companies, about the importance of their getting influential and well-paid jobs, without being accused of speaking up for capitalism, competition and political conservatism?[64]

As Swedish feminism drifted, the significance of the marketplace equalities already achieved too grew ambiguous. As the individual income tax reform of 1970 indicated, Swedish policy had aimed to "eradicate" the "principle of the man as a chief wage earner in the family." But did this mean that women were to become capable of earning enough to be a family's chief wage earner? No Swedish politician or feminist pronounced this goal, for the plain reason that it opened the prospect of men finding it easier to withdraw from family responsibility, the prospect of a Sweden filled with mother-headed families. Then was the new policy meant to produce families supported by two-wage earners? families requiring the wages of two earners? No politician or feminist ever quite announced this goal either, for the obvious reason that it contradicted on its face the general commitment of the nation to ever greater abundance and an ever-rising standard of living. But statistics could well have begun to reflect such a policy. As young Swedes more and more abstained from marriage, they were not necessarily more and more living alone. On the contrary, a higher proportion of women were living with a man, married or not, in 1980 than in the previous half century. Few Swedish feminists extolled separation from men. Few offered discourse on the superiorities of lesbian affinities. Yet just what was the inwardness of the new modes and mores of living together in egalitarianized Sweden? For all the exhaustive discussion of part-time versus full-time jobs, of parental leaves, of gender-skewed union councils, a strange discretion seemed to prevail on the ultimate relations between men and women. Swedes had won easy access to contraceptives in the 1960s, and programs of sex education had become universal in the schools, but on sexual relations, "openness, candour and honesty [do] not seem particularly widespread in Sweden."[65] It was possible that change was underway. In 1976, when various changes in the laws on rape were proposed, women's groups demanded and got the appointment of a commission to study the whole question. By the late Seventies wife-beating had been taken up for public discussion. The decade saw a kind of minor efflorescence in women's autobiographical writing. Yet it was just as possible that, in the mini-revolution young Swedes had already wrought, loosening the tight bonds of marriage in favor of consensual unions, they were seeking to hold off confrontation. The first people in history freed by economics and politics to give first priority to the dramas of private life, Swedes may have sensed reasons to quail from the prospect. They may have begun to suspect that in the depths of sexual intimacy still more monsters of inequality and power politics lurked, ones no schemes of social insurance or housework-sharing could pacify. Strindberg would have understood. So did Ingmar Bergman.

Confronted by the reluctance of women themselves, Wistrand might have decided to settle for the strategy of invigorating women to larger aspirations. Instead, with "decision-making bodies" in mind, she turned to another tactic—quotas."Everyone agrees that quotas should not be the first resource in achieving certain goals," she agreed, but then proceeded to list reasons why quotas sometimes were justified. Quotas could assure a "wide range of background experience," but she herself had observed that Swedish women had not been forward in "staking out their own domain," and of course she had urged them to adopt men's goals. Another reason was that "there is no way to make the process of individual selection objectively valid," but since she had no case to make that quotas were any better, this was at best wholly a negative argument. A third reason was that quotas could be "the only way to effect a desired change," but Wistrand had had to wrestle with the fact that Swedish women had not registered desire for a change. As for men, she agreed that "of course" quotas would be "hard" on "those men forced to leave their positions to make way for women." One who clearly did desire the change was Wistrand. She was not deterred by the fact that she found herself in a small minority. The idea of equality through coercion had finally penetrated to the heart of militant Swedish feminism. The last of her arguments still stood apart, on its own, irrefutable: quotas might "insure justice for various population groups."[66] But Wistrand's own generalization of the issue, beyond women to "various" groups, illustrated the political problem: which groups? who would choose them? Feminism had had its roots in real history, and had addressed itself to real societies. Here it was becoming abstract.

6 Soviet Russia. Suppression

Feminists before the Revolution

As Richard Stites has shown, Russian feminism flourished in the years 1905–7.[1] When the Czar's autocracy seemed about to yield to parliamentary government, feminists won support from the liberal landlords' Kadet party; from the Trudoviks, the non-Marxist workers' party; and from the peasant-oriented Socialist Revolutionaries. The aristocrats' Octobrists remained hostile. So did the Marxist Social Democrats, Menshevik and Bolshevik alike. Only the extremes, on both right and left, rejected feminist initiatives. Had the broad center had its chance to thrive, feminism would almost surely have thrived with it. With at least three leading factions of their own, feminists were neither monolithic nor homogeneous. They differed on the same issues feminists differed over in the West. Yet something like unity prevailed on one issue, the suffrage. Had the promise of 1905–7 for parliamentary government survived, Russian feminists might very likely have resembled their American sisters in leaving their differences for later resolution while pursuing together the goal of entrée into political life. The vote actually was won for women in one part of the empire, Finland. Finnish feminists, identifying with Finnish nationalist demands for still greater autonomy within the empire, had become, by early 1906, the first feminists in the world to claim, with justification, that by their own efforts they had won suffrage for themselves. This victory just next door constituted a powerful stimulus to the feminists of St. Petersburg and Moscow. The largest Russian feminist group, the Union for Women's Equality, reached out to link hands with the International Women's Suffrage Alliance, founded by American and English feminists in 1902; in 1906 Russian feminists attended the IWSA's congress in Copenhagen. Russian feminists were breaking out of their isolation.

With the quenching of liberal hope by the reassertion of police and autocracy, feminists between 1908 and 1914 found even simple sisterhood difficult. Proselytizing was out of the question. Even so, one of the feminist groups managed to hold an All-Russian Women's Congress in St. Petersburg in 1908. It ended in uproar, anger, and walkouts. While the government had been by no means helpful, the cause for disruption came from the left. Although the leading woman Marxist, Alexandra

Kolontai, had left Russia fearing arrest, her Social Democratic col-leagues attended the congress as a "labor group" in order to attack the feminists as a bourgeois movement irrelevant to the problems of work-ers. Feminists were thus the target not only of the Czar's reasserted autocracy, but of the increasingly ideological revolutionaries. Should the Czar's autocracy collapse, feminism might flourish once again, but not without enemies.

Bolshevik Feminism

The responsiveness of the Provisional Government of March to No-vember 1917 to feminist hopes and demands revived and sustained feminist organizations, but feminists were granted no chance to test the Left.[2] The inchoate yet powerful impulses toward liberation among peasant women remained beyond their reach. The fact that it was a woman, Maria Spiridonova, who emerged from a Czarist prison to head the Left Socialist Revolutionaries, tended to foreclose opportunities for liaison, since Spiridonova remained a revolutionary of the old breed, intent on social, economic, and political revolution and—still—a de-fender of terror. At the same time the Social Democrats, with Kollontai prominent among them, agitated persistently among working-class women against the feminists. As the Petrograd Soviet moved toward a focus on workers' politics, the thesis that women's interests depended on class interests took concrete form, for the workers dominant in the Soviet could not possibly be denigrated as the source of women's oppres-sion. Thus, although its enemy to the right had collapsed, Russian feminism's enemy to the left loomed as a more powerful adversary even before the Bolsheviks seized power. As Lenin and his colleagues liqui-dated political opposition, the last supports for feminism were under-mined.

Among the Bolsheviks seizing power in Russia in November 1917, there were women of stature: Lenin's wife; his sister; his long-time friend Inessa Armand; the party functionary Elena Stasova, "Comrade Absolute," armed with her ever-ready briefcase, keeper of party rec-ords; and Alexandra Kollontai, a Menshevik won to Lenin in 1914 by his stand on the war, and one of the conspicuous Bolshevik speechmak-ers on the streets of Petrograd in the hectic weeks before November.[3] There was also a returnee or two from exile, like Lenin—Angelica Balabanoff, for example. Some, such as Stasova, wanted a career in the party, but not necessarily in a position involved with women. Others such as Krupskaya, Lenin's wife, clearly held women's concerns first in their hearts but just as clearly took it for granted that Marxist doctrine was correct: women's concerns would be met in the context of the larger concern. Still others, Balabanova among them, held the classic, romantic, genderless revolutionary view that general justice would mean general freedom.

The youngest of these women, Kollontai shared all these outlooks to a degree, but also another. Kollontai had found from experience, dating back to her first associations with the Social Democrats in 1905 in St. Petersburg, that the men in the party needed to be urged to support political work among women. Their orthodoxy on feminism led them to think about women only in the future, after the revolution, not in the present, when the revolution was still to be made. Kollontai pressed her Bolshevik colleagues to set forth an active mobilization of women. Lenin was reluctant. The plans Kollontai urged upon him in 1919, for going directly to women in the name of women's own concerns, struck him as feminism revived. In 1920, however, he agreed to establish a Women's Department—*Zhenotdel*—over the objections of some skeptics.[4] The department was not granted the sort of autonomies Kollontai had wanted for it, and, as if to underline that fact, Lenin appointed his friend Inessa Armand to head it, passing over Kollontai. Armand's mission was to sell Bolshevism to women by direct propaganda and, indirectly, by services helpful to women, whether in factories, villages, or domestic relations courts.

Upon Armand's death in the cholera epidemic of September 1920, Kollontai finally received the post she wanted, clear evidence of the credibility she still enjoyed in Lenin's eyes. Propagandizing women was wholly to Kollontai's taste. But propagandizing alone was not enough. Women's problems were special and she could not resist turning to them. Concerned over hundreds of thousands of women left destitute by the wars, Kollontai gave a speech to regional heads of the Women's Department, "Prostitution and Ways of Fighting It."[5] She expounded a traditionally socialist environmentalist outlook. But what was to be done? Since prostitution would no longer exist under socialism, could not the government simply ignore it in favor of building socialism as fast as possible? By no means. The women needed help. Nor should the prostitutes be treated as criminals. They should be regarded as persons who ought to be put to productive work. Little was exceptional in Kollontai's speech, but it won scant favor. The commissars on the Central Committee thought that the task of the Women's Department was to recruit good Communists, not unfortunates. Were prostitutes likely to make good Communists? Good Communist women were lean, brown, "sturdy and high bosomed," as a novel of the time portrayed them, "striding forward to victory," and committed to "multiply fiercely and rapidly."[6] Prostitutes were not good material for the Communist

New Woman. Talking with the German Communist Clara Zetkin, Lenin had already made the party's attitude clear when he criticized Rosa Luxemburg's work with prostitutes in Hamburg. "Are there really no industrial women . . . in Germany who need organising . . . need a newspaper . . . should be enlisted? This is a morbid deviation."[7]

Kollontai was pressing Lenin and his Communist colleagues at a point where their own theory was thin. Few Marxists had ever spoken thoughtfully in public about sexuality and sex. Following the publication of August Bebel's *Die Frau und der Sozialismus* (Woman and Socialism) in 1883, Marxists considered the topic adequately dealt with and then forgot it. Sexuality under socialism, Bebel had argued, would be freed for its natural, undistorted expression.

[The] individual shall himself oversee the satisfaction of his own instincts. *The satisfaction of the sexual instinct is as much a private concern as the satisfaction of any other natural instinct.* . . . How I shall eat, how I shall drink, how I shall sleep, how I shall clothe myself, is my private affair,—exactly so my intercourse with a person of the opposite sex.[8]

But this formulation had not offered guidance for sexuality before the revolution. Nor did it help guide revolutionaries in the midst of their revolution. Among some good Communists, sexual relations were already being regarded as purely private matters, nobody else's business. Lenin, however, disapproved. To Clara Zetkin he waxed indignant at some comrades' sexual indulgences. He "sprang to his feet, slapped the table . . . and paced up and down the room," Zetkin wrote.

The revolution [he said] calls for concentration and rallying of every nerve. . . . It does not tolerate orgiastic conditions. . . . Promiscuity in sexual matters is bourgeois. . . . The proletariat is a rising class. It does not need an intoxicant . . . neither of sexual laxity or of alcohol. . . . there must be no weakening, no waste and no dissipation of energy.

In fact, Lenin's outlook included more than just the question of how good Communists must behave during the revolution. He contradicted Bebel's famous description of liberated sexuality. "I consider the famous 'glass-of-water' theory as completely un-Marxist and, moreover, as anti-social. It is not only what nature has given but also what has become culture . . . that comes into play in sexual life." Yet when he went on to reveal what he thought to be an admirable kind of sexual life, Lenin forsook Marxism's historical, cultural outlook in favor of his own idea of what was natural and, by plain implication, universal. "One love affair after another" was not right in revolutionary times; it never would be right. The culture that should shape sexuality would be directed to the needs of young people:

Healthy sports, such as gymnastics, swimming, hiking, physical exercises of every description and a wide range of intellectual interests is what they need. ... This will be far more useful to young people than endless lectures and discussions on sex problems and the so-called living by one's nature.

Neither Zetkin nor Lenin seemed conscious of any incongruity in his citation of that supreme formula of classic bourgeois, cold-water, Christian asceticism, *Mens sana in corpore sano*. Thus when Lenin chided Zetkin—"Really, Clara, is this the time to keep working women busy for months at a stretch with such questions as how to love or be loved, how to woo or be wooed?"—he was not simply postponing the time for such questions.[9] He wanted these questions postponed for all time.

For Kollontai, such an outlook undercut any hopes for freedom for the Women's Department. It registered a spirit quite closed to what for her was foremost. Socialism was important not simply because, in its provision of justice and freedom for all, it would provide them for women. There was more to it than that. Women had a special need for socialism. Women were different from men, and in that difference their need for socialism rooted.

The old Bolsheviks—now renamed Communists—who dominated the Politburo were not any more interested politically in sex and sexuality than was Lenin. Late in January 1922, after only fifteen months, Kollanti was fired as head of the Women's Department. With the party still open to debate, Kollontai had joined in the attack on Lenin by the Workers' Opposition group some ten months earlier. The Workers' Opposition argued that the party, instead of presuming to instruct and lead the industrial workers of the Soviets, ought rather to be taking its lead from them. It should be less interested in unity than in democracy. For Kollontai the issue ran parallel to her view on women. In each case her impulse was to immerse herself in a collective life in the here and now. Her old struggle with bourgeois feminism had registered her sense that it resisted collective life in favor of promoting freedom for individual women. In the same way, Lenin's democratic centralism resisted real collective life in favor of control exerted from above.

Lenin rejected the Workers' Opposition sharply, and to Kollontai he responded with a special twist. Some years before, in Norway, Kollontai had been sexually involved with one of the Workers' Opposition leaders, Alexander Schliapnikov. In answering Kollontai, Lenin alluded to this one-time "unity" of her own. Talking with Clara Zetkin, Lenin allowed himself another allusion that could hardly have had anyone but Kollontai as its target: "I will not vouch for the reliability or the endurance of women whose love affair is intertwined with politics, or for the men who run after every petticoat and let themselves in with every young female. No, no, that does not go well with revolution."[10] These were cheap shots. When Kollontai joined the Workers' Opposition, her personal relationship with Schliapnikov had long been over. The "inter-twining" of love with politics most notable in Kollontai's life had been her defense of her husband, Pavel Dybenko, an erstwhile Bolshevik naval commander, against charges of dereliction of duty back in 1918. Since Lenin had gone on to appoint her head of the Women's Department, obviously he had not found her altogether unreliable. Kollontai's loss of support among her Communist colleagues followed from her inability to abandon what occupied the center of her own imagination, the linkage between socialism and sex.

As for the Women's Department, under one of Kollontai's successors, Sophia Smidovich, and her successors in turn, the department went about a standard political task assigned it by the Politburo: to propagandize Moslem women. In the effort to prevent their new Soviet Union from disintegrating into its constituent ethnic parts, the Bolsheviks regarded no area as more ominous than Moslem Central Asia. Differentiated from Russia by race, religion, and culture, the whole vast region had no obvious reason for embracing Communism. Moreover, Marxist theory offered no purchase on the problem. Neither an urban working class nor a rural proletariat existed with whom to ally. However, if Moslem religion was, as it seemed, the oppression of all women by all men, then Moslem women could be viewed as, in Gregory Massell's formulation, a "surrogate proletariat."[11] In the campaign to enlist them, agents of the Women's Department in Central Asia had remarkable careers. Some won adoring women followers. Some were martyred by enraged sons of Allah. Whether Communist success in heading off secession owed much or little to the women of the Women's Department would be difficult to calculate. The assignment nevertheless clearly showed the department's status as a political tool of the leadership. In 1930 Joseph Stalin, finding no more work for it to do, abolished it.

Alexandra Kollontai: The Myth and the Quest

During the hectic Petrograd summer of 1917, Alexandra Kollontai was a conspicuous figure.[12] At forty-five, though no longer young, she radiated health and vivacity. Befitting her cultured girlhood, she dressed with style. Neither then nor later did Kollontai ever affect the standard image of Bolshevik womanhood—grim, lean, short-haired, rifle in hand. All photographs show a beautiful woman, elegant and graceful. One can only speculate that, for some, her fusion of political and sexual vitality was hard to take. Lenin proved to be one, eventually. Another was a twenty-eight-year-old would-be politician, Pitirim Sorokin, whom she apparently bested in open debate. During the hectic summer of 1917, he retaliated in his diary:

Yesterday I disputed at a public meeting with Trotsky and Madame Kollontai. As for this woman, it is plain that her revolutionary enthusiasm is nothing but a gratification of her sexual satyriasis. In spite of her numerous "husbands" Kollontai, first the wife of a general, later the mistress of a dozen men, is not yet satisfied. She seeks new forms of sexual sadism.[13]

In a few years, as some of her writings trickled out to the West under such provocative titles as *Wege der Liebe, La bolchevique enamorada, Red Love,* and most misleading of all, *The Autobiography of a Sexually Emancipated Communist Woman,* Kollontai earned notoriety. As various Western visitors brought back reports that a sexual revolution had followed upon the political, social, and economic ones, she came to appear almost the symbol, even the impresario of uninhibited sexual self-expression, greeted with delight by some, with horror by others. It was all myth-making, slanderous on the one hand, glamorizing on the other. Kollontai was in the right job as commissar of charities and public welfare. She was a social mother. John Reed saw her with "tears streaming down her face," as she arrested striking functionaries in order to get the keys to the door of her ministry in November 1917. But she was not Soviet Russia's Jane Addams. For Kollontai, the solution to the sexual question was not to be found in giving up sex.

Ironically, as her myth grew in the West, her own frustrations mounted. "Now began a dark time in my life," she wrote, looking back from 1926.

There were differences of opinion in the Party. I resigned from my post. . . . Little by little I was . . . relieved of all my other tasks. I again gave lectures and espoused my ideas on "the new woman" and "the new morality." The Revolution was in full swing . . . much of what was happening did not fit in with my outlook. But after all there was still the unfinished task, women's liberation.[14]

The dark time was personal as well as political. During the months of her involvement with the Workers' Opposition that led to her dismissal as head of the Women's Department, her second marriage, to Pavel Dybenko, was also foundering. Yet if Lenin and the revolution were failing her, Kollontai knew that it was she who was failing Dybenko. "[I] know that I cannot give you full happiness . . . I am not the wife you need."[15]

Daughter of a general, Mikhail Domantovich, and married young to Vladimir Kollontai, a man who would become a general, Kollontai had left husband, home, and soon Russia itself for the unsheltered life of radical politics. Barbara Clements has suggested that, in her embrace of Marxism, Kollontai manifested the impulse of a generation more than some personal rebellion. "Marxism was modern, it was European, it was systematic, it was sophisticated, and it was revolutionary." Of course only a tiny minority of the generation took to Marx. Moreover, of those women who did, many if not most—Elena Stasova, Claudia Nicolaeva, Concordia Samoilova, Nadezhda Krupskaya herself—proved reliable and comradely political helpmates whose deepest motivation evidently was to serve. Kollontai was not like that. Her own recollection of her farewell to domesticity was sharply focused: "I loved my husband, but the happy life of a housewife and spouse became for me a 'cage.' "[16]

After Kollontai left home at the age of twenty-six, she spent a decade immersing herself in radical politics in Russia, Germany, and Scandinavia. She apparently avoided any serious relationships with men during those years. A polemic she inserted into the essay she prepared for the confrontation with feminists in St. Petersburg in 1908 hinted at one possible reason why. Her primary targets in the essay, "The Social Basis of the Woman's Question," were of course the feminists themselves and then, implicitly, her own Marxist colleagues, so reluctant to think about the woman question at all. But then she singled out Sweden's Ellen Key. Key said all the right things about marriage: it should be based on no material motives; mutual inclinations alone should sustain it; and if it led to motherhood, motherhood should be socially guaranteed. But Key refused to give up the family. Indeed, Key was suspicious of socialism itself, especially of any "socialized" child-rearing, as a danger to the variability of personality. In effect, Key left the sexual relations of individuals disconnected from society, whereas for Kollontai the whole point was what social revolution could do to transform sexual relations.

Soon Kollontai was expounding openly on new possibilities between the sexes. In "Sexual Relations and the Class Struggle" (1910), she noted that new sexual ideals seemed to be bubbling up everywhere in modern society.

History [she wrote] has never seen such a variety of personal relationships—indissoluble marriage with its "stable family," "free unions," secret adultery; a girl living quite openly with her lover in so-called "wild marriage"; pair marriage, marriage in threes and even the complicated marriage of four people.[17]

While by no means giving her imprimatur to all these arrangements, Kollontai clearly welcomed the spirit of experiment and freedom they evinced. At no point did she stop to brood over the obvious fact that the society generating these experiments and those freedoms was not socialism. Only socialism could fulfill the new ways, she insisted again. In reviewing, with warm approval, a book by a German feminist psychoanalyst, Grete Meisel-Hess's *The Sexual Crisis* of 1910, Kollontai ignored standard Marxist materialist criticism of bourgeois marriage in favor of a far more psychological analysis of her own. Modern bourgeois marriage was impelled not by material but by spiritual want.

Because of their loneliness men are apt to cling in a predatory and unhealthy way to illusions about finding a "soul mate" from among the members of the opposite sex. They see sly Eros as the only means of charming away, if only for a time, the gloom of inescapable loneliness.[18]

These essays were written between 1909 and 1911, while Kollontai was in the midst of her first liaison since leaving her husband. Almost certainly her lover was the highly trained economist Peter Maslov, a fellow quasi-Menshevik and fellow exile. Apparently Maslov was prepared to divorce in order to marry her. She ended the affair late in 1911, however, unwilling to become a stepmother to Maslov's several children. But apparently there were other reasons, too.

In 1926, just after the last political activity of her career and during the marriage law debates of 1925–26, Kollontai at fifty-four wrote a brief sketch of her life. Ninety percent at least of the forty-five small pages was devoted to politics. But the few passages that she did devote to her personal life were striking. She disposed of her first marriage with the brief comment that, while she had loved her husband, she found housewifery a cage. The passage in which she most fully unburdened herself had to do with her life later, after she had gone out into the world "to work, to struggle, to create side by side with men." It had to do with the relationship between that work and love. Before "I talk about . . . my intellectual existence," she wrote, "I still want to say a few words about my personal life."

The question arises whether in the middle of all these manifold, exciting labors and Party-assignments I could still find time for intimate experiences, for the pangs and joys of love. Unfortunately, yes! I say unfortunately because ordinarily these experiences entailed all too many cares, disappointments, and pain, and because all too many energies were pointlessly consumed through them. Yet the longing to be understood by a man down to the deepest, most secret recesses of one's soul, to be recognized by him as a striving human being, repeatedly decided matters. And repeatedly disappointment ensued all too swiftly, since the friend saw in me only the feminine element which he tried to mold into a willing sounding board to his own ego. So repeatedly the moment inevitably arrived in which I had to shake off the chains . . . with an aching heart. . . . Then I was again alone.[19]

Wanting not the "human being" in her, only the "feminine," Maslov had threatened her extinction as a personality. Self-defense, not love, had come to inhabit the interior of the relationship. What the sexual dimensions of this affair had been, Kollontai most likely revealed in an essay written a year or two after she and Maslov parted.

The normal woman seeks in sexual intercourse completness and harmony; the man, reared on prostitution, overlooking the complex vibrations of love's sensations, follows only his pallid monotone, physical inclinations, leaving sensations of incompleteness and spiritual hunger on both sides.[20]

While this may have been unfair to Maslov, whose failings, such as they were, did not appear to include a coarsening of sexual sensitivities, it distinctly implied a new revolutionary agenda. Already attuned to "completeness and harmony," women did not need to be changed. But men did. A new society, a revolutionized society, was necessary so that men might become different.

In an earlier essay written in 1913, "The New Woman," Kollontai had projected a rather different solution. A long review of some thirty-odd novels published mostly in Western Europe over the previous ten years or so, the essay was a departure from Kollontai's usual product, being neither theoretical nor, in a standard socialist mode, a systematic empirical survey full of tables, graphs, and "data." In "The New Woman" Kollontai responded to the novels as though to a documentation at once too elusive for statistical treatment and too deep for theory to appreciate. Her voice was celebratory, annunciatory, lyrical. Again, what elicited this response had nothing to do with standard radical socialist politics.

A "wholly new" type of young woman had begun to appear, Kollontai wrote. Hitherto unknown, this new type had superseded the pure, nice girl and also the long-suffering wife of bourgeois idealism, both the dry old maid and the priestess of love of bourgeois decadence. Her most salient feature was not so much a trait but a fact of relationship. The new woman was on her own, alone, single. In the past "there was no place in either literature or life" for the single woman, but "life does not stand still," and now in 1913 the single woman was to be found everywhere, in offices, in libraries and laboratories, in factories and schools. It was not necessity that had made her single. She was proud of her inner strength, her self-reliance, her single state. She would not have it otherwise. She was in charge of herself.

The crucial dimension of this single state Kollontai spelled out exactly:

Love ceases to form the only substance of her life . . . it is allotted the subordinate role it plays with most men. To be sure, for the new woman, too, there come periods in her life when love—love, the passion—holds her soul prisoner, when her mind, her heart, and thereby all other interests are eclipsed and thrust into the background. At such times the new woman can experience the crassest dramas, she can enjoy and suffer like the woman in the past. But the stage of being in love is but a transient period in her life.[21]

The new woman did not live for love and passion. The "holy" which she served was "the social idea, science, creativity. At her work, her ideal is for her . . . in most cases, more important, more valuable, holier than all the joys of the heart, all the delights of passion."

In this scenario men would not have to be changed to match women. Women were being changed to match men. The key was in learning, like men, not to care too much about passionate relationships. Sex was not to be repressed but subordinated. The new woman took her sexual joy when it came, drained it to the dregs, then passed on without regret or recrimination, back to work. The contrast between this annunciation of 1913 and her 1926 lamentation over men's inadequacies suggested that Kollontai had not succeeded in becoming a new woman herself.

She probably tried. If a new woman swore off engulfing love in order to safeguard her independence, perhaps she could risk herself again in a more limited way with a different sort of man. During her wartime years of exile in Norway, Kollontai lived with Alexander Schliapnikov. While almost nothing is known of the inwardness of this affair, one fact is plain. Whereas both Vladimir Kollontai and Peter Maslov were men of culture, like Kollontai's father, Schliapnikov was the son of workers, not at all preoccupied in the manner of the classic intelligentsia (as was Maslov) with culture. That Kollontai could collaborate with Schliapnikov years later in a purely political enterprise may or may not tell us in what spirit the affair ended. She herself never said. We can only guess that with Schliapnikov a sexual relationship had not entailed the kind of dependency she had suffered with Maslov. A "giant, bearded sailor," as John Reed saw him, Pavel Dybenko too was a son of the people, his parents being peasants. Moreover, he was only twenty-eight when he married his forty-six-year-old wife in 1918. No doubt some suspicion of the motivations of a sophisticated, elegant, cosmopolitan but middle-aged woman in joining herself to such uncomplicated youthful energy seemed justified to such another young man as Pitirim Sorokin. Yet ideologically, both Schliapnikov and Dybenko confirmed Kollontai's romantic and populistic faith in the working masses, in contrast to Lenin's cadre of expert professionals. At the same time, such men might meet Kollontai's need to affirm her sexuality without losing her personality.[22]

As her confession in the autobiographical fragment of 1926 suggests, however, she had not found the new woman's way of love adequate. Whether her divorce from Dybenko was in itself a disappointment we cannot be sure. Quite possibly she had found Dybenko looking to her for a mother while she still wanted a lover. In any case, she felt impelled to reaffirm her original ideological insistence that personal answers to the profound personal problem she found within herself were impossible without socialism. In "Theses on Communist Morality in the

Sphere of Marital Relations" (1920) she let the new woman fade into the undifferentiated. What mattered was that the collective become strong so that the individual cease to need individual relationships. "The closer the emotional ties between the members of the community, the less the need to seek a refuge from loneliness in marriage."[23] In the last of her essays on sex, love, and socialism, "Make Way for Winged Eros" (1923), she sought to dissolve sexuality itself in the warmth of the social. By then she was long out of the Women's Department, had lost her battle against Leninist democratic centralism, and had accepted a minor diplomatic post in Sweden as a kind of polite exile. But the unfinished task of women's liberation remained and she was going to have her say about it, fully and unimpeded, at last.

She began with history, a sketch of what she believed had happened to Eros in Russia during the desperate years of war, revolution, civil war, and wartime Communism:

The men and women of the working classes were in the grip of other emotions, passions and experiences. In those years everyone walked in the shadow of death. . . . In face of the revolutionary threat, tender-winged Eros fled. . . . There was neither time nor a surplus of inner strength for love's "joys and pains." Such is the law of the preservation of humanity's social and psychological energy. As a whole, this energy is always directed to the most urgent aims of the historical moment.[24]

Here Kollontai was being untrue to her own experience. She at least had had the energy for both love and revolution, Dybenko and the Central Committee. But her reasoning brought her to the real confrontation with her most serious opponent, Lenin:

Men and women . . . came together without great commitment and parted without tears or regret. . . . "wingless Eros" consumes less inner strength than "winged Eros," whose love is woven of delicate strands of every kind of emotion. "Wingless Eros" does not make one suffer from sleepless nights, does not sap one's will and does not entangle the rational workings of the mind.[25]

Lenin had argued just the contrary. Wingless Eros, an equivalent to the glass-of-water theory he scorned, did divert energy from the revolution, he insisted, and must be rejected in favor of that love in which culture comes into play. Except in some totally hydrological theory of sexuality, there could hardly be any doubt that Lenin was wrong, Kollontai right. Sex on the run had not hurt the revolution.

But Kollontai now made it utterly clear that such sex had nothing to do with socialism. It was merely a phenomenon of the transition. Winged Eros was another matter entirely. And it was now time, with the revolution victorious to think of such love again:

It is time we separated outselves from the hypocrisy of bourgeois thought. It is time to recognize openly that love is not only a powerful natural factor, a biological force, but also a social factor. . . . Even the bourgeoisie who saw love as a "private matter," was able to channel the expression of love in its class interests. The . . . working class must pay . . . attention to the significance of love as a factor which can . . . be channelled to the advantage of the collective.[26]

This began to sound like Lenin; he too wanted to deprecate natural love in favor of love shaped by culture. In "Theses on Communist Morality" Kollontai herself had squared the circle on the question of natural sexuality, nearly repeating Bebel at one point—"The sexual act must be seen . . . as something which is as natural as the other needs of a healthy organism, such as hunger and thirst"—while at other points berating the "bourgeois" attitude that sexual relations were "simply a matter of sex." In "Winged Eros" too her language often blurred rather than sharpened her meaning. "Obviously sexual attraction lies at the heart of 'winged Eros,' " she wrote, and asserted that, in the new world of socialism, "the accepted norm of sexual relations" would most likely stress "free, healthy, and natural" attraction.[27] If this would indeed be winged Eros, it was hard to understand just what the wingless kind had been after all. Nevertheless, beneath the verbal confusions there subsisted a unifying vision, and Kollontai insisted on it.

In proclaiming the rights of "winged Eros," the ideal of the working class at the same time subordinates this love to the more powerful emotion of love-duty to the collective. However great the love between two members of the collective, the ties binding the two persons to the collective will always take precedence, will be firmer, more complex and organic. Bourgeois morality demanded all for the loved one. The morality of the proletariat demands all for the collective. The blind, all-embracing, demanding passions will weaken, the sense of property, the egotistical desire to bind the partner to one "forever," the complacency of the man and the self-renunciation of the woman will disappear.[28]

Since Lenin and other conventional moralists could still read this as promoting promiscuity through the trivialization of sex, Kollontai remained vulnerable to their criticism. Both Krupskaya and her Women's Department successor, Smidovich, still regarded her as part of what they considered a breakdown of manners and mores. But Kollontai herself was wise enough to realize that her views exposed her to objectors far more important than ascetic old Bolsheviks. From the standpoint of any hopes for a popular democratic socialism, the youth who had been wrenched loose from old sureties, eager to know whether in the chaos and suffering there was hope for genuine freedom, mattered far more.

. . . . I can hear you objecting, my young friend, that though it may be true that love-comradeship will become the ideal of the working class, will this new "moral measurement" of emotions not place new constraints on sexual relationships? Are we not liberating love from the fetters of a bourgeois morality only to enslave it again?[29]

It was the pathos of Kollontai's career as a theorist that, though she had the polemical nerve to respond to this challenge, "Yes, my young friend, you are right"—going on, of course, to urge the attractions of a world where love "in the present sense of the word" would not mean as much—she had not convinced herself. Love in "the present sense of the word" meant the love that had entangled her with Vladimir Kollontai and Peter Maslov, the longing to be understood, the hope for completeness and harmony in the arms of the beloved. The hope that such completeness and harmony was to be had in socialism had sustained her through her time of troubles. But when, resigned from politics at last, she came to write her autobiographical sketch, she conceded a terrible point. She insisted proudly that "to work, to struggle . . . side by side with men" had been her chosen way, that she had never let her feelings, "the joy or the pain of life take . . . first place," that "creativity, activity, struggle always occupied the foreground." Even so, the blind, demanding passion kept arising. Its source was not really sex, sexuality, healthy nature at all. She could struggle with an "aching heart" to shake off the chains, even knowing that once again she would be alone. But then, "the greater the demands life made upon me, the more the responsible work waiting to be tackled, the greater grew the longing to be enveloped by love, warmth, understanding."[30]

Ultimately, for Kollontai, socialism was not the solution to the problem of love, but a source of the problem. Her perception, back in 1908, that Ellen Key, rather than bourgeois feminists and antifeminist Marxists, was her most dangerous antagonist, had followed from the deepest fear in her heart. Nothing ever would quench her own glowing individuality. Socialism, with its constructed wholenesses and harmonies, would only make the ache of individuality worse. Kollontai knew very well that life was indeed "creativity, activity, struggle," and that any life so led quite naturally generated the longing to be enveloped by love, warmth, and understanding.

Alexandra Kollontai: The Last Charge

Lenin boasted that Bolshevism had done more in one day to liberate marriage and sexual life than bourgeois Western liberals had been able to achieve in decades of trying.[31] Marriage was taken from the church; a secular contract, it needed only to be registered at state offices; it had no more links to property. Old prohibitions on divorce were lifted;

divorce became a matter for the partners in a marriage to decide. These reforms were not socialism, of course. Socialism would build the nurseries and clinics, the day-care centers and schools, the canteens and centers for rest that would socialize the heart of the family, which was child-rearing. But these decrees did deliver, as Western liberals had not, on the principle that when it came to sexuality, people should be in charge of their own lives.

In 1920, bans on abortion were lifted. Even more than the new divorce law, this lent color to lurid Western equations of Bolshevism with sexual license, even with the "socialization of women." For Lenin and his colleagues Bolshevism meant just the opposite. Although obviously more honest and moral than the criminal abortions tolerated under Czarism and in the West, legal abortion was but a negative good, a recognition of need but not an invitation. Obviously preferable to the abstract, anti-individual divorce codes of the West that forced persons who had come to abhor each other to remain shackled, the new divorce laws also were negative goods, intended to discourage marrying lightly while allowing a legal end to marriages already ended in spirit.

Western visitors got the impression of a kind of vast effervescence going on in sexual life in Russia in the early 1920s. Practically every observer commented on it—Bessie Beattie, Maurice Hindus, Dorothy Thompson, Fanina Halle.[32] One of the most attentive was a 1915 Swarthmore graduate, Jessica Smith, who had worked for suffrage in New York after college, and then worked in the Intercollegiate Socialist Society. She visited the Soviet Union in 1922 with the American Friends' famine relief service, spent a year in Moscow, and after two years back home, returned in 1926 for a second extended visit. In *Women in the Soviet Union* she reported more copiously on the Women's Department and on the debates in 1925–26 over proposed new marriage and divorce laws than any other traveler of the day. Smith was aware that no ideological consensus had been pronounced on all the issues of marriage, family, sex, love, and private morality. She was convinced, hence, that the ferment was real and that "the new moral code is still a dynamic thing."[33] "No mold has yet been set." She praised what was going on, even though its upshot could not be told. She did so by directing contempt at what she did understand, the Western scene, then praising the Soviet scene in contrast.

The new moral code is being shaped by more important influences than . . . endless lectures and discussions. . . . The new demands and interests of life are the determining factors. There is no leisure class of young men and women creating standards of dress and hair cut and conduct for the rest to ape. There is no mass of young people absorbed in sex as an escape from boredom, spending their lives on the business of heightening their sex appeal by a thousand artificial means, encouraged by the advertisements that scream at them from all sides. There is no such thing as "general education" in the colleges of Russia, turning out annually a huge crop of "half-baked intellectuals" to swell the ranks of the idle and discontented. . . . Their interest in sex is neither as an escape, nor as an end in itself. It is therefore far more vital, more brutal if you will. They are concerned with fitting it into its proper relation to the rest of their lives.[34]

In his famous book, *Humanity Uprooted*, based on a visit in 1923–24, Maurice Hindus was less sure that socialism had released some new spirit. Much of the candor and unself-consciousness in relationships between the sexes that delighted visitors from Anglo-Saxon lands particularly, had, he observed, roots back in old prerevolutionary Russia: "[Neither] chivalry nor puritanism had [ever] secured the clutch on Russia as they had in other lands. . . . The relations of the sexes in [the] midst [of the Russian intelligentsia] remained always close, simple, unaffected. Even more is it true of the peasantry."[35]

The debates of 1925–26 were particularly hard to understand.[36] Why, if the decrees of 1917–18 and 1920 had been so obvious, did they have to be changed now? The debate was genuine; the party itself had generated no orthodoxy; the New Economic Policy was generating new perspectives on family and marriage; for practically the last time, something like popular opinion was heard in the Soviet Union.

On the Bolshevik party left, one participant, the economist Evgeny Preobrazhensky, said that by 1925 some young people had emerged ready for no law at all, for total freedom at last. "Marriages differ, there is already one sort of marriage which heralds the marriages of the future. People concluding such a marriage do not consider registration necessary because they know that neither party will harm the other."[37] But this was more a kind of orphic dictum than a contribution to policy, Preobrazhensky conceded. "There are few such people," and even he, though a proponent of crash programs designed to storm the future in preference to the NEP's molecular progress, agreed that laws had to take general, not elite, psychology into account.

On another side, voices were heard complaining about the license all too prevalent since the revolution. Nadezhda Krupskaya deplored legal abortion as contributing to "unbridled passion, casual pregnancies . . . and [a] general disrespect for women, love, motherhood, and the family." She was seconded by Kollontai's successor as Women's Department head, Sophia Smidovich, who expostulated upon "African passions" welling up among Soviet youth. The idea that Smidovitch was speaking for "a Party leadership that was in this instance singularly united," voicing some reaffirmation of the Bolshevik puritanism of Lenin, runs up against the facts: first, in excoriating immorality, she went beyond

Soviet youth to question the character of certain good Bolsheviks themselves; second, the reforms agreed upon by no means reinstated asceticism.[38]

Abortion was not recriminalized; divorce was made easier. The reason was that the debates of 1925–26 did not turn on morality at all but on economics. The 1917 divorce law had prompted a surge of divorces, which then subsided. But divorce began rising rapidly again after 1922. To the large population of single women was added a population of divorced women, commonly with children. Even worse was a swelling population of mothers who could not get a divorce. Multitudes of peasants still identified marriage with the church; they failed to register their church marriages; their marriages thus had no legal status, and such a wife—a common-law wife in Western terms—had no legal protection, should her common-law husband abandon her. Some of the urban working class also had been accustomed to nonchurch common-law marriages; so had many of the intelligentsia. It was the marriage law, not the divorce law, that was at fault. The reformers of 1925–26, then, meant to throw up walls of protection around women of broken common-law marriages. They also sought to improve the status of legally divorced women. The issue was particularly thorny among peasants living in the old extended family, the *dvor*. Their communal property was already liable for the responsibilities of a divorced man among them; with reform, it would be liable for divorces between common-law partners, too. But what constituted a valid common-law marriage? The reformers were reminded of the possibilities of fraud. The point of making divorce even easier was to encourage more persons to contract legal marriages in the first place.

It was the intervention of Alexandra Kollontai in this tangled debate that most vividly revealed how thoroughly the new Soviet family code had been captured from theory and given over to pragmatism. Returning from her quasi-exile, Kollontai confronted the disputants with one last chance to embrace socialism.[39] What, she argued, could be less socialistic and communistic, more blatantly individualistic and bourgeois, than assignment of responsibility for the welfare of a divorced woman and her children to one individual man, and precisely that one man who least wished to support her, the ex-husband who had abandoned her? Kollontai had always insisted that all children deserved to be free of the vicissitudes of depending upon any particular individual. No child should suffer because of the failures of a father. The same argument of course applied to their mothers. But it was going beyond injustice to the point of outrage, she insisted, for mothers with children to be dependent on alimony. For a woman to be shackled by divorce itself to a man she abhorred mocked justice. How could any socialist imagine that Russia had really got beyond bourgeois hypocrisy, as Lenin had boasted, when it proposed to extend such injustice? What was the proper answer? In principle, Kollontai still held to the full vision of society's responsibility for all mothers and all children. As Preobrazhensky had suggested, in a truly free society no laws at all were needed. Marriages would be contracted within the heart, and divorces, too. In the circumstances of the debate, however, she offered a lesser solution. Let there be no alimony law at all. Instead, let divorced wives and their children be supported by the community by means of a fund sustained by a tax paid for that purpose. Then, and only then, she argued, would free marriage exist, based upon the heart; then and only then could free divorce exist, severed from money and property. Then winged Eros might fly freed of the cage of the couple.

Of all proposals during the marriage law debates of 1925–26, Kollontai's was the least likely to be adopted. Preobrazhensky's utopian wish for no law at all at least cost no money, whereas Kollontai's plan would cost a lot. Peasants and workers, as well as the Left, Right, and Center of the party's committee, all lacked the stomach for its cost. Implicitly, Kollontai had said that in socialism mothers and children come first. No one agreed. Kollontai went back to her post, wrote her brief autobiographical *cri de coeur*, and settled into exile.

Stalinism's Women's Assignment

When in 1930 the unrivaled leader of the Communist Party, Joseph Stalin, abolished the Women's Department, no protests were heard. If asked for, no explanations were given. The Women's Department had constituted a social welfare service woven into the activities of the party. It had dispensed food to the hungry, policed sanitation, pressed public health campaigns, coped with orphans, monitored school facilities and housing, and responded to family crisis. It had been the embryo of a vast system of social housekeeping manned by women. Now it was gone. Above all, it had been, as Richard Stites has said, an "engine of mobilization." Bolsheviks had never visualized themselves presiding over an inert population. Their persistent claim to being a "democratic" political force derived from their constant drive to induce active political consciousness among the masses, consciousness determined by the party. Very possibly, by 1930 Russia's women were more highly mobilized in political consciousness than the women of Italy, Sweden, or the United States, and that was in considerable part due to the Women's Department. But whether this represented, as Stites for one has asserted, the climax—and end—of a "Proletarian Women's Movement" that had first risen among the workers and intellectuals of St. Petersburg around 1906, is quite another question.[40] The impulse to the mobilization of women pursued by the Women's Department from 1922 to 1930 was to be found in the Central Committee of the Communist Party, not in any proletarian women's organizations, any women's sections of free trade unions, or any Bolshevik feminist groups, since none of these existed. The best answer to why the Women's Department was abolished in 1930, is that Stalin and his aides no longer wished to incite political consciousness among women. In no way was this evidence of some rise or resurgence of residual antifeminism in Communist leadership. After 1928, with the First Five-Year Plan for industry and collectivization of the countryside, Stalin had no wish to incite further political consciousness in men either. The engines of mobilization were accelerated even more, but now ever more surely for an army of labor.

In May 1936, as Stalin was preparing the first great show trials of his old Bolshevik former colleagues, new decrees were announced on marriage, divorce, and abortion.[41] Stalin's house sociologists, notably Samuel Volfson, explained the new decrees as testimony to the continuing progress of socialism. So long as people still lived under even the residual influence of capitalism, Volfson explained, as presumably many Russians still did in the 1920s, divorce and abortion had been necessary out of respect for individual freedom. But once socialism had shaped people, as presumably it had by 1936, divorce was no longer necessary, since no one any longer had to marry for capitalistic reasons, that is, out of economic need. Accordingly, divorce was put out of reach for all but a few Russians, effectively, the richest Communist Russians. Similarly, once bourgeois influences no longer impelled girls into unwanted pregnancies, abortion no longer was needed. Accordingly, abortion was effectively recriminalized for all but the few most privileged Communist Russians.

No such widespread debate as had preceded the new laws of 1926 was invited in 1936. For reasons that are not certain, a few opinions were expressed in one party newspaper, *Izvestia*. Since *Izvestia* was edited by Nicolai Bukharin, these comments may have been his last service to a Russia fast being reduced to "teleology," before going to his own trial in 1937 and to execution by Stalin's courts. Clearly registering popular feeling, these comments protested the abolition of legal abortion:

I consider that the projected law is premature. . . . Very often it is the lack of living quarters that is the reason behind an abortion. . . . in our village . . . the creches . . . are constantly full up. . . . A categorical prohibition of abortion will confront young people with a dilemma: either complete sexual abstinence or the risk of jeopardizing their studies and disrupting their life. . . . It must not be thought that the majority of abortions are the result of irresponsible behavior. ... a woman resorts to abortion as a last resort. ... Abortions will become obsolete ... when knowledge of human anatomy spreads, methods of birth control are ... used and—last but not least—when housing conditions are improved.[42]

While the May decrees had been labeled "preliminary," such public reactions did not stop them from being installed.

Until Soviet archives yield more of their secrets, historians can only speculate with as much logic as they can assemble on the motives of Stalin's planners in issuing the new decrees. The obvious speculation is that they were addressed to a demographic crisis. By 1936 the cohort of surplus young women left without mates because of World War I were into their thirties and forties, beyond prime baby-bearing ages. The crucial cohort of younger women, between eighteen and twenty-five, was in balance with young men, but this cohort, while balanced, was small, for as young children between 1914 and 1920 they too had died in large numbers from war, hunger, and disease. The prospect then was for a cycle of fewer workers and fewer babies. Stalin was already responding to the prospect of fewer workers by drawing ever higher proportions of women of all ages into the work force. With the 1936 decrees he acted for more babies. The decrees on abortion and divorce framed six other decrees aimed directly at stimulating baby production. Subsidies were announced for seventh and further children, and for maternity hospitals, nurseries, and kindergartens. A budget of several billion rubles was projected.

It is hard to imagine that Stalin and his planners were thinking of the next war, which Stalin had already evoked to justify his crash program of industrialization. Boy babies born in 1937 would not be ready for war before 1955 or so. The prefigurations of another war that would threaten Russia long before 1955 were perfectly apparent to Stalin by 1936. The demographic policy announced in 1936 registered the more general teleological policy of striving for total control on a long-range basis, not so much for specific purposes as for its own sake, for the principle of submitting society to science. In 1926, people still retained much freedom to order their sexual lives; from 1936 on, sexuality would be directed into approved channels.

The new policy was accompanied by adjustments in ideological mobilization. The plainest such case was that of Samuel Volfson himself. As it happened, Volfson had written a book, *The Sociology of Marriage*, in 1929; he had expounded familiar old socialist doctrine on the family, doctrine laid down by August Bebel, echoed on occasion by Lenin, and embraced by Kollontai: the family was a bastion of capitalism; socialism meant the "extinction of the family" and the liberation of personality from the family's crippling clutches. In 1936 Volfson apologized.[43] All this was quite mistaken, he said. One of the evidences of socialism's superiority over capitalism consisted exactly of the fact that socialism nourished, while capitalism corrupted, the family. In *Pravda*—by contrast with *Izvestia*—veritable pastorales on young Soviet familyhood were published:

Fatherhood and motherhood have long been virtues in this country. This can be seen at the first glance. . . . Go through the parks and streets of Moscow . . . on a holiday . . . see not a few young men walking with pink-cheeked, well-fed babies in their arms. The rise in the standard of living has brought the joy of parenthood within the reach of all adults. . . . The birth-rate is rising . . . the mortality rate . . . [is] down.[44]

A certain effort was required to disguise the point of greatest tension over the new policy. Stalin could not conceal a note of peremptory warning to those who would bear most of the burden, young women. "We need men," he had announced earlier in the year, very possibly in the same kind of bathos as had overtaken Mussolini. He went on:

Abortion which destroys life is not acceptable in our country. The Soviet woman has the same rights as the man, but that does not free her from a great and honorable duty which nature has given her: she is a mother, she gives life. And this is certainly not a private affair but one of great social importance.[45]

The touch of menace here was faulty; so was the hint that in the Soviet Union a bit of suffering was appropriate. Volfson found the right tone, one of triumphalism, of celebration:

This tragic cleavage where woman has to choose between productive work and the family does not exist in the U.S.S.R. In socialist society . . . conditions are created which allow women to combine harmoniously . . . productive and social life with the performance of her family functions, her duties as a mother. . . . In the U.S.S.R. woman's productive and social work does not in the least interfere with motherhood but is beautifully co-ordinated with it and with the stabilization of the family.[46]

In socialism, women could be both mothers and workers harmoniously.

To Leon Trotsky in foreign exile, all this appeared as the plainest evidence for the bankruptcy of the regime:

It proved impossible to take the old family by storm—not because the will was lacking, and not because the family was so firmly rooted in men's hearts. On the contrary, after a short period of distrust . . . the working women, and . . . the more advanced peasants, appreciated . . . the socialization of the whole family economy. Unfortunately society proved too poor . . . the bureaucratic government . . . acknowledged its bankruptcy. . . . The revolutionary power gave women the right to abortion. . . . [Now, having] revealed its inability to serve women . . . with the necessary medical aid and sanitation, the state makes a sharp change of course. . . And . . . makes a virtue of necessity. . . . The triumphal rehabilitation of the family . . . is caused by the material and cultural bankruptcy of the state. . . . the leaders are forcing people to glue together again the shell of the broken family.[47]

Probably Kollontai, now ensconced in Stockholm as Russian ambassador—the first woman to be an ambassador, another world's first for Communism—agreed. But we can only assume it; she never said so publicly.

Trotsky's scorn for Stalin's economic performance was not quite ingenuous. Long before Stalin, he too had insisted on crash industrialization, and nothing he said explained how he but not Stalin, could have afforded the heavy costs of a socialized family economy. Moreover, exile stimulated his sensitivity to the sexual as well as political and economic decadence of Bolshevism's commanding heights:

. . . . nice apartments, automobiles . . . personal affairs [arranged] without unnecessary publicity and consequently without registration. . . . On the heights of Soviet society . . . prostitution takes the elegant form of small mutual services . . . even . . . the aspect of "the socialist family" . . . vices which power and money create in sex relations are flourishing . . . luxuriously. . . . [the] "marriage of convenience" . . . is now fully resurrected. . . . It is useful to have as a father-in-law a military commander or an influential Communist.[48]

Still, Stalin's decrees themselves showed what was missing: sharply increased budgets for retail shopping, for household goods and household services, for housing itself. "The mere struggle for a room unites and divorces no small number of couples every year in Moscow."[49] Had Stalin's commitment to the family been a high priority, his budgets would have reflected that fact. As it was, it seemed reasonably apparent that Stalin expected his policy of babies and workers to be paid for in the same way his collective farms and his new industries were paid for, by sacrifice, especially by women.

Early in May 1936, *Pravda* carried the report of "A Remarkable Conference." More than three thousand "activist wives," it appeared, had met in "the magnificent hall of the great palace of the Kremlin" to discuss what they could do to help their country. An address to the assemblage by Comrade E. M. Vesnik, describing "the work of the wives of the engineers and technical workers of the Krivoi Rog metallurgical combine" made clear what this was. The wives of Krivoi Rog had set up child-welfare clinics, nurseries, crèches. They had fitted them out with linen, tablecloths, sheets, and towels, all made by themselves. They had also organized a canteen for the engineers' club, and then taken over the combine restaurant as well. They had started a poultry farm. They set out to upgrade the local workers' hostels, opening rooms for mending clothes, laundries, and barbering. Six months earlier, one wife "was still paying calls on her neighbors, from old habit, to play cards and gossip." But today "she is saying with tears in her eyes: 'How I wish the restaurant of our guild were better than all the others and our hostels the most beautiful and civilized.' "

Pravda warned its readers that while some might look upon these wives and be reminded of the charity ladies whom Bolsheviks had justly scorned in prerevolutionary days, now they must realize that, though "not themselves employed in the enterprises and establishments," these women too were "active builders of socialist society." Moreover, *Pravda* noted, this movement of the wives "sprang up spontaneously."

In a climax to their remarkable conference, the wives of the managers and engineers of heavy industry at Krivoi Rog issued an "Appeal to the Wives of Managers and Engineers of the Soviet Union":

... everyone of us has already found her place, however small, in the common effort.... The large world of interests in which our husbands live, has become ours, too.... All that was petty, futile and humdrum in our domestic life has disappeared.... We remember the words of the great Stalin that we are the mothers, the teachers of youth.... We are needed in the schools, ... in the hospitals, the canteens, the clubs, the hostels, the study groups.... Cheerful green settlements for workers, well-provided canteens, the joyous laughter of children, healthy mothers who give heroes to their country.... Comrades, we have seen Stalin. Our heart is full of inexpressible joy, of great happiness.... Comrades, our work is appreciated ... the wife of a leader of industry can fight for socialism side by side with her husband.[50]

In effect, Stalin and his planners intended to get their social services for nothing. The billions of rubles scheduled for the elaborate network of facilities that would ease the task of the new mother-workers were not spent. Whether, as Trotsky said, the Soviet Union was simply too poor or whether Stalin simply chose to direct its resources elsewhere, the result was the same. It was gilded with the rising ideology: "The housewives, who only yesterday spent their lives in a circle of narrow family cares, have today become partners in the great work of Stalin."

That this ideology meshed perfectly with a crucial category of young women, Masha Scott's example testified.

Masha was typical of a whole generation of young Soviet women who ... became professional women whereas their parents were barely literate. This group ... were steeped in the slogans of equality of opportunity for women. They had been raised on the propaganda of the twenties about the elimination of the bourgeois family as an institution. They wanted to have as little as possible to do with cooking, washing dishes, and changing diapers.[51]

Yet we can only guess at the real feelings of the wives of Krivoi Rog and of managers and engineers everywhere in the Soviet Union, women who might well have had other ideas of their own about the use of the time their husband's status and income had begun to allow them. Precisely that stratum of women who in Italy, Sweden, the United States, and everywhere in the West provided the vanguard of feminism, was being actively denied any voice of its own.

In 1944 still more new decrees on marriage, divorce, abortion, and reproduction were announced.[52] By then, as Soviet tanks were forcing Nazi invaders westward, it was clear that Russia had suffered another demographic disaster. Once again a severe imbalance in the gender ratio of a generation was destined to reverberate for thirty years through the schools, the economy, the army. Once again the skew was greatest where it was most alarming, in Russia proper and the Western republics by comparison with Moslem Central Asia, where youth remained more nearly in balance and families large. The Moslem peoples showed no disposition to seek work in the industrial centers, however. A more and more self-consciously "Russian" leadership did not encourage them to.

People's courts were told in 1944 to discourage petitions for divorce; divorce became effectively unobtainable. Legal abortions, already nearly unobtainable, were now hedged practically to the vanishing point. New inducements were offered for baby production, now of a more far-reaching and sophisticated sort. By subsidizing only seventh and successive children, the 1936 planners had really assumed that the source of baby abundance remained the countryside. Young urban wives had hardly been addressed. Now, with subsidies beginning with the third child and increasing step by step after that, the planners were addressing families most inclined to stop after one or two children.

Easily the most striking feature of the 1944 decrees was their singling out of a category ignored in 1936, unmarried mothers. It could be assumed that, owing to the shortage of men, thousands of women would indeed become unmarried mothers. Such women were now offered special economic support. An unmarried mother was now scheduled for subsidies for her first and second babies as well. Moreover, she would be able to have her children brought up at state expense in "children's institutions."

Historians have not been able to learn Stalin's exact intentions in issuing these decrees. One authority, Rudolph Schlesinger, who edited all Soviet marriage laws for Western edification in 1949, speculated that the 1944 decrees contained the germ of a truly radical policy, one at last taking up the mission to "socialize the family economy" dear to the hearts of Bolsheviks such as Trotsky, Kollontai, and presumably

Lenin himself. He pointed out that the logic of child subsidies suggested that a mother's support should not be cut off when her last child reached twelve, as was scheduled for the unmarried. Moreover, her support should equal the earnings of other women at work, since reproduction was certainly as crucial as production to society. The subsidies should be adjusted to costs, so that in Moscow, say, where expenses were higher, motherhood would not be penalized by comparison with motherhood on the kolkhozes. Finally, motherhood should guarantee lifetime support. This might mean, for instance, that mothers with empty nests would proceed into jobs as nursery matrons or kindergarten aides. The further logic hidden in the decrees would become explicit:

.... motherhood could be regarded as a profession like any other, bestowing not only social prestige but also a standard of life comparable with that obtainable by any other kind of not specially skilled labor. . . . it seems evident, on the basis of Soviet experience, that a State can combine the demand for large families with that for social equality between men and women only by removing from the husband's shoulders . . . the responsibility not only of his children, but of his wife also, if her fulfillment of the duties of motherhood prevents her from earning her living in some other way.[53]

If only on the basis of the fact that the regime showed no signs of undertaking any such scheme by Stalin's death in 1953, it seems unlikely that the planners had it in mind. One further feature of the decree probably tells what they did intend. In 1926 the new decrees had tried to provide legality for unregistered common-law marriages. Now, in 1944, once again all but state-registered marriages were deprived of legal status. Even surreptitiously celebrated church marriages, if unregistered, were stripped of legality. Almost certainly the planners were anticipating a rise in unmarried motherhood. That status, while granted new subsidies, was at the same time burdened with a new shame. No longer could the place on a child's birth certificate for "father's name" be filled in; it was to be left blank. The ancient "search of paternity," founded on the old insistence that the economic responsibility for an illegitimate child be borne by its natural father, was prohibited. The child would bear its mother's name. Only the ban on abortion provoked as bitter feeling as this decree. It seems unlikely that the planners meant to force more women into this status. They evidently meant to force more couples into registered marriage and, insofar as this succeeded, to keep the roster of unmarried mothers at the minimum the demographic skew dictated. But very definitely the unmarried were to have babies. Once again, the regime hoped to get both production and reproduction at least expense. That was one definition of Stalinism: cheap labor.

Enigma Wrapped in Ideology: Modern Soviet Women

Censuses of 1959 and 1970 clearly exposed the spreading postwar Soviet demographic reality: marriages of two working persons were producing one, sometimes two, children. In 1975 Leonid Brezhnev made his call on the Twenty-fifth Party Congress for an "effective demographic policy." This was easier asked than done. No one spoke of once again prohibiting abortion. Stalin's restrictions had been canceled two years after his death, in 1955; there had been a surge of illegal abortions in the bad old bourgeois way during the years before. No one spoke of again tightening up on divorce. Stalin's restrictions had been canceled as soon as was seemly after his death. The prohibition upon establishing paternity for children born out of wedlock was not abolished until 1968, however, suggesting that it had indeed offered certain practical benefits to the regime, despite popular feeling. No one spoke of some large new plan to socialize child-rearing. After six years of figuring, in 1981 the planners came up with a schedule of modest new subsidies. They were intended to tease the modern urban Russian couple to go on to a second child, then a third, while offering no incentive to families in the Moslem borderlands to go on to an eighth, ninth, or tenth. Drama and melodrama had faded from the demographic story in favor of a kind of endemic low anxiety.[54]

By the 1960s, as Gail Warshofsky Lapidus has pointed out, Soviet experts—economists, sociologists, demographers—were investigating Soviet women's lives in a new detail.[55] They found that, like the vast majority of Western working women, most Russian women worked in gender ghettos. This, more than anything else, explained why Russian women too earned on average about 65 percent of men's average income. Russian women went further in schools than Russian men, thus were more often overqualified for their jobs. Russian women were found over a wider span of the occupational spectrum than were Western women, but when it came to management levels, they too were vastly outnumbered by men. Were Russian women discontent with any of these conditions, as were many Western feminists? There was no way to tell. Studies agreed that in Soviet Russia women spent about two and a half times as long at housework as men did, about twenty-eight hours versus twelve. Many outside observers suspected this was a source of discontent. Polls, however, revealed no widespread wish among women to ease their double burden by giving up outside work. Asked in 1970 whether they would quit work for full-time devotion to home and children, were that possible, no less than 77 percent of a group of women in Moscow said no; only 19 percent preferred full-time domesticity.

Another poll in 1974 showed similar overwhelming preference. Nineteen percent was, however, a far higher proportion of women than were in fact engaged in full-time work at home. In 1970 some 33,000 young working women were asked about their intentions and their wishes for children. Fifteen percent said they intended to have only one child; 52 percent, two; 31 percent, three or more. But for an "ideal," 57 percent said three or more, while only 1.5 percent said only one. If a focus of discontent lay in the contrast between 31 percent intending to have three or more and the 57 percent who wanted three or more, or if unresolved tensions existed between disdain for full-time domesticity on the one hand and desire for more children on the other, no one asked.

Soviet ideologists remained at work. Their basic theme echoed the theme of all socialist triumphalism: under socialism all things combined in harmonious unity. Repeating sociologist Volfson's paean of 1936, a 1975 book intended for Western consumption systematically described Soviet women's lives as conflict-free progress toward "fully developed personality." Soviet historian Z. A. Yankova offered "proof of the existence of a harmonious link between the family and society." Philosopher Y. Z. Danilova noted the "harmonious combination of features common to all humanity and to those that are typically feminine." Another philosopher, V. S. Yazykova, noted that, whereas the Soviet state had once had to concentrate on "drawing women into production and public activity," now it faced the opportunity "to promote the harmonious development of woman's intellectual requirements (in creative labour, education, in setting up a family, making friends, recreation, caring for and bringing up children)." These new harmonies and unities were to be found not only between sectors of the system, between family and job, between politics and marriage, but within home and marriage themselves. Yankova cited a study that counted the frequency of four "types of family structure." These ran from the old authoritarian, man-headed family to the new family of "complete equality," the middle two being ranged in between. No fewer than 65 percent of families in Moscow were found to be the fourth, fully equal type; 53 and 51 percent of families in two smaller towns belonged there. Only 5 percent of Moscow families remained the old bourgeois capitalist authoritarian sort; in the other two localities, only 10 percent. Indeed, another study showed that only 43 percent of the families interviewed even thought they had a "head of the family." The other 57 percent professed to have no head at all; husband and wife guided the family equally in harmonious unity.

Close reading came upon certain themes that roughened the surface of this harmonious progress. Thus, despite a general disposition to say that men, if not yet doing so, certainly should be carrying more of the household's duties, Yankova said it was the mother who "largely determines the psychological and emotional atmosphere" of the family, while Yazykova, expounding on the importance of "the tenor of cultural and intellectual life in the family," proceeded to explain that mothers "determined" this. Historian Y. D. Yemelyanova, noting that women were far outnumbered by men in the party, the soviets, and all high offices generally, said this was a consequence of the fact that their "sociopolitical" activity had not been allowed to interfere with "their prime social function," that of "being mothers." Then, typically, Yemelyanova hastened to add that the gap would narrow as communal facilities grew. T. N. Sidorova used the same argument to explain women's lag in scientific reasearch, then commended efforts to reduce their domestic load as a solution. Darker suspicions welled up on occasion. Danilova said that "old customs and bigoted morals" in "everyday life" in the family were the greatest obstacle to change. "The survivals of the past in social consciousness are most tenacious in relations between man and woman, which, because of their intimate nature, are less amenable to public regulation than others." Such warnings could hardly be explored, however, for fear the picture of harmony and unity would prove but a façade, some new Potemkin's village, behind which the reality of life had been hidden. Still more dangerous was sudden apprehension that disharmony, contradiction, and conflict existed, not as "survivals of the past" but as functions of the new society itself. Yankova noted that teachers, psychologists, and others found that small families were centered "solely on the children." "In such a family a woman devotes a vast amount of time to her child and the satisfaction of its egoistic demands." While a rising material standard of living in the Soviet Union "does not stimulate the growth of consumer psychology," this might not prove to remain so much longer, were more and more Soviet children to grow up mother-spoiled and egoistical.[56]

Such occasional anxieties were but froth on hidden reefs, the shadow of dim monsters beneath the surface of Soviet self-congratulation. Westerners eager to know how Russian women really felt got little from Soviet social science. More spontaneous hints were precious. A short story published in Moscow in 1969, "A Week like Any Other," by Natalia Baranskaia, was seized upon by a host of observers as just such a hint of feelings unaccommodated by ideology. The heroine of "A Week like Any Other," Olga, was a modern postwar Russian career woman.[57] A university graduate with an advanced degree, she had a job in a scientific lab with a promising future. She had a husband, two children, a home. She was twenty-six years old and already drawn, drained and tired. Living two full-time roles, she was being torn by the strain of it, and, looking ahead, could see no early change in her situation. One solution for Olga might have been to give up her job and career, assuming her income was not absolutely necessary. Some Western observers guessed that this could well become an attractive option for many Soviet women:

Whereas abroad the feminist quest has encouraged the right to work, in the Soviet Union some women would nonetheless press instead for the right and ability *not* to work. Elsewhere, this has characteristically been a middle-class demand; and perhaps, as the functional equivalent of a middle class develops ever more clearly in the USSR, this demand (assuming it can be afforded) will be more loudly and widely voiced.[58]

Baranskaia's heroine hardly gave it a thought: "I value my independence." Other students felt sure that many would agree.

I sense that in spite of their double burden of work, women by and large accept the Soviet government's claim to have vastly improved the lot of women and opened to them the doors of professional life.[59]

Of course for Olga it was too late to remain single, but to young women reading her story that option might seem worth some consideration. But few if any Western observers felt that this was a serious option for Russian women:

I see no sign that young women at any level of society are even considering the ideal of remaining single as an acceptable alternative to marriage. Marriage is central to young Russian women for life without a husband seems senseless; everyone wants to get married, even those girls . . . of the intelligentsia.[60]

In Baranskaia's story, Olga's husband was not castigated for failure to share household duties, and it is not clear whether he did or did not in fact share them. Presumably, husband and wife still loved each other anyway. It was an attractive option for Western students to single out Russian men, however, as culprits in the story of women's two roles. Historian Alexander Dallin characterized "the Soviet man" in general:

Whereas all sorts of technical and organizational "solutions" to [the problem of women's overload] are discussed, the central issue underlying the widespread demand for new "division of labor" between male and female in the house and in child-rearing, is the attitude of the Soviet man. This, and not communist doctrine, is the real problem of ideology that confronts Soviet women.[61]

Earlier, the author of the first major American study of Soviet women, Norton Dodge, had laid responsibility at more specific feet: "Lenin's call to liberate women from the tyranny of husbands and the home has had few strong advocates within top Party circles . . . equality in the home for Soviet women continues to be far less evident than equality in the workplace." Richard Stites preferred this wider focus: "Soviet

men . . . are not really ready to grant complete equality to women."[62]
All this, however, was more nearly an expression of Western, perhaps
peculiarly American, liberal feminism than of Russian views. Even
Soviet apologists recoiled from the picture of Soviet man over the stove.

The communist mode of life presupposes not an equal sharing of "slavish"
functions, but the abolition of "domestic bondage," not the equal division of
housework between wife and husband, but the transference of the most unproductive, the most dulling chores to public services.[63]

Unfortunately, this finessed the more existential fact, clear to Western
observers, that the "domestic bondage" was worse in Soviet Russia
than in the West:

Child-care and housework are considerably more burdensome for Soviet than
for American working women. . . . Soviet women grumble about the "second
shift." Although child-care facilities are much more extensive . . . the supply
does not meet the demand. The availability and quality. . . of household machinery. . . fall far short.[64]

Thus, while Soviet men did not share any more than Italian or Swedish
or American men, Russian women were worse off than their sisters.
Baranskaia's story could of course hardly dwell upon this.

"A Week like Any Other" was that rarity in Soviet literature, a story
without a lesson. It offered no solution, and was all the more revolutionary in Soviet contexts for that. Western observers might wonder,
however, whether the Olgas—and the Mashas—told as much about
modern Soviet gender psychology as the masses of women at work in
their gender ghettos. If marriage remained the hope for all, perhaps
for most that hope set priorities:

Most Soviet women appear to be eager to marry and to stay married. Most
seem to attach much greater importance to their families than to their jobs. . . .
the things women like or dislike about their jobs may often merely reflect the
extent to which the job demands mesh with or complicate the family situation.[65]

In Baranskaia's story, Olga appeared to want not to have to choose, and
Soviet ideology declared, as had Volfson, that Soviet women did not
have to and did not want to choose. Yankova cited still another poll in
which women were asked which of two tasks, "public activity" or "child
care and managing the household," was primary. Eighty-six percent
replied, "Both tasks are primary." But women who did have a priority
of marriage over job might then generate discriminating demands on
the economy, adjusted to both their marriages and their work.

[Some] Soviet women do yearn for a Western model—but it is the model of a
part-time housewife with part-time employment, or even a full-time housewife. . . . To some Soviet women, the division of labor between the traditional

Western middle-class family appears, rightly or wrongly, to be a luxury they hope a rising standard of living ultimately will afford them. Within the present Soviet context, such women prefer a narrowly defined, 40-hour-a-week job to the kind of commitment to career—let alone . . . Party. . .—that usually is necessary for administrative promotion.[66]

For an Olga this was of course unacceptable. She was doomed to go on being Superwoman, trying to do it all, exhausted.

Paradoxically, women's attachment to marriage and home suggested that women might be happier than men with the Soviet system. Colette Shulman offered one such speculation:

It is my impression that for most Russian girls the identity process is not particularly aggravated by their images of their future roles. . . . Exempt from the harsh school of military service and for the most part from the pressures of political infighting for promotion to high jobs, with their lives rooted in caring for home, husband, and children, Soviet women retain a wholeness of spirit and a capacity for belief that makes them less vulnerable than men to disillusionment and cynicism.[67]

The contrast between men and women, then, was that women really cared less about the system, about the party and its monopoly of power, about the campaigns for accelerated performance, about the connivances of this manager and the dynamics of that. Men, whether they wanted to or not, had to confront the realities of the system, and disillusionment and cynicism followed from their helplessness in it. Women thus were more "harmonious" with the system. They were indeed, as Joel C. Moses found, the proper guardians of loyalty within the party.[68]

On December 10, 1979, a new magazine, *Women and Russia*, appeared among the intelligentsia of Leningrad.[69] It was an unofficial magazine, hence illegal. Its editors, Marina Oulianova and Tatiana Mamonova, were feminists, hence illegal. They printed essays, poems, and autobiographical fragments from a dozen or so other women. They dared the censorship to let them be heard.

One of the striking things about *Women and Russia* was its diversity of views. Though an exercise in dissent, the magazine did not belong with the dissident movement, already familiar in the West, composed mainly of male intellectuals and artists. This dissident movement, known for its literature circulating underground, had never concerned itself with women's issues. Not only had it "never raised the question of women and feminism," Oulianova charged, but "it was phallocratic, like the whole organization devoted to Samizdat." As she saw it, dissident women were on their own. But they were at one only in their dissidence, not in their theory or in their grievances. Thus, while Oulianova herself was as hostile to the old Orthodox church and religion as any old Bolshevik, both Svetlana Sonova and Tania Sororeva, raised in atheist schools, anchored their criticisms of the regime in an awakened Christian faith. Most contributors simply ignored religion.

One strong feeling did thread its way through most of the pieces: Russian women suffered much more than men from Soviet society. No consensus emerged, however, as to whether this condition followed mostly from Soviet practices or from the residue of pre-Soviet practices. More of the writers still revered Lenin while blaming Stalin for Soviet woes than judged Lenin himself responsible. In their utter specificity, some of those woes simply transcended decades of ideological debate. Vera Natalieva, a Leningrad resident, repeated laments about housing that the Italian ambassador had noted seventeen years before, and that Trotsky had glossed forty-three years before. Natalieva's emphasis was upon forced sociability: only one oven, one stove, one kitchen for several families, and only one laundry. The bad old days of only one faucet and one toilet had been ended for many—though by no means all—but Natalieva lamented lack of privacy. She gave it a "class" note: when one was an intellectual in a community apartment, one met neighbors' suspicion, scorn, and even fear. Natalieva was not ready to charge that Soviet housing plans were calculated deliberately to check privacy, to promote harmonious sharing, although that had been the guess of Maurice Hindus fifty years before:

Large apartments for a single family will never again be built in Russia while the present regime remains in power. Home never again can be a physical or any other kind of castle. There is no need, say the Russians, for large homes, because so much of the life of the family has already been transferred to outside places.[70]

Home was the place where "egoistical" personalities were hatched, disharmonious with the communal and the social. Natalieva for one had here stepped forth, as a feminist, lamenting the absence, not the tyranny of home, and she did so not in the name of traditional domestic virtues, but as a feminist desiring intellectual and psychological freedom.

Perhaps the most common lamentation from the contributors to *Women and Russia* focused upon Russian men. Western observers had been intrigued to sense no animus toward men even among Russian women discontent with their lives. Gail Warshofsky Lapidus has written: "From a comparative perspective, Soviet writings are conspicuously devoid of overt hostility to men, even though male behavior is a frequent target of criticism." Bernice Madison agreed: "Soviet women are not man-haters"[71] The contributors to *Women and Russia* did not quite confirm this view. Oulianova asserted that alcoholism raged as a veritable plague: "The women buy the vodka, the men drink it, then the men beat the women." Struck by the spread of what she called the "maternal family," Natalia Malakhovskaia traced it partly to wives' desire to rid themselves of "their drunken husbands." Liudmila Nobatova went so far as to speculate that one reason Russian women were so eagerly sought for jobs was that Russian men were so prone to drink on the job. Masculine drinking could be seen as a symptom of deeper things. In a psychoanalytic study, Tatiana Goritcheva argued that Soviet Russian men sought a mother in their wives, and therefore often married women older than themselves. Tania Sororeva agreed: "Soviet men have a very infantile psyche."

Complaints and alarm over Russian men's drinking, particularly in the countryside, had been a staple of reformist literature for 150 years. The regime itself, concerned at evidence that the habit had spread widely into factories, had tried standard methods of direct and indirect discouragement but not checked the blight. In *Women and Russia* Tatiana Goritcheva offered a broad sociological analysis of the malady that the regime could not have accepted. In the Soviet Union, she said, women had not really been emancipated. Instead, men had been reduced to the status of women, reduced to the passivity and dutiful routine that had characterized traditional femininity for centuries:

In a society like ours, man cannot be independent, cannot confront life with actions, cannot construct his own life consciously and freely. While in the family (ravaged by widespread alcoholism), as in industry, women constitute the foundation. At present, they are obliged to.[72]

It was the sense that something was sadly wrong not with Soviet women but with Soviet men, *Homo Sovieticus*, that most nearly unified the voices in *Women and Russia*. Their attestations to the troubles of women, their anger at the indifference of male dissidents, their evocations of the martyrdom of women were sharp, but no more heartfelt than their sense that Communist Party politics had cut to the heart of life, into the heart of life, into the nexus, the bond, the union between men and women, and had harmed it, perhaps mortally. Here was feminism as subversion indeed.

Within days of the publication of issue number one of *Women and Russia*, KGB men came calling. Tatiana Mamonova recalled some of the interrogation:

KGB: "Do you deny you are the editor of *Women and Russia*?"
TM: "I do not deny it. I'm happy about it, since with our signature on the Helsinki Accords of 1975 we can at last receive and send information."
KGB: "You publish disinformation. Aren't you ashamed? Pitiful stuff. . . ."
TM: "We'll try to do better in the second issue."
KGB: "And why don't you publish officially?"

TM: "I'd be happy to publish officially. Will you help?"
KGB: "That's not our business."[73]

Issue number one proved to be the last issue of *Women and Russia* in Russia.

By no means were the feminists of *Women and Russia* "representative" or "ordinary." How to tell just what voices were typical remained a problem beyond solution. Still, it seemed likely some women were satisfied with Soviet policies. Perhaps the most poignant group among postwar Soviet women were those who, in their own sixties and seventies during the 1950s and 1960s, had found in jobs provided by the regime solace for their blighted private lives, whether as widows, divorcées, or most common of all, never married. In the cities such women served as floor monitors in the hotels, as concierges, the eyes and ears of the police in the great new housing blocks. Most of all they were to be found in the countryside:

Mysovsky turned his head. . . . On the other side of the street a whole detachment of elderly women were striding along in single file one after the other. All very smartly dressed in their Sunday best—just as in the old days they used to set off to church. . . . "Where are you off to in such fine order?" "What, don't you realise this is *our* day. . . . ?" "You mean you're off for your pensions?" "That's it, that's it. . . . We are grateful to the present authorities. . . . If I could write I'd send a letter to Moscow itself. They did not forget us in our old age."[74]

No more than in Italy, Sweden, or the United States can the story of women in Soviet Russia be summarized in aphoristic concision. Nor can it be compared with those other stories as to relative progress, achievements, and failures. It can, however, be consulted in pursuit of a hypothesis: "where the individual is engulfed in the social, equality can be achieved without freedom."

Conclusion

For Anna Maria Mozzoni and her peers, the prime need of Italian feminism was friends and allies. Had Giuseppe Mazzini presided over the first years of Italian unity, it seems reasonable to guess that able and dedicated women would have shared in guiding it. One of them could well have been Mozzoni herself. Nothing told her that, as a woman, she lacked any of the qualities required for civic, public life. Under Mazzini, women like Mozzoni might have used the new powers of the state for women's benefit. But Mazzini was to be the saint, not the organizer, of Italian nationhood. Cavour and his heirs gave priority, not to the cultural and spiritual ambitions inspiring Mazzini, in which women might count, but to economic and diplomatic ambitions, in which they did not. Thus, although the early governments were anti-clerical, they had little reason to extend significant favor even to anti-clerical women like Mozzoni and other feminists.

Hope for Italiam feminism, then, had to rest in growth in the numbers of those who, like Mozzoni, being educated, free of the ideologies of the church, and ambitious, might come to constitute a meaningful mass. But the faltering Italian economy did not begin to underwrite growing numbers of such women. Insofar as a middle class did emerge, it remained heavily Catholic. When Mozzoni herself turned to the new Socialist Party, it was from lack of alternatives, and the alliance with socialism would prove frustrating, too. The obvious opportunity for the masses of Italian women was to share with the masses of Italian men in political democratization: most men as well as all women still lacked the vote. But Socialists feared the majority of Italian women: their political leaders were the priests. Thus when Giovanni Giolitti pursued his politics of incorporation to the point of democratizing the suffrage, no one prodded him to include women. By the time the Socialists finally resolved their ambivalence in 1919, it was too late. Luigi Sturzo's Popular Party too supported suffrage for women, but the Popolari and the Socialists canceled each other out. No alliance emerged to head off Benito Mussolini with his quite special kind of feminism. Perhaps it had been inevitable in Italian history that the split between state and church would be overcome; when it happened, in 1930, it buried a feminism already dead. Whether the fundamental reason for the failure of early Italian feminism derived simply from the fact that there were too few feminists cannot be affirmed, however. Even a more flourishing feminist movement would have found great difficulty in escaping maceration in Italian politics, hungering as that politics was for what it could never capture, economic success.

Early Swedish feminism suffered a quite different fate. In Sweden too, feminists remained few. That preindustrial Swedish life itself prompted visions of sexual individualism on the one hand, and of matriarchal community on the other, Almqvist and Bremer showed. But such utopianisms were soon chilled by the breakup of that older life. The early feminists were themselves part of the old elite establishment, hence quite uninspired to search out new allies, let alone imagine feminism as a growing popular movement. Some of Strindberg's animus against early feminists followed from his sense exactly of this elite, privileged status. As parties took shape, only the party of the new farmers openly resisted women's progress. Had the Liberal Party, under Karl Staaff, won stable dominance in Swedish politics, women would have benefited, for Staaff's party was committed to women's as well as men's universal suffrage. What liberalism might have meant for women in the marketplace was another matter. On the one hand it might, in the tradition of *Hertha*, have opened the way for women in town governments, perhaps even the parliament and the state. On the other hand, being solicitous of craftsmen and small entrepreneurs, it might have tended toward perpetuation of old Sweden's guild privileges, which had reserved craft skills to fathers and husbands. The pervasiveness of the assumption that women would share in a new Sweden showed itself when the Conservatives, not the Liberals, voted in woman suffrage, at least partly in echo of the Bremer Society's original elite ties.

The final step in this assimilation of feminism into parties came with the rise of the Social Democrats. Feminists who had rejected the Bremer Society for its elitism in favor of the unions and the SD were of course then forced to face the question whether feminism had a place within socialism. If feminism was indeed a bourgeois movement, adapted to the wishes and ambitions of educated, ambitious, talented middle-class women, what did it have to do with the problem of the workers? But the Swedish Social Democrats' rapid abandonment of ideological nicety in favor of Swedish nationalism quickly eased tensions, and the interests of women entered the agenda of the SSD well in time for the party's long domination. What this meant, of course, was that feminists within the unions and the SSD would never be free to evolve consciousness of their interests on their own. Always, they would have to think and act with the policies of their great friend in mind.

For American women, there would be no such experiences as those of these early Italian and Swedish feminists. American feminists, unlike the Italian, would find no shortage of educated, ambitious women to become feminists, and thriving feminist organizations would find allies among temperance people, church people, and the rising exponents of a new evangel, social science. Feminism would be a far more vital movement in all that "third party" of reform that flourished in America but not in Italy. On the other hand, American feminists would have no such friends as the Swedish court, the Liberal Party, the Conservative Party, or finally the Social Democrats. Whigs, Democrats, and Republicans alike would maintain indifference. The result of this isolation would not be Italian-style helplessness, however, but rather a vitalizing freedom that Swedish feminists were denied. American feminists had their own sphere in which to evolve, women's sphere, subsidized by the flourishing of middle-class life based on a flourishing democratic capitalism.

In the Soviet Union, bourgeois feminism was simply extinguished by suppression and exile after Lenin's revolution in 1917. But Bolshevik ideology had nothing against women either in the marketplace or in posts of power. Whether Alexandra Kollontai's fall from such positions of power registered a failure on Lenin's part in living up to his ideology, a failure of prudence and tactics on Kollontai's part, or some sociology inherent in Lenin's practice of party dictatorship that made gender discrimination inevitable, can hardly be decided once and for all. Still, Kollontai's fall did not bring down the Women's Department. Until 1930 an agency did continue to exist, however strongly directed by party leaders, that sought to ameliorate harsh conditions and promote consciousness among women. Here was the shape of what might be labeled "Communist feminism." Even during its brief life, however, this Communist feminism did not enjoy enough freedom to debate, for instance, whether the New Economic Policy might hold promise for women greater than that offered by crash industrialization and rural collectivization. Those Russian women who were directly involved in the NEP, whether in farmers' markets, shopkeeping, or even factory work, as well as wives and daughters, were strictly forbidden any organizations of their own. Hence, suppression of the grass roots of feminism had begun years before Stalin's liquidation of the Women's Department. Nevertheless, it is useful to speak of the condition of feminism in Soviet Russia, if only as a kind of ghost, in order to ask exactly what it was that feminism did and did not lose as a consequence of Communist political monopoly.

Asking the question from Kollontai's perspective, we can see that Russian feminists lost the chance to link the marketplace and sexuality. Kollontai had strongly urged that sex, sexuality, and sexual relationships be relegated to a secondary, even minor, place in women's lives.

That, indeed, was a primary motive for her demand that women work. Lenin of course agreed. But with the suppression of feminism in Soviet Russia, debate over this linkage was suppressed. Pronouncements on the proper linkages between sexuality and marketplace, home and work, private and public, issued at the time of the decrees of 1936 and 1944 had nothing to do with feminism. They followed from calculations of Stalin's labor market managers and demographers. At the same time, the lack of feminism in Soviet Russia did not cost Russian women jobs, careers, life beyond the home. On the contrary. As post-World War II Russian women went on to still higher levels of training, of professional opportunity, of administrative responsibility, they did so still without the impulsion of any feminism at all. By every coherent index, a higher proportion of Russian women held more jobs and pursued more careers than their Swedish and American sisters, where feminism had never been suppressed, and more too than their Italian sisters, in whose country feminism, after suppression, had been reborn. Had this happened because, under Communism, feminism was unnecessary?

While socialist ideology had always criticized feminism on class grounds, it had never explained why, under socialism, a feminist movement had to be suppressed, made illegal, criminalized. The criminalization of feminism under Soviet Communism followed from political motives, not socialist ideology. Stalin's crash industrialization, whether justified by reference to Russia's enemies or utilized as a means to complete the dictatorship, required every worker available. Women were eminently available. The true parallel between the Soviet Union's full employment and the West was with Western nations at war: then capitalism too drew heavily on women. Neither historic Western feminism nor socialist feminism had ever addressed the issue of full employment through national mobilization; Russian feminists were not allowed to. By the late 1970s Soviet husbands, in echo of the call in the Swedish sex-role debate of the late 1960s, were being asked to think about sharing in the housework. It was impossible to tell whether such calls were coming from feminism's ghost. Certainly such an idea would have repelled both Kollontai and Lenin. The idea of Communist Man doing the dishes fitted none of their visions. But as Leon Trotsky had long ago observed, Joseph Stalin's Communism had made mockery of the old idea of abundance through socialism. Women had not been freed from housework. They had just been given a second full-time job. The suppressed debate in Soviet Russia had to do with other questions. How many people might like to have another child, if they could afford it? What would it cost to help women cut down on the hours they spent on family duties? How many women might like to work only half time? How many would like not to have to work at all? How many women presently at work could the economy spare as full-time homemakers? Essentially, these questions reversed the perspective of feminism in Sweden and America; in Sweden and America they were not discussed because they seemed the reverse of what concerned most women most. In Soviet Russia they were not discussed because of politics.

As Italian feminism struggled for rebirth after the disaster of Fascism and war, pathos rather than tragedy came to characterize it. Nothing could have seemed more obvious in 1945 than that Italy's first and urgent need was for economic revival. Italian women would be borne up on its rising tide along with their men. No conceivable inequalities between men and women, no conceivable grievance of women as women, could diminish that hope. As women had shared with their men in the debacle of defeat, so they would share in recovery. Yet Italian feminists could not follow that elementary and powerful logic. They were trapped. The agency plainly destined by no later than 1948 to preside over any economic recovery that might commence was also antifeminist. Whatever ambitions Alcide De Gaspari may or may not have nursed for reviving the kind of lay, nonclerical Catholic democratic party that Luigi Sturzo had led, free of obedience to the church, he could not resist the Vatican's constant presence, supplemented by American diplomacy. The DC's women's organizations were creatures of the party. On the other hand, Palmiro Togliatti's Communists had no commitment to an economic miracle. Proceeding on the standard ideological assumption of an eventual breakdown of the economy from its "contradictions," the Communists set about building their mass opposition for an indefinite wait for power. Thus any and all Italian women in the tradition of Mozzoni, talented, ambitious, secular-minded, free of Catholic imprint, had no place to go. They could hope that enough of an economic boom might be inspired to begin to multiply jobs, careers, and professions, but they could not make the case for women in such positions except in isolation. Should the economy flourish, they might begin to constitute an interest group on their own, but they would have to hope for some decline in the polarization of politics, some rise in the fortunes of parties in between.

Meanwhile, such women had little ground from which to compete with the Union of Italian Women linked to the PCI. Inheriting from Turati's Socialists a tension between the interests of its hard-core of blue-collar male workers and some ideology of full employment, the PCI found it expedient to perpetuate Gramsci's visions of a traditional Catholic-Communist family, utterly at odds with any hopes and ambitions of young women like Mozzoni, as well as Kollontai, individualistic, wholly disinclined to sequestration in the roles of wife and mother, eager for public responsibilities and power. Once the economic miracle itself faded, undercutting hopes for sheer material opportunity, and once the tiny secular, free-trade parties of the center grew even tinier, the logic was set for blowup. But the repudiation of the PCI by the young radical feminists of 1968 and thereafter left them even more homeless than before. For some of these young women, this provided the opportunity for pressing feminist self-consciousness beyond issues of equality and into issues of sexual relationship; many called for separation, *separatezza*. But most turned again to utopianism. They followed Gramsci's path of looking for some vision of ultimate harmony, health, and stability in Italy, a vision not of parties and churches and intellectuals but of the people, that hard-working, essentially pious but anti-clerical, communal, and moral people that had already carried Italy through its centuries of captivity before the Risorgimento.

All this proceeded in complete contrast to Sweden's story. There, once the sorting out of the political parties was over by the late 1920s and early 1930s, Swedish feminism enjoyed a home, safe and secure and powerful, against which it would find it hard to protest. Social democracy would neither press women to work, like Stalin, nor encourage them to stay home, like the Vatican. It neither prescribed a women's sphere as women's proper place nor embarked upon public programs to socialize the home. One result was to lend feminism in Sweden a muffled quality. An Elin Wägner might grow anxious that, in the technically skillful pursuit of economic abundance, some quality of community was being lost, a quality that Ellen Key had embodied, of motherhood manifested not out of sociological necessity and women's subordination but from within women's deepest spirit. On the other hand, an Eva Moberg might suddenly realize that the supposedly egalitarian unions and Socialist Party were doing nothing to prevent a traditional male monopoly of power and leadership from persisting. But just as Wägner found it hard to imagine a more family-centered politics than the Social Democrats', so Moberg found it hard to get beyond criticism of the bosses to the question why women and feminists had not already allied for equality.

Neither of these situations would characterize post-World War II feminism in America. For one thing, postwar feminism in the United States would have to get itself reborn. Why had it disintegrated? No Fascism had suppressed it. No Stalinism had suffocated it. One of postwar American feminism's most basic problems would be to reckon with its peculiar past. Similarly, postwar American feminism would enjoy no such capable bearer as the Swedish Social Democrats. On the contrary, as its most likely helper, the postwar Democrats, staggered and foundered, feminists would find themselves for the first time faced by a political party hostile to feminism and unsympathetic to the problems overtaking a steadily growing number of women.

Similarities might be emphasized over contrasts in the stories of Italy, Sweden, and Soviet Russia. In none of the three countries did women win new status in politics. Can this be interpreted, then, to say that no connection existed between workplace status and power? While the answer to the question can only be more "yes" than "no," the question is more useful as it points beyond itself. Clearly, for women equality with men might be achieved along several routes. The feminist route took for granted that women ought to rise to men's level and, hence, share the powers men had enjoyed and women had not. But equality could also be achieved through the process of men's loss of power. In that case, feminism would have to rethink its own goals and tactics. Ultimately, the most critical power for feminism was its freedom and resources for thinking about itself. From that perspective, workplace equality mattered most exactly as it stimulated or undermined feminism. Here the contrasts were far more compelling than the similarities between Italy, Sweden, and Soviet Russia.

Part III The American Case

I have divided the American story differently from the stories of Italy, Sweden, and Soviet Russia. Instead of first presenting the course of American political economy to the present, I have halted at 1920, in order to look next at American feminism to that date. The historical reason obviously is that 1920 marked a climax in the history of American feminism. Such a reason might have justified a division in the Italian story too, for in an important sense, 1919 marked a kind of high point for Italian feminism as well, followed by a decline comparable to that of feminism in America. But my fuller reason for dividing the American story is to highlight the daunting problem for American historians of explaining feminism's decline after 1920. The historian of Italy need do no more than point at Fascism. But feminism in the United States rose in the context of the powerful democratic capitalism of the early nineteenth century. It sustained itself through the powerful industrialization of the last half of the century, and moved on to its suffrage victory through the progressive years of political and economic consolidation. No obvious events in political and economic life after 1920 seemed to decree the withering of feminism. Although I am hardly unaware of the profound changes and episodic vicissitudes within both political and economic life in the United States since 1920, I have preferred to emphasize the even more powerful continuities, precisely in order to emphasize the dramatically different story of feminism and women's consciousness. Chapter 9, therefore, on American political economy after 1920, while in no way perfunctory, is deliberately short, to set off its longer counterpart that follows.

7 Early Wonderland

Machines and Democracy: The American Stimulant for Men Only

Twenty-four years after declaring independence, seventeen years after a victorious peace, eleven years after installing a sturdy frame of government, the United States remained shaggy, muddy, nondescript. This was so of Puritan lands as well as of the slavery-cursed South: "in spite of more than a century and a half of incessant industry, intelligent labor, and pinching economy Boston and New England were still poor." Though "great planters lavished money . . . on experiments to improve their crops and their stock" in Virginia, they did so, as Henry Adams noted, "in vain." Some of the basic needs were understood: "If Americans agreed in any opinion, they were united in wishing for roads."[1] Yet somehow roads did not get built. Antidemocratic conservatives blamed democracy: popular publics refused to pay. Similarly, the technology of steam engines, already widely applied in England, seemed to leave Americans indifferent. First John Fitch, then Robert Fulton, were treated as foolish cranks. When the capital was transferred in 1800 from sophisticated Philadelpha, Benjamin Franklin's town, to a "fever-stricken morass" on the banks of the Potomac, the nation's future seemed sealed. The new President, self-consciously democratic, spoke of enough "room" to the west for a "thousand years" of agrarian simplicity. Soon, perhaps realizing that a thousand years were not enough to accommodate the hundred generations he had foreseen, Thomas Jefferson contracted for the Louisiana Purchase, doubling the national acreage. A farmers' democracy seemed certain.

Among the defeated antidemocratic Federalists, Alexander Hamilton in particular had been sure that the new United States could not be both a great and an agricultural nation. Hamilton had urged that, since the democratic majority was obviously going to be preoccupied with land, crops, and the West, deliberate measures be taken by the new national government to promote industrial growth. Let a national bank be established to make loans to entrepreneurs. Let duties be set to protect American enterprises from English competition. Let taxes be levied to pay for improvements. Let the wartime debt be funded in order to create a class of creditors with a stake in a strong government. Above all, though, Hamilton wrote a "Report on Manufactures" for the House of Representatives in 1791, in which he revealed the key to a mighty future.

Almost surely challenging a distinction favored among the philosophers of the century, namely, that what was "natural" counted as rational, reliable, and desirable by comparison with what was "artificial," Hamilton hailed machinery as "an artificial force brought in aid of the natural force of man . . . an increase of hands, an accession of strength." Of course the increase Hamilton most welcomed was not that of "hands" but of minds, heads, hearts. The liberating power of machines lay not in their production to meet men's needs, but in their stimulus of new needs. Manufacturing "creates a demand for [articles] such as were [previously] either unknown or produced in inconsiderable quantities." Inciting new demands, machinery multiplied itself. With such an expansion of wishes and desires, the "bowels as well as the surface of the earth are ransacked for articles which were before neglected," and animals, plants, and minerals "acquire a utility and a value which were before unexplored."[2] In effect, earth itself would be transformed, "nature" and the "natural" coming to be understood not as "form" but as activity, in reciprocity with the transformative activity of man-the-machine-maker.

This Hamiltonian vision of an industrial America itself carried a powerful democratic charge. One of the fundamental facts about mankind as a whole, the Treasury secretary wrote, was its "diversity of talents and dispositions." Men were different from each other. But how could an agricultural society ever liberate this diversity? Where farming prevailed, most talents went unchallenged, most imaginations unawakened. On the other hand, "when all the different kinds of industry obtain in a community, each individual can find his proper element, and can call into activity the whole vigor of his nature."[3] Agriculture meant conformity, industry meant variety; agriculture meant routine and repetition, industry meant innovation, transformation, change, new products, new lives, new hearts and minds.

Hamilton got his bank, his funded debt, a few taxes and some duties to his taste, but these were overwhelmed by politics. English goods might be discouraged by tariffs, but Americans would not be discouraged from land. Even John Adams, a fellow Federalist, found Hamilton's vision abhorrent; a stand-patter, Adams wanted to protect the old New England Way against democracy, not undermine it with planned innovation.

Had Hamilton been less suspicious of democracy, he need not have feared the results of Jefferson's victory. However raw and ragged the country was in 1800, Henry Adams later felt its future already assured, not in the endless acres treasured by Jefferson but in the "national character." In America individuals had been relieved of the burden of institutions—of "church, aristocracy, family, army . . . political intervention." In effect, in America human nature had at last been liberated. "Reversing the old-world system, the American stimulant increased in energy as it reached the lowest and most ignorant class, dragging and whirling them upward as in the blast of a furnace." In the United States men put their pasts behind them. Nor were they controlled by the poverty of the present. "The poor came, and from them were seldom heard complaints of deception or delusion." Americans lived for the future. From "the mere contact of a moral atmosphere," ordinary men "saw the gold and jewels, the summer cornfields, and the glowing continent."[4]

Adams was echoing Alexis de Tocqueville. Arriving in 1830 for a long and careful visit, Tocqueville found "a social state in which neither law nor custom holds anyone in one place." The result was "feverish ardor," "restlessness of temper," a whole people "in a hurry." Since neither nature nor politics set a limit to human endeavor, "the American lives in a land of wonders." The greatest wonder was the unlocking of human nature. Animals, Tocqueville observed, "only know how to satisfy their primary and coarsest needs," whereas we human beings "can infinitely vary and continually increase our delights." Here was the promise Hamilton had linked to machines, now defining a society.

The universal movement prevailing in the United States, the frequent reversals . . . the unexpected shifts . . . all unite to keep the mind in a sort of feverish agitation which wonderfully disposes it toward every type of exertion and keeps it, so to say, above the common level of humanity.[5]

Tocqueville did not hesitate in emphasizing the general truly egalitarian dimension of this temperament. Choose any American at random, he said, and you will find him "a man of burning desires, enterprising, adventurous, and, above all, an innovator." True, one category of men were left out, blacks, whether slave or free, and Tocqueville made clear that by "democracy" he meant only the North, not the South where "spiritualized despotism and violence" reigned. He could foresee terrible conflict arising between North and South. The "atrocity" of slavery had not checked the enterprise and exertion of the ordinary white man in the North, however. So powerful had the stimulus of opportunity become that Tocqueville found Americans transcending the usual psychology of needs altogether.

Chance is an element always present to the mind of those who live in the unstable conditions of a democracy, and in the end they come to love enterprises in which chance plays a part. This draws them to trade not only for the sake of promised gain, but also because they love the emotions it provides.

Americans did not take up land in order to settle down, or make money in order to store it up.Their passion was for "a sort of gamble, and they enjoy the sensations as much as the profit." "For an American the whole of life is treated like a game of chance, a time of revolution, or the day of a battle."[6]

By 1830 the country was no longer the primitive place it still remained at the beginning of the century. The Erie Canal had been built. Steamships were on the rivers. Roads had been cut and hardened. Towns were multiplying, city life growing richer. Tocqueville came too soon to observe large-scale industrialization and factories, and his observations of the flourishing local manufactories were sporadic. Trade impressed him most, and he could foresee trade becoming "a national interest of the first importance." As yet, Americans bought manufactured goods from England for the simplest reason: "low cost is the supreme law of trade," and the English sold cheap. But already, in addition to "the innumerable multitude of little undertakings," industrial enterprises of "extraordinary" size were being founded. A grand final prospect opened. "I cannot help believing that one day [the Americans] will become the leading naval power on the globe.They are born to rule the seas."[7]

Tocqueville's sense that industrial expansion in the United States was linked with democracy reflected history.[8] The principles of large-scale industrial activity had been perfectly well understood in 1800. Eli Whitney had extrapolated one great principle, that of the division of labor, into another, that of interchangeable parts, at his New Haven gun factory in 1798. At Waltham, Boston men built a factory in 1812 that demonstrated the integration of several different manufacturing processes under one roof. Yet the few factory towns of early nineteenth-century America—Providence and Fall River, Waltham and Lowell, Troy, Cohoes, Utica, Hamilton's Paterson—were more conspicuous as exceptions than as heralds. The most important industrial growth proceeded in hidden ways, carried out in households by families, in small mills along a thousand streams, in small shops harboring a heterogeneity of artificers, all exhibiting that "peculiar aptitude for mechanic improvements" that Hamilton himself had recognized as a democratic trait. Such local manufacturing surged in the 1820s, perhaps by as much as 50 percent; it continued to grow in the 1830s, then boomed again in the 1840s at the highest rate yet. By 1840 steam engines, welcomed at last, were producing more horsepower—760 thousands—than in Britain (620 thousands). British industry still far outproduced American, but in America a far broader and deeper base was being laid. North of slavery, little engines proliferated. In another ten years the American lead over Britain had reached 400 thousands of horsepower.

Although American artisans often feared factories, they were consistently progressive in improving their tools and methods. They themselves patronized a thousand local mills and forges. The European guild, with its compulsion to protect secrets and defy innovation, had not crossed the Atlantic. Tocqueville worried about the tendency of industry to degrade craft workers, throw up a few rich men, and produce a multitude of the poor, but he doubted that these new rich could become a stable class, with a stable and coherent class interest. Factory workers, however, constituted a more serious problem; they were in danger of becoming "stationary," a special case of people in the midst of general mobility, at the mercy of their employers. Although Tocqueville had praised the American habit of getting together to get things done, he said nothing about the possibility of labor unions, referring this problem instead to "the particular attention of legislators."[9] Otherwise it was clear to Tocqueville that American economic growth proceeded inextricable from popular democratic interests. Agriculture itself, the interest of the vast majority, was thoroughly implicated. Agriculture, trade, industry, the three went together. The blast furnace of the "American stimulus" was melting fixity, structures, classes, and interests into a general interest.

Tocqueville explicitly named what that interest was. "The love of money is either the chief or the secondary motive at the bottom of everything the Americans do." He was not being critical. Americans did not pursue money because they were greedy but because they were democrats. Democracy and money had logical connections. Democracy threatened always to disintegrate into mere anarchy, a welter of individualism. How could men be got to hold back from sheer short-run opportunism? How could any kind of society and community be sustained in a democracy? Rank and deference had been repudiated; authority and power had no legitimacy except as democratized. One way remained: "The cooperation of each . . . can only be obtained by paying for it." Praising the quickness with which Americans combined for every kind of goal and task, the trait historians would label an "associational" impulse, Tocqueville unflinchingly located it not in any such vague concept but in economic self-interest. In a postfeudal, postaristocratic, posthierarchical, postdeferential, post-Puritan nation, money would inevitably be far more important than in the old predemocratic life. There, for the vast majority of men, money had hardly mattered, certainly not as the center of aspiration. But in a democracy, for every man to aspire a standard was needed. Money provided the means for keeping score: where "men are no longer distinguished by birth, standing, or profession, there is hardly anything left but money which makes very clear distinctions between men." Tocqueville saw also that money had an indefinitely transformative power suitable to democracy. The "cooperation" upon which men entered on the basis of being paid, that is, on the basis of their hopes for money, "infinitely multiplies the purposes to which wealth may be applied and increases its value." In a democratic capitalistic society, more and more things became interchangeable in money terms. Land became money, ships, grain, wood, books, art, space, time, men themselves. Exchanges could be set up for translating the multifariousness of reality into a common language, a common currency, enabling every man to venture, gamble, speculate, risk himself. Money, like the language of poetry, could intensify the original passions attached to land, ships, produce, manufactories. Earth itself could be made to sing of money, China tied to Boston, New York to California. Money bound men to each other who had never met, never would meet, in loyalties more certain than creed, race, nation. The new nation founded at the Revolution had had no medium like this, no negotiable language of aspiration and salvation. Not until the nation embraced money as its fundamental language would Americans, as Tocqueville said, "nowhere" see "any limit placed by nature to human endeavor."[10]

The particular psychology Tocqueville set at the center of American economy came to be expounded by Joseph Schumpeter as one of the key engines driving capitalism:

Prizes and penalties are measured in pecuniary terms . . . promises are strong enough to attract the large majority of supernormal brains. . . . They are not proffered at random; yet there is a sufficiently enticing admixture of chance: the game is not like roulette, it is more like poker. . . . Spectacular prizes much greater than would have been necessary . . . are thrown to a small minority of winners, thus propelling much more efficaciously than a more equal and "just" distribution would, the activity of that large majority of businessmen who receive in return very modest compensation or nothing or less than nothing, and yet do their utmost because they have the big prizes before their eyes.[11]

One might expect the irrationality implicit in this scheme to have been realized by more and more men, over time, with a subsequent reduction of stimulus. But it was Tocqueville's point that in America the gamble appeared worth it, the odds better than in old Europe. Capitalism would flourish in America, not because everyone could win the spectacular prizes but because everyone could get in the game.

The local, decentralized, small-scale nature of the early decades of industrialization not only stimulated large numbers of men to think of themselves as enterprising, innovative, and adventurous; it was also laying the foundation for what would eventually emerge as the central feature of the American economy. While Americans were still buying cheap English manufactured goods, the best customers for small American mills, shops, and factories were other Americans. The American market was beginning to grow, and it would not be long before that market would be the strongest stimulus to production. Soon, mass production for a vast market would seem to be the American system. Let English iron producers concentrate on specialty items; let Europeans send over lace and fine carpets. American mills would turn out the rails and rough plows, the broadcloth and sacking. The American market was being generated in such a way that it would become by far the largest market in the world. American production would be shaped to its demand.

Although in such predictions as America's eventual naval hegemony Tocqueville showed that he expected the United States to evolve as a society and a nation, essentially he identified its sociology with its psychology. Here and there were to be found external limits on that psychology: slavery and the racism that appeared to accompany it; the class conflict potential in large-scale industry; the necessity for getting free of dependence on cheap English goods. Yet these were of but secondary and probably temporary significance. Far more compelling was the psychology of enterprise that had already transformed all structures and institutions into expediencies. American society was not a social order but a process. Oriented not to past or even present but to future, Americans were not really "socialized," for the society they inhabited remained to be created. But would they ever create any society at all? Tocqueville took note of the most conspicuous scene where new societies were being built, supposedly, only to renew his basic argument:

Ohio was only founded fifty years ago . . . nevertheless, the population of Ohio has already started to move west. . . . These men had left their first fatherland to better themselves; they leave the second to do better still; they find prosperity almost everywhere, but not happiness. For them the desire for well-being has become a restless, burning passion which increases with satisfaction.[12]

What if there would be no place for men to stop?

Masculine Transcendence: California and New York

As the American stimulant whirled men upward, many tried to cling to familiar stanchions. With his sense of old New England as having a fully matured identity already, John Adams tried to hold off Hamiltonian innovators, defending the old colonial constitutions of the separate states against reform. Dutch patroons defended their antique privileges against democratic farmers, while local iron magnates in Pennsylvania and the Jersey bogs viewed the onset of consolidated operations with fear and trembling. Craft workers of every persuasion were sensitive to the threat of rationalized production. Perhaps the most interesting attempt to restore fixity, however, was the most paradoxical, for nowhere more than on the frontier did the dynamic of transformation seem more surely at work. Yet as Henry Nash Smith has told us, in many men's minds the West was envisioned under the haze of a myth of stability, that of a "Garden" of sturdy, independent farmer-republicans. This was Thomas Jefferson's myth, and one of the central fault lines in the history of American democracy would be the association of Jefferson, the prophet of equality against privilege, with this static vision of society.[13] Insofar as Jefferson hated cities, shrank from money and finance, and deplored the multiplication of material desires, his eminence as champion of democracy inhibited ready acceptance of the idea that democracy's task in the United States was to embrace and not repel money, cities, and material efflorescence.

As Smith has pointed out, however, even myths of the Garden could be schizoid. Had Daniel Boone gone west to plant Virginia and civilization in the wilderness, or to flee Virginia for freedom in the wilderness? Tocqueville comprehended one dialectic that integrated both. Men were not hungry for wilderness, but on the other hand they were not embracing freedom only in order to foreclose on it. No more than merchants were making money only to store it up, were farmers taking up land to settle down. It was the hazard of new fortunes that drew them, and this they expected to be renewable. As Constance Rourke portrayed more than fifty years ago, in the first great scholarly effort to grasp American culture as popular and democratic, the archetypal, larger-than-life heroes generated in the pre-Civil War popular theater were preeminently rootless.[14] While one, the Yankee pedlar, had an incipient affinity with emergent merchant capitalism, his most salient capacity was to transmute his Puritan past from object of solemnity into one for mockery and stylized comedy. He registered a definitive liberation, not just from institutions but from the very ethos of community-based morality, and could, therefore, serve quite rightly as the progenitor of generations of American brokers and salesmen and promoters. Similarly, in the theatrical backwoodsmen, of whom Davey Crockett was only the most famous of many, the point was not to record some regression to "natural" freedom—half-man, half-alligator—but rather to display the facility with which ever new and unbounded identities could be put on and off, like masks, in explicit affirmation that all identities were masks, and that freedom grew therefore in the ability to present as many of them as possible. Of all the archetypal figures, that of the black minstrel manifested this certitude best, for his ability to dissolve the constraints of language itself in music-sustained non-sense lyrics registered itself against the background of the most horrendous socialization of all, slavery. Tocqueville himself reasoned that democratic energy would show itself first, so far as media were concerned, on the stage, where popular audiences had the best chance to show immediate approval or the reverse,[15] and nothing could have more vividly displayed the emergent hegemony of democracy than this theater that Rourke categorized as "American humor."

Still, if democratic psychology had come to prevail, that would be seen finally in its capacity to inhabit and dominate a place with its process, for not even the United States, despite Jefferson's illegal purchase, was infinite. In one melodramatic leap, by which the methodical step-by-step process of Western frontiering was left to pedestrian convention, such a place was found.

The new empire haunted the popular imagination, this was the greatest of the nomadic adventures. In the East, the music halls and variety and minstrel shows were filled with songs and stories about California for at least two decades. The American impulse toward autobiography sprang to life in California, and innumerable narratives of personal adventure poured from the press, to be eagerly seized by eastern readers.[16]

Perhaps no observer was more open to the psychic meaning of the California gold rush than Bayard Taylor, reporting to the *New York Tribune.* Having no "exciting dreams of trade" of his own, he said, and "troubled by no dreams of gold," Taylor was free to experience the greater excitement—as Tocqueville had been—of trying to explicate unprecedented lives. Realizing that his subject was the experience of glamour, he tried hard to render it with as much of its physical immediacy as he could.

A better idea of San Francisco, in the beginning of September, 1849, cannot be given than by the description of a single day. . . . The mist which after sunrise hung low and heavy for an hour or two, has risen above the hills. . . . The crowd in the streets is now wholly alive. Men dart hither and thither, as if possessed. . . . You speak to an acquaintance—a merchant, perhaps. He utters a few hurried words of greeting, while his eyes send keen glances on all sides . . . he is off. . . . It is impossible to witness this excess and dissipation of business without feeling something of its influence. The very air is pregnant with the magnetism of bold, spirited, and unwearied action, and he who but ventures into the outer circle of the whirlpool, is spinning, ere he has time for thought, in its dizzy vortex.

A "marvelous" place, San Francisco exhibited this quality because of the transformation it wrought in ordinary men:

The most immediate and striking change which came upon the greater portion of the emigrants was an increase of activity, and proportionately, of reckless and daring spirit . . . men hitherto noted for their prudence and caution took sudden leave of those qualities, to all appearance, yet only prospered the more thereby.

Despite the "apparent" recklessness, some deep logic was at work, as though these men understood very well what was at stake:

Perhaps there was at bottom a vein of keen, shrewd calculation, which directed their seemingly heedless movements; certain it is, at least, that for a long time the rashest speculators were the most fortunate . . . nothing is more contagious than this spirit of daring and independent action, and the most doleful prophets were, ere long, swallowed up.

So marvelous was this psychology that it seemed only appropriate that its setting too could partake of contrivance devised for magic:

The appearance of San Francisco at night, from the water, is unlike anything I ever beheld. The houses are mostly of canvas, which is made transparent by the lamps within, and transforms them, in the darkness to dwellings of solid light.

It was just as impressive, however, that this remarkable psychology could flourish against the grain, so to speak, of physical staging.

Towards the close of my stay, the city was as dismal a place as could well be imagined. The glimpse of bright, warm, serene weather passed away, leaving in its stead a raw, cheerless, southeast storm. The wind . . . blew a heavy gale, and [a] cold, steady fall of rain. . . . The mud in the streets became little short of fathomless. . . . One could not walk any distance, without getting at least ankle-deep, and . . . it was impossible to stand still for even a short time without a death-like chill taking hold of the feet.

The chill was at least part of the context of the dominant sociological fact of a single-sex society.

Think of a city of thirty thousand inhabitants, peopled by men alone! The like of this was never seen before. Every man was his own housekeeper. . . . Many home-arts, learned rather by observation than experience, came conveniently into play.

With some friends he visited a pond near the old Presidio:

Several tents were pitched on its margin; the washmen and gardners had established themselves there. . . . The washerwomen, of whom there were a few, principally Mexicans and Indians, had established themselves on one side of the pond and the washmen on the other. The latter went into the business on a large scale, having their tents for ironing, their large kettles for boiling the clothes and their fluted wash-boards along the edge of the water. It was an amusing sight to see a great, burly, long-bearded fellow, kneeling ... and rubbing a shirt on the board with such violence that the suds flew. . . . Their clear-starching and ironing were still more ludicrous; but, notwithstanding, they succeeded ... and were rapidly growing rich.

Taylor could not resist thinking ahead to improvements, including correction of the sex ratio: "If every married man, who intends spending some time in California, would take his family with him, a social influence would soon be created to which we might look for the happiest results." But it was obvious that for Taylor these happy results were not to include any leaching away of the glamour, let alone some feminization, of the essential spirit of the place. In San Francisco's "social intercourse" he found "something exceedingly hearty, cordial and encouraging," "a bluntness of good feeling" that allowed the "ordinary forms of courtesy" to be "flung aside." He found an exact precedent for the kind of society California might become: "I was constantly reminded of the stories of Northern history—of the stout Vikings and Jarls who exulted in their very passions and made their heroes of those who were jovial at the feast and most easily kindled with the rage of battle."[17]

The California gold mines themselves would soon be taken over from the forty-niners by corporations; the mystical canvas-sided cubes would evolve into merchant mansions; and native sons would appear—Josiah Royce was one—to mock the myths of golden glamour as but tawdry flights from social responsibility. Yet no matter how far incorporation, rationalization, routine, and hierarchy might overtake them, the early days of unrestricted individualism generated a power for mythmaking that would not die from organization. The rush to California was more a chapter of American psychological than of economic or social history, and it was not going to be the last.

If gold was quite literally the object of passion in California, its symbolic power presided with even greater force where men were drawn by the prospect of creating it out of thin air. California really only fed the emergence of New York as the alchemical center of the new economy. New York had already seen the emergence of men manifesting the Tocquevillian psychology in a quite specific occupation, international trade. The New York lawyer George Russell, writing an introduction to Freeman Hunt's two-volume commemorative collection, *Lives of American Merchants*, in 1857, echoed some of Tocqueville's language:

The American merchant is a type of . . . restless, adventurous, onward going race and people. He . . . stocks every market; makes wants that he may supply them . . . scarcely has the intimation of some obscure, unknown corner of a remote sea, when [he] is consulting his charts, in full career for the "terra incognita."[18]

According to Jonathan Goodhue, author of the tribute to one of these merchants, the attraction of business had a very clear resemblance to religious self-discovery:

Commerce is dangerous. . . . Money is "perilous stuff" . . . the merchant occupies a post of peril . . . is to live in constant excitement, with anxiety, hope, fear, adventure, risk . . . [can] expect little tranquillity of mind . . . [must] deal directly with . . . the most seductive, exciting, and treacherous commodity in the world; that which most tempts integrity . . . absorbs the faculties, chills the human affections. . . . But let him . . . recognize . . . that the possible moral advantages of a position are proportioned to its moral perils.[19]

Many of the thirty-seven men memorialized by Hunt gained fame as family founders: Brooks, Perkins, Peabody, Lawrence, Lorillard, Astor. Almost all were identified, in the years of their ascendancy, with the old Federalist, the new Whig, often explicitly antidemocratic element in New England and New York. But they would have no power to check the emergence of more powerful forces. New York would not be organized around established families. To a degree, their own drives helped establish the city as a financial even more than a commercial or industrial center. In his Phi Beta Kappa oration to Harvard audiences in 1856, Henry Bellows, pastor of New York's Fifth Avenue Unitarian Church, elevated New York's central preoccupation into a religion for— and of—America. As Bellows saw it, New York, impelled by New Englanders who had been swarming into the metropolis for a generation, had taken over national spiritual leadership from Boston. He too saw the merchant as a kind of conjuror of things unseen: "Might you penetrate that inner counting-room, the merchant's brain, you find at work there an Imagination, whose familiar sweep circumnavigates the globe, penetrates the policies of distant cabinets, and anticipates the prospects of remote kingdoms." But his attention was on the Yankee in general, as a type whose reputation as merely "utilitarian, material, money-loving" was misguided:

Our people are characteristically . . . a highly ideal race; living an unconscious life of intense thought; experimenting with human nature; and far more engaged with the processes than the results of their activity. Their own passions and inward life are infinitely more interesting to them than any of the external possessions or material comforts they acquire.

The point was not that "our people" disdained money. On the contrary. Dismissing those who deplored Americans' "accursed hunger for gold," Bellows insisted that "money is a great ally of freedom in our country," not only in the social sense that a "vastly wealthy" nation was capable of far more good deeds than a poor one, but in regard to individual psychology. "Men everywhere seek money as the general representative of desirable objects, but especially as the equivalent of independence."[20]

For Bellows, as for Hamilton and Tocqueville, material progress amounted to the liberation of male human nature. Animals, Tocqueville had said, "only know how to satisfy their primary and coarsest needs, whereas we can infinitely vary and continually increase our delights." It was this human capacity for imagining new delights that was the democratic engine in American capitalism. Almost certainly with a famous essay of Emerson's in mind, Bellows made the same point from the other side:

The savage and the saint show a kindred impotency in the simplicity of the wants and usages they boast. Too lazy or ignorant to cope with Nature, they affect to be her children when they are only her slaves. . . . Nature, if she has a conscious soul, is well pleased with this submission, which leaves her ancient dominion complete, and permits her to take the human clay, whose erectness seemed to threaten rebellion against beast and clod, back into her bosom, undistinguished from that of the ox . . . or the bird.[21]

In order to maintain himself erect, then, man repelled nature's bosom and embrace and tyranny. The United States, thus, with its "extraordinary combination of material comforts and splendors . . . such a subjugated and subsidized world, as history never before saw in the hands of a whole people," far from being "Nature's Nation," was really "History's Nation," a place in which human nature at last—male— had been liberated.

Nationality has done its best work for society. Its day is waning . . . patriotism is giving way to philanthropy, nations to man. . . . What makes [America] the goal of exiles from all lands, forbids it to be a competitor in the race of nations. . . . it is representing man's essential independence of everything but justice.

In an obviously deliberate reference to the most famous Phi Beta Kappa oration of all, Emerson's "American Scholar," Bellows scornfully rejected aspirations to a "national Literature and a national Art":

We are working in America at a very different problem from that of a national literature, art, or even character; a problem higher and deeper than any nationality; the question of *human* equality, liberty, and brotherhood. Ours is a representative people; its interests are not its own, but those of the race. . . . *American* literature, *American* art! Heaven save us from them![22]

Bellows was perfectly sure of the link between money and this cosmopolitan destiny. It was not simply the fact that the United States was democratic, but that it was an abundant, prosperous, economically overflowing democracy that had earned it its role as humanity's representative.

No matter how corporate and bureaucratic American capitalism might become, California and New York would remain, literally as well as symbolically, the one a permanent frontier, the other a furnace that never cooled, sustaining the promise of life as a matter of creation. It was only logical that this should be so. The promise of American life registered in California and New York was not one that would be surrendered even grudgingly to the worst of economic and social calamities. Having touched the heart of human nature, it would resist every circumstance that seemed to deny it. Interruptions of economic growth would be regarded as merely temporary, the evolution of economic methods as incidental, by comparison with the reduction of all institutions and all organizations to servicing the passion for innovation. Tocqueville saw that preachers and the churches had retreated from the marketplace, if not always in full allegiance to the separation of church and enterprise, then prudently, aware that in any test church would lose to marketplace. It was clear to him that American political parties were agents of interests, in no way interests in themselves. They were flexible, malleable, practical, opportunistic. They no longer debated the virtues and vices of democracy; both were democratic, if indeed there was any real party around in 1830 to oppose the party of Jackson and democracy anyway. Just as he had come too soon to observe the first days of large-scale industrialization, so too had he come too soon to observe the rise of a community of reformers who would find both political parties unacceptable; but that body of reformers would themselves, as a kind of third party, espouse democracy even more insistently as an ideal beyond debate. Among them, the passion for gambling would mount higher even than in the goldfields of California or in the counting houses of New York. Among them, perfection itself would seem legitimate as the beacon for history.

Masculine Immanence: America as Community: Men and Women Together

Hamilton had doubted that industrialization and democracy were compatible. In America the democratic majority was made up of farmers, and intuitively farmers understood that capital accumulation for industry would be at their expense. Farmers were unwilling to wait through the epoch of industrial buildup for it to benefit them. A linkage between ambitions to industrialize and a suspicion of democracy persisted. It came to one kind of climax in John Quincy Adams's presidency.[23] Without being as openly skeptical of democracy as his father and his father's party, the Federalists, John Quincy Adams nonetheless had clearly believed in the virtues of leadership by the modern-minded, enlightened few. Adams wanted a sharp upgrading of science in America. He wanted a national university located in Washington. He wanted the government to establish uniform standards for the general benefit of enterprise. Indeed, Adams wanted the government in Washington to become the stimulus of modernization; he wanted the United States to be centered on a truly national government. While Adams's hopes were not focused in industrialization itself, his vision of a superintending state clearly challenged any idea of politicians simply following popular self-interests. But Adams's program was not founded on wide popular demand—on the contrary. His overwhelming defeat in 1828 was regarded as a victory, not just for his opponents' policies, but for democracy itself.

Nonetheless, despite the surge of Jacksonian populism, skepticism about its capacities for rational leadership persisted. The Whig Party itself had no choice but to join in on the politics of myth, symbol, and personality, but independent anti-Jacksonians like the lawyer and editor Daniel Raymond, the engineer Jacob Etzler, the historian Richard Hildreth, and others feared that the logic of democracy guaranteed that government would remain at the mercy of the immediate self-interest of heterogeneous interest groups.[24] Most of all, democracy would promote the spirit of individualism, whereas the hopes for a modernized, rationally progressive, industrial future depended on long-term calculations, collaboration among groups of diverse origins, planning. Democracy would lead to scenes of hectic anarchy, as in California, to whirlwinds of speculation, as in New York. Rather conspicuously, neither California nor New York were centers of industrial enterprise.

The most interesting effort to reconcile popular government and economic progress came from Henry C. Carey.[25] Carey had family reasons for exalting a democratic United States. A political refugee from Ireland, his father had flourished in the New World as a publisher. Not only did his son find in his father's success a validation of American democracy; during a long life he regularly excoriated English society and the British economy as the exemplar of all things exploitative and undemocratic. From his first book, on wages, published in 1835, Carey emphasized the immense productivity and abundance already achieved in the United States. This was not due to the good fortune of an abundance of land or natural resources. It was due instead to the freedom of ordinary men to exert themselves naturally. Carey took it as axiomatic that unfettered human nature was productive. In the United States, man had been allowed to be himself. Carey insisted that no conflict of interests could possibly emerge where men were free. His most revealing title was *The Harmony of Interests Agricultural, Manufacturing, and Commercial.* He wrote his book on wages to disprove the gloomy logic of Thomas Malthus and his English colleagues, who in effect argued that mankind as a whole could enjoy no progress, owing to the constant pressure of population on subsistence.

Soon, however, Carey began to argue that Americans were not exploiting their freedom correctly. Instead of concentrating their efforts in such a way that agriculture and manufacturing sustained each other, they were spreading out over vast territories, abandoning old communities for new frontiers. Carey found this dispersion antithetical to human nature. "The natural tendency of man is to combine his labours with those of his fellow man." "It is not good for man to live alone, and yet throughout this country, we find thousands and tens of thousands of men flying to the West." Man is "everywhere disposed to remain at home, when he can," Carey insisted, and this disposition would, if encouraged, conduce to the highest economic development.[26] In essence, Carey's program consisted of encouraging production and consumption to proceed in closest proximity. He cited the expansion of the coal and iron industries of eastern Pennsylvania as an example; the result, he said, was to stimulate local farmers, carpenters, bankers. He expected textile mills to move in. The kind of extensive agriculture that had arisen in the West was not only wasteful in itself; it required the growth of transportation facilities, the proliferation of wagoners, porters, sailors, "most of whom have scarcely any home but the tavern." Carey did not criticize factories; he wanted factories that served neighbors. He did not criticize bankers; on the contrary, he believed the development of credit profoundly beneficial, as a stimulus both to enterprise and to trust between men. These banks, however, must not be located in New York but in the local community. All this was linked in Carey's mind with another issue, the question of risk. "The whole tendency" of the economic system of long-distance trade, he said, "is to the production of a gambling spirit."

No set of men can now feel any confidence in erecting iron-works, cotton-mills, or woollen-mills; and until all shall feel full confidence, the little capitalists cannot get to work, and the business must remain in the hands of great ones, who can run great risks.

The system that Carey had come to deplore was, quite simply, that of free trade, which he saw as sucking American farmers into calculating their interests according to prices in Liverpool, and American manufacturers into having to reckon with the imports from foreign low-wage factories. Carey had come to demand protection, so that the country could benefit from "the work of the millions of little men . . . the little farmers, and little mechanics, and litle shopkeepers" in evolving the integrated, harmonious local communities in which modern industrial development would fulfill itself at its most efficient and beneficent.[27] Soon, having once praised the freedom of small towns to pursue their own prosperity without interference, Carey was insisting that government must intervene to some significant degree as equilibra*or, coordinator, even innovator, precisely to avert the rise of centralized large-scale enterprise. While "natural," association nonetheless required protection, stimulation, encouragement by an agency with the power to overrule contrary forces. Politically, this drew Carey to the Whigs, if only because Democratic leaders of the 1850s seemed to have embraced the kind of hectic economic expansion he was sure could lead only to eventual class warfare.

While the Whigs themselves proved the embodiment of futility in a democratic politics, Carey's optimism was renewed with the rise of the Republicans. With the federal government's success at mobilizing industry for the Northern war effort, the politics of a long-term, government-impelled program of controlled economic development strengthening organic community seemed affirmed. Carey was soon to be bitterly disillusioned by the postwar party's identification with the interests of New York bankers and Eastern capitalists eager to establish domination over the whole country. His general point of view he would not yield, however. The ideal of a national policy deploring conflict, promoting the harmonious integration of all groups, celebrating community over individual, and operating on the mandates and methods of social science, would constitute the spiritual heat of a kind of party of public spirit, a third party objecting not just to the positions of the two major parties but to their very principle of existence, the assertion of special self-interest. Not for one minute would Carey have agreed that his outlook partook less of basic American character than the outlook distilled by Tocqueville. Yet while Carey and those who came after him, Lester Ward and Herbert Croly, John Dewey and Josiah Royce, always emphasized the identity of their ideas of collaboration and supervision with democracy and America, they could never show that they had the support of democratic majorities. If Tocqueville himself had exaggereated, in ascribing burning desires, adventurous innovation, and the spirit of romantic risk-taking to "the" American, it would be equally questionable whether "the" American wished rather to carry with him into the modern world assurances of harmony, community, and solidarity if these seriously jeopardized individual opportunity, expansion, and abundance. Men like Carey were the ultimate American optimists. Believing that in the United States all traditional values—community, democracy, social harmony—could be saved while pursuing new ones—mechanization, prosperity, opportunity, innovation—such men made it more difficult to consider whether in fact the nation did face hard choices.

Woman's Place in the Real Wonderland

According to Tocqueville, democratic wonderland was restricted to men. On the farms, of course, women continued to work as partners in perpetuation of a functional unity as old as the history of agriculture. Women could be found hard at work in bootmakers' workrooms, too, around grinding mills and nail works, as well as in shops and taverns over all the northeast. The growth of democratic capitalism from grassroots craft labor did not draw on masculine energy alone. But the spirit of trade, in which Tocqueville located the principle of infinite innovation, was not that of craftsmanship. Craftsmanship was hands, and a host of anti-industrial critics would bemoan the destruction of honest hand labor by mechanization. But it was trade, not labor, that incited the love of gambling, and Tocqueville saw quite clearly that gambling was for men only. Trade, capital, investment, risk-taking, the marketplace, money—all these were "gender-specific." As the realm of trade and enterprise grew, more and more men spent their work time among other men, not with their women. Their women stayed home. A class devoted neither to labor nor to inherited privileges was being born, a class between these others, a middle class. In the middle class, husbands and wives would not work together.

In years to come, sociological historians would explain all this as the result of industrialization and modernization. The industrialization of work required that it be taken out of the household into the factory. In the morning a man left home to go to his work, while his wife stayed home to do her housework. In those cases where the first factory workers were women, which was the case in the United States just as in Italy, Russia, and Sweden, they were young unmarried women. This was exactly how Hamilton had visualized the start-up phase of American industry, drawing on country girls working in the streamside mills while they waited to get married. When a working girl married, she went home.

Tocqueville, however, did not utilize this modernization model. In the first place, he saw relatively few factories and dwelt little upon their significance. The capitalism (a word he never used) seen by him was that of trade and banking, not of industry. In the second place, as he examined America he was not interested in how it too might be experiencing the same transformation being undergone by other nations. His interest from the start was in what distinguished America, its democratic politics and institutions. This meant in turn that he was interested in how Americans made democracy work. The segregation of the sexes was one of the ways they made it work.

Tocqueville's language was perfectly explicit in assigning the separation of woman's from man's sphere not to some indeterminate force of social evolution but to policy. Americans had decided that things should be that way. He compared them to certain other people who wanted things otherwise.

In Europe there are people who, confusing the divergent attributes of the sexes, claim to make of man and woman creatures who are, not equal only, but actually similar. They would attribute the same functions to both, impose the same duties, and grant the same rights; they would have them share everything— work, pleasure, public affairs. It is easy to see that the sort of equality forced on both sexes degrades them both, and that so coarse a jumble of nature's works could produce nothing but feeble men and unseemly women. . . .

That is far from being the American view. . . of democratic equality. . . between man and woman. They think that nature . . . clearly intended to give their diverse faculties a diverse employment. . . . The Americans have applied to the sexes the great principle of political economy which now dominates industry. . . .

In America, more than anywhere else in the world, care has been taken constantly to trace clearly distinct spheres of action for the two sexes.

Thus, far from registering mere sociological determinism, Americans had taken charge of their destinies in this realm, too, as much as, more narrowly, they did so in politics and the economy. "You will never find American women in charge of the external relations of the family, managing a business, or interfering in politics." The American woman "never leaves her domestic sphere."[28]

For American women, the challenge would be whether to accept this separate sphere or not. Why should not women too respond to the American stimulus? Women's imaginations too held infinitudes waiting to be unleashed. Tocqueville himself never really tried to explain why women ought to accept their segregation. He tended to highlight loss. "In America a woman loses her independence forever in the bonds of matrimony." As though aware of the peculiarly American dilemma he himself had identified, he turned to a non-American simile: after a girlhood of freedom in her father's house, an American wife found her husband's "almost a cloister."[29] Americans were Protestants; Puritan wives had been partners, helpmeets, not nuns. It might be hard for some American women to accept an alien immurement.

Perhaps women would be offered compensations. In the United States,

Tocqueville wrote, "the highest and truest conception of conjugal happiness" had been conceived. Then perhaps women would be reconciled to their separate sphere in the rewards of their marriages. But Tocqueville himself undercut such a prospect. It was perfectly true that American men, preoccupied with the marketplace, "set great store on obtaining" at home "that type of deep, regular, and peaceful affection which makes life happy and secure." But they did not get it. American wives, he judged, were not "tender and loving companions," but "chaste and cold."[30] He was less clear on the reason why than his traveling companion, Gustave de Beaumont. Actually, Tocqueville's research into American women's psychology was always handicapped to a degree by his felt fidelity to a fiancée waiting back home. He tended to rely for his information on manners and mores on such well-traveled persons as the aged Swiss-American ex-Treasury secretary Albert Gallatin, the young German-American Francis Lieber, and the cosmopolitan Joel Poinsett.[31] But most of all he turned to Beaumont, who felt free for a certain amount of participant observation. Beaumont found American girls obsessed with the marriage market and the result marked strongly on their characters: "Women, so tender by nature, take on the imprint of that prosaic, rational world. . . . American women merit your esteem but not your enthusiasm."[32]

Tocqueville traced American women's chaste self-control to the education that had been extended to them, obviously by the American men who had installed the sexual sociology he admired. Ultimately, however, the responsibility for the lack of the "deep, regular, and peaceful affection" wanted by the men rooted not just in the sociology of the system but in American men's own psychology. They simply had "neither the time nor the temperament for tender sentiments or gallantry." This followed rigorously from men's involvement in the marketplace:

The disturbed and constantly harassed life which equality makes men lead not only diverts their attention from lovemaking by depriving them of the leisure for its pursuit but also turns them away by a more secret but more certain path . . . the mental habits of the industrial and trading classes . . . [which are] calculating and realistic.[33]

Thus, however chaste and cold their women might—or might not—have been, it was the men who were the cause. The men were following out the logic which Graham Barker-Benfield has described as a "spermatic economy," "saving" themselves for their work.[34] The basic principle of the economic wonderland, abundance, had not been extended everywhere. The infinite expansion of wishes and delights had not yet commenced in sexuality. Beaumont portrayed one result in a quick sketch of married young America.

The American, from earliest youth, is devoted to business. . . . The lot of the young girl is not the same. . . . This young man and young girl, who are so dissimilar, are united one day in marriage. . . . In the evening the man comes home, full of care, restless, overcome with fatigue. . . . He asks for his dinner, and offers not a word more; his wife knows nothing of the affairs that preoccupy him; in her husband's presence she is still isolated. . . . In American eyes, the wife is not a companion.[35]

Such a marriage hardly seemed compensation for encloisterment. Yet women who might want to resist the sphere being offered them would find paradox and dilemma attaching to every tactic for sexuality. If the price to be paid for passionate involvement with the marketplace was sexual repression, why were not sexually repressed women just as fit for such involvement as their men? They were just as intelligent, just as imaginative as men. The education given girls in America was premised on that equality. But it was precisely Tocqueville's point that the passions of the marketplace were so strong that, if allowed, they would engulf and "capitalize" sexuality. Money, that most dangerous element, must not be allowed to come into contact with women, love, marriage, sex. Tocqueville revealed his anxieties on this point by an indirect hedge of his judgment that American men were fully socialized into the sexual system of separate spheres. While he said on the one hand that the lack of deep affection in the home was an "evil," but only a "secondary evil," elsewhere, he noted one way by which this evil might itself be compensated. Democratic equality, he said, would tend to produce both "a great many honest women" and at the same time "a great number of courtesans."[36] Tocqueville did not doubt that sexuality was a powerful drive in women as well as men. It seemed clear to him that if women were admitted to the marketplace and the "turmoil of politics," those European "disorders of society" from which Americans were free because of the separate spheres would arise to haunt Americans too. Honest women would remain so no longer. It was not a matter of some weakness inherent in women. Implicitly, Tocqueville was saying that neither men nor women could be blamed were sexuality to become one more medium, like intelligence, energy, daring, imagination, cunning, strength, and perseverance, for competition in the marketplace. The only means women would have for countering this outlook would be to enter the marketplace and prove, in the face of testing—one day to be called "sexual harassment"—that they were in fact sexually insusceptible. This would be far in the future.

But one powerful and essentially irresistible force was already at work making for stability rather than change in the separation of the spheres. As David Potter pointed out in the last chapter of *People of Plenty* (1954), American economic abundance directly affected American child-rearing, home, and family. Potter tended to emphasize changes in housing, food, clothing, and so on in twentieth-century America, but the changes were underway even as Tocqueville toured. Philippe Aries has shown that the impulse to disentangle the family from public life for private cultivation had been manifest among the middle orders of Western Europe for at least three centuries.[37] It was part of their struggle for self-definition and freedom. In the United States, with the democratization of this impulse, women, first as mothers, then as housewives, became its crucial bearers. In her meticulous study of Utica, New York, between 1790 and 1865, Mary P. Ryan has traced this gradual emergence of a private family, detached from productive work, more and more under the influence of the mother, among the new commercial middle classes.[38] Tocqueville had said that, while granting women their special sphere, Americans never supposed that "democratic principles should undermine the husband's authority and make it doubtful who is in charge in the family." But there were good reasons why such a disposition would not last, and Henry Carey noted the change some years later. Yes, he said, a man remained master in his house but in practice a man handed its management over to his wife, "whose control, within doors, is complete."[39] Indeed, nothing stood in the way of a man turning over everything but the moneymaking to a managerially talented wife.

Tocqueville himself, mesmerized by the spectacle, not of the fruits, but of the pursuit of moneymaking, missed all this. Though well aware that some American men had got rich, he felt sure rich men could never congeal into a class, and, besides, he was more impressed by what he took to be the constant fluctuations in men's fortunes. So far as women were concerned, he deduced simply that they were prepared for the downs as well as the ups in their men's lives. But other visitors of the time were more struck by the realized affluence in many women's lives. Traveling between 1833 and 1835, Michael Chevalier several times noted how well dressed American women were. Mechanics' daughters compared well with merchants' wives. Chevalier found it admirable: "What a contrast between our Europe and this America!" Women were exempt from all heavy labor. "Since the man earns enough to support the family, the woman has no other duties than the care of the household, a circumstance still more advantageous for her children."[40] None of this beguiled Harriet Martineau. The indulgence of women in the United States, she agreed, was "large and universal, instead of petty and capricious," but it was still indulgence. Adversity, she said, had put thousands of England's women to the test of their own resources. "[The] prosperity of America is a circumstance unfavorable to its women."[41] American women were not being tested. Some years later, visiting from

Sweden, Fredrika Bremer would agree. A "hothouse luxury" had over-taken too many American women, to their detriment. Perhaps women observers—including England's Frances Trollope, too—sensed a danger less visible to men. Yet the very terms of such criticism defined the route to stability. The prosperity that might underwrite frippery and orchidaceous luxury also underwrote better, more convenient family housing, more complex, stimulating, and intense relations between children and grownups. The family's material resources multiplied. Perhaps history would locate turning points. Catherine Beecher's portrait of the American housewife of 1840 as a sickly incompetent might or might not prove accurate. Her point picked up the deeper history, however: there was a new world of resources, both material and intellectual, waiting to be mastered by the housewife. This enrichment of the supplies of domesticity—all the way from better houses, better kitchens, better furniture to better dietetics, better schools, and better child psychologies— constituted an empowerment of those in charge, that is, women. That Tocqueville imagined that American women did in fact "sacrifice" themselves in accepting their separate sphere followed in part at least from the fact that this new abundance remained invisible to him, partly because of its less obvious nature, partly because its most copious outpourings lay ahead. But at no point did it ever occur, and at no point would it ever occur, to American women, let alone American men, to oppose such abundance just because it did enrich and heighten life for women in their separate sphere. As the supplies of domesticity swelled in decades ahead, perhaps to a climax in the 1950s, women would face the danger of finding their own powers taken over by their suppliers. Not every new appliance worked. Boxes and cans could depersonalize eating. For those, such as Charlotte Perkins Gilman, who despised cooking and hated the cathexis of food, this would be only to the good, but for far more housewives, it would take struggle to maintain autonomy and power precisely against the abundance that had increased that autonomy and power. But all power was by definition engaged in struggle to sustain itself. Mothers finding light and guidance in new psychologies of child-rearing had to struggle to prevent their mothering being taken over by the psychologies and psychologists. But it was precisely in such struggles—"dialectic," if one wishes—that the significance of the abundance of American capitalism was measured. Puritan mothers had had no such struggles; their tasks were prescribed by tradition and doctrine perpetuated by poverty.

While to women, then, the new economy of democratic capitalism did offer new opportunities, new challenges, new powers, and not just the chance to be sacrificial, still this did not deflect the most important process at work as a consequence of the separation of men's from women's lives. On the contrary, it deepened it. Just as women, with their newly abundant supplies, grew more richly and emotionally involved in their sphere, they grew even more different from their men. In Italy, just as in Sweden and Soviet Russia, women shared with their men most of the basic political and economic experiences of their nations. They shared the poverty. They shared the convulsions. They shared the revolutionary and reactionary politics. In America, however, men, fired by visions of personal opportunity, impassioned by the prospect of limitlessness, were becoming a sort of person which their women were not. American women, too, were becoming something new. They were not remaining creatures of tradition while their men were becoming self-creating creatures. Women, too, had come to hold powers of self-creation. But the stages on which each engaged upon this self-creation differed so basically that their performances could easily head toward contrast rather than complement, toward conflict rather than harmony. While finding the wives of male pioneers in the West to be "resolute," Tocqueville also found them "sad." On her own tour of the West, Margaret Fuller found the eastern wives hauled by their men to Wisconsin unhappy, consumed with memories of what they had lost. The historian Annette Kolodny has found in the letters of pioneer women feelings, thoughts, and hopes utterly different from those of their men.[42] Henry Carey would have understood. He thought the epic of "O Pioneers" was a mistake from the start. Mankind was basically home-loving, in his view, and the views of historians suggest to us that the pioneer women were indeed. The difficulty was obvious: it was hard to carry out the separation of the spheres on the way west.

None of this meant that where the separation of the spheres prevailed, contradiction and dilemma could not flourish, loss could not be suffered. Ryan, following historians Daniel Scott Smith and Linda Gordon, observed how sexual abstinence, reinforced by new ideologies about women's purity, appeared to spread as the rationale for fewer children spread. Understandably, relations between husband and wife grew "exacting" and "tense." Some of the impulse toward creation of that "female world of love and ritual" compellingly portrayed by Carroll Smith-Rosenberg no doubt arose here.[43] The logic of separate spheres could cut into families. With fathers steadily more intent upon the marketplace, obviously mothers would be spending more time with the children. These included sons. But how were mothers to know what boys needed to become effective men? Historians have noted the rise of a new maternal pedagogy stressing love as the proper means of a mother's suasions, but no one quite explained how maternal love prepared a boy for the challenges of the competitive democratic marketplace. Too long provided, a mother's love might soften a young man. It did not occur to Tocqueville to ponder this relationship. Once having noted that democratic opportunity undermined fathers' authority over sons, he commented on mothers' influence over daughters only. Again, he had come a bit too soon to witness the fuller elaboration of the new sociology. Had he been more prescient, he might well have tested his judgment of that system's stability by looking further into parent-child relations. What protection had been installed against a wife's compensation for the inadequacies of her marriage in her mothering of her sons?[44]

Tocqueville did however clearly identify one escape from such tensions already fully available. He saw nothing but good in the special relationship between American women and religion. This drew in the first place on the clergy's own self-interest: since they could not interest men impassioned by the marketplace, women were their reliable constituency. Since the symbiosis of women and clergy guaranteed that American "mores"—essentially, its sexual culture—would continue to be severe, and, hence, politics and the marketplace left untroubled by "the instability of desires," Tocqueville applauded. But he did not ever explain just what good the relationship did for women. Touring in 1835–36, Martineau saw the same alliance but came to a diametrically opposite judgment. The clergy themselves Martineau found deplorable, "the most backward and timid class in the society . . . self-exiled from the great moral questions of the time; the least informed . . . the least efficient." Connection with such men could lead only to morbidities:

I cannot enlarge upon the disagreeable subject of the devotion of the ladies to the clergy. I believe there is no liberal-minded minister who does not see, and too sensibly feel, the evil of women being driven back upon religion as a resource against vacuity.[45]

Purely as a compensation, then, religion could compound, not ameliorate, women's lack of power.

The great feminist individualists would attack religion. After being rejected in her wish for harmony with the greatest religious prophet of the age, Margaret Fuller would launch out on life unaided. Elizabeth Cady Stanton would attack all churches. But the logic of affinity was too powerful to resist. It could draw some women all the way to taking over the realm themselves. Frances Willard forged a mass women's reform organization out of the mores religion had sponsored. Mary Baker Eddy would go so far as to compose her own evangel and construct her own church with the largest daring of all, for Eddy presumed that her mission would not be of interest to women only but to men too. The production of further difference between the sexes would be would be promoted by all such ventures. Fuller and Stanton called women to lives like men's, but Willard, Eddy, and the expositors of woman-derived religion emphasized women's special differentiating features. The peak of their power was to imagine men changed to resemble women—less drunk, less material, less sexual. These initiatives would remain ambivalent to the end. Examining records of the mid-eighteenth-century religious revivals, the early nineteenth-century revivals, and the temperance movements late in the century, Barbara Leslie Epstein found signs of antagonism to men in all of them. What then was the salvation for women? To be released from their sphere? or to be able to make it prevail?[46]

That unappeasable restlessness Tocqueville found in American men everywhere—in Utica as much as in New York City—was by no means absent from women, then. But for women the expression of it was harder. To men the direction to follow was reasonably clear: opportunity awaited and they had but to seize it. But for women, choices were not clear-cut. Identify with family and home, plunge into housework? or seek as many larger activities as possible? Escape the tensions of marriage in abundant mothering? or in the warmth of sisterhood? Indulge the pleasures offered by affluence for personal display? or translate money into household improvement? The fluctuation between religion as escape and religion as power took place inside individuals as well as in public. Ultimately, for American women, basic orientation followed from what they felt and imagined about American men. Were men women's jailors or their providers? Was there a victor in every man? or a drunkard— and worse? The logic of the separate spheres prescribed what thoughts were best. Best to think of American men as still, first of all, at heart, fathers, husbands, loyal brothers, family men. If this became increasingly difficult, then let them be thought of as what many apparently wanted to be, great boys, grown to manhood but still free to embark on enterprises and speculations. Then, finally, if their faults, their undue and unwelcome appetites, their proneness to drink grew undeniable, let them be thought of as reformable. This would, of course, be to fail to see American men and think of them as they saw and thought of themselves. Perhaps the hardest thing for American women would be to understand the men whose lives they were no longer sharing and that country in which the men were living and they were not.

Industrial Apotheosis and the Basis for Democracy for Everyone

By 1860 the economic momentum built up during the previous thirty years was overshadowing anything like Henry Carey's policy.[47] Promotion of the highest degree of integrated self-sufficiency possible in every community and region was succumbing to sectional specialization. Pressing the growth of technology and manufacturing within, not against, the community structures of the past was yielding to vast homogeneous zoning. Carey's own favored Whigs had collapsed. The famous American System of Henry Clay, cobbling together East, South, and West in a purported harmony of specialized functions, failed in its own terms by failing to keep slavery safely sealed off as a problem local to the South. With the rise of the Republicans, sectional conflict of some sort was imminent, for the Republicans had nothing to offer Southern slavery but slow death. Following the war, after brief and inadequate efforts at reconstituting the South, Republican policy left it to molder away in colonial subjection, while turning to arrange financial and monetary policy to facilitate rapid accumulation of capital. The party collaborated in the completion of the coast-to-coast railroad network. Then it retired from the field, leaving private capital to plunge pell-mell into development of large-scale industry. The statistics of American industrial preeminence to be cited in twentieth-century schoolchildren's textbooks were generated in the thirty-five years after Appomatox. Indefinitely stimulated by the war, the prewar iron industry evolved a steel industry; steel production multiplied eightfold in the twenty-years before 1900; a towering national entity, the United States Steel Corporation, capped the process. Within thirty years of the discoveries at Titusville, a wholly new industry, oil, reached into every home as well as into every other industry. At century's end, still another new energy system, electricity, was being installed. New quintessentially industrial cities were springing up mushroomlike, large and small, across the old northwest—Cleveland, Gary, Homestead, Braddock, Weirton and Clairton, Youngstown and Akron. Commercial old Pittsburgh had been overtaken by coal, furnace, and smoke. The hub of a completed railroad ganglion, Chicago became a center for speculation and finance more feverish than Wall Street.

Once, during the Civil War, a few men had imagined, as George Frederickson among others has noted, that the whole process of economic development might be pursued under superintendence.[48] The victory of the North, after all, had attested to the efficacy of central planning. During 1861, romantic fantasies of quick victory through dashing military energy had deluded men's minds, but the realities of Bull Run and other early battles quickly dispelled them. The Northern war effort depended upon planners, men coordinating the purchase of war supplies, coordinating the work of war suppliers, coordinating the operation of the railroads as one single national network. Quartermasters, working anonymously in government agencies, became the key figures upon whom the generals and the armies depended. At no point before in American history had rational thinking been applied to economy and society more thoroughly: logical sequences, feedback loops, integrated systems directed the lives of millions.

Numerous women found places in this enterprise.[49] In the medical and other caring services a Katherine Wormeley, a Mary Phinney, a Cornelia Hancock, a Clara Barton discovered the advantages of system and organization. A Women's Central Association of Relief for the Sick and Wounded evolved into the famous United States Sanitary Commission, and while the Sanitary Commission's top officers were men (headed by Henry Bellows himself), men often of upper-class traditional outlook, they were but façade. The commission's work was done by women of a modern, practical, organizational outlook. Most symptomatic was the commission's preference for professional women over volunteers: professional women were paid. Here was by far the nation's largest exercise in social mothering and social housekeeping to date. Numerous Sanitary Commission women did move from war work into postwar philanthropic and charity work, with a plain emphasis upon efficiency, management, and professional administration generally, by contrast with the more spontaneous and improvised style of prewar reform associations. Had the managerial outlook of the Republican war effort carried over into the postwar economy, gender segregation might still have excluded women from the larger sectors of planning and superintendence, yet there would have been less of a contrast in style between women's work and men's. Women would have been seen to practice the same sciences of control and coordination practiced by men. Separate spheres would not have signified separate psychologies.

In the event, however, the postwar epoch proved to be one not only of economic boom and bonanza, but of devastating business cycles and raw social violence, as well as of pervasive economic inequality. Picking up on prewar efforts, no fewer than 650,000 workers joined a National Labor Union; the Panic of 1873 devastated it. The Knights of Labor won 750,000 members before it too collapsed after the Haymarket riot of 1886.[50] These efforts at forging working-class solidarity might well have succeeded in time, so far as any inner logic of the ongoing economic expansion was concerned. In those years many of the new workers were drawn from the farms and small towns of old-stock America. While they had imbibed all the hopefulness Tocqueville had found in Jacksonian America, they were by no means prepared to let hope alone justify the lives they found in the raw new cities. Business money subsidized Dwight Moody in his efforts to reconcile these Protestant down-and-outers to their defeat, but the very shallowness of Moody's revival suggested that it could not have long availed.[51] Politically, native

American workers were trapped, however. The Republican Party was not yet ready to gamble on the full-dinner-pail tactic inaugurated in 1896 by Mark Hanna, whereby elite workingmen were promised larger cuts of the pie in return for loyalty to capitalist growth.[52] On the other hand, the Democratic Party had been heavily invested by Irish politicians, whose city machines put the linkage between party and labor on a basis quite impossible for old-stock workers to accept.[53] Most important, however, by the last decade of the century, huge numbers of new immigrants were pouring in to lend the American working class its special ethnic and religious heterogeneity. Indeed, it would be this ethnic diversity that would challenge Marx's argument, based on observing the ethnically far more homogeneous English working class, that, under the impact of the methods of production, all ethnic, religious, and racial consciousness would be burned away in favor of class consciousness. No merely abstract argument would ever resolve that issue. In the United States the facts of history would show that the methods of production never did subordinate ethnic, religious, and racial self-consciousness to class.

Thirty-five years after Marx, while conceding that the United States did still seem to be obeying some law of social evolution other than the one Marx had discovered, Friedrich Engels was repeating the same theme:

America after all is the ideal of all bourgeois: a country vast, rich, expanding, with purely bourgeois institutions unleavened by feudal remnants of monarchical traditions, and without a permanent and hereditary proletariat. Here everyone could become, if not a capitalist, at all events an independent man, producing or trading, with his own means, for his own account. And because there were not *as yet* classes with opposing interests, our . . . bourgeois thought that America stood *above* class antagonisms and struggles.[54]

For Engels, the Haymarket riot signaled that this apparent classlessness of bourgeois America had at last broken down and could be treated as the delusion it always had been. But for one new American, Haymarket had precisely the opposite effect. In his youth, Samuel Gompers explained in his autobiography of 1926, he had thought that class struggle against capitalists offered workingmen their only hope. Change in "the present social and political systems" to "their very foundations" was a necessity. Yet Gompers became precisely the kind of labor leader criticized by Marxists, one who sought advantage for his constituents within the system, one who wished the system well because of its ability to serve the welfare of its workers. Gompers's major assumption about the American economy undergirded his leadership: the economy could afford to pay good wages. Operating on this assumption, Gompers paid no attention to politics. Rather, he concentrated purely on establishing, through solidarity, credibility for the union at the bargaining table. He felt contempt for ideology: "We must build our program upon facts and not theories."[55] The leading fact was that the route to labor prosperity lay not through polarization or revolution but through bargaining.

The fact that the workingmen for whom Gompers worked were craftsmen, men of classic skills gathered into brotherhoods of similar men— the fact that Gompers's American Federation of Labor did not reach into the ranks of the new factory workers themselves, the machine-tenders rather than the machine-makers, or into the multitudes of unskilled diggers and haulers and carriers—meant that Gompers's essential optimism about the economy remained untested in his lifetime. Yet the very success of the AFL meant that when a much more serious testing time arrived, with the Great Depression, the chance that Marx and Engels would be proved right at last had already been much diminished.

Meanwhile, the sufferings of the industrial and unskilled laborers ignored by the AFL were suffused and inflected by the particularities of a dozen different histories. The impoverished Italian peasants arriving in their tens of thousands every year up to 1914 stimulated New York City's economy. Italian men dug the subways cheap. Italian girls worked for miserable wages in the ready-made clothing factories; the girls who jumped to their death in the Triangle Fire of 1911 were Italian and Jewish. For all the grimness of their condition in their new world, however, the Italians were engaged in a vast enterprise of their own. While many had come as individuals, planning to send money back home and return there themselves one day, most were involved in a reconstruction of family. Italian women quickly began shaping a new family by reducing their rate of reproduction, but this was in no way a repudiation of family claims. Indeed, by comparison with what was happening to southern Italian peasants on their native ground, their uprooting, migration, and relocation in urban industrial America strengthened family ties and enlarged family significance. All the newly invented institutions of Italian-American life—the clubs, the newspapers, the burial societies, the local church itself, which had to be wrested from Irish domination—all clustered round the family nucleus. Never had the family seemed more utterly the fruit of nature than surrounded by all the artifice of hyphenated culture. The idea of a circumambient "system," of which to become "conscious" in all its exploitative power, could not be brought to focus even among the most self-conscious of the new community's leaders, for their primary task was obviously to assure that community's solidity, not to criticize its host.[56]

An analogous process took place in the West, in the countryside. Young Swedes rejecting their degradation in the rationalization of the fields in Sweden generated a family life, nurtured by churches, far stronger in the American Midwest than what they had been able to afford in Sweden. So did other Scandinavian immigrants. Peasants from Catholic Germany established farm communities with interlock between family and economy tighter than they had known in the old country.[57] As a sheer economic phenomenon, the post-Civil War surge in agricultural production was as impressive as that in industry. Nearly five times as much corn was produced in 1910 as in 1850, more than six times as much wheat. Butter, milk, beef, pork, chicken, apples, pears, oranges, lettuce, carrots, beets: many of these multiplied even more. Shipping, refrigeration, wholesale and resale efficiencies, not to mention banking, all flourished on this agricultural base. The 1.5 million farms of 1850 had quadrupled by 1910, at which time rural Americans still outnumbered urban Americans.[58]

Henry Carey, for one, had deplored this development. He felt sure that the temptation to rapid agricultural expansion using methods of extensive cultivation would lead to trouble. Staple farmers, he warned, would soon find themselves hostage to international markets. Of course he proved right. Many farmers, he said, would find themselves pushed by various market forces toward mere subsistence. This was happening widely by 1890. Moreover, he predicted, extensive methods of agriculture would exact ecological costs of indeterminable but vast dimensions. Carey proved a prophet here, too.[59] But the fact that Carey's hopes for an intensive agriculture oriented to local markets were disappointed did not mean that the farmers had no recourse. By the 1880s farmers locked into the great commodity crops—wheat, corn, and cotton—were being whipsawed by the market, but their response, the independent, third-party politics of Populism, clearly declared a determination to save the essence of agricultural life. Symptomatically, the first entrance of farm women into widespread quasi-political activity was among the farmers' Alliances of the 1880s, in both the Southwest and the West. They took part in Alliance programs as wives and mothers.[60]

As the Populist movement put a sharper definition to the Alliances' more diffuse cultural efforts, the farmers' irreducible demand became clear. Railroads were no longer to be allowed to charge rates to ship farmers' crops to market that spelled bankruptcy for the farmers; railroads were to be put under regulation; indeed, railroads were to be nationalized—socialized—if necessary. And not only railroads. Bankers were to be prevented from exploiting farmers. So were millers. The manufacturers of the machinery farmers needed were not to be allowed to raise their prices while the prices farmers got for what they produced fell. The Populist farmers' defense of the family farm had not required the assistance of Swedish and other immigrant farmers. That addition helped assure, however, that those pressures of the marketplace of which Carey had warned could be deflected. Ironically enough, intensive techniques were gradually applied in agriculture, but on the factory farms of the California Central Valley and on Eastern truck farms. This was hardly the sort of enterprise Carey had had in mind. It echoed the slave economy, the central horror of which he had appreciated—its destruction of family ties.

Whether the historian is to argue that it was by fortuity and accident, then, or by some profound inner logic that family ties were strengthened, not weakened, in the process of American industrial takeoff, has not been answered by consensus. Yet few historians have doubted that a "middle-class" mind grew more, not less, pervasive between the Civil War and the century's end; that for all the facts of conflict, patterns of class conflict had not become habitual; and that the basic mood of the millions of newcomers, who in their poverty and diversity were sometimes imagined to threaten a wholly new epoch in American history, was that of the natives whom they joined—one of optimism about their future.[61] The fears felt in middle-class circles themselves about the growth of Big Business and—as they saw it—Big Labor, were an echo of Henry Carey's fears of an economy given over to private passions, an economy racing forward without a driver, an economy without political direction, lacking governor and government. As these fears assembled slowly into what would regard itself as a movement and label itself "progressivism," it would respond once again to the possibility of subduing conflict in favor of harmony, of moderating competition in favor of collaboration, of preferring community over self-interest, society over the individual.

By the end of the century, thirty years of intellectual work had culminated in the creation of a new science, a science of society itself, "social science," offering those made anxious by uncontrolled change the prospect of control. Historians once saw in progressivism men anxious to protect an older world against further change: local manufacturers alarmed at the competition from industrial megaliths, small-town bankers uneasy at Wall Street, small-town editors, lawyers, doctors humiliated at the shrinkage of their eminence—Henry Carey's sort of men. Then historians discovered that many of those who were actually forging huge new corporations, manufactories, law firms, and newspaper chains, saw this as a perfectly rational, logical, cost-efficient, productive evolution, and wanted to rid it of irrationalities, needless competitions and duplications, self-defeating legal restrictions.

Both groups found individualism antipathetic. Individualism strained the fabric of local integration. Individualism worked athwart the principles of corporative endeavor. Both found promise in social science. Both looked to government as aide and ally.[62]

Debate between defenders of old localities and advocates of new efficiencies concealed what would soon seem the major fact about the new economy: it was beginning to produce for direct mass consumption. Much of the production of the 1870s and 1880s continued to be for capital plant—for more factories, mines, mills, bridges, railroads, ships—in other words, "production for production." But at the same time the processing and packaging of foods, the manufacture of men's ready-to-wear clothes, and the bottling of various "medicines," was already attaining mass status, "production for consumption."[63] New meanings were being attached to old products. By 1900 soap signified far more than mere cleanliness. Some new inventions already in mass production, notably the electric light and the telephone, spoke less to individual consumers as such than to an enhanced and expanded staging for richer private lives in general. This social consumption facilitated private consumption. As "utilities," phones and lights were quickly absorbed into the moral background, being unquestionable improvements just as much as were the new sewage systems, indoor plumbing, and street cleaning services that distinguished the postwar from the prewar cities. Americans were the first people to begin to take for granted a manufactured environment.

Yet, remarkable as this achievement was, it concealed a further and more revolutionary potential. As late as 1900 the market had not yet come to be dominated by new machines for truly personal use, machines providing the self with extension, expansion, and stimulus, "pleasure machines" in the ultimate sense glimpsed by Hamilton and affirmed by Tocqueville. Their appearance was under way. By 1900 bicycles, the new, easy-to-ride safety bikes rather than the old, awkward, dangerous giant wheelers, had become objects of mass purchase. Bikes could be put to practical application: grocery delivery, getting the kids to school and workmen to work. But bicycles' appeal was far more psychological than utilitarian. They hardly improved on any prior kind of transport. They were not improvements upon the horse or the buggy, let alone the train. Their true predecessor had been roller skates, and it was the sheer lyric heart of roller-skating that persisted in bicycling. Of course bicycles were instantly gathered into the tension between the generations, into courting, sexual culture, sexual issues. Their successor was to be the car.

Progressive-era anxieties that the automobile, as a rich man's toy, would exacerbate class feelings and weaken democracy, were logical

but soon allayed.[64] Henry Ford's solution to the problem of the automobile for a time obscured the basic point. His famous Model-T, cheap,
black, angular, appeared an eminently practical machine, adapted to
"getting the farmer out of the mud." But as Robert and Helen Merrill
Lynd were to find in studying Muncie, Indiana, in the mid-1920s, the
citizens of Muncie bought cars not because they needed them but
because they could not resist them. People in Muncie did not need cars.
Walking—or bicycling—to work was cheaper, healthier, altogether more
rational for most. And by any prior rational reckoning, most people
could not afford cars. The Lynds found that many Muncie families
sacrificed housing to buy cars; some undoubtedly cut down on food
and clothing in order to "afford" one.[65] Cars had been immediately
recognized for what they were: enhancements of the individual, means
to more exciting lives, larger experience, wider horizons. A democratic
culture would insist that they be available to more than the wealthy
few. Advertising was needed for none of this. Advertising followed, it
did not create.

The other new pleasure machine, the Kodak camera, invented in
1888 and widely known by 1900, had also, like the car, not yet become
a mass product but, unlike the car, it was free of early suspicion of being
an undemocratic plaything of the rich. What prior need the hand-held
Kodak camera met, no one ever explained. Rather, it arrived as practically an attachment to imagination, a translation into quasi-auto-
matic machinery of the inner meaning of art. The camera's transactions
with reality taught that reality existed exactly in transactions, with the
seeing eye as active as what it saw. Again, Hamilton had proved right:
the camera, a machine, invigorated the mind.

Once pleasure machines seemed affirmed as the logical ultimate
product of industrial production, private demand took over as engine
of the system. The fatal weakness of small-town capitalism would stand
revealed: it could not promise mass abundance. At the same time, the
parochial nature of the farmers' radicalism would stand revealed. The
ever greater production of the farmers did not interest consumers, for
enough wheat was enough, while the farmers' readiness to socialize
industrial production for their own sake promised only to inhibit mass
production of pleasure machines. At the same time, inclinations to treat
industrial workers as a class apart undercut the stimulus of demand
upon such mass production. It would take time for this logic to work its
way forward, but its power was already clear before 1914 and World
War I. No serious effort was made to preserve the social order of local
capitalism, for that would have required severe constraints imposed
upon the new national corporations, and the price of that was too high:
choking the cornucopia. At the same time, though, rule by the men

who had generated the new corporations—the Carnegies and the Morgans, the Hills and the Clarks, above all the Rockefellers—was resisted, by means of the revivification of politics, above all of the presidency in the person of Theodore Roosevelt. Indeed, in Roosevelt it was possible for the great new public of consumers to believe that no hard choices need be made.

The Promise of Democratic Capitalism: Theodore Roosevelt and Family-Centered America

From 1868 to 1896 the two major political parties served special interests within the nation rather than any particularly coherent concept of the national interest itself. Repeatedly politicians of both parties showed themselves more inclined to parasitic exploitation of their positions than to any faithful representation. Keeper of the symbols of Civil War victory, the Republican Party enjoyed its greatest infusion of new legitimacy as the only true national party with the maturation of the Civil War veterans themselves in the late 1880s and 1890s, who, through their organization, the Grand Army of the Republic, repristinated the façade behind which the party pursued its mundane manipulations of tariff, money, and various subsidies to private enterprisers. All that impulse toward national superintendence summoned by the Civil War, so compatible with supervisory women, subsided quickly. It was hardly surprising that crisis should arrive first for the Democrats, lacking as they did even the façade of national coherence. With the nomination of William Jennings Bryan, the party laid claim to the heritage of the farms and small towns of old America. Unfortunately, this left out the factories and cities of new America. It also proceeded simultaneously with the Southern wing of the party installing racism at its worst, legal Jim Crow. The riposte of the Republicans, Mark Hanna's "full dinner pail," was powerful. Hanna did not so much win labor for the GOP as stigmatize the Democrats. McKinley and Hanna were not plausible as the exponents of a truly national party, but they had guaranteed that debate over basic national policy would emerge only among the Republicans.

Of course Theodore Roosevelt's accession to the presidency was a matter of political accident. Still, his subsequent success in establishing himself as the dominant political figure on the national scene for the next dozen years suggests that he came to register, more than he created, a basic political public by the time his career was over. That modern large-scale corporate capitalism could serve the interests of a democratic middle-class culture seemed by no means sure in 1900.

That it should have come to seem far more assured by 1914 followed, at least in part, from the fact that Roosevelt had revived interest in the presidency and made it the focus, not so much of politics itself but of national identity. From a preoccupation with the powers of vague but vast and looming entities such as "trusts" and "monopolies" and "organized labor," political publics were refreshed with a spectacle of personal confidence that even the largest social conflicts could be controlled. Bryan had preceded Roosevelt in this repersonalization of politics, but in his hysterical evocation of malign forces crucifying innocence, Bryan seemed to be registering weakness, not strength.

From the start, Roosevelt had no intention of trying to actually break up any of the large economic combinations held to be a threat to the old moral order.[66] Neither Big Capital nor Big Labor seemed to him evil simply for being big. Trust-busting constituted his holding action, in a first term when he understood that some comprehensive plan for inducing collaboration among all the major economic interests had no consensus behind it. His trust-busting was always opportunistic, expedient, symbolic. This had nothing to do with any hidden readiness to serve the new big corporations and bankers. Roosevelt had no particular regard for them. Though a rich man—indeed, the first rich man to serve as President since George Washington—Roosevelt's personal fortune did not begin to compare with those of a John D. Rockefeller or an Andrew Carnegie or a J. P. Morgan or a James J. Hill. His money was that of the old Dutch families of Manhattan who had, by and large, refused to plunge into the turmoil of industrial expansion and join the new capitalists. Roosevelt frequently expatiated on the dangers of wealth. Decadence, passivity, luxury, and a feminized softness awaited those who succumbed to its temptations. It is difficult to read simple envy into these sentiments. Roosevelt himself had enjoyed every imaginable benefit from his father's resources. He had never had to go to school as a boy, being provided with tutors and instructors in everything from Latin to horseback riding. At Harvard he spent the modern equivalent of perhaps $25,000 a year on himself. He never particularly tried making money. It was not how money was made but how it was used that mattered. Roosevelt always understood that the expenditure of money was legitimated in the creation of self. Out west, in his early adulthood, he spent large sums fitting himself out as a ranchman. Hats, shirts, boots, buckles, belts, neckerchiefs, and gloves all served the presentation of self in the photographs he sedulously accumulated from all his trips. So did the horses and saddles, the English shotguns and pistols, the American rifles and revolvers and knives, always of the best.[67] Roosevelt's adventure in Cuba was an extremely expensive affair. He personally fitted out not only himself but his company of Rough Riders.

Other performances, such as that of New York City police commissioner, might require less personal expenditure but still more public staging. At the bottom of all this was Roosevelt's realization that neither Big Business nor Big Labor, neither industrial production nor mass abundance, in and of themselves generated personality and manhood. This in turn had a political dimension: neither businessmen nor labor leaders, neither bankers nor farmers, would of themselves generate national visions and national leadership. They would always be limited by their partial perspective as special interests. Roosevelt had no doubt that national interest inhered in character.

Ironically—if not tragically—Roosevelt's legacy faded most where his vision was clearest. Reading the rise of the Kaiser's Germany for what it was, the beginning of the end of British patrol of the world's seas, Roosevelt set out to ready the United States for the role Tocqueville had foreseen, as Britain's heir in responsibility for world stability. Roosevelt's deeds were large. He intervened in the Far East. He prepared for digging the Panama Canal. He built up and displayed American naval power. One can only speculate that, had he returned to the presidency in 1913, his vision might have been installed as American foreign policy. The basic stake of the United States in the European balance of power might have been defended in time. As it was, Roosevelt's significance as man and politician remained confined to the domestic stage. In his years as President, Roosevelt's strength drew on style more than substance. Or rather, his style was substance. American presidential politics had had few if any men who testified, in their very personalities, that the ordinary preoccupations of personality might be in any way relevant to the larger issues of democratic capitalism. The most common of Presidents, Andrew Johnson, had been a disaster. A hero for but not of democracy, Jackson had been more icon than person. The roots of Lincoln's psychology remained elusive from first to last. Roosevelt not only appeared to, but did offer himself copiously to public view.

His most compelling stage was his family. Still young enough as President to have small children, he let the White House be seen as a resort for active young boys and a showcase for one of the first of the new young women of the age, his oldest daughter, Alice. Sagamore Hill too, the family's "private" domain, became familiar to a generation of magazine-reading Americans.[68] Here a sunny, modern domesticity, healthy, active, child-centered, competitive, exuberant, egalitarian, seemed to reign. Utterly unequipped for the old Victorian patriarch's use of dignity and distance for authority, Roosevelt vividly enacted a wholly new model of father, identified without tension as manhood. The country could not get enough. When Roosevelt warned against "selfishness" and "self-indulgence," his meaning was clear. His warning had nothing to do with an exaltation of work, let alone of self-denial, but rather with the correct use of abundance. The vigorous family life modeled by the Roosevelts was expensive: big houses, trips, games, costumes, lessons, subscriptions, tickets, doctors, graduations, parties, weddings. Yet none of this registered as luxury, materialism, decadence. Life at Sagamore Hill was well beyond the means of most Americans—beyond Roosevelt's means, too, in the less affluent afternoon of his life—but it was imitable, and besides, it spoke directly to the hopes of the majority of Americans of becoming better off all the time. His example lent indisputable point and meaning to the economic abundance that had become the most obvious characteristic of American life.

Roosevelt's style of consumption suggested that women would have even less need to forsake their assigned sphere. As mothers, wives, and domestic superintendents generally, women would have a realm far more complex, enriched, and stimulating than had been theirs in 1830, when Tocqueville commented upon their segregation. Roosevelt's own wife, Edith Carow Roosevelt, while often understood to provide the emotional counterweight to her husband's boyish enthusiasms, never once undertook social work or public activity, let alone the slightest intervention into her husband's realm of politics. Yet it was Roosevelt, far more than any other major political figure of the age, who welcomed women onto a larger stage.[69] Roosevelt knew strong-minded women all his life. He grew up with them. His mother's sister Anna, his own older sister Anna—"Bama," "Auntie Bye"—and his younger sister Corinne he knew as eager and interested intellectual advisers and comrades. Neither Roosevelt's mother nor his first or second wife was in this mold, but it is clear that he forced no sentimental image on other women in idealizing these. His Harvard senior thesis topic— "The Practicability of Equalizing Men and Women before the Law"— was most interesting for showing his interest in the topic, rare among the men of his class. It revealed deep impulses more than deep thought. After shuttling back and forth between conceding and denying the "practicable" implications of what he took to be the leading problem, women's lesser average physical strength, he managed in the end to convey the idea that new legal rights were needed, even if he did not say exactly which. He grew clearer with the years.

By 1885 Roosevelt had welcomed women who were active outside the home in settlement houses and charity work, starting up schools, parks, libraries, and other civic amenities, and in "service" generally. Obviously he believed that the women of his class, provided with abundant domestic help and often unmarried, could not and ought not to be expected to let their talents lie idle. Roosevelt took his own political problems regularly to Bama. By the time of his presidency he had become thoroughly alerted to that new creation, the independent, modern-minded American girl, in the person of his own daughter. When Roosevelt declared in 1905 that, for the vast majority of women, home would—and should—remain the proper sphere, he was not rejecting careers or public service for any woman. Rather, he was reacting to the horrors of factory and sweatshop life. In an address of 1911, "The Conservation of Womanhood and Childhood," he showed familiarity with the findings of recent survey studies of conditions in Pittsburgh and other industrial cities. He commented with indignation on recent decisions in the New York courts that struck down protective legislation. He rejected as purely abstract the "freedoms" these courts pretended to defend. Many feminists agreed with him completely.

In 1911 Roosevelt came out for woman suffrage—the first major American politician to do so. Certainly his act was expedient: he hoped to steal a march in his difficult task of defeating an incumbent President, William Howard Taft, for the party nomination. But it was a gamble that did not violate his convictions. Typically, Roosevelt could not consciously dissemble. He offered his support for woman suffrage, yes, but only "tepidly," as he put it. His campaign drew support from many strong-minded and able women, however, and he welcomed them. Indeed, the third-party Progressive campaign of 1912, with its emphasis upon the need for a national economic and social policy under the mandate given a popularly elected President, to be carried out by trained administrators and social scientists, practically fulfilled the spirit of rationalism and the wish for the harmonization of national life that William Leach has shown had come to be pervasive in post-Civil War feminism. Roosevelt's experiences in 1912 warmed him up; as he said in his *Autobiography*, written in 1913, his support for suffrage soon became "zealous." "My association with women like Jane Addams and Frances Keller, who desire [the vote] as one means of enabling them to render better and more efficient service, changed me." Even this was not quite as conservative as it sounded. Bravely, he affirmed larger rights, too: "Women should have free access to every field of labor which they care to enter, and when their work is as valuable as that of a man it should be paid as highly."[70]

Still, for years Roosevelt had professed an alarm about falling birthrates. A high birthrate he associated with "virile, manly virtues." A lowered birthrate he linked with vices:

Any man who studies the statistics of the birth-rate among the native Americans of New England, or among the native French of France, needs not to be told that when prudence and forethought are carried to the point of cold selfishness and self-indulgence, the race is bound to disappear.[71]

But this anxiety was not linked to some emotional or ideological objection to women in public life. Just as it had come to inhabit some prosuffrage feminist circles, a degree of social Darwinist racism inflected Roosevelt's thought. He was not prepared to accept some decline among the white Anglo-Saxon Protestants of the Northeast, compensated by the high birthrates of immigrants from Catholic and Jewish Europe. Nor, even though he had invited Booker T. Washington to the White House, was he prepared to face down American racism on the occasion of the Brownsville riot of 1907. Roosevelt's presidency, in both policies and personality, remained addressed to WASP America, and so were all his ideas and impulses about women. Roosevelt tried to calculate how many babies "the married woman able to have children must on the average have," and decided the number was four.[72] The Swedish Social Democrats' Alva and Gunnar Myrdal were to arrive at the same number a generation later, from more or less the same motive. What was the point of trying to build a better Sweden, if the Swedes were going to die out? What was the point of a New Nationalism, if the people who had created the nation were going to fade away? That there would be plenty of white Anglo-Saxon Protestant women still available for public and political service, whether because they remained unmarried, or could not have children, or had raised their quota of children, or could combine raising children with public service, Roosevelt took for granted. He never tried to count them.

The record of women during World War I impressed Roosevelt. Jane Addams's pacifism disappointed him deeply, but the tens of thousands of women, including those in his own family circle, who in 1917 rushed to the Red Cross, the nursing corps, government bureaus, and war-production factories proved to him that women could understand why men fought and could back them up. Roosevelt came to his most extreme views in 1918, not long before his death. In a blistering appraisal of his former party, he declared that New York machine politicians were quite incapable of solving modern social problems. Let the New York Republican machine, which he himself had once entered holding his nose, be replaced by women![73] Further than this, no politician had gone. Further than this, none would ever go.

Had Roosevelt lived on into the 1920s, into his own sixties, he would have had the chance to ponder whether the managerial, collaborative, coordinated, balancing methods of the New Nationalism that he had espoused in 1912 were compatible with the renewal of economic boom. Growth, not planning, had characterized the American economy since 1830. Boom, not balance, had sustained the investment of energy by millions of enterprisers. Streets of gold, not the greenery of parks and public virtue, had attracted the immigrants. No doubt Roosevelt had taken steady growth for granted in his New Nationalist campaign. No doubt most of the new-style businessmen who had joined him, men of a "national" outlook, identified with the new big banks and the new integrated corporations, meant to have steady growth. Yet all this constituted a new idea and would require testing by experience. It was not Hamilton's idea. Hamilton had meant to use government to get things started in the first place, to provoke industrialization where "natural" conditions discouraged it, to get a boom going that could then take off on its own. Such a boom had been got going, if not by Hamiltonian means, and now the question was, whether it could be taken in hand without cooling it off and reducing the growth rate. It was possible that the New Nationalism, with its emphasis on security and predictability and its "search for order," would not prove long to be in the interests even of the new managers and coordinators, should it begin to run athwart the logic of mass production for mass consumption. Neither old small-town progressives nor new corporate progressives were necessarily going to offer emotional welcome to a marketplace thronging with newcomers, let alone to blacks, the perennially excluded, but they might find it hard to confine to themselves the fruits of an economy they had generated on a democratic basis. Theodore Roosevelt himself had shown that the moral life required abundance. To reserve that abundance to some while denying it to others would require a political counter-revolution.

For women, the temptation posed by a managerial, state-centered, housekeeping politics like the New Nationalism was strong. Segregated from the marketplace, detached from the drives and engines that had originated the boom and sustained it through its heyday, women might find a new politics of supervision and consolidation profoundly fulfilling of their own different heritage. They might also find themselves contributing to cutting the boom short of its full expression. Theodore Roosevelt himself, of course, had no fears of some feminizing of life. He was sure strife and conflicts aplenty awaited to challenge unencumbered masculinity. He himself was one of the first in the age of Darwin to imply that, if challenges were not forthcoming, it would be the art of life to invent them. In principle, the strenuous life need never end. But he too left the question unasked, whether there was any alternative for the United States to keeping economic expansion going until it had reached into every backwater, infused every ethnic strain, enriched every church and temple, endowed all races, blessed every child in every family.

8 The First Feminism

Daughters or Sisters of the Promised Land?

How far back can we reach for the beginnings of feminism in America? In 1891 the feminist Helen Campbell, a home economist and friend of Charlotte Perkins Gilman, published a biography, *Anne Bradstreet and Her Time*. Without ever arguing that Bradstreet had been a feminist herself, Campbell opened up the case for regarding her as one. Persistently, literary scholars would read Bradstreet as "representative." In 1967 Robert Richardson presented "her finest work, 'Contemplations,' [as] a splendid and coherent expression of what was best in New England Puritanism." Next year, the literary historian Hyatt Waggoner claimed Bradstreet for his enterprise of finding out "what's American about American poetry." Commenting on those beginning to write of Bradstreet as "a woman poet," Sacvan Bercovitch claimed that the "best of these critics," particularly the poet Ann Stanford, actually were studying her "as a woman" in order to highlight "the representative quality of her work." Bercovitch reasserted his own assumption: "Ann Bradstreet was neigher a conformist nor an individualist, but a Puritan."

Campbell, however, had not written her biography to show how Bradstreet represented either Puritanism or America. She assumed that studying Bradstreet would show something different, not familiar, about American history. "[No] woman's record remains of the long voyage or the first impressions of the new country." Campbell was intrigued by the fact that for Bradstreet the passage to America had not had that triumphalistic quality lent it by Governor Bradford of Plymouth or Governor Winthrop of the Bay. Her heart had "risen" against it; she had hated it. Nor did Campbell miss the fact that Bradstreet had commented on men who criticized women poets. She found that Bradstreet had identified with the great Queen who had loomed over her girlhood. It was Bradstreet's difference, not Bradstreet's typicality, that interested her. Campbell nursed a dramatic hope: "Grave doubts," she said in her preface, "at times arise as to whether America has had any famous women." Perhaps she could show in Bradstreet that such doubts were unjustified.

On occasion a historian or two has picked up on Campbell's lead. In his *Builders of the Bay Colony* of 1930, Samuel Eliot Morison agreed that "the story of the settling of America has been told largely in the terms of men," leaving the "dark" history of the American pioneer woman unwritten. For "puritan women of gentle nurture," taming the wilderness might not have offered the same "release and creative joy" it did to men. But since Morison's goal in *Builders*, in a spirit of overt ancestralism, was to rescue the Puritans from their 1920s critics and restore them as good fathers, he could not truly tell a "dark" story and did not. He could not very well have chosen Anne Hutchinson for his chapter on women without showing such darkness, so in treating of Bradstreet he treated her as at one with her culture, revealing certain warm and appealing dimensions in that culture that might otherwise not be appreciated. A later Harvard study, Edmund Morgan's *The Puritan Family* (1944), drew briefly on Bradstreet for the same purposes, to show ungloomy, normal, "human" qualities in Puritan life: "[The] Puritans were neither prudes nor ascetics. They knew how to laugh, and they knew how to love."[1]

By 1977 a coherent feminist perspective on Bradstreet was available to Emily Stipes Watts as she compiled her anthology, *The Poetry of American Women from 1632 to 1945*. Inevitably, Watts too, in her search for what defined, characterized, and typified, would engage in reduction. But she would be free of mistaking what was "Puritan" in Bradstreet for the "finest" of Bradstreet, what was "American" in Bradstreet for what was significant in Bradstreet. Watts quite explicitly raised alternative possibilities. Had the Puritans explored the special relationship of mother and child? No, but Bradstreet did. Was it Puritan to ignore fatherhood, as Bradstreet did? Was not the critic Roy Harvey Pearce right in noting that Bradstreet never affirmed "the communal experience"—the heart, after all, of "the New England Way"—and right, therefore, in saying that Bradstreet was not a true American Puritan? Was not Bradstreet's pride in her sex also found in the English women poets of her day, and did this not mean that in this she was better understood as more English than American? Was it not interesting, too, that in the famous "Contemplations," rich with imagery from nature, the nature Bradstreet borrowed from was all English? She had not yet "seen" America. And then was it not interesting that this Puritan never testified to having had some experience of mystic certainty of God? After all, Edward Taylor did. "I never saw any miracles to confirm me," Bradstreet wrote to her children. Would John Winthrop have said this, or John Cotton? In the end, Watts was able to avoid reducing Bradstreet even to the frame of "American woman poet." She noted that Bradstreet's "amatory verse" to her husband would not be found again in American women's poetry for nearly three hundred years. Textually based, Watts's Bradstreet emerged as neither particularly radical, dissident, nor feminist, but neither did she fit nicely some inclusive, coherent social (or even literary) canon, such as "Puritanism" or "the New England Way."[2]

With Bradstreet studies (and Anne Hutchinson studies[3]) as a guide, it seemed less likely that feminism's beginnings would be pushed further and further back, than that women's studies would sooner or later erode the clarity of the colonial story. That would not happen easily, however. While neither Bradstreet nor Hutchinson were good or representative Puritans, their importance did not follow from that fact. They were important for their achievements. Bradstreet wrote lasting poems. Hutchinson mounted a political challenge that resonates to this day. The problem for both feminist history and women's studies would be to make sense of the fact that between Bradstreet and, say, Emily Dickinson, no powerful woman poet appeared. After Hutchinson, no woman mounted challenges to established powers for two centuries. The long interval by no means attested to women's passivity or adjustment, let alone contentment, but it attested to the difficulty posed for historians, who lacked achievements by specific individuals to analyze.

Examining the Revolution, Mary Beth Norton and Linda Kerber have shown how politics itself shook a long evolution.[4] With a new nation to worry about, Americans felt pressure to call all resources to its aid. The role of mother was hardly new, but the self-conscious exercise of that role as "republican mothers" was urged upon women. For such a role to stimulate further consciousness, however, was quite another matter. Such fathers of the Revolution as John Adams, Thomas Jefferson, and George Washington persistently professed their wish and yearning for home life. Both Adams and Jefferson commented invidiously on French women by comparison with the home arts, "chaste affections," and unspoiled simplicity of their own. The wish registered by Abigail Adams, in her famous admonition to her husband working away at constitutional matters in far-off Philadelphia, to "remember the ladies," was not for the encouragement of republican motherhood. When Adams was in Paris, temporarily enthralled by the women there— "To tell you the truth, I admire [them]. They are handsome and very well educated. Their accomplishments are exceedingly brilliant"—his wife responded in envy: "I regret the trifling, narrow, contracted education of the females of my own country. . . . [Here], you need not be told how much female education is neglected . . . how fashionable it has been to ridicule female learning." Abigail Adams was not talking about the usefulness of education to mothers wishing to rear republican children. In England, sometime after the Revolution, while Adams was busy with statesmanship, she enrolled in a course of public lectures on science. It was "like going into a beautiful Country which I never say before, a Country which our American Females are not permitted to visit or inspect." To a woman friend Abigail Adams, while affirming her own agreement that woman's province was the household, also confided her aggrieved feeling that "even some men of sense have been illiberal enough to wish us confined [there].[5]

It was true that in the decades after the Revolution men of "liberal" views on women were few. Perhaps the only one of explicit and insistent purpose was the novelist Charles Brockden Brown who, in six novels published between 1795 and 1802, presented the case for property rights, political rights, and education for women. Women should have no less of these than did men. But the problem with other men was not their "illiberality." The fathers of the republic themselves had no particularly coherent ideology about women at all, certainly not in any collective sense. Benjamin Franklin wanted all women to be taught a trade, but for neither liberal nor illiberal reasons. Ever the practical observer, he had noted how often women were thrown on their own resources by widowhood, spinsterhood, or other circumstance. Hamilton's sense of women ranged across a whole spectrum of society, from the underemployed farm girl he hoped to see busily employed in factories to his glittering socialite sister-in-law, Angelica Church, after whom he had yearned, not to forget such demimondaines as Mrs. Reynolds with whom he did adventure in dark places. Quite apart from any questions about Sally Hemings, Jefferson's own personal ties with women were so charged with conflict that, had he ever tried to expound sexual ideology, he would have confronted a crisis of consciousness.[6]

It was precisely their fascination with elegant foreign women that reciprocally impelled both Jefferson and Adams to compensatory praise of their own simpler womenfolk, but this was not yet enough to induce a whole rhetorical strategy. Franklin, who, though in his seventies, learned how to flirt with the ladies in Paris, brought home no lingering regrets. As would Jefferson, he simply took it for granted that the great task for the American future would be peopling the wilderness. That was understanding enough as to the role of women. As Catherine Albanese and others have argued, the revolutionary generation can be understood to have consolidated its experience into a new "civil religion," that of the nation itself, with Freemasonry its semisecret cultic church.[7] Enrolling the greatest of the revolutionaries, Washington, and the greatest of the new type of American democratic manhood, Franklin, the Masons constituted a pantheon made up of Fathers in a continuous succession of fathers, sons of the original first founding Pilgrim Fathers. In Masonry women were not confronted with illiberal confinement; rather, they were adjuncts, auxiliaries, "General Washington's

Sewing Circle," their place so obvious as to need no ideology. The pervasive plausibility of this condition was such that C. B. Brown's novels fell as into a well. Having written them in hopes for popular success, Brown turned to other things and ended up identified with the new nationalism.

Lawrence Friedman has suggested that something like a persistent, deliberate, systematic ideology of "true American womanhood" began to emerge only with the postheroic, even unheroic generation, the generation of Noah Webster and Parson Weems, of David Ramsey and James Kirk Paulding, not only sons with prodigious fathers against whom to measure themselves, but sons humiliated and wounded by the War of 1812.[8] Now commenced that "patriotisme irritable" that would strike visitors from abroad for the next generation. The ideology of a womanhood manifest in ever more conspicuously "feminine" characteristics provided dialectic tension for the assertion of heroic masculinity. As the eagle began to scream, women were expected to stand guard over the hearth. Their greatest task would be that of rearing sons fit for the task of expanding the nation.

Here emerged a matrix for the creation of consciousness—feminist consciousness. A great deed had been achieved, women sharing in it, though hardly as equals. Who could doubt that men of the people's militias at Saratoga and Valley Forge, at King's Mountain and Yorktown had played the leading role? But women had been conscious and recognized participants. Now another great task was at hand, that of lifting the nation from independence into a "rising glory." But was the logic of different roles as obvious in peacetime as during war? By 1848 the women at Seneca Falls would deliberately echo this national history.[9] There must be, they said, a Second Declaration of Independence, another Revolution, another victory. Yet it was also obvious that the analogy, if pressed very far, would not clarify wishes. The women at Seneca Falls had no intention of separating from men, as America had separated from Britain. They had no intention of mobilizing a women's army against the forces of men. They had been told their major task was motherhood. Would they reply that they had not been given the freedom and resources to carry it through successfully? They had been told that the conspicuous, bold, public tasks were reserved for men, because men and women were different kinds of beings. If so were not women's special qualities bound to draw them into moral restraint of the growingly uncontrolled nation? Feminine qualities actually heightened concern for the unfortunate, the sick, the lame, the blind. Slaves were beginning to impel men into protest; women were even more likely to comprehend slavery's horror. They were tuned to its degradation of home, family, motherhood, femininity itself. On the other hand, if it was not really true that women and men were different kinds of beings, different in temper, character, mind, and soul—if a woman with the same education and the same rights as a man displayed much the same range of character, tastes, abilities, and ambitions—why should there be any task assigned to women as a whole at all? Let some enter the marketplace like men, as individuals.

Whether or not Tocqueville had been right, that in 1830 American women had willingly and rationally surrendered to the role prescribed for them by the ideology of True American Womanhood and separate spheres, the Seneca Falls Convention showed that the harmony he had admired had ended. The ending of harmony through consciousness and self-consciousness hardly guaranteed direction, however. The wish for independence was itself a guarantee that independence had already begun, but its growth would depend no longer so much on the flux of external change and "material" conditions as on the clarification of wishes. The moment had arrived for the appearance of a powerful single consciousness, capable of offering others the spectacle of her own struggle.

Two Lost Leaders: Waldo Emerson and Margaret Fuller

Margaret Fuller sought herself in men's worlds. Radical thought, social analysis, romantic politics drew her. Yet before she died, she had undertaken her most thorough liberation in private life, in love, marriage, and motherhood. She had reached the point where she repudiated her own most famous feminist lament, over women as victims. She ended up no victim. Had Fuller been fully appreciated by Ralph Waldo Emerson, American intellectual history at least would have been different, for Emerson, as the most radical individualist of his generation, might have helped mediate the way to radical individualism for women. Emerson was not ready for this—not, as I believe, from flaws in his ideas, but rather from wounds of the heart. How different feminism might have been had Fuller lived and Emerson been happy, we can only guess, but their specific potential is a part of the record.

The Eager Heart: Fuller to Emerson

In the summer of 1843, thirty-three years old, Fuller, with her friend Sarah Clarke, toured the West. Escorted to Niagara Falls early in June by Clarke's brother James, the two women proceeded by lake steamer to Chicago, where another brother, William Clarke, conducted them into the wilds of northern Illinois. Later the women traveled to Milwaukee and into Wisconsin territory on their own. After nine days or so at an annual encampment of Indians on Mackinaw Island in August, Fuller returned to Boston in September. Next year she published a book, her first, on her trip.

Summer on the Lakes was Fuller's first attempt at extensive objective, reportorial writing. Much of the time during her trip she had been unhappy. During two weeks in Chicago, she said, "of me, none asked a question. . . . I have not been led to express one thought of my mind with warmth and freedom since I have been here." Westerners were "all life and no thought," action without reflection, bent wholly on money. But Fuller self-consciously strove not to judge the region by its failure to be interested in her.

I have come prepared to see all this, to dislike it, but not with stupid narrowness to distrust or defame. . . . I trust by reverent faith to woo the mighty meaning of the scene, perhaps to foresee the law by which a new order, a new poetry, is to be evoked from this chaos.[10]

Writing up her book from her travel diary, she did keep out the laments and complaints she had sent in letters to friends back east, Emerson, William Channing, and others. *Summer on the Lakes* proved a display not of the famous Fuller personality but of an analytic, empathetic observer.

Fuller understood that what she saw in Illinois and Wisconsin was but a phase, a region in transition. Its meaning would be revealed in the future. Its present—crude, rude, "the sweetest forest glades" blackened by the campfires of new settlers—constituted one of those harsh necessities by which finer times are funded. But Fuller could not but hope that some things would not be lost. In "Milwaukie," on the pier, "I see disembarking the Germans, the Norwegians, the Swedes, the Swiss." Might not their "old legendary lore" survive, "their tales of the origins of things" mingle with those of the native Indians? Fuller did not offer apostrophes, in the style of Walt Whitman, to glorious democratic literatures. The vision of some wholly new world sweeping away what was affecting and delightful in the immigrant pasts repelled her. Those who finally attracted her most were the natives, the Indians, to be found everywhere, lurking on outskirts, camped beside small lakes, ghosts haunting the new world that preferred to believe it had no past. Her days at the Mackinaw encampment were her happiest. "I liked very much to walk or sit among them." After some pages of fond description, she turned to the futility of missionary efforts at making the Indians over, then elided into melancholy: "nature seems like all else to declare that this race is fitted to perish." She hoped only that "there will be a national institute containing all the remains of the Indians." "I have not wished to write sentimentally of the Indians," Fuller concluded, but she could not avoid saying that, had those who had taken the country "been truly civilized or Christianized," the conflict of races might have been avoided.[11]

But one group at least she hoped would not succeed in preserving its past. These were the wives of the American settlers, particularly those of the better sort, the "ladies," who she saw were by and large miserable in the West. Going west "has generally been the choice of the men, and the women follow as women will." They were "doing their best," Fuller wrote, but "too often in heartsickness and weariness." To some degree victims, and victims of men, these women nonetheless did not draw Fuller's sympathy. "Their grand ambition for their children is to send them to school in some Eastern city. . . . Their culture has too generally been that given to women to make them the 'ornaments of society.' " Perhaps the girls would grow up "strong, resolute, able to exert their faculties," but if so, only after "a great deal to war with in the habits of thought acquired by their mothers from their own early life."

Summer on the Lakes was a strong book, clear in its judgments about a large and variegated social scene, the best promise of what Fuller might have gone on to write for thirty more years, had her life not been cut short off Fire Island. She showed a strong sense of history: whole peoples found themselves threatened with destruction by historical processes; other peoples found opportunity for new beginnings; men and women could be divided by the same experiences. The book was no unified exercise in personal self-consciousness; it was not focused on the grievances of women. The most pointed judgment Fuller offered reflected her utter lack of sympathy for those Eastern wives trying to bring some of their culture to the West. She noted the trouble and expense to which some settler families had gone to lug a piano with them: "The guitar . . . would be far more desirable for most of these ladies."[12] But Fuller really objected to these pianos in the East, too, as functions of only "ornamental" womanhood. The West thus offered some cure for the artificialities of Eastern womanhood, and Fuller appreciated that.

Nevertheless, Fuller's objective reportage of the West resolved none of her own problems. Certainly she herself was not going to learn the guitar. She had already rejected the "petty intellectualities, cant, and bloodless theory" she had grown up with in Boston and Cambridge; now she knew that this Western "land of go ahead," from which the Indians had been evicted, was also not for her. "Truly there is no place for me,"[13] she wrote Emerson, then returned not to Boston but to the astonishing new world of New York City, reporting on it for Horace Greeley before going off to Europe and Italy in 1846.

Of course Margaret Fuller once had very much hoped to "find a place" in the intellectual world of Boston and Cambridge. Educated like a precocious son by her father, she had had full access to the most advanced circles of eastern Massachusetts's liberalizing philosophy, theology, psychology, and literature.[14] She had been determined to become the confidante of the emerging eminence of transcendentalism, Waldo Emerson. Fuller visited the Emersons for several weeks in their Concord home during the summer of 1836, when she was twenty-six, a year after her father's death. Her relationship with the Emersons was reaching its climax in 1840–41, exactly as Emerson was writing his most isolating and individualistic essay ever, "Friendship." From this climax their friendship cooled, never to be warmed again.

From the start, Emerson had found that Margaret Fuller took some getting used to. "I once," he recalled in 1840, "fancied your nature and aims so eccentric that I had a foreboding that certain crises must impend in your history that would be painful to me in the conviction that I could not aid even by sympathy." Fuller, however, would not be rebuffed. Lidian Emerson grew particularly fond of her. Fuller was free to radiate her own enthusiasms, and Emerson himself soon relaxed. She, he saw, was "an extraordinary person. . . . It is always a great refreshment to see a very intelligent person. It is like being set in a large place. You stretch your limbs and dilate to your utmost size." Fuller was able to persist, and Emerson to find accommodation, as he wrote in 1840: "You have your own methods of equipoise and recovery, without event, without convulsion, and I understand now your language better, I hear my native tongue, though still I see not into you & have not arrived at your law."[15]

Settling in Concord with his bride in 1835, a year before they met Fuller, Emerson had soon been offered the society, friendship, and admiration of several young persons, including Fuller—Caroline Sturgis, for one; a girl named Anna Barker for another, no intellectual but of such beauty in form and grace as to occupy symbolic status; and "Raphael," Samuel Gray Ward, Anna Barker's fiancé. To these happy few, Emerson sometimes added favorite correspondents, notably Thomas Carlyle, a British friend named John Sterling, and a onetime mistress of Johann Wolfgang von Goethe, Bettina, whose collection of spurious materials on her friendship with Goethe Emerson had read on Fuller's prompting. Emerson had written a fan letter, to which Bettina had responded.

Emerson's confession to Fuller in 1840 of his early ambivalence toward her turned out to be explosive. In August, 1840, speaking for both herself and Caroline Sturgis, Fuller had "taxed him with a certain inhospitability of soul inasmuch as you both were willing to be my friends in the full and sacred sense & I remained apart critical, & after many interviews still a stranger." As Emerson put it in his journal, Fuller complained that their relationship was "not friendship, but literary gossip." Emerson had thought his relations with both Fuller and Sturgis sunny and serene. His response was not to deny their charge; instead, he incorporated it into a familiar Emersonian dialectic, in an eight-week exchange of letters. First, to Sturgis he wrote two letters, thanking her for telling Fuller "that you were sure of me," then expounding on relationship generally: "I hate everything frugal and cowardly in friendship." He then reaffirmed their particular relation— "As we, dear sister, are *naturally* friends"—and concluded with a marvelous dismissal:

So, dear child, I give you up to all your Gods—to your wildest love and pursuit of beauty, to the boldest effort of your Imagination to express it, to the most original choices of tasks and influences and the rashest exclusion of all you deem alien or malign;—and you shall not give me so great a joy as by the finding for yourself a love which shall make mine show cold and feeble—which certainly is not cold or feeble.[16]

To Fuller, after offering thanks for her letter—"I shall never go quite back to my old arctic habits"—and pretending that the crisis between them had been caused by Anna Barker's incipient marriage to Ward, Emerson concluded as though all was well: "Write to me from any mood." But soon, after he admitted having been intimidated by her at first—"a great court lady with a Louis Quatorze taste for diamonds & splendor"—Fuller wrote in a challenging mood: "How often have I left you despairing and forlorn. How often have I said, This light will never understand my fire. . . . did you not ask for a 'foe' in your friend? Did you not ask for a 'large formidable nature'?" Fuller may not have known exactly what she wanted, but she knew what she did not want, Emerson's dismissal: "my soul, in its childish agony of prayer, stretched out its arms to you as a father."[17]

If Emerson did not wish to play father, it could have been because of his impersonal conviction that the modern intellectual must refuse to perpetuate dependency and followership. Certainly he must stop being "authority." But neither could he be "influence." He must wean, not seduce, his hearers. Yet this was never exactly the point he made to Fuller. Through the rest of the month he temporized, handsomely: "You have a right to expect great activity great demonstration & large intellectual contributions from your friends. . . . Can one be glad of an affection which he knows not how to return? I am." But propitiation would not suffice. Fuller insisted: there was something wrong that could be righted, if Emerson would only change. And he could change—she knew it.

If he could have, he would not, and finally he brought things to climax. "I have your frank & noble & affecting letter" (a letter which has never been found), he wrote her, "and yet I think I could wish it unwritten." I remain ready to be your friend, he told her, but he was no longer ready to talk about their friendship. He did not want to analyze or measure it. He offered her a model to follow: "A robust & total understanding grows up resembling nothing so much as the relation of brothers who are intimate and perfect friends without ever having spoken of the fact." He then presented her with what was no doubt the most stunning gift he could have offered, a bit of naked confession: "Tell me that I am cold or unkind, and in my most flowing state I become a cake of ice. . . . It may do for others but it is not for me to bring the relation to speech."[18] At bay, Emerson left nothing to Fuller's imagination, concluding with an open warning:

Up to this hour our relation has been progressive. I have never regarded you with so much kindness as now. . . . I honor you for a brave and beneficent woman. . . . Let us live as we have always done. . . . Speak to me of everything but of myself. . . . I see very dimly in writing on this topic. It will not prosper with me. Perhaps all my words are wrong. Do not expect it of me again for a very long time.[19]

Of course we cannot know what difference a more accessible, a warmer, a more flowing Emerson might have meant for Margaret Fuller. At most, perhaps, an equal friend with whom to explore, on occasion, the roots of self, the means whereby to hold off the death of individuality threatened in rationality, science, society, social science, organization, and the collective. Though Fuller was to prove she could break forward into her own autonomy without Emerson, his help could hardly have harmed her. His help could hardly have harmed others to whom he denied himself. Emerson was America's foremost explorer of romantic individualism, the fullest intellectual expositor of Tocquevillian democratic man, but his personal relations with other romantic individuals were frozen. In his essay on "Friendship" he wrote:

I do with my friends as I do with my books. I would have them where I can find them, but I seldom use them. We must have society on our own terms. . . . I cannot afford to speak much with my friends . . . though I prize my friends, I cannot afford to talk with them and study their visions, lest I lose my own.[20]

Emerson agreed that "these things may hardly be said without a sort of treachery to the relation," yet he did not deny it. Friendship had an essence, a kind of "entireness, a total magnanimity and trust," that was not finally compatible with self, and self came first.

The Heart Chilled: Emerson and Ellen Tucker Emerson

There was nothing in "transcendentalism," however, nothing in "Emersonianism" that decreed personal alienation. Historians who understand the root of history in individuals are prepared to recognize that not all potentials realize themselves. Ralph Waldo Emerson was not a kind of Inevitability-Machine, not a deductive explanatory principle. He too had evolved from beginnings, had had a history, had not always been "self-made."

Emerson's first wife, Ellen Tucker Emerson, had not been a standard preacher's wife. She was not a helpmeet. Mary Moody Emerson, Emerson's admiring aunt, had urged her to be:

The man that God has blest you with is devoted to the highest and most urgent office. Lean not on him for improvement which is going on for Heaven. Be yourself a ministering angel to him and society . . . I hope you don't paint nor talk French.[21]

But this was neither Emerson's idea nor his bride's. In their short married life, Ellen Emerson traveled some weeks for her health, spent her only summer with Emerson in a summer house, and was sick a good deal of the time at home in their Boston apartment. In any case Emerson's widowed mother, Ruth, lived with them and managed most things.

Here I sit in my own little domicile & realize that I am Mrs. Emerson to the full for Betsy and Nancy and Martin must have their daily and nightly tasks allotted—and Mr. Such a one with his wife are in town and they must come to tea tomorrow—no cake—bless me how many eggs? how much sugar? and there are those brasses and the spare chamber bed must be attended—only imagine the careless, one eyed skittish.Ellen Tucker in this situation & send her a little fairy Order to tap with her wand upon the household duds and ease me of my woe—Do I alarm you?

Certainly she had not been raised to be a ministering angel or helpmeet:

[She] led a gay life. There were rides, drives, music, parties, callers, visitors, excursions to the country. Ellen was interested in clothes and fashions. She wore the latest thing in sleeves, and had her hair curled in a fashionable manner.[22]

Her stepfather—her father had died when she was nine; her mother remarried four years later—bringing five children of his own to join the widow Tucker's three, seems to have been an affectionate man able to indulge daughters without spoiling them. A sense of fatality may have been ingrained in this generous clan. One brother and one sister had died of tuberculosis before Ellen's marriage, and another sister, close to Emerson, died in 1832. Her mother died in 1833 of the same scourge. Before Emerson met her, when she was seventeen, Ellen Tucker had already recognized her proneness to the dreadful malady. She was not an invalid when she married, but quite clearly she was not going to be turning the beds for "Mr. Such a one" and wife.

Emerson, so he said, had not been stirred by girls. "I was a hermit whom the lone Muse cheers,/ I sped apart my solitary years,/ I found no joy in woman's meaning eye." Yet he had been alerted to "the law all laws above,/ Great Nature hath ordained the heart to love. . . . To every mind exists its natural mate." Prompted by this knowledge, "eagerly I searched each circle round,/ I panted for my mate."[23] Although in this poem his finding Ellen appeared a kind of instantaneous illumination—"the star broke through the hiding cloud"—in fact Emerson went through at least a brief period of worry that "sentiment" was overthrowing "reason," and he never did lose some sense of doubleness in his attitudes toward her.

Her own emotional singleness may have been a source of appeal. This sunny indivisibility allowed her to treat Emerson with an intimacy that was quick and fresh, still delightful for historians to read. After a first, hesitant, but determined, shy tease—"I am resolved tonight to let you peep into the deep well of my heart. . . . Oh I never thought that I should draw aside the veil thus from the sacred places of my soul. . . . (Oh the metaphorical droppings of a girl in her teens)"— Emerson's young fiancée gave herself over to her will to trust and simply released her "gleeful heart." She called him "my lord," "my king," "your lordship," the "Rev. R.W.E.," finally "Grampa" and "Grandpa." She thanked him for his letters, expecting one every day. We do not have Emerson's letters to her and can only infer their kind. "Waldo says," she wrote, presumably quoting one, " 'Are not the affections in your own power?' I say No!—Every day I say—No!—." Her point—the sudden swoop on his solemn puritanical position could hardly be called argument—had been anticipated in an entry in her notebook, evidently triggered by her first acquaintance with him.

Riding at the circus for days the restrained canter of some of the horses I cannot but compare to my affections . . . curb them and their strength shows itself in certain uneasy motions disagreeable very to the rider. . . . So my affecs—being often curbed for want of room they do render me disagreeable to others and vastly uncomfortable myself—.[24]

She clinched her point—and added spice—by an obvious comparison:

"I wrote so to somebody once who was vexed that I could not *try* & love him—." It seems plain that she sensed in Emerson a stale residue of old Puritan fears. She wanted to be sure:

Notwithstanding Grandpa my heart is a stranger to the tender passion—yet I do feel too much regard for you to allow you to be shocked by what I know should displease you—there rest a minute—take a short nap—[25]

Emerson's sexual hopes had been excited. He wrote his brother Charles of a stopoff with Ellen at a Shaker village:

Mother Winkley or Sister Winkley hath given Ellen & I a long & earnest sermon on the "beauty of virginity" & striven to dissuade us from our sinful purpose of "living after the way of manhood and womanhood in the earth" but I parried her persuasion.[26]

With this girl Emerson could feel that the otherness of sexuality need not limit but could exhilarate consciousness.

It was of course always possible that, on longer testing, the exhilarations of courtship and young marriage would fall back into conventionality. Honeymooning, traveling to Philadelphia, the young couple composed a rhyming trip journal, Emerson's highfalutin contribution showing undertones of strain:

O Broadway O Broadway where beauty parades
In the splendor of pain, lace, plumes, flowers and brocades
O Broadway of fashions & Broadway of trades
My Mind is unequal thy pomp to unfold
Thy wealth & thy folly, noise, motion & gold
Howbeit thy beaux
Made me turn up my nose
And if I told my sincere tho't
I fear that thy belles would love me not.[27]

Ellen Emerson described herself "blushing like a country miss/ To see the utter nakedness" on New York's streets, but later, not joking, in a letter to Charles, wrote: "I dislike N York more than ever and am surprised at the difference in the sensibilities of the fashionables of B & NY." In this letter to Charles, Emerson concluded: "As to Ellen, she is pretty well but I would rather see her a grain more robust before I go away." Then Ellen added a postscript registering a sense of anxiety in Emerson:

Really!—I have given him leave yea have urged his going away *now*—for he is every whit as much out of his element at *Concord N.H.* [her home]—and (oh tell it not) not a text has he expounded not a skeleton of a sarmint has he formed not a sonnet has he perpetuated since he turned his back B ward.[28]

Plainly the story was being darkened already by her tragic curse. Pregnancy must have been regarded as a deadly peril. We can only try to imagine.

At all events, whatever the future might have been, Emerson for one brief season did compose his life with another consciousness that he did not want simply as a useful "friend." Even in this short period he apparently revealed something in himself never incorporated in his later "self-reliance," something his seventeen-year-old lover discovered with sympathy but also with a slight touch of concern:

... why Grandpa you're growing young again! ... you've gone back and hope to retrace your steps quietly I suppose till you come to the sweet sunny places of childhood—Grandpa you may go back and you may find the spots again and your cheek may be springing with richness and your eye bright with health but your spirit knows too much—that cannot be free as in days past.[29]

This man was not yet Ralph Waldo Emerson, and his bride realized he did not want to become that. Had Siri Strindberg realized the same about her husband? But Siri lived, Ellen died. Strindberg could spend the rest of his life retracing his steps, keeping young.

Four years after Ellen Emerson's death, Emerson remarried. Lydia Jackson Emerson was a helpmeet. In a letter of their courtship, Emerson signed himself "Waldo Emerson," "for whom I hope you will be able to find a more affectionate name than Mr. E."—but Lydia Emerson never could. She had recognized from the start that he was a great man, and she herself had been one of those New England girls—already thirty when she met him—practically reared for the manse. Still, she eventually found herself hoping for something more. She asked her husband for one letter just for herself, a "private" letter telling her there was part of him just for her.

"Ah you ask me for that unwritten letter . . . always unwritten, from year to year, by me to you, dear Lidian . . . always due and unwritten by me to every sister and brother of the human race." Obviously this was not what Lidian had meant at all. "I have only to say that I also bemoan myself daily for the same cause—that I cannot write this letter."[30] And Waldo Emerson never did, never could.

Staying home while he toured, lectured, received acolytes, enjoyed the sights of the West, Lidian Emerson eventually became what the classic helpmeet never had been, a domestic dissenter, somewhat sly, sarcastic, sardonic, casting strange light on her husband's views as she understood them.

As historians anxious to make amends for their craft's ancient omission of women now contemplate three women in particular—Margaret Fuller, Ellen Emerson, Lydia Emerson—obviously they will give their fullest pages to Fuller, not only as an autonomous individual but as one who produced books, letters, articles, and in general works enough to sustain the historian in claiming Fuller's autonomy and right to historical presence. But the historian averse to mere external principles of selection will wonder if guilt at the omission of women can be repaired while omitting Ellen and Lydia Emerson. Lydia Emerson was a martyred woman, useful to a story of women victimized, and in her case doubly so. For not only did Emerson disappoint her on her own terms; those terms with which she came to her marriage can be construed as themselves a cause of her crippling. Ellen Emerson, on the other hand, was not Emerson's victim, only nature's. Ellen Emerson, like Fuller, had autonomy, quite unlike Fuller's but by no means the less for that. At the very least, Ellen Emerson belongs somewhere near mainstream history for her particular relationship with a mainstream man: she exerted force over Emerson, influence, power. Ellen Emerson tells us what a major American—and his movement—might have been. Since we know of her what we do because of her relationship with Emerson, historians can conclude that a major reparation for the omission of women in telling history will often be to tell of women in the lives of their particular men.

Of course we cannot be sure how Waldo Emerson would have differed had Ellen Emerson lived. Would he have written "Friendship," had Ellen's gaiety filled his house? Would he have felt less threatened by Margaret Fuller? Perhaps Fuller might have taken something from his happiness with Ellen lacking in his marriage to Lidian. All can only be speculation. In any case it was sad that Waldo Emerson, who wrote of everything, wrote of women only conventionally, never expounded on the logic, resources, and democracy of romantic love, never contrasted it to the rational love of old Puritanism and the sentimental love rising like groundwater sapping foundations in his own lifetime. For the greatest expositor of individualism and the self to have left sex muffled was to leave it open to capture, first by the tribal panics of the Young Men's Christian Association and Anthony Comstock, then by the sciences and languages of hygiene, medicine, "community," and "cooperation."

Fuller in the World

Meanwhile, after returning from her first plunge into the reality of democratic America in the West, Margaret Fuller took time out, before resuming journalism, to revise an earlier article already published under the title, "The Great Lawsuit—Man versus Men; Woman versus Women." "I felt a delightful glow," she wrote W. H. Channing when she had finished, "as if I had put a good deal of my true life in it."[31] In fact, she had taken a step backward. Had she left "The Great Lawsuit" as it was, and moved on directly from *Summer on the Lakes* to her New York City journalism for Greeley, she would not have blurred her image in the history of feminism. She would have been seen more clearly not as the spokeswoman of a class of persons victimized and oppressed, but as a female exemplar of individualism.

It seems clear that in *Woman in the Nineteenth Century* Fuller was able to say things she had not been able to say in her earlier article. In his biography, Thomas Wentworth Higginson explained the peculiar title of the first version as due to Fuller's eagerness "to avert even the suspicion of awakening antagonism between the sexes."[32] In "The Great Lawsuit," the struggle she had celebrated was not that of the sexes with each other, but of the individual against the multitude, of the spirit against conventionality. That this individual might be a woman simply paralleled the fact that such an individual might be a man: "Woman versus Women, Man versus Men." But in *Woman in the Nineteenth Century* the basic struggle was not that of Woman, the individual, against unawakened common life, but of Women as a sex against Men as a sex. "Knowing that there exists in the minds of men a tone of feeling toward women as toward slaves," she wrote, women had to expect that "measures are not likely to be taken in behalf of women" until women insisted on them. The nature of these measures became clear in *Woman in the Nineteenth Century*.

Men have . . . been for more than a hundred years rating women for countenancing vice. But at the same time they have carefully hid from them its nature. . . . it has been inculcated on women for centuries that men have not only stronger passions than they, but of a sort that it would be shameful for them to share or even understand.[33]

The fundamental inequality in the relationship of men and women had consisted, then, of this supposed inequality of passion, installed in the institution of marriage itself, where the inequality reigned supreme.

Fuller's solution to this inequality was not the familiar transcendentalist insistence that women were just as well endowed as men. On the contrary, in this particular inequality women constituted the norm, men an excess:

On this subject, let every woman who has once begun to think examine herself; see whether she does not suppose virtue possible and necessary to Man, and whether she would not desire for her son a virtue which aimed at a fitness for a divine life and involved, if not asceticism, that degree of power over the lower self which shall "not exterminate the passions, but keep them chained at the feet of reason."[34]

Declaring that "a great part" of women looked upon men "as a kind of wild beasts," Fuller proceeded not as though this were simply a mistaken if understandable view, but as though men indeed were beasts and therefore to be tamed. She saw in prostitutes the emblem of women's slavery to men, in marriage a disguise of prostitution. If women were to marry, "early marriages are desirable," but a woman should "never be absorbed by any relation." Fuller praised women who did not get married at all, "old maids," mystics, saints, "women of genius," great actresses. As for men, taming them was in fact possible. She commended the Peace Party. She lauded vegetarianism. Temperance movements pleased her. "The praises of cold water seem to be an excellent sign of the age."[35]

Here was a program for feminism that would not lack practitioners over decades ahead: on the one hand, withdrawal from men in the most crucial relation, the sexual relation; on the other hand, expansion of woman's sphere in ways that would impinge upon men, control and contain them. Fuller's idea that the trouble with marriage inhered in "inequality of passion" followed more from her goals than from observation. Vegetarianism and cold water were not needed to cool men off; Tocqueville had noted that democratic capitalism itself had already done that. But Tocqueville saw cool marriages as logical parts of the separation of spheres against which Fuller struggled. For her, the point of cooling off marriage was not, as in Tocqueville's sociology, to make marriage less interesting to men, but rather to make it less interesting to women. Marriage reform, in Fuller's America as in Hertha's Sweden, would mean a new single standard, women's standard.

A later feminism, following up on this demand for a reduced sexuality, could easily miss Fuller's real point, for she smothered it herself in *Woman in the Nineteenth Century*. Fuller had no interest in simply improving woman's sphere, enforcing women's morals, and leaving it at that. She wanted out where men were. Although she had found "no place" for herself in American society, east or west, high or low, her driving passion remained that of finding a real place, of identifying herself, as she already had in German philosophy, with mighty forces, of being part of large histories. Her anxiety at any new sexualization— or "re-"sexualization—of marriage seemed to anticipate Charlotte Perkins Gilman's attack on the "excessive" sexualization of everything. But Gilman would not be Fuller updated, even though Fuller herself made it easy to think so.

Fuller's own final plunge into history was to make her biographies high-risk enterprises. She left America. She evidently behaved in ways she had deplored in *Woman in the Nineteenth Century*. She behaved in ways that surprised herself. Nathaniel Hawthorne's imputation to her of a "moral collapse" might be assigned to his own moral complacency, but by far the best case in a new "lawsuit" would have been made by Fuller herself—not against men but against common opinion. Her biographers would be tempted sometimes to casuistry:

Fuller made herself vulnerable by advocating standards of purity and celibacy—for women and men both—that she herself later did not live up to. . . . However, at the time she wrote *Woman in the 19th Century* she *was* practicing what she preached; and, during her liaison with Ossoli, she no longer discussed personal morals. At no time did she recommend chastity and live unchastely.[36]

Of course what was wanted was what tragic shipwreck denied, a new look at women in the nineteenth century, a fresh feminism, an autobiography. Happily, she had at least begun all this not only in life but in available letters.

The passion Fuller unleashed in Italy was in the first place political, in service to that most perfect of men, Giuseppi Mazzini, in company with such marvels of feminine independence as the Countess Belgioioso, for that most admirable of ends, the rescue of Italy from its oppressors. There seems little doubt that the visionary, desperate rising of Italian patriotism in 1848–50 drew out some of the deepest drives of Fuller's mind and soul. Not only were those egotistical displays that had repelled so many when she was conducting her "Conversations" in Boston gone. Gone also were the attachments to pale vegetarianism and androgynous "peace parties" in *Woman in the Nineteenth Century*. In the heat, dust, and blood of combat at Rome, Fuller found that men too were victims, but that the answer to victimization was not lament but courage. She subordinated herself eagerly to the struggle, never questioning whether her individuality or womanhood was being lost. Surrounded by heroes, Fuller found herself flinching not from heat, dust, and blood, but from some necessary deeds.

Rome is being destroyed; her glorious oaks,—her villas . . . the villa of Raphael, the villa of Albani, home of Winckelmann . . . all must perish, lest a foe should level his musket from their shelter. I could not, could not! . . . I know not how to bear the havoc and anguish. . . . I rejoice that it lay not with me to cut down the trees, to destroy the Elysian gardens, for the defense of Rome; I do not know that I could have done it.[37]

Almost certainly one of the losses from the Fire Island shipwreck was what Fuller might have taught women about "regeneration through violence," about the inevitable subjection of all values, including women's values, to the destructions and reconstructions of history.

Most of all, though, almost certainly Fuller would have been heard "confessionally," from her heart, on her husband, her son, and America's need for larger imagination in personal life. Fuller knew very well she would be expected to explain herself back in America. In the midst of all the high political striving in revolutionary Rome, she had met a man, Giovanni Angelo Ossoli. At first she had not taken him seriously. Then she had. She became his lover. She had his child. She married him. Later, she asked herself why she had done these things:

Our meeting was singular, fateful I may say. Very soon he offered me his hand through life, but I never dreamed I should take it. I loved him, . . . but the connection seemed so every way unfit, . . . He, however, thought I should return to him, as I did. I acted upon a strong impulse. I could not analyze at all what passed in my mind. I neither rejoice nor grieve, for bad or for good, I acted out my character.[38]

To "act out" one's character: here was a principle for "personal morals" worth expounding—an Emersonian principle, expounded in relations Emerson never got to.

Fuller realized she would have to explain not only herself but her husband, too.

I presume that, to many of my friends, Mr. Emerson for one, [Ossoli] will be nothing, and they will not understand that I should have life in common with him. . . . I have expected that those who have cared for me chiefly for my activity of intellect would not care for him.

Ossoli lacked one gift that Fuller herself as much as any had made famous: "About him, I do not like to say much, as he is an exceedingly delicate person. He is not precisely reserved, but it is not natural to him to *talk* about the objects of strong affection"[39] "He is very unlike most Italians," Fuller wrote of her new husband, "but very unlike most Americans too."[40] In *Woman in the 19th Century*, in struggling to imagine how someday the sexes might meet and marry without oppressing each other, she had imagined a "Whole" that would be created by ideal relations. Yet she never really described this whole as made up of some ideal pair; instead she was far more emphatic in describing the whole of each individual in the ideal new day:

Male and female represent the two sides of the great radical dualism. But in fact they are perpetually passing into one another. Fluid hardens to solid, solid rushes to fluid. There is no wholly masculine man, no purely feminine woman.[41]

This then raised the question, what were the "mutual needs" of such fluidities? Fuller appeared to live her way into this new fluidity in her relation with Ossoli, seeing herself sometimes as a husband to her husband—he playing wife—as well as father to her son:

Ossoli sends his love to you. I may say of him, as you say of your wife, it would be difficult to [do] other than like him, so sweet is his disposition, so without an effort disinterested, so simply wise . . . so harmonious his whole nature. And he is a perfectly unconscious character, and never dreams that he does well.

. . . Ossoli has always outgone my expectations in the disinterestedness, the uncompromising bounty of his every act. He was the same to his father as to me. His affections are few, but profound, and thoroughly acted out.[42]

At the same time, Fuller unhesitatingly—"out of her character"— affirmed the natural, the biological, the antitranscendental, nonhistorical basis of the "radical dualism" underlying reconciliation. She affirmed her motherhood. Even more, she did not suppress self-conscious delight in the sex of her baby:

As was Eve, at first, I suppose every mother is delighted by the birth of a man-child. There is a hope that he will conquer more ill, and effect more good, than is expected from girls. This prejudice in favor of man does not seem to be destroyed by his shortcomings for ages. Still, each mother hopes to find in him an Emmanuel.

Not hesitating to affirm feelings a later egalitarianism would find offensive, in the very process she would also affirm a sexual difference. Difference need not mean some rigid polar identity:

. . . I do not know what to write about him: he changes so much, has so many characters. He is like me in that, his father's character is simple and uniform, though not monotonous. . . . He is now in the most perfect rosy health, a very gay, impetuous, ardent, but sweet tempered child. . . . I wash and dress him; that is his great time. He makes it [last] as long as he can, insisting to dress and wash me the while, kicking, throwing water about, full of all manner of tricks that I think girls never dream of.[43]

What kind of feminist child-rearing Fuller might have come to urge we can only guess, but here, in attributing her son's deliciously protean masculinity to herself, she almost suggested that theories of environmental egalitarianism would be irrelevant. In *Woman in the Nineteenth Century*, she had quoted Charles Fourier to that effect:

Fourier had observed [the] wants of women, as no one can fail to do who watched the desires of little girls or knows the ennui that haunts grown women. . . . He therefore, in proposing a great variety of employments . . . allows for one third of women as likely to have a taste for masculine pursuits, one third of men for feminine.[44]

For her son, Fuller's hope was that he "be neither a weak nor a bad man." Ossoli himself was both a good and a strong man, if in neither case in American terms. But Fuller could see herself too, quite naturally, as her son's father as well as mother, and could identify with a father's feelings. To Marcus and Rebecca Spring, the New York couple whose money had subsidized her long trip to Europe in the first place, she wrote:

I thank you warmly for your gift. . . . I have learned to be a great adept in economy by looking at my little boy. I cannot bear to spend a cent for fear he may come to want it. I understand how the family men get so mean.[45]

Though American feminists welcomed *Woman in the Nineteenth Century* as the first great tract in the gospel of victimology, they never thought to identify themselves as a "Margaret Fuller Society," as Swedish feminists identified themselves in their Fredrika Bremer Society. *Woman in the Nineteenth Century* was less expressive than eccentric in Fuller's life, for she throve in the mainstream of democratic American romantic individualism. Ann Douglas has noted that Fuller, in the later years of her life, was becoming increasingly suspicious of "art" in America, of "words," rhetoric, eloquence, as diversions from the real, urgent issues of the day, a diversion to which women were especially liable in their sphere, itself removed from those urgencies and realities.[46] Fuller had begun to believe the right literature was history, and presumably carried in her luggage—the luggage lost on the beach at Fire Island—a "History of the Struggle for Italian Liberty," the manuscript for which Henry David Thoreau searched, combing up and down the beach. But what mattered most was not so much Fuller's disgust with the evasions of sentimental Victorian culture (to which she herself contributed in *Woman in the Nineteenth Century*), but the promise that, fully ready to "act out of her own character," she would have had much to tell American women, and Americans generally, men and women, of the exceptional resources available in their own remarkable new culture for their own struggle for liberty. Not that transcendental reportage would be lacking from others, telling, as she might have, of the romantic richness of Manhattan as well as of the West, of capitalism as well as of the Civil War, but Fuller's voice might have been just as powerful as Walt Whitman's while more accessible, demotic, and "popular," especially for women. American women, American feminists, the whole nation needed a great genius to prove in her sex that American democracy did not depend on the gender-divided sexlessness Tocqueville had said it did.

American Women in Their Separate Sphere: The Coils of Religion

American women had a special relationship to religion, Tocqueville felt. This was true, first, because religion had a special relationship to American men. For one thing, democracy held dangers for religion. Where power shifted from one party to another, "any alliance with any political power whatsoever is bound to be burdensome for religion."

Clergymen were well advised to step back from partisan conflicts. A subtler danger threatened, too. "[If] the Americans, who have handed over the world of politics to the experiments of innovators, had not placed religion beyond their reach," how could religion escape damage from "ebb and flow" and from "agitation and instability"? But finally it was religion's abstention from economics that counted most. American men lived for money, exerted themselves in "a passion for well-being." "It may be that, should any religion attempt to destroy this mother of all desires, it would itself be destroyed thereby." Clergymen in America understood: they stayed aloof from party conflicts and "let themselves go unresistingly with the tide of feeling and opinion." Religion in America was "a world apart in which the clergyman is supreme" but one which he is "careful never to leave."[47]

The special relation religion bore to American women followed. Women were not involved in politics or in the pursuit of wealth. Nothing then prevented religion and clergymen from entering into close relations with women. What Harriet Martineau deplored, Tocqueville found a basic structural strength in American sociology. The reason the American marketplace, passionate as it was, and independent of religion as it was, nevertheless proved stable and solid, was that it was quite free of any disturbances from the realm of manners, morals, and domestic life. Nowhere was domestic life as pure or mores as strict as in America. This was because in America women were in charge of mores, morals, and domestic life, and they discharged their trust in conjunction with religion. If religion was "powerless to restrain men in the midst of innumerable temptations which fortune offers," it had influence elsewhere. "It cannot moderate [men's] eagerness to enrich themselves . . . but it reigns supreme in the souls of women, and it is women who shape the mores."[48]

The simplest relation in this alliance of women and clergy would be for women to be the auxiliaries and customers of the clergymen. Their auxiliary service might grow to such heroic dimensions as foreign missions, their consumption of clerical products as conspicuous as in Henry Ward Beecher's Plymouth Church flourishing in Brooklyn, where women outnumbered men by two-to-one. But the alliance of women and clerics could become tense. Barbara Berg has pointed out that, while many of the voluntary women's societies devoted to moral reform in the epoch 1820–60, were indeed auxiliaries in a clergy-led "benevolent empire," the most vigorous and far-reaching of these, the American Female Moral Reform Society, rooted in New York City but drawing adherents over the Northeast, "strenuously resisted clerical objections" that it was overstepping its boundaries. Most notably, the Female Moral Reform Society extended its hand to prostitutes, and when (male) religious leaders objected, the society denounced them by name. Here was conflict, women demanding more power within their own sphere as against their supposed allies. Berg has read this as the seed of something larger and more powerful. Going beyond prostitutes, the female reform society reached out to other unfortunates—victims of alcoholic husbands, of wife-beaters, of deserting husbands, of indigence, of scabrous rooming houses, of loneliness, old age, high rents, and low pay. Here, Berg says, was an outlook that "subtly suggested a unity of all women emerging from the common bonds of oppression." The reform societies were inducing a sense of "the unity of all women" that in turn prompted "the growth of a feminist consciousness."[49] Here was the birth of feminism in felt oppression, the feminist as victim.

Historian Ann Douglas has examined a quite different expression of the dyad women/religion in the same period, this one a case of collaboration, not of tension. She has shown how a whole roster of liberal clergymen, theologically softened descendants of the hard old Puritanism of their grandfathers, entered into symbiosis with a comparable roster of women, the granddaughters of that old heritage, in the elaboration of new arts, values, and lives. "Changing and exchanging roles," these "Ministers and Mothers," passively accepting their exclusion from the masculine realms of politics and economy, spun out the threads and webs of a "sentimental" culture.[50] In examining how this soft, passive, essentially derivative outlook harmed powerful writers and critics of commercial life, Douglas credited this alliance—and hence its women—with great power. Effectively subverting the emergence of a vital critical "romantic" force, the women and clergy were allied in a "feminization" of American culture, defining the new role that would keep women confined in their sphere in the future, that of "consumer." While Douglas deplored sentimentalization, and hence regarded the women it engulfed as victims, at the same time she did not assume that to be a victim was to be simply weak, exploited, suffering. The alliance between women and religion generated power. That power could, however, defeat itself by continuing to accept its confinement to a sphere.

The essentially dialectical nature of an alliance between women and religion within a self-enclosed sphere, could be seen in the contrasting tactics of women who rejected the alliance. For Catherine Beecher science, not religion, offered women their future. Beecher accumulated evidence that, she said, showed American women to be in a bad way—debilitated, ailing, sickly. But her prescription was not more religion. Presumably Beecher believed religion had failed American women as it had failed her personally. But Beecher did not prescribe feminism.

She agreed entirely with Tocqueville's analysis of American sexual sociology: women did have their separate sphere. But what women needed in order to take possession of it effectively was a scientific approach to all their tasks. Beecher spelled out this approach in her *Treatise on Domestic Economy* of 1841. In this, she provided practical advice on nearly everything—the kitchen, the clothes closet, the garden, food in winter and summer. She was particularly concerned that women should understand their bodies. She discussed lungs, the legs, the heart, omitting almost nothing but those parts that made a woman a woman. Eventually apotheosized as "domestic science" and "home ec," what Beecher offered women was an outlook freed of the tutelage of any men, let alone clergymen. Of course she left all the dilemmas in her outlook unstated. A fully efficient Catherine Beecher housewife would presumably get her jobs done quickly. What was her spare time to be used for? Was it possible that the point of modernizing housework and body care was to make it fill up rather than save time? At all events, here was a strategy by which women could gain freedom from their religious ally and his tendency toward domination, while at the same time preserving the basic form of the separation of the spheres. How the fruits of scientific womanhood would eventually be distributed, whether in richer elaborations of woman's sphere, or in efforts at expanding it, or finally in trying to break out of it, could be left to the future.[51]

Not only Catherine Beecher dispensed with religion. At least one antebellum abolitionist feminist, Sarah Grimke, would assail not just clergymen but biblical authority itself for its discouragement of reform.[52] Many women would be made indignant at Massachusetts clergymen's denunciation of women's activities in 1838. Like Grimke, many women giving themselves to the moral reform of slavery would be made into feminists by the condescension of male abolitionists, typically clergymen. The route from the snub of women at the world antislavery convention in 1840 to the feminists' Seneca Falls declaration of women's rights would be direct. Still, the line taken by Sarah Grimke would remain exceptional. It would eventually be taken up again by one of the young women of Seneca Falls in her grand old age. A long lifetime of heroic self-liberation would be required for Elizabeth Cady Stanton to get there, but one day she would. She too would locate women's oppression in the Bible, the man-written, man-translated, man-manipulated absolute of manners, mores, and morals, and offer a variation of her own. Tocqueville had never imagined such a thing. That women might seize the opportunity offered them by their separate sphere to question the universality and fixity of religion would have been to imagine the foundations of democracy shaken. Of course by the time

Stanton offered feminism the chance for religious independence, feminism itself had become political, committed to its project of winning the vote, therefore fearful of alienating new allies, including religious allies whom Stanton would be sure to offend.

Just what women stood to lose from alliance with religion did not remain for distant debate. Mid-nineteenth-century democratic culture did not fail to suggest it. Like volcanoes bursting through the supposedly secular and rational crust of commercial capitalism, two super-patriarchies took shape with all the saturation of society by religion that had characterized the first Puritans' unitary states. It was as an "afterclap" of Puritanism that Ralph Waldo Emerson saw Salt Lake City and the Mormons during a stop on his train trip west to California.[53] But Mormonism was not necessarily so anachronistic. It had absorbed the central principle of capitalism into its Puritanism and allowed it to dictate mores, that is, marriage, sex, and domestic life. "Mormons were obsessed with the quantification of life," their most recent student has said; "they posited a plurality of wives, a plurality of gods, and a plurality of worlds." In Mormonism, the logic of reward in expansive capitalism was carried all the way: the more money a man had, the more wives he could have. Lust did not justify a plural wife; a poor man might lust till he burned, but he would burn with only one or none. It was exasperating to moral-minded tourists to find the Mormons successful at attracting women from several lands, including democratic America. Evidently no scruples innate to femininity restrained them. Evidently some women responded to an evident logic: the rich man is the better man; why prefer the lesser and poorer man, when one could share the better? As Louis J. Kern has pointed out, all this induced in the Mormons a classic hope of the marketplace: "[The Gentiles] may break us up, and rout us from one place to another, but by and bye we shall come to a point where we shall have all the women, and they will have none."[54] When Eastern feminists, outraged to realize that Utah's enfranchisement of women mocked their own assumption that the women's vote would mean women's power, found those women defending their suffrage, anger, not reflection, followed. Utah's women had to be victims.

Back east, at Oneida, in New York State's religiously burned-over expanses, John Humphrey Noyes's communitarian "socialism" combined business, politics, production, and reproduction into one unified process, as completely cooptive of the individual as any theoretical utopia of the day proposed. Sexual transactions at Oneida were conducted under the direct superintendence of the patriarch, who participated in them more actively than any of his aides. It was not so much the positively Franklinian spirit of practicality that mattered most at

Oneida, pervading everything—dress, machinery, housing, sexual relations, government, art. Rather, it was that this calculated spirit prevailed only with the blessing of the patriarch, infusing his strength
and security in every new departure.[55] Unimaginable in any other
nation, Noyes and Brigham Young—together with Joseph Smith—were
"representative men" in Emerson's sense. Not remotely typical of any
kind of population, they nonetheless registered powerful tensions derivative from the central experiences of the new democratic society. It
was against still more sweeping, if no doubt less sensational and exaggerated, regressions and reversions—afterclaps—into patriarchy that
the separation of the spheres was pitched. So long as women had that
shelter, they would be safe from such eruptive superpatriarchies as
Oneida's Perfectionism and Mormonism's quantification of the eternal.

A deeper protection was possible, however. In their very gigantism,
Smith, Young, and Noyes strongly suggested that real patriarchy, patriarchy on a truly convincing scale, was not a democratic possibility
but reserved only for the few. Most men might prefer to remain brothers,
collaborate in dismissing fathers, and count on women to keep home
ready when it was time to return from play. The most powerful possible
exposition of such an outlook would come from one capable of explaining it all in the highest terms, religious terms, a religious man who did
not want to be a patriarch at all and could explain how patriarchy
could be got rid of.

Unconscious America and the Nurture of Manhood: Horace Bushnell

Pastor at Hartford's North Church from 1833 to 1859, Horace Bushnell, despite his long tenure in that office, was far from being a classic
pastor of Puritan descent. These historic figures, often presiding over
their flocks for twenty-five, thirty, even fifty years, were being memorialized as a vanishing breed, beginning precisely in the year of Bushnell's own retirement, in William Sprague's massive *Annals of the American Ministry*, eventually published in nine volumes. But Bushnell himself
had already modeled a new type.

Had these remarkable community shepherds been great pulpit ora-
tors? By no means; nor was Bushnell. Had they been scholars, theologians, Biblicists? Such had been rare. They were, preeminiently, pastors, fully accessible and richly individual personalities to whom each
member of a congregation could relate, as a precise modern slang would
have it, one-on-one. Bushnell, however, totally lacked this quality also.
He had great difficulties with "pastoral duties." "He acknowledged
this to have been a defective branch of his service, and that for which

he had had least aptitude." As partial remedy for his deficiency here, "it became a custom with him and Mrs. Bushnell to make the annual visitation together."[56] The last thing Bushnell ever wanted was to have to intervene in the spiritual life of another individual.

It seems reasonably evident that Bushnell had never wanted to be a clergyman at all. A country boy from a poor farm family, in 1823 he had arrived late, at twenty-one, at Yale, where college freedoms quickly absorbed him. By graduation his "religious life was utterly gone down." Though his mother "felt the disappointment bitterly," Bushnell went on to study law, and proceeded to New York City to work on the *Journal of Commerce*. By twenty-seven he was ready to go west as a lawyer, with politics in mind. "We are tempted to imagine what a different man he would have become as a Western lawyer and politician," his daughter was to write, and any historian is tempted, too. Though agreeing that in a political career some of her father's "fineness and poetry and spiritual insight" might have been lost, Mary Bushnell could not help wondering "from his public addresses what a power he would have wielded in matters of national importance, and how fearlessly he would have supported the right cause."[57]

Then why did he not go west, become a territorial governor, a congressman, join the new Republican Party, become a major statesman? His daughter cast a haze of mystic predetermination over the story: "[His] life, unconsciously to him [was] swayed by the faith hidden in his mother's heart. She knew him better than he knew himself, and turned him to the higher purpose he did not recognize." Writing at the end of his life, Bushnell himself told it somewhat differently. His mother had, he agreed, avoided anything like explicit direction. But in 1829, when he was about to leave for Ohio, she came out into the open. She remonstrated, "very gently, but seriously." "I saw at a glance where her heart was, and I could not refuse."[58]

Bushnell's success with his Hartford congregation seems reasonably evident. Many of them were dissidents from an old-fashioned, orthodox, law-giving Puritan preacher, Joel Hawes. Hartford's swelling middle class had little patience with orthodoxy's fossil language and psychology and its continuing assumption of the privileges of punitive dictation. The same dissidence had welled up eighty years before in the Connecticut Valley, when another congregation of merchants' families had objected to their pastor's determination to search out inner lives and convict them of error. But while this exercise of Protestant democracy had only spurred Jonathan Edwards on to formulate still more rigorous philosophies of God's transcendence and man's dependence, Bushnell, inheriting the rigid Hawes's protesters, went on to a quite different adjustment.[59]

By Bushnell's time the triumph of evangelical revivalism seemed irresistible. The numerical expansion of the two most rapidly growing Protestant denominations, the Baptists and the Methodists, was based on verbal, emotional, dogmatic evangelism. The revival had invaded even Boston, where such defenders of the old logical, systematic faith as Lyman Beecher had begun to avail themselves of the new manipulative methods. Bushnell despised it all. He deplored the very assumptions of "revival." With its playing on guilt, its use of fear, its hypnotic repetitions, its "anxious seat," the revival encouraged inner drama that highlighted the individual's boundaries, his atomistic contingency, his separateness. Bushnell attacked this individualism. All individuals, he said, were inextricable from origins, childhood, parents, circumambient sustenance. The revival concealed this. What true Christianity should be doing was to exploit the endowment of childhood. "Growth, not Conquest, the True Method of Christian Progress," was his retitling of an article first published more biblically as "The Kingdom of God as a Grain of Mustard Seed." And God had appointed that agency best placed to nurture such growth—the family.

Although Bushnell also included state and church as "organic powers" in God's work, it was in the family that his argument came to focus. Bushnell's discussion of the family in his book *Christian Nurture* (1847) was not part of the sentimentalization of Motherhood nowhere more copiously expounded than by his Hartford neighbors, Catherine Sedgwick and Lydia Sigourney. Bushnell hardly mentioned mothers in the book. Nor did he offer family as a kind of balance wheel providing stability to a tumultuous society, as a haven in a heartless world. The whole purpose of the family was to serve character, Christian character, which Bushnell defined in a special way. Christian character was to be "graceful," "gracious," "natural." The "gracious or supernatural character," he said, "possesses the peculiar charm of naturalness." For the "highest moral beauty," this naturalness was necessary. Christian character, that is, was not "learned," not the product of a "conversion," of a revival, but of growth. A principal reason Christians so often lacked "character, or outward beauty" was that "piety begins so late in life, having thus to maintain a perpetual and unequal war with previous habit."[60]

It only followed then that, in fulfilling its task, the family too must be natural, gracious, graceful. Bushnell was emphatic in deploring ideology in the family, any undue self-consciousness in the parental function:

A power is exerted by parents over children, not only when they teach, encourage, persuade and govern, but without any purposed control whatever.

The bond is so intimate that they do it unconsciously and undesignedly—they must do it.[61]

Catherine Beecher to the contrary, there was to be no "science" of parenthood, no professionalization of domesticity, no psychiatric formulas for the heart.

Bushnell's vision of family followed from wish, not experience. The life—the "natural" life—he might have led, had his mother not diverted him, he soon began to live anyway as a kind of shadow of his "real" life. When as early as 1835, two years after his ordination, he began to suffer the "throat trouble" that would nag him the rest of his life, he chose travel as his cure. His first trip was to the White Mountains of New Hampshire, alone. Next he vacationed on eastern Long Island in the summer of 1838, also alone. He wrote his wife: "The surf roars. . . . This is the place for me. I begin to feel alive. . . . I am afraid you can hardly imagine how very comfortable it is here. . . . I was never so much away from home in my life."

What Bushnell found away from home was often the roar, the excitement of conflict. Writing his wife of some theological debates he was attending in Boston in 1839, he noted first how he had restrained himself, then confessed that he wished he had displayed more "moral courage," like Luther, and had plunged in. From Washington, D.C., he wrote her in 1844 with the same ambivalence: "This is a most wretched and contemptible place. . . . I hear a furious debate. . . . I am getting acquainted very fast with men, and faces, and affairs. I should be quite a politician if I remained here long."[62] Back home, his excitement over politics having subsided, he resumed his studied detachment from all reforms. In a few months "the breakdown in health, threatened for so many years, actually came." Ill health then earned him a year's sabbatical, on full salary (paid by his sympathetic congregation), for a year alone in Europe, where he soon recovered his vitality. After a few months, for no particular reason than the venting of his own combative impulses, he won notoriety for a gratuitously insulting "Letter to the Pope" (Gregory XVI).

Bushnell thanked his wife for allowing him these escapes. His first paean to wifehood came from Boston early in 1844.

I have had no little enjoyment of my dear wife and children this afternoon. Sitting here over my fire alone . . . [never] did I realize so convincingly the great power you have over me . . . I am sure . . . there is nothing more beautiful, and more to be envied by the poets, than this same charm of power by which a good wife detains her husband. It is not an ambitious, noisy power; it is silent, calm, persuasive, and often so deep as to have its hold deeper than consciousness itself.

The crucial point was that, while a wife might "detain" her husband, she "does not take him away from the rough world and its drudgeries—does not make him less than a man." She allowed him his early retirement, at fifty-seven. He got to Cuba and California. He faced the storms of the Minnesota prairie. The gospel of his ill health was maintained to the end, more often obscured by his adventures than otherwise. At sixty-six, deep into "retirement," Bushnell explored the Adirondacks. "Though an invalid, he walked and climbed, and fished, after a fashion that would have exhausted many men who boast of perfect health." He and a guide climbed Mt. Marcy. From the top, racing with the sunset, "the two old men proceeded to coast down the steep incline, clinging or catching as they might. . . . [The] travellers appeared, staggering with fatigue, but jubilant."[63]

In commending the "unconscious" processes of family nurture, Bushnell was not only rejecting the old orthodox psychologies of sin and conversion, but also expounding his felt assessment of America. In 1849 he delivered the annual patriotic sermon to the New England Society of New York City. Its title: "The Founders, Great in Their Unconsciousness." In this panegyric, Bushnell first of all repudiated all ideas of the "conscious design" or "sagacious forethought" of the Puritan fathers:

They are not to be praised as a tribe of successful visionaries, coming over to this new world . . . to get up a great republic and renovate human society the world over. They propound no theories of social order.

He then quite explicitly attacked the Lockean "social compact" theory of the American states as, so far as it was true, trivial, and insofar as it was not true, profoundly hurtful. American independence had been achieved, not by deliberate compact, but by growth, as he observed of Connecticut in 1776:

Here was, in fact, a little, independent, unconscious republic, unfolding itself by the banks of the Connecticut . . . so that when the war came . . . it stood ready. . . . the people had never set up for independance. . . . they had . . . actually grown apart, unconsciously.[64]

The Founding Fathers had handed down no specific social order to be followed, no maxims, no principles, no creed to be obeyed. They had handed down their example, but that example was quite other than prescriptive. "The very greatness of [our New England fathers], as it seems to me, is their unconsciousness." Each generation had its own equal relation to divinity, each lived by its own "secret laws," which consciousness could only discern on occasion dimly, never master, never organize. Tocqueville had already argued that democracy had undermined the authority of the father in any traditional guise. If fathers wanted to get along with sons, they could rely only on "confidence and affection," on relations "more intimate and gentle." Democracy "loosens social ties, but it tightens natural ones." Sociologically, Bushnell saw this process reaching to institutions as well. Those early anxieties about power that had led the Fathers to devise various structures and mechanisms, to divide and separate functions, to arrange a "constitution," were fading as the republic evolved in organic growth:

All kinds of progress . . . work together in our history . . . till finally [the race] is raised to its true summit. . . . And when that summit is reached, it will be found that, as Church and State must be parted in the crumbling and disintegrating processes of freedom; so, in freedom attained, will they coalesce again, not as Church and State, but in such kind of unity as well nigh removes the distinction.[65]

One could be sure that in this process of coalescence the family would be not so much integrated as apotheosized.

In extending to his wife the qualities he could only wish his mother had had, Bushnell was completing the portrait of ideal America. It is at least interesting to remember that Tocqueville omitted discussion of mothers and sons in his analysis of child-rearing in the great democracy; of mothers he spoke only as to daughters, just as he had spoken of fathers only as to sons. Tocqueville's omission may have registered sensitivity to an unsettling issue. How could mothers separated from "real" life raise sons appropriately? It is interesting too to note how modern social science was to confirm, even while modifying, Bushnell's vision of a motherhood "organic" within America. The professional anthropologist Margaret Mead, writing in 1942 to explain how Americans should fight World War II, identified a crucial contribution of motherhood:

[The] American mother, watching her three-year-old learn to make his way among other children, is faced with a very real dilemma . . . in America, mothers and nurses are . . . impressed with the dangers which little boys will encounter. . . . in her mind's eye . . . the American mother sees . . . a crude melee of frontier battles, gangster battles, tong wars, feuds, Indian attacks, and hijacking. American history mixes with the front pages of the tabloids. . . . Her baby boy is going out to face this world of violence. . . . If her small Jimmy . . . is going to get along in this world and be more successful than his dad—and for what else did she bear him?—he'll have to be a good deal tougher than his dad. . . . it is women, the mother and the nurse and the sister, who exhort the baby boy to be tough.[66]

Here, of course, Mead was urging that mothers do deliberately what Bushnell had hoped they would do "naturally," while, moreover, training their boys to be what he thought boys were by nature. But the difference was not as great as it might seem, for Mead thought American men had been badly damaged. They had been demoralized by the Depression, weakened by the New Deal; their manhood was in danger. Thus, in the great opportunity offered by Pearl Harbor, American men had the chance to resume their "nature," especially if their women realized it. As a professional anthropologist of orthodox modern views, Mead naturally could not explicitly affirm any notion of a "natural" masculinity, but her identification of an American tradition of manhood was so strong as to render the distinction trivial.

A few years later the professional psychoanalytic historian Erik Erikson was to repeat Mead's observations on American motherhood, with a clearer echo of Bushnell's exaltation of organic unconsciousness:

> We suggested that the mothers of the Sioux and of the Yurok were endowed with an instinctive power of adaptation which permitted them to develop child-training methods appropriate for the production of hunters and hunters' wives in a nomadic society, and of fishermen and acorn gatherers in a sedentary valley society. The American mother, I believe, reacted to the historical situation on this continent with similar unconscious adjustment when she further developed Anglo-Saxon patterns of child training which would avoid weakening potential frontiersmen by protective maternalism. In other words, I consider what is now called the American woman's "rejective" attitude a modern fault based on a historical virtue designed for a vast new country, in which the most dominant fact was the frontier, whether you sought it, or avoided it, or tried to live it down.[67]

Obviously, Erikson too was not propounding any idea of some "natural," biologically ordained masculinity. But in his case, the vision of motherhood was even more mystical, even more magical than Mead's, and partly just because of a mystery he himself raised: why, if the American mother had reacted with such marvelous "unconscious" accuracy to the conditions of the nineteenth century, had she failed to react in the same way in the twentieth?

Bushnell at least, in his own double-edged tributes to his wife, had left some opportunity for historians to guess why such unconscious organic unities and harmonies as he yearned for were not really likely. On one occasion, for instance, in 1861, when he was fifty-nine, two years into what would prove his long and far-traveling retirement, he wrote his wife:

> I shall probably be with you some time this month,—think of it, this month! I feel a kind of sad interest in going home this time, as it bears a look of going home for the last time, till I go to the final home of all. The experimenting seems to be going by, and the sitting down, to wind up all, appears to be all that is left me.[68]

What message Mary Apthorp Bushnell took from a letter like this we do not know. We do not know much about her at all—what she thought of her marriage, felt about her husband, about his illnesses, about his trips, her children, her life, herself. Nevertheless we can see, in the fullness of her husband's work, in his reconceptualization of religion, in his relocation of the family, his criticism of ideology and contract and "conscious design," his praise of the graceful and natural, as well as in his private person, how seductive Bushnell's views could be. His very last sermon, preached when he was nearly seventy, showed how far the regression in Puritan Protestant America might carry: "Mary, the Mother of Jesus." Of course, not long before, he had published his book on woman suffrage, a "reform against nature."

Unconscious Women: Religion as Aggression

An immense activity surged among American middle-class women under the aegis of religion. It was not what Tocqueville had imagined or Martineau saw. Yet it too, for all its energies and all its various forms, remained within the logic of separate spheres, and all of it subsided back into inertia.

Women began going out on foreign missions before the Civil War, then after the war went in growing numbers and as single women rather than as missionaries' wives. A whole roster of separate women's denominational boards and societies were founded in the two decades after Appomattox. Every woman on mission was backed by scores of women at home, administering, educating, fund-raising. The women's boards often raised more money than the old established boards. Theological seminaries still refused to open their doors to women, but dozens—probably at least sixty—missionary training schools were opened to women, sometimes women only. "Many restless, ambitious and devout women from small . . . towns and farms escaped . . . by sailing to the mission fields.[69]

After World War I these thriving women's organizations were "consolidated." They were merged into their denominations' general missionary organizations. Although promises were made of equal status in the newly "integrated" organizations, most missionary women understood the disaster, and the "disaffection of Presbyterian women was so apparent" that it provoked a report on the "causes of unrest" among the women of the church. Its authors noted how reasonable it was for women to feel distress "when a great organization which they had built could be autocratically destroyed by vote of male members of the church" without consultation or debate.[70] One feminist historian, Barbara Welter, has equated women's missionary careers with other examples of women being allowed entry into fields where men were no longer interested, but the collapse of women's missions was rather a reassertion of control by men, a control that was to persist into the epoch of Billy Graham and the television preachers of the Moral Majority. Of course the collapse of women's missions only preceded by a little the collapse of foreign missions in general, for reasons quite independent of any questions of gender equality within the churches, but that collapse nicely registered the fact that all the energies that had been invested by women in their own efforts had not won them autonomy.

But women's religiousness had by no means to be limited to a faithful service to others. It could reach out to self-interested theologizing. Mary Baker Eddy showed how. Tocqueville himself had predicted that religious imagination in democratic America would move, in theology, toward "pantheism":

As conditions become more equal, each individual becomes more like his fellows, weaker, and smaller. . . . The concept of unity becomes an obsession. . . . Not content with the discovery that there is nothing in the world but one creation and one Creator, he [seeks] a . . . system which teaches that all things material and immaterial, visible and invisible . . . are only . . . the several parts of an immense Being . . . in the midst of the continual flux and transformation of all that composes Him.[71]

It was only logical by this sociology of belief that women, socially weaker than men, should make up the vast majority of followers of "spiritualism," that fad, fancy, and philosophy in the popular fermentation of ideas before the Civil War. Spiritualism's assertion of mind's preeminence over matter inspired countless "demonstrations" that showed how blurred the line had become between religion and entertainment. But it took one woman's particular genius to transform diffuse ideations into cult.

Of all the forms of matter over which the powers of the mind would be most welcome, none surpassed ailing, suffering, sickly flesh. Discovering the "Science of divine metaphysical healing" in 1866, Mary Baker Eddy (still Mrs. Patterson then) found no instant fame and fortune. She did not do what revivalists did, go out on the highway and preach the Gospel. She wrote a new gospel. For nine years—she was already forty-five in 1866—in circumstances of poverty and loneliness, she worked on her book. The first edition appeared in 1875. She founded the first Church of Christ (Scientist) in 1879, and Eddy (who married Asa Gilbert Eddy in 1877) was on her way to status as myth, fully meriting virtually the longest entry in the entire three-volume dictionary of *Notable American Women*.

Christian Science remained a small if conspicuous denomination, numbering hardly 100,000 at Mrs. Eddy's death in 1910, and never enrolling much beyond a quarter of a million at its later peak. Mrs. Eddy was too combative, the running of her church too rigid, its rites and practices too expensive for Christian Science itself to become a mass church. As with the similarly expensive Communist Party, far more people entered and left than were members at any particular time. But Christian Science was only the most famous focus of a whole congeries of churches, movements, organizations, philosophies, cults, and therapies flourishing in the late nineteenth-century airs. William James discussed the whole complex under the label "mind cure," cure by means of mind—or Mind. There was New Thought, Unity, Divine Science. Multitudes of believers found no need to leave their old church homes in order to benefit from the new. Still, the effective heart of mind cure was in the proliferation of new organizations. It was here that mind cure's conspicuous correlation with women translated into action. Old churches opened few doors to women, the new ones many.

Not only was [mind cure's] most famous exponent a woman, scores of its lesser exponents were women, as founders, writers, preachers, teachers, healers. Mind cure gave jobs to women by hundreds and thousands. The clear majority of Christian Science practitioners were women. The majority of preachers in the proliferating Unity churches were to be women.[72]

Here was a woman-impelled, woman-controlled, woman-serving religion at last, an escape not just from the pallid seducers despised by Harriet Martineau but from all "unconscious Fathers" as well. Rooted in deep needs of a growing sector of the late-nineteenth-century middle classes, mind cure clearly had the potential for displacing old evangelical Protestantism, as the less existentially acute forms of liberalism and modernism were already showing themselves incapable of doing.

But mind cure carried the seed of its defeat within itself. Mind cure's preoccupation with healing and health left it vulnerable to competition from "real" science—both the material science of modern medicine, just on the verge of its breakthrough into its own miracles, and that far more elaborate science-of-mind to be known as psychotherapy. Also, mind cure's preoccupation with sickness and health left it politically passive. Indeed, "it was the genius of mind cure to discover how the weak might feel strong while remaining weak."[73] Mary Baker Eddy's own life was the model. To those without power, without a future to be seized, without comrades to join, becoming sick offered a project for identity. Mastering one's sickness demonstrated a strength otherwise unavailable. For women, the irony of mind cure was that it only anticipated, but did not prevent, women's delivery of themselves over to men again, not preachers or pastors any more but doctors, and to all that preoccupation with the dramas of sickness and health, doctors and hospitals, diets and medicines, that would inflate the American health industry into by far the largest in the world, a key part of American popular middle-class culture and, eventually, a significant cause of the destabilization of the economy through inflation. Christian Science, Science of Mind, Unity would have been cheaper. Of course these would have left women where Tocqueville had found them, locked in their separate sphere, locked out of the great marketplace where real science, real power, real health, and real death held sway.

No doubt women's religious vitalities surged the highest, and wrought the most, where they did seek to act, not just on themselves as in mind cure, but on others, and not just on other women, as in the foreign missions, but on men, and, to boot, American men. The Women's Christian Temperance Union aimed to stop men from doing something those men obviously enjoyed doing and meant to go right on doing because they enjoyed it. But if men enjoyed it, women did not. It was the first direct challenge by a mass of women to a mass of men in American history, indeed, in modern history. While the two competing woman's suffrage associations were enrolling about 13,000 dues-paying members, and the General Federation of Women's Clubs around 20,000, the WCTU could count 150,000 members, with another 50,000 in its young women's union. It was the first autonomous mass woman's organization in the country, in the world.

Historians have sometimes tried to find some correlation between the rise and fall of temperance/prohibition movements and measurable rise and fall in the use/abuse of alcohol. The WCTU fit no such correlation. Its origins drew directly on a so-called women's "Crusade," supposedly flaming up spontaneously in Hillsboro, Ohio, just before Christmas of 1873, then spreading rapidly across the upper Midwest until, by March 1874, first the national religious and then the secular New York press began to take note. The movement then achieved firestorm, touching nearly one thousand communities, no longer only in the Midwest but in New Jersey, Pennsylvania, upstate New York, New England, and the Western territories (though hardly at all in the South). The Crusade of 1873–74 remained confined to small towns and villages, where, by comparison with the big cities, the abuse of alcohol was presumably neither notable nor growing. We have no evidence that alcohol was being abused in Hillsboro, Ohio. What we do see is that what were being abused by Hillsboro's saloons were the feelings of the ladies who marched against them that December day.

All this was a switch from the great tradition of evangelical temperance and prohibition movements before the Civil War. Then, the heart of the enterprise had been the personal horror story told by the evangelist himself: "I am resolved to free myself from the tyrant rum!" This had been the pivot of the life of John B. Gough, famed for years as leader of the prewar "Washingtonian" antiliquor movement. Presenting himself as having been saved from drink, the evangelist sought to convert others into ex-drunkards and enlist them too into prohibition circles. The effort was one among males by males directed at males. The WCTU was not at all simply a female parallel to this. Neither Annie Wittenmyer, the WCTU's first president, nor Frances Willard, its leader from 1879 to her death in 1898, were ex-drunkards. Presumably neither ever took a drop. No leader of the WCTU, national, state, or local, ever presented herself as a reformed alcoholic. Nor were many of them victims of drunken fathers or husbands or brothers or lovers. One of Willard's nephews was an alcoholic, but Willard never dwelt upon his example nor did she ever suggest she had been drawn to temperance by personal experience. (If any man ever "abused" her in life, it was a Methodist preacher, her ex-fiancé, who as president of Northwestern University harassed her from her post as Dean of Women and then, years later, as a Methodist bishop saw to it that she was denied a seat at the Methodist General Conference; so far as anyone knows, the bishop was a teetotaler.) True, the head of the largest local WCTU chapter, Matilda Carse, had lost a son under the wheels of a drunken carter's beer wagon, and a few others were probably wives of men who drank too much. But certainly the cutting edge of the WCTU was not the great story of self-reformation but of reforming others.

Within two years of her accession to its presidency, Frances Willard had the WCTU on record in favor of woman suffrage. Her predecessor, Annie Wittenmyer, left, certain that the temperance cause would suffer by such association. Willard's victory in this fight was fateful. The most recent and meticulous historian of the WCTU, Ruth Bordin, has examined Willard's insistence, in her 1889 autobiography, *Glimpses of Fifty Years*, that temperance came first for her, and only then suffrage and feminism. Implicitly, this was to say that the vote was a means to achieve an end that women were unlikely ever to win without it. Linking temperance itself to "home protection," the suffragist could then advertise the vote for women as defense of the home. Bordin has judged Willard's claim dubious:

Willard's primary commitment may not have been to temperance. From the beginning, women's rights probably commanded her deeper loyalty. Evidence suggests that Willard's first allegiance was to the women's movement and that temperance provided her with means rather than ends.[74]

One could question whether even this goes far enough. While Willard went on beyond suffrage to urge still more women's issues on the WCTU— raising the age of consent (still as low as ten years in some states);

reform of women's prisons; free kindergartens; employment centers for young women; foster homes; industrial training schools for girls—her ideas ran far beyond these boundaries into a larger vision. By 1886 she had the WCTU in regular touch with the Knights of Labor. Soon she was breaking with the conventional evangelical view of intemperance and blaming it on overwork in the industrial marketplace, on dangerous work, poorly paid work, and no work. After trying for some years to arrange links between the WCTU and the National Prohibition Party, by 1892 Willard was trying to ally prohibitionists with the new Populist Party. Soon the WCTU was hearing from its president about Christian socialism, the need to abolish poverty in America, the need for a socialist America. In all of this, the original woman-oriented focus of the organization had been expanded to embrace issues no longer conventionally gender-inflected. Women's rights were simply among general human rights.

Since the WCTU, after Willard's death, rapidly sloughed off all these "Do Everything" issues in favor of the old, single focus on temperance, it is easy to emphasize Willard's failure. But she had prevailed in one crucial respect. While her successor, Lillian M. Stevens, entirely concurred in the abandonment of all Willard's social issues, she did hold fervently to the necessity of woman suffrage. Without the suffrage, women could not impose prohibition. In 1904 the suffrage association itself came to be headed by the woman who had headed Willard's suffrage division in the WCTU, Anna Howard Shaw. At the same time, the WCTU became overshadowed in the temperance movement by the clergy-led Anti-Saloon League. Suffrage thus became inextricably linked both with the temperance movement and the evangelical movement. Suffrage leaders themselves, racing from one state referendum to another, came to identify their one critical foe as the organized liquor interests. Only in the South, where the rights of women continued to be linked invidiously with the rights of blacks, did this complex of woman suffrage/prohibition/evangelicalism fail to jell. Thus, the Eighteenth and Nineteenth Amendments to the Constitution were to seem twinned in the imaginations of a new generation, which sensed that in evangelical prohibition there was at work not some eternal gospel or some psychology of compassion and caring, but a grasp for power.

Ruth Bordin's argument that Frances Willard did not mean what she said applied to the WCTU itself. It too was not what it seemed:

[Once] the Crusade gained momentum in Ohio, it tapped the growing, if frequently unconscious, need of women everywhere to assert themselves. . . . [Beneath] the surface, what gave the Crusade its thrust and its real importance was that these women were experiencing power. . . . [The] radical and public methods they endorsed represented a real if only partially conscious commitment to the idea that women could legitimately function in the public realm. . . . Temperance became the medium through which nineteenth-century women expressed their deeper, sometimes unconscious, feminist concerns.[75]

Not only were those who sought power "unconsciously" vulnerable to capture by allies more awakened than themselves. They could also find themselves in confrontations that they were not ready for and perhaps had not even unconsciously wanted. As an "effective pressure group," the WCTU had "in many instances . . . succeeded in forcing a male-dominated society to do what [women] wanted, at least temporarily."[76] Was it confrontation that Willard herself had really wanted? Was it confrontation that the ladies of Hillsboro had wanted on their December march? If it was inconceivable that the women of Hillsboro might learn to enjoy a cobbler or a fizz or even a collins or grog now and again, Willard had not been a Hillsboro matron. She had become a modern American, knowledgeable in the arts of organization, of salesmanship, of personal promotion, mobile, flexible, and "political" beyond all anxieties about "role conflict" and "identity" and "place." Was not the future of such women to include the glass of wine, the sherry, the sociable martini? Of course the issue was general. If the "deeper" concerns of women were to remain unconscious, they could only remain hostage to Hillsboro. If they were to become conscious, they would have to ask whether Hillsboro, all dried up, closed down, "feminized," was what they really wanted.[77] Frances Willard spent only a few months of the last four years of her life in the United States, preferring friends in England, as though things were closing in on her in America among her adoring followers. She may well have been on the verge of a plunge into new if chillier waters, far better than the one she suffered, in death, too young, at only fifty-eight.

Perhaps nowhere more than in their relations with religion did American women, and American feminists, differ from their Italian, Swedish, and Soviet Russian sisters. In America, religion was a realm for rich creative endeavor for women, for feminists at once a challenge and a trap. No such realm existed in Italy, Sweden, or the Soviet Union. Officially banned in the Soviet Union, it was left to unofficial underground life, increasingly strange and out of touch for younger generations. If by 1980 some young Russians were showing signs of interest in religion as relief from official ideology, any special implications for women remained to be seen. Underground Russian feminists were as likely to reject as embrace historic Orthodoxy. In Italy, religion confronted women as authority; in the Catholic church's outreach to women, all the initiative was retained by a male priesthood, and those Italian women and feminists rejecting such leaders had to reject religion itself in favor of secular politics. Only as the link between feminism and Communism broke down in the 1960s did a kind of autonomous women's religious movement show itself in Italy, in freedom from both church and party, partly as protest, partly as deep political hope. In Sweden, popular nineteenth-century protest against the official state church found women emerging as participants and leaders in autonomous evangelical revival, but it was these elements that made their way to America. Labor unions and community groups counted for far more in Swedish women's twentieth-century lives than church or religious activities did. In contrast, in the United States, precisely the vitality and richness of woman's sphere provided security for women's religious initiatives. As Frances Willard's career indicates, however, breaking out of woman's sphere on such initiatives was another matter. The question implicit in the story of the WCTU had not been answered by 1920: could a mobilization of women under the banners of religion ever translate into mobilization independent of religion? Women's political mobilization went further in Russia, Sweden, and even Italy than in America: American women's religious mobilization may in the end have inhibited larger rallyings.

American Women in Their Expanding Sphere: The Coils of Social Science

Male Retreat: Josiah Royce and the Attack on Lyric Freedom

In 1886 Josiah Royce, a son of California born in 1855 in the Sierra Nevada mining town of Grass Valley, published his first book, *California*, a work of history. Royce was destined for a career as philosopher, and this was to be his only venture into history, but *California* neatly anticipated his mature philosophic stance. Nominally intended to justify the action of downtown San Francisco businessmen vigilantes in taking over responsibility for law and order in the hectic city of early gold-rush days, his story was meant to exemplify a much larger one. The history of early California, Royce explained,

begins with the seemingly accidental doings of . . . individuals, and ends just where the individual ceases to have any very great historical significance . . . and where the community begins to be what it ought to be, viz., all important as against individual doings and interests.[78]

Tocqueville had warned against precisely the kind of history Royce was setting out to do. As he had said, democracies were not going to be easy for historians to write about: "in periods of equality . . . causes . . . are infinitely more various, better hidden, more complex, less powerful, and hence less easy to sort out and trace." One reaction to this challenge was all too human: "[The] historian is soon tired." But another was even more dangerous. Unable to follow the "trace of individuals," historians were "left with the sight of the world moving without anyone moving it." Troubled by this mystery, historians were then "tempted to believe that this movement is not voluntary and that societies unconsciously obey some superior dominating force." In short, "historians who live in democratic ages . . . are led to link facts together to make a system."[79] Royce indeed was determined not to concede the "trace of individuals" in California, but to make his story show system. When, in 1856, following the assassination of a reform-minded newspaper editor, James King, by a San Francisco supervisor, James Casey, the businessmen-vigilantes took over, they proved that the "steady, conservative forces" of mankind, working through "three very well-known and commonplace forms, namely, . . . the family, . . . the school, and . . . the church," had taken over, and that California's truly modern history had begun.

Of all the "conservative" institutions of mankind, Royce's later philosophy was to suggest that the school, that is, the modern university, was preeminent. Perfect symmetry in his career would have been achieved, had he stayed at his alma mater, Berkeley, making it into the conservatizing Vatican of the Golden State, instead of going off to stale old Harvard, which did not need conservatizing. Where more than in the West were the virtues needed of "loyalty," of loyalty to loyalty itself, of fidelity to the collective enterprise of science, thus to impersonality, objectivity, self-abnegation, submission to method, and the willing sacrifice of self to the beloved community? Still overcast by the glamorous haze of frontier romance, of gold-rush magic, of extreme romantic individualism, the West awaited Puritanizing. But if Royce personally could not resist the lure of the settled Cambridge commune with its still unshaken foundations in old Puritan repressions, he could at least leave with a blast at the very sources of the myth of Golden California. *California* aimed to show not just that, after an early phase of accidental anarchic individualism, the eternal conservative forces of community and maturity had taken over. Rather, Royce meant to deny the historical legitimacy of that early phase itself. He would show it had never existed. He would reveal the myth as purely a case of delusion. "Any chance number of an early newspaper would tell you more about the pioneer community than the boastful and reckless old pioneer will tell in a month." Presumably the newspaper would, as the romanticizing old pioneers would not, tell of the families, the schools, the churches. But Royce knew this was a cheap shot. The myth of Golden California had not waited for old men in their dotage to invent it. It had been invented on the spot:

> Even in so early a book as the *Annals* [of San Francisco], published in 1855 . . . one finds the life of 1849 and 1850 regarded in dream-like and unsubstantial fashion. . . . in California . . . young men of 1854 already talked of the days of 1849 as they might of a romantic and almost forgotten ancient history.

In the finest passage of his book, where Royce intended to dispel the lyric, golden, marvelous California of myth by irony and detachment, he succeeded only in showing why mere irony and criticism could not prevail:

> Everybody . . . used to gamble: so one seems to remember. And gambling in the big saloons, under the strangely brilliant lamp-light, amid the wild music, the odd people, the sounding gold, used to be such a rapturous and fearful thing! One cannot express this old rapture at all! Judges and clergymen used to elbow their way, so one remembers, to the tables. . . . The men in San Francisco who did not thus gamble were too few to be noticed. If you condemn this gambling . . . that is because you do not know the glorious rapture. . . . But one's memory does indeed reach beyond this respectable amusement; and is equal to the description of decidedly worse things, in which of course everybody was also engaged! There were some women in the city in 1849, but they were not exactly respectable persons, yet they were the sole leaders of society. They too gave it even in later years a certain grace and gaiety that makes one speak of them, with a curious sort of reverence. . . . Just as one cannot easily remember who the men were that did not gamble in those days, so one fails to recall in looking back on the early years the women who were respectable.[80]

The brilliant lamplight, the wild music, the sounding gold—rapture, rapture! It was owing only to Royce's perhaps unconscious integrity as a historian that he could expound so acutely the allure beside which his "steady, conservative forces" as the key to American history could only seem pallid.

Where had Royce learned that these conservative forces had in fact been at work in California all the time? From his mother's "diary," detailing her own early days in the state. But since Sarah Royce wrote this diary at her son's suggestion, we can guess that he already knew what it would contain. As John Clendenning has pointed out, Royce's father, Josiah, Sr., provided his family no stability, no security, no sure place, no roots.[81] Royce, Sr., was not a farmer or a storekeeper or a mailman or—inevitably—a traveling salesman, but all these alternatively, and in San Francisco, a fruit peddler "too garrulous to make a success." Sara Royce provided all the stability the family enjoyed and the philosophy to go with it—belief in the necessity of perseverance, sacrifice, and toil. With a shift in perspective, Royce might have seen his father as one of that company of free-spirited itinerants and wan-

derers celebrated by Constance Rourke in her portrait of popular masculine democratic culture in *American Humor.* That he did not, that he
obviously admired his mother while deploring his father, does however
tell us of the potential for new alliance between feminists and reform-
minded men. Although by going to Harvard he forsook the task of
conservatizing California, Royce did not really mean to restore old
Puritan patriarchal authority; the age of fathers was over. Instead, he
proposed his new vision of science as the sacred circle of community.
Of course it was outrageous to proclaim that the community "ought to
be . . . all important as against individual doings and interests," unless
that community merited such importance. Many—if not most—communities were bigoted, narrow, suffocating of the individual. A community was beloved not, as mere tribalists of all ages maintained, just
because it was communal, but because it truly did incarnate superin-
dividual virtues. These were not the virtues of patriarchy, however, but
rather of the capacity for reason in all persons, certainly including
women. All persons could be scientists and philosophers. But they could
not be these if they still harbored, as did many Americans in the late
nineteenth century, a secret, nostalgic conviction that, "whatever its
faults, 'after all, their wild and pleasant life [in California]' " had not
been " 'so very, very wrong.' "[82] Although we cannot be certain exactly
why he thought so, Royce was sure that that life had been very, very
wrong and was sure history would say so. But history has not.

The Alliance: Sociology as Women's Science

As historian William Leach has shown, in *True Love and Perfect
Union* (1980), the entanglement of feminism with social science began
soon after the Civil War. Among the founders, in 1865, of the American
Social Science Association was a leading feminist, Caroline Dall. Some
of the men in the new ASSA brought with them exhilaration at the
wartime successes of systematic management of large-scale military
operations. Some hoped the postwar Republican party would become
the champion of national planning. After the dashing of such hopes,
after 1872, the ASSA served to focus feelings as critical of democratic
politics generally as they were critical of the two familiar parties.
Democratic politics was part of the problem, not a solution. Disorder,
convulsive change, inefficiency, corruption, as well as injustice and
human suffering, were apparently endemic in the postwar political
economy. Finding themselves shut out from the major institutions of
economy and politics, the men of the ASSA did not, as had earlier
generations of preindustrial notables, retire in disdain. Their fortune
did not lie in the past but in the future, in the powers of a new method,

a new technique, the new methodology of a new science, a science of society itself. Unlike the romantic, individualist reformers of the prewar decades, these new visionaries dreamed of positive government, government enlarged to the measure not just of the spreading maladies of the nation but of nationwide opportunities for modern social development. They were heirs of Henry Carey.

Late-nineteenth-century American social science came to one climax in a man notably friendly to women, the sociologist Lester Ward. Then it arrived at its largest climax in a man, John Dewey, who, while never himself emphasizing feminism, women's issues, or any mission special to women, nevertheless enjoyed a kind of automatic rapport with women leaders of Jane Addams's generation. The basic lure for women consisted essentially in the "philosophy" of social science rather than in its "powers": its vision, essentially utopian, of the kind of world social science could—and would—create. It would not be the world of Emerson and Fuller. It would most certainly not be the world of laissez-faire. It would not be the world of the political parties, dominated by assertive self-interest. It would not be the world of popular culture, whether in its old Yankee village form or its new, lyric, "Californian" styles. As Leach has explained, the ASSA vision of the ideal world stressed "equilibrium, symmetrical harmony . . . interdependence."[83] Unities, integrations, and wholes constituted its norms. Its master metaphor was the "body," construed as a smoothly harmonic integration and interdependency of parts. Naturally, "health" defined its finest state. Dewey would gather this whole complex itself up into one unitary metaphor, his philosophy of education construed as the facilitation of "growth."

For feminism, struggling to resolve its inheritance of woman's sphere, all this could be deeply attractive. To protest and reject woman's sphere was to invite all the uncertainty, disorder, conflict, danger, incompletion, struggle, disharmony, asymmetry, disunity, and disease of man's life into woman's life. Why not, then, if woman's sphere had originally been defined by prefeminist masculine self-interest, embark upon the adventure of expanding that sphere from purely private into public life, inviting those men to join who seemed to agree that the public world of economy and politics was in disorder, in need of reform, of control, and of housekeeping. That this logic was powerful came to be emphatically revealed when that most masculine of public men, famous for his pursuit of manly self-expression in all the classic locations—the political back rooms, the frontier, war—Theodore Roosevelt himself, welcomed his phalanx of women in the campaign of 1912 and went on explicitly to declare that women might well be handed the job of keeping New York's house in order, since the old-line politicians were not up to it. The central task of woman's sphere was, after all, to tend bodies, to facilitate growth. The reproduction of the race hardly ended at the exit of new life from mothers' wombs. It proceeded through all those practices and institutions granted to woman's sphere for child-rearing. Health, harmony, interdependence—these had been watchwords of woman's sphere long before a new social science had begun to exalt them. Here was a marriage preordained by democratic history.

This alliance seemed to contain fewer dangers than the first alliance in which feminists had risked themselves. Abolitionism had been the entrée to public life for many of the women who had soon found themselves declaring their own independence at Seneca Falls back in 1848. Indeed, in his seminal study *Beginnings of Sisterhood*, historian Keith Melder has argued that women did not generate a clear, explicit, insistent feminist language until they had undergone their experience in the female antislavery auxiliaries, written their abolitionist petitions, run their bazaars for abolition work. Women discovered their own condition by discovering that of others. "In striving to strike *his* chains off," Abigail Kelley was to recall, "we found most surely, that we were manacled ourselves." Working to liberate blacks, Lucy Stone had said, women discovered themselves "plunged in degradation," too.[84] But women abolitionists had not worked with blacks, they had worked with white male abolitionists. Certainly white male abolitionists were neither manacled nor degraded. In his recent close analysis of abolitionism on its molecular, "small-group" level, Lawrence Friedman has noted one ironical result. The female "auxiliaries" of the 1830s gave way to "co-missionary" equality and gender integration in the 1850s, and as they did so,

[as] male [abolitionists] increasingly embraced women colleagues in the mission to the slaves, [both white men and women] were withdrawing from a modest co-missionary tradition with free blacks. It appeared that expansion of gender contacts required contraction of bi-racial contacts.[85]

Whether gender expansion "required" racial contraction or not, the alliance between male and female abolitionists was bound to end, once abolitionism succeeded. Women then were left with nothing but a demand to be rewarded for their services. This was to ask male abolitionists to undertake something they had never contemplated. The bitterness with which even the most farsighted feminists received the request that they step back in favor of "the Negro's hour" after the Civil War did not conceal the fact that abolitionism had ended up making women feel sorrier for themselves than for blacks. One day this withdrawal of concern for blacks would allow some white Southern women to commend woman suffrage as a means for serving white Southern racist arrangements.

No such dilemmas and ambivalences seemed to underlie an alliance between feminism and a body of emergent middle-class reformers concerned with new ideas of institutional management and social control. The appeal of this alliance became stronger when it became clear just how it might serve one of the deepest needs felt by its female partners, that of finding in social science answers to what postwar feminists agreed was the question of questions, the marriage question, which was to say, the problem of sex. It was only appropriate that this question should be not only answered, but brought to apotheosis as the very foundation of feminist social science, by nineteenth-century feminism's last and climactic leader.

Wild Cow in a Tame Universe: Charlotte Perkins Gilman and the Pathos of Feminist Utopia

Born in Bushnell's Hartford and raised well aware of her formidable female relatives—her grandmother Mary Beecher Perkins, and her famous great-aunts Catherine Beecher, Harriet Beecher Stowe, and Isabella Beecher Hooker—Charlotte Perkins grew up with strong and articulate women in her family culture.[86] Nor did her father, Frederick Beecher Perkins, attempt to discourage this heritage. Frederick Perkins separated from his wife not long after Charlotte's birth, but, rare though meetings were between the two, he remained a presence in his daughter's life until his death. Of her father's preference for literary, intellectual women his daughter had no doubt; like Margaret Fuller, in becoming such a woman Charlotte Gilman was fulfilling, not rejecting, a tradition familiar among intellectual nineteenth-century American men in New England.

But the Perkins's marriage had been a disaster. Marrying at twenty-nine, Mary Westcott, the petted, indulged daughter of a Providence merchant family, was prepared for sheltered domesticity, not for hardships. Yet Frederick Perkins, an intellectual without a calling, had married while saddled with debts and only succeeded in increasing them. The Perkins family never really had a home, only temporary quarters in boarding houses and with relatives. Two of the four children Mary Perkins bore in eight years died in infancy. But as a single parent with two young children, Mary Perkins did cope, in a peripatetic existence following no easy rules. Frederick Perkins's financial support kept the little family just above poverty. When Charlotte Perkins was fourteen her mother moved into a Swedenborgian community household, made up heavily of persons like herself, divorced women with children. When her daughter was eighteen, Mary Perkins agreed to let her attend the Rhode Island School of Design. For a variety of reasons, RISD did not prove to matter much, but, still living with her mother, Charlotte Perkins clearly had her own life among numerous friends associated with Brown University, earning bits of money here and there, tutoring, baby-sitting, and selling a little art to supplement her father's contributions. Contrary to her own statement in her autobiography, Charlotte Perkins did read and enjoy novels with her mother, played chess with her mother, sewed, gossiped, and kept up the household with her mother, with no special tension, until she was twenty-four.

Gilman's latest—and first thoroughly informed—biographer, Mary A. Hill, has pointed out how dramatically different Gilman's girlhood and young womanhood appear in her autobiography, written late in life, compared to her diaries and letters written at the time.[87] In the former one finds a victim, an isolate, a martyr growing up in friendless solitude, denied love by a damaged mother, chilled by an elusive father, tormented by an older brother. "Girlhood—If Any," was the seventy-year-old's choice as heading for her chapter on herself at sixteen. But in the diaries and letters an exuberant, self-confident, self-enjoying, bumptious, often flip and witty young person appears, by no means disinterested in valentines, flirtations, and frolics with friends of both sexes. At nineteen Charlotte Perkins was a devotee of William Blaikie's physical fitness program and, as such, a dedicated jogger; she had always been physically strong and vital as a young girl, and in her self-exultation had emphatically included body as well as brain as part of self. Not even Gilman's autobiographical reconstructions could deny all this record. In recalling herself at twenty-one, she recalled the "Power and Glory" she had felt: "My health was splendid, I never tired, with a steady cheerfulness."[88] Of course this particular passage was meant to contrast with what came next, her breakdown in marriage, but it sheds light backward, too, onto that "girlhood—if any." For a girl wanting to be free, it had been ideal.

Walter Stetson met Charlotte Perkins early in January 1882 and asked her to marry him seventeen days later. Charlotte Stetson always blamed her husband for his haste. He had known only "the beauty of the body and its sexual attraction" during those seventeen days; he had not got to know her character, her mind, her real, deeper, true self. She generalized her feelings in an article, published in September 1885, "On Advertising for Marriage." But in fact the two married only after no less than two years and three months had gone by after Stetson's proposal. The bride was then two months shy of her twenty-fourth birthday, no helpless bud. This marriage was a disaster. Baby Katherine arrived in March 1885, and by October Charlotte Stetson was on her way to California, alone.

Just how Charlotte Stetson—later, Charlotte Gilman—continued to put the blame for her marriage, not so much on her husband as on a whole social order, rather than on herself, we may not be able to tell. She had been completely successful in getting Stetson to wait a year before any engagement was announced. Many nineteenth-century girls terminated such courtships short of engagement and so could she have. Then, she had been successful in getting him to accept an engagement of more than another year. Many nineteenth-century girls terminated engagements without marrying and so might she have. Retrospect shows that the bride had been, to say the least, ambivalent about marrying at all. Had she married on the rebound? For more than a year before meeting Stetson, she had pursued an emotionally intense relationship with a longtime friend, Martha Luther. According to her biographer, "Charlotte had the confidence to scoff at 'Philistines,' to state openly that her sensuous love for Martha was superior to the love of any man."[89] But when Martha Luther began showing signs of responding to another suitor, Charles A. Lane, Charlotte Perkins's efforts to outcompete proved her confidence mistaken. Still, marrying on the rebound usually is a hasty affair, and the twenty-seven months between proposal and marriage demonstrated someone's caution, resistance, restraint.

When the ministrations of the Beecher women's family doctor, S. Weir Mitchell, proved unavailing, back in Providence during a reconciliation, Charlotte and Walter Stetson separated for good, Charlotte moving to California, now with her three-year-old daughter, in the autumn of 1888. She had gone on writing and publishing in Providence: "Why Women Do Not Reform Their Dress," "An Appeal for a Ladies Gymnasium," and columns in the local labor newspaper that supported suffrage. She might have had a career in Providence. But more than just a career was needed.

In California for the next several years, Charlotte Stetson made her way first in the Los Angeles area, then in San Francisco, in that women's world of clubs, organizations, newspapers, conventions and congresses and leagues, churches and neighborhoods and houses, that had grown up in California as elsewhere in the nation. Not neglecting her own improvement—French lessons, the gymnasium, great books—writing pieces every week for local papers, she began to travel, giving talks and speeches, and found herself popular. In 1890 she wrote her "awful story," the nightmarish tale of a woman's nervous breakdown, published as *The Yellow Wallpaper*. In this story, despite every device of husband and doctor, the martyr-heroine disintegrated. This was not a description of her own marriage. "Walter says he has read it four *times*, and thinks it the most ghastly tale he ever read. Says it beats Poe, and Doré!"[90] In her autobiography Gilman characterized the marriage in her story as "beginning something as mine did," then explained that "the real purpose of the story was to reach Dr. S. Weir Mitchell." Mitchell's prescription for her back in Providence had been home and passivity: "Live as domestic a life as possible. . . . never touch pen, brush or pencil as long as you live."[91] Stetson was determined to show him that he had misdiagnosed her; she was suffering not from too much but from too little activity, not from too much but too little brain life.

In 1893, as her divorce became final, Stetson decided to send her daughter, by then eight, to live with her ex-husband, who soon married her erstwhile best friend, Grace Channing. Her purpose was not to free herself so much as to save her daughter Katherine from fatherlessness. In coming years Katherine spent much time with her mother as well. But the arrangement did leave Charlotte Stetson homeless, and she began changing addresses about as often as her own mother had during her childhood. She had already found a new deep attachment, to a journalist named Adeline E. Knapp, in Oakland. After Katherine went east, Stetson moved to San Francisco to live with the writer and feminist, Helen Campbell, "Mother Campbell," twenty-one years older, the biographer of Anne Bradstreet. In 1896 she cut loose from California for a fully peripatetic life as lecturer, writer, feminist, celebrity in the women's world. One important stop was in Chicago at Hull House with Florence Kelley, Alice Hamilton, Ellen Gates Starr, Julia Lathrop, and Jane Addams, a woman's enclave that seemed to be the promise of a whole new Chicago, a women's world expanding into the whole world, especially as the best of men—Richard Ely, John Dewey, John Peter Altgeld—seemed to signify that that women's world was really what men too at their best might desire.

On August 31, 1897, in Laconia, New Hampshire, Charlotte Stetson began a book, "Economic Relation of the Sexes as a Factor in Social Development."

The first day I wrote 1700 words. . . . The second day 2400 words; the third, 3600; the fourth, 4000. "Doing finely," says the diary. I well remember that 4000-word day, the smooth, swift, easy flow—. . . the splendid joy of it—I went and ran, just raced along the country road, for sheer triumph.[92]

She wrote in Laconia till September 6, then overnight in Boston on a visit to Providence; she wrote in Hingham, Massachusetts, on September 16 and 17; then back in Boston; during a visit to Norwich, Connecticut; in New York by October 2. On October 8: "Finish book, 356 pages." *Women and Economics* proved to contain twice the number of words she had written "in seventeen days, in five different houses," but she had got her "argument . . . method and style" all down in that one surge of inspiration. Published in May 1898, soon translated into German, Dutch, Italian, even Hungarian and Japanese, *Women and Economics* made Stetson an international figure.

It was symptomatic of her book thatStetson offered no headings for her chapters, fifteen in all. The book circled around a single theme, repeated throughout. "Excessive sex-indulgence is the distinctive feature of humanity. We, as a race, manifest an excessive sex-attraction . . . The human animal manifests an excess in sex-attraction."[93] Although it is conventionally emphasized that Stetson owed the intellectual framework for *Women and Economics* to the sociologist Lester Ward, Stetson mentioned Ward only once. While she was no usual scholar bound by standard scholarly proprieties, if she really did owe much to Ward, this scant recognition of her debt was surprising. She had met Ward in January 1896, had been immensely flattered at his praise of a poem of hers, and did seize upon Ward's famous *Forum* article of 1888, "Our Better Halves," published five years after his major statement, *Dynamic Sociology*, as precipitant of her own views. But far from simply expounding Ward, in *Women and Economics* Stetson had brought her own life experiences into focus. In arguing the biological superiority of the female sex, Ward had not been concerned with "excessive sex-indulgence" in the human species, but rather emphasized that, given the great test of nature, the ability of a species to reproduce successfully, the female sex clearly mattered more than the male, or at least, so the evidence he chose to cite seemed to indicate. Stetson's preoccupation with excessive sex indulgence was based on neither a necessary nor a logical inference from this idea of Ward's.

The reason for excessive sex-indulgence in the human species, Stetson explained, was women's economic dependence on men. Responding to their dependency, women competed for men by highlighting and exaggerating their sexual features. Naturally, this in turn led to women's becoming stereotyped, as in the nineteenth-century expression, "the sex." In pursuing this notion, Stetson filled the book with ambivalences. One of its striking polemics was the author's intense dislike for the conventional modern woman. Physically weak, passive, emotionally childish, intellectually vacuous, the female product of "sexuo-economic" dependency might have seemed best understood simply as victim, but Stetson clearly grasped the degree to which this feminity had found its own forms of power, and she despised them. That nature decreed a quite different kind of female she was sure:

To make clear . . . the difference between normal and abnormal sex-distinction, look at the relative condition of a wild cow and a "milch-cow," such as we have made. The wild cow is a female. She has healthy calves, and milk enough for them; and that is all the femininity she needs. Otherwise than that she is bovine rather than feminine. She is a light, strong, swift, sinewy creature, able to run, jump, and fight, if necessary. We, for economic reasons, have artificially developed the cow's capacity for producing milk. She has become a walking milk-machine.[94]

This comparison of the "wild" with the tamed and civilized hardly fit with Lester Ward's—and Stetson's own—"reformed Darwinism," with its emphasis upon the evolutionary advantages of mind, purpose, plan, control, the advantages, that is, precisely, of civilization over the "wild." But far more revealingly, it contrasted with Stetson's polemic on the male of the species. Here, it seemed, civilization had indeed worked all to the good. By "nature" the male was destructive, power-hungry, competitive, individualistic, "spending," "scattering," and ferocious. But as a consequence of civilization, the human male had become constructive, cooperative, productive. Under present conditions men were actually superior to women. In the most crucial terms of all: "He has been made the working mother of the world."[95]

True to a scientistic ideology of "objectivity," Stetson professed to find this history of woman's fall and man's rise no occasion for lament but for acceptance: "Women can well afford their period of subjection for the sake of a conquered world, a civilized man." It was enough that now women were about to escape their temporary historical sexuo-economic subjection. And why?

This change is not a thing to prophesy and plead for. It is a change already instituted. . . . Neither men nor women wish the change. Neither men nor women have sought it. But the same great force of social evolution which brought us into the old relation—to our great sorrow and pain—is bringing us out, with equal difficulty and distress.[96]

Here again, this was no disciple of Lester Ward. Such determinism had been exactly what Ward had striven to refute. But that determinism served Stetson well: what she described as inevitable she did not have to reveal as her own heart's desire.

What this was she made completely clear five years later, in what was by far her most characteristic book, bold, blunt, sarcastic, merciless, *The Home*. By then she had married again. Her new husband, her cousin Houghton Gilman, seven years her junior, appeared in her autobiography abruptly, without introduction, on her wedding day.

The beauty of [our] honeymoon was somewhat marred by my trying to read *Human Work* to Houghton! He bore it nobly. If one marries a philosopher or a prophet there are various consequences to be met; Xanthippe loses her temper over it, Kadijah does not, I believe.

Thirty-four years of marriage ended with his sudden, unexpected death from a cerebral hemorrhage. "Whatever I felt of loss and pain was outweighed by gratitude for an instant, painless death for him, and that he did not have to see me wither and die—and he be left alone."[97]

By her autobiographical accounting, Gilman started *The Home* before this marriage. It was evident in any case that in marrying she was not contracting to create a home. Already, in *Women and Economics*, she had stigmatized the homemaker as practically the last "primitive," premodern laborer. Modern work was specialized work, whereas the homemaker did a bit of everything, all badly. Far better that this work be divided up and done by experts. By far the most sensational of the professionalizations of homemaker that she recommended was motherhood. Quite simply, mothers in the modern world of sexuo-economic dependency were bad mothers: "pathological," "morbid," "defective," "diseased," "too female for perfect motherhood!"[98] Experts in mothering were as needed as experts in making clothes or steel.

But if the nursery was to be evicted from home, so also was the kitchen; food perhaps even more than babies inspired Gilman's highest emotional pitch. Of course one fault of home-cooked meals was their dietetic deficiency. Nutrition was a modern science. "The selection and preparation of food should be in the hands of trained experts." Again, the homemaker and housewife could not in justice be expected to be an expert on everything. But Gilman's feelings about food were not really centered on the claims of modern nutritional science. What she assailed was the linkage of food with certain emotions:

Our general notion is that we have lifted and ennobled our eating and drinking by combining them with love. On the contrary, we have lowered and degraded our love by combining it with eating and drinking. . . . The stomach should be left to its natural uses, not made a thoroughfare for stranger passions and purposes; and the heart should be approached through higher channels.

The last phrase was surprising. If the "stomach" represented hunger for food in its "natural" form, then surely the "heart" was not the proper organ of reference for love, or, as she elsewhere put it, "sex-attraction." But it was not sex phobia that unified Gilman's view of home. She assailed emotional attachments to food on other grounds also: "The limitless personal taste developed by 'home cooking' fears that it will lose its own particular shade of brown on the bacon, its own hottest of hot cakes, its own corner biscuit." Raised by a mother who cooked only for sustenance, accustomed herself to eating out in a dozen boarding houses, at the homes of a hundred friends, in station cafés and at church socials, Gilman had no existential investment in food and obviously had no intention of catering to any in Houghton Gilman. "As cooking becomes dissociated from the home, we shall gradually cease to attach emotions to it; and we shall learn to judge it impersonally upon a scientific and artistic basis." In *The Home* Gilman pressed these feelings on to implacable conclusion. Cooking must be science. "This is forever impossible at home. Until the food laboratory entirely supersedes the kitchen there can be no growth."[99]

What remained a mystery, both in *The Home* and in *Women and Economics*, was why there should be any home at all, or any marriage. Once stripped of kitchen, dining room, and nursery (as well as of library, studio, game room, etc.), what remained? Bedroom? To the "natural" nature of "sex attraction" Gilman several times referred. But never did this natural drive issue in any relationship or institution devoted to sanctioning just that attraction. One of the most obvious evils of "excessive" sex indulgence was prostitution; like Margaret Fuller, Gilman urged women to include prostitutes in their drive for freedom. Consistently, in evoking a "normal" sexuality successive upon the epoch of the excessive, she celebrated monogamous marriage, paradoxically as the "natural" order intended by evolution, despite evolution's evident age-old inability to enforce it. Yet this monogamous marriage did not appear to rest upon sex attraction but rather upon its "purpose," which was children. Husband-and-wife were, by "telic" logic, inherently father-and-mother. And since mothering—and presumably also fathering—were to be made scientific and professionalized, marriage itself was not really the focus of child life.

Yet "every human being needs a home," as Gilman had already declared in *Women and Economics*. The real problem concerned those not married at all. Already, she had noted, most men spent ten years or so getting started in business before they married, and as more women went to work, they too would wait. Thus more and more "individuals" were living as "detached persons," and theirs was the need for home that most stood out.

What the human race requires is permanent provision for the need of individuals, disconnected from the sex-relation. . . . Married people will always prefer a home together, and we can have it; but groups of women or groups of men can also have a home together if they like. . . . [For women, the] knowledge that peace and comfort may be theirs for life, even if they do not marry—and may still be theirs for life, even if they do—will develop a serenity and strength in women most beneficial to them and to the world.[100]

If the emphasis here was upon the advantage to women of same-sex homes, Gilman also noted the propensity of men, in pursuit of "real rest and pleasure," to recur to each other, too, in "the distant camp in the woods, the mountain climb, the hunting trip." The "delightful companionship" Gilman evoked as one of the home's rewards, "at the end of the day's work," by no means had a primarily heterosocial or even androgynous focus.

In the end, not even Tocquevillian motives for home seemed relevant. Gilman never obscured that what for her counted most in life was work. It was in work, true work, modern work based on modern principles of professionalization and specialization, that men had most fully developed themselves, and women would, too. In such work human beings were not male or female but simply human. To the extent that they were human, at work, they were less male and female, less masculine and feminine, more what they had in common. It was here, in fact, that Gilman's greatest political polemic fixed. Although men might have been civilized by civilization, the male-dominated world of work nevertheless was not in good order. "In the economic world, excessive masculinity, in its fierce competition and primitive individualism," still prevailed, wreaking "more evil than good."[101] This only went hand in hand with the tendency of "excessive femininity" to induce habits of "inordinate consumption." In criticizing "fierce" competition and "primitive" individualism, Gilman did not mean to laud "mild" competition or "sophisticated" individualism. She wanted collaboration and team spirit. Her explicit avowal of herself as a kind of "socialist" was enough to make that clear. So long as the world remained "masculine," women would not be humanized by entering it. Gilman made this clearer in *The Man-Made World* of 1911.

Advocates of football . . . proudly claim that it fits a man for life. Life—from the wholly male point of view—is a battle, with a prize. To want something beyond measure, and to fight to get [it]—that is the simple proposition. This view of life finds its most naive expression in predatory warfare; and still tends to make predatory warfare of the later and more human processes of industry.[102]

Gilman took care to agree that so long as masculine sports were clearly labeled as such and did "no harm to the more important social processes," they might be allowed a place in the better world, but, in summarizing what sorts of petty and idle feminine activities too would disappear, she evoked, by a clearly unconscious process, a scene in which football also would have no place: "Genuine relaxation and recreation, all manner of healthful sports and pastimes, beloved of both sexes today, will remain." Similarly, she dismissed "all the old religions made by men" as having been "forced on the women" whether they liked them or not.[103]

Only with Gilman's own novel *Herland* before us, might we think the logical conclusion of her emotional development obvious: why not get rid of men altogether? Presumably Lester Ward, in arguing the evolutionary primacy of the mother over the mere impregnator, the father, had provided the scientific foundation for such a fantasy. Gilman's emotional life inspired its existential legitimacy. The ability of the all-female inhabitants of "Herland," her utopia, to reproduce by parthe-nogenesis, echoing Mary Baker Eddy's earlier vision of "amogenesis," was a mere technicality. Although its story or plot is the least of *Herland*, on purely plot grounds the central mystery in the book is why its collective heroine, the entirely self-sufficient, unanimously female cit-izenship of Herland, should entertain any thought of readmitting males to their society at all. Gilman's almost surreptitious answer, that the three male intruders—American college-boy types—represented "a chance to re-establish a bi-sexual state for our people." conveyed neither emotional nor intellectual conviction so much as the implicit conces-sion that a wholly female utopia could only be a propaedeutic and educational, but not a serious political ambition. Yet a serious political ambition was not concealed. Admission of men into this female world required changed men, as one of the college boys, Vandyke Jennings, attested:

I found that much, very much, of what I had honestly supposed to be a phys-iological necessity was a psychological necessity—or so believed. I found . . . that my feelings had changed. . . . And more than all, I found this—a factor of enormous weight—these women were not provocative. That made an enormous difference.[104]

Given such a change, men became eligible to consort with women. That Vandyke Jennings found his wife, Ellador, withdrawing after a presum-ably procreative transaction, into a "good comrade," "sorry, honestly sorry" at his subsequent presumably male "distresses," and full of "thoughtful suggestions" as to how he might relieve them, simply ratified the principle that for the women of Herland sex meant, and meant only, motherhood.

But it would be a mistake to identify some phobia as to men, mas-culinity, and sex as the center of Gilman's imaginative reconstruction of the world, let alone to see her as prefiguring later bisexual or lesbian feminisms. Her biographer, Mary Hill, finds reason in her diaries and letters to suggest not only emotionally warm and even "sensuous" relationships with other women but a readiness to consider herself as possessed of "sex attraction" for men too during her years as unremar-ried divorcee in California. What Gilman seems to have most wanted to be, however, hardly had reference to men at all or to women. She wanted to be light, strong, swift, sinewy, a creature able to run, jump, and fight, too, if necessary. She wanted to be a wild cow, not a milch cow. She did not want lesbian relationships rather than heterosexual relationships. She did not want any heavy relationships at all. Certainly her marriage to Houghton Gilman was not heavy. Gilman wanted to be free, curiously not unlike Josiah Royce's own homeless, happy father in early California.

Gilman, however, could not find means for projecting this ideal in straightforward ways, anymore than Fuller had. The truly striking feature of *Herland* was not its exclusion of men, but of men's work. In Herland all the orchards were planted, all the houses built. In Herland, " 'There's no dirt. . . . There's no smoke. . . . There's no noise.' " History had ended in Herland; only housekeeping remained. "Everything was beauty, order, perfect cleanness, and the pleasantest sense of home over all." Where society itself had become home, it only followed: "There were no adventures because there was nothing to fight." With these assertions Gilman came very close to abandoning her reform Darwinism altogether in favor of a return to the simple affirmation of inherent, eternal traits, those of men and of women, and in the process came close as well to betraying a sense that the United States did indeed belong to men, that the United States could never be Herland. Herland "was as neat as a Dutch kitchen." In Herland, every road was "as perfect as if it were Europe's best."[105]

Thus it was only as a kind of frustration of imagination that Gilman expounded the new philosophies of the professionalization of everything, embraced social science, affirmed managerial progressivism (as "socialism"), deplored competition, wrote as a kind of sister of John Dewey and Thorstein Veblen if not as a daughter of Royce. It was not at all clear that wild cows were wanted in Herland. Lacking original literary talents herself, Gilman found no genres or languages prepared for portraying light, lithe, nimble, self-reliant, self-supporting womanhood in the actual circumstances of American life, even though she herself had lived that way. Instead, she turned to and immensely inflated, to the level of world-historical evolution, the tale of woman as victim.

Other new lives were already being led and told. Owen Johnson's slightly sensationalistic novel of 1913, *The Salamander*, celebrated a new type, the American flapper. A vivid creature, despite—or because of—her Midwest roots, the flapper sought adventure hungrily, flaunted individuality, and plunged into the fires of New York, confident she would not be consumed. As Lewis Erenberg has shown in *Steppin' Out*, a meticulous study of turn-of-century New York City, a whole array of new social inventions and arts were at last filling a gap left by the extremes of post-Civil War society.[106] Right into the 1890s, the scenes for social mingling of the sexes were restricted to, on the one hand, the great private mansions of Fifth Avenue and, on the other, the rough

saloons and music halls of working-class appeal, where, in fact, the only mingling was between male patrons and female providers. Something like this polar distribution prevailed in smaller communities, too. By 1900 new kinds of acceptable public places where the two sexes could consort had begun to proliferate: hotels with many more public rooms, restaurants, cafés, night spots. For the first time the sexes could drink in public together, here and there smoke together. New music, new kinds of musical instruments, new kinds of dancing invited associations heretofore either confined within private walls or regarded as abusive of feminine reputation. A new realm, neither that of work nor that of home, was being enhanced and enlarged, explicitly intended to enhance and enlarge the potentialities of self in both sexes.

Charlotte Perkins Gilman remained uncomprehending of the young women of this new generation:

They remain . . . the slaves of fashion . . . lifting their skirts, exhibiting their legs, powdering their noses. . . . I have no objection to legs. . . . The one-piece bathingsuit is precisely as right for women as for men. It is an exhilarating sight to see men and women, swimming together, walking or running on the beaches together, free, equal, not stressing sex in any way. But these gleaming "nudes," in the street-car for instance have no *raison d'être*. . . . I have seen legs . . . with knee and thigh in full evidence, which so far from being desirable were fairly repellent. . . . There is a splendid stir and push among our youth, what is called a "revolt" . . .—but what have they to propose instead? So far there has not been put forth by all this revolted youth any social improvement that I have heard of.[107]

For Alexandra Kollontai too, in Russia, escape from the sex in self was the promise of socialism, but she too, like Gilman, was essentially a privileged individualist. In Italy the simple premodern sexuality that Gramsci praised in man-the-worker would remain rather more necessity than virtue so long as Italy remained poor. In Sweden, where an ancient permissiveness had preceded the welfare state, there was little for youth to revolt about.

The flapper was neither a sentimental nor a romantic figure. There would be times when, as Paolo Valera saw of the girls of Milan, it might be hard to be sure no edge of mercenary interest had not come to characterize her. Yet the flapper would never manifest that "rational" love commended by the late-nineteenth-century social-science sex reformers, the love which, as William Leach has shown, seemed to many feminists to be their escape from the constrictions of their separate sphere with all its sentimental furnishings. New York City love would not be rational love, would never quench sex attraction in work let alone socialism, would not deprecate masculinity. New York City love would have little to do with that loyalty toward Beloved Community that

Royce had prescribed as the cure for individualism. No doubt it too would be susceptible to sentimentalization. *Guys and Dolls* would promulgate stereotypes as comforting as *Little Women*. But as the story of the most famous of all the flappers, Zelda Fitzgerald, would show, incineration, not just excitement, remained as the price that might have to be paid for being a salamander.[108] Love as risk, not as security, marriage as exposure, not as comfort, had begun to be sensed as a promise in American life.

Individualistic Feminism: Elizabeth Cady Stanton versus Religion and Social Science

Ironically, as the most promising alliance for women seemed to be coming to fruition, it was already withering. With the diffuse circles of the American Social Science Association consolidating into professional specialties, housed within the emergent new graduate departments of the universities, theory and practice combined, as Rosalind Rosenberg has shown us, in opening doors there for women.[109] Theory—the theory of Ward's sociology, deepened by the findings of anthropology, psychology, and a more empirical sociology than Ward's—led to underwriting with evidence what idealists had previously had to affirm by faith, that women's apparent deficiencies were not functions of feminine nature but of environment, education, upbringing. John Staurt Mill was confirmed. Practice, warmly encouraged by men like the James Angells, father and son, W. I. Thomas, George Herbert Mead, and especially John Dewey, found young women entering graduate work in social sciences in new equality, notably at Chicago but also at Cornell, Columbia, and Clark. Even a man like Franklin Giddings at Columbia, as Rosenberg has shown, still skeptical of women's capacity for full equality in public life, nevertheless opened the way for Elsie Clews Parsons, while out-and-out opponents of women's graduate work such as James Cattell found his own student, Edward Thorndike, demanding that a woman graduate student in psychology be given faculty status.

Yet by the 1920s it was clear that the old vision of the American Social Science Association had evaporated. As the social sciences grew more scientific, they grew away from their links with reform. Great reform-minded founders of a science, such as Lester Ward, became objects of derision for their lack of method, their giving priority to social change, their subordination of science to society. As the first priority of the social sciences came to be precisely to become sciences, the fact that some social scientists now happened to be women lost all the meaning it would have had, when social science and feminism supposedly enjoyed inherent affinities. And as it happened, the numbers of women entering the social sciences quickly leveled off. In the career of the most famous of them, Margaret Mead, feminism would always remain problematic. But the great disaster of social science was that it cut off the potential for the reemergence of a feminism focused unambiguously in individuals of power, autonomy, and genius. As the career of the most remarkable of the organizational leaders of nineteenth-century feminism indicated, Margaret Fuller's spirit was ready for revivification. On January 18, 1892, a stout old lady of seventy-six had offered the purest claim upon equality yet enunciated, that of individuality.

Elizabeth Cady Stanton had fought the good fight for over fifty years. A bride of twenty-five at the London Anti-Slavery Convention of 1840, she had been among those who were enraged by the condescension of male abolitionists, and who went on to take the lead at Seneca Falls in the women's rights convention. The historic honor attached to that otherwise obscure place derived from the fact that it was the home of Henry and Elizabeth Cady Stanton. From then on for a quarter century, few months went by when Stanton was not involved in political action of some sort somewhere. Politics aroused her. Horace Greeley's abandonment of the woman suffrage cause in 1867 at the New York State Constitutional Convention angered her. The abandonment of women in favor of blacks by the Republican Party, busy passing the Fourteenth Amendment, enraged her. (She was to be guilty of occasional racial remarks as a consequence.) Victoria Claflin Woodhull's candor during the suffrage convention of 1871 in New York thrilled her; she developed an attachment to Woodhull that appalled her more cautious sisters. Late that same year the response she drew from Mormon women to her talk on women's rights in Salt Lake City delighted her. There was little doubt about it: Stanton was by nature, constitutionally, an enthusiast.

She was favored in life. The $50,000 she inherited from her father in 1859, when she was forty-four—the equivalent today of $500,000 at the very least—lent her a security few other feminist leaders enjoyed. Money mattered. Stanton bore and raised seven children, a fact that won her immense credibility as she came to confront her audiences with more and more advanced, radical views. Henry Stanton continued to provide her with husbandly presence and approval to his death in 1887, when she was seventy-two. All this was good fortune, luck, grace.[110] Harriet Martineau and Sweden's Fredrika Bremer had judged that prosperity had softened and captivated American women, but Stanton made use of it. Stanton had no sense of identity with her class. Eagerly, she reached out to working women, for contact with unions. Eventually she quenched irrational racial tics. She refused to observe prudence on the marriage question, confronting it in its sexual heart: wife abuse, venereal disease, abortion, prostitution, "marital rape." Though Stanton explicitly insisted that women were as sexually appetitive as men, when she defended "free love" she meant not some extramarital prodigality but the abolition of unwilling or forced sexuality within marriage. She insisted that the cleansing of marriage of all coercion demanded divorce as a relief available without humiliation to all spouses.

Stanton's enthusiasm for reforms got neither herself nor reforms anywhere. The alliance of women like herself with working women got nowhere. Pressing the marriage question in league with Woodhull led to fiasco and the backlash from the Young Men's Christian Association, Anthony Comstock, and the U.S. Congress, which passed laws against free speech and free practice on matters sexual. Most other feminists backed off from even egregious instances of injustice inflicted by the legal system on women who had "fallen." Stanton gave up the suffrage association then as politically hopeless. She did not go home, however. Instead, at fifty-seven, she launched out on the national lecture circuit, dragging through the nights in stuffy railroad cars, waiting out the Mississippi's ice floes, putting up in a hundred spare bedrooms in strangers' homes, a decade before Frances Willard's similar and somewhat more comfortable odyssey. It was the making of Cady Stanton. She learned self-sufficiency. She became a professional. She earned her own money. She learned about the presentation of self as a Lyceum star.

It was this Elizabeth Cady Stanton who addressed her sisters in 1892. She had accepted the presidency of the suffrage association somewhat dubiously in 1890, not at all sure she fit into what had begun to become a role controlled by organizational needs. Now, as she resigned, she saw no reason not to offer existential, individual, personal truth rather than expedient, prudential, political, organizational, social truth. "The talk of sheltering woman from the fierce storms of life is the sheerest mockery," she said, for those storms "beat on her from every point of the compass, just as they do on every man."[111] Some in her audience might have wondered whether, protected by her inheritance, by her successful husband, by her good health, by her long comradely sisterhood with Susan B. Anthony, Stanton could justly claim to have earned her insight by hard experience. But this would have been to deprecate the power of inner experience in favor of the externalities of social-science theory. Stanton had the courage to refrain from claiming that she had ever suffered storms personally from father or mother, husband or children, poverty or patriarchy. She was not a victim. Yet, being victimless had not meant harmony, equilibrium, sisterhood, community, unity, peace. She felt free to recall a fact existentially pertinent to all women:

Whatever the theories may be of woman's dependence on man, in the supreme moments of her life, he cannot bear her burdens. Alone she goes to the gates of death to give her life to every man that is born into the world; no one can share her fears, no one can mitigate her pangs.

Stanton was hardly commending these facts; they simply were.

The great urgency of women's equality was that, being just as exposed as men to the "fierce storms" of life, women had been less prepared for them and thus suffered "more fatal results":

An uneducated woman trained to dependence, with no resources in herself, must make a failure of any position in life. But society says women do not need a knowledge of the world . . . but when for the lack of all this, the woman's happiness is wrecked, alone she bears her humiliation; and the solitude of the weak and ignorant is indeed pitiable.

But the final overmastering fact was common to men and women—the ultimate "solitude and personal responsibility" of "individual life":

To appreciate the importance of fitting every human soul for independent action, think for a moment of the immeasurable solitude of self. We come into the world alone, unlike all who have gone before us, we leave it alone, under circumstances peculiar to ourselves. No mortal ever has been, no mortal ever will be like the soul just launched. . . . There can never again be just such a combination of prenatal influences . . . just such environments. . . . Nature never repeats herself. . . . our most bitter disappointments, our brightest hopes and ambitions, are known only to ourselves. Even our friendship and love we never fully share with another. . . . there is a solitude which each and every one of us has always carried with him, more inaccessible than the ice-cold mountains, more profound than the midnight sea; the solitude of self. . . . to it only omniscience is permitted to enter. Such is individual life. Who, I ask you, can take, dare take on himself the rights, the duties, the responsibilities of another human soul?[112]

The plea here was not to men to lift their oppression of women, but rather to women to take counsel with themselves.

After her retirement from the suffrage association's presidency, Stanton went on to produce one of American feminism's remarkable works, her *Woman's Bible*. On occasion Stanton granted that some Protestant clergymen were friendly to women, even to feminists. Some had invited her into their pulpits. But from as early as 1850 Stanton had been criticizing Protestant clergymen for antifeminism. She found the post-Civil War growth of Protestant fundamentalist, Bible, and missionary societies ominous. Her hostility to the churches hardly stopped at fundamentalism. She despised Henry Ward Beecher, the adulterous preacher of Brooklyn's Plymouth church, at once the softest of the new liberal exponents of a religion of feeling and an antisuffragist. From the 1870s on, stimulated by postwar biblical scholarship, Stanton began urging critical analysis of the Bible itself as not just antifeminist but antiwoman. A longtime friend of temperance, nevertheless she came to deplore the links between suffrage and Frances Willard's WCTU precisely because it was the Women's *Christian* Temperance Union. Finally, in 1895, when she was eighty, she brought out *The Woman's Bible*, essentially her own more or less polemical commentaries on those passages, 10 percent or less of the whole, touching on women. Not only did she portray Old Testament Jewish culture as a violent patriarchy. She took the occasion to reject the divinity of Jesus and to label the doctrine of Mary's virginity "a slur on all natural mother-hood." In 1896 the delegates to the annual suffrage convention were invited to exculpate themselves from any and all responsibility for *The Woman's Bible*. Though upset by it herself, Stanton's oldest friend, Susan B. Anthony, begged the delegates not to take so "narrow and illiberal" a step, but they did, fifty-three to forty-one. The new, younger leaders carried the day, trapping suffrage with temperance, leaving it vulner-able to xenophobia and racism. "Much as I desire the suffrage," Stan-ton wrote, replying to criticism of her Bible from church groups, "I would rather never vote, than to see the policy of our government at the mercy of the religious bigotry of such women."[113]

In effect, Stanton sensed the disaster impending for feminists in finessing the questions of class, race, and religion in order to concen-trate on the vote. Stanton's anticlericalism did not express some famil-iar rationalist spirit, or even that "religion of humanity" being ex-pounded by some of the new prophets of social science. The greatest such prophet, John Dewey, would one day expound the virtues of a *A Common Faith* as the all-embracing myth of a scientifically energized society, but this was not Stanton. Stanton did not even recommend religion to the self-in-its-solitude. "Each soul must depend wholly on itself." To the extent that religion could strengthen and not weaken that self-sufficiency, well and good, but no further. So far as women were concerned, Christianity and Western religions generally had failed so badly that, like Mrs. Eddy, Stanton saw value in construing a femi-nine dimension in God. She was, moreover, eager to see women take over the boards and ministries of the churches. But all this was not to promote either harmony or health, but to arm women for their lives: "Seeing, then, that life must ever be a march and a battle, that each soldier must be equipped for his own protection, it is the height of cruelty to rob the individual of a single natural right."[114] In the end, perhaps, Stanton sniffed in religion the ultimate source of illusions: illusions of harmony, equilibrium, organic oneness. Here was the dan-ger of "pantheism," against which Tocqueville had warned, now show-ing itself in both preachers and philosophers as well as social scientists. Here was the greatest danger for women. The life of woman's sphere itself was supposed to be harmonious, a life of organic connections, a life promoting equilibriums. What could be more obvious than perpetuating women's exclusion from "real" life by burdening them with dreams of harmony everywhere, by fitting them only to recoil from the real world rather than to enter it, struggle in it, flourish or shrivel in it, there or not at all.

Feminism was thus caught in a bind. Its most remarkable figures— Willard, Gilman, Stanton among them—fully autonomous in their own lives, had to either muffle their real message to the point of smothering it, as did Willard, or surrender it to utopian visions of method and harmony, as did Gilman, or settle for heroic isolation, as did Stanton. These women made no mistakes. There is nothing we can say they ought to have done that they did not, or did not do that they ought to have. It is up to us to recognize their autonomy. Their lives help us better understand the crucial locus of the history of the struggle for freedom, which can occur only in what are real, not abstract, individual minds.

Feminism on the Eve of Victory

By 1900 American feminists were concentrated on suffrage.[115] The old division between pure suffragists and those who saw suffrage as but one item on a whole menu of reforms had faded. Effective organizational leaders of the second generation were taking over. The transition had a deeper logic. Ideas of social reform, let alone of socialism or of *Revolution*, as Stanton, Susan B. Anthony, and their friends had titled their magazine, provoked basic opposition. But there could be no long-term effective opposition to suffrage. As Jane Camhi and Carl Degler have noted, the organized antisuffrage movement was staffed and impelled by women.[116] But these women based their opposition on the same ideology held by many, almost surely most nineteenth-century feminists and suffragists too: women were different from men, in significant ways superior to men. It was the suffragists, not the antisuffragists, whose argument made sense: how could women expect men, different as they were, indefinitely to protect women and advance their interests? Implicitly, antisuffrage women were challenging, not so much prosuffrage feminists for their betrayal of true womanhood, as men, to rise above basic manhood. It was in the temperance movement, filled with women dubious about feminism, only temporarily mesmerized by Willard, that the antisuffragist logic crumbled. Temperance women wanted the vote to enforce their superiority. This was why, then, the chronological propinquity of the Nineteenth with the Eighteenth

Amendment was "no accident" but, instead, resistered deep affinities, to the loss of both.[117]

But focus on suffrage implacably diminished inquiry and debate on other issues. It was obvious that, taken in their totality, American women led drastically different economic lives, for instance. What was the right approach to this fact? Comfortable women in New York City did their best to help the city's poor working girls in the needle trades to organize.[118] But the girls proved unorganizable. The comfortable women then went to the legislature for protective laws. But did not such laws presume a basic inequality for women in general in the marketplace? The deeper irresolution inhabited feminists themselves. Just what did the Puritan-descended white women of the Northeast, Midwest, and West Coast really want? What would they use their votes for? The sort of autonomous individualistic life prefigured by a Fuller or a Stanton was by no means to be found the secret desire of large numbers of women, even of young women. The suffrage movement itself could not resist co-optation by the rising anti-immigrant movement of the late nineteenth-century in the North or by the new Jim Crow system being installed in the South.[119] White Protestant women would use their votes to defend Anglo-Saxon civilization. Once Theodore Roosevelt had welcomed public women, it was overwhelmingly likely that women's vote would reenforce, not challenge, familiar social, economic, and religious solidarities.

The issue on which women's use of the vote appeared most conflicted was that which some feminists once, back in the early 1870s, had labeled "the marriage question," that is, sexuality and sexual relations in all their dimensions. A great reduction of freedom had quickly overtaken this realm. With Congressional passage of the Comstock laws of 1873, Americans lost their right to debate matters of profound concern to all who had sexual lives. Not only the articles, but discussions of birth control and contraception, were criminalized. During the same years, by action of most state legislatures, abortion, too, was criminalized.[120] Modern feminist historians sometimes tend to tell these stories as ones of outright loss for women, but women were far from united in opposition to these deprivations. Feminists not only were divided but never could, in their own debates, formulate a clear defense of sexual freedom. How could they have? The prefigurations of sexual freedom in the lives of a Fuller or a Stanton were really functions of personal character, of an almost privileged if not aristocratic sort, comparable to the freedoms enjoyed by such a real aristocrat as Cristina Belgioioso in Italy or that daughter of privilege in the Soviet Union, Alexandra Kollontai. Far more indicative was Gilman, with her certainty that before women could embark upon larger lives they must be freed from the need to use their sexuality for economic security. For Gilman, this meant a drastic reduction in sexuality. How could Gilman, without immense utopianism, have urged repeal of the Comstock laws and a return to legal abortions? And indeed, among all those advocates of "free love" portrayed by Sidney Ditzion in his breakthrough study of 1953,[121] many, perhaps most, meant by that free love the freedom of women (and men) to refuse any but freely chosen sexual relations. This might well mean less, not more, marital sex. It meant favor for liberalized divorce laws, and here in fact the existence of widespread popular wishes for more liberty won the start of slow reform. But otherwise the route toward freer sexuality still seemed to lie through haunted forests. Why might not contraception and abortion mean greater, not less, submission of women to men?

Change was under way. The logic generating greater freedom for the young to invent new forms of heterosexual sociality was at work in the democratic capitalistic marketplace. The economic wealth for supporting coed high schools and colleges continued to swell. The pleasure machines for thrilling new sociabilities were proliferating. Artists like Charles Dana Gibson were catching the materials for new gender icons. The Gay Nineties were real. But all these potentials for a fully eager exploitation of American abundance still had to confront the forces of resistance. It was feminism's ironic fate to let itself, even as it mobilized for its triumph in the Nineteenth Amendment to the Constitution, remain entangled with those forces of resistance. To have given up its fixation on suffrage in order to debate just what women ought to use their new votes for would have been to forsake feminism's basic strength. Sisterhood could not, it seemed, safely be given up until the competitive, lyric, acquisitive, emotional, expressive, and, above all, romantically individualistic ethos of the men who had excluded women from that ethos—the feminists' own fathers, husbands, brothers, and sons— had been extinguished. Let rational management, social equilibrium, communal harmony prevail. But this only meant that the force surging on toward the victory of 1920 had rendered itself vulnerable to disintegrative defeat. While Carrie Chapman Catt and the panoply of suffragist leaders pursued their course of political manipulation brilliantly, they were being transformed into anachronisms. Democratic culture, funded by capitalism's own unchecked transformations, was generating new manners and mores and institutions increasingly attractive to the new generation of women. Since women and feminists of the past, in their separate sphere, had for long been excluded from democratic capitalist culture, and had never understood it, the alienation was understandable.

9 Wonderland as Old Faith and New Reality

American Capitalism and Expressive Abundance: The 1920s

During World War I the federal government intervened vigorously in civilian life. It pursued a vigorous propaganda campaign. It coerced suspected persons and organizations. Late in 1917 it took over the economy. Controls were fastened on industry. Rationing was applied to food and fuel. Credit was controlled. Strikes were headed off. It was a remarkable display of the immense managerial competence that had been generated in American business and government. No less than in the Civil War, the much briefer achievements of 1918 attested to the potential for a nationally rationalized economy, a "political economy," in the United States.

Once again, the wartime example was dismissed for peacetime. Federal intervention into civilian lives persisted for a bit in the form of harsh interference with left-wing political life and sweeping roundups of persons variously suspected of "Bolshevism" and "anarchy," but with Democrats already in disarray under a sick President, there was no one to make the case for, at the least, managing the transition. Once escaped from a brief but sharp post-war inflation and recession, the triumphant Republicans, behind the façade of President Harding's slogan, "Less government in business and more business in government," undertook to stimulate business and resume the historic boom. The new Treasury secretary, Andrew Mellon, one of the richest men in the country, got the newfangled income tax reduced. The new Commerce secretary, Herbert Hoover, set about encouraging businessmen to think of their interests from the perspective of new trade associations. Although Harding had announced that the United States would stay out of Europe's affairs, he encouraged Hoover and the State Department to push foreign trade. The administration encouraged wide-open development of resources in the West. It discouraged labor unions by means of Justice Department injunctions. On the other hand, it watched without protest as Congress, strongly urged by labor unions themselves, cut off the historic flow of immigration in 1921 and 1924; immigration had been surging again once the war was over. Something like the

ethnic, religious, and racial proportions of the population were thus fixed for the first time in American history, not to be much changed until supplemented by the great Hispanic infusions half a century later. All the last great ethnic newcomers were set for their evolution through second and third-generation adaptation, culminating in the 1950s.

With far less need to produce for production, the economy of the 1920s found its prime stimulus in the vast consumers' market.[1] Production swelled of the new electric housekeeping machines, of radios, cameras, sporting goods, of records and victrolas, of ready-to-wear clothes in far greater variety. But the key product by far was the car. It was in the Twenties that Detroit became the quintessentially American industrial city. Instantly attractive to young men of all ages, cars renewed the American male's intrigue with machines. They spoke of competences at tinkering and of speed as exhilaration. One effect was to reanimate, not so much the old division between the spheres, but the old sense that the sexes were different beings with different fascinations. With most cars still having to be crank-started, women were at a disadvantage. At the same time, though, young women could go for rides in cars with young men, in a different sort of relationship than on bicycles, side by side. As General Motors' bright new vehicles drove Henry Ford's old black ones off the road, the car's status as family center grew. Cars incited vast new corollary industries. Apart from Akron and tires, as well as the manufacturers of highway equipment, of gas station fittings, and of fuel itself, cars prompted the mushrooming of roadside lodgings, of tourist attractions, of parks. The vacation on wheels was emerging as an expected right of family life in a fashion never possible in the age of horse and train.[2] Millions could not afford cars, but their deprivation did not prompt a politics of protest. As cars grew cheaper they seemed more accessible, one day, as a plausible expectation. Historians who collapse all this into "consumerism" have generally been unable to enrich our understanding of how the spreading culture of democratic affluence worked. The preeminent advertising man of the Twenties, Bruce Barton, for instance, had no demonstrable ability to induce people to want things they did not already want. A man of still vital religious background, Barton validated the new affluence by linking it with themes of personal vitality already affirmed in the liberal Protestantism of his father.[3] Far from manifesting some spreading passivity, vacations and the new family life generally registered a spreading readiness to pursue experience adventurously.

The most impressive demonstration of American capitalism's productivity appeared, not in things, however, but in institutions. Enrollment in colleges and universities soared in the 1920s. While already large indeed, by European standards, before the war, the great land-

grant universities of the Midwest and West grew toward truly democratic and even mass dimensions only after it. The famous private
colleges and universities grew, too, if not by as much. Not only was the
withholding from the labor market of the several million students
testimony to the ability of the economy to do without them. The educational facilities themselves—faculties, plants, libraries, laboratories,
by far the largest in the world—were expensive. But the American
economy could afford them. Their implications for culture dramatically expanded what had already been under way in the post-Civil War
growth of high schools to near ubiquity among middle-class young
people. High schools had been providing social space for young people
for decades, but on a severely restricted basis. High schools were day
affairs; students returned home to their parents each afternoon. Moreover, teachers oversaw students *in loco parentis*. The colleges of course
drew older students. Overwhelmingly the colleges and universities
were residential. Moreover, it was in the Twenties that, with the spreading professionalization of all disciplines, university faculties abandoned parental surrogacy in favor of their own research. College faculties were not far behind. Effectively, a whole new age cohort had been
granted a moratorium during which to explore tastes and experiences
on its own.[4] A much higher proportion of young men had left home
young to go to work in the nineteenth century; their sisters had stayed
home till they married. Now young people of both sexes mingled for
four years between home and marketplace, between home and marriage.

Almost by definition, as children of the favored middle classes, these
young people made new demands on the machinery of production for
consumption. They would have much to do with shaping the culture
of abundance. What was happening by no means testified to some
growing split between generations, let alone some generational conflict
or struggle. The deeper permissions had long been in the making. The
parents of the college students of the 1920s had grown up in the 1890s,
the "Gay Nineties." They were already clearly recording the demand
that the new industrial plant be put to the service of broad democratic
cultural elaboration (rather than, say, to the support of a new luxury
class, or to the pursuit of various vast public works, or to the creation
of a new military force). What the college cohort of the 1920s enjoyed,
their parents would have been happy to have had for themselves. They
paid their children's bills gladly. Their children would be more decisive
than they were in generating a distinctively modern culture.

Historians have had trouble writing about the Twenties. They have
not been able to resist viewing the decade in the lurid light cast by its
end. Since the Crash on Wall Street was so palpably the predestined

conclusion to an uncontrolled frenzy of speculation, was not the decade itself guilty? At the very least, since men of supposed probity and substance utterly failed to foresee the crash, were they not guilty of delusion and self-delusion? Elementary economics has charged that the Twenties collapsed because those who enjoyed it most would not share it enough: too many hard-working people got too little wages to keep the factories operating. More refined analysis shows that the story was hardly that simple. There were many soft spots during the boom, in construction and agriculture, for example. Accommodating Winston Churchill's determination to return Britain to the gold standard and diplomatic preeminence led to malign rigidities in the world money system. The German war debts took on a nightmarish circularity that no one could stop. And so on.[5] But the real problem for historians has been, not to identify causes for the Crash and for the Depression that followed it, but to understand the Twenties severed from the Crash, as though just possibly the decade had a life and meaning that were not swallowed up in the crash, let alone predestined to it.

The task has not been eased by powerful writers. In John O'Hara's *Appointment in Samarra*, the destruction of Caroline and Julian English's marriage proceeded within the shell of the first year of the Depression as though constituting its very meaning. Julian English's suicide—"It was *time* for him to die"[6]—temptingly summarized the triviality of the country club culture that had flowered like dandelions during the decade. Of course, writing in 1933, O'Hara wrote with the historian's advantage of hindsight. Far more intimidating has been Scott Fitzgerald's *The Great Gatsby*, arriving as the decade still had its most hectic years to run. While Fitzgerald visualized his hero, no less than Henry James his Christopher Newman half a century before, as the emblematic American, it was the 1920s boom that conspired in Gatsby's excess and in the notion of the Twenties as the end rather than the beginning of a culture. Able historians came to write books with such titles as *The Illusions of a Nation: Myth and History in the Novels of F. Scott Fitzgerald*. Yet ultimately the most telling aspect of *The Great Gatsby* was its freshness and vitality of language and art, and it was the teeming of such vitality, not only in all the "high" arts but in the new media of radio, records, and movies, in newspapers, in the fads and follies of pop fashion, in the successful combination of innovation and mass production of the pleasure machines, and in the adaptation of psychology, the social sciences, and theology to a variety of popular uses, that told something other than a moral tale of disintegration. The tendency of popular expression in the 1920s to run to extravaganza, all the way from the Ku Klux Klan and Al Capone's bootleg wars to the sports spectacles held in giant arenas, reaffirmed the spirit that had overtaken the popular theater a century before and that Constance Rourke was just then reconstructing. It was very much 1920s culture that Rourke had in mind as she argued that modern Americans could be confident they did indeed constitute an integral culture.

Moreover, just possibly it was in the 1920s that a beginning was being made on meeting that single greatest threat to national integrity, racial discrimination. Black artists had generated a music that would prove inexhaustible in its significance, not only for the black artists and their black audiences, but for growing numbers of white Americans (and quickly, white Europeans as well). The injustices of race would soon infest jazz and its popular variations as well, but the root of the music in the experiences of a race would remain undoubted. Popular music's growing significance for the self-definition of each new generation would draw race into themes of mainstream, middle-class social character, undermining and overriding the Jim Crow system of separate spheres. Linked with sexual abandon, primitivism, and even "barbarism," jazz would often enough be used to re-enforce racial stereotypes. O'Hara's Julian English would spend his last moments of life "screaming with jazz." But historians themselves one day would realize that they could not very well condescend totally to the Twenties when it had been the point of emergence of a major art from esoteric confinement into mainstream popular culture.[7]

The most remarkable book on the Twenties was written with the sounds of the Crash still reverberating. Paul Carter has suggested that the "enduring charm" of Frederick Lewis Allen's *Only Yesterday* inheres in its art of offering its readers what still seems "fresh and alive" rather than "frozen into history." In suggesting that "it is not too much to say that the Twenties were really the formative years of modern American society," George Mowry has offered the same clue to the book's enduring appeal.[8] In his most famous chapter, "A Revolution in Manners and Morals," Allen proffered the metaphor that would challenge all subsequent narrations. In that chapter it was clear that the revolution had special meaning for women. Starting out by observing a prototypical Mr. and Mrs. Smith at breakfast sometime in May 1919, Allen first noted that Mr. Smith would still look pretty much the same in 1930: "The movement of men's fashions is glacial."[9] But for Mrs. Smith, in 1919 a revolution impended. Still abjuring rouge, still wearing a veil, still showing no more than an ankle below the hem of her dress, still preparing for the beach with an outer tunic worn over her knitted swimsuit, plus of course long stockings, Mrs. Smith in 1919 still much resembled her older prewar sister. She attended no beauty parlors. She did not smoke or drink. But within months, by 1920, she would begin shortening her skirts. In two years, the weight of clothing worn by a woman was cut in half; by the mid-1920s, by two-thirds. Textile-producing capitalists suffered. Corset manufacturers went bankrupt. No amount of advertising, no salesman's guile mattered. Cosmetic manufacturers soon were making millions. Long hair fell onto busy barbers' floors.

The symbolism of all this was at once powerful and ambiguous. Charlotte Perkins Gilman herself had wanted to relieve women from the burden of their nineteenth-century garb. But she was not pleased by the new modes. She had dressed the citizens of *Herland* in light tunics, at once functional, deindividualizing and nonprovocative.[10] By no means were the new costumes of the 1920s without provocative and individualizing intent. By no means was their point simply convenience. Inevitably, historical revisionism would blur the sharp focus of the story Allen told of a few years after 1919. Valerie Steele and others have argued cogently that, on the one hand, the old Victorian styles were by no means intended simply to conceal and repress. After all, they had often exaggerated women's "secondary" sex characteristics. The bustle was for display. Far from constituting simply defensive armor, corsets had been worn because they made women feel "pretty and charming."[11] On the other hand, the flapper's costume could not be traced to some American revolution; as body type and costume, the flapper had emerged from the inner logic of fashion, still headquartered in Paris. In fashion as in literature, in the view of Harold Bloom, some environing set of social conditions mattered far less than the previous style.

Still, while fashion itself may have approached the condition of an autonomous flux, unconnected with anything outside itself, the changes wrought between 1919 and 1922 were definitive. The experience would be shared in all Western nations. It was in the United States, however, during the Twenties, that the symbolism of the flapper would be given democratic force, notably in the movies. The central theme was not, despite Gilman's fears, provocation and flaunting, but demystification. The female body ceased to be an object of reverence, awe, and fear. Dating from 1920, the first Miss America contests saw young women presenting their bodies like objects as any producer might present a creation. Bodies were for their possessors to control. The early Mack Sennett Bathing Beauty movies made an unprecedented point: female bodies could be linked with comedy, visual puns, play. That women by the time of the Great Crash were freer and more in control of themselves than in 1919 was part of the revolution Allen described. Paula Fass has made the point in her study of college girls of the 1920s learning how to use lipstick, smoke, and conduct themselves on dates. Far from giving themselves over to heedless hedonism, they were learning a new etiquette, a better etiquette because it was more honest and because it aspired more to new experience.[12]

Through jazz, the revolution in manners and morals would link race and sex. The combination, explosive, bitterly resisted, invincibly fascinating, would help guarantee that decades could pass before its potential would begin to be plumbed. This would be part of what it meant to say that the Twenties were the beginning of modern America. But it was possible even in the 1920s for writers to realize that new kinds of stories were waiting to be told about men and women together. Love had rarely been a tragedy in American imagination. In *The Great Gatsby* and *Tender Is the Night* Fitzgerald told American tragedies. Henry Carey had never been ready to believe that the great American boom, properly superintended, could possibly lead to tragedies. That was because Carey had deplored and fought individualism. The economically integrated local community, succoring and enfolding, would extract from all individuals the poison of their aloneness. Tocqueville, on the other hand, had never imagined any relation between man and woman important enough to merit tragedy. In the 1920s the separate spheres were crumbling with breathtaking rapidity. Young men and women were learning their new etiquettes as fast as possible. A Fitzgerald realized that some of them might learn that no etiquette, no mere social code, could tame awakened hearts.

Women's Share in Defending the Faith: The 1930s

Herbert Hoover and the Republican Party were not quite such blind and feckless entities as a hostile electorate would soon find them. The Smoot-Hawley Tariff of 1930, effectively destabilizing world trade, was indeed a blind and terrible act, but it represented a pattern less than an incapacity. In the first year of the economic decline, when few men believed it would prove more than another of capitalism's evidently inevitable business cycles, Hoover did sensible things. By cutting some taxes, beefing up public works expenditures, and easing credit, he, a Keynesian before Keynes, tried to stimulate the economy. Whether it was wise of him to urge businessmen to keep both prices and wages up is not as clear; had they obeyed, some of the "natural" processes by which the business cycle reversed itself might have been inhibited. Unfortunately, those processes took place anyway, without reversal. By 1931 a deflationary collapse impended, now fed by the disaster threatening to take the banks of Germany under. If they went, so would go the banks of France and Britain, and then America's. No one had won World War I after all. Hoover's grant of a moratorium to both Germany and the ex-Allies was intelligent, but too little and too late. Under the financial pressures, world trade disintegrated; each nation was left to itself. *Sauve qui peut.*

Whether Hoover and his party could have done better in trying to head off the world depression has never been plausibly argued. Marxist analysis has been irrelevant: further animadversions upon why the revolutionary moment failed to arrive in America has less to do with economics than with politics. That Hoover's "Keynesian" stimulants had been too mild was not made obvious by the failure of the New Deal's stronger stimulus. Besides, in 1932 Hoover had increased the dosage through his Reconstruction Finance Corporation, which had not worked either. Ultimately, the argument against the Hoover administration's efforts had it that the government's money was being put into the wrong hands. It was not so much that the hands that should have had it were those that needed it most, although it was true that Hoover's apparent preference for banks and institutions over individuals added a reputation for callousness to one for stupidity, an idea confirmed for good when he proved willing to feed farm animals but not farm people. Hoover's point was simple: the dole can corrupt people; it cannot corrupt horses or institutions. But the institutions were people too, and these, the bankers and businessmen who got the RFC's loans, were often quite rationally unable to see, in light of the disaster around them, the point of building more plants that would then join those already idle.[13]

Soon Franklin Roosevelt and his New Deal were getting money into the hands of several million people who did badly need it. Multitudes of Americans had lived on government checks before, but never simply as "relief." This was the New Deal's radical departure. Demonstrating administrative agilities not even the Bolsheviks had exhibited in their own days of improvisatory crisis, the New Dealers dispensed their alphabet soup—AAA, CCC, PWA, WPA, and more—to millions in need of it. Like his cousin before him, Franklin Roosevelt was able, as Hoover was not, to persuade democratic publics that what was happening to them was within the competence of energetic men of good will to fix. Whether he and his men ever quite imagined that they knew what was going on in the economy has never been clear. Having declared that fear was what must be feared most, FDR had nonetheless gone on to strike fear into those who presumably made more difference to the economy than anyone else, the New York bankers and big-time industrialists whom he stigmatized as "economic royalists." Then, in 1937, as the economy seemed to have been restarted at last, the New Dealers cut government money off, as though inflation, not deflation, had become the menace. Promptly the country fell back into another bad recession.

By the campaign of 1940, issues of war and peace, of production for defense, and possibly of war itself, had taken over. Had the Depression been ended by then? Again, only refined speculation can answer. The war years made clear what the New Deal had not been able to: The American economic plant, in the widest sense, had all along been capable of producing far more than it had ever produced before, far more than it had in 1929, let alone in 1940. What was required was political consensus. That consensus existed after Pearl Harbor. Roosevelt brought Republican Wall Street lawyers and Republican businessmen to Washington to run the economic war program. They succeeded.

Nonetheless, Roosevelt's greatest achievements were political. Probably the most crucial one came with some reluctance on Roosevelt's part. Labor was admitted to the marketplace as a major player. Roosevelt had no high opinion of the leaders of organized labor that he knew. He did not want strife but collaboration on the industrial front, and opening the way for organizing workers in the great nonunion basic industries was no obvious way to labor peace. But the Wagner Act (1935) was passed, and American labor entered its new era with the successful efforts of the CIO. In postwar years organized labor would enter into near-Saltsjöbodenlike negotiations with organized industry, the result being the creation by the 1950s of by far the most prosperous blue-collar workers in the world. Often of second or third-generation ethnic background, usually Catholic in faith, these workers, beholden to the New Deal, would constitute, in their well-provided-for families, the completion of the immigrant drive toward social reconstitution, the lost homes of Europe reconstituted in America. But, though beholden to the New Deal historically, blue-collar union labor would have no more than practical commitment to the Democrats. By the very fact that labor won much of its gains by its own efforts at bargaining, the idea of government as a perennial and necessary part of the economic process was veiled. Labor's test of future governments would be simple: were labor's wages, were labor's families safe?[14]

For others, the heritage of the New Deal would be simplicity itself. Having failed to share the 1920s prosperity, farmers had come to seem an intractable problem. The New Deal took the most direct step: it offered direct government support. The paradoxical result for the political future was that this support came to seem untouchable once Thomas E. Dewey paid in defeat in 1948 for the Republicans' supposed intention to reduce farm supports. After that, the farmers were safe and could abandon the old New Deal coalition whenever the time seemed right. Meanwhile blacks experienced paradox unmediated. While the New Deal never did anything for them directly, and while their historic enemies, Southern whites, constituted a major element in the New Deal, blacks nonetheless forsook the party of Lincoln for the Democrats in 1936 and fifty years thereafter. Southern blacks found the trickles seeping down from the Triple-A's program in the South far better than the nothing they had known before. Northern urban blacks found some crumbs in the WPA. Black women working as domestics for rich anti-Roosevelt matrons funded Father Divine's Heavens that fed and sheltered starving black men. For blacks, the basic hope was to become part of a political coalition that would consider their interests as legitimate as anyone else's.[15]

At no point were women, or any particular sector of women, thought of as a part of the New Deal coalition. The great women of the New Deal—Eleanor Roosevelt, Frances Perkins, Molly Dewson—all persisted in their efforts at protection for women at work.[16] The Depression rendered their basic perspective still more cogent: women worked because they had to, and they should have the help of the state. The Depression also brought out further the contradiction inherent in their outlook; women were attractive as workers because they were cheap, but protection would make them more expensive. With considerable symbolic force, the New Dealers' discouragement of two government workers in one family (a policy introduced under Hoover) made plain their essential vision, of a work force of men paid enough to support a family. The millions of unemployed included women, but the focus of policy and imagination was upon the man in the breadlines, the man selling apples in the street, the man riding the freights for the Central Valley, Florida, the wheatfields. In some communities married women schoolteachers were fired. As Lois Scharf has told us, organized women's groups monitored New Deal legislation.[17] They protested against lower wage scales written into the NRA codes. They urged repeal of the 1932 "married persons clause." They searched out and protested inequities built into the new Social Security system. At the same time they pointed out, to those urging women to step back in favor of men, that few women workers competed with men, since the overwhelming majority of women workers worked in gender ghettos, poorly paid and dead-end. Here and there in some sectors, as Winifred Wandersee has noted, some middle-class women did find jobs to supplement their husbands' salaries, presumably in an effort to keep up with the new higher standards of expectation generated in the 1920s.[18]

Most women were on the defensive in the 1930s, but there was no way the decade was going to be conceived as peculiarly hard for women.

It was hard for men, too. Perhaps more distinctly than in any decade in American history, men and women shared directly, but what they shared would be of no particular advantage to women. At the same time, from noneconomic perspectives, the Depression appeared to favor women. Studying Muncie ten years after their first visit, Helen and Robert Lynd found women's morale higher than men's.[19] The pressures of unemployment, underemployment, and lowered income called on virtues still traditional to most women. They could scrimp, patch, make do, keep the household going, hold the family together. It was anthropologist Margaret Mead's impression, upon returning to the United States in 1939 after eight years in the South Seas, that Americans had been hurt badly by the Depression, hurt not so much in pocketbook as in self-image, self-confidence, faith in themselves. She meant the men:

A whole generation of fathers have faced their growing children with bowed heads because they had somehow failed; a whole generation of children have grown up under the shadow of that failure, believing in many cases that someone—the Federal Government, or somebody—should do something about it, anxious for a panacea which would assuage the guilt and unhappiness of their parents or anxious for some scapegoat on which to vent their resentment.[20]

In Mead's view, while it had obviously helped people, the New Deal— a "government for the people, but often not by the people"—had not really addressed this deeper damage. (Actually, Mead felt damage to men had been inflicted earlier, too, in the Twenties, in the national failure to accept world leadership after 1919.) One result was that fathers began to cease providing sons with adequate models. A mother was left to cope with preparing her son by herself:

[She] looks across at her husband, belt unbuttoned, slumped comfortably, reading the sports news. He hardly ever gets angry, doesn't half stand up for his rights, could have had a raise years ago, but didn't like to start a row about it. If her small Jimmy, standing with toes turned in, looking very small in his new overalls, is going to get along in this world and be more successful than his dad—and for what else did she bear him?—he'll have to be a good deal tougher than his dad, who lets himself be pushed around. Which means that if she thought in theoretical terms, she would say, "His inheritance of aggression isn't enough. If he follows his father, he won't be strong enough."[21]

From this perspective, any call for equality for women had been rendered irrelevant. One of the salient sociological features of the Depression decade was a negative: the troubles of the time provoked no religious revival. Millions of Americans, both men and women, though far more men than women, were uprooted by the Depression, but for even more millions there was shelter from the storm, not in the New Deal, not in politics, not in God, often not even in communities, but in families. While tens of thousands of Americans retreated from the cities back to rural homesteads, perhaps the supreme symbol of the age would be John Steinbeck's Joads, picking up roots for California with Ma Joad as the heart of the family.

As the Republican Party was reduced to national minorityhood by the Depression, as the New Deal elicited a majority coalition, women came to have less, not more, access to and reliable association with parties and politics. The potential for women within the Republican Party, as old as its birth in 1854 as heir of abolitionism, a potential renewed for brief life after the Civil War, then renewed again with Theodore Roosevelt's progressivism—a potential founded ultimately on the solid fact that the GOP found its basic strength where feminism had found its, among the Protestant middle classes—once again shriveled. Reduced to its heartland, the Ohio-to-Iowa Midwest, the GOP became more tribal, more defined by the ancient local culture of town and country rather than of city and corporation. This was indeed the culture of woman's sphere, but no longer a culture where woman's sphere might expand, evolve, deepen itself. The Protestant Republican heartland had become defensive, its women no longer encouraged into social housekeeping. Moreover, as the tribal party faced its minorityhood, the national party's attempt to escape irrelevance offered no better prospects to active women, since that meant the revitalization of the East, of Wall Street, of banking and an international outlook, symbolized in the candidacies of Wendell Willkie and Thomas E. Dewey. This wing of the party too had little interest in a League of Women Voters or a Professional Women's Federation.

Meanwhile, as the younger heirs of the suffrage struggle moved on to Albany, then Washington, they generated no heirs of their own. As Susan Ware has shown us, the peak of women's participation in the New Deal, such as it was, was reached by 1936. After that, the interest of women at large in the New Deal and the Democrats was simply as wives and daughters of the farmers, the labor union members, the urban blacks, and others who made up the New Deal's coalition of interest groups. The stronger the ethnic coloring of the New Deal grew, the clearer it was that the New Deal meant mostly the restoration of family stability, uniting men and women, and nothing for women in particular. Here was the fundamental reason why the leading New Dealers, liberals and reformers though they were, felt no compulsion or guilt over equality for women. That would have been to single women out. Something else was of far greater urgency. In sum, in contrast to the long economic boom, Depression and New Deal together induced, not deliberately but as by a kind of osmotic suction, the reabsorption of women back into the prepolitical, molecular realms of life, helpmeets again, often much more directly, to their men, far more than sisters in their separate sphere.[22]

Gathering the Fruits of Faith: A Home for Everyone

With her sense that the Depression had badly damaged the American psyche, Margaret Mead very much hoped the war could be seized upon to restore morale. Pearl Harbor had been another shock, leaving the American people "like children afraid of the dark," wanting "Washington to tell them what to do." But, Mead felt sure, it would not be enough for each American to be told how many bonds to buy or how much to produce. Each American "with the people of his town or his township, his block or his union local or his ship," must demand the right to do more, to use his own imagination and devotion, his own initiative, as well. Americans must participate deeply. "Out of their local brains and guts, out of their hearts and purposes," they must know that "they themselves are forging the weapons of war."[23]

It never occurred to Franklin Roosevelt that the United States might fight World War II this way, an expression of Henry Carey's grass-roots populistic capitalism. When he called Henry Stimson from New York to Washington to head the War Department, he was recognizing the headquarters of the economy in the capital of corporate finance, not in the spirit of the grass roots.[24] The men who ran production in wartime were chieftains of the national corporations and law offices. They succeeded. For all the restless shifting of lines of command, of War Production Board into Office of War Mobilization, of bond drives into tax increases, a prodigy of production was achieved. Factory production doubled in the war years. With 15 million men inducted into the armed services, Depression era unemployment soon ebbed away. Women went to work, 5 million of them signing on from 1941.[25] Though many replaced men in various tertiary jobs, and many helped swell the ranks of the federal bureaucracy, many also went into direct war production. Rosie the Riveter and others helped build bombers, cargo ships, ammunition and machine guns, as well as produce uniforms, K-rations, medical kits. Still, by comparison with Russian women, American women did most of their work at home. Not many more than one-third of all women took jobs during the war. The figure testified, not to women's need or wish, but to the immense capacity of the American industrial system. Drawing on the facilities left idle during the Depression, the system was capable of rapid expansion of more facilities in the last great surge of American "production for production." So vast did the system's capacity prove to be, when properly stimulated, that the war years did not require civilians to scrimp. While rationing, particularly of gasoline (to save rubber), caused endless irritation, Americans of working-class background especially found the war and returning prosperity simultaneous. The postwar boom began before Pearl Harbor. Marriages soared between 1940 and 1943, partly of course because of the draft, but partly also because of the end to the Depression.[26]

Little if any of all this manifested the spirit of popular identification with the war effort so urgently recommended by Mead. In the elections of 1942, millions did not vote. Many, at war work far from home, were disenfranchised by the residency requirements that American states defended as a remnant of local autonomy. Many, as the bite of the Depression eased, felt no prompting. The election was a triumph for the two basic tribes of Americans least affronted by either Depression or war, the small-town Midwest Republicans in their heartland, and the white Southern Democrats. Their control of Congress after 1942 effectively declared what the President would announce explicitly only later, that the New Deal was dead. That Franklin Roosevelt failed to defend the New Deal during the war by no means implied that, had he chosen, he could have saved it. The New Deal majorities of 1934–40 had been based on negatives. With the greatest negative, the Depression itself, removed, the stability of the New Deal coalition came into question. It would not follow automatically that the Republican Party would benefit. But, far from evoking that kind of national restoration of self-confidence for which Mead hoped, the war intensified political division. Implicitly, the resurgent anti-New Dealers of 1942 wanted only one thing from the war: victory. Roosevelt played into their hands by subordinating all other political issues, including the survival of the New Deal, to that end. He knew better. He knew that the very war itself had rooted in the failure of the United States and its allies to concert a supervision of the world after the victory of 1918. For the United States to return home once again, after victory over Nazis and imperialist Japanese, would compound disaster. But Roosevelt never found the right words. We must "say frankly," Margaret Mead urged, "that we are fighting in order to get the chance to set the world in the kind of order that we want,"[27] but she meant something more substantial, less ethereal than the Four Freedoms, something less implausible than the Four Policemen, a commitment less wishful and shallow than that for the United Nations. As it was, the politics of wartime told unambiguously that the wish of most Americans was to get the war over with as fast as possible in order to project the wartime boom into peacetime.

The war itself redounded to the prestige of men as soldiers, in reality and in popular image, in veterans' organizations, and as an age cohort crucial for the start-up of the postwar economy. In Russia, World War II confirmed the absolute necessity for the universal participation of women in the workplace. In Italy, wartime disaster, aside from confirming the absolute necessity of the family, also provided women the myth of the Resistance, in which women shared. Sweden's women knew neither gain nor loss from their country's neutrality. On a comparative basis, one might well conclude that, all things considered, American women won less from the war than either Italian or Russian women, while undergoing a far more hectic drama than women in Sweden. They had been left to muddle through. For all the quasi-official summons to war work, neither federal nor local governments had come forward with day-care centers to ease the burdens of working mothers; enhancement of medical and health care was erratic; certainly provision of housing for workers in wartime boom towns had been lacking. One student of the period, William Chafe, has observed: "With strong, determined leadership, a solution might have been found." The real problem was that any solution would have contradicted the terms of the problem. What most Americans wanted from World War II was, first, victory, and, second, a perpetuation of the prosperity it had already brought. They did not want a changed America. Margaret Mead's call for a popular mobilization had in no way implied some radical rearrangement of gender roles. But Mead's insistent attention to motherhood did imply a new national consciousness of the importance of mothering to the reproduction—or revivification—of historic American national character.[28] Only mothers fully aware of the war and of the postwar need for an American commitment to remake the world could do their job properly. No merely sentimental mothering would do. Motherhood focused on the national task did imply a symbiosis between family and politics, mothering and policy, private and public. None of this had been any part of wartime management either.

Ideas about national planning were rejected with ideological passion by the Congress, but Congress gladly collaborated with the administration and the war boards in averting a postwar slump.[29] A clear pattern emerged: postwar prosperity would be sought through stimulating consumption. Housing offered the chance for a vast synergy. With cheap mortgages prompting sprawling housing projects on the peripheries of the great cities, the need for cars, for gasoline, for concrete and steel for the roads to accommodate the cars carrying about the new suburbanites would compound. A decision to let the railroads, worked to exhaustion during the war, go unrepaired followed logically. Invited to pass an act declaring full employment a national responsibility, Congress flinched, but a G.I. Bill passed in 1944 offered not only housing subsidies to veterans but also subsidies for education that would keep many of them off the job market for at least a few years. Women workers, who had been encouraged to think of their war jobs as "for the duration" only, were encouraged to return home. Many did not wish to, and after a few years it would become clear that the postwar boom would accommodate a greater number of women at work than in 1940. But in 1945 Congress refused to pass an equal-wage act, mostly out of a sense that women workers would be competitive with the returning veterans. The G.I. Bill did provide men an advantage over women: few women were veterans. It also provided white men an advantage over blacks: blacks were a lower proportion of veterans and fewer black veterans were in a position to make use of G.I. loans or educational opportunities.

The war stored up some problems. The divorce rate spiked, at over 18 percent of the number of new marriages in 1946, compared to just over 14 percent the year before, and under 14 percent the year after.[30] But the marriage rate also spiked in 1946. The United States had the highest marriage rate of any country in the world from 1944 to 1948. Economist Richard Easterlin has pointed out that the Depression-born babies of the 1930s had an advantage in the postwar economy.[31] They were few and thus in high demand. Young men found jobs and careers easy to get in the 1950s; they found getting married economically easy. They became the fathers of the baby boom. However, the marriage surge of 1944–48 could not yet have registered the impact of the postwar boom, which did not get securely under way until 1947. The young marrieds of 1944–48 were still 1920s babies. What the early marriage boom bespoke was a set of pent-up expectations, nursed through Depression and war, never surrendered. Young women born in the 1930s would enjoy the finest marriage market. Relatively scarce, and still marrying young men somewhat older than themselves, they would enjoy the larger number of young men born in the late 1920s as suitors. It was this match that impelled the boom of marriage based on great expectations rather than on experienced realities.

The economic realities of the fifteen years after 1945 were by no means in the nature of an American economic miracle.[32] The miracle had already been wrought during the war. Yet a first and fundamental task was achieved: no depression. The recessions that punctuated the epoch did not begin to resemble the 1930s. A disturbing peak of 7.6 percent in unemployment early in 1950 fell off to 2 percent late in 1953, primarily because of the Korean War, but while there were later peaks of over 6 percent, inflation had overtaken unemployment as the prime concern of policy makers by the last of the 1950s. Yet the unemployment figures contained another disturbing trend: each bottom in the rate rose higher, from 3 percent to over 4 percent, then to over 5 percent in the recession of 1959–60. Moreover, the rate of growth in the gross national product in the first years of the 1950s fell off in the last, from a little under 5 percent to a bit more than 2 percent. The rate for the decade, 3 percent, fell well below the rate during the 1920s, 4.7 percent, and below that of the forty years before, 3.7 percent. An emergent bargain seemed to be in process: slower growth in return for more stability, a smoothing of the business cycle at the expense of rapid surges. The stability drew on the heritage of the 1930s and 1940s: government contributed more to the economy. As a percentage of all employees, federal workers grew little; two million were added to the rolls of state and local government, however, primarily owing to the expansion of the suburbs. The federal government's contribution came in money spent for the military. Here were shock absorbers built into the system. The Republican administrations of the 1950s showed no particular commitment to a deliberate policy along these lines. While the money managers held the reins tight, Dwight Eisenhower and his advisers held to the "classic" concept that that budget is best which is, first, balanced and, second, least. The fact that the Republicans were not able to balance or reduce the federal budget as they wished meant that their administrations did prove a stabilizing and, moderately, a stimulative influence, but it also meant that the 1950s saw still further shriveling in any New Deal start on social welfare. Three expansions of the New Deal–originated Social Security system were passed, for political, not economic, reasons, but further discussion of pensions, as well as of health and sickness insurance, paid vacations, unemployment insurance, job-retraining programs, education-equalization programs, maternity leaves and benefits—all the staples of European political debate—were left to private bargaining by labor unions.

World War II saw a second wave of successful labor organizing, following that of 1937–39.[33] Organized manufacturing workers achieved a peak in real wages in 1944 that they would not surpass before 1955. After the New Deal and wartime surges, union members constituted about 35 percent of all workers (farms excepted) in 1945. Their proportion held steady, then began to decline, to about 33 percent in 1960. By 1955 or so the united AFL-CIO had for all practical purposes ceased trying to organize new workers. Unionization confronted not only the Taft-Hartley Act of 1947. A South determined to protect its regional edge in low pay made discouraging territory. With fewer large plants to unionize, costs went up in trying to proselytize in small enterprises. But, most daunting of all, the growing numbers of new workers were to be found in locations never penetrated by the classic craft and industrial unions—in offices, in government, in service enterprises of all sorts. More and more of the new workers were women, and women had always been hard to unionize even in industry. Only one woman in seven in the labor force belonged to a union in 1958. (Since most unions practiced racial exclusion, black men, too, were left outside.) In effect, by the 1950s union labor comprised a kind of elite of blue-collar males in steel, automobiles, the chemical, rubber, and electrical industries. Its significance for women was plain, for it was here that the family wage, with growing fringe benefits, constituted a standard unmatched in the world. Blue-collar families were partaking of abundance. But their position was precarious. The elite workers of the 1950s had bene-fited from their low numbers; the younger ones among them in partic-ular were able to marry young in near-assurance of high wages. Such labor scarcity would not last long, however, as the first baby boomers entered the market in the mid-1960s. Moreover, the high family wage of the 1950s echoed America's continuing dominance in the postwar world economy, but those wages constituted a heavy charge against the costs of production, which offered opportunity to low-wage foreign competitors. The labor unions themselves would be no help. Increas-ingly isolated as one interest group among many, they would find few natural allies for a broad political movement. For the new workers, the labor unions' increasingly defensive posture, protective of past gains rather than alert to coming challenges, offered little. Indeed, by the end of the 1950s it was reasonably clear that the surge of baby boomers destined to enter the labor market soon could not be accommodated at the decade's low rate of economic expansion or at the high level of wages enjoyed by the elite industrial workers. Thus the new workers, with women increasingly numerous among them, would not find much strength or guidance from labor unions. They would be on their own.

It was in the 1950s also, perhaps more than at any time since the 1880s, that the two major political parties lost autonomy.[34] While each twice nominated men—Dwight Eisenhower and Adlai Stevenson—of notably national, nonparochial status, neither could assemble an ef-fective new majority. Trying to hold as much of Franklin Roosevelt's New Deal coalition as possible, the Democrats needed more poor peo-ple, but in the case of the most conspicuous, the more they were pursued the more dangerous they were to the old coalition. White Southern Democrats in particular were not enthusiastic about the slowly grow-ing attention of Northern liberals to blacks, whether as voters in the South or as working men in the North. On the other hand, the Repub-licans, although they could nominate and elect a hero above politics, could provide him a Republican Congress only once in four tries. The party could expect to benefit only from the crumbling of the Democrats' inherited majority, and in order to hold itself ready to do so had to avoid major new departures in policy for the national economy. Both parties thus were likely to be impelled far more by their inheritances from the past than by any effort to analyze portents in the present for the future. The Republicans would proceed as though the long historic boom had been only temporarily checked and had been resumed, perhaps at a more measured pace, but all the more surely because of that. The Democrats would assume the boom needed the stimulus of justice, mediated by their periodic intervention. That the United States might not any longer be in more or less complete control of its own economic destiny was an idea that attracted no one.

Destabilization and Women's Surge into the Marketplace

In 1960 John F. Kennedy promised to get the nation moving again. The razor's edge by which he won over an unattractive opponent suggested that no broad consensus existed for such an effort. But Kennedy's chosen economists, drawn from the most prestigious university departments in the country, read the signs of the 1950s: slowing growth, rising unemployment, rising inflation.[35] Kennedy brought with him the standard Northern Democrat's concern about unemployment. He had plans for expanded spending on defense, particularly to escape the Eisenhower administration's undue emphasis on nuclear weapons because they were cheap. Many of his advisers urged large expenditures on social goods—health, education, culture, recreation, and moderation of the slowly but surely growing ranks of the poor. A vigorous growing economy was needed. With a second tax cut in 1964, following the first in 1962, strong growth persisted into 1966, for the longest and best expansion in the twentieth century. The great American boom seemed to have been reignited.

But hardly were the 1960s over before a Republican president, Richard Nixon, felt he had to intervene in the economy in ways that would have been anathema to the party's orthodoxies of the past: he set prices, fixed wages, and took the dollar off the international gold standard. By the late 1960s the international monetary system set afoot by the Bretton Woods Conference in 1944 was beginning to stagger. That system had worked through the years of the United States' overwhelming postwar dominance in world markets. Those years were coming to an end. Basically, the cause was America's postwar success.[36] The huge balance-of-payments deficits destabilizing the monetary system followed from prosperous America's heavy imports, which in their turn were a major part of the surging recovery in the economies of Western

Europe and Japan. So long as the United States held to some reasonable degree of free trade, those newly recovered economies were in a position to begin to outcompete basic American industries. Similarly, although the oil shock of 1973 had roots in American foreign policy, its larger source was in the immense appetite for oil generated in the Western and Japanese economies. When circumstances invited, the oil producers in the Middle East were able to boost prices once again, in 1979, to unimagined levels. In the United States, organized labor in basic industry particularly felt the temptation to close American markets; a Trade Act of 1974, while holding the way open for new international negotiations to reduce tariffs, also cleared the way for "quotas," "trigger prices," "trade adjustment assistance," and other disguises for renewed protection. The Democratic Party was whipsawed. Organized labor had been one of its major constituents since 1936. It could hardly watch passively as gates to historic South Chicago steel mills swung shut, as auto workers in Detroit saw their neighbors driving cars made by auto workers in Japan, as the smell of rubber vanished from the air of Akron. Yet the free market had been an essential part of the party's foreign policy since 1944, and besides, cheap imports pleased a vast array of consumers just as important to Democratic successes. When a mid-1970s recession ebbed, the Carter administration revived the evangel of free trade, but it ended in a paroxysm of skyrocketing inflation, interest rates, and unemployment, echoed by the intransigent hostage crisis in Iran. The economy's vicissitudes strongly suggested that the United States was becoming a more reactive, than active, power.

The new Republican president, Ronald Reagan, conceded none of this. Echoing Kennedy, he proposed to get the economy surging again, by means, on the one hand, of a massive tax cut and, on the other, a massive increase in government spending, specifically for armaments.[37] Presumably, the deficits and consequent hyperinflation this combination seemed to promise would be averted by the surge in economic activity, on which a lower tax rate would yield higher returns. This theory was excused from testing, however, by a more traditional assault on inflation, a deep recession, precipitated by the Federal Reserve Board's grim restraint on the money supply. Once inflation had been wrung out, the lineaments of a new economy became clearer. While taking steps, such as quotas on auto imports from Japan, to avert total collapse of smokestack America, the Reagan administration rejected protection as a policy in favor of impelling the national economy ever faster into its postindustrial exploitation of new technologies and the postwar growth of metropolitan suburbs. This was a straightforward gamble that the energies of the huge baby-boom cohorts would flow into multitudinous new small-scale enterprises and swell the ranks of communications and finance. By 1986 the verdict was not in on economic Reaganism. A low-inflation, low-interest-rate environment had been substituted for the high-inflation, high-interest-rate environment that had seemed about to burn out of control under Carter. But an official unemployment rate of 7 percent refused to decline; large numbers of young farmers were being driven to bankruptcy by debt; commodity producers from oil to copper were faced with a world glut; and the stability of banks, from small farm-town institutions to Manhattan goliaths implicated in the woes of Mexico, was being maintained as much by positive thinking as by assets. The postrecession recovery had slowed, by late 1986, almost to a standstill. American statesmen found themselves asking Japan and West Germany to provide the stimulation once considered a task the United States alone could fulfill.

All this was accompanied by a transformation in the job market. The baby boomers initiated a surge in college enrollments from the mid-1960s. Young women enrolled as often as young men. For reasons demographers and social historians will be long in teasing out, young people began to manifest a shifting ethos. Demography alone spelled a marriage squeeze. The first cohort of female baby boomers far outnumbered the pool of males three to five years older. These young women were entering the marriage market by the late 1960s. The last cohort of male baby boomers would well outnumber the pool of females three to five years younger. Marriage market thus linked with job market in encouraging baby boomers to defer or to forgo marriage. They would improvise a new kind of private life, adapted to the unmarried in their twenties and early thirties. The numbers of doctors, lawyers, and other professionals grew, impelled not by demand but by supply. Young women became an ever-growing percentage of practitioners.[38]

Between 1973 and 1983, women's degrees in computer and information services rose from 15 percent of the total to over 36 percent, in data processing from 13 percent to 41 percent. Women graduating with degrees in banking and finance rose from not quite 4 percent of the total to nearly 33 percent. Women were getting 63 percent of the degrees in advertising in 1983, 62 percent in journalism, just about 50 percent in personnel management and slightly less in accounting, all in a dramatic rise during the previous decade. Women made up 35 percent of the delegates elected to a Small Business Conference held in Washington, D.C., in 1986. Women entrepreneurs were particularly notable in the business service sector. Women remained absent from the board rooms of old-line industrial America, but in banks and law firms their advance could be measured as a function of their first surge into the professional schools. In effect, for the first time in American history the economy saw a significant number of women on their own, earning high salaries and promotions, and even, slowly but surely, going into business on their own. Tocqueville would have recognized a revolution. Their most conspicuous impact, however, appeared not in economic, let alone political, but in cultural terms. As one-half of affluent professional and business couples, they shared in modeling a style of life far beyond the standards of the suburbs, intimately linked with the new technology.[39]

Most of the new jobs generated in the postindustrial economy were not high-paying, not full of promise for the future.[40] In offices, in shopping malls, in clinics, in art galleries, in travel and insurance agencies, in hospitals and cleaning establishments, jobs paid far less than a family wage. Such jobs were hardly expressive of aspirations to success and independence. The wives of unemployed blue-collar union men sought work out of plain necessity. Young working families required two wages to make up one family wage. For women, this new job market intersected with other social trends. After its 1946 spike, the divorce rate had descended to a twenty-year plateau, but then started to rise again after 1968, until divorce became the prospect for half those getting married. Logicians might argue whether women's work led to divorce more often than divorce led to women's work, but the results were evident. The numbers of women—divorced, never married, widowed—raising children on their own earnings grew steadily. The "feminization of poverty" had as one consequence the impoverishment of children. The United States had long exhibited the greatest disparity of incomes among Western industrial nations, the top one percent owning an immensely disproportionate share of the national wealth, the bottom 10 to 20 percent grossly less. As the wealth of the wealthy swelled in the 1970s and 1980s, the want of the poor increased, and the proportions of these poor who were women and children also increased.[41] The wives of rich men had always led vastly different lives from the wives of poor men, but the contrasts in the new economy were still more striking. While there were yet few women wealthy from their own enterprise, the new generation of successful women were quite unlike the wealthy wives of the past. It would challenge the ingenuity of ideologists to compose theories according to which they resembled, simply by being women, the struggling single mothers and impoverished divorcees more than they did their young male counterparts.[42]

To a feminism committed to opportunity, every "first" for a woman had been an occasion of celebration: the first doctor, lawyer, merchant, chief; the first head of an advertising agency; the first partner in a Wall Street firm, the first general. But it was reasonably obvious that in the new economy the vast majority of new women workers were not on tracks opened up by pioneers. They were in traps. The traps may have been their best option, but there were no doors opening up to freedom.

Unions offered no help to women.[43] By the 1970s the various subsidies available through government to women in need were understood to be at once overly intrusive and inadequate. Neither political party had a policy notably helpful to women. However few their numbers, women in Congress, working with a few women in government, had been influential in the passage of Title VII of the Civil Rights Act in 1964, then in passage of the Equal Employment Opportunity act, enforcement of Title VII by the EEOC, and in submission of the Equal Rights Amendment by Congress to the states.[44] From all this a general disposition of women activists to look to the Democratic Party made sense, with liberal Democrats obliging in the rules changes that brought far more women—and blacks—to the nominating convention of 1972 than ever before.[45] But as the presidential vote of that year showed, not only was there no majority in the making for a new liberal left program, there was no evidence whatever that women were any more interested than men. With the Reagan administration's open hostility to affirmative action and ERA, the vision emerged once again of a woman's vote, if not so much pro-Democratic, then certainly anti-Reagan, only to be decisively dispelled in 1984. Quite apart from women's wide involvement in the antiabortion movement and the religious Right, the fact was that the Democrats' incoherence on the economy could be felt to be threatening to the prospects of the new generation of successful young professional and business women. Although women remained scarce in Washington and the upper levels of politics, their numbers were growing in state and local politics, and they were quite as likely to be found in Republican Party circles as in Democratic. Indeed, in some of its classic old precincts—labor, the South, Irish wards—the Democrats retained a more or less explicitly masculine style, long abandoned in the sleeker more technocratic suburbs.

A basis far more solid than that of womanhood, let alone of women's solidarity, had been established for women's growing presence in the marketplace: personal need. It seemed likely that, so far as the further advance of women in politics was concerned, to the point where some women might exercise great power, this prospect would improve precisely as the solidarity among women further disintegrated and as the economic future continued to partake of uncertainty.[46]

10 The Second Feminism

A Strange Death: Feminism after Suffrage

Winning the vote was a great victory. No other feminists ever won one so great. In Russia women were handed the vote by triumphant Bolshevik ideologues. In Sweden women got the vote as much from Conservative Party panic as from Liberal or Social Democratic efforts, and, in any case, from few promptings of feminist politics. Woman's suffrage came to Italy as part of the rebirth of democracy in Fascism's wreck. In the United States, by contrast, a long political campaign had been conducted. Thousands of rallies had been held. Hundreds of thousands of men had been canvassed in referenda in a score of states. As the number of state victories slowly grew, major politicians were won over—Theodore Roosevelt, Charles Evans Hughes in 1916, finally, against his own reluctance, a president, Woodrow Wilson. Feminists pressured Congress, then state legislatures for the final prize, an amendment to the nation's Constitution. Then what happened?

As Estelle Freedman has pointed out, when Arthur Schlesinger, Sr., declared in 1922 that women were standing on the threshold of a "new era," later historians of the decade inclined to agree. Writing as early as 1927, Charles and Mary Beard portrayed a shift in power. "Already potent by that time, [women's] influence in politics was immensely enlarged when the ballot was placed in their hands." While the Beards never did quite go on to demonstrate this influence, they did lay out a larger pattern of women's advance. American women, they wrote, had won "an amount of economic power and leisure that was the envy of their sisters in every other land." Although the Beards did not neglect comment on jobs, their emphasis was upon freedom "from the necessity of working for a living." Women "were the chief spenders of money." In consequence, "they called the tunes to which captains of industry, men of letters, educators, and artists now principally danced." Moreover, women had won greater rights in private life, evinced in both the statistics of divorce and the steady accumulation of greater "rights in their children." Characteristically, the Beards did not fail to conclude with a mordant twist. While women were advancing, men were in retreat: "[The] father, in losing his prerogatives, lost few of his obligations; indeed they were multiplied rather than diminished, especially for the male of the upper classes." As objects for purchase compounded, he had to earn more so his wife could buy them. "And his wife, besides defying and divorcing him, could still secure alimony. . . . The 'lord of creation' appeared to be on the verge of an eclipse."[1]

As Freedman has pointed out, strong exception to such a view was taken as early as the 1930s, not so much by historians, however, as by social scientists—notably the University of Chicago social welfare specialist Sophonisba Breckinridge in 1933, and Ernest Groves, an exponent of a new specialization, "marriage science," in 1937. But Breckinridge's study, *Women in the Twentieth Century,* far more detailed and penetrating than the Beards' few pages on women (in what was otherwise a massive book), forsook the Beards' implicit focus on middle and upper-middle-class life for sectors obviously far less fortunate. Groves too, writing of "the feminine side of a masculine civilization," ignored what the Beards stressed, the Twenties as a decade of change, in favor of his own stress on women's continuing subordination.[2] In effect, while persuasive as far as they went, both Breckinridge and Groves finessed confronting the Twenties portrayed by Frederick Lewis Allen, a time of "revolution in manners and morals." Without trying to judge whether Allen's portrait was right or wrong, they simply ignored it and presented another portrait. Thus they left the way open for historians to continue to judge the 1920s as a decade of gain for women, perhaps great in some ways, not so great in others, but a decade of true significance in the history of women, a special time, an epiphany, maybe even a "kairos," a season of great opportunities. The advantage of this approach was that it allowed feminist and women's history to proceed in tandem with standard mainstream history. The problems of feminism would not have to be sought in the decade of prosperity and the liberation of manners and morals. The collapse of feminism would not have to be found dialectically in the climax of the long American boom. It could be located syncretically in the collapse of the boom, in regression, in the Great Depression.

But this picture of the Twenties would not be acceptable, once self-consciously feminist history revived. The problem was obvious. How could a decade in which feminism itself foundered be left uncriticized? In 1959 Robert Smuts, in *Women and Work in America,* laid out data showing women's indifference in the 1920s to politics, professional careers, jobs, to feminist groups themselves. Having won their great victory, Smuts suggested, feminists had suffered a slump in motivation.[3] Six years later, an English observer, Andrew Sinclair, in *The Emancipation of the American Woman,* offered ruminations on the four decades since suffrage to something of the same effect. He devoted his last chapter to discussion of the fact that "despite the trends of industrialization, Victorian patterns of behavior have persisted," patterns separating men and women, containing women in their separate sphere, encouraging women to think of themselves as different, higher, special. Why were American women clinging to this old scheme when objective conditions no longer required it? Sinclair was not quite ready to echo the argument Betty Friedan had offered two years before, in *The Feminine Mystique*. Friedan had presented American women as victims of such ideologists as women's-magazine editors and pop psychoanalysts recycling in new guises the old doctrine of women's natural domesticity.[4] Sinclair inclined to locate the drama within women's own minds. The "mass ladies' magazines," he said, had no initiatory power; they followed, they did not lead. In effect, American women had found themselves brought to the "quest to become free in mind and spirit," but they were flinching from it. Sinclair was not sure just why. He oscillated between stressing the temptations posed by the suburbs, with their big comfortable houses and tidy comfortable churches that had a comfortable god inside—all in echo of the old laments of Harriet Martineau, Fredrika Bremer, and others that American affluence was bad for American women—and, in contrast, the hard work and uncertainties and fears inherent in the quest for free minds and spirits. Nor did he share Friedan's plain assumption that liberation from the disenabling mystique would take the form of liberation from home for the marketplace. "Some wives, unable to use their leisure to improve themselves, have gone back to work in their middle age."[5]

In 1971 William O'Neill, in *Everyone Was Brave: The Rise and Fall of Feminism in America*, in effect disposed of the problem of the 1920s as misleading. Feminism had failed long before it got the vote. Once, O'Neill said, some feminists at least had understood that "the heart of the woman question was domestic and not legal or political; that woman's place in the family system was the source from which her other inequities derived." But feminists had let themselves be frightened off the questions of marriage, home, sex, children, understandably, no doubt, in view of the state of American culture at the time, but with sad results. Since this defeat of feminism in its realist "radical" form occurred as early as 1870 or so, most of the history of nineteenth-century feminism had been that simply of futility. Even such heroines of radical insight as Gilman had come up short: "[She] apparently believed it possible to have socialized homes in a capitalist society."[6] But it was not really inadequacies in feminism so much as inadequacies in American society that best explained American feminism's fate. It was American society that had failed. O'Neill seemed to think of 1900 as the approximate point of the beginning of declension, a process only accelerating as the century wore on. "For all their problems," he wrote, the cities of America "seemed at the turn of the century to be alive with possibilities for new and better ways of living." It was perhaps this prospect that had nerved Gilman's optimism, and on that account she could be excused for her naïveté:

What she could not have guessed in 1898 was the extraordinary affection Americans would demonstrate for the detached, self-contained, single family dwelling. The retreat to suburbia had already begun, thanks to the streetcar, but in the twentieth century it became a rout. World War II, the G. I. Bill, the Federal Housing Administration, and similar developments made it possible not only for the middle but for the regularly employed working classes to enjoy the benefits of suburbia. Housing projects snaked out from and around every major city, laying waste the countryside and erecting in place of meadow and woodland acres of identical domestic boxes and forests of utility poles and TV antennas.[7]

At this point, certainly, where the problem of judging feminism dissolved into the problem of judging America, feminism itself got lost to view except on the thesis that for some reason men's affection for suburbia had surpassed that of women. If suburbia had undercut new possibilities, it had done so for both men and women. In the end, O'Neill wished that feminists had taken up a stance of radical criticism of the nation even though there had been little hope of its effect.

Women are not operationally equal to men anywhere in the Western world, but they are more nearly so in the welfare states than in socially underdeveloped nations like the United States.
    In retrospect it seems clear that some kind of socialism, whether democratic (Sweden) or not (U.S.S.R.), is essential to women's full emancipation. Socialist ideology commits left-wing governments to equalitarian practices.

What was not clear was whether O'Neill was under the impression that the "equalitarian practices" of the welfare states reached to the "heart of the woman question," that is, "the family system," marriage, sex, home, children. As it was, since he himself agreed that the odds against socialism in the United States were "desperately high," the odds against "thoroughgoing feminine emancipation" could only have been "astronomically high."[8] The optimistic, liberal, yea-saying motivation Schlesinger had generated for writing women's history here stood contradicted. What the motivation for further history so desperate might remain to be seen.

In *The American Woman, 1920–1970* (1972), William Chafe simply finessed the question of feminism's success or failure. Implicitly dissolving the question "What happened to feminism?" into an emerging new one, "What are the chances for the new feminism?," he took for granted that neither the suffrage nor nineteenth-century feminism had inaugurated some new era. Nor did he measure society since 1920 according to some abstract model of equality. Seeking to discern deep structural forces and broad social trends playing upon women, he necessarily appeared to run the chance that no forces or trends would be found favorable to women's chances for progress, but happily, Chafe did find forces and trends justifying optimism. He was particularly impressed by the wartime appearance of married women in the job market. That, it appeared, registered a permanent breakthrough. But however reassuring the discovery of economic and sociological trends favorable to women might have been, that left the new feminist history still confronted with the mystery of a prior, apparently triumphant feminism that either had or had not inaugurated a new era, had or had not been futile, had or had not been in tune with the deep currents of American history.[9]

Militant new feminist history itself demanded a sharper focus. Distilling Friedan, Sinclair, and O'Neill into a decisive rejection, in *Womanhood in America: From Colonial Times to the Present*, in 1975, Mary P. Ryan described the disintegration of the old "homosocial bonds of the nineteenth century" under the pressures of institutional change within capitalism. The morbid fruit of these pressures was a new imperative, a "heterosexual imperative":

In the first half of the twentieth century, American men and women were sold an ersatz sexuality and a spurious privacy. Under the banners of fulfillment and intimacy, a new breed of domestic ideologues, best represented by psychotherapists and advertisers, had insinuated themselves into conjugal and sexual relations. Exacting new standards of womanhood and manhood were set up in the remotest recesses of American life and personality. What passed as privatization in the twentieth century . . . most resembled privacy in its profitability to the private sector of the economy, especially to psychologists, advertisers and the manufacturers of consumer goods.[10]

The discussion to which this passage served as peroration showed that Ryan did not really mean, by the "first half of the twentieth century," 1900–1950, but 1920–1970. Hers was the final step in the process of reading the postfeminist period of American history as hostile to women. Once again women had been made into victims. That, by her accounting, men too had been victimized signified little; practically all Ryan's analysis bore upon the damage to women. Like Tocqueville, she judged that American marriages were far less than they might have been in emotional satisfaction, but whereas Tocqueville had judged this tolerable for men, she judged it intolerable for women. Women should be free not to marry.

In 1979 Estelle Freedman brought this historical argument to final focus. Feminism had died in the 1920s because feminism itself had been dependent on those old "homosocial" bonds. The old temperance sisterhoods had been coopted by the male-led Anti-Saloon League. The old missionary auxiliaries had been coopted and/or left to wither away. The sisterly outreach to working-class women, such as it was, notably in the Women's Trade Union League directed at the Italian and Jewish girls in the needle trades in New York City, had fallen short. The implicit promise of community in social science had shriveled under specialization and professionalization. Most of all, of course, the suffrage sisterhood had been undermined by its own success. Carrie Catt's attempt to supply a successor in the League of Women Voters never began to suffice: what issue did the League ever have remotely as clear and compelling as the vote? As for the wider circumambient spiritual sphere in which nineteenth-century women counted, it had been chilled at its very heart. The rise of a raw fundamentalism in the Protestant heartlands introduced a spirit intensely hostile to the kind of soft liberal indulgence of emotion and sisterhood that had lent Henry Ward Beecher rank as the outstanding cleric of his day. At the same time, liberal Protestantism itself was in disintegration, its missionary nerve cut, its investment in Prohibition questioned from within its own family, its shrinkage to a cult of positive thinking more and more apparent. Though feminism itself had been far harder and more political than the host culture that had sheltered it, it had, presumably, drawn upon it and depended upon it. Now, that saving host had been withdrawn.[11]

Yet in this final reckoning what faded from view was the decade itself, the 1920s in all their specificity. Certainly, if the Twenties amounted to no more than the elaborate con game Ryan saw in it, selling the ersatz and the spurious, its lethal impact on feminists might well seem plausible. Having spent their lives sheltered in the securities of sisterly homosociality, women would be easy marks for the heterosexualizing advertisers and psychologists. But so also might feminism have faded, had the 1920s been what the Beards and Frederick Lewis Allen thought them, a rather remarkable surge of democratic culture. Indeed, the Beards had taken note of one phenomenon that did not fit neatly into Freedman's story. The old General Federation of Women's Clubs had not disintegrated in the Twenties. It had grown. Of course the Federation had never been a prime feminist organization, but its persistence told of energies still at work among women; de-emphasizing its familiar attention to literature, the Federation of the Twenties put more stress on foreign affairs, laws, applied education, and so on. It was almost as though these women thought the new era had begun and they were free to explore it.

Finally, even feminism's death in the Twenties from forces hostile to it required no postulation of hostility to women. It was Charlotte Perkins Gilman who was hostile to the young women of the 1920s. If they were indifferent to her, and to feminism in general, it was because of what she and the nineteenth-century feminists had made of themselves—persons who could not respond to the rising new age of abundance. It would not be through advertising and the lucubrations of pop Freudian psychologists that democratic capitalism would be shaped. The mass market had been generated long before, in the very politics of democracy itself. That this market would flourish in symbiosis with the most intimate strivings of personality had been clearly understood by Hamilton, perceived by Tocqueville, long before. It was hardly surprising then that nineteenth-century women were not prepared for the 1920s. But it would be of no use for them to rail against the times. They themselves had realized there was no point in the fantasy of saving themselves in "socialism." The process of responding to the unprecedented new opportunities for personal abundance in the rising economic abundance was showing itself in just those parents of the new college generation of the Twenties. Born in the 1870s and 1880s, they were permitting and facilitating the revolution in manners and morals that their children born after 1900 were bringing off.That one result of this revolution was the disintegration of the old homosociality, with its separation of spheres, constituted part of the opportunity.[12]

Life without Feminism in Depression, War, and Peace

The attempt to explain the disappearance of feminism by reference to various ideologies, mystiques, imperatives, and stereotypes not only assumed a degree of passivity in mass audiences that could not be demonstrated, but ignored the major realities of the 1930s, '40s, and '50s as well as those of the 1920s. Whatever theory might compose as alternatives to the New Deal, most Americans were left in the Depression to cope by their own devices. Despite all the hundreds of thousands of men impelled to ride the rails in flight and search, the epoch rewarded solidarity between the sexes. When there was a family to go to, people went to it. Where a marriage promised mutual aid, it prospered. Among the classic Midwestern Protestant middle classes, woman's sphere was at once reconstituted and transformed—reconstituted as a source of morale and means of mutual aid, and transformed in adjusting its life away from a separate service to women and toward a service to coping by all. In all this, any possible spark to feminism had no straw to ignite. Insofar as women were often psychologically more prepared to cope than men, their services were welcomed. The discriminations contained in New Deal and other government rules and actions could hardly be regarded as ideological. Neither of the two major parties had much to gain from singling out women. None of the parties on the left singled out women. Sen. Huey Long's Share-the-Wealth movement did not single out women, nor did Dr. Francis Townsend's old-age pension movement. In every case the reason was the same: everyone was in the same boat. Few women even among the handful of feminist-successor organizations ever tried to trace the Depression to women's inequality; even fewer ever blamed the Depression on men as men.[13]

Basically the same logic applied equally during the war, then far into the postwar years: everyone was in the same boat. In Margaret Mead's hope that Americans would seize upon World War II as an opportunity to restore American idealism and self-confidence, women had a special part, for it was men's loss of self-confidence that most mattered. The last thing appropriate during the war was for women to make any claims for themselves separately. Feminists during the Civil War had hoped to be rewarded for women's service afterward; feminists during World War I demanded it. But their services in war had earned them nothing; everyone had served; there was no reason women deserved a reward for doing their duty. Their disappointment after the Civil War had embittered some feminists; their success after World War I had left them quite unprepared for what would follow. World War II prompted a modest flurry in the parties; the Republicans in 1940 and the Democrats in 1944 composed words friendly to the idea of constitutionally recognized equality, although not to the specific Equal Rights Amendment that had been urged for years by the Women's Party. Activist women were still divided. Soon the wartime flurry subsided. Late in 1952 the Democrats abolished their women's division; so did the Republicans. Why did women need a special division? Were they not men's equals already?[14]

Late in the war, in 1944, in one of those performances that defy neat synthesis, the Swedish economist-sociologist Gunnar Myrdal published his study of American race relations. In *The American Dilemma* Myrdal spelled out in copious detail how far short the United States had fallen in allowing black people to share the opportunities of American democracy. As a survey, his study could only have been profoundly discouraging. Yet he concluded on a note of optimism. Americans, he said—obviously meaning white Americans—would not forever fail to live up to their own ideals. They would not forever tolerate feelings of guilt and shame. Just why the eighty years since Appomattox were to be discounted Myrdal did not explain. In an appendix, he turned to women. Raising the old parallel between women and slaves, he implied that women too might hope for justice.[15] For whichever women were listening, Myrdal's linkage itself might have been discouraging. Had not women already broken beyond the plight of the black race in their suffrage amendment? The linkage recalled painful memories: was it wise for women to seek allies among the weak? Better, perhaps, for women to strike bargains with the strong.

If the wartime boat in which"everybody" was being borne along was transformed with peace, that did not mean that commonality of experience declined in the years from Hiroshima to the Test Ban Treaty. It was quite enough for commonality that among the fortunate cohort of the young more were marrying than ever before, and marrying younger than had their parents and grandparents, and finally that, almost unanimously, more were having babies young. It was in the 1950s that a new medium moved from curiosity to necessity in American life generally. Hardly more than 5,000 TV sets were produced in 1945; by 1950, 7 million sets were sold. Early television had a homogenizing impact. Tied together by the old radio networks, stations broadcast the same programs. Early programming relied on old formulas. The power of the audience over programming was vast: overwhelmingly, television audiences were made up of families. Families accustomed to going to the movies once or twice a week, perhaps dividing up in doing so, watched television at home every night.Eventually the mass audiences of early television would begin to crumble around the edges, being wooed segmentally by age, by sex, by day of the week and on weekends, through a steady diversification of programming. But the 1950s were the years par excellence when Marshall McLuhan's vision of a television-based"global village" appeared plausible. Henry Carey's America once again glimmered forth, now as the maximum of decentralization based on the maximum of centralization. Yet even in the 1950s the spectacle of a centrally programmed culture was misleading. Not all family time was spent before the tube. All the new suburbs had to be perfected, their raw edges smoothed, their parks planted, their schools monitored. Women preeminently did these things. As in the new satellite apartment towns of Sweden, women in the new American suburbs found themselves leading public lives. Many of the mothers engaged in parent-teacher association politics, leaving the way clear for older married women to take jobs, some of them women who had stepped aside only half-willingly in 1945. The steady rise in the ratio of women working for pay steepened a bit in the 1950s; few of the new workers were out for careers; the ratio of women getting advanced degrees had declined in the small cohort of baby boom mothers; those who worked did so for the pay. Where would feminism come from in this vast scene?[16]

The Fifties hardly practiced silence on ultimate matters. The two Kinsey reports on sexual behavior, on men in 1948, on women in 1953, impelled a revolution in popular American discourse. Morality had still dominated public discussion of sex through World War II. Now statistics would. Eventually even television would show sunny mainstream myths yielding to the presentation of diversity. But the Kinsey reports blighted prospects for renewed romantic realism even more than traditionalist morality had. The great "finding" of the reports was that Americans behaved as they did sexually, not out of sexual differences, but from class, age, racial, regional, educational, and religious differences. The "liberatory" aspect of the reports was their tacit conclusion that sexual behavior did not cluster around poles of normality and deviance but occupied a variety of spectrums. Everybody belonged to some kind of sexual minority. Everybody was to be tolerated. While this would serve to invite greater public tolerance, it had almost nothing to offer to individuals in the midst of real-life dramas. Insofar as it was a thesis of feminism that women were the more likely losers in real-life dramas, the Kinsey reports contained danger for women.[17]

The Kinsey reports provided rhetorical protection for the new venture of a young Midwesterner, Methodist in background, with commercial ambitions, the founder in 1953 of *Playboy* magazine, Hugh Hefner. Bringing female nudity down from classical art and up from the pornographic underground, Hefner was able to combine it with advertisements for standard appurtenances of a new affluence: sports cars, stereos, scotch, tweeds, travel. *Playboy* broke out of the family complex. Not a family magazine, it was a "magazine for men," in principle unmarried men. Drawing on Eric Dingwall and other historians of sexual customs, Hefner eventually equipped *Playboy* with a "philosophy," the point of which was the injustice and stupidity of all laws interfering with sexual behavior between mutually consenting adults. Hefner was right: the revolution of manners and morals of the Twenties had been delayed. Young Americans of the 1950s still found sex entangled in a welter of archaic rules, mores, inhibitions, and censorship. More liberty was overdue. The Kinsey reports had only implied as much. *Playboy* made the case openly. Women had as much at stake as men. Everyone was in the same boat. *Playboy* soon became a formula magazine. It never tried to pioneer new sexual frontiers or render the sexual experiences of individuals. Its essential message was that sex constituted a consumer product like any other. Its roots were in a style of life, a standard of living. Sex was vested in objects, not minds, in sex objects, not passions. One day *Playboy*, like its eventual competitors, would be assailed by a new generation of feminists. In the years of its rise it would by no means constitute a spur to feminism.[18]

Feminism Reborn: A Many Splendor'd Thing

In 1957 Betty Friedan, a 1942 graduate of Smith College, sent a questionnaire to some 240 of her classmates. Bored with her own life as a suburban matron raising three children, Friedan had taken up free-lance writing as an escape. She hoped to get an article from her survey. She got a book.

By the time Friedan published *The Feminine Mystique* in 1963, the federal government had come forth with important works. Esther Peterson, head of the Women's Bureau founded back in 1920 in response to woman suffrage, persuaded the new Kennedy administration to sponsor a Commission on the Status of Women. Peterson was from the labor unions. From his days in the Senate, she knew Kennedy to be open to labor's interests. Peterson was thoroughly committed to labor's traditional support for protective legislation. Like other labor leaders, she opposed the Women's Party's Equal Rights Amendment. Kennedy had been persuaded somehow to support the ERA. Peterson felt sure this was a mistake. All Peterson wanted was a commission to demonstrate the need for equal pay, extension of the minimum wage, and other measures of immediate practical import for women workers, and to head off the ERA as the fetish of an elite of professional women. She got it. As for Kennedy, evidently he regarded the commission as adequate recognition of women, for he offered no more political favor to women thereafter.

The commission's report in 1963 provided data on women workers that women's rights groups would use for years to come. Because of momentum generated by it, an Equal Pay Act was passed the same year. Few women did the same work as men, hence few were covered, but the act held considerable potential. As Patricia Zelman has pointed out, when courts interpreted it to mean equal pay for "substantially" equal work, its reach was considerably extended.[19] Congress may very well have proven reluctant to embark upon any further reforms, but, following the President's assassination, the soon-to-be famous Article VII of the Civil Rights Act of 1964 passed easily, a keystone in Lyndon Johnson's vision of a Great Society. Gender was added to race among the prohibited grounds of discrimination. Article VII thus affirmed another of Esther Peterson's hopes, broadened access to jobs and careers for women. The following year, the Equal Employment Opportunity Commission (EEOC) was created and funded. Thus, even before Friedan called the first meeting of the National Organization of Women (NOW) in 1966, formidable levers of power had been devised of great significance for women. No such levers had ever been available to feminists or women before. So long as the consensus behind the Great

Society persisted, feminists would have friends in Washington. The EEOC might pry open realms of endeavor long closed, overcome inequities in pay, promote greater job security. NOW's role would be to mobilize women in support, to grow, and to stick together.[20]

In its Statement of Purpose, NOW embraced a familiar ideal of equal rights. Women would demand full participation in American society, exercising all its responsibilities and enjoying all its liberties in equal partnership with men. Like the women at Seneca Falls in 1848, NOW's founders proposed to take their stand on the mainstream values of the nation. But in 1968 Ti-Grace Atkinson, president of NOW's New York chapter, the largest in the country, resigned in a flurry of recriminations. Friedan's comments three years later nicely capsulized the issue. Atkinson, Friedan said, had become unduly preoccupied with issues extraneous to NOW's main aims. As the Statement of Purpose had said, NOW proposed to win greater access and greater equality for women in the marketplace. Atkinson by contrast had attacked the "institution of sexual intercourse." NOW was not interested in issues of marriage and sexuality. Atkinson was preoccupied with abortion. NOW was not. NOW did not find the roots of women's oppression in their private relations with men. Atkinson did.[21]

Atkinson's resignation did not represent New York or any large number of NOW members anywhere. Yet the schism threatened NOW on a fundamental basis. Could women's progress toward equality really be achieved through political action aimed at economic conditions alone? Indeed, were women's demands to be economic and political alone? Atkinson brought up the marriage question that had haunted and bedeviled the old feminist movement, which had first tried to contain it, then to escape it. It had paid the price after 1920.

Friedan saw a still further challenge. Though inclined to suspect Atkinson of an old-fashioned ambition for personal power, she realized that Atkinson was objecting not only to NOW's agenda of issues but to its internal organizational structure. NOW itself, Atkinson said, was constructed according to the hierarchical principles of the offices and headquarters into which its members hoped to enter. Women ought to strive to eliminate hierarchies.[22] As another of the seceders, Carol Freeman, wrote, women, at the bottom of the pyramid of power, must not try to climb up the pyramid. They must get it off their backs altogether. Friedan was frank: NOW was interested in power. NOW hoped to see more women scaling the heights of power. NOW was after participation in the system, not some new egalitarian system. NOW did not claim that women held the secret of some new, better system.

As NOW struggled to control its own agenda, by 1970 it had become clear that a far deeper feminism than any it had anticipated had awakened. In effect, NOW had criticized the suburbs as simply women's sphere modernized. But Atkinson, Freeman, and the early dissidents were not complaining at having been left sequestered in a sphere of their own. They were complaining of what their lives had been like, not cut off from men, but in the most direct relationship with men. Nor were these relationships only sexual. From a variety of sources in the late 1950s, a "New Left" had emerged, energized by students—almost unanimously young men—contemptuous of what they saw as the impotence of the Old Left, whether Marxist or liberal. As black protest grew and the Vietnam War took shape, this impotence of the Old Left showed itself not only on both those issues, but more broadly in a kind of inertial surrender to the drift of the nation into suburbanized complacency. New Left leaders offered a more "spontaneous," "open," and instinctive style of politics, often attractive to young women, too. Some tried to add sex to war and racism on the New Left's agenda. They felt women could be as spontaneously political as men. Some of them felt women had a special contribution to make in the New Left's reinvigoration of political debate.

They were met with condescension worse than that customary among the Marxist orthodox. As early as 1964 Stokeley Carmichael, president of the black Student Nonviolent Coordinating Committee (SNCC) gave his famous reply to Ruby Smith Robinson's paper on "The Position of Women in S.N.C.C.": "The only position for women in S.N.C.C. is prone." But the response was not peculiar to blacks. At a National Conference for a New Politics in Chicago in 1967, sponsored by Students for a Democratic Society, Shulamith Firestone, a spokeswoman for a group of women seeking to link women's with other New Left issues, was refused the podium, the chairman kindly explaining that issues far more important than those of women awaited debate. Firestone's group left the convention.

In 1970, when one of these women, Robin Morgan, published an influential anthology of new feminist writing, *Sisterhood Is Powerful*, she included a reflection on her own experience in the New Left:

[When] I began to work on this book, I considered myself a radical woman who regarded the Women's Liberation Movement as an important "wing" of the Left; as a tool, perhaps. . . . I was a so-called "politico," who shied away from admitting . . . that *I* was oppressed. . . . This left me conveniently on top. . . . I . . . nurtured a secret contempt for other women who weren't as strong, free, and respected (by men) as I thought I was. . . . Especially threatening were the women who admitted that they were simply unable to cope with the miserable situation we were all in, and needed each other, and a whole movement to

change that. Well, somewhere during that year, I became such a woman. . . .
Somehow . . . this book seems to have been most responsible. All of us who
worked on it . . . had to read and think and talk. . . . I couldn't believe—still
can't—how angry I could become, from deep down and way back, something
like a five-thousand-year-buried anger.[23]

By the time Morgan published her 1970 anthology, a host of groups
and grouplets and cells and associations had taken a kind of confeder-
ational shape as a Women's Liberation Movement.[24] Some practiced a
kind of street theater, others a politics of symbolism. At Atlantic City
in 1967 a group of women staged a counter-Miss America show, mocking
the pretensions and sexism of that stale rite. One group labeled itself a
Society for Cutting Up Men (SCUM), another W.I.T.C.H. In Boston an
influential Cell 16 published a journal, *No More Fun and Games;* it
organized classes in judo and karate. In most of this ferment, as though
in recoil from the complacent assumption of male leadership in the
New Left, an open hostility to men came through loud and clear. Its
explicit sexual meaning was, however, by no means clear. One of the
leaders of Cell 16, Roxanne Dunbar, commended "asexuality": "Considering what one must go through to attain a relationship of whole to
whole in this society, or any other that I know of, the most 'normal'
person, the most moral, is the celibate."[25]

What did any of this have to do with NOW's stated goals? Women's
liberationists might have gone on to argue, turning Marxism upside
down, that NOW's economic and political goals could be achieved only
by effecting some kind of revolution in sexuality first. Dunbar expounded the theoretical basis:

Feminism is opposed to the masculine ideology. . . . Some women embrace the
masculine ideology, particularly women with a college education. But most
women have been programmed from early childhood for a role, maternity,
which develops a certain consciousness of care for others, self-reliance, flexibility, noncompetitiveness, cooperation, and materialism. . . . If these "maternal" traits . . . are desirable traits, they are desirable for everyone, not just
women. By destroying the present society, and building a society on feminist
principles, men will be forced to live in the human community on terms very
different from the present. . . . [Feminism] must be asserted, by women, as the
basis of revolutionary social change.[26]

Dunbar here drew on the old doctrine of the spheres for her psychology
of women: women were indeed, not by nature but by education, training, programming, different from men. But they were also better than
men. The practical meaning of that was not that they must be sheltered
in their sphere, as old nineteenth-century doctrine had had it, but that
their sphere must become the men's sphere, too. Men must become like
women.

But women's liberation too confronted challenge. When the radical feminists of women's liberation—and the liberal feminists of NOW—reached out for contact with black and Hispanic women, they met a strong rebuff. Of all women in America, working-class black and Hispanic women might benefit most from NOW's lengthening menu of demands for affirmative action, child-care facilities, job training, housing allowances, pension equity, health care, along with equal pay, pay based on comparable work, and greater women's presence in politics and unions. NOW's program did attract a number of activist black women. Yet some black women leaders confronted both NOW and, especially, the exponents of women's lib with the fact of a deep existential difference. Black women were not like the Italian and Jewish women workers of 1900 whom feminists had once tried to help through the Women's Trade Union League. Young Italian, Irish, Jewish, Polish, and other working girls had shared with their men in working their way up. But black women shared an oppression. Black women carried a double mandate: to combat not just their own oppression as women but that of "their" men, too. "Our husbands, fathers, brothers and sons have been emasculated, lynched, and brutalized."[27] To expect black women to share in some general indictment of "patriarchy," "masculine ideology," and men in general would be to ask them to repudiate their most compelling historic experience.

The same point could be made even more positively when it came to conceptualizing the vast ranks of the most economically and politically oppressed women worldwide as "third-world" women, most conspicuous in the United States as Hispanic women. One Hispanic woman leader, Cherríe Moraga, presented the issue to her radical peers sweepingly:

The most important thing about third-world feminism is it emerges out of identity politics. . . . White women don't always realize that third-world women are not just anti-racists, but pro our cultures. That's an important distinction. The ways that third-world feminism can be different is that it's coming from a real belief and commitment to the integrity of our own race and culture, and keeping that. The white women's movement tried to create a new form of women's culture that on some level has denied where people come from.

Moraga took pains to show that she was not criticizing simply some preference, perhaps "lesbian," perhaps homosocial, among women for their own company.

[There] are lots of women who weren't lesbian separatists who talk about women's culture. Whether the women were Irish or German or came from working class or Jewish backgrounds, the desire to have a women's culture suddenly become devoid of race, class roots, what you ate at home, the smells in the air. Third-world feminism is talking about the vital, life-giving necessity of understanding your roots. . . . You don't need to cut off an arm for a movement.[28]

Chicano feminists were not attracted by a future without Chicano men. Their grievance was against a system that exploited Chicanos, both men and women.

The problem here for white middle-class radical feminists was old. Margaret Fuller had lamented that there was "no place" for her. For nineteenth-century feminists the solution had been their culture in woman's sphere, then redefined by radicals like Gilman as a model for the nation, with women becoming social mothers. With the crumbling of woman's sphere, this recourse had become empty. What sounded like echoes of the old way were in fact not. "There must be something you dug about how your mother raised you,"[29] Barbara Smith asked of the white women's movement, but in fact there was not. For lack of vital roots, the smell of home cooking, the sense of a whole culture at one's back, some of the new radicals had already begun looking for pasts they could adopt. When Adrienne Rich published *Of Woman Born: Motherhood as Experience and Institution* in 1976, she recalled her childhood in south Baltimore. She had had in effect two mothers, one her biological, white mother and the other her emotional, black mother. Social taboo had taken her black, warm, true mother from her. "When I began writing this chapter I began to remember my black mother again."[30] In *Woman Power: The Movement for Women's Liberation* (1970), Cellestine Ware condensed all American history into the frontier and then repudiated it. In frontier America, "experience was transformed to fit . . . the strong, silent frontiersman. The wellspring of passion and sensibility seemed dried up in this grim process." Then where might feminists turn in their quest for passion and feeling and sensibility? "There had been all along in America a population that . . . had been excluded from frontier society. . . . the black community and its art forms." Ware also praised the beatniks of the 1950s and their 1960s siblings: "A generation had discovered that deep feeling and spontaneity were delightful."[31]

As white middle-class feminist historians began rewriting American history in the late 1960s and 1970s, they thus faced a fundamental question. Was the America described by Tocqueville part of women's heritage or not? Had the America of democratic capitalism evolved somehow simply as an environment hostile to women, against which they had constructed their protective sphere? Had that formidable system then finally broken through their self-protective sphere to impose upon them an "ersatz" life, a "spurious" culture? If so, the purpose of rewriting that history would have to be made acutely clear. Oriented essentially toward the future, feminist history would have to ask whether a future could be constructed which "on some level . . . denied where people come from." Obviously this would not be of interest to those who affirmed where they had come from, namely, men.

For NOW the problem ran deep. Committed to pressing for women's equal participation alongside men in the marketplace, it could hardly at the same time indulge in rejection of the very foundation of that marketplace. If women were to become men's marketplace equals they would have to meet marketplace tests, become the kind of people effective in the marketplace. This meant refraining from drawing upon women's experience in women's sphere as justification for asserting standards for revamping the marketplace. Even more compelling, in committing itself to the pursuit of marketplace equality NOW had effectively denied itself fundamental criticism of nonmarketplace relationships. Of course it could criticize any number of abuses and wants clearly harmful to women in the marketplace: not only lack of day-care facilities and sexual harassment on the job but also such manifest damages to individual efficacy as wife abuse, unfair divorce settlements, rape, even restraints on access to abortion and contraception. But the fundamental issues of private sexual relationships were not contained in these palpable abuses but in the very "institutions" of heterosexuality, love, marriage, family, and so on, and Friedan's response to the schisms of 1970 showed plainly enough the strong wish of marketplace feminists to steer clear of these whirlpools.

Swedish feminists had a powerful sense of a certain kind of Sweden with which they identified; when the Swedish Social Democrats affirmed it, the partnership of feminism and party was affirmed. In Russia, the early feminists of Bolshevism of course rejected the past, though it was not a past of "men" but of autocracy; the future they affirmed was unambiguously that for both women and men. Italian feminists most nearly found themselves in a position comparable to the Americans: the past they rejected was notably one in which men held dominance, yet at the same time, as Gramsci showed, that past contained powerful traditions no purely feminist utopias considered rejecting. In the United States radical feminists appeared trapped. They could not join NOW in attempting to enter the marketplace. The old realm of a separate sphere had disintegrated and the new one in the suburbs was repellent. Freed of the need for prudence, fueled by outrage, energy for utopian purity and dizziness had been released. Yet by the same token, energy had been released for the purest dialectic, of seizing the masculine past for women's own final liberation, as Shulamith Firestone exhibited in *The Dialectic of Sex: The Case for Feminist Revolution*, in 1970.

The Future as Abolition of the Past:
Shulamith Firestone's Dialectic

One of the victims of the New Left's male chauvinism, Shulamith Firestone spent no time on complaints. Questions of short-run political tactics, of organization outreach, of middle-term strategy did not concern her. To Firestone it seemed clear that all feminist tactics and strategy would remain trapped within a constriction as old as history itself. She rehearsed a long invariance:

[Women] throughout history before the advent of birth control were at the continual mercy of their biology—menstruation, menopause, and "female ills," constant painful childbirth, wetnursing and care of infants, all of which made them dependent on males (whether brother, father, husband, lover, or clan, government, community-at-large) for physical survival.
[A] basic mother/child interdependency has existed in some form in every society . . . and . . . has shaped the psychology of every mature female and every infant.
[The] natural reproductive difference between the sexes led directly to the first division of labor.

It was nature, then, not history, that underlay the inequality between the sexes: "Half the human race must bear and rear the children of all of them."[32] It was these "oppressive power structures set up by nature" that constituted women's deepest difficulty.

But how was this difficulty to be overcome? Firestone was unambiguous. It was to be overcome in the same way other oppressions of nature had been, by science and technology. "Now, in 1970, we are experiencing a major scientific breakthrough . . . in biology, biochemistry, and all the life sciences . . . in genetics . . . on the origins of life. Full mastery of the reproductive process is in sight." The most precious specific fruit of this scientific progress was evident: "Childbearing could be taken over by technology."[33]

Firestone did not imagine that women—or men—would welcome artificial childbearing easily. Much of her book was in fact devoted to examining the "past traditions and psychic structures" that had been erected to "reinforce" the oppressive structures of nature. These were of two major sorts: basically, the Bible's harsh realism in warning women they must bear their babies in pain and suffering, and modern liberalism's counter sentimentality, concealing pain in myths of love, family, tribes, and races. She then devoted effort to point out the vast advantages for both men and women in further scientific advance. For men, too, warned that they must live by the sweat of their brows, the Bible's brutal realism would be denied by automation. With freedom from biological oppression, love truly could become universal rather than a luxury confined to brief moments and dark spaces.

A work of brilliant sweep and consistency, yet Firestone's book won no significant following. Trying to guess why, Alison M. Jaggar repeated themes Firestone herself had raised: women were trained in technology; women blamed technology for such evils as medicalized childbirth, pollution, war; women thought of technology as masculine. More sweepingly, in 1986 a feminist philosopher, Sandra Harding, in *The Science Question in Feminism*, challenged the whole apparatus of Western science itself as "androcentric," innately hostile to "women's experience."[34] But Jaggar added a further speculation:

The final problem with Firestone's theory, from the perspective of many radical feminists, lies perhaps in the fact that she does not hold men responsible for the system of male dominance . . . men appear in her theory as being ultimately women's protectors.[35]

Whatever Jaggar's own view might have been, this was a misleading simplification. Not only did Firestone blame men for their psychic and social reinforcements of nature's inequality, but she blamed them for obstructing science itself: "new scientific developments that could have greatly helped the feminist cause [have] stayed in the lab." Science, that is, was by no means some autonomous force, beyond the influence of gender, beyond good and evil, but deeply implicated in all the traditions and psychic structures that sustained inequality. Yet in essence Jaggar's point was correct. Firestone pointed at a history that had been essentially that of men and argued that women must identify with it. She reached out to quote the most relevant possible authority for her view, Simone de Beauvoir. De Beauvoir rejected appeals to some possible past of maternal or simply feminine dominance or even simply equality as a guide to history.

The devaluation of women [under patriarchy] represents a necessary stage in the history of humanity, for it is not upon her positive value but upon man's weakness, that [woman's] prestige is founded. In woman are incarnated all the disturbing mysteries of nature, and man escapes her hold when he frees himself from nature.[36]

Matriarchy never had been dominance for women but simply men's worship of Nature through women precedent to their learning how to conquer nature. Women, too, must try to free themselves from nature. They must join men in conquering nature. The historical past with which they must identify was men's past, that of accumulation of power for transcendence. Firestone was de Beauvoir's one unshaded disciple in America.

It was of great significance for the condition of modern American feminism that Jaggar, in using the standard vocabulary for labeling different groups in the feminist movement, could identify the feminists most averse to Firestone as "radical." From a perspective independent of feminism little might have seemed more radical than Firestone's support for an all-out development of modern reproductive science. That her lack of radicalism inhered in her failure to stress "the need for a political structure against male power" in itself constituted a comment on the nature of that struggle as radical feminists conceived it. Its essence was utopianism: oscillation between dreams of a past that never was (in the United States and the Western world at least) and a future that no one could explain how it could ever be.

The Female Body: Natural or Historical?

No longer—if they had once been—worshipful of women's bodies, what had men in their liberated patriarchal state come to feel about them? In *Of Woman Born*, Adrienne Rich did not shrink from the worst: men still feared women, dreaded their bodies, hated their works: "The ancient, continuing envy, awe, and dread of the male for the female capacity to create life has repeatedly taken the form of hatred for every other female aspect of creativity."[37] It was reasonably clear that Rich conceded no such idea as Simone de Beauvoir's, that men in freeing themselves from primeval feelings about women had thus advanced. Men always had felt and still did feel the hateful envy, awe, dread. Similarly, in finding a "universal" dread of women among men, the feminist theologian Mary Daly clearly included modern as well as primitive man:

The universal and irrational belief that there is a "base element" in femaleness reflects "man's underlying fear and dread of women. . . ." More and more evidence of this fear, dread, and loathing is being unearthed by feminist scholars every day, revealing a universal misogynism which, in all major cultures in recorded patriarchal history, has permeated the thought of seemingly "rational" and civilized "great men"—"saints," philosophers, poets, doctors, scientists, statesmen, sociologists, revolutionaries, novelists. A quasi-infinite catalog could be compiled . . . revealing this universal dread.[38]

How had men acted upon their fears? For Rich, a gifted poet, one project seemed evident: to smother women's true voice. For Daly, the main result had been the concoction and imposition of giant religious apparatuses smothering women's true religiousness. Bad as these results were, though, and stimulating as they might be to feminist countermeasures, there was another male response at once far worse in intimate impact and far less obvious as to countermeasures. Susan Brownmiller's *Against Our Will: Men, Women and Rape* (1975) spelled it out.

Rape had been the personal crime par excellence about which no feminist politics had yet been generated. Even feminists had rarely yet publicly spoken of it. One cannot doubt that Brownmiller was fully aware of the irrefutability of a simple charge: rape had been ignored, underestimated, repressed not only by historians, supposed discoverers of truth, but by those who might be able to do something about it in the here and now, by lawmakers, judges, psychologists, teachers, preachers, the police. Rape was a crime that exposed the victim to further victimization by the law. Rape was a crime that victims were afraid to report, lest they be stigmatized as the cause of it. Rape was a crime the possibility of which was denied by most women precisely because of their sense of helplessness. In defiance of all old taboos and inhibitions, rape must be put on the feminist agenda. Rape must be exposed to the public light.

Brownmiller did not content herself with such an eminently worthy—and long overdue—enterprise. She had larger game in mind. "From prehistoric times to the present, I believe, rape has played a critical function. It is nothing more or less than a conscious process of intimidation by which *all men* keep *all women* in a state of fear."[39] While not utterly explicit about the deepest reasons for this male process, Brownmiller most likely had in mind that men raped in order to repel their fear of women. This would not have been utterly incompatible with a kind of dark parody of Beauvoir's basic thesis: men raped in order to make themselves powerful.

That men suffered from an "ancient, continuing," "universal and irrational" dread of women's procreativity might be a thesis to be pursued through symbol and myth, through the archives of art and science, the practices of law and medicine, but rape was also, presumably, a matter of statistics. Or did Brownmiller mean rape simply as something universally potential—a kind of Hobbesian threat ever immanent between any man and any woman? She had literal rape in mind, certainly. That historians had neglected rape as a historical phenomenon she had no difficulty in pointing out. Millions of rapes had been committed on a mass basis throughout history during wars. German soldiers had raped widely in Poland and Russia during World War II; Russian soldiers raped in Germany. Pakistani soldiers had raped widely in Bangladesh in 1971. She noted what American historians practically never did, that rape had been committed during the American Revolution. In all this, point was added to a theme traditional in feminism: women wanted peace, hated war, wanted safety; men wanted violence. Yet what had been the "meaning" of the rapes committed during wars? In Bangladesh, Pakistani soldiers had had the political blessing of their leaders. In Russia, German soldiers raped, not women, but the members of subhuman races. In Germany, Russian soldiers revenged the violation of their sisters. Politics was at stake. Nor did Brownmiller's thesis work out as mere matter of fact. Lee's soldiers raped no one in Pennsylvania. War was hell, but Sherman's soldiers raped no one while devastating Georgia. Nor were other linkages of rape with history automatic. Brownmiller noted the rape of black slave women by white men in the Old South; presumably such rapes did not mean the same thing as rapes of white women by blacks in newly independent Congo.

Once finished with reports from wars and mass behavior, Brownmiller turned to rape in its more usual image, as an assault by one man on one woman, hidden, in isolation. Again, she began with provocative rhetoric: "The typical American rapist might be the boy next door." Since this had force only as a contrast with popular notions to the contrary, Brownmiller immediately dulled her point by adding quickly that this was so only if "next door" was a slum or ghetto. But she was hardly aiming to reassure those of her readers for whom "next door" was a tract house in a standard suburb or a dormitory on a coed campus. Shifting to psychological from sociological terrain, she asked whether the "typical American rapist" was a "weirdo, psycho schizophrenic, beset by timidity, sexual deprivation, and a domineering wife or mother?" The implications of this cliché were particularly hateful: some woman had dominated this rapist, some woman had emotionally starved him; such a woman belonged in the web of those responsible for rape. Again, she declared the cliché untrue: such psychologizing was only a little more sophisticated than the familiar old sneer that somehow the rape victim herself had "asked for it." Brownmiller insisted: men were to blame for rape. The fact that they were monsters in committing rape was not due to some other prior monstrousness: "The typical American perpetrator of forcible rape is little more than an aggressive, hostile youth who chooses to do violence to women." The operative word here, presumably, was "chooses." Men were not driven to rape by irresistible impulses, whether biological, sociological or psychological. Rape was a "conscious process."

As a good journalist, Brownmiller could not help but let data interfere with her stated thesis, even though it undercut her polemic. Having insisted that rape was a crime of violence rather than of sexual passion, she conceded: "But there is no getting around the fact that most of those who engage in anti-social, criminal violence . . . come from the lower socio-economic classes." Only urgent prior needs would have wanted to "get around" such a fact. At least that outlook offered a clear mandate for social policy directed at reducing—though hardly eliminating—rape: improve the condition of the lower socioeconomic classes. A further concession offered a rather less clear policy. Drawing from anthropologist Margaret Mead, Brownmiller noted that some men did not rape at all: the Arapesh. At the very end she professed that eradication of rape would require "the understanding and goodwill" of "many men" as well as of women, without, however, any hint that such eradication would require the revolutionizing—the Arapeshization— of American men. All this fitted awkwardly under the title of that last chapter: "Women Fight Back." How? "Kick him in the balls, it's your best maneuver."[40]

As reform of rape laws came before dozens of jurisdictions, other physical affronts to women were brought to focus in the growing heat of feminist self-consciousness by the late 1970s. Wife abuse. Child abuse. By the early 1980s pornography had been brought to political focus. By no means all of this scrutiny presumed to be indicting "men" in general, or "masculinity" or "male psychology." The issue that haunted most discussions was historical: was child abuse growing or not? Were battered wives more frequent? Or had about the same proportion of husbands battered their wives everywhere, always? Were there not non-wife-battering societies? Had there not been a time in American history when wives were not battered? Surely wives had not been battered more often in the nineteenth century, say, just because they had lacked the vote. And surely there was some kind of lesson in this for feminist tactics, feminist strategy.

The most interesting issue from the standpoint of historical analysis was pornography. Possibly the historian could prove that before a certain date no American men had access to any pornography, indeed, that before another certain date pornography did not even exist. Yet in the same demythologizing spirit as Brownmiller, one of the feminist leaders against pornography took special pains to argue that pornography was not consumed by "bad" but by "good" men: "Why So-Called Radical Men Love and Need Pornography."[41] The suppression of pornography, thus, would by no means make men better in any fundamental way; it might remove an affront to women in the marketplace and deprive men of the sanction of legality for their prurience, but it would not change their hearts. Just exactly why pornography constituted an offense to be dealt with by law remained at issue. If pornography could be shown to provoke rape, the logic was clear. But were "radical men"— or even "so-called" radical men—the rapists? Brownmiller had not singled them out. If pornography did not provoke rape, and if it did not interest women, then it might be thought a part of masculine culture, a phenomenon of man's sphere. But even then it told, presumably, something about men's minds, and antipornography feminists were angry at those minds.

From this point feminism found several routes, practically around the compass. Firestone's, the embrace of technology to replace the organs of reproduction, won no support; indeed, Firestone's vision was susceptible to attack from the antipornographers. Freeing the sexual body for experiences uncompromised by an "end" in reproduction exposed women to men's sexual fantasies even as they were invited to explore their own. In a kind of sequel to her book on rape, Susan Brownmiller confronted this trap in her 1984 book, *Femininity*. Systematically surveying how women had, over the ages, manipulated their bodies, their hair, their clothes, their voices, their skin, the way they walked, stood, sat, and moved, all in obedience to fluctuating norms of what was natural, proper, right, appropriate, decent, attractive, Brownmiller concluded that a woman with the same ambitions for life as a man carried a nearly hopeless burden. She was compromised from the start by a self-consciousness about the most basic aspect of daily life; she arrived at moments calling for maximum effort and concentration already drained by her efforts at managing her appearance. Brownmiller told how she had, in the mid-1970s, true to the feminist tradition announced at the anti–Miss America action in Atlantic City, affected the unadorned face, rejected the ritual shaving of legs and armpits, shopped for only convenient clothing. But that had been a passing moment in feminism. "My unadorned face, the free-spirited look of a decade past, now appears stick-in-the-mud, frumpy and prim: I am the dowdy feminist, the early Christian, the humorless sectarian who is surely against sex and fun." Women bore a burden heavier than the fear of rape: the need to appear feminine, attractive, presentable. Underlying the use of cosmetics was not feminine vanity but "feminine insecurity, an abiding belief that the face underneath is insufficient unto itself." In the end, Brownmiller had little help to offer. "It was probably inevitable that the anti-makeup forces should lose."[42] With a last conventional reference to "radical restructuring" of the social order, she seemed to signal some slight hope. But she never promised that in the restructured order women would not still feel the need to paint and primp.

Brownmiller only carried further, into intimate ultimate recesses of preoccupation, what had already been mounted, an attack upon women's preoccupation with dieting. In 1981 the writer, diet counselor, and feminist Kim Chernin published *Obsession: Reflections on the Tyranny of Slenderness*. Chernin's subtitle neatly encapsulated her theme. Even such a feminist as Charlotte Perkins Gilman had despised the standard woman's body of her time as too plump, too rounded, too maternal, lauding the lean, the quick, and the strong. But in 1981, Chernin said, it was obvious that many women were suffering in their pursuit of the slim line and ultimate fitness. Ample breasts, generous hips, capacious pelvises, solid buttocks and thighs—were these after all not the appointments of womanhood in healthy races? "Fat" was the upholstery appropriate to the female frame in its amplitude and splendor. In *The Hungry Self: Women, Eating and Identity* (1985) Chernin went on to offer a psychoanalytic explanation of such severe disorders as anorexia nervosa: anorexics were best understood as daughters struggling with their mothers. In contrast to Gilman, Chernin prescribed a revival of the "childhood kitchen" with its first-loved foods. Not the detachment of emotions from eating, but eating with the right emotions, was the route to growing up with a self-approving body identity.[43]

Victims of men's dread as well as of men's lust, victims of rape and victims of pornography, victims of the need to have a pretty face and a slim figure, women might well find the rationale for feminism crumbling from a sense of futility. One logical response was Chernin's: convert the sense of victimization into a sense of celebration.

Adrienne Rich too agreed that body was a source of woe to women:

I know no woman—virgin, mother, lesbian, married, celibate—whether she earns her keep as a housewife, a cocktail waitress, or a scanner of brain waves—for whom her body is not a fundamental problem: its clouded meaning, its fertility, its desires, its so-called frigidity, its bloody speech, its silences, its changes and mutilations, its rapes and ripenings.

But Rich refused to accept this as anything other than invitation to dispel the cloudiness and discover saving truth:

I have come to believe . . . that female biology—the diffuse, intense sensuality radiating out from clitoris, breasts, uterus, vagina; the lunar cycles of menstruation; the gestation and fruition of life which can take place in the female body—has far more radical implications than we have yet come to appreciate.

Though devoting her book to motherhood—as "experience" rather than as "institution"—Rich had no intention of confining the significance of women's physicality to reproduction. Women's bodies had veritable philosophical significance:

Physical motherhood is merely one dimension of our being. We know that the sight of a certain face, the sound of a voice, can stir waves of tenderness in the uterus. From brain to clitoris through vagina to uterus, from tongue to nipples to clitoris, from fingertips to clitoris to brain, from nipples to brain and into the uterus, we are strung with invisible messages of an urgency and restlessness which indeed cannot be appeased, and of a cognitive potentiality which we are only beginning to guess at.

Herewith women were provided the ultimate freedom they needed, freedom from men. Men might dread, envy, fear, lust after, or exalt women's bodies, but they would—could—never know what it was like to be a woman, and all women need do was affirm their bodies. This was the route to women's liberation. What still blocked women's liberation was simply women's attitude toward themselves: "[The] fear and hatred of our bodies has often crippled our brains."

Some of the most brilliant women of our time are still trying to think from somewhere outside their female bodies—hence they are still merely reproducing old forms of intellection. There is an inexorable connection between every aspect of a woman's being and every other; the scholar reading denies at her peril the blood on the tampon.[44]

Just what form of intellection greater sensitivity to their bodies might encourage in women Rich did not make clear. Certainly not history: nothing she said encouraged the least need to distinguish between, say, Russian, Swedish, Italian, and American men in their dread of women's bodies; Russian, Swedish, Italian, American women in their cognitive potentials. The mode of analysis was universal. Perhaps its most plausible content was religion.

A New Heaven for a New Earth:
The Flight to Radical Theology

When Elizabeth Cady Stanton wrote "The Christian Church and Women" and "Has Christianity Benefited Women?" as well as her *Woman's Bible,* she was not working out personal problems of faith or resolving personal relationships with any particular church. Like many late-nineteenth-century males of liberal Protestant background in the Northeast of Protestant America, Stanton had one day found herself free of dependence on religious symbols and practice. Personal faith had simply vanished, like the colds of childhood. When she questioned Christianity, it was with no anguish.[45] The Christian churches became, for her, forces to be scrutinized as sharply as any political party or economic interest, and as little sacred.

No such cool secularism emerged from the ferment of women's liberation. True, some feminists of standard Protestant background could well ask the point of any denominational allegiance. By the time of the rebirth of feminism in the mid-1960s, Protestantism's smorgasbord had grown even more lavish than in the late nineteenth century, but none of the offerings seemed particularly salient for feminists. On the other hand, a spreading fundamentalistic television evangelism of overtly antifeminist animus was beginning to make the old main-line denominations look passive, socially inert. Perhaps there was some reason to welcome feminism as a way to recover mainstream vitality. Georgia Harkness, longtime professor at Methodism's Garret Bible Institute, and a woman who said that she herself had been "extraordinarily well treated in the churches," offered her "historical and theological" inquiry, *Women in Church and Society*, in 1972, encouraging a broad advance of women within the churches. To the anthology of the Women's Caucus of Harvard Divinity School, subtitled "No More Silence!," Krister Stendahl, dean of the divinity school and already author of *The Bible and the Role of Women* (1966), offered the plainest of solidarities:

I feel quite awkward when asked to bring a male perspective to these essays. . . . I doubt that I am the right person for this assignment, because it all seems so simple and obvious to me. . . . The . . . question is . . . one of justice and equality. . . . Basic justice is simple. It is right.[46]

Compared with Stendahl's unclouded certitude that gender justice was indeed compatible with historic Protestantism, the contribution of William E. Phipps attested to the complexity of history. After protesting accusations of misogyny and antifeminism against Paul as anachronistic, Phipps did agree that Jerome and Augustine had gone badly astray. Worst of all was John Knox. Himself a Presbyterian "whose highest degree came from Knox's University of St. Andrews," Phipps had to confess: "It is embarrassing for me to present this study on Knox."[47] There was simply no apologetics to be concocted for Knox's *First Blast of the Trumpet against the Monstrous Regiment of Women*, for his *Second Blast*, for his antiwitchery, for his sexist bigotry generally. The most that might be said was that Presbyterianism was better than Knox. The explicit terms in which Phipps recorded his dissent from the standard hagiographical biographies of Knox, lauding his contributions to Scottish freedom and dissenting democracy while ignoring his bigotry, offered one promising route for faithful Protestant feminism. Faithful Catholic and faithful Jewish feminism could take it too. Let John Knox or Pius XI or Rabbi Eliezer be openly identified as what they were: unawakened misogynists. Keep the tradition but purge it.

But purging the tradition was not as powerful as forging beyond tradition. Having sought theological implications in the New Left of the late 1960s (*The Radical Kingdom*, 1970, and *Liberation Theology*, 1972), Catholic Rosemary Radford Ruether stressed the "Misogynism and Virginal Feminism in the Fathers of the Church" in a 1974 anthology, *Religion and Sexism*, but her deeper impulses were still celebratory, not critical. In *Mary—the Feminine Face of the Church* (1977) she called for "the humanization of the church," presumably still the church of historic Christianity. In *Womanguides: Readings toward a Feminist Theology* (1985), all the "Foremothers of WomanChurch" remained familiar Biblical and Christian figures. How WomanChurch could be anything less than a revolutionizing of the old historic church was hard to see, but no explicit call yet appeared. At a Catholic Boston Women's Ordination Conference in the spring of 1980, the tug of the tie to history was more openly avowed. "Most—but not all" of the participants "were in favor of deciding to stay" in the church, "despite the cost," in a belief "that there is something of great worth here, that remaining is a matter of love and faith and belonging."[48]

For Jewish women the idea of abandoning historic faith for some new sisterhood roused special conflict. They still labored under disadvantages in religious courts, in studying law, in sexist observances in the synagogue. In a way, orthodox historic Judaism was the very spring of Western patriarchal domination. Yet history had bound Jewish men and women together in a special way:

Jewish women do not need to hate men in order to liberate themselves; nor should Jewish men be seen simply as crude oppressors of women throughout history. For most of our history, both Jewish men and women suffered from outside persecution and hostility, and their mutual solidarity carried them through. Instead of polarizing, we must try to liberate men. . . . We must . . . liberate men Jewishly.[49]

True, there was Judaism and Judaism. Reform Judaism had been making moves toward equality for decades, whereas Orthodoxy remained basically unchanged, but, as Blu Greenberg observed, Reform's greater sympathy to feminism followed, not from its sense of Jewish treasures, but from its embrace of "liberal, modern" values. If there was something of "great worth" in Judaism, worthy of feminists' loyalty, it could only be, instead, in what was, not what was not, Jewish.

Conflict for Jewish feminists was rooted in another, perhaps still deeper, Jewish heritage than the law and anti-Semitism, however. Judaism was not a religion of the church. Jewish synagogues and temples were not analogues of Catholic cathedrals and Protestant churches. The Jewish community was the temple and within that community, the family was a "miniature sanctuary." With their Old Testament "Jewish" self-identification, the Puritans in America had stressed the significance of the family too, but never except in hierarchical subordination to the church, and never with such organic fusion with the faith as in Judaism, where the family was sealed to God not just by the Bible but by Talmudic prescription. Never were Puritan men bound to the home as were Jewish men: home ritual gave Jewish men a key place in the kitchen and in shopping. Even "sisterhood" would have only an ambivalent appeal to Jewish women, as a potential threat to the tie of man and wife. Thus, for Jewish women in particular "socialist feminism" could pose a special challenge insofar as classic orthodox Marxist socialism identified the family as the locus of women's oppression. A new faith might provide Jewish women a new family, a sisterhood, a WomanChurch, but it would utterly lack the core of ancient Judaism.[50]

Celebration of new faith could and did burst the bonds of historic identities, nowhere more dramatically than with Mary Daly. A Catholic, a professor at Boston College, Daly published in 1968 a harsh criticism of the Roman Catholic church, *The Church and the Second Sex*. In a title echoing Simone de Beauvoir's, she rehearsed the evidences of Christian religion serving as an "instrument of the oppression of women." Though noting that the church owed some of its misogyny to its Jewish and Greek roots, she found nothing in its later history to relieve a continuing nurture of "sexual prejudice." While "winds of change" had risen around John XXIII's Second Vatican Council, reaction had set in with Paul VI. Yet for all her indignation, her pessimism, her harsh intellectual honesty, in 1968 Daly still wrote from within, not from outside. She could not follow de Beauvoir. De Beauvoir had, of course, rejected not only the church but religion. She was an atheist. She had in effect adopted the "religion" of her father, an unbeliever, in place of that of her mother, under whose influence she had grown up pious. De Beauvoir belonged to the congregation of modern men who had forged science in place of religion. Hardly anywhere more than in her passages on women and religion had de Beauvoir revealed her own sense of herself as utterly different from most women. She did not write as one of a sisterhood. Daly agreed that de Beauvoir's atheism was a great aide to courage and acuity in historical thought:

It is probable that Simone de Beauvoir's psychological detachment from religious belief is a reason for both the vigor and clarity of her criticism of the Church's role in the oppression of women, and of its limitations.[51]

But Daly had no such detachment. When she did finally break with the institutional Roman Catholic church, it was not in the name of some secular philosophy. Leading an "exodus" from Harvard's Memorial Chapel where she was the first woman to preach at Sunday service, in 1971, she issued her call: "Sisters: the sisterhood of man cannot happen without a real Exodus . . . we cannot really belong to institutional religion as it exists. It isn't good enough. . . . Our time has come. Let us affirm faith in ourselves." Spelling out some aspects of this faith in

Beyond God the Father (1973), she declared that the alternative to the "phallic morality" of the old religions would be, not some new church, but an Antichurch, not a "cosmic church," but a "cosmic covenant." Only thereby would all that was evil in modernity, particularly "The Most Unholy Trinity: Rape, Genocide, and War," founded as it was on the "sexual caste" system integral to all patriarchal religions, be overcome.[52]

For Daly's American Protestant readers, her most striking chapter no doubt was that directed against "doctrines concerning Jesus." The ideal of imitating the historical Jesus, she declared, had entangled Christians beyond numbering in a "web of inauthenticity and hypocrisy." On the other hand, worship of the sacrificial Jesus—Christ on the Cross—had provoked Christians, not to humility, but to contempt and hate for all those who failed to join the worship, Jews especially. Christianity had been tribalism. The deficiencies of Jesus worship had not been overcome by the "myth and cult" of Mary. Though supposedly exalting her with its dogmas of Immaculate Conception and Assumption, the church had never admitted her into its pantheon. At the same time, as a figure beyond imitation of real women, Mary tacitly degraded them all. Protestants at least had had the courage to expel her. In sum: "Jesus Was a Feminist, But So What?"[53]

With paths thus broken, it became easier for feminists nominally still within their churches to press nearer their own boundaries. Judith L. Weidman, an ordained Methodist clergywoman, and editor of *Christian Feminism: Visions of a New Humanity*, declared in 1984 that the contributors to her anthology did still "hang in with the church," even though it was "at great price."[54] Yet key selections in the book hardly bore this out. In a chapter on Bible interpretation, assigned intriguingly enough, not to a Protestant, but to a Catholic scholar at Notre Dame, Elizabeth Schüssler Fiorenza dismissed all efforts to reread the Bible that still sought to find "universal" and "normative" authority in some texts if not in others. How must the Bible be read? Feminist Bible scholarship "places biblical texts under the authority of feminist experience."[55] Protestant women in the pulpit had already avowed the meaning of this explicitly. To Peggy Ann Way, her authority as a minister was not "rooted in the Scriptures" but in "experience," and was thereby "freer" than the ministry of her masculine colleagues.[56] Whether feminist Bible criticism went further than had the great heroes of Bible criticism might be argued, but few of them had been so explicit. If historic Puritan Protestantism's reliance on the Bible had long ago been petrified by fundamentalism into Bibliolatry, the new feminism clearly stood in confrontation with an important past, without yet quite confessing it.

In "The Feminist Redemption of Christ," Rita Nakashima Brock, a theologian at Valparaiso University, argued that classic orthodox Christology had fed a dualistic imagination that projected all that was fearful within oneself onto others, hence, far from promoting love, had promoted the hatreds so conspicuous in Christian civilization. "The feminist Christian commitment is not to a savior who redeems us by bringing God to us. Our commitment is to love ourselves and others into wholeness. . . . That healed wholeness is not Christ; it is ourselves.[57] Still other Protestant feminists followed other leads, which, while professedly still "hanging on" in the church, far more clearly looked ahead to a church that had never yet been. Letty M. Russell, a theologian at Yale and active in both the National and the World Council of Churches, offered a comprehensive theology from "a feminist perspective," but the experiential roots of Russell's theologizing were in outreach, her years of ministry to Puerto Ricans in East Harlem, her acquaintance with blacks in the civil rights movement, her knowledge of India in the YWCA. Russell's vision was of a kind of Sabbath of Humanity, a church "open to the world," "open to others," "open to the future." Her outlook was far from that of the nineteenth-century missionaries. Since the "others" were all already "dearly beloved brethren" "in spite of their denominational affiliation," the Christian church itself was simply one subdivision of humanity at large. Humanity at large was already "under God's grace."[58]

Sheila D. Collins, active in an interdenominational publications agency, wrote of "herstory," a new history that would "exorcise the patriarchal demon" at the heart of the old history. So far as church identities narrowly were concerned, Collins was straightforward: "The Protestant Reformation, which promised so much and gave so little to women, may represent a step backward for the female of the species." But "herstory" had little to do with nuances in Christian history per se. Collins touched on various theories, including de Beauvoir's, attempting to identify the deepest reason for the oppression of women in history; but writing "herstory" would be not so much a rewriting of history as a new history altogether, "revelatory" history, history revealing sisterhood. In the end, Collins's position was Daly's. She cited approvingly Daly's ultimate justification for feminism itself: the women's movement was "very possibly the greatest single hope for the survival of religious consciousness in the West." History—the history of patriarchy—was precisely the story of the decline of religion; "herstory" was the prophecy of the revival of religion, true religion, the religion of the "sisterhood of man."[59]

The issue hovering over and circling beneath all feminist theology was men. In the "sisterhood of Antichurch," in the sisterhood of "cosmic covenant," would men be welcome? Would the new "language" of feminist theologizing be appropriate to men as well as women? Presumably the answer in each case was "yes." Even Mary Daly referred repeatedly to "androgyny." Yet the new feminist theology offered no reasons for expecting such sharing. Feminist theology aimed at restoring what once had been, to reclaim what had been stolen, but not in any essential way to change what mattered most, women in their essential sisterhood. The new religion would amount to women coming into—or returning to—their inheritance, not in any reform or conversion or revolution of women. On the other hand, were androgyny and the "sisterhood of man" to be installed on earth, men did have to be reformed, converted, revolutionized. The issue was not whether such a reform of men might be merited or justified or necessary, but what it had to do with men's history. Why should anyone expect such a change in men?

One reading of history—not "herstory"—suggested a possibility. According to Sheila D. Collins, Rosemary Radford Ruether at least once had speculated, on "a cue from Jung," that once upon a time, men, in order to achieve self-consciousness and transcendence, had identified nature as an object to subdue, conquer, control, and in so doing, had lumped women in with it.[60] Here was a version of de Beauvoir's approach, seeing in men's view of women a "project" of their own self-creation, a self-creation that took the form of patriarchy. Feminist theology then might confront in straightforward fashion the implied question: could not women, aspiring to self-consciousness and transcendence themselves, legitimately hope that men would gradually realize that their own project of self-creation would be helped and not hurt, deepened and not deflected, by active, self-projecting women? Perhaps the history of men—"the patriarchy"—could be rewritten, not to iterate and reiterate women's oppression, but to demonstrate the shortcomings and failures of men's enterprise in its own terms. But Ruether did not follow out this line, nor did Collins, nor did feminist theology. Instead, they focused on the contrast between patriarchy and sisterhood, to the point that the contrast itself began to seem "universal" and "normative," a fact not of history but of nature, issuing finally in the theme that indeed what most differentiated women from men was precisely their attitude toward nature, their "gynecology," their collaboration with rather than conquest of nature, their immanent rather than transcendent relations with nature. De Beauvoir was turned upside down, her concern to explain why women had not become self-conscious egos and transcendent activists dissolved into celebrations of women as nontranscendent, nonindividualistic, noncompetitive, nonegoistic, and nurturing. Desire to celebrate sisterhood fed upon the mystification of men, not as brothers but as creatures in dread of women. Creatures in dread of women, creatures impelled by a propensity to rape women, creatures in need of pornographic simulacra of women obviously merited no conciliation from women. Proclamation of men's misogyny served as the basis for women's courage. Knowing from inside what it was like to be a woman, women knew women's strength and, knowing that men did not, understood the need for self-reliance. In the process, women rejected the possibility of collaborating with men in the projects men had pioneered, that of becoming stronger, freer, more individual, less religious, more history-making.

Sexuality: Nature or History?

If men were rapists by nature and theocrats out of irreducible necessity, no politics of equality was likely to flourish. If the old politics of accommodation to the oppressor could no longer be accepted, then only a politics of separation appeared logical. Separation had already been practiced in the nineteenth century, as both Tocqueville and Henry Carey had described it. That had of course been only a partial separation: women were excluded from man's realm but men still ruled in woman's, at home and in the bedroom. If the crucial oppression of women was, as modern women's liberation affirmed, in the sexual relationship, then separation had to proceed to that. Partly in conjunction with the emergent Gay Liberation movement among men, partly from independent impulses, lesbian women had begun "coming out" in the late 1960s, but in 1969, when Betty Friedan felt that lesbian women were attempting to gain influence in NOW, she stigmatized them as a "lavender menace" and conducted a purge. Lesbianism had arrived in women's politics.

Female homosexuality had always enjoyed a kind of haze or penumbra or even fog of indulgent mystification in the late nineteenth century as one sort of sisterhood, a not surprising condensation of the homosociality of woman's sphere, its physical expression construed less as a passion than as a sentiment. Since emotional attachments between females had interfered with no important male interests, they had hardly required definition, let alone persecution or prosecution. For some women, notably Jane Addams, Bryn Mawr's Carey Thomas, and especially Charlotte Perkins Stetson, "loving and living with other women, within the separatist environment of women's colleges, settlement houses, and reform organizations," the separation meant lives without men.[61] No one made ideological points about it. Jane Addams never distinguished homosociality from homosexuality; the very vocabulary had not reached her. Gilman never discussed lesbianism. In urging her Bryn Mawr girls not to get married, Carey Thomas had not been thinking primarily of sexuality; she had been thinking of the waste of their intellectual energies in domesticity. A powerful writer, Willa Cather, could live with a female friend for forty years without ever writing a word in illumination or justification of homosociality or homosexuality.

Carroll Smith-Rosenberg has discussed the chilling of this misty idyll by language alone.[62] "Science" began to make distinctions. That the science was heavily medical lent it special prestige. Expounded by men like Havelock Ellis, "sexology" traced both male and female homosexuality to disturbance of normal, natural maturation. Ellis's purposes were liberal: he aimed to blunt traditional views that male homosexuals were simply immoral. On the contrary: they could not help being that way. For women, however, the effect was to isolate one category of behavior that had been left undisturbed and uninspected. The result was not so much the labeling of particular women as of a style of life. Pursued with discretion, "Sapphic" love might persist unharassed in privileged enclaves such as Greenwich Village, but the prospect of a woman's sphere more completely separate from men's, with institutions and power of its own, was blighted. It was linked with the "unnatural." While male homosexuality was left to the dubious justice of police vice squads, female homosexuality faded behind curtains of social irrelevance.

After Friedan left the presidency in 1970, NOW reversed gears and adopted a civil liberties approach to lesbians. If, as one feminist indicated, "most lesbians experience their sexual preference as innate and involuntary," let them be treated like any other "minority" group.[63] Denying them equal rights in the public marketplace on account of their private sexual preferences could not be justified. So far as NOW was concerned, this tactic resolved its problem. Few NOW members professed to be lesbians;. although NOW's goal of equality for women in the marketplace could not harm and might help lesbians, lesbians themselves, once equal within NOW, could pursue whatever other goals they might wish elsewhere. Implicitly, NOW hoped that lesbianism would once again fade into the background within feminism at large.

Among the hundreds of local groups and in the pages of the dozens of short-lived journals of women's liberation, however, lesbianism became far more than a civil liberties issue.[64] The Daughters of Bilitis, an organization formed back in 1955, showed that consciousness had been consolidating among lesbian women years before, but the lesbian issue in the new feminism rose directly from the political debates within that feminism itself. Some lesbians began presenting themselves not as an oppressed minority but as the logical vanguard for women's liberation generally. In their 1970 manifesto, "The Woman-Identified Woman," the "Radicalesbians" noted that the charge against lesbians—that they were not "real women," that they were "dykes"—assumed that the status of being a woman was defined in relation to men. In heterosexuality, "the essence of being a 'woman' is to get fucked by men." "As long as the label 'dyke' can be used to frighten a woman . . . keep her separate from her sisters . . . then . . . she is controlled by male culture."[65] Carried thus far, and no further, here was affirmation that, should a woman happen by prior "innate and involuntary" constitutional endowment to be a lesbian, she ought to be so in dignity. Moreover, she could claim special feminist credentials. But that logic also contained the basis for an evangelical lesbianism. If lesbians were the most liberated of women, why ought not other, nonlesbian, "straight" women take heed? Asking, "Is Women's Liberation a Lesbian Plot?" two lesbian writers spelled out how lesbian life did constitute the kind of independent life many feminists professed to want:

If you do not have a man around, you must be prepared to take total responsibility for your life. [A woman] must . . . study opportunities for promotions and pensions, and learn about real estate, insurance, politics, banking, and stocks. She will also have to respond to the smaller challenges like caring for a car, understanding simple mechanical and electrical appliances, painting, carpentry, and doing the budget. . . . Life becomes greatly expanded. . . . Because the lesbian was not trying to interest men and probably rejected much limiting and damaging advice, she has an advantage over the feminist. She knows how to survive as a loner.[66]

The Radicalesbians asserted this linkage of lesbianism with a sense of single responsibility almost in echo of Elizabeth Cady Stanton's "solitude of self":

She is forced to evolve her own life pattern, often living much of her life alone, learning usually much earlier than her "straight" (heterosexual) sisters about the essential aloneness of life (which the myth of marriage obscures).[67]

In addition to this appeal to feminism's most heroic tradition, lesbian feminism also drew strength from feminism's most powerful intellectual case. Why could not sexual preference too be understood, not as a matter of innate and involuntary urges, but as historical creations? Marriage, the home, family already had been. Gilman had shown the "sexuo" half of the "sexuo-economic" relationship between men and women to be a historical phase in social evolution. Why should not both heterosexuality and homosexuality be conceptualized as matters of culture, not biology? In that case, preference for one or the other would follow from choice. Rather than lesbianism being imposed by nature on some unknown proportion of women, any woman choosing the values of feminism might well choose to be lesbian.

Demographic trends may have contributed to the confrontation. As late as the 1890s some 20 percent of American women did not marry, but by the 1950s this figure was falling to around 5 percent. If lesbian preferences did follow from innate and involuntary predisposition, what percentage of women experienced such predisposition? Margaret Fuller's citation of speculation that perhaps one-third of women felt strong inclinations to masculinity was not really any help. The evangelical lesbians of 1970 were not interested in being "dykes," in being "she-men," but in loving mutuality. Whatever the proportion of "innate" lesbianism might have been, more women obviously found themselves in the relation of heterosexual marriage in the 1950s than in the 1890s. But if some such approach was compatible with NOW's, it went unspoken. More commonly, the civil liberties approach was formulated in such a way as to at once obscure and facilitate the evangelical:

People must come to realize and admit openly that there are varieties of sexuality, of which heterosexuality happens to be the most popular but not necessarily the most valid. Women's liberation must promote the issue as a non issue of no more importance than a person's preference for Swiss or American cheese.[68]

Cheese manufacturers aside, preferences for Roquefort over Emmenthaler, Gorgonzola over Wisconsin were indeed matters of taste, not politics, but no cheese was more "valid" than another. The preference for a separate, nonheterosexual life on the other hand might indeed be based on what seemed more valid.

In *Quest: A Feminist Quarterly*, Emily Medvec outlined an alternative to seeking equality in the marketplace. Entitling her article "Money, Fame, and Power," Medvec made clear that she found little validity in money, fame, and power in the male world. Instead:

We must extend our focus to the new arena of creating our own political and economic base: establish banks and credit unions, publishing companies, an independent strike fund for working women, more diverse feminist businesses, technological research and development centers, a feminist political party, TV networks, feminist hospitals and universities, and so forth.[69]

The route by which women might arrive at such a choice could well be far more a matter of experience than of some innate, involuntary biological predisposition.

In a feminist novel of 1977, Marilyn French's *The Women's Room*, the heroines, a gifted, favored, fortunate few, have, after heroic effort, broken their way into one of the classic bastions of male dominance, no less than hierarchical, competitive, Puritan old Harvard itself, dispenser of credentials for entrée into the established marketplace of power, prestige, and money. Clarissa, Mira, Val, Iso, Kyla—each was on her way to a Ph.D., professorships, consultantships, and insider status in worlds of influence, each on her way to success. Harvard was the empowerment par excellence for realizing NOW's demand for women's rightful equal share in the American wonderland. And what were their feelings, on the brink of success? "We hate . . . Harvard." "We hate the political, the economic, and the moral structure of Harvard." Like the Catholic church, like General Motors, like the U.S. government, Harvard lived by patriarchy, hierarchy, power, male bonding. What price equality in such a heartless world?

And I thought: Christ! For years I worked in the civil rights movement, in the peace movement, . . . I worked with the committee on Somerville schools . . . on Cambridge schools. All this while, I'd been thinking—people, or children. But half the people I was trying to help were males. . . .
    I belong to all women's groups now. I shop at a feminist market, bank in a woman's bank. I've joined a militant feminist organization, and in the future I will work only in that. Fuck the dissertation, the degree, Harvard.[70]

The Women's Room was not a paean to lesbianism. Its heroines were not lesbians. But they might become lesbians. Their recoil from Harvard was not from some innate aversion to heterosexuality. It was rather from Harvard as hierarchical power structure. It was then by an act of imagination that the heroines attributed that structure to heterosexual men. Whether such a rejection of the world in which NOW aimed to place women as equals would lead to lesbianism was a separate question. There were more alternatives open to women who rejected Harvard than lesbianism's separation. There was solitude. There was trying to change men. But lesbianism might seem preferable to these somber and difficult alternatives.
    The subsidence of lesbianism as a storm center during the first decade of the new feminism hardly followed from any resolution of the challenges it posed. Lesbians would certainly not disappear, but as women's liberation itself lost any semblance of a unified movement in favor of a multiplicity of voices, the way was open for NOW to take the lead it had hoped to have from the start. However many ambitious young women may have been disappointed by Harvard, lesbianism was hardly likely to provide a rallying point for the vast majority of such young women flooding into the colleges and graduate schools intent upon careers and success in the marketplace as it existed. Private relationships with men could be adjusted far more easily in straightforward personal accommodations: casual relations with men, living together with a man, postponement of marriage, postponement of chil-

dren. All these grew mightily in the 1970s. Even less was lesbianism likely to offer much to those multitudes of women, young and not-so-young, taking jobs in the 1970s for straightforward economic reasons. Many of these reasons were linked closely to the cost of getting married, the cost of keeping a family going, the cost of children. Here, if anywhere, a backlash against career-minded feminism could take shape. In such a backlash, of all varieties of feminism, lesbian feminism would seem the most threatening. Deep in its own logic lesbianism, like NOW and like nineteenth-century feminism before it, continued to assume, on a level of unconsciousness that testified in itself to its dependence on the larger shape of American history, that abundance would prevail in American life. All its visions of a separated "Herland" took for granted the old capacity of the economy to expand, proliferate, spawn new communities, new suburbs, new frontiers. To the growing numbers of women in most immediate contact with the realities of the job market, of wages, of prices, of men laid off, of the costs of raising children, such an assumption seemed obtuse. Lesbianism carried the stigma of a luxury product. Presenting lesbian love in the most desperate circumstances of poverty and oppression, as in Alice Walker's *The Color Purple*, only sharpened, in its untransferable exoticism, the reality for most women: their bed had already been made; they had to sleep in it.

A New Man: Comrade, Playboy, Colleague?

In September 1971 NOW set up a "Task Force on the Masculine Mystique." A young sociologist, Warren Farrell, was put in charge. Farrell set out around the country lecturing and seeding male consciousness-raising groups. A National Conference on the Masculine Mystique was held in June 1974 at New York University. Scores of "facilitators" were sent forth, both to stimulate more rap groups and to plan actions, as well as to begin to construct a national network. A flurry of books on men's liberation appeared in 1974, Farrell's own *The Liberated Man* conspicuous among them. Perhaps men could change. Perhaps their age-old propensities too were not innate but historical. Perhaps they need not dominate and fear women's bodies, or rape them, or monopolize God forever.

The men's liberation program abandoned the old idea of the Seneca Falls Convention that women deserved equality as a matter of American justice. Gunnar Myrdal had revived that view in 1944, prophesying that American whites would ultimately live up to their own values of justice with respect to blacks, and then invoked the old analogy with women. But in obvious parallelism with Betty Friedan's *The Feminine Mystique*, the men's liberationists proclaimed that men too, like women, were victims. Like women, they too labored under the burden of a mystique that circumscribed their behavior, cramped their self-images, smothered their feelings. Incarnate in John Wayne, the Dallas Cowboys, and the war in Vietnam, unliberated masculinity was called upon, not to liberate others so much as itself.

This parallelism with the feminine mystique suffered from ambiguity from the start. Basically, Friedan—and implicitly, NOW—did feel that women had been damaged psychologically by their mystique. They had been caused to lack self-confidence. They had learned not to be aggressive. Displays of high intelligence had been discouraged. Let women then learn to be more self-confident, more aggressive, more openly intelligent. Let them approach more "masculine" behavior. Men's liberation turned this about: "To the extent that women have been conditioned to . . . exclusive passivity, they have been maimed. The same can be said about men who are conditioned to exclusive activity."[71] Let men learn a degree of passivity. Let men approach more "feminine" behavior. The androgyny implicit in Friedan's attack on the feminine mystique grew more explicit in the attack on the masculine mystique. Ordinarily, men were taught how to conceal their emotions, but it was better to be able, as women were, to reveal oneself. Men were taught how to give orders and exert control, but it was better to deal with people in a nonhierarchical, noncontrolling, consensual way, the feminine way. Men could not cry; it was better to be able to cry. A man projected sexuality, but sexuality constricted and limited affective expression; sensuality, women's way, was better.[72] The more explicit such formulations became, however, the more it appeared that characteristics clustered at the feminine pole were good and those at the masculine pole bad, thus undermining any logic of some androgynous mingling in a half-way ground between. The whole issue of decreasing the stereotypical polarization of masculinity and femininity was further confused by the effort of some of the new male consciousness-raisers to locate the springs of a less exaggerated masculinity. According to Don Clark, a California clinical psychologist, "homosexual self-understanding" was a "necessary facet of male liberation."[73] But tracing a masculinity friendlier to women to male homosexuality rendered any parallelism completely incoherent.

The asymmetry between feminine and masculine mystique served to obscure a far more important contrast. Though a sociologist, Farrell drew by far most of his documentation from psychological and psychiatric literature, as did his counterparts, Jack Nichols, Marc Feigen Fasteau, Clark, Jack Sawyer, Sidney Jorard, and others. But it was ultimately sociology, not psychology, that undergirded Friedan's attack on the feminine mystique. However psychologically constricting, what the feminine mystique had cost women most were jobs, status, careers, success, prestige, money, power. However psychologically constricting, mystified masculinity had cost men none of these things. Perhaps women would have to cry less, give orders more, learn aggression in order to fulfill NOW's program. But why should men risk losing money or power by becoming more passive, more emotional, more feminine? Men's liberation had no answer. Indeed, by wholly evading the question, men's liberation hardly got started before it stalled. But the essentially expedient, opportunistic quality of male lib was to be seen best in its remarkable amnesia. An exactly opposite evangel to male lib had flourished and come to popular climax hardly ten years before. In Myron Brenton's *The American Male* of 1966, Hendrik Ruitenbeek's *The Male Myth* in 1967, and other such tracts, alarm had been raised, not over some obsession with aggression in the American male, but over his decline into passivity.[74] Lamentation over a deterioration in American masculinity had popped up during World War II. Margaret Mead had waxed anxious over American men. Just previously Philip Wylie had castigated a generation of "Moms" for castrating their sons, and army psychiatrists brooding over draft deferments under Section 8— psychiatric unfitness—agreed with him.[75] In the 1950s, hammering home his own certainty that American manhood had suffered internal hemorrhage, Norman Mailer had commended to white males immersion in the dangerous elements of black jazz, hipster drugs, impulsive violence.[76] The advantage of any of these animadversions for feminism was problematic. Perhaps feminists could agree with Wylie that moms were the unhappy product of women's frustration, but his ideal of masculinity was not necessarily that of the friends of women's rights. Similar ambiguities seemed to lurk in Mead's outlook. As for Mailer, it would prove easiest, as Kate Millett would do in 1970, in *Sexual Politics*, to simply categorize him as a hostile misogynist. Yet dialectic rather than simple confrontation remained a possibility in this concern over damaged masculinity. In *The Feminized Male* (1970), the sociologist Patricia Sexton attacked the school system as a feminized enclave. "Teaching has not been a manly profession, nor school a manly occupation for boys."[77] The feminized male was the boy who satisfied the schools' essentially feminine mandates. Since Sexton's ultimate point was feminist—that society would be better off with women sharing power and "power centers" with men—the coherence of her book depended on linking the feminized male with this goal, but this she failed to establish. It was not at all clear that rescuing boys from the schools would help advance feminism. Yet Sexton did succeed in raising the issue of whether feminism would be advanced by prompting some feminization, or at least some demasculinization, of men themselves, along the lines of male liberation. If the contribution of defeminized schools to a collaboration of masculinity and femininity in the power centers remained mysterious, the contrast of such collaboration with androgyny was clear.

The attempt to win men by persuading them of their own self-interest in feminism thus tailed off into laments and complaints quite different from those of Brownmiller, Rich, Daly, and others who saw men as essentially predatory on women. In 1983 the feminist writer Barbara Ehrenreich sketched out a history of what she labeled a "male revolt" dating from the early 1950s. She noted the Beat Generation of poets, novelists, mystics, musicians, bohemians, and wanderers famous for its subversions of the suburban myth, but she found Hugh Hefner's *Playboy* more significant. Its commercial success suggested a more pervasive sensibility. In effect, *Playboy*—and the Beats—had anticipated NOW's male liberationists by twenty years. *Playboy* had projected a whole new style for younger men, replacing the old buttoned-down, uptight corporate repression. Its invitation to women had of course been ambiguous from the start. Were they simply one of the playboy's expenses? or were they, too, self-supporting playgirls? In any case, the upshot had been, after a quarter-century, a spread of self-indulgence among men, a decline of old models of responsibility to wife, marriage, children, family. While hardly intent upon resurrecting the 1950s suburban idyll, Ehrenreich did not deny herself a bit of melancholy: "If we accept the male revolt as a historical fait accompli . . . [are] we not acquiescing to a future in which men will always be transients in the lives of women. . . ?" Presumably, for feminist separatists, lesbian or not, such transience would be more than welcome, but for feminists still heterosexual in their expectations, it left troubling prospects. Ehrenreich found nothing but bare hope to offer, with a surprising twist: "I would like to think that a reconciliation between the sexes is still possible," she concluded, but on a basis that had no linkage to any history, before or after the male revolt: perhaps as "brothers and sisters."[78]

This was obviously unsatisfactory, and Ehrenreich, together with Elizabeth Hess and Gloria Jacobs, returned to the issue again, in *Re-Making Love: The Feminization of Sex* (1986). Women too, it appeared, had had their revolt. While much of the book presented the facts of a sexual liberation among women in the 1960s—birth-control pill, vibrators, validation of clitoral orgasm, and so on—its polemic was aimed to call feminists to the defense against a "counterrevolution," a sexual backlash threatening the new freedoms. Women should not let themselves be pushed back into repression. But this still left the matter of life with men as murky as ever. Basically repeating Charlotte Perkins Gilman's old thesis that women's sexuality had been distorted by the economics of the marriage market, Ehrenreich reversed Gilman's hope for a minimization of sex in favor of more abundant, less calculating sexuality. But there was no reason why this would not spread, rather than check, transience in relations with men. Precisely such transience had been the point—and the hope—of Alexandra Kollontai's vision of a socialism in which all women would be free of any economic need to bargain with their sex. Kollontai's hope, however, had derived from her fear that women's sexuality left them ever in danger of being psychologically engulfed in any deep sexual attachment. One of socialism's virtues, then, was that it made sex less important, less crucial a constituent of character and personality, less linked to meanings beyond itself. Ehrenreich, too, was defending the disentanglement of sexuality from bargaining and dramas of stereotyped masculinity and femininity. But she had already clearly noted in *The Hearts of Men*, how simple sexual liberation more easily promoted exploitation and separation between the sexes than some new equality, freer, more spontaneous, more intimate and trusting and, yes, loving. Just as one of the key features of the Women's Liberation Movement had been the self-validation of lesbians, so one of the key features of the male revolt had been the assertion by male homosexuals of the legitimacy of their subculture.

For those still yearning for a "reconciliation between the sexes," Ehrenreich's celebration of "pleasure" as the legitimation of sexual freedom could only deepen melancholy into darkness. Not only had the authors of *Re-Making Love* circled back to the old myth of some natural sexuality to be revealed once all historical burdens and barnacles had been scraped away, but they had short-circuited feminist efforts to convert such concepts as femininity and masculinity into terms of history rather than of nature. And, finally, they had done so while finessing the question whether the different sexual physiologies of male and female made for different psychologies. Susan Brownmiller's thesis on the rapist to be found in men was not to be answered by a new myth of Eden.

The National Organization of Women: Realism and Pathos

Embrace of genetic engineering; polemics against rapists; celebrations of the body; theological prophesying: these were brilliant and penetrating contributions to American imagination. They hardly made, together or separately, a "movement." The early leaders of theNational Organization for Women assumed that levers of power had to be pressed if women were to advance toward "full participation" in American society, toward a share in "all its responsibilities" and enjoyment of "all its liberties," as NOW's Statement of Purpose had urged. Friedan's impulse to ostracize lesbians followed from her sense that they would prove a liability in a movement hoping to win power: NOW's later tactic of accepting the civil-liberties dimension of lesbianism while ignoring its larger issues nicely displayed the organization's will to practicality. It followed also that NOW would not welcome attacks on men, even though its own flurry into male liberation contained an implicit judgment that women would find it easier to share power with certain kinds of men than with others. In no way had NOW been a grass-roots organization in its origins. Created by a handful of political women in Washington, D.C., as a device for putting pressure on a government agency, the Equal Employment Opportunity Commission, it more nearly resembled a lobby than a movement. Yet the early activists understood that their effectiveness would persist only as it was clear that a real and growing constituency for women's rights did exist. The rights in which Friedan and her associates were interested had nothing to do with patriarchal priests or playboys. They were marketplace rights. As Friedan's successors in NOW's leadership set about preparing the organization for effective political leadership, they could look to great opportunities. As the 1970s opened, the first large groups of young women of the baby boom were leaving college, intent on jobs and careers rather than marriage. They were a natural constituency for a movement dedicated to widening access to the marketplace, demanding equality in salaries and wages, in promotions, in fringe benefits. Moreover, the general macroeconomic benefit to the nation of the new cohorts of marketplace-oriented young women had become clear. It seemed that NOW and feminism were at last, as William Chafe said, moving with, not against, the "underlying trends at work in the society." "No longer was feminism irrelevant to most people's daily lives."[79]

NOW's leaders therefore welcomed the efforts of Congresswoman Martha Griffith of Michigan in 1970 and 1971 to get the Equal Rights Amendment reported to the floor of Congress. The ERA could become the rallying point for a broad mobilization. Women who might differ in the particular needs to which they gave first priority could unite behind the great symbol—women's equality explicitly sealed in the nation's Constitution. The point was not that any great changes would follow automatically upon ratification of the ERA: "There are not any acute problems women currently face which the ERA will solve." Important advances had already been won without constitutional amendments. Perhaps the most dramatic change in the condition of career women had been brought about in university faculties through use of an executive order issued by Lyndon Johnson in 1967; other such gains were imaginable, ERA or no ERA. But, as Jo Freeman explained, the ERA's value would lie exactly in the political energy its pursuit would inspire and the "psychological victory" its passage would bring. True, there was a risk. Writing in 1975, Freeman warned that if "ratification efforts drag on and on for years," the ERA would turn out "to be a losing proposition," but she, for one, registered no pessimism.[80] Pursuit of the ERA made political, psychological, and ideological sense.

No one would be able to prove, upon the defeat of ERA, that its pursuit had been a mistake, since no one could prove that, without it, feminism would have won the prominence it did in the 1970s and early 1980s. Nor could anyone prove that NOW had not been working in accord with "underlying trends," for no logic decreed that underlying trends automatically won out in the political marketplace. The political market, like any market, was imperfect; countertrends could disrupt it, minorities paralyze it, emergencies overload it. The response of many feminist leaders, to assume the defeat was a function of a temporary deviation from a basic trend, recalled the response of earlier feminists to early defeats in the struggle for suffrage: if not now, then eventually. Yet the defeat of ERA prompted reflection in one particular direction that feminism itself had tended to neglect. Feminism's fundamental case was that the ultimate cause of women's subordination was—could only be—finally, men, but it was by no means clear that ERA had failed as a consequence of men's opposition. Women had opposed ERA too. Some anti-ERA women, such as Marabel Morgan, author of *The Total Woman*, (1973), simply reasserted, for reasons of their own, old ideals of separate spheres. But in the feminist Barbara Ehrenreich's view, there was another focus of anti-ERA feeling of a far more practical sort. The animus of some women appeared to be directed, not so much against feminism and "liberated" women themselves, as against "liberated" men availing themselves of the new gender equalities to enjoy sex while avoiding responsibility for wives, children, family. Ehrenreich quoted the most conspicuous anti-ERA woman leader, Phyllis Schlafly:

Should a husband have the legal right to stop supporting his faithful wife of twenty or thirty years by the simple expedient of saying, 'I don't love her anymore; I love a younger woman'? Even though love may go out the window, the obligation should remain. ERA would eliminate that obligation.[81]

It was of course demagogic to say that ERA would automatically preclude alimony. Yet new divorce laws in various states, dedicated to greater equality, were already proving to have left growing numbers of ex-wives in penury. One of the arguments used by Warren Farrell, aimed to entice men to give up their traditional masculinity, had been that women earning good salaries took the pressure off men.

The case for ERA had been pressed in context of the growing numbers of women in their thirties making their way in the professions, the banks, the insurance companies, the universities, in real estate and the entrepreneurial realm of services and communications. But all this appeared to take for granted what feminism itself had not yet validated, let alone a wider political consensus, namely, that women were in fact to be expected to support themselves by jobs in the marketplace. What had begun as a demand and an aspiration appeared to have become a compulsion and a duty. Of course the strongest force rendering women's work a compulsion had risen in the marketplace itself, seconded by the demographics leaving more and more women with no choice but to work. But ERA had never been urged primarily as a response to the problems of women in the marketplace. In Friedan's original impulse, and that of the young college-trained generation, it had been linked to a rejection of domesticity. ERA thus was easily stigmatized as a ratification of trends making life harder, not better, for all those whose goal in going to work was to meet the harsh challenges of necessity. Perhaps at no point in American history, for instance, had husband and wife been more bonded by economic pressure than were husbands and wives with college-age children from the late 1960s through the last of the baby boomers graduating in the early 1980s. But ERA spoke far more clearly to the young college graduates themselves.

Similarly, while ERA itself spelled out no concrete implications of the equality it asserted, feminists preoccupied with women's marketplace position had frequently called for expansion of facilities for the day care of working mothers' young children. Yet, no matter how many studies might be cited affirming that day care wrought no ill effects on children, the call for day-care centers had not followed from any debate. It took for granted what in the lives of many women—and many men as well—had been experienced as harsh necessity. Once again, ERA appeared to ratify what for many persons appeared to be compulsion, necessity, pain, defeat. The fact that ERA was more likely to help than to harm struggling single mothers, women with underemployed husbands, even Schlafly's middle-aged wife abandoned by a liberated husband, was beside the point. ERA had not been advanced for those causes, nor had feminism nourished itself on these problems.

Finally, feminism's own inner split could only have contributed to prompting opposition. Although the original sponsor of ERA was the National Organization of Women, with its prime regard for women's access to the marketplace, the feminists of women's liberation, with their prime regard for women's culture, women's sphere, women's bodies, women's sexuality, had no reason to resist ERA and, indeed, obvious reasons to support it. But insofar as the specific goal of an ERA was linked with this more heterogeneous feminism of women's liberation, ERA, once again, could be stigmatized as taking for granted what had not remotely won consensus among women at large. Insofar as the locus for some of the greatest tensions between men and women was in the black community, ERA's association with the thesis that women's basic quarrel was with men suffered from a handicap extraneous to its backers' real purposes, but one they could not reject.

Ironically, it was among ERA's most natural supporters, too, the young college-educated career women of the baby boom generation, that the methods of women's liberation lost appeal. Their ambition for the marketplace drew from no animus against men. Their postponement of marriage did not register any impulse toward separate lives; soon it was evident that the new generation of career women expected to combine career with marriage, childbearing, and family. Keeping score on each new social invention—unisex kitchens, his-and-her bank accounts, contracts for cohabitation, half-time careers for two, along with flex time, commuter marriages, home care versus day care, and so on—far more closely reflected a new ethos of experimental collaboration than one of challenge. Of course many of the newly successful, quite in accord with the ideology of success they had assumed, quite predictably attributed their success, as men did, to their own efforts, in implicit deprecation of feminism and sisterhood. It was thus a further irony that, while feminism and NOW could quite accurately point to remarkable fulfillments of the Statement of Purpose, they would not necessarily be credited for them.

ERA also suffered from bad luck. There was nothing that decreed the Supreme Court must strike down antiabortion laws in 1973, just as the campaign for ERA was getting into high gear. The linkage was emotional and symbolical, not logical. Conceivably, a supporter of ERA could also believe abortion should be illegal. But certainly once antiabortion forces became coherent and politically insistent, NOW and feminism could not withdraw from the issue. Yet abortion rights had not been prepared for by wide democratic debate, let alone by feminist debate. Pressed by a small number of civil libertarians, the court's decision could then be counted another advance in the process of securing individual liberties against all intrusion, whether backed by a majority or not. But antiabortion quickly emerged as a means for the mobilization of feelings already inflamed by the rapid social changes in the United States since the 1960s. It offered self-validating moral condensation to the audiences already assembled by the militant fundamentalism of Protestant television evangelists, and for the first time in American history this meant that Protestant and Catholic popular tribalism were in collaboration. But in addition, the abortion issue specifically, like the playboy syndrome generally, linked into feelings of resentment against men. The feminist Deirdre English discovered one concentration of antiabortion sentiment precisely among women who sensed in abortion another encouragement to male irresponsibility. Once again, feminism had no easy counter to such feelings.

To the burden of defending the Supreme Court's abortion decision was added that of facing the majorities for Ronald Reagan. Reagan's long ideological rigidity came to be rewarded at last by the twin accidents of the old Republican Party's continuing disintegration, and thus, vulnerability to capture following the disaster of Richard Nixon, on the one hand, and the Democrats' climactic collapse under Jimmy Carter. Translating the 1980 vote against Carter and the Democrats into a new stable Republican majority would be no simple task. Since Reagan and his California sponsors were sure that, in a capitalist economy, rich men should be freed from restraints on becoming richer, the route to majority support had to include identification with the "social issues," among which abortion was preeminent. Certainly the new administration had nothing to gain from wooing feminists. By withdrawing support from affirmative action, the administration effectively linked explicitly feminist issues with the difficult social issues. Reagan's prolonged and careful abstention from pressing the abortion issue to confrontation nicely defined his own, as well as his managers', priorities, but feminists could take little comfort in that. Much of their own constituency, as well as their antagonists', held to the very same priority: economics first, then national defense, and, finally, once these were secure, justice. The history of the twentieth century attested to the prudence and wisdom of that.

But bad luck was not the ultimate reason for the political defeat of ERA, let alone of feminism generally, in the mid-1980s.[82] It was not that feminists and the supporters of ERA were still a minority. Nineteenth-century feminists had always been a minority, to their day of triumph, yet had triumphed by 1920. While a minority, however, they had been a decisive minority. The majority of women had continued to be women of the countryside, of the farms and farm towns of East, South, and West. But the women of the growing middle classes of the commercial and rising industrial towns and cities had seized their historic opportunity, formed their local associations, forged their sphere, a sphere that, on opportunity, could take on national dimensions, as during the Civil War, with its need for the care of soldiers. They could forge their nationwide temperance societies. Black women among the freed slaves emerged in the culture of black churches; immigrant women from a score of nations held to ethnic and religious identities incomprehensible to the native white Anglo-Saxon Protestant heritage of woman's sphere. Yet, however outnumbered, white Anglo-Saxon Protestant women of the rising capitalist-based middle classes had remained coherent and decisive. As Theodore Roosevelt, among others, registered, they were not to be denied: they deserved civic equality precisely as protectors of their sphere.

But no such single coherent and influential sector of women emerged in the "second" feminism after 1965. Women frustrated by suburbs of the 1950s were at odds with women for whom the suburbs fulfilled a long social climb. Women who enjoyed the luxury of being able to reject men, whether as patriarchs, playboys, or rapists, were at odds with women whose men had been rendered jobless. Such solidarity as might prompt sisterhood between black and white women was persistently undercut by the radically different problems of black men from white. Dramatically different relationships with men divided women on social issues, most conspicuously abortion, but even, as new laws proved faulty, divorce. Perhaps the most poignant difference emergent was that between married women who chose not to have children and those who chose to do so. Here above all profound contrasts in outlook and self-interest could easily be imagined. Still, the crucial fact was not difference itself. Difference had been evident in the nineteenth century. It was, rather, the absence of any such decisive group as the white urban middle-class Protestant women who had created woman's sphere and had then moved out into feminism in the nineteenth century. Certainly the new generation of upwardly mobile, highly successful women in the marketplace did not constitute such a new dominant group. If anything, their own future was obscure. Inevitably, by the 1980s their new status had prompted the discovery-creation of new maladies. Books such as *Smart Women/Foolish Choices, Women Who Love Too Much, Men Who Hate Women and the Women Who Love Them,* and *Why Do I Think I Am Nothing without a Man* offered a focus in pop psychology and private life the reverse of any vector toward translating personal marketplace success into public political influence.[83] NOW's own effort to establish itself among the women of the new underpaid and overworked postindustrial work force, while fully justifiable in terms of its own Statement of Purpose, also constituted tacit acknowledgment that the women moving up in the higher careers and professions fell far short of making up a sufficient, or even necessarily coherent, interest group. "Class" was too simple a concept for clarifying this situation, but the better words for doing so were still only in process of generation.

Paradoxically, with no great triumph to enjoy, analogous to the suffrage amendment, feminism's survival was more assured. Its "way," its route, its bearing had been rendered much less clear, but in the very debate over what these should be the remarkable vitality generated over the previous twenty years had plenty of channels to pursue.

Conclusion

Nineteenth-century American women—Northern, white, Protestant women—led lives increasingly different from that of their men. In old small-town America, eighteenth-century America, Henry Carey's America, they had shared life with their men. The economics of small-town life had drawn on men and women in organic partnership. The politics of colonial America had remained reserved for a few men; most men shared with all women an apolitical routine. Democratic capitalism undercut this old order. It generated a realm of entrepreneurial energy that split men from women in a dozen ways. The psychological was by far the most important: men became emotionally concentrated on what women barely understood. Democratic capitalism also generated modern politics as a realm of men and men only. No longer would government and local community collaborating with family and church in the old Puritan way predominate. Politics and economy came to constitute a kind of realm of their own, generating visionary new stages reserved for men—California and New York City. None of this may have been inherent in capitalism. Capitalism might have been contained within the frame urged by Carey. If the eighteenth-century economy was capitalist, it had been so contained. But if Tocqueville was right, that democracy had already unleashed the infinitude of human nature, then the kind of expansive, more or less hectic, more or less uncontrolled emergence of a male world of enterprise was inevitable.

Women then found themselves with a special space, a sphere more or less explicitly and self-consciously reserved for them. Basically, this sphere consisted of the residue of the old small-town community left behind as democratic capitalism wrought its transformations. The simplest definition of woman's sphere was "home," soon made abstract as "domesticity." But just as in the old integrated community, women remained in touch with one another beyond the boundaries of their individual homes. Indeed, once men began responding to the stimulant of the growing marketplace, and spent less time sharing work and community with their women, women began spending more time with each other. Soon, as historians have shown us, they were busily engaged in "associations." Men's associations depended on money; women's depended on womanly attributes. Democratic capitalism underwrote these white, Protestant, middle-class women's activities through the rest of the century. No economic desperation made their employment in the marketplace necessary; their husbands earned enough to support both home and women's free time for associating. As the sharpest focus of consciousness in this women's associational world, feminists too benefited immensely from democratic capitalism. No ideology or political jealousy prompted them to try becoming capitalists. On the contrary, by maintaining watch over the mores, as Tocqueville said, women made it possible for men to commit themselves still more completely to their own wonderland of speculation and self-transformation. There was positive symbiosis in women's taking heed for "community" in order that political economy might thrive. Many early feminists found subsidy from a father, others from a husband. Soon a Frances Willard could make a self-supporting career within woman's sphere itself.

All this was quite in contrast to what happened in Italy, Sweden, and Russia. In none of these countries did feminism enjoy the steady and lush growth of a woman's sphere. The point at which men's and women's lives were most dramatically disrupted was the point also at which they had most emphatically shared, in the destruction of the peasant villages, then in the dislocations of industrialization. Moreover, where old patterns of sharing persisted, in the Italian family, inhibitions against woman's sphere increased, for it was precisely in her service to the family in its narrowest sense that the Italian wife and mother continued to be valued. In Soviet Russia, where the old family had been smashed by politics, women's condition in the new industrial economy offered not the slightest chance for a woman's sphere, since their new condition was that of workers in that very industry. Only on the new collective farms was any space offered for Russian women to generate a sphere of their own, and that would be totally cut off from any possible contact, through association, with the rest of society. Such a sphere as they might concoct would have little, if any, feminist potential at all.

In the United States, then, women had what women in Italy, Sweden, and Russia did not: space, time, and resources of their own to define themselves. To tell this story in such a way as to cast the women concerned as victims, as passive clay onto which was stamped some hegemony by men, is to perpetuate Tocqueville's temptation to resolve the puzzle of why women accepted their sphere with the answer that they were saints. We do not have evidence to that effect. Feminism tells us that women did not accept passivity but rather realized the opportunity handed them for great activity and seized it. The question was, to what end? Activity for its own sake can rarely be found in history. Tocqueville came close to suggesting that this was the condition of American men, and in a certain sense Constance Rourke confirmed it:

the heart of popular male culture in the age of Jackson was self-enjoyment, the irresistible response to the freedom to mock old identities and pursue the unprecedented—all things new! Women were not granted such a range of freedom. On the other hand they were not coerced into a mold. Their identification with home and domesticity was an ancient one. They were being offered the chance to convert that identification into one with a "sphere" that, centered on home and domesticity, might expand to include what once had been part of the community shared with men—good works, works of charity, of motherliness for the unfortunate, the abandoned, the real victims of the new scheme of things.

One day historical measuring tools may be able to tell us how many women experienced the transition from eighteenth to nineteenth century, from Henry Carey's ideal America to Tocqueville's ideal America, as suffering, deprivation, coercion, and how many experienced it as relief, opportunity, gain. The tools will have to be refined. It does not follow that women who embraced home and domesticity narrowly were narrow or afraid. What the historian needs are tools to tell him how many women had generated hopes and ideals for mothering that were frustrated in the integrated communities of the eighteenth century. How many Puritan wives had yearned for escape from their husband's headship precisely in order to provide the tender loving care he frustrated and forbade? Until we can tell the story of the emergence of home and domesticity as one of aspiration, we cannot tell it as one of deprivation and compensation. The "heartless world" is to be seen long before woman's sphere emerged.

By the same token, sensitive tools are needed to disentangle motives and ideals at work when other women undertook their associations to expand woman's sphere beyond narrow domesticity. What was the truth about Frances Willard? Did she use temperance as a front for her real interest, feminism? If so, what did she want from feminism? Did she see feminism as the means, through "socialism," to change men and thus make possible women's breakout from woman's sphere into the great wide world? All this might be so, but it need not be true that all those women who after her death failed to follow on where Willard had led, those who fell back from "socialism" and feminism into straight temperance, did not also share the very same goal of changing men, and hence of breaking down the division between the spheres. It was not a weakness in woman's sphere, or in feminism, that they should have generated such differences. Quite the contrary. Northern white Protestant women enjoyed the luxury of a hundred years of opportunity to think about themselves and what they wanted to be.

No such luxury was enjoyed by women in Italy, Sweden, or Russia. Quite apart from the grueling fate of ordinary peasant women, such women of the middle strata as there were never enjoyed the kind of long historic updraft provided their American sisters. On the one hand cribbed in by a traditionalist church, boxed off by welfare politics, confronted by the coercions of one-party dictatorships, the middle strata of Italian, Swedish, and Russian women were on the other hand offered alliances with men they could hardly refuse, in unions, parties, religious movements. They had little chance to ferment hopes among themselves. The very leitmotif of woman's sphere in America was in effect denied women in Italy, Sweden, and Russia. The business of making the nation homelike in Sweden was taken over by great patriarchs leading a patriarchal, male-dominated party. In the Soviet Union the Communist Party took unto itself all rights to supply social mothering. Only in Italy did the aspiration for an "American" future of democratic capitalism flourish, but in Italy the aspiration fell short, and home remained what it had already been, insurance against failure, a haven in a mediocre world.

In the United States, as women reflected upon themselves in their sphere, they saw themselves leading quite different lives from men. It was hard not to begin to think they were quite different from men. At just this juncture a few unusual women made a break. Margaret Fuller did not truly think of herself as different in nature from the best men around her. She wanted Emerson to be better than he was, but not more womanly. Abstraction vanished from Fuller's imagination. In Italy she felt no restraint in following a man, Mazzini. She did not pretend that she was capable of all it took to wage war, but in her life with Ossoli she ignored standard sex roles without fear. She had already shown herself eager to observe and write about the larger America beyond women's roles, men's America. But while it is easy to wish that there had been more Fullers, a hundred thousand Fullers, and to judge that, because there were not, most women's lives must have been repressed and blighted, such an approach leads nowhere. Far better to comprehend Fuller thoroughly: she herself could not escape the undertow back into woman's sphere and lamentation over women's victimization. She herself succumbed to the discourse construing men and women as by nature quite different kinds of beings. Thus it is not so much the weakness of other women compared to Fuller's strength that illuminates women's world, as the power exerted by woman's sphere over women's minds, a power so great that it deflected Fuller's.

We can see the same practically gravitational influence in other exceptional individuals. Charlotte Perkins Gilman never could unchain the eager, lithe, lean speculator and adventurer within her from the warm and reassuring limits of progressive womanhood. Stanton's case remains the most fascinating. Clearly, at the end of her long life Stanton was saying plainly that women must think of themselves as men did, ultimately on their own, dependent finally on themselves as individuals for their salvation. It was remarkable even more for someone of her age than of her sex to say so, and some such developmental psychology as Erik Erikson's might one day inspire the biography showing that it was exactly this project, of gradually coming to full consciousness of her autonomy, that brought Stanton into a hale and liberated old age. Yet what was it in her case but her long life in woman's sphere at its most attractive that had delayed her final self-affirmation?

Again, the point of grasping the power of exceptional women is not to then judge others, but to establish the strength of the influence of woman's sphere. Northern white Protestant women, coming to think of themselves as different from men, many of them coming to think of themselves as superior to men, hence as even more deserving of the suffrage than the original egalitarian-minded suffragists had thought, could not comprehend American men. While smoking out Emerson's profound aversion to intimacy, Fuller never broke through a purely external sense of what American men were about before she lapsed back into woman's sphere with *Woman in the Nineteenth Century,* in which there were no American men, only "Man-in-general." Stanton was excused from feeling little more than recurrent rage and outrage at American men for their refusal to accept her offers of political alliance, and it was to the accompaniment of resentment and indignation, if not rage, that more and more women pursued their final goal of the suffrage. Presumably the modern men upon whom Gilman commented were American men, but she could not decide what they were like. At one point, when criticizing women for submitting to primitive seclusion at home, she declared that men were the truly socialized sex, indeed, that they had become the social mothers. At other times, when gripped with indignation at women's slavery to sex, she railed against the competitiveness and excessive individualism of men. As though somehow women, not men, had created the new world of orderly industrial production, she declared that men were out of phase with modernity, ill-adapted for the sort of collaborative sciences of society she celebrated.

While there is no reason to think that, just because of their unusual qualities, Fuller, Stanton, and Gilman were more rather than less likely than other women to comprehend American men, we can only respond to the record. At no point in history did nineteenth-century American feminists show any sign of understanding the interests of American men. It was as though they were living in some generic Nation. In Italy feminists always understood the basic preoccupation of Italian men— to get Italy launched on its career as a modern nation. No feminists in

Soviet Russia could possibly doubt the basic commitment of the Bolsheviks and the men of the Communist Party. Sweden's feminists were
at all times aware of the competition of parties in shaping a new modern
Sweden. But in the United States feminists thought of the nation as
already defined. There was no constitution to be forged, no social
democracy to be saved, no revolution to be forwarded. In confronting
their isolation from men, women at large and feminists in particular
turned to certain sorts of men, men who themselves faced isolation and
impotence in the marketplace, specifically, preachers and reformers.
On the whole, this was ultimately to run athwart men. As Josiah Royce
showed, the emergent exponents of social science were hostile to the
political economy and male culture that had produced New York City
and California. Consistently, at their very best, from Chauncey Wright
to John Dewey, the social scientists lauded the social over the individual, control over initiative, community over conflict, the rational over
the romantic, as though choice between these poles was necessary
rather than a dialectic choosing both. All this was profoundly compatible with woman's sphere.

Questioning whether nineteenth-century American feminism was a
success or a failure leads nowhere. By the time the vote was won in the
United States, many of the most powerful women in woman's sphere—
from independents like Gilman to college presidents like Bryn Mawr's
Mary Carey Thomas, from social workers like Jane Addams to doctors
like Alice Hamilton—had wrought for themselves one logical possibility for women in woman's sphere, life without men so far as any vital
economic or emotional needs were concerned. The fact that this New
Womanhood led to no second generation, left no successors, was hardly
in itself failure. The point of any new social creation is not simply to
perpetuate itself. New Womanhood constituted a new historical point
of reference, of usefulness to all persons in the future interested, for
whatever reason, in further thought about possible new arrangements
between the sexes. In the same way, the fact that women's votes prompted
no revolution—or even reform—in politics or the economy was hardly
a failure. Suffragists had never announced a program for women voters.
The one largest political ambition among women—temperance—had
already been installed in the Prohibition amendment. By the time that
amendment was repealed, the responsibility had long ceased to be
women's. The disintegration of feminism itself was in no meaningful
sense a failure, any more than the disappearance of the horse and buggy
was a "failure," when automobiles appeared. Woman's sphere itself
had disintegrated. That its disintegration entailed the loss of certain
embodied values was certain. Later historians in distress at their own
societies might try to locate the origins of the "loss" of what they find

missing. But that would not mean that the 1920s are best understood in terms of loss. Times were not better for women before 1914. The years between 1920 and 1963 were not "decades of discontent" because of the absence of feminism. Certainly those years cannot in any way be thought of as functionally parallel to the disintegration of Italian feminism after 1920 or the disappearance of Bolshevik feminism after 1926 or 1930, let alone as parallel to the fading of bourgeois Liberal feminism in Sweden in the 1920s, premonitory to the rise of Social Democratic feminism. All these others were the function of powerful external political and economic transformations. Feminism's disappearance in the United States was a function of new cultural forces. Rising from deep within both American popular culture and the nineteenth-century generation of a domestic mass market for capitalist production, they would catch nineteenth-century feminists unprepared. As the crumbling of the century-old separate woman's sphere proceeded rapidly, even as suffragists mounted their final campaigns for the vote, sharply new options were being opened up that neither suffragists nor feminism had anticipated. The United States clearly had moved far to the forefront in its elaboration of a broad democratic culture based on advanced media and a consummated industrial productivity. No such crisis was presented to feminists or women in Italy, Sweden, or Russia. In England, too, feminists were confronted with no challenge of such a broad and massive force. American feminists found themselves uniquely engulfed.

For the feminists of the Second Awakening, after 1965, this particular history of feminism, peculiar to the United States, presented a unique context for new choices. First, would feminists of the Second Awakening strive to reconstitute woman's sphere? If that sphere had so well sustained feminism in the nineteenth century, and if its collapse had, as some feminist historians soon would argue, explained the shriveling of feminism after 1920, perhaps there was a case to be made for reviving it. But the feminists dominant in the organization of NOW obviously rejected any such choice out of hand. They rejected nineteenth-century feminism. Indeed, according to Betty Friedan's argument, women of the 1950s had somehow found themselves entangled in a new separate sphere, suburban isolation, and had begun to protest against that isolation in favor of a straightforward share of public marketplace life alongside men. They must learn to compete like men. But the difficulty with this outlook soon revealed itself. NOW's demand for marketplace equality finessed any real analysis of all those relationships and institutions that had been submitted to broad popular experimentation at least from the 1920s, if not from the 1890s—sexuality, courtship, marriage, home, family, parenthood, childhood, that is, non-marketplace life, "private" life. Quickly, the voices of women's liberation over-whelmed this attempted finesse. Feminists thus faced another option: should they address themselves to a thoroughgoing critique of private relationships?

Of course, for women whose lives did not tell them that anything was wrong with private life, there was no need to choose, but for feminists, by definition conscious of inequities and injustices, the real question was not whether reforms were needed, but how to pursue them. If the basic ills of private life were rooted in the structures of the economy and politics, then to address those private ills directly would be to become preoccupied with the symptom, not the cause. But wom-en's liberation soon showed its basic choice: the injustices of private life were to be pursued directly. Those institutions in which women and men collaborated in the most immediate way, as different sexes, were to be confronted without mediation. Nothing in American politics or economics promised any "solution" to these private injustices. No American party resembled the Swedish Social Democrats or the Italian Communist Party. But the rapidity with which the feminists of women's liberation occupied strongly defined critical positions showed that their choice did not derive in any significant way at all from the mere absence of socialism as a meaningful option in the United States. It derived from accumulated experience. This was unmistakably experience that had induced profound aversion to the suburban idyll, aversion to the same feminine mystique already rejected by Friedan and NOW's lead-ers. Thus, NOW and women's liberationists were at one in their refusal to abide woman's sphere such as it had come to be by the 1950s. In effect, both had judged that the "revolution in manners and morals" of the 1920s had soured, whether or not it had ever had the potentials some, such as Frederick Lewis Allen, had imagined.

But this unity in negation was no basis for unity in march. Repelling lesbians in the first place for fear of their political costs, Friedan at the same time was responding to a more general issue. Rejecting the sub-urban idyll as in practice the imposition of a "heterosexual impera-tive," lesbians were for practical purposes proposing that women indeed turn to a woman's sphere, but a new woman's sphere, the nineteenth-century diffuse homosociality strengthened by winning far more eco-nomic independence for women than they had had back then. Ironically, lesbian feminism projected needs for access to jobs and careers in the marketplace far more compelling than NOW's: it looked forward to women supporting themselves quite independent of men. But the early split between NOW and lesbians was deeper than any expedient pa-pering-over could conceal. NOW's implicit assumption that women not only must be allowed to compete in the marketplace, but would prove ready, eager, and effective in doing so dismissed differences between men and women as essentially irrelevant to feminism, whereas women's liberation, including its lesbian cohorts, pressed the discussion of such differences toward the center of feminist debate. For all their differences, women's liberationists were at one on a fundamental point: women did not need to change. They rejected Charlotte Perkins Gilman's persistent tendency to suggest that the greatest transformation to be wrought in a gender-equal world would be in the depths of women's conceptions of themselves. The feminists of women's liberation were far more likely to search out the womanhood neglected by historians, celebrate it, and criticize the manhood that had subordinated it. Those to be changed were not women but men. Thus, still another option opened to modern American feminists. It concerned men directly: ought they to be changed? or accepted as they were? if the latter, ought women to seek to emulate them? or, so far as imaginable, do without them?

For NOW this issue was tricky. Accepting the challenge of trying to compete in the marketplace risked the discovery that some marketplace challenges, such as the peripatetic lives of top executives, might prove peculiarly difficult for women. On the other hand, to demand equal opportunity while demanding at the same time changes in the rules of the game in itself constituted a concession of the importance of differences. Women's-liberation feminists had little problem with this issue: the marketplace should be reformed in whatever way necessary to allow women better chances at independence. For women's liberation the issue of men was far more charged outside the marketplace. All women's-liberation feminists agreed that women's sexuality had been harmed by the suburban idyll. But women's sexuality had been released from 1950s repressions in the 1960s and 1970s; as much as anything, the agency of release was access to contraception. Here, feminism found itself in the position, not of having to make a revolution, but of having to make up its mind whether it approved of the one it faced and, to a degree, had called for.

Of course convinced lesbian feminists assumed a basic incompatibility between the sexes; if women's sexuality commonly appeared as more humane, more loving, more social, indeed more human than men's, that did not mean that change in men could be hoped for. Separation was necessary. It was where the exaltation of women's sexuality did induce hopes for change in men that visions of androgyny arose. Enhanced relations between the sexes would follow from a reduction in the differences between the sexes, wholly through changes in men. But feminists uninclined to androgyny on either temperamental or political grounds had to construe the question of men another way. Unwilling to abandon the new heterosexual freedom, they could not ignore the fact that that freedom seemed not to automatically promote more harmony, equity, and intimacy between men and women, man and woman. Just as men could well interpret women's new marketplace successes as reason to reduce their own responsibilities for supporting women (and children), so they could interpret women's new sexual freedom as reason to avoid limitations on theirs. Here, on one of its frontiers, feminism then did generate an idea of identity between the sexes. Women had just as much capacity—some said more—for sexual pleasure as men, just as much "need" for it, just as much right to it. There was inspiration in this idea. If the roots of the political and economic inequalities between men and women were to be found in their sexual relations, then a radical equalization of their sexual relations might at the least open the way to an attack on political and economic inequalities freed of the drag of sexual issues. By no means could the solution of political and economic inequalities be assumed to follow automatically from sexual equality. But the linkage of the realms would be reversed. Of course the implications of sexual equality remained to be seen—and imagined. Presumably marriage would cease to have a sexual motive. Presumably the role of the family in shaping and inflecting sexual expression would dwindle. Feminism's deepest task, that of historicizing women's lives, that of showing that women's subordination had not been founded on nature but on history and the power of men in history, would be much facilitated. With such institutions severed from their supposed roots in the biology of sexuality itself, history could capture them fully.

But the cost would be immense. The extrication of sexuality from power relationships in the name of pleasure mystified sexuality. The fundamental discovery of modern psychologies was that the most powerful sexual organ was the brain. The approach to sexuality through biology—or zoology, as in the Kinsey reports—in effect reawakened the idea particularly precious to Marxist eschatology, that there remained to be discovered, buried beneath the burdening overload of history, a natural sexuality. Disentangled from history, the sexes could collaborate in pure equality untroubled by power relationships. Psychology itself had lent some credence to this dream of Eden. By expounding much of the brain's impact on biology as neurotic, psychotic, or otherwise abnormal, it could imply that a healthy brain might well facilitate a healthy natural sexuality, a sexuality freed from the brain for its own innate expressiveness. But Freud, along with other psychologists, insisted that the brain never would be freed of conflicts, in which its associations with sexuality would always be critical. The vision of a sexuality liberated for natural expression had the further implication that sexuality would be denied to the individual as one resource for her own, and his own, individuality. As Alexandra Kollontai had said, once sexuality was detached from political and economic fate, the self would no longer suffer from those immersions in sexual relationships that threatened to sweep it away; the self would be immersed instead in the collective.

It was in American life that such questions could take on political importance for feminism. Kollontai's visions ran up against the sheer economic shortfalls of Communism. America was far richer. But it was in America that feminism had the fewest political allies. Particularly as the economy of the 1970s and 1980s called on political agents for response to the destabilization of the long historic boom, the prospects for any kind of deliberated public policy aimed to explore the potentials of sexual equality shriveled. Feminist sexual egalitarians themselves, even while deploring the threats of a rollback of women's sexual freedoms, could hardly fail to see that theirs was the situation of a privileged minority. Given the new access of highly equipped women to jobs and careers in the affluent marketplace, the chances for working out problems on a private basis with personal resources had actually improved. But little of this meant much to the larger numbers of women, some of whom needed far more public help than they were getting to cope with their responsibilities, others of whom were becoming far more outspoken in their hostility to an economy in which there seemed to be fewer men on whom women could depend. But just as in the nineteenth-century feminists had remained a minority, yet got what they aimed for, so in the feminism of 1985, after twenty years, it was not the minority or majority status of feminism that mattered most, but feminism's own basic goals. In sum, these still could be said to add up to "equality," by 1985 clearly declared to mean equality in all things—political, economic, social, sexual. But the feminism of the second awakening had effectively demystified equality. Equality meant equality with men, but this could only mean real men in real history. Feminists still had to decide what kind of men they wanted to be equal with.

In the Soviet Union the most powerful creation of men was the party-state. Soviet women had no choice but to accept their subordination, along with most of their men, to that mighty institution. In Italy, perhaps the key theme was the inability of men to create stable new forms of power, particularly as older forms deteriorated, with the consequence for women being, on the one hand, a perennial frustration of feminist hopes for new freer lives, and on the other, the importance of preserving such older sources of stability as the traditional family. The most powerful creation of modern Swedish men was, through the agency of unions and a social democratic party, the extrapolation of an older society and culture into coherent and stable modernity, in which women were provided both support and opportunity in such a way as to co-opt feminist imagination. In the United States one of men's powerful creations was the economy, persistently if often cyclically expanding. But men's most powerful creation of all was themselves. Lenin and his Bolsheviks called fervently for the creation of a new Soviet Man, and Soviet ideologists proclaim his existence today. But Soviet ideology defines this new man as the creation of the Soviet system. Italians of the Risorgimento eagerly anticipated an Italian rescued from foreign despotism and thralldom to economic backwardness and poverty, an Italian recalled to rationality and vigorous independent humanism. Yet one of the main symptoms of Italian political and economic mediocrity was in the deepening conflict between types of Italian manhood. As for Sweden, the deepest determination of the successful Social Democrats was to save old securities and old identities, not forge new ones. Swedes had asked for nothing more than the freedom to be Swedish ever since they put Charles XII behind them. But as Tocqueville spelled out, the single central power rising in the new democracy in North America was that of a new psychology. To a degree, the American psychology he described had been carried across the ocean: American men wanted what in Europe only the privileged few had been allowed to have, riches and power. But the diffusion of aristocratic motives to the many—"Every man a King"—itself transformed the psychology. For American men, society dissolved from hierarchy and structure into activity. American men's sense of self did not include limits defined by other men. They saw themselves as the engine of their own lives.

But nineteenth-century American feminists had not had to try to imagine themselves equal with such men. In the sociology of democratic capitalism they had been assigned their sphere apart from men. They had gone about making themselves into quite different kinds of persons from men. The terms of the one collaboration between men and women, sexual collaboration, had reflected this division. Men's sexual passions were cooled by their preoccupation with the marketplace, women's by their prudence. The sexual tie did not threaten separation. As feminism deepened and expanded woman's sphere, it did not so much invade men's proper sphere as occupy the ambiguous zones of men's excesses as slave owners, as drunkards, as patrons of prostitutes. Only then, as the vision of a general feminization of society began to take shape, climactically in Charlotte Perkins Gilman, did confrontation commence. Feminists found alliance with men hostile to the old Tocquevillian male psychology. Religious leaders, in the first place, then philosophers of community such as Josiah Royce, finally, visionaries of applied social science, such men had no reason to exclude women from their efforts. The application of religion, philosophy, and social science to politics and economy stressed, in consistency with woman's sphere, community rather than competition, sharing rather than possession, the bonding of selves rather than self-expression. And certainly the pursuit of the beloved community was far from reawakening sexuality from its cool restraint. It was as though woman's sphere was about to be nationalized.

Yet, if this was a moment of high potential, it was even more a moment of crisis for feminism. Had the partnership with social philosophy— with Lester Ward and Josiah Royce, Thorstein Veblen and George Herbert Mead and, above all, John Dewey—prevailed, feminism would finally have succumbed to woman's sphere rather than finding it a kind of privileged sanctuary from which to mount sorties on the larger society. Feminists of autonomous individuality such as Margaret Fuller and Elizabeth Cady Stanton had never accepted woman's sphere as the source of identity and a model of social order anyway. Neither had Charlotte Perkins Gilman, however extreme her assault on the emotional resources of individuality. The problem was not simply one of contrasting values. When a man like Theodore Roosevelt offered alliance to women as social mothers, it was reasonably evident that he had no intention whatever of abandoning lyric, competitive, expressive, Emersonian masculinity. He wanted to save it from extinction in industrial bureaucracy by redirecting it to new realms. Roosevelt's trap was the more seductive exactly because, in affirming the perpetuation of the old masculinity, he had no intention of weakening the bar against awakened sexuality. His ideal manhood remained boyish, preadolescent, sensuous but not sensual. The alliance of feminism with social philosophy promised a new collaboration between the sexes that at the same time would remain cool, ordered, contained, collective. For emotional warmth, each sex would withdraw on itself, just as Gilman had recommended.

Neither party to the new alliance, then, neither the feminists nor the social scientists, neither the Theodore Roosevelts nor the Gilmans, was prepared to respond to what was happening within its own broad middle-class constituency. The pretensions of both parties to possessing the key to social control proved empty in the face of the continuing vitality of a popular democratic culture. The plain evidence of the Gay Nineties that the middle classes were interested, neither in woman's sphere nor community philosophies, but in individual life was suppressed until it could not be resisted in the 1920s. By then, the price feminism would pay for papering over its inner tensions with the campaign for suffrage was obviously going to be higher.

The great difference between the first and second feminisms in the United States, between feminism before 1920 and feminism since 1965, has been that, whereas in the first feminism these inner tensions, dilemmas, polarities, contrasts, and even contradictions tended to get suppressed, in the second feminism they have been asserted, expounded, pursued, developed, insisted upon. The basic reason in social history seems clear. From first to last the existence of a real woman's sphere provided feminism its most powerful orientation; it was almost irresistible that feminism often think of itself exactly as woman's sphere equipped with new rights and power. But the most fundamental issues for women were not those of winning power for woman's sphere but those of the costs paid by women for their seclusion in that sphere. The basic issues were those linked with new kinds of relations women might strive to achieve with men. For the feminism since 1965, the problem of woman's sphere had been solved. Insofar as such a sphere still existed, it had been fragmented, deeply invaded by outside forces of the marketplace, more and more undermined by women's entrance into the marketplace out of economic motives, and, most of all, completely infiltrated by the new sexuality, repudiating the old reserve and self-denial of the nineteenth-century separation of spheres. In effect, feminism had no opportunity to evade issues.

The vigor with which issues were pursued almost literally within months of the reemergence of self-conscious feminist initiatives in 1965 testified to the pressures built up within women in a variety of circumstances. But the basic task for feminist consciousness was not to be fulfilled simply in releasing these pressures, in venting feelings long smothered, in praising womanhood and demanding rights. That task was, instead, to think about men. By 1986 it was obvious that many American women had scored many notable successes. Women were to be found in high places in the anti-ERA Reagan administration as well as in liberal circles of the floundering Democrats. Women were to be found as partners in Wall Street law firms and brokerage houses as well as in welfare and child-care work. Women were to be found producing television and radio programs full of sex and violence as well as documentaries on wife abuse, child abuse, the travail of women workers. The feminist expositors of social mothering allied to the Progressive Party in 1912 would have had no difficulty in distinguishing between these kinds of success. Women who pursued quick fortunes on Wall Street, women who defended corporations against antipollution regulation, women who rationalized "authoritarian" regimes into anti-Communist friends of the United States, had nothing to do with feminism and the triumph of women's values. Yet even nineteenth-century feminism had clung to the banner of equality from first to last. As the Swedish feminist Birgitta Wistrand had asked: Why should not fifty-fifty obtain anywhere and everywhere? Why should women have to defend their right to make a million or become a general? To such women as Fuller and Stanton, nineteenth-century feminism's easy answer had been suspect even in its own time. Yet modern feminism manifested nothing like unity on this point. It still included women who asserted the virtues and values of women, often with far greater fervor than even the most dedicated loyalist to woman's sphere back in the nineteenth century, because they were freer to talk about bodies. If some modern feminists, such as Shulamith Firestone, conceptualized women's bodies as problems to be solved, others, such as Adrienne Rich, celebrated them as founts of special wisdom and knowledge. If Firestone's point of view anticipated a complete equality with men, emphatically including equality in sexual intercourse, Rich's reasserted the need for difference and separation. The unqualified pursuit of fifty-fifty, in short, inevitably meant equality with different kinds of men, some of whom nineteenth-century feminists, together with their modern heirs, had always deplored. It meant that, for some women, equality meant becoming like men, for others, men like women.

It was in American history that feminists—and women generally—faced these challenges. Nothing had decreed fixation of American society by centralized planning, by welfare politics, or by continuing economic shortfall, as in the Soviet Union, Sweden, and Italy. By 1986 the way was open to American women for success in all sorts of arenas of competition. It was in this sheer variousness, underwritten by the continuing capacity for self-transformation in democratic capitalism, that American feminism found its new challenge. The fact that women remained far short of fifty-fifty success was no longer the overriding issue. From its origins, feminism had always nourished feelings of self-esteem as well as grievance. It had never fully embraced John Stuart Mill's condescension of saying that women were indeed as inferior as common opinion held them but it was not their fault. Although fluctuating from time to time and person to person, feminism had always proclaimed: Let women be women. Even Fuller and Stanton, while urging women to expose themselves to the same realities faced by men, never forsook a sense of women's particular endowment. It was the torment of modern American feminists to have to face the challenge of rapidly spreading opportunities to become like men. Soviet Russian women had had no choice. They had been deprived of the challenge to create themselves. In Italy, from its ill fortunes, and Sweden, from its good fortunes, feminists found the challenge muffled. It was in its conflicts, its frustrations, and its indecisions on how far and in what ways women should become like men that modern feminism in the United States displayed, not only its deep symbiosis with its own particular kinds of men, but also its long-term vitality.

Part IV The Genius of Individuals

In this final section I have tried to unleash individuals to the maximum. Of course writers, moviemakers, philosophers, too, work within the limits of specific experiences, specific languages, specific addresses, and I have meant to make out particularly Italian features in D'Annunzio and Sibilla Aleramo, identify what we must know of Sweden to best comprehend Strindberg, note what Kollontai and her successors wanted from Russia, inquire how Kate Chopin and Willa Cather, Stephen Crane and Henry James responded to America. But in this section I hope national boundaries yield to a more general perspective. The figures I have chosen seem to me to have, whether deliberately or by accident, trenched against boundaries, subverted limits, speculated upon the new. It follows that my point is in no way to tease out some larger, transnational language for the further exploration of sex and power. Nor is it to discern various myths and discourses. Students of the mythopoetic in literature, such as Leslie Fiedler in *Love and Death in the American Novel*, have forged powerful instruments for the diagnosis of culture. I have no thought of contributing to that. If some of the artists in these final chapters, such as D'Annunzio, do embody culturally powerful myths of sexuality, that could well be as a consequence of crisis in the myth. It is the crisis, not the myth, that controls these chapters. I believe that writers and moviemakers who press into crisis tend to merit study on literary and "artistic" merit also, but I have not hesitated to include a writer such as Harriet Beecher Stowe, who, although by no means secure in any claim to literary power, nonetheless drew art from the deepest crisis of her society, the disappearance of the American Father.

The lack of the systematic in these chapters, then, is wholly calculated. Neat endings in history are discouraging. History should resemble that exploration of wonderland that Tocqueville found to be American men's passion. History should demonstrate that there can be no end to expeditions into new wonders.

11 Italy

Italian Literature: Condescension or National Service?

Antonio Gramsci had more than one explanation for the failure of Risorgimento Italy. True, the new realism of economics and Marx yielded the fundamental reason, the failure to institute an agricultural revolution in the south, the failure of Italy to undergo a French Revolution. But this was after all abstract, mere Marxism. No politics had ever been remotely likely to have followed such a course. Gramsci's hope that, given this original failure, its deficit could be made up in the factories by the urban man-of-work, in the shop councils, was earnest enough. But it left him with little to do but watch, report, praise, and pray.

Since Gramsci was, by innate vector, an intellectual, his most heartfelt lament over the fate of Italy focused on the condescending attitude of Italy's intellectuals, the attitude of her artists, writers, poets, and philosophers toward their countrymen. Gramsci singled out the scripture of Italian patriotism, Alessandro Manzoni's *I promessi sposi* (The Betrothed), published in three volumes between 1825 and 1827. The heroes of *The Betrothed* were two simple, humble Italians, a young peasant and his young peasant girl, in love and eager to marry, but whose hopes were constantly frustrated by a local magnate and disappointed by their timid priest. Set in the ambiance of a popular rising against Austrian rule in seventeenth-century Milan, the book radiated its implicitly nationalist drama: Italians had only simplicity and honesty with which to combat the oppressions of alien politics and armies. The sweetness and charity of Manzoni's own imagination seemed to place his book beyond reach of any mere partisanship and to establish its *italianità* similarly, on a level transcending mere politics. As Gramsci analyzed it, however, *The Betrothed* also displayed something less satisfying to a modern democrat. "For Manzoni, 'the people' have no inner life, no profound moral personality; they are simply what they are, like any simple animal." Gramsci linked Manzoni's outlook to that of an "aristocratic" Catholicism toward its own people: "condescending benevolence rather than a shared humanity."[1] Gramsci argued that the "traditional stance of Italian intellectuals" toward the people was summed up in the expression often attached to Manzoni's country lovers—*gli umili*. (In English, "the humble" lacks the right connotations; "the little people" comes closer.) To Gramsci, Italy had no "national-popular" literature; its national literature had no popular roots. Italian intellectuals, in effect, had written not so much from a class position as from a position that simply deprived the people of status as real participants in Italian culture and, ultimately, in Italian politics. Paradoxically, they had done so in a way that removed that culture even further from ordinary Italians: some years after the first edition, Manzoni undertook his rewriting in the more highly "finished" prose of Tuscany, effectively fixing cultivated Tuscan Italian as the language of Italian high culture. (A further paradox, this laid the ground for the achievements of those later writers, notably Giovanni Verga and Grazia Deledda, who brought dialect back into Italian with liberating force.)

While Gramsci's efforts to establish this point by comparisons with France, England, and even Russia were perfunctory, he offered a larger context. The fault of all Italy's high culture was its lack of local address. For the mind acting to free itself for creative activity, Gramsci said, Benedetto Croce's humanistic devotion to the universal value of "spirit" proceeded on a level far above any real life of people and nation, too far above to help them. Croce's humanism had become really nothing more than the self-perpetuation of an increasingly more isolated intellectual elite. Thus Gramsci's political point, that Risorgimento Italy had failed because the new state had not promoted an agricultural revolution in the south, was equivalent to his cultural argument that the nation's intellectual leaders had treated Italy's peasants—the *contadini*—not as people with a culture but as an inert mass, victims at the very least, but not citizens. The duty of the intellectual then was clear: to become an "organic" intellectual, his work consciously linked with the culture of the people.

A Sardinian, Gramsci never forsook his sense of Italian country people as strong and vital, but he knew very well they had been crippled culturally as well as economically. Certainly those hundreds of young women who had set out as schoolteachers to overcome illiteracy were doing their duty, but obviously this was a paltry enterprise. And was it not further condescension? Would not Sardinian peasants likely use their literacy to try to escape Sardinia—as indeed Gramsci himself had done—and to seek better lives in the new Italy, however poor, of cities and money and bought culture? Were intellectuals to tell them nay? It was the old problem of Marxism: must not bourgeoisification precede the revolution? Let the traditional culture of condescension fade away. But must not an epoch of literature for the market intervene, sentimental, even sensational perhaps, before the organic intellectual could begin to prevail? Gramsci reacted to such literature in his years as a drama critic in Turin, but while it was obvious what he thought of it then, he never made clear whence a better literature might come.

Women's Literature: Tradition as Barrier

For nineteenth-century Italian feminists, the problem of avoiding male condescension was not easy. Quite apart from economic and political conditions generally, the backwardness in which most Italian women lived also involved the laws, manners, and mores of marriage and sexual relationships. Italian women may not have been as subservient as those women in Moslem Central Asia whom the Bolsheviks of the Women's Department tried to liberate, but they too appeared passive in their acceptance of subordination and subjugation to father, husband, priest. Perhaps a Mozzoni-style feminist, individualistic and egalitarian, committed to reason and science, should try to awaken such women from their sleep. She needed promises that could be honestly made.

A Mazzinian republican, Mozzoni had no investment in the Roman Catholic church, and as a rationalist she regarded the church as morally as well as politically corrupt. Mozzoni kept her private life private. She had relations with men and bore a daughter while unmarried. When she later did marry, she kept her maiden name. She offered no general reflections about the private relations between men and women. The fact that she was never made to suffer for her private life testified to a tacit Italian bargain: so long as private lives were kept private, Italians privileged by class were excused from abiding by official standards. In Princess Cristina di Belgiojoso's case, aristocratic status covered private unconventionality; in Anna Kuliosscioff's case, the indulgence was granted foreigners in exile.[2] Lacking such familiar sanctions, so much the deeper was Mozzoni's privacy. Still, her silence followed from more than personal prudence; it was quite enough for Italian feminism to raise its political and juridical demands without adding matters of private intimacy. If the marriage question proved intimidating in pluralistic America, how much more so was it in Italy. For Mozzoni and others, socialism offered a release from the dilemma. Once socialism had arrived, these relationships would not have to be talked about, since, freed of the distortions of church and capitalism, they would then be conducted according to nature. In effect, what could not be discussed would never have to be discussed.

Literary culture discouraged bringing the private to voice. Some sense of the limits within which women writers writing of women operated can be gleaned from the response to their work by Croce, the literary as well as intellectual critic of the age. Croce, far more than any other man, sought self-consciously to speak for a renewed humanist Italy. He wrote little about women writers, but what he said clearly conveyed his sense of them as a special category. He praised one of the early novels on prostitution, *Una fra tante* (1878), by "Emma" (Emilia Ferretti Viola), for its "less sentimental" investigation, and welcomed its argument that the church's continuing reliance upon charity had become an obstacle to humane reform. He admired another novel of the same year, *In risaia*, by the "Marchesa Colombi" (Maria Torelli Viollier), not only for the author's rendition of the hard life led by the rice workers but for her command of folkloric detail. Croce did not despise such works of a sociological or local-color cast. But when he wrote about the young poet Ada Negri in 1906, he distinguished between art and theme, form and substance. Negri, one of the first women writers of working-class background, had, he noted, been praised for her "antiliterary" qualities, for her realistic materials, for her "sincerity." But what she needed, he said, was not sincerity and "serious feelings," but art. In poetry, at least, form was all. Negri's early work had carried an unmistakable socialist as well as feminist charge.

In contrast, when Croce wrote of "Neera" (Anna Radius Zuccari), he praised her precisely for her sincerity, "the best part of her art." The equivocation was unconscious: what was clear was that Neera's work, unlike Negri's, carried no political, let alone feminist charge:

[The] best of her books offer a panorama of feminine love, in its ideal and its reality. . . . Neera acknowledges . . . a predilection for the theme of women who have sought but failed to find fulfillment in love, marriage, motherhood. In this fruitless search, in this hope eagerly sought but never achieved, the passion of love shows itself at its strongest because violently repressed and yet not annulled, speaks in cries of anguish, locks itself up in sadness, or diffuses itself in kindness.[3]

This was not wholly unlike the ideologies of passion familiar enough to Italians in their Foscolo, their Leopardi, and certainly Donizetti, Rossini, Verdi. But Neera seemed to be working to another point altogether. Italian lovers did love unhappily, time after time, but usually to the end of writing poems about their lost loves—commonly dead by then—whereas Neera's heroine appeared to be a character even less dignified in Italian writing than elsewhere, the spinster. How many of these spinsters, she said, could—had they the courage, did they not blush at being mistaken for married—tell stories of urgent desires of which no one had known, of scorching ardor that could never speak. Here at least was the point of entry for drawing a new category of person into the humane exploration of love, even for drawing Italian literature into consideration of sexuality itself.

But Croce was having none of that. He emphasized rather Neera's "antifeminism." What Neera aimed at in portraying her spinsters was not simply, in the naturalistic spirit of Zola, the sheer fact of their subjective sexuality, but far more the means by which they reconciled themselves to their fate, that is, in her own phrase, "platonic love." Croce approved. Here was a "spiritual" solution to a problem no doubt "material" in its origins but requiring—or having—no material answer. Somehow this linked up with feminism's "false concept of material equality." Neera, as Croce paraphrased her, believed that women were "made for the family and not for the council chamber or the streets."

But were there not women who found no one to marry?—I pity them, they are unhappy (Neera replies) . . . There are women who don't find total satisfaction in maternity. —Unfortunately—. There are those without husband, child, family, who must busy themselves somehow, in politics, philanthropy, literature.— Poor souls, treating their pains with bandaids and aspirin: "But aspirin and bandaids are never means to the ideal, only petty remedies used in secret in hopes for the time they won't be needed."—There are women of genius born for success, for politics, for art, for science.—Exceptions—.[4]

That Croce could cite these judgments of dying traditional moralism without a sense of absurdity, irresistibly implies that he had exposed himself to feminism and had recoiled. In a telling passage he summarized his case against feminist egalitarianism:

All human beings tend to spiritual unity, toward repose in what had absolute value; but to gain this high satisfaction, the goal of human life, there is no purpose in the female becoming male, or the male female. This would be the same as to say that the poet, in order to become fully human, also had to become philosopher, mathematician, statesman, soldier, explorer, farmer, customs officer, or tax collector. . . . Everyone is a fragment of humanity, a microcosm. It is not necessary for the farmer to lay down his hoe to matriculate in philosophy or theology in order to share in the divine. And it is not necessary for woman to imitate the material exploits of men in order to raise herself spiritually.[5]

The philosopher's grant of spiritual equality to the farmer was no doubt serious, sincere, and democratic. But that Croce was in the grip of unconscious needs in his reference to the "material exploits"—"le azioni materiale"—which men need not agree women should emulate also seems likely, as he moved on by elision to Neera's praise for "platonic love." "Platonic love, say the sly, doesn't exist; every love has the sexual instinct for its ultimate motive." That Croce should attempt to dispose of modern ideas about sex by assigning them to "i furbi"—the sly, the cunning, the crafty, wily, artful, obviously prurient, sexually self-seeking, the "materialistic"—was a comment on the condition of elite Italian culture. Croce of course could not bar women's way into the magazines and publishing houses, or the audiences being prepared by the new "social science" and by socialism and by the slow but visible emergence of an inchoate middle class, with women among them, if still mostly only as readers, consumers. But he registered a sense that, if women were to enter the realms of culture and freedom, they must be purged of sex. A Negri had the potential for achievement, but a Negri must forgo the use of her art for sexual protest.

One Woman's Story: Literature as Self-Creation— Sibilla Aleramo's *Una donna*

No doubt the best-known woman writer of the period was Mathilde Serao. Serao wrote what might well have been categorized as "women's literature," stories of a sentimental bent. Still, in perhaps the best of these stories, she managed to break with sentimentality while sticking to the central theme of girls in love. A Neapolitan, Serao often saturated her stories with the sociology and economics of the real Naples. In one, two girls competed in friendship for the same young man, only to lose out to a third because they themselves were both desperately poor. Girls employed in a telegraph office found romantic hopes spoiled by having to work on Christmas day. In the teacher-training schools, girls' brains and ambition met petty rules, rebuffs, and indifference. Although when Serao tried for pathos or philosophy she failed, when she wrote of the slums and the new working girls she spoke with precision and force. Her best book was probably a tract, *Il ventre di Napoli*, written in both indignation and melancholy, about the grandiose schemes of politicians for "redeveloping" Naples, and about their perennial failure. In an appreciative essay, Croce did her the justice of not reducing her to "woman writer" or "women's writer." Serao identified with no women's causes, let alone feminism. She obviously saw herself as a successful professional, and feminism as a kind of self-limitation. At the same time she embodied the possibility that women, like men, could rise to public levels of insight and moral imagination. Whether something other than Croce's patently condescending attitude toward women writers would have helped, if not Serao, then young writers yet unheard, to arm themselves for still more compelling revelations, can only be guessed.[6]

Henry James feared that Serao would squander her talent on tales of "passion." "Beautiful," he agreed, "are the exhibitions of grinding girl-life in the big telephone office and in the State normal school."[7]

Serao was at her best, he said, "almost in direct proportion as her characters were poor." But when she turned to stories of passion—as she too often had—this "robust and wonderful Serao" drifted into noisiness, agitation, a "high pitch," vulgarity. The problem was one of the "salience" that "the type of fiction commonly identified as the 'sexual' " had achieved in recent years, and though James found fault with Gabriele D'Annunzio too on exactly the same score, he associated this kind of fiction with "the ladies," "the female hand," women writers. It was entirely possible that, with their interest in "man's relation to himself, that is with woman," women writers, in the name of describing love, would drain literature of its attention to the character and the "breathed air" of those who loved. For himself, as an example of the writer who understood the virtue for art of "hanging back" when it came to passion, James cited Jane Austen. Whether this, implicitly, was to imply that English culture could hang back while Italian could not, James left unstated. It was a loss to literary history that he did not comment subsequently on a writer, both Italian and a woman, who found a way to write a sexual fiction without hanging back, yet who avoided the high pitch, in a psychological study under control from first to last.

In 1906 the Crocean barrier to a realistic literature by women was broken when *Una donna*, by "Sibilla Aleramo" (Rina Pierangeli Faccio), appeared. It was easily the best Italian novel yet written by a woman. Croce did not write of it and the reason seems evident. It was at once a fully realized work of art and a clear case of a woman—Woman—pleading a case for women.[8]

Aleramo was by no means an unknown when she published her first novel at thirty. She had been writing articles, notices, and stories for a decade; had edited a journal in Milan, *L'Italia Femminile*, founded by the feminist Emilia Mariani; and was known in Milanese intellectual circles where Ernesto Teodoro Moneta taught that socialists might allowably be interested in such specific reforms as women's rights and pacifism. She was acquainted with broad European currents of change and discontent. She described her heroine as having been awakened from "infinite solitude, silence, the loss of faith and hope" by a book sent her by her father, Guglielmo Ferrero's *L'Europa giovane*. Through Ferrero she discovered a sense of her solidarity with a whole generation of European youth. *Una donna* had international success—in England with a translation in 1908, in Spain, in eastern Europe, in France, most of all probably in Germany. Without having to wait to be told, many Italian critics, writers, and readers also recognized what they had before them.

Una donna was the story of a miserably unhappy marriage as told by the wife. That wives in Italy were often miserable had not been easy to explain to reading audiences even in united Italy. Neera, for instance, in *Teresa* (1886) and again in *Lydia* (1887), had shown how young women were made unhappy unto death by attitudes and customs that frustrated true love, but in each case she saw to it that the victim never married at all. To confront unhappy marriage was to confront not just the canons of mate selection but the institution of marriage itself. But far more compelling in *Una donna* was the heroine's decision: she abandoned her marriage. The obvious literary ancestor of the novel was Henrik Ibsen's *A Doll's House*. It was as though Nora had undertaken to tell her story in her own words. August Strindberg, who despised Ibsen's play as a piece of "gallantry," might have found more to think about, had he had a Swedish translation of *Una donna* to read before his death in 1912. *Una donna* had a dimension that Ibsen's play left only in shadow. Like Nora, the heroine of *Una donna* was a mother, but unlike Nora she linked motherhood with marriage in her effort to understand how her tragedy had come about.

At the age of eleven the heroine had come with the rest of her family to a small provincial town on the Adriatic, where her father was to build and supervise a chemical plant. She was radiantly happy. Her father had raised her by the principles of the late-nineteenth-century scientific enlightenment; she knew she was his favorite, and she delighted in being allowed to spend time helping in the factory offices. By contrast, her mother was a woman wholly alienated from her husband, deeply depressed, unable to take an interest in her family or the town.

An old woman came to help mama with the house. Chattering away, she would say how when I was married with children I'd look on being a clerk in the factory with a smile. Calmly, I told her that I wasn't going to get married, because I couldn't be happy unless I was free to work, and I told her that every girl should feel the same way. Marriage was a mistaken institution. Daddy had told me so.[9]

But she did get married. Soon, when fifteen years old, she was taken, in a kind of seduction-rape, by an employee at the factory ten years older than she, who had been courting her for two years. "Did I belong to him, then? I believed it after days of a bewilderment I couldn't name. . . . What had I become? What would happen next? My life as a girl had ended."[10] From this point on, it was easy to imagine the heroine as the victim of a very specific Italian culture, that of the Mezzogiorno with all its retrograde concepts. Had she never left Milan and not been identified as, in effect, the richest girl in town, had she met only other young Milanesi interested in books and ideas and politics, perhaps this would not have happened. Soon, the link between psychological and sociological horror became more explicit. Two years or so later, a man in town made overtures to her; her husband away, her marriage in shreds, she felt her need for love aroused, but she nonetheless repelled him. Still, enough suspicion was generated that a local notable—of the clerical party—made capital of it against her husband's faction, the democrats. Her virtue became an issue in local politics: negotiations were conducted toward the production of an actual document in which the clericals' leader, backing down, would offer written attestation to her "complete respectability." Ironically, here the "private" indeed became "political" in a way that reversed the demands of a later feminism. Surely in an enlightened society such private tortures were nobody else's business. Yet these more or less specific sociological references were not the heart of the book.

Nor indeed were those circumstances that defined the heroine's dilemma as mother. Had her problem been that simply of a wife, the laws of Italy would have mattered less. Divorce was unavailable to Italians, despite the state's presumed freedom from the Catholic church, but separation was a recourse in a variety of degrees. In the case of separation, however, Italy's laws, still rooted in ancient Rome, granted custody of minor children automatically to the husband. The heroine of *Una donna* had a son whom she adored, and her husband would not surrender his right. The heroine therefore had a terrible choice: stay in a marriage that was destroying her, or leave both husband and child. But here too the novel had other than sociological business. No more than *Anna Karenina* was "about" imperial Russia's divorce laws, was *Una donna* "about" the perpetuation in modern Italy of the ancient father's right. The heroine understood this. Her real topic was not backward, provincial, southern Italy as distinguished from Milan, or indeed Italy at all. It was universal, about woman's heart.

At this point, one can imagine literary history putting its finger on the explanation for *Una donna*'s success. Its author, Rina Faccio, writing her novel in Rome in 1903 and 1904, had undergone all the experiences of the heroine in her book. Like her heroine at the end of the book, she had left her husband and child. But she had left them hoping that by one means or another—law, pleas, miracle—she would get her son back. The writing of *Una donna* in Rome became her effort to explain to herself how she could have done what she did, and why. She made her true decision in writing the book: to give up hope. It was now that, following the intuition of a friend, she recognized a new self in herself. She gave it a new name, "Sibilla Aleramo." Writing her book from the perspective of a first-person narrator, the author realized she had converted herself into her own fiction, her own creation.

Something in me woke again . . . a need for tenderness . . . poetry . . . music . . . a languorous dream of ecstasy. . . . In a frenzy I clasped my boy to my breast. . . . He fixed me with his sweet eyes questioningly. . . . Why was I bringing my suffering to this little creature, asking for what he couldn't give? Why was I demanding from him the love missing from my life?

Then should she not sacrifice her desires? The answer to this became clear: "Why do we exalt maternal sacrifice? . . . What if once mothers didn't suppress the real persons in themselves, and their children learned about life from them?"[11] The heroine recognized a bitter truth: so long as she remained with her husband, she could be only an embittered, suppressed person and hence a bad mother, just as her mother, who had stayed in a bad marriage, had been. She had no real choice. She must leave not only for her own sake, but for her child's sake, too. That this realization came to her only after she had left, simply added to the power of the message: messages so bitter could be understood only after, not before, desperate action.

It then became possible for the author to confront another question. Why did men behave toward women as badly as the heroine's husband behaved toward her? "How can a man who has had a good mother be cruel toward the weak, betray a wife he has loved, play the tyrant over his children?"[12] He did not really love his wife, yet he imprisoned her. The only truly intimate emotion he felt for his wife was jealousy. On this issue the heroine's introspections approached truly revolutionary thoughts for Italy. Was it possible that, in a land where illustrious mothers, Marias, and mammas had flourished as the very embodiment of all that was high and deep, the consequence was the production of spoiled men, men who became bad husbands and fathers?

With the publication of *Una donna*, Sibilla Aleramo fell silent for thirteen years. After her famous novel, this must be the most interesting fact of her career. As years of prior polemical feminist writing had shown, silence was not her preference. Evidently she felt she had cheated. She had meant to be utterly honest in her book, yet she had failed to make one thing clear: when she had left her husband, she was already in love with another man. She explained this at last, in 1919. It was also true that no mere book, no matter how complete in itself, could purge all anguish and guilt over an act whose reverberations would not end: she still loved her son, and her son would grow up without her. Aleramo had already gone to work among the denizens of the Agro Romano, a district of desolation outside Rome where uprooted victims of modernizing Italy's rationalizations took refuge. Like young idealists going to the people in the Czar's Russia, like Yankee schoolmarms going south in post-Civil War America, Aleramo sought meaning and hope in schools for the forgotten. Concern for feminism, any special attachment to women in particular as victims, faded.

It was true that, in abandoning her child—far more than in leaving her husband—Faccio/Aleramo had incurred a debt essentially unpayable. But as her book made elaborately and insistently clear, she owed a debt also for some of the strength she had found to do what she had done. After all, most Italian wives reconciled themselves to their fates. The heroine's own mother had gone to her doom without any but passive resistance. Perhaps worse, many Italian wives might have felt no rebellion at all. This wife was different.

I was the oldest. . . . My father showed I was his favorite. . . . I felt a boundless adoration for him. . . . Out on walks around town with him, hand in hand, I felt buoyant, on top of everything. He told me stories . . . about when he was little. . . . when he was eight he saw French soldiers enter Turin "when there wasn't any Italy yet." A magical, mythical past!

In her case at least, then, one man, who like all other men had had a mother, had been neither cruel nor indifferent. This man's prestige in her eyes eventually contributed to her downfall. After some years of more or less futile wooing, the young man who was courting her told her that her father had a mistress. She was shocked, felt betrayed. From a purely external standpoint, from this time on the heroine's father became a more and more opaque figure in the novel, callous to his workers, his wife, his children, yet obviously still emotionally needy, capable still of reawakening his unhappily married daughter by his gift of Ferrero's treatise. Eventually, as a worn-out old man retired in Milan, he lost all his glamour, yet remained the obvious source of his daughter's strength. He had given her absolute foundation:

I was twelve years old. . . . Sometimes daddy gave me little jobs to do, that I carried out with scrupulous exactitude. "What about being my secretary when we get everything ready?" I felt my old timidity challenged by a new confidence. . . . I remember a photo of myself. . . . I still had my curls in front but short in back, like a boy, I had given up my pigtails. . . . I no longer thought of myself as a girl, but not as a woman either. I was an individual, busy and responsible. I felt useful.[13]

The possibility that her repugnance for sex with her husband was due less simply to his rape of her than to her sense of betrayal at the revelation of her father's mistress, entailed in its turn the heroine's sense of her mother. "A good mother mustn't be like my mother, self-sacrificing. She must be *a woman*, a real human person." But this was no answer to the other question, why men with good mothers treated their wives badly. The implied answer was clear: a good mother, who was not self-sacrificing but "*a woman*, a real person," would also be a good wife. A good wife would not let her daughter be enchanted, then betrayed, by her husband. But this implicit logical answer was overlaid by the far more potent story of the heroine's effort to summon the strength to sacrifice herself for the sake of her son. That effort cast no light at all on the utopian hope that good mothers would be good wives in the first place, real women, real persons. Certainly, if men were to treat their wives as equals, all might be well, for as the heroine asked, in extenuation of her own weak, defeated, depressed, and useless mother: "how could she be a woman if her parents gave her, ignorant, weak, unequipped, to a man who wouldn't take her as an equal . . . ?"[14] In that case, let women be educated to grow up equipped, intelligent, strong, as Anna Maria Mozzoni had urged. But Aleramo, unlike Mozzoni, was working at the roots of personality and identity, and never evoked such social, political answers to private, psychological anguish. In *Una donna* the heroine derived her strength precisely from the combination of her father's magic and her mother's weakness. The bind was double. Back of the novel there hovered the figure of the missing strong mother, whose effect was to induce in her sons only the emotion of possession, with jealousy at the first prospect of losing her its strongest expression. There was no feminist lesson in *Una donna*.

Immersing herself in the Agro Romano, in surrogate children, Aleramo also embarked upon a succession of lovers, younger as she grew older. In Sweden, Ellen Key was just then hailing relations between younger men and older women as the "new European love," but Aleramo never tried to sing such loves, obviously sure she could summon no such artistic concentration as she had for *Una donna*. As Croce had admonished Negri, art lived in form. The prose voice of *Una donna*, abrupt, self-conscious, tense, yet naked and insistent, registered the twin incertitudes of terrible recollections and a terrible future, rendering consciousness forging itself while haunted by a logic still too dark to be fully elucidated. No Italian had yet written this way, let alone an Italian woman. It was unlikely that such a voice would encourage others. *Una donna* would not germinate Gramsci's "popular-national" literature. Aleramo had not presented herself as an organic intellectual.

Stimulated by Gaetano Salvemini, Aleramo undertook a notable inquiry into the schools of Calabria. When Mussolini marched on Rome, she was in Paris. When Croce drew up an anti-Fascist manifesto in 1925, she was one of those to sign. But she had to live. Her writing, increasingly florid tales of love that editors rejected, left her in poverty. In 1930, in an article entitled "La donna italiana," she identified Mussolini as the reawakener of Italian motherhood. She subsisted on a state pension until the regime's collapse, then became a member of the

Communist Party in 1946. Her last important writing, *Dal mio diario, 1940–44*, traced this conversion, negotiated in company with her last lover, a young poet-scholar-intellectual of twenty. She wrote for the party until her death at eighty-four.

Self-Created Masculinity: Gabriele D'Annunzio

Far more organically related to its time than Aleramo's investigation of private torment was a final assertion of unfettered masculinity, in symbolic rupture of the impasse that Giovanni Giolitti could preside over but not master. Because he did believe that politics, not just art, could break the impasse, Mussolini, not Gabriele D'Annunzio, ended up as Italy's *marito-maschio*. Yet D'Annunzio, daring poet, impetuous novelist, connoisseur of women, and flier, more surely perpetuated a classic type for whom politics had to be transcended. In D'Annunzio the private became the public, in a compelling demonstration of how sexuality—obviously masculine—could offer itself as the very axis of a culture. Had Italy been a nation like other nations—like the France, Britain, Germany, or America it aspired to equal—its modern literature might have quickly become more sociological. Social comedy might have flourished. As it was, Italy's high literature perpetuated, not so much the condescension Gramsci deplored, but reliance upon distance, irony, eventually bitterness, from Giovanni Verga and Luigi Pirandello through Italo Svevo and on to Moravia, Pavese, Silone, Vittorini, Morante. By contrast, D'Annunzio crowded close, practiced oratory and postures of commitment. Of all the persons discussed by Croce in his *History of Italy* from the Risorgimento to World War I, D'Annunzio was the only man not a statesman to draw repeated mention as the Hegelian historian struggled to place and yet to exorcise him. In the last volume, *Il novecento*, of the magisterial modern nine-volume *Storia della letteratura italiana*, the first and longest chapter is devoted to D'Annunzio.[15]

D'Annunzio was thirty-four when he ran for parliament in 1897. His candidacy was symptomatic of the condition of Italian politics, for he ran—and won—as the candidate of no party. He had no issues except for the greatest issue, Italy's purpose, mission, reason for being. D'Annunzio barnstormed the district, evoking for large crowds the long-ago Italy of great art, splendor, and genius. D'Annunzio probably could not have won a democratic franchise. In his native city, Pescara, however, he was already famous, and his campaign had a kind of credibility for more than the privileged few who could vote. By 1897 Italians well knew that cultured Europeans, crucially the French, had tendered D'Annunzio a respect and enthusiasm accorded no Italian writer for a century past. He was united Italy's first international success. But in addition he existed as a personality, as a man, and that on a more or less sensationally Italian model, a hero of eminent boudoirs as well as books. Croce conceded the heart of the matter, that D'Annunzio was a brilliant writer, but had he been only that, had he not attested to some basic spring of energy capable of feeding more than art, his raid on public status in 1897, then later as a war leader, and finally as ruler of the republic of Fiume, would have been merely ridiculous. In running at all, D'Annunzio displayed both contempt and hope for parliament and the politicians' Italy. He took his place in the house on the extreme right, but then, when occasion offered, switched to the extreme left, not, as he said, from any respect for socialism per se but from agreement, as he thought, with revolutionary readiness to bring down the whole order of things. More subtly, he was manifesting his own identification with Italy's basic problem, which was still to settle into a sound identity, and even the process by which that identity might be forged, not one of violent seizure of power, but of poetry, persuasion, and language.

When D'Annunzio returned to Italy in 1915, after five years in France, he started preaching war. The only reasons he offered for war were inextricable from his own eloquence. Perhaps the high point of his literary achievement had been reached some years before, during his liaison with Eleanora Duse, which ended in 1904. After that, some years of extravagance had helped drive him to France, where he had found admirers but not creative rebirth. Back home in 1915, he adopted Italy itself as his art project, an Italy that must not skulk through the world's greatest drama in ignominious neutrality but seize the occasion to display its *italianità*. War was to win not possessions but self-possession, to defeat not foreign enemies but the inner enemies of lassitude and mediocrity. In an important sense, D'Annunzio was responding to the problem that some of the older heroes of the Risorgimento had brooded over. Italy had not finally won its independence through heroic struggle, but by devious diplomacy and French arms. The final achievement, the winning of Rome in 1870, had been a kind of unearned luck. The wars in Libya and Ethiopia had been at once sordid and humiliating. Italy's need to prove itself in real struggle remained.

At fifty-two, D'Annunzio demonstrated physical courage again in the war. He had exposed himself to death before, in duels. At the front he suffered wounds and lost an eye in behavior which no one could doubt was completely sincere, without ulterior motive—in the language of a later moral psychology, "authentic." He had a deep, earned, professional interest in the linkages between death and creative energy. Death—as idea and in risk—had stimulated him personally and helped impel his genius. War might serve as a kind of mass democratic school, too. As such, it might stimulate the nation to higher creativity.

D'Annunzio's exploration of beauty and death were both linked with sex. From the start his achievements as poet, novelist, and playwright were inextricable from his achievements as womanizer, seducer, lover. In these achievements too, D'Annunzio was authentic. His letters, yet unpublished, to which biographers have gone as they might go to the private letters of any canny statesman, confirm that, for D'Annunzio, no divide existed between private and public life.

Mia divina, mia bella, mia buona, mia santa. . . . Volevo la tue lettera, l'ho trovata, l'ho baciata, l'ho aperta tremando. . . . Reprimi questo fuoco che te uccidera, e uccidera me con te, o unica mia, unico mio sospiro! Tuo sempre sempre sempre sempre sempre tuo tuo tuo Gabriele tuo tuo.[16]

As Philippe Jullian notes, such a letter might easily have been put to music for an Italian opera. The girl to whom he sent this letter when he was eighteen, was the girl back home. Two years later D'Annunzio married someone else. But this proved no lack of sincerity in his first protestations of love, any more than the collapse of the marriage not much later discounted his wife's subsequent attestations to a year of overwhelming happiness. For D'Annunzio much of the intoxication of love derived, not from its object—lover, wife, mistress—but from the fact that love could be transfigured into a project, an art, freedom. Love consisted in large part of a relationship to language. Women with whom he was in love were occasions for the release of language. D'Annunzio did have many requirements; not just any woman would do. But he had a powerful appetite for aspects of women's lives that can only be regarded as generic, dimensions requiring no particular woman but that only women could display. Women's clothes, cosmetics, perfumes, jewels: on all these he was an expert. A latter-day sophistication, sniffing out homosexuality in such fascinations, would miss the point. D'Annunzio was engaged in rescuing masculinity from its decline into the antiheroisms of the politicians, of the new business and capitalism, of socialists and social priests, rescuing it from a middle-class future of mere materialism, predictability, peace.

Croce argued the reverse, that D'Annunzio himself represented "materialism," the merely sensate. "With him," Croce said, "a note which had hitherto been absent was sounded in Italian literature, sensual, decadent, brutal." Conceding D'Annunzio's genius, Croce explained that with old religions and old rationalisms no longer binding European moral consciousness, industrialization and power politics had produced "an uneasy state of mind," "lust for enjoyment," a "spirit of adventure and of joy in conquest," yet also "restlessness and withal lack of enthusiasm and indifference." D'Annunzio had, that is, occupied a vacuum. This argument was forced, however, and not fully considered, as Croce himself could not but reveal. He did not conclude that these broad European diseases raged most in Italy, but least: "Even in unsentimental and practically-minded Italy, the enemy of all fanaticism, such tendencies had taken root." This was equivalent to categorizing D'Annunzio as a European rather than an Italian writer, and this was not Croce's point. Almost despite himself, for Croce could not help sensing "sensuality" and "sadism" in D'Annunzio, and some connection between this sadism and the war, Croce did grasp the larger drives in D'Annunzio's career. "Materialism" and "sensualism" hardly described them.

The aim of his art was the joy of the eye, the ear, the touch, the smell, indeed of all the senses, and if he had an individual aim, which stood for him as an ideal, it was to develop a new universal sense, different from those which the human animal had hitherto possessed.[17]

Here Croce grasped the logic of the salvation D'Annunzio was offering to modernity. The threat posed to spirituality by modern industrialization emerged when industrialization invaded minds to install there the same principles of operation manifest in the new factories: standardization, routine, predictability. D'Annunzio's inspiration was to recognize the point on which to offer maximum resistance, the sensorium, the body itself as the very temple of the individual. Minds were collective, bodies irreducibly individual.

As Philippe Jullian and others have pointed out, D'Annunzio perhaps more than any other man of his time abstracted out from the totality of modern industrialization exactly those elements that offered transcendence over its anti-individualistic, socializing forces. He loved airplanes and cars. He loved speed. Speed was not available to societies and nations, except metaphorically, only to individuals, physically. Obviously, it also carried with it new ideas about death, and thus of life in dialectic with death. The airplane's Icarian associations included death but also the sun, and D'Annunzio's lifelong poetic use of sun imagery prefigured the liberatory dimensions of industrial society rather than simply echoing old myths. If the early Italian automobile industry, with Giovanni Agnelli, had its special associations with racing, speed, and death, so obviously did Italy have a special potential relationship with an industrial society's search for the sun. The progressive twentieth century's exposure of the body to the sun would constitute a radical comment on the bundled-up nineteenth.

Between Croce's idea that life must not be divorced from its center, "that center being for man his moral and religious consciousness," and what he could see in D'Annunzio, there was no final contradiction. The key element in D'Annunzio remained poetry and language. D'Annunzio did not just speed but wrote poetry about speed. He attested at every point that without language there was in effect no experience, or else, no more than the mere sensualism that Croce feared. Croce himself never responded to the experiential side of industrialism; like the socialists, he remained preoccupied with production. D'Annunzio realized that the fate of industrial man would derive from the side of consumption. When focused on production and work, consciousness remained puritan, ascetic, collective, anti-individualistic, antipoetic, whether production existed under social democracy or capitalist plutocracy.

It was reasonably evident to all that, for D'Annunzio, women too were objects, like airplanes and cars, even the sun itself.[18] They too were "sacred" objects, sacred because they were the necessary occasions for experience, language, poetry. It was one of D'Annunzio's great services to overcoming an Italian—and European—tradition of love as old as Dante, that he insisted on real women of real flesh, real sex organs, in place of those Beatrices and Lauras of the more spiritual tradition in which the most precious love object was ordinarily dead anyway. This "materialization" of women was not a tacit reduction of their status to procreation, in the direction of Mussolini's Fascism-to-come. In vivid poetry written before he was even twenty, D'Annunzio had celebrated the ecstasies of heterosexual fellatio, and letters written thereafter show his continuing gratification from that experience. In its liberation from the demographic anxieties of the old order, modern industrial society would take up the challenge of sex and sensuality as a realm for far more autonomous and individualistic explorations, and the key to its success here too would be in language, the ability to free experiences from sociological norms. The arguments of Michel Foucault on modern sexuality as "discourse" have made the point, only backward. There was no natural sexuality waiting to be released from thrall by philosophical criticism, only new sexuality created by new discourse, new poetry.

If D'Annunzio returned women neither to maternity nor to inaccessibility, he did not emancipate them. He had no interest in their civic status. In the poor education of his Trasteverine beauty, Barbara Leoni, he saw no occasion for tutoring; what interested him was her classical physical beauty and her emotional ardor. It did not matter to him that she never evolved. On the other hand, he feared nothing in the sophisticated culture of Duse or of his French admirers and mistresses, for theirs was education that simply enhanced and intensified the opportunities for love. He had no interest in women outside his personal relations with them. In these relations he was interested most of all in what made for his art. His women were materials for a purpose.

Ironically, neither Croce nor any other Italian of the age was ready to criticize D'Annunzio on this account. Mozzoni, seeking allies Risorgimentos for the pursuit of equal rights, never included passion among those rights. Nor did any other feminist or feminist organization. If no Italian feminist developed Charlotte Perkins Gilman's idea that women's freedom required less, not more, sex and sexuality, none attested to any suspicion to the contrary, and when Italian feminists, like their counterparts in America, Sweden, Russia, England, and elsewhere, turned on prostitution as a social evil, it was with a due sense of the failure of society to insist upon enough repression. Croce too preferred that platonic love preached by "Neera," supposedly antifeminist, yet criticized by no feminists but Sibilla. The danger in D'Annunzio did not appear in any tacit subordination of women to the purposes of art or even, ultimately, of sexual gratification. In the aristocratic bohemias and elite decadent circles he frequented, a certain sexual equality often did obtain. Female as well as male adventurers found the Paris of the Third Republic a theater for their affairs. Mazzini's supporter, Cristina di Belgiojoso, once had been such an adventurer, as were women from America, Germany, Russia, England, and Sweden then and later. Some were lesbians, such as the American Nathalie Barney of Cincinnati and Paris, making another kind of affirmation of the autonomy of sex. Some were great artists, such as the American Isadora Duncan of California and Europe, using sex for the sake of another language. Duncan engaged in a kind of sexual duel with D'Annunzio, flattering herself on her victory.[19] Thus, perhaps paradoxically, D'Annunzio was not necessarily vulnerable to charges of supporting or favoring sexual inequality. Often enough he showed his own readiness, even eagerness, to be an "object" for women.

For feminists, what was most challenging about D'Annunzio was the power of his art, seeming to validate his affirmation of the senses as the media through which freedom would be won in a modern society. For Catholic moralists and the church, D'Annunzio posed no challenge: he was simply shocking, his works to be put on the Index and he himself assailed as an immoralist. For socialism too, D'Annunzio appeared simply as an apologist for privilege, hostile to any hopes for social justice and equality. Such straightforward repudiation was less simple for Croce, who understood that the refreshment of culture could not be left simply to criticism but required joy. Yet Croce had found no reason to trust that Italy—and Western culture at large—could give up an authoritative center and survive. For him that center was philosophy and the university, and for the university D'Annunzio's example was troublesome indeed.

But feminists were tied neither to the university nor to the church. A female D'Annunzio? Practically unthinkable. Yet to reject D'Annunzio totally was to cut short the effort to break with the ideologies in which women had been kept passive, ideologies still sustained by both university and church. Once again, socialism seemed to offer itself as the alternative, but with D'Annunzio in view, feminism had to ask itself whether the equality socialism constantly promised also promised liberation. Feminists had repudiated cultures that denied them equality. They needed dialogue with a culture in which not equality but freedom was the issue. If D'Annunzio too, to an extent, registered the weakness of any middle class in Italy, he also clearly registered the fact that those Italians least bound by the past were not interested in settling for equality. The son of a *piccola borgesia* himself, D'Annunzio registered a popular hope that modernity would liberate the senses, unleash the imagination, empower the individual. For feminism to oppose this rising eagerness for the future would be to blunt its own demand for release from the past. D'Annunzio's art followed the logic of his passion. Certainly he wrote in hopes of making money, but he did not write poems for a court or novels for an experienced readership or plays for critics. In passion, ulterior motives were fatal. D'Annunzio wrote on the assumption that he would find his audience in people eager to see a man be himself. The absurdity of the figure D'Annunzio often cut in the eyes of strangers was itself testimony to his refusal to be ruled by hostile or indifferent eyes. This affirmation of the self as authentic performer seconded feminism's own struggle to escape roles and statuses.

Finally, D'Annunzio challenged feminism to confront the body in its most tormenting aspect. As objects of passion, as bearers of jewels, clothes, and perfumes, D'Annunzio's women were forms of art. A work of art was an object, passive, to be enjoyed. Women made themselves beautiful, into objects to be admired and enjoyed. Yet it was clear that for D'Annunzio beauty mattered as an invitation to activity, to making art. The relation grew dialectical: a woman was made beautiful by her lover, her beholder. In effect, in the vigor of his insistence upon the rights of passion, D'Annunzio rejected beauty as a kind of attribute of an object and located it in relationship. For feminism there was no reason to reject this view. It relieved women of the one inequality that feminism consistently ignored, the inequality of beauty. Escape from this inequality was not to be found in relativizing beauty to social stereotypes. It was no solace for a plain girl in Italy to be told that her features would be regarded as having dark beauty in Sweden, or for an ordinary Swedish blonde to be told of the enthusiasm awaiting her in Italy. However ignored by feminism, these too were social formations weighing upon women, therefore to be criticized and dissolved. D'Annunzio had defined a process toward that end, a process opening up the prospect of a world in which all women could be beautiful.

A New World: Milan in 1920

In 1922 Paolo Valera published the fourth edition of his famous *Milano Sconosciuta* (Unknown Milan). Valera was that rarity, a writer, journalist, and intellectual from genuine lower-class origins. His father was a street vendor of matches, his mother a seamstress. Valera had published *Milano Sconosciuta* first in 1879. It was a scathing, raw, realist exposé of Milan's population of beggars, prostitutes, smugglers, thieves, wandering halfwits, underpaid ballet girls, and low life generally, all loosely held together by a kind of anarchist-socialist indignation. Second and third editions had followed in 1898 and 1908, with Valera's original, self-consciously antibourgeois style somewhat downplayed in favor of a more systematic inquiry into Milan's problems. The 1922 edition, the work of a seventy-year-old, turned back to the tone and style of the first, presenting an impassioned, often hectic, consistently vivid portrait, mingling scenes of fifty years, with the author's "participant-observation" technique again strongly visible. One of Valera's new chapters was "Le nuove femminile e i nuovi maschi" (The new women and the new men):

The life of the new women, girls from sixteen to twenty, is taken up by trifles. Cocktails, fortune-telling, races, cars, dance halls, expensive and indecent. . . Spectacular dances like "il foxtrot, two-steps, il tango." . . . At intervals they take off for the lakes, the sea, the mountains. Somewhere there is always some amusement. They squander and they make things squandered.[20]

New Milan had reawakened the old anarchist's morality, his old socialist's asceticism, the proletarian artist's disgust at the shapelessness of decadence.

But Valera's observer's eye triumphed over antique moralism. He had always been at once fascinated by and anguished over Milan's "sellers of love," his anguish reaching out to include those who revealed the ultimate horror of prostitution, women plying the trade into their thirties, forties, fifties, in pathetic mimesis of what at best was a young woman's slavery. But these new girls, he agreed, one could not count among *"le vendetrici d'amore."* These girls had no need to sell themselves. "They work. You find them in banks, law offices, business offices, government offices. They are typists, stenographers, translators," honest working girls. What caught Valera's eye was their complex new outlook, their new manners, their daring new morals. Though self-supporting, they accepted gifts—gloves, silk handkerchiefs, a hat in the latest fashion, a meal in a grand restaurant, even a couple of weeks in the mountains. Valera could see that these lives were being led on a different route. "It's a life that doesn't get to marriage easily." Pursuing the sociology of it, Valera entered ultimate ground:

The parents? The parents know nothing; or pretend to. They pretend not to know their pay is not enough for the silk stockings, the two-hundred lira shoes . . . the chiffon parasol. . . . It's by working overtime, say the honest mammas. They live in narrow circumstances. The whole family sometimes in one room. . . . No one protests if one or the other stays out on the streets for diversion. The mothers and fathers have known too much suffering themselves to impose it on their children.[21]

Valera had got hold of a great theme. The Italian folk were abandoning their ancient resignation, their acceptance of suffering as fated, and they were doing so at a most crucial juncture, in the form not of children rebelling against parents but of parents extending permission to children, above all and most strikingly to daughters.

Valera's inability to pursue his observations and develop his guesses followed perhaps simply from the inability of an old man to shake off all old preoccupations. He fell into an elegiac, resigned mood: the war has changed everything. No one ever has enough money. There's always more in the shops than you can possibly afford. You can't find a delicatessen anymore, or a fruit stand, or a wine dealer, where they aren't out to skin you. Women are irritable. Today's prostitutes, if younger, are smaller and skinnier than those of the good old days with their more flexible bodies, fuller mouths, healthier laughs. But even as he watched the thirteen and fourteen-year-olds "dancing negro dances" at the Luna Palace, he knew better.

In my time hypocrisy reigned, the lie, the good woman who obeyed the rules and pretended not to notice how her perfumed curls had somehow got loose. . . . No more. The epoch of the lie has fallen. . . . Last night at the Palace . . . there were mothers who knew their role. . .sitting along the edges of the hall, watching their darlings fondly. . . .They danced in a kind of general massage, rubbing together incessantly. They are a strong generation. People without prejudices. Probably they could laugh at a relative's funeral. . . . Making families doesn't interest them. One thing is certain: much independence is in them.[22]

In Russia Alexandra Kollontai had already written her paean to the "new woman," based on the novels beginning to appear everywhere, it seemed, in Western Europe and even Russia itself. In the United

States the flapper had already been invented, Owen Johnson had written of his "salamander," the girl who, burned once, might be burned yet again and again but never destroyed. Zelda Fitzgerald was to see herself as a salamander after the war. The Twenties would be a distinct new epoch in America, as Valera anticipated for Italy. In the life of the new generation, in dance halls and night clubs, but even more in colleges and universities and in the movies—Valera noted the movie houses that had come to Milan, although he did not see the movies themselves—a new consciousness would be forged. But not in Italy.

Whether, without Fascism, Italy too might have had its "Twenties," shaped perhaps by D'Annunzian motifs, responsive to a slowly unfolding middle class, remains one of those questions history alone can formulate. Perhaps the greatest difference for Italy would be that, in the 1960s and 1970s, it would have no Twenties to recall. Fascism itself could not afford a Twenties. Between D'Annunzio and Mussolini a kind of haze of tension and misunderstanding gathered. With the younger man in power, the older man's fantasies were awkward and obtrusive. The regime did not please the poet. It was becoming realistic. Fascism was not about to pay the sheer economic bills for romantic illusions. D'Annunzio was pensioned off to his Lago di Garda eyrie. Fascism proceeded with its mystifications of marriage, womanhood, sexuality, ruralized, fertilized. It ignored Milan.

Gramsci's Dream: Italy as Utopia of the Popular

To Antonio Gramsci all this was irrevelant. Gramsci never contemplated the prospect of a growing new middle-class bourgeoisie in Italy. But Gramsci was by no means indifferent, let alone hostile, to sexual issues. And in what he did say, he often displayed his usual freedom from mere orthodoxy. Between 1916 and 1920 Gramsci wrote brief theater notices for the Turin-based Socialist paper *Avanti*, once edited by Benito Mussolini. In March 1917, Henrik Ibsen's *A Doll's House* came to town, with one of Italy's best-known actresses, Emma Gramatica, in the lead. Before a glittering first-night audience, "thick with cavaliers and their ladies," the company had hopes for a success. Gramsci's reaction to the play was like that of any good liberal bourgeois feminist. He admired it. *A Doll's House*, he said, was a true work of drama, because it expounded "human individuality" undergoing suffering in its struggle for autonomy. Gramsci's appreciation of its dramatic pleas for individuality was unshaded; so was his approval of the heroine's choice of herself. The Risorgimento ideal of sacrifice he rejected. Nor did any alternative socialist ideal of sacrifice suggest itself to him. Here, as often, Gramsci showed himself a humanist in the classic line, affirming individuality.

But the audience, Gramsci noted, had another view. It applauded happily after the first act, and then again after the second, but as soon as it realized that Nora Helmar, "that superior being," was not just bluffing but actually would abandon house, husband, and children "in order to find herself, to find the roots of her moral being," it turned cold and hostile. Gramsci turned his review into an attack upon this audience, "our bourgeoisie, great and small"—a specifically Italian audience incapable, he said, of accepting the play:

The only form of women's liberation understood in our culture is that of the woman who becomes a coquette. . . . The woman of our [Latin] countries, the bourgeois woman, remains still a slave, without depth of moral life, without spiritual needs, even more a slave when she takes up the only liberty granted her, that of intrigue. She remains the female of the species suckling her young . . . succoring the sick . . . most exalted when least attentive to her duty to herself.[23]

In vehement and explicit insistence in this review upon the peculiarly Italian and Latin nature of this decadence, Gramsci was undercutting any general thesis of class determination of sexual ethics. The review could be read almost as a compliment to Norway and Northern culture for having generated Ibsen and his ideal heroine, as though Ibsen had not despised the decadent bourgeoisie of Oslo. Gramsci compounded his incoherence by then locating the "superior," "more spiritual," "less animal" ethic, which the Italian audience rejected, in a "universal morality," universal because "profoundly human, because made up of spirituality rather than of animality, of soul more than of economics, nerves and muscles." These unhistorical, "transcendental" conceptualizations were hardly Marxist.

After having castigated the Italian bourgeoisie, Gramsci concluded his review with a tribute to those who lived the story of Nora daily, those who worked, women who knew they were not mere provocations to voluptuous pleasures, the women of the proletariat:

I know two proletarian women, women who have no need of the law or divorce in order to rediscover themselves and create a life in which they are more themselves. With the full consent of their husbands, men who are not cavaliers but workers, simple and without hypocrisy, they have left their families to live with men who are more truly their "missing halves," yet without breaking the ties of intimacy with their children. All this has happened without any of those Boccaccio-esque snickers of our bourgeoisie. Such women do not laugh at Ibsen's heroine. They see in her a spiritual sister, artistic testimony to the meaning of their own lives . . . full of interior life and the exploration of one's own personality rather than of vile hypocrisy, the itch of morbid flesh, the gross animality of slaves become masters.[24]

Although Gramsci reviewed practically everything that came to Turin, including the new "theater of the grotesque," Pirandello, and all the foreign plays—Ibsen, Shaw, Wilde, Turgenev—his favorite theme remained the lightmindedness of the Turin playgoing audience. In Dario Niccodemi's *La maestrina* early in 1918 he saw sentimentality as a mask for the audience's prurience. Because the Turin bourgeoisie was not interested in white-collar heroines, Nino Berrini's *Una donna moderna* failed in 1917, as it had at its premiere five years before. Postwar plays about noble soldiers betrayed by heartless wives were popular because they appealed to low impulses. In 1920, reviewing a play of Leonid Andreev, he prognosticated, as a replacement for the bourgeois audience that had rejected it, a new, better audience, "rougher, more open, honest, sincere," a "proletarian audience."[25]

Although it is by no means clear that Gramsci ever actually knew any coquettes or became sufficiently acquainted with any bourgeois young women to learn whether they had any "interior life" or not,[26] at least he had the Turin theater from which to draw inferences about the Turin aristocracy and upper bourgeoisie that constituted its patronage. What did he really know of the Turin workers? His projections onto proletarian women of Ibsen's ideals for Nora obviously contained peculiarities. Certainly Nora had not wrung her ideals out of working-class experience. In dealing with the Turin workers politically, observing and interpreting their efforts to win control over their own lives on the factory floor, Gramsci thought of them as pioneering a new, more democratic means of production. But had they evolved a working-class culture? A new sexual culture? The growing practice of common-law marriage and of bearing children without benefit of wedlock among the young socialist women of Turin no doubt testified to the palsying of old Catholic controls, but this was hardly evidence for the rise of a new audience for such playwrights as Ibsen, Shaw, Andreev, and the others, rooted as these were in bourgeois experience. The route from factory work to modernist culture remained a figment of hope and wish and desire, not of analysis.

Not long before watching *A Doll's House*, Gramsci had gone to a rather different kind of performance, a recital by the exhibitionist actress Lydia Borelli. "In the beginning there was sex," his review began. Then: "In the beginning was the word. . . . No, in the beginning was sex." After this ironical note, Gramsci went on to an explicit rumination on the place of sex. Though he had heard of Borelli's elegance, her dramatic powers and hypnotic appeal, he had, he said, found himself unmoved. What then did it mean to say that sex came before all? Dante's celebration of sex had drawn on the "necessary," the "inevitable" motion of one half of humanity toward the other half. Together, they (by

Dante's Italian logic) would produce a whole. But today, Gramsci said, we find halves embracing not another half but two or three or more halves. "Some could be a half for all men." People said they admired Borelli for her art, her sincerity, her acting. But she had no art. The verse she chanted was best when it had no sense at all but its sounds. "This woman is pre-historic, primordial." "Borelli is *par excellence* a film actress, for in film the only language is that of the human body in its ever-renewed plasticity." On the modern stage, imitating cinema, sex had raped intelligence. "The Borelli case . . . is not comforting. . . . Man has worked hard to reduce the factor of 'sex' to its proper limits. To let it grow now, to the damage of intelligence, is evidence of brutalization, not of spiritual elevation."[27] Rarely did Gramsci reveal himself more clearly as a traditional Italian intellectual, being as orthodox in his sense that, at the heart of Italian life, mind exercised hegemony over body, as all the perennial spiritual celebrators of Dante.

But Gramsci knew that a cultural impasse had been reached. Writing of Carlo Veneziani's *La finestra sul mondo* in December 1918, he repeated a familiar theme: sex is what interests Italians most, therefore Italian playwrights write only about sex, and the theater that results is a merely commercial phenomenon. Then he went on:

Until now the Italian theater has presented sexual life in only two or three ways, either to stimulate and provoke erotic thrills or to wax romantic and sentimental, according to the aphorism, "After making love, every animal feels sadness." But because the Italian theater had already perfected these approaches a third became necessary. (Three is the mystic number of Christianity and Masonry, which have done so much to shape Italian morals.) This third way was excogitated by Pirandello, Chiarelli, Antonelli. Confronted by sexual life, the personages in their plays adopt a critical outlook, an attitude completely intellectual, introspective.[28]

For Gramsci the Pirandellian subjection of sex to intellectualization, introspection, decomposition, structuralization, and detachment generally, though a merited assault on both sensual and sentimental modes of perception, constituted a dead end. Surely Pirandello was not a playwright for the proletariat. A voice "beyond hypocrisy," his was also a voice beyond acculturation in any movement toward a new society at once democratic and productive.

Then where were democratic voices to be heard? The voice that Gramsci never listened to was the same voice that had at once intrigued and appalled Paolo Valera. One of the most schoolmasterish essays Gramsci ever wrote was his chastisement of his fellow intellectuals over "the problem of Milan." Why have we failed in Milan? he asked. It was not enough, he said, to point to the objective conditions—Milan's infinitude of small factories, its lack of big factories, its multitude of shops, its hosts of clerks and secretaries and office workers. We ought to have understood Milan better.[29] But it was precisely these new kinds of voices Gramsci himself had not listened to, those of the new young women in white collars, just as hard at work as the men in the factories.

In prison, Gramsci experienced an urge to "do something *für ewig*," which in March 1929 he clarified as a project in writing history. First, he would work on nineteenth-century Italian history, particularly on intellectuals. Second, he would work on "theory of history and historiography." Third, he would work on "Americanism and Fordism." In effect, Gramsci had in mind an integrated treatment of Italy's past, present, and future. Its past, a failure, was susceptible to research. Its present was a matter of "theory," that is, of will. It would be possible to study its future because that future was already present in the United States. In "Americanism and Fordism" Gramsci offered his most abstract discussion of sexual themes, reaching out beyond Italy to an analysis based on function.

Gramsci's attention was attracted to the United States because there the basic methods of modern industrial production, as he understood them, were most fully installed. The United States was in the van of modernized countries essentially because there had been no feudal inheritance to be overcome. Gramsci regarded the anti-Americanism widespread among Italian (and European) artists and intellectuals as itself a feudal residue. Pirandello himself, with his lament that "Americanism" was "swamping" European culture, was an example of this retrograde outlook. In prison, Gramsci found the fundamentally new phase of historical development in America, and he found its essence in the America identified with one man, Henry Ford.

The Ford who interested Gramsci was not the inventor of the assembly line. For the actual sociology of industrial production—the assembly line—Gramsci credited Frederick J. Taylor. But Ford, Gramsci thought, understood the need for a modern psychology of production. He was interested in far more than the shop-time efficiency of his workers; he was concerned with the total pattern of his workers' lives. A new kind of man, a new kind of personality and character structure was necessary, if the new kind of work was to get done: "The attempts made by Ford, with the aid of a body of inspectors, to intervene in the private lives of his employees and to control how they spent their wages and how they lived is an indication of these tendencies." Ford's efforts had proceeded along with the American experiment with Prohibition. To Gramsci that was logical: "the most dangerous agent of destruction of labouring power" was indeed alcohol. But there was another danger, too: "Abuse and irregularity of sexual functions is, after alcoholism, the most dangerous enemy of nervous energies. . . . It is worth drawing attention to the way in which industrialists (Ford in particular) have been concerned with the sexual affairs of their employees and with their family arrangements in general."

Gramsci was intent that Prohibition and sexual policing not be mistaken as "puritanical." That would be to see them simply as residues of America's own preindustrial past, and to imply perhaps that Ford and his fellows, under the influence of history, had some interest in the humanity or spirituality of their employees. At stake was the creation and preservation of an efficient work force: monogamous men, moderate, sexually orderly:

The truth is that the new type of man demanded by the rationalisation of production and work cannot be developed until the sexual instinct has been suitably regulated and until it too has been rationalised. . . . It seems clear that the new industrialism wants monogamy: it wants the man as worker not to squander his nervous energies in the disorderly and stimulating pursuit of occasional sexual satisfaction. The employee who goes to work after a night of "excess" is no good for his work. The exaltation of passion cannot be reconciled with the timed movements of [production]. . . . This complex of direct and indirect repression and coercion exercised on the masses will undoubtedly produce results and a new form of sexual union will emerge whose fundamental characteristic would apparently have to be monogamy and relative stability.[30]

But Gramsci never explained why Ford's intervention in the private lives of his workers was necessary. Tocqueville had shown a century earlier that American men already were monogamized, moderate, sexually disciplined. Then was it because Ford's workers were a new, less-disciplined breed? recent Catholic immigrants? blacks? If so, Gramsci did not say so. Indeed, it was notable that, in claiming his own Italians—plus the Slavs—as a people given to work, he was citing a Catholic people. In fact, Gramsci knew very well that a work ethic prevailed in America more widely than in Italy. If the ordinary Italian was a man of work, the rich Italian was not, whereas in America, even the millionaires worked. "This, for the average European, is the weirdest American extravagance."[31] The America of mass production was rooted in America's special past; how then could it predict Italy's future?

On another level Gramsci contrasted Italy and America to Italy's advantage. America had no experience of those residues from feudalism, true, had none of that frivolous and hedonistic aristocracy that patronized the Turin theater, but certain changes in "bourgeois" sexual morality were overtaking America as a consequence of its success:

It would be interesting to know the statistical occurrence of deviation from sexual behavior officially propagandised in the United States, broken down according to social group. It will show that in general divorce is particularly frequent among the upper classes. This demonstrates the moral gap in the

United States between the working masses and the ever more numerous elements of the ruling classes.

But Gramsci then quickly overlaid this class category with a sexual category that effectively cancelled it:

The male industrialist continues to work even if he is a millionaire, but his wife and daughters are turning, more and more, into "luxury mammals". Beauty competitions, competitions for new film actresses (recall the 30,000 Italian girls who sent photographs of themselves in bathing costumes to Fox in 1926), the theatre, etc., all of which select the feminine beauty of the world and put it up for auction, stimulate the mental attitudes of prostitution, and "white slaving" is practised quite legally among the upper classes. The women, with nothing to do, travel; they are continually crossing the ocean to come to Europe, escaping prohibition in their own country and contracting "marriages" in a form barely disguised in fragile legal formulae.[32]

All the confusions in Gramsci's thinking about "Americanism" and in his attempt to link sexual ethics with industrial production derived from his Italian populism. So long as he held to a quite normal liberal—and Marxist—view of Italy as backward—"Italian democracy still exudes the atmosphere . . . of a society not yet revolutionized by industrial capitalism, not yet infused with the valiant ambitions of economic individualism. . . . It remains . . . lacking all impulses to initiative and ambition. . . . is still essentially 'Catholic' "[33]—he could indulge himself in criticizing those who feared Italy's Americanization. "What is today called 'Americanism' is to a large extent an advance criticism of old strata which will in fact be crushed by any eventual new order and which are already in the grips of a wave of social panic, dissolution and despair. . . . " Let Italy too be individualized, democratized, Protestantized, as America has been for a hundred years. But in the end, Gramsci could not accept the idea of Italy following the model of another nation, or even the abstract model propounded by Marx for all nations. He determinedly resisted any idea that Italy could not find answers to its problems in itself. In this light Americanism suddenly did become a danger: "But it is not from the social groups 'condemned' by the new order that reconstruction is to be expected, but from those on whom is imposed the burden of creating with their own suffering the material bases of the new order. It is they who 'must' find for themselves an 'original', and not Americanised, system of living, to turn into 'freedom' what today is 'necessity'."[34] This "original" system of living was to come, of course, from the ordinary Italian man-of-work, the peasant and his wife, whose sexual culture, since it was already integrated with regular work, was already adapted to industrial capitalism. If Marxism stood for anything, it was for the linkage between basic social character and the basic forms of production, but Gramsci explicitly denied that, in Italy, the change from agriculture to industry would decree a change in basic character: "The new type of worker will be a repetition, in different form, of peasants in the villages."[35]

The source of Gramsci's populistic faith in the particular traditions of humble Italy can only be debated. No doubt at some important level of his imagination, he, like so many other supposedly scientific Marxists, surrendered to the hope that, in Italy at least, the prescribed stages of social evolution would not have to be ground through implacably before utopia dawned. No doubt, for all the ambiguous compliments he paid the United States, he hoped that the repulsiveness of Ford's hegemony could be skipped over in an Italy forewarned. But there is need also to consider that at an equally important level Gramsci's imagination flinched at sexual specters. To trace these to one "puritan" source or another in his own background would be less interesting than to find such specters generated by his own radical logic. Marxism of course provided him with no tools for defying them. Its myth of a natural harmony between the sexes that would accompany socialism neither spoke to the gender and sexual issues of the interim nor satisfied minds truly radicalized by the thought that there was no such thing as a "natural" sexual stability such as Horace had celebrated. Gramsci himself was evidently unprepared to generate some reconciliation to sexual contingency superior to that offered by Bebel—let alone Lenin. Far better, and easier, to find the defense against sexual disorder already immanent in Italian life, in the culture of the Italian worker, first as peasant, then as factory worker. Thereby, "sex," sexuality, and "the sexual question" could and should be finessed as topics dangerous and irrelevant to the pursuit of industrial democracy. True, Gramsci never denied that a new kind of woman was and must be in the making. "The formation of a new feminine personality is the most important question of an ethical and civil order connected with the sexual question."[36] But this very formulation shed more light on the combination of fears and wishes that controlled his thinking on that question. The need for a "new" feminine personality obviously simply contradicted his faith in the survival of the steady old wife of the countryside, free of "little games." But it just as plainly picked up the fear he registered in his look at America, that, while men might very well go on as hard-working beings in the age of affluence and consumption, women might not. They might become "luxury mammals." That the danger was great in Italy, those "30,000 Italian girls who sent photographs of themselves in bathing costumes" to an American film studio all too painfully proved.

Although Gramsci never spelled it out, the obvious answer to his problem was for women to be kept at work, work presumably as demanding as the work of the peasant's wife, work as a rosary of daily humanization. But the peculiar abstraction of Gramsci's outlook could be seen in his lack of interest in the young women studied by Paolo Valera. They were not luxury mammals or idle housewives, but poor working girls, and they were hardly evolving as the new feminine personality for which Gramsci hoped. Nor was Gramsci able to ask himself whether the new "national-popular" culture that he hoped would succeed upon the old condescending culture of the traditional intellectuals was in fact taking form before his eyes. He recoiled from the movies, dismissing film as a language "only" of the body, a grammar threatening to release sex from the containments within which civilization had laboriously—and necessarily—sought to confine it. Such resistance simply registered what he himself declared, that even opening the issue of changing sexual culture was dangerous:

Until women can attain not only a genuine independence in relation to men but also a new way of conceiving themselves and their role in sexual relations, the sexual question will remain full of unhealthy characteristics and caution must be exercised in proposals for new legislation. Every crisis brought about by unilateral coercion in the sexual field unleashes a "romantic" reaction which could be aggravated by the abolition of organized prostitution. All these factors make any form of regulation of sex and any attempt to create a new sexual ethic suited to the new methods of production and work extremely complicated and difficult.[37]

One can only guess that the continuing neglect of Sibilla Aleramo's *Una donna* on the part of Italian literary editors registers their agreement with Gramsci that, indeed, in Italy, some things were simply too dangerous to let out of the bag.[38] Would it be surprising, perhaps, to find the same inhibition at work to explain why there were so few such "romantic," confessional, individualistic, "unilateral," "unhealthy" novels written by modern Italian women? Not just in the Fascist 1920s and 1930s, but in the liberated 1970s and 1980s. It is worth noting that the constant theme of Italy's finest postwar woman writer, Natalia Ginzburg, has been the hopelessness of marriage. Young women of the towns and countryside all yearn for it. All are disappointed in it. None have any warm sisterhood in which to escape it. Ginzburg's telling is always cool, detached, objective. This is simply the way things are.

Eternal Italy in the Movies: Rossellini and Fellini

In the 1930s Fascist bureaucrats tolerated, indeed welcomed, a certain mass culture of the heart, sentimental, formulaic. So long as it did not incite unappeasable material appetites, it suited the essentially theatrical nature of the regime. But new African wars, then the disaster of alliance with a far more implacable Fascism, brought chaos. The postwar Italian novel conveyed, if not a broken, then a somber and brooding heart. Fascism, war, defeat, utter collapse had made Italy's case too pathetic for Pirandellian and Svevian ironies and satires, and many Italian writers, though not all, found themselves irresistibly drawn to portray an Italy as inertial as any Egypt, an Africa, an India, neither Sweden nor Argentina, nor, even, "Mediterranean," but, say, Chinese. Others looked with more eager minds to American literature, spring of fresh words, fresh hopes, new forms as alien to old Italy as the notion of jazz and cars for everyone, and all the more valuable for that. But the art form of the movie emerged with far more force, no doubt just because it was more adapted to facing truth while holding off despair. Yet the great Italian directors ended up resisting, rather than affirming, Italy.

Cameras were turning before the Nazis fled Rome. Roberto Rossellini's *Roma città aperta* appeared in 1945.[39] The "neorealist" methods of *Open City* may or may not have been a fruit of the Resistance. After all, Rossellini had made films in the Fascist Thirties perhaps equally neorealist; one, *La nave bianca*, was suppressed by the authorities in 1941 for its pacifistic tone. But the neorealist mode seemed right for postwar imagination. In *Open City*, the long take, in steady recording of unemphasized action, in a world of gray and shadow and cobbled pavement, enclosed the characters as in some claustral catacomb. Anna Magnani's face and body and voice defined one final screech: Rome, Italy, Italians once again Europe's victim, a void open to all. In *Paisan*, in 1946, the method seemed even more appropriate. Simple people shown with "simple" means—the steady long take, no fancy cutting, no lighting, their motions more often awkward, cramped, comic than elastic or firm, faces registering lifetimes of caution, suspicion, naïveté—the affirmation was unmistakable, the objectivity and detachment clear, with the kind of constant irony of the observer who knows he is no better than those he observes but who knows he observes, an irony beyond pity. Perhaps here again was some hint of the Manzoni of *I promessi sposi*, one more condescension to humble Italians. In *Open City* the personae of the main players themselves, the "everyman" Aldo Fabrizi and the "elemental" Magnani, almost demanded that they be seen as undivided simple persons, he homogeneously a "character," she all sheer sentience and passion. Antonio Gramsci might have disapproved.

From these two famous populistic movies, Rossellini moved to a sequence of films of more or less explicit mythmaking. One portrayed Italy's own ultimate saint, *Francesco, Giullare di Dio* (Francis, God's Clown), another Italy's own martyr-genius, Galileo. Even *Stromboli*, starring Ingrid Bergman, identified Italian passion as elemental, volcanic passion, capable of heating up even Swedish purity. But the last of these films, *Anno uno*, seemed, in the extremity of its didacticism to register some sense that mythmaking had to be carried into exhortation. Evidently aimed at acquainting a younger generation with the greatness of Italy's postwar leader, the perennial Christian Democrat prime minister Alcide De Gasperi, the film crossed the line into propaganda, as though trust in Italy's own resources was, after all, not enough. A strong man still was needed.

Perhaps more than that of other directors, Rossellini's career might be adequately explained in terms of peculiarly personal sources, but in conjunction with others it was hardly merely eccentric. Federico Fellini, a writer on Rossellini's first three postwar movies, directed his own first movie in 1952, and then, in 1953, *I vitelloni* (The Gang, The Boys, The Good Old Boys).[40] With *I vitelloni*, Fellini was his own man, in a harsh, implacable revelation of mindlessness in the young men of a provincial town. This was no implicitly liberal movie, eliciting sympathy in the name of environmental determinism, open to suspicions of condescension and sentimentality. *Il bidone* (The Con Men) in 1955 was even more savage, not only in its presentation of worthless swindlers, but also of their victims, poor miserable peasants, greedy and credulous, physically as well as psychologically ugly. Fellini cast the leading swindler with an American actor, Broderick Crawford, wholly unpersuasive physically as an Italian. Perhaps Fellini thought a standard Italian actor would blur the existential point for an Italian audience. Skilled at playing a priest in the gang's callous stings, the Crawford character was shown finally experiencing a kind of sickness unto death at his own contemptibility as man and father, but the effect was one of contrivance, as though Fellini really had no convincing means to convey remorse and contrition in a character truly Italian.

Fellini had made two quite different films in alternation with *I vitelloni* and *Il bidone*, *La strada* and *Le notte di Cabiria*. Starring Giulietta Masina—Fellini's wife—as one of a pair of dubious traveling minstrels, *La strada* was the first of his films to present the artist as hero, as an entertainer confident of his audience's readiness to conspire in the creation of illusion, a magic holding off and replacing reality. In *La strada* reality was symbolized in the immense empty landscapes of Lazio and the Abruzzi, emptiness capable of invading hearts. Perhaps only Fellini's cinematic virtuosity kept *Le notte di Cabiria*, again starring his wife, this time playing a "simple" soul, a prostitute uncorrupted by her metier, from simple sentimentality. Then, in a final alternation, Fellini turned again to sociological savagery, in *La dolce vita* of 1960, a more elaborate movie than *I vitelloni* or *Il bidone* and an assault, not on the immemorial meanness of the small towns and countryside, but on the postwar economic miracle, then, in 1963, in *8½*, to the hero-artist, whose hero, a film director faced with a drying up of the springs of invention, makes a movie about revivifying the springs of invention. Far more unbound and open than *La dolce vita* in its modes of presentation, *8½* made final Fellini's prime commitment, the perpetuation of creative energy.

With *Amarcord* (I Remember), the fusion of both his manners and modes, Fellini was able to offer the least mythologized truth of modern Italy. Perfectly balanced between the viewpoint of its protagonist, Titta—obviously Fellini himself as a boy in Rimini—and the viewpoint of the camera, once again detached, objective, resourceful, and inventive but never moralizing or expostulatory, the film reanimated the great tradition of Italian art. Its rendition of Rimini in the 1930s was probably the definitive study of Italy under the Fascist regime in its gathering senility. All of a "normal" provincial Italy was there—the young hero's whole family, *la bella famiglia italiana*, along with the standard roster of the small town going nowhere, from the soiled beauty to the vain movie-house manager, from the flowery lawyer to the skinny Fascist chiefs. The unmistakable note of melancholy, at times of anger and bitterness, differed notably from the harsh contempt for "the boys" in *I vitelloni*. Lumpish, unattractive, prurient, and oafish as they were, the hero and his friends were simply callow and untended, capable of hopes as gaudy and immense as the fantastic ocean liner gliding along Rimini's shores, as bedazzling as the white ship that lured James Gatz of Minnesota. It was a cause of bitterness that only the accident of genius should allow any of those hopes to be fulfilled, that no doubt all Fellini's boyhood friends in Fascist Rimini still lived lives little better in De Gasperi's Italy than those Mussolini had confined. *Amarcord* swelled out far beyond the precincts of Fascist Rimini and postwar Italy. Its land was just as its title said, the ego-creating memory, just as in *8½* Fellini had presented, not dreams, but dreams created. The transcendentalizing ego still lived in Italy too. Yet universal as the movie was, it was also irreducibly Italian, above all in the premium it placed on the sheer necessity of transcendental re-creation.

In all his movies, Fellini presented a "modern" woman only once, in *La dolce vita*, and there again he used a foreign player, the Swedish actress Anita Ekberg. His desacralization of sex knew no limits. In *Amarcord* the crazy uncle, escaping from his family on a picnic, climbing a tree, howling like a dog, or, rather, like a mangy monkey, "I want a woman," "I want a woman," was a figure of grotesque, not condescending, comedy. The women in *Amarcord* were gelatinous, hairy, caky with makeup. The wraiths, phantoms, balletlike sprites of *8½* figured as

Beatrices now understood only as poetic vapors. Whether vastly fleshy or ethereal, women were a category, almost a breed or race, unequivocally, "eternally" different from men. No slightest hint of equality was ever at issue in a Fellini movie. Equality between different principles would be simply, nearly metaphysically, absurd. Only, possibly, in the relation of illusionist to illusionist, artist to artist, actor to actress, as in *La strada*, might some equivalence have been obtained, but even then, not as an affirmation of the possibility of the communion of two bodies, the marriage of two souls, but as a professional partnership. Fellini perpetuated and sharpened the theme of solitude. He was hardly any longer a "traditional" intellectual, hardly any longer "patriarchal," but feminism could find little comfort in such ministrations.

It is tempting to find the movies of Michelangelo Antonioni the self-conscious condensation of the darkest side of Fellini, with modern actresses—notably Monica Vitti—portraying modern women far more evident.[41] In *I vinti, Le amiche, Il grido, L'Avventura, La notte, L'Eclisse*—the remarkable achievement of a single decade of work—solitude as the issue of a modernized life was rendered obsessively. That this may have had a special incidence among Italian women he appeared about to insist, but he soon generalized his theme beyond Italy's case, rendering, in *Blow-Up* and *Zabriskie Point*, his theme on non-Italian stages as though he meant to be irradiating a universal, not an especially Italian, malady. A historian can only guess that in this extrapolation he lost touch with his own roots of creation.

Vanished Italy in the Movies: Pasolini

Another director, Pier Paolo Pasolini, reasserted the Italian frame as the anguish still held off in Rossellini's early movies, and still deflected by Fellini's, poured forth in greater flood. Pasolini had no fixed home. Born in Bologna, he had been taken by his parents—his father was a military officer—from one place to another across the north. He spent the war years as a boy in Friuli. "It was through Friulian that I came to understand some of the real world of the peasantry."

While the peasant world has completely disappeared in the major industrialized countries like France and England . . . in Italy it still survives. . . . In the immediate post-war period the peasantry still lived in a completely peasant world just like it was one or two centuries ago.

Pasolini wrote poetry in Friulian dialect during the war. Since he had grown up learning standard Italian, Friulian was for him an artificial language, but the effort signaled his lifelong sense of homelessness. Eventually he would repudiate "literary language" altogether.

Pasolini had been raised without a standard Roman Catholic education. Though his father, a good Fascist, had attended church, he was an unbeliever, and his son never showed any symptoms of returning to the faith. Instead, he began to read the Gramsci of a "national-popular Italy" and for a time thought he had found a new church.

In the immediate post-war period the *braccianti* [day-labourers] were engaged in a massive struggle against the big landlords. . . . For the first time I found myself faced with the class struggle. . . . I sided with the *braccianti*. . . . The *braccianti* had red scarves around their necks. . . . I embraced communism, just like that, emotionally. Then I read Marx.[42]

But this embrace of the Communism of the countryside too, like writing poetry in Friulian, was more reflex than answer. In 1950 Pasolini moved to Rome, where he spent the rest of his life making art.

From the standpoint of art, Pasolini's problem was to find the medium for expressing his own personal need for union with some culture, for uncondescending solidarity with a people. He could not make good his repudiation of his father's Fascism without trying to fulfill what Fascism had not fulfilled, an effort to provide Italy with unity and authenticity. That he failed might be inferred from the restlessness of his movement among forms—from poetry to short stories to novels, to movie scripts, movie acting, directing movies, playwriting. No single one of Pasolini's works in any medium ever won tribute as a masterpiece. Each was regarded as evincing some undigested contradiction or forced rhetoric. Yet the very shape of his career revealed a general challenge to all Italian artists in a way those more complete in their crafts did not.

In Rome, Pasolini worked on movie scripts from 1954 on (once with Fellini on *Le notte di Cabiria*). But his most important works were two novels, *Ragazzi di vita* (1955) and *Una vita violenta* (1959), the first of which was the reason for his movie work. Almost as though updating Valera's sketches of late-nineteenth-century Milanese low life and Matilde Serao's telling of the truth about late-nineteenth-century Naples—and as though anticipating Maria Antonietta Macciocchi's updating of Serao—Pasolini wrote his novels about the low life and slum life of Rome. In Rome all this was new. The center of the old Catholic city remained more or less unchanged—despite Mussolini's "improvements"—but as the economic miracle grew, the outskirts began piling up in monster *barrachi*, instant slums, suburbs without trees, parks, lawns, or greenery, not long after to be converted into high-rise slums, the population densities rivaling those of Naples, to the immense profit of postwar construction speculators linked to the Christian Democratic Party. Here was that category of persons, growing in numbers, who eluded orthodox Marxist categories and, as Macciocchi was to proclaim in Naples, likewise eluded Palmiro Togliatti's postwar Communist Party. Here were the "subproletarians."

Communist Pasolini's attitude toward the Communist Party was an instinctive, emotional contempt, utterly clear in its bearing:

Togliatti's policies . . . were tacticist, diplomatic, authoritarian and paternalistic. The PCI leadership always had a paternalist attitude towards the rank and file, never going to the bottom of problems, wheeling and dealing with the political enemy. . . . I have always been against Togliatti's policy.[43]

Penniless when he arrived in Rome, Pasolini had found space in one of these new peripheral slums, "where lots of pimps and petty thieves and whores live." Fellini hired him to provide verisimilitude for his prostitute-heroine Cabiria's experiences. But for Pasolini the attraction was deeper.

The process he saw at work in postwar Italy, and hated, was simple enough—the destruction of an old communal world by a new acquisitive one. "[Objectively,] what is happening is that the North is colonizing the South and transforming the peasants into petit bourgeois, turning them into consumers. Italy as a whole is moving towards a consumer civilization, it's turning into a horrible petit bourgeois world." Pasolini was himself, as he said, petit bourgeois by rearing, and at the heart of the petit bourgeois horror was exactly what continued to infest the Italian Left of the Communist Party—"moralism." "My hatred for the bourgeoisie is not documentable or arguable. It's just there. . . . But it's not a moralistic condemnation; . . . it is based on passion, not moralism. Moralism is a typical disease of part of the Italian left, which has imported typical bourgeois moralistic attitudes into marxist, or at any rate, communist ideology."[44] The subproletarians of Rome's Ponte Mammolo had not yet been overtaken by *consumismo*, were not yet shrunken by moralism; they still displayed passion, the straightforward embrace of life that Pasolini saw in the real Italy.

Pasolini gave up being a writer to become a moviemaker. "[Gradually,] as I worked in the cinema and got more and more into it I came to understand that the cinema is not a literary technique; it is a language of its own." He preferred the new language over the old because literary language had become politicized:

[The] avant-garde, and all the left-wing linguists and university professors who had been churning out the old rhetoric about Italian Unity being achieved through the integration of the artificial language based on Florentine, through the integration from below of the popular languages, the contribution of the dialects, etc. . . . [all] . . . has been proven false.

Thus Italian itself, as a language, had become morally repulsive:

I had instinctively given up writing novels and then gradually . . . poetry, too, as a protest against Italy and Italian society. I have several times said I would like to change nationality, give up Italian and take up another language.

But Pasolini discovered not only that cinematic language was indeed another language but also a transnational language. The point was less to abandon Italy than to offer Italy—and all mankind—a better, liberating language:

[At] first I thought [the language of the cinema] was a protest against my society. Then gradually I realized it was . . . more complicated than that: the passion that had taken the form of a great love for literature and for life had gradually stripped itself of the love for literature and turned to what it really was—a passion for life, for reality, for physical, sexual, objectual [*oggettuale*], existential reality around me.[45]

What kind of movies might express this "passion for life"? Rossellini's two remarkable celebrations of life, *Stromboli* (1950) and *Viaggio in Italia* (1953), both with Ingrid Bergman, had not kept him from ending up in the implicit despair of *Anno uno*, counseling Italians to revere the only reality they had, the "tacticist and authoritarian" priest-politician, Alcide De Gasperi. Fellini's celebrations of life continued to come forth, of course, but, as *Amarcord* was to testify, only on the tight wire of a perfectly balanced inner creativity rather than on some vision of home or of some authentic Italian community.

   In his first movie, *Accattone* (1961), Pasolini, using the Roman subproletarian world, sought by various means to argue the religious and indeed transcendental dimensions of this society: the music of Bach accompanying scenes of casual violence, the hero's dream of death and an afterlife. But Pasolini's insistence that these registered some prebourgeois, preindustrial, mythic elements in subproletarian life was effectively discounted in his next movie, *Mamma Roma* (1962), which displayed the same subproletarians now betraying signs of corruption. Pasolini's indecision over whether he had been right or wrong in using the actress Anna Magnani for his "mamma" was echoed in his wavering between describing his characters as "subproletarian," or as a subproletariat "tending to become" petit bourgeois, or as "an upper subproletariat, so to speak." "I wanted to bring out the ambiguity of subproletarian life with a petit bourgeois superstructure."[46] The specious sociological precision of such language, comparable to that of collectivizing Bolsheviks trying to decide which peasants were high, which middle, and which low, may have interfered with Pasolini's attempt to embrace "cinematic language." But this was less important than the evidence that he could abandon some hope for a true Italian embodiment of life and passion, even as he saw Italy drawn more and more into the transnational world of "horrible" bourgeois consumer culture.

Pasolini's efforts at a way out led him into far more interesting cinematic experiments in the mid-1960s, in movies that combined elements in a fashion easily eliciting the label "surrealist" without necessarily promoting confidence that the organizing intelligence behind it was at all times in command. After *Il Vangelo secondo Matteo* (The Gospel according to St. Matthew, 1964) and *Edipo Re* (Oedipus Rex, 1966), Pasolini filmed two famous classics of straightforward celebration of "passion for life, for reality, for physical, sexual reality," *Decameron* (1971) and *I racconti di Canterbury* (Canterbury Tales, 1972). To those who imagined Pasolini was simply selling out for commercial success through a kind of "classic" salacity, he had provided the answer before he made the movies: ordinary Italians were free of the repressions that responded to salacity and pornography.

Ordinary Italian people are not very repressed, from a sexual point of view: in fact they are very free. If you want to talk to the ordinary people about sex you can do so extremely freely. . . . Repression [in Italy] is not so pathological as it is in other bourgeois societies which don't have Catholicism, which is basically not a rigid religion. There hasn't been a Protestant revolution in Italy, in fact in a sense there hasn't been a religious revolution at all: Catholicism has superimposed itself on paganism, particularly among the ordinary people, without changing them in the slightest.[47]

Decameron and *Canterbury* were meant as revivals of this original, natural, spontaneous spirit of the unspoiled people. (For all the backhanded compliment to Catholicism, Pasolini took care to preserve all the anticlericalism of the originals in his movies.) Presumably, the English folk of the fourteenth century had loved life, physical reality, and sex no less innately than did the fourteenth-century Italians of the *Decameron*. If modern Italians had an advantage, it derived from England's "success" in becoming a modern, industrial, Protestant country at the expense of the passion for life. In *Decameron* Pasolini made his Italian point by once more transposing all the dialogue into dialect, of Naples now rather than Friuli; the characters displayed their simple, unrepressed vitality in their own tongue.

Artistic and/or commercial success aside, Pasolini's two cinematic transformations of literary classics indicated that he had given up any party politics in favor of a politics of timeless myth. His art no longer served his personal quest for unity. That he could now find only in life, not art—in personal life, obviously, since there was no politics anywhere worth commenting on. Another movie, *A Thousand and One Nights*, once more based on an even more timeless classic of passion, added to fears that Pasolini's new fantasy, of redeeming the modern world through sex, had got out of control.

In 1975 Pasolini made *Salo o le 120 giornate di Sodoma* (Salo or the 120 Days of Sodom).[48] Transporting Sade's fantasy of sadism from its timeless castle to the last days of Fascist rule in the "Italian Social Republic of Salo" in late 1944 and early 1945, he had become familiar with and meant to use the most frightening details of Nazi degradation. Sade's sadists became Fascist sadists, the exercise of their sexual fantasies the demonstration of what pure political power, unmixed with any responsibility or love, unchecked by any countervailing power, converted sexuality into. Pasolini's political insight drew him to isolate out and emphasize one dimension along which this unlimited sadistic power would express itself, the dimension of the generations. The helpless victims in *Salo* were—again, in echo of Sade—adolescents of both sexes, that is, persons still waiting to be initiated into history, but brutalized, tortured, slaughtered, and murdered instead. Possessing what only history could grant, power itself, sadists possessed only the power to end history.

But could one combat evil by depicting it? Pasolini's courage had allowed him to realize that Sade's fantasies were paralleled by documentable history. It had always been a mistake to censor history. Whether history's truth could be told in the special language of the movies was the question. By Pasolini's own account, literary and cinematic languages were radically distinct. In translating Sade's literary horror into cinematic terms, he faced a challenge far greater than that posed by Boccaccio, Chaucer, or the narrator of the Arabian Nights. Could Sade's "meaning" truly be served, protected, and contained in cinematic language? Or would the worlds that in Sade's pages prompted readers to exercise their own imaginations be betrayed, when the moviemaker invented images of his own to display? The rape, torture, blood, violence, sadism, and excrement were all to be found in Sade, but as ideas, not moving pictures. Sade relied on a limiting device Pasolini could not use. His readers could stop reading, then resume. But Pasolini's viewers were trapped. His movie seemed to have registered an ultimate despair, not over a reality to which he attested, but over his inability to win enough distance from that reality to give himself room to make art.

The impression that Pasolini sought death and found it, in another

tawdry periphery of ancient Rome, at the hands of a young male prostitute, deepened the darkness of his last work. It was as though Pasolini
had come to equate power, the power that displayed itself in sadism,
with masculinity, as though for him the well of life, in passion, had
been poisoned at its source.

With Pasolini the reliance upon the immemorial endurances and
stoicisms and integrities of the Italian folk, still registered by Gramsci,
Rossellini, and Fellini, had evaporated at last. But any possibility that
the kind of "postpeasant" individualisms of *Una donna* and D'Annunzio
might be converted from their histrionic excesses into realistic drama
of, say, bold brave girls in Milan, perhaps in a literature and cinema
directed to Milanese audiences, won no exploration at all.

The startling work of two new women directors gave no more credence to any such possibilities. In several films full of the passion of
sex and love, the director Lina Wertmuller essentially renewed an
operatic Italy, extrapolating Aleramo and D'Annunzio into comic or,
alternatively, pathetic melodrama. But no doubt the film most "liberated" for analytic psychology was Liliana Cavani's *Il portiere di notte*
(The Night Porter) of 1974, with its story of the postwar reunion between
a wartime victim of Nazi sexual sadism and her tormentor.[49] The almost
enchanted compulsion by which both victim and sadist resume their
relationship, with full recognition and self-consciousness, and this time
to death, could have been assigned to a political context: "War releases
the sadomasochism latent in us all." Even the movie's implicit sexual
stereotyping, the woman masochistic, the man sadistic, could have
been contained within a political logic: women's sadism is suppressed,
and men's invited, by war. But Cavani's movie offered no such easy
reconciliations, inciting instead the idea that sadism and masochism
were perennial forces, not easily suppressed by mere politics. When the
militant feminist women of the late 1970s marched through the midnight streets of Rome on their mission to defy rape, confront sadism
and violence, and "take back the night," they were announcing plainly
enough that, whether or not sadism was latent in men, and especially
whether or not masochism was latent in women, they were prepared
to repress these forces, to deny and defy them, ready to resist cooptation
into any social order that relied on them.

But like the last movies of Pasolini, Cavani's was not really soluble
even in feminist politics. The great tradition of Italian humanism was
proving brittle. Gramsci had warned that sex ought not be let out of its
cage at the domestic fireside. Such movies as *Salo* and *The Night Porter*
could only have been judged deleterious by Gramsci for having been
made at all.

Starting Over: Young Love in Modern Italy

In 1976 the bookstalls of Rome and elsewhere carried stacks of the "sexual-political diary of two adolescents," a "pornographic" best-seller, *Porci con le ali* (Pigs with Wings). *Pigs with Wings* was the love story of Rocco and Antonia, Dante and Beatrice reborn, Petrarch and Laura, Romeo and Juliet, Renzo and Lucia. The book began in a new way, however: "Cazzo. Cazzo cazzo cazzo. Figa. Fregna ciorgna. Figa-pelosa, bella calda, tutta puzzarella. Figa di putanella."[50] The heroine, Antonia, is repeating the dirty words in imitation of herself when she was young—she is now sixteen—when just thinking and whispering them was enough to prompt her to masturbation. Rocco too, also sixteen, also thinking back on his sexual initiations, uses the same words. These are the "real" words, the words of popular life, not the words of medical textbooks, moral tracts, sentimental novels, or poets.

Rocco and Antonia meet at a political demonstration of comrades, all grave and stern. Antonia wants reality here, too:

I felt like a dog. Worse than a dog. Like the last of a mangy breed dying out for lack of a reason for living. Looking for one pair of human eyes I encountered Rocco's. . . . I had never seen him so upset, not even after the coup d'état in Chile. I would never have imagined he could make a spontaneous gesture, one not prescribed for the behavior of your basic militant.

On their first date she asks immediately:

"Listen, what do you think of me? I mean, I'm not fishing for compliments or anything. I'll go on living if we just talk about anything. . . . But I'd really like to know. I mean, did you call me up because you felt something special about me or just because you wanted a girl?"

Rocco replies:

No . . . I could have called any girl. . . . That day at the demonstration . . . it frightened me a little. . . . It's crazy, knowing you for two years [at school] but not having the faintest idea what you're like. Look, mostly, for me, you're someone in the collective who they say has already made love, so she's more cool. A feminist. I don't know what.[51]

Rocco and Antonia make love. Their love moves fast. Does Rocco care for Antonia or for what he does with her? In his boyish anxiety he seems not to understand her readiness to surrender. He seems to be willing to rape her when he could have seduced her. "After sodomy, can there be love?" Feeling humiliated, Antonia finds it hard not to humiliate him publicly, by flaunting another lover. Quickly, their love becomes their past.

Dear Rocco: I loved you. . . . You were the sweetest boy in my life. . . . I loved you because you were not arrogant . . . because you loved me (Tolstoy said that, I think, about Anna Karenina, about us women) . . . because when you were sad it didn't make you mean . . . because you didn't pretend to be older or cooler than you are. . . . Now it's over. Not because of Lisa or what you did to me that way when we couldn't look into each other's eyes. Just because it's over. Games end. And I guess I believe that that's what love is—just a game. . . . I hope you will love this letter; I loved writing it.

Dear Antonia: It's me. Tomorrow I'm going off on my vacation. . . . I can't get out of my mind what we talked about doing when we'd go on a vacation. . . . Now we won't have our fucking vacation, we won't get to make love in a tent, go swim in the nude and all the other stuff. . . . Leaving . . . gives me the sense for the first time that it's over, we won't get back together. . . . I've been thinking about the things you said to me. . . . Things I thought were clear, like my love for you and when I felt tenderness for you, were really confused, beautiful things mixed up with ugly things, very ugly, like being violent . . . not thinking of you as a person, and so forth. . . . Maybe someday a new Rocco and a new Antonia, full of love and beautiful things, can make love for its own sake, and can talk to each other in words that mean what they say and nothing else.[52]

Of course both these young lovers had oppressive parents and underwent their passion against the background of an oppressive culture. They saw themselves as victims of an oppressive system. But in *Pigs with Wings* this oppressive system was as much that of the Communist Party as of the Catholic church. The oppressive parents were good Communists, the oppressive culture a Marcuse-ified Marxism. The party lecturer lectures:

"Rock music, having first functioned as a collective outlet for and a collectivizing of the erotic energies repressed by civilization, a civilization that 'kills love in the name of the reality principle,' (shame, shame), is today only consumer's goods, part of the obscene market in the superfluous." ("Induced needs," he adds, with the air of wanting to make everything perfectly clear.) "On the other hand, we find it in the ambiguous role of a meta-language." (Meta-language?) The confusion among the seven or eight still listening—people hoping to go into culture work—was universal.[53]

Marcello, the university Communist, dilates upon "della disgregazione delle masse giovanile," upon the "decelerazione dei processi conoscitivi," upon the "depauperamento cultural," like any Puritan preacher engaged in lamentations, like Croce defending the heights of humanism, like any Pope. When Marcello finds his high Marxist language losing his audience, he moves to a lower level:

[Marcello] shifted in his chair . . .: "Listen,"—he speaks fondly, as colloquial as a good old-fashioned parish priest—"when you get together, to smoke, etc., do you talk? or do you listen to music?" Paolo squirms . . . if he answers he'll look like some ordinary character who smokes pot and listens to records with his friends instead of meditating full-time on the plight of the workers.

Italian Communism too is a churchly world, as encompassing, safe, secure, and suffocating as an old country family. It even has its "Protestant" biblicism:

"Come in, come in, my boy. . . . I'm happy to see you . . . away from those political debates in school—so alienating. I don't know why I keep on doing those things, just because the Party asks me to. Saying no of course you get called an 'uncommitted intellectual.' But certainly that's not the way one gets to be an organic intellectual. If only they would at least read their Gramsci." For a minute I was scared that he was going to ask me how many times I had read my Gramsci.

When it comes to sex, the party's priestly, paternal, university wise men avail themselves of the same official dictionary language as the Latinizing intellectuals of yore:

Now, you for instance, are you on good terms with your penis? I mean to say, how goes it with masturbation? . . . Oh, excuse me. I should have told you that I'm not embarrassed and sometimes I forget others might be. . . . Embarrassment is, after all, a bourgeois residue, isn't it. But if you prefer, we won't talk of these things.⁵⁴

Rocco of course talks of "these things" endlessly, as does Antonia. For *pene* (penis), *cazzo, biscotto, pistolotto, filetto, cuccello, pisello*. Masturbation? Not *masturbazione* but *sega, segatura*. The dirty words are not the words of sex scientists, sex counselors, or marriage counselors, of Marxist sociologists, positivist social psychologists, or humanist poets, but of the hungry young themselves. Sexual intercourse? *Scopare; una scopata; una chiavata; cazzo;* maybe *fare l'amore*. A girl's organs? *Figa; fica; figapelosa; griletto; porcellino*. Marcello's solicitude for Rocco's sex life is merely a power play, a homosexual seduction. Later the same Marcello takes Antonia. Marcello is bisexual, androgynous, modern, empty.

With *Porci con le ali*, the revolution arrived at its dialectically inevitable destination, becoming for the young, in its righteousness, its call upon duty and asceticism, exactly the same incubus as its predecessor had been. It inspired the same desperate and, if courageous, certainly reckless need for fresh air, fresh faces, fresh language, inspiring the same "blasphemy" and "obscenity." Those who postponed life beyond the revolution mimicked those who postponed life beyond life.

Feminism beyond Politics

In any modernizing democratic society, sex was bound to loom ever larger on the agenda of cultural elaboration. Individuals being steadily released from old forms of social containment were certain to find the most compelling experiences of freedom where their own capacities for experience were most immediate. The control over sex by church, state, and mores had never been convincing. Were sex not policed, sex police would lose their jobs: sex police might well exaggerate the importance of their duties. In a society like Italy, where sexual discipline appeared seamlessly interwoven into the entire fabric of life, individualistic challenges to that discipline could seem less threatening than merely eccentric. A powerful force—the Italian past—operated to discourage singling sex out as a kind of topic separable from social order. Thus, while excoriating the sexual self-indulgence of the decadent Turinese bourgeoisie, Gramsci hoped the new sexual morality of a democratic industrial society would remain as orderly and routine as the old. Instead of exploring the implication of his own view that sex really should not be added to the agenda of modern politics, for fear of the 30,000 nice Italian girls who had sent pictures of themselves in swimsuits to Hollywood, Gramsci preferred the same condescending Manzonian fantasy about the humble people, that they had no pent-up romantic passions, that their inner drives too were modest.

For feminism it was an impoverishment to be inhibited from straight-forward consideration of sexuality. Not that feminism as a movement could have provided greater resonance for, say, Sibilla Aleramo. Her book made a sensation; the fact that it inspired no further books in Italy was hardly a comment on Italian feminism, but on dominant Italian culture that could find no place where it fit, it was. A confessional, individualistic women's literature was not likely to grow from a political movement. Italian feminism's larger impoverishment derived from its entanglement with the myth of a new, natural sexual order consequent upon general social revolution. While suppressed during Fascism, the recrudescence of this myth after World War II tempted Italian feminists to ignore some of the most powerful renditions of postwar Italy's deepest problems, just as they had ignored the attempt of a D'Annunzio, before Fascism, to reassert sexual order by a histrionic exaggeration of one element of traditional sexuality, heroic masculinity. As a social and political ideal, equality was simply irrelevant to the challenges posed by D'Annunzio, just as it was to the conditions confronted by Rossellini, Fellini, Pasolini, and the postwar moviemakers. The feminists' equality for women would have solved none of the issues faced by Sibilla Aleramo's heroine. Her own solution was not to become equal but to become an individual, autonomous and self-aware. At the same time, D'Annunzio's cult of ego clearly limned what it would take for women to be equal: they too could risk their bodies in fast cars, their hearts in heedless love, their brains in true poetry. D'Annunzio for one did not oppose them.

That postwar Italian feminism did not resist seduction by the myth of a natural egalitarian socialist sexuality can be explained by the political and economic facts of postwar Italian life, and indeed by those facts of culture too that revealed women to be still subordinate. When feminism did turn directly to sexuality, from the late 1960s on, it did so in consistency with the myth. In the great divorce and abortion refer-enda, women rose to protest their victimization. The protest marches against rape drew on victimization. The demands for withdrawal from men obviously drew on views of women as men's victims. All this was to perpetuate feminism as a politics. That sexuality was a source of victimization few ever denied, and that women's victimization sur-passed that of men by orders of magnitude always carried credibility. Yet it was this approach that foreshortened feminist imagination. Po-litical language itself suggested another perspective: the route to overcoming women's weakness in relation to men was not to reduce men's power but to increase women's. That, however, was not a route to be pioneered by politics but by acts in the first place of individualistic assertion. Certainly the relationship was dialectical. Winning equality in the movie industry would be as political a task as winning power in the state, but in modern Italy it was probably more important for women to win power in the movies than in the state. It was probably more important for Italian feminists to follow Sibilla Aleramo than Antonio Gramsci.

12 Sweden

Sex as Swedish Icon:
Carl Michael Bellman's Ulla Winblad

The emergence of a modern psychological literature in Sweden, capable of penetrating private life, would not be easy. A sense of provinciality had impelled eighteenth-century circles of earnest readers, in both Stockholm and rural gentry circles, to consume French, German, and English books. A church that had settled comfortably into privilege generated no language of private inquiry that might one day be secularized into novels that would search the heart. With no Jonathan Edwards, Sweden had no Benjamin Franklin either. No Hawthorne was waiting in Swedish religious psychology to be born. The greatest religious figure of the age, Emanuel Swedenborg, simply converted archaic language into language even more orphic, cryptic, mystifying, and obscure. When the monarchy, under Gustav III, in 1792, resumed the sway it had lost after Charles XII, that sway was, by Gustav's intent, French. Courtly, elegant, elevated, Gustavian culture suppressed Swedish experience and Swedish individualism. Anna Maria Lenngren, trying to write of a real Sweden, country Sweden, the common life of Sweden, hated the court and the Frenchified aristocracy. But she found her own spring of language soon dry. Swedes well placed to demand a more practical language—merchants, reform-minded gentry, civil servants, some scientists, liberal politicians—would need time and confidence before thinking of themselves as private individuals with demanding hearts.

Without a language, private life could seem terrifying, a well of dark and disintegrative forces, best shunned or fled or denied. Carl Michael Bellman's genius was to realize that it could be faced if it was sung.[1] Some eighty of Bellman's songs were collected and published in 1790 as *Fredmans epistler* (Fredman's Epistles), and more the following year as *Fredmans sånger* (Fredman's Songs). Bellman drew Fredman from a real Stockholm personage of the 1760s and 1770s—the bewigged royal watchmaker, a dandy fond of French toilet waters. He was also fond of the grape. He married, for money, a widow who later sued him for embezzlement. He died a pauper, buried in a pauper's grave. Fredman's story—and the stories of many other Stockholm characters as well—

was told in the poetry Bellman composed to accompanying music drawn from the countryside. In the contrast between the familiar forms of the music and the highly subtle forms of the poetry on the one hand, and the disintegrating lives they narrated on the other, Bellman achieved an effect neither moralistic nor sentimental but realistic and fatalistic. In his remarkable analysis, Paul Britten Austin has observed of Bellman: "His metaphysical gaze is utterly candid. He sees both the glory of the senses and their nothingness."[2] Bellman realized that the music of the folk and country Sweden would not head off the horrors of individualism and urban life. As "Sweden's Mozart" he generated a gaiety intended to enclose, not repress, decay and death.

One female figure appeared in Fredman's songs. She was Ulla Winblad, derived, like Fredman, from a real-life person of Stockholm. Maria Kiellstrom, daughter of a street sweeper, employed in a silk factory at nineteen, was seduced at twenty by a young nobleman, bore a baby, and lost it. The sort of young woman who would be ground into the statistics of Stockholm's delinquencies by visiting pastors and sociologists a few decades later, Kiellstrom served quite a different purpose for Bellman. Not in the least did her story suggest to him the need for better pay in the silk factories, or the sexual injustices of class. Nor did it prompt him toward the cadences of pathos. Bellman arranged her first appearance in the epistles as Venus herself, riding Stockholm harbor's glittering waves on a summer morning. Tritons and dolphins, cavorting, accompanied her. She was a goddess.

The allusions, obviously, were classical or, more precisely, as Austin has classified them, rococo. One might expect to find Ulla Winblad in a Roman fountain of the Renaissance. Through the language of classicism the Renaissance painters—and poets—had indeed brought erotic female flesh back to the attention of early modern Europe. As long as the setting remained mythological, the flesh that of a goddess, and her relations disguised in swans, showers of gold, and a Paris conducting a beauty pageant, the existential power of her flesh would remain checked. Ulla Winblad's world was Stockholm's own Lake Malären. When she moved about, it was on Stockholm's own streets, with their seedy vicissitudes. Appearing once "clad in a black embroider's bodice,/ So trim and neat,/ in petticoats flouncing their frills and laces," she was promptly arrested by the police for violating sumptuary prohibitions against poor but pretty girls dressing above their station. Far from constituting some principle of beauty incorruptible by history, Bellman's Venus had a density of local identity just as vulnerable to disintegration as was Fredman. But no one could doubt the necessity of responding to her radiance. She was the local girl as Eternal Feminine.

The popularity of Bellman's songs was not undercut by the collapse of Gustav's court, for which he had composed them. They would live on, particularly as drinking songs, sung on the holidays on the lakes, in the forests, and on the sea islands of summertime, time of the sun's return and exposure of the body. One day that other Stockholm writer, August Strindberg, would break through the iconic, impersonal, escapist practices of Swedish drinking and eroticism with his radically psychologizing art, revealing, as by a bolt in the night, the precariousness, even among the holidays, the songs, and the drinking, of the emergent new middle-class individual. Meanwhile Bellman's songs held off panic. Like Mozart's, his ultimate appeal was to art as a specific against self-analysis. Bellman shaped Swedish into an instrument for song rather than for novels. The preference for escape rather than analysis would persist. Erotic nudity in Swedish movies would have nothing to do with some liberation from repression. Like Ulla Winblad, the great iconic female movie stars would embody a perfection wished for but not attainable. But Strindberg would never write about or describe erotic beauty. He never counted it as significant in any human relations. For him, language would serve the exploration of panic, not its transcendence. This would entail an assault on Swedish culture more than an evolution, and for feminism, intimidation as much as opportunity. Yet Strindberg would be offering what no Swede yet had done, the means to individuality.

Utopian Sexual Equality: Carl Almqvist's Sara Videbeck

Between Bellman's and Strindberg's nightmarish places, however, another Sweden would briefly emerge, gentle, bucolic, as Lenngren would have wanted, a land for quite a different kind of woman than Bellman had celebrated or Strindberg would deplore. After years of labor over a dozen mannered styles, Carl Almqvist at last, by 1839, came forth in the plain, pure, affective prose of his masterpiece, *Sara Videbeck*. The story of a simple country girl and a simple soldier boy, creating by their own openness to each other a new way of love, of sexuality, of living together, it constituted a Swedish idyll out of time, beyond history.

Leaving Stockholm on a steamer bound for Arboga on Lake Malären, a young sergeant named Albert met a young woman, Sara Videbeck. The sergeant soon found himself off balance. The young woman seemed delightfully fresh and innocent, yet amazingly at ease and self-possessed. During a brief snack onshore, she paid for her own raspberries. At the end of the run, in Arboga, Sara watched over their luggage while

Albert hurried into town to find lodgings for the night. Only one room could be found at the inn. Sara made it plain that he need not spend the night in a hayloft: "If you remain here, I shall not mind it at all!" At first impressed by "such a wonderful and simple freedom, such pure and unfeigned virtues," the sergeant then grew depressed. Did he mean nothing to her? Was he no more than a fixture, a bedpost? His night was spent in a chair. The next morning, resuming their journey by horse and wagon, they began to tell each other their lives. She told of her dead father, her sick mother, her dreams—of Albert, the previous night! He told of his origins, his prospects, his opinions of her: "Whether you wear silk wimple or a hat, I like you just the same." The narrator summarized where this was heading: "the journey afterward did not progress so rapidly, on the whole, as Albert and Sara had first calculated."

As they approached Sara's home in Lidköping, after four more nights' lodging, Albert listened in amazement at Sara's plan for them to live together:

"I shall never, never take anything that belongs to you or interferes with your mode of living. . . . I don't intend to give up my trade . . . if we set about to have a mass of unnecessary things in common . . . I might be cross. . . . If you love me with your soul—then I am happy and have all I want . . . and beyond that I shall take care of myself entirely, be merry, satisfied and industrious. . . . To take things lightly and wisely, just as they are, Albert, is half the battle." [3]

The honest sergeant could not help protesting, but Sara had answers for each of his objections. When the time came, he realized that he loved the real Sara, ideas included. " 'Will all this do, Albert?' . . . in the whole expression of his face was the answer: 'It will do.' "

In an epilogue Almqvist disavowed any intention to illustrate a thesis. Europe had already suffered too much from theses, general ideas about the "good." Only by solving the mystery of happiness would the mystery of morals be solved, and "good morals do not spring upon earth from annihilation and violation of what is individual." He had offered his book as a mere "sketch," portraying two individuals who were looking for happiness with each other. Sara Videbeck herself was, however, much given to moral generalizations, perfectly consistent with the views of her creator.

My belief is that a man and a woman should never live together, because people who are in love provoke, irritate, and finally ruin each other more quickly than those who do not care so much about each other.[4]

Thus the absolute priority of the individual over the general, the social, the communal, carried right into that most compelling of relationships, two individuals drawn to each other by love. It would be Strindberg, not Almqvist, who would analytically dramatize the horrors of parasitism, dependency, and violence generated between two individuals whom love had shackled together. Almqvist contented himself with sketching the possibility of freedom in love.

One contrast between Almqvist's and a comparable heroine, Henry James's Daisy Miller, brings out some of the Swedish dimensions in this consideration of love. Like Sara Videbeck, Daisy Miller presented herself with fresh candor. She too was self-conscious about her individuality. She too asked for acceptance of herself as she was. Both scorned a concern for appearances in favor of motivations. But Sara Videbeck had one thing Daisy Miller did not, a job. She earned her own daily bread. She was a glazier, expert in the cutting, fitting, and care of glass in doors and windows. As it happened, she practiced this craft only by a kind of special dispensation. Her father had been a glazier, and it was his daughter's right, by old guild rules, to go on practicing it as sole support of her widowed mother. Otherwise glazing, like many other crafts, was closed to women. Almqvist certainly meant to oppose such discrimination against women, but his choice had been to portray, not women victimized by it, but a woman enjoying economic independence. It was that kind of woman who interested him. Nor did Sara Videbeck have the least intention of losing her economic freedom upon her mother's death. She expected to open a shop and sell glass boxes and little mirrors. Moreover she had, she informed Albert—with whom she spent more time talking about putty, trowels, and the secrets of glazing than she did about philosophy of life—discovered a unique art of mixing chalk and water, so as to produce a putty so superior that all the masters "will want to buy . . . once they know about it." Before opening her shop each morning at ten, she would mix this special putty for sale to the master glaziers: "It will be good business and a happy life!"

James's Daisy Miller had no such source of independence. Her independence remained wholly psychological, characterological, funded by wealth she never earned or commanded. As James proceeded on into his later, greater speculations about the influence of wealth upon feminine personality, his conclusions grew increasingly dark. In his final test of the issue, *The Golden Bowl*, Daisy Miller's descendent, Maggie Verver, the immensely rich daughter of the immensely rich founder of American City, found herself suffused not only by the corruptions of Europeans around her but by corruptions and malice infiltrating her own soul and the love she held for husband and father.

For Almqvist's Sara Videbeck, the question was whether Sweden would allow utopian possibilities such as hers to take root and flourish, or whether Sweden too might, in a surge to affluence, generate the sort of condition James took as peculiarly American, wherein individuality had to risk destruction not by want but by excess. Sara Videbeck was certainly a young entrepreneurial capitalist in the making. Might her own energies defeat themselves, or could they be held to the service of what finally mattered, happiness? That Almqvist himself understood the larger issues implied in his heroine's economic freedom, he demonstrated by showing his hero, Sergeant Albert, in a determined, "typically Swedish" attempt to comprehend Sara by "placing" her in some social category. First, struck by her poise, he thought she might be a girl of the upper middle class. Then, caught by a detail of dress, he wavered, uncertain whether she is "really of the higher or lower class." Piqued, he sought certitude by consulting the ship's register, where he found her listed as a "glazier's daughter." This did not really settle matters, though, and later, knowing she would not be a loyal lamb of the state church, he tried Dissenter, but that failed, too. In the end she was what she was:

Yes, she is what I took her for—a daughter of the middle class, yet not of the lowest grade. A charming and remarkable intermediate! Not a country girl, not at all a peasant girl—nor yet entirely of the better class. What is the real status of such an individual? How shall I address her? There is something about this intermediate state.[5]

Anomalous as a glazier, Sara Videbeck was also anomalous as a personality. The one "place" the two lovers thought they might enjoy was only a small port stop on the steamer run from Stockholm. Its charms stemmed as much from negative as from positive reasons. " 'How I like this little town,' [Sara] said frankly. . . . 'It is so different from Stockholm.' "

Everything is unpretentious . . . crooked, narrow lanes . . . [rather than] arrogant straightness . . . no marks of aristocracy, none of the superiority of the higher peerage, none of the nobility of wealth in the rich and proud middle class, no signs of that primitive distinction found among the independent peasantry . . . no, here are to be seen only civic conditions of the unpretentious kind. One gets the impression that all the houses belong to skippers, glaziers, brushmakers and fishermen.[6]

Herewith, most of old Sweden and new were dismissed as incompatible with individual happiness. Yet was not Strängnäs, the little town, doomed? Changing the old guild rules to let women like Sara Videbeck join men as glaziers and brushmakers, carpenters and shoemakers, might help underwrite such love as she and Albert had arranged, but what was to happen to glazing and brushmaking and all the old crafts themselves, once the winds of economic progress blew through the musty old Swedish economy? Having to compete with English workers, Swedish workers would be compelled to modernize. To avert national decline, Sweden would need to industrialize. Strängnäs would become out-of-date, old-fashioned. Its future would be no more secure just because its glaziers included women.

Whether the ideals Almqvist had sketched in *Sara Videbeck* were detachable from preindustrial craft economies such as still survived in the Sweden of 1840 he did not go on to discuss. The reaction to *Sara Videbeck* hurt him; moralists, judging it immoral, forced him out of his school postings. Several of the new newspapers then springing up offered him an outlet, and he continued writing for the next decade on questions that would become staples for feminist debate: property, inheritance, electoral and economic rights for women. He spoke explicitly on sexual issues, deploring a double standard, deploring any new "asexual" single standard, deploring legal approaches to prostitution. But Almqvist's cutting edge remained his doctrine of the individual.

In proceeding to his most radical point, arguing that, just as husbands and wives should not live together, neither should mothers and fathers, Almqvist protected his central insistence that individual happiness cannot be sacrificed to transindividual demands. When it came to those individuals who were children, Almqvist obviously believed they should not be brought up where structures of power and authority dominated, that is, in families where fathers held sway. Certainly they should not be brought up by collective methods, where social rules held sway. In the United States, as in Sweden, modern twentieth-century feminists would work for an egalitarian two-parent family, fathers sharing with mothers, neither the head of the other. Almqvist had rejected this arrangement already, in *Sara Videbeck*, as corrosive upon the love that had drawn the partners together in the first place. There was no organized feminism in Almqvist's time to ask him to defend his plan that mothers, funded totally by state-collected taxes, should oversee child-rearing. His obvious lifelong assumption that an original, matriarchal epoch of humanity had been disrupted to humanity's loss by subsequent patriarchy, might not have seemed to justify assigning women to a task that left men free for lives that women might be legally but not practically free to live as well. Yet his views and visions had not derived from France or from some historically detached outlook of abstract professional utopians. Almqvist felt himself in touch with Swedes as a people. It seemed to him that, still free of "arrogant straightness," of class pride, of priestly morals, they had a real chance at simple happiness.

The Individual (Female) versus Sex:
Fredrika Bremer

Almqvist's *Sara Videbeck* might be thought of as an answer, seventeen years in advance, to Fredrika Bremer's "Great Mother" novel of 1856, *Hertha*. The exchange of one authority for another—of matriarchy for patriarchy—would avail nothing to the happiness of individuals. Actually, the novels to which *Sara Videbeck* could have been an answer had been written already by Bremer in the 1830s. In these family novels, apparently so dependent on sentimental detail, Bremer had betrayed the anguish that had foreclosed any such optimism as Almqvist registered and that led her instead to the new tyrannies of *Hertha*. Daughters writhed in torment in *The Family* of 1833, in *The President's Daughters* of 1834, in *The Home* of 1838. There were three of them in the first, four in the second, no fewer than five in the third, as though, suspecting that she had hidden rather than revealed her deepest emotion, Bremer imagined she might succeed by repetition. Even this was not enough. She threw in daughter surrogates, waifs, stray orphans, nannies, "House-Counsellors." Although all, daughters and daughter surrogates alike, suffered, the novels were exercises in evasion, for the fathers, father surrogates, and father substitutes who were the ultimate engines of this suffering were left only floating into and out of focus in their daughters' imagination.

In one novel, however, Bremer did find control over her real material—inner life, not domestic detail. Daughters did not dominate *The Neighbors*. The scheme of this book differed wholly from the other three. The attention of the narrator, self-described as "little—and good," was held fully by her formidable mother-in-law, "*ma chère mère*." Through this medium—a narrator's fascinated but detached observation, instead of narcissistic brooding—Bremer created the one character in her early writings who appeared to live out of inner resources:

See, then, a tall lady, of a large and handsome growth, whose figure in youth must have possessed both symmetry and strength . . . never . . . tight-laced . . . with the mien and bearing of a general . . . a very friendly, pleasant smile . . . but when this sentiment is less friendly . . . such stern determination as is not pleasing in a woman. . . . Ma chère mère has a rough voice, speaks loud and distinctly, makes use sometimes of extraordinary words, and has a vast many proverbs at her tongue's end. She walks with great strides, often in boots, and swings her arms about; still, whenever [she wishes] she can assume a style of the highest and most perfect breeding . . . her word is worth as much as a king's . . . the universal opinion . . . is that she is prudent . . . to be relied upon, and a steadfast friend.[7]

"*Ma chère mère*" ruled alone. General Mansfield, her husband, had been a handsome man and a brave soldier, but at the same time extravagant, domineering, and willful. He inquired but little after his children and lavished away his properties. When he died, leaving his sons penniless, his wife arranged for them to come into a "certain annual sum" from her own funds, meanwhile taking over as manager of her dead husband's debt-ridden estate.

In short, compared to the bad father her husband had been, his wife was a good father. She made up for the deficiencies of her husband's Swedish upper-class self-indulgences with her own Swedish practicality and determination. Compared to General Mansfield, with her "mien and bearing" she was the true "general." Patrolling her stables, barns, and fields, she was all that a good patriarch was supposed to be.

Bremer could not help betraying the urgent importance for her of separating this potent figure from material sexuality. When *ma chère mère*, "young, rich and proud," had married at the age of twenty, her husband had already had a wife who had died, leaving him with four sons. These sons his widow, *ma chère mère*, would proceed to raise after his death. While this was quite enough to make clear that *ma chère mère* was indeed to be thought of as mother, not as wife or even bride, there was still more distancing in the division of the General's four sons. His first wife, it seemed, had been a widow when she married the General, and a mother of two sons. Thus *ma chère mère* raised not just her husband's two real sons but his two step-sons also. *Ma chère mère* could mother everyone. That no marriage was actually portrayed in *The Neighbors* simply repeated what had been true in Bremer's previous stories. Now, however, there was no fatherhood, only motherhood.

Bremer wrote approvingly of this tall, large woman who spoke loudly with a rough voice, moved about, booted, with great strides, and combined the style of the highest breeding with the mien of an officer. To no other character in all her stories—including *Hertha*—did she ever devote the details of dress, speech, behavior, and ambience that she expended on Fru General Mansfield. Had the book consisted simply of this admiring portrait, it would have stood as a finished whole, unique among all Bremer's work, and a nearly irresistible invitation to believe that here Bremer had shown what she herself wanted to be and to be like. But the book did not confine itself to such a portraiture. As though aware that she was concealing the costs of what it took to be a dominant matriarch, Bremer threaded another tale into her story of *ma chère mère*. It appeared that the elderly General Mansfield and his young bride had filled their procreative roles at least once, producing a son of their own. "His birth nearly cost the life of the mother." Since this birth agony only made the infant "more precious than life itself," its mother forswore those practices of the effete women of the aristocracy who found nurses for their babes among the poor girls leaving their own at Stockholm's foundling hospital: "She suckled him herself; scarcely would permit any one besides herself . . . to touch him." "He slept in her bosom." "Many a time" the young mother was found "on her knees by his cradle, as if worshipping him." "Thus the relation between mother and son was extraordinary . . . they were the lioness and her cub . . . a union of savage strength and deep tenderness, combat . . . and caress at the same time." Since this extraordinary union could hardly have been apparent at the time to the ten-year-old who later narrated it, we must assume it was apparent primarily to Bremer.

Such a union could not last. "One day, as she laid him . . . to her breast . . . he bit her severely with his young coming teeth." In surprise and pain, "the mother gave him a blow. The child let go the breast, and refused from that moment ever to take it again." Since this mother at least could not stand seeing her baby at a surrogate breast, she promptly weaned him. His revenge came seven years later. When, upon witnessing a piece of misbehavior, his mother set out to administer a "well-deserved correction, he turned like a young lion and struck her." "Unable to live together or apart," the two went on alternating scenes of "combat and caress." Only the influence of "a child, a little girl," Serena, "lovely, quiet, but sickly," exerted restraint upon Bruno's course toward extravagance and dissipation. A climactic confrontation with his mother sent him out into the world. He had been gone, heard of only in rumors, for seventeen years, when the narrator began her portrait of his mother. Sailing the oceans wild, gambling, killing other men in duels, even—according to one report—tearing children from mothers' arms as a slave trader—Bruno had indeed gone wild. Was it his mother's fault? Upon his sudden, unheralded return, she went blind from shock. (An earlier character too, surrogate daughter Elizabeth in *The H-Family*, had suffered the same seizure, though for different cause.) The taming of Bruno, his "socialization" to Swedish norms, would not be brought about by a woman blinded by her own works. The process of this taming was left unexplored in *The Neighbors*. Though quiet, gentle Swedish Serena would profit from it, and supplant the impassioned Oriental woman he had brought with him, Bruno appeared to succumb more from exhaustion than to any practiced wiles.[8]

It was to Bremer's credit that, having written of so many girls suffering from fathers, she had not moved next to imagining girls taming their lovers. Instead, she transmuted her suffering girls into a powerful matriarch. But as her heroine's psychosomatic blindness signified, this only further concealed the problem of sexuality. Waiting for their men to come home satiated from foreign wars and Viking wandering may have been the habit once of Swedish women, but Bremer realized that a girl's escape from subordination had to be negotiated in psychosexual depths, not in accidents of sociology. It took her long years of voice-lessness, but she did finally confront her theme directly, for in telling of Hertha she told not only of Hertha's struggles with her father and of Hertha's rise to power in her hometown, but also of Hertha and a young man who loved her and of Hertha's love for him.

During Hertha Falk's emergence to sway over Kungsköping, many of the ladies in town found her feminist preoccupations turning her "dark and plain," but one young man, Yngve, felt otherwise. Yngve appreciated her for her inner self: "How handsome you are, Hertha! I am not talking about mere external beauty." Hertha had prepared herself beforehand to resist. She "had said in her heart, 'I will not love a man; I will not give my soul and happiness into the power of a man.' " She had not prepared herself enough, however. Rejecting men in general was one thing; rejecting a specific man, another. "What had happened to her? That which . . . happens to the most ordinary woman from the most ordinary man; her feelings had awoke under the burning ray of the kiss of the beloved." "Was she displeased by his bold advances? No, in reality, not." Here was a stage for straightforward confrontation: feelings or feminism, burning kisses or burning commitments? At this exact point, the author intervened in equivocation: "This [kiss] is never displeasing to a woman on the part of the beloved, when she knows that the fire which burns in it is not that of earth."[9] Had Yngve's burning kiss then not been "of earth"? If Hertha had responded as any "ordinary woman" would have, did ordinary women too prefer their kisses not of earth?

Instead of elaborating upon differences between profane and earth-less love, however, Bremer advanced her story by simpler means. She started to keep Hertha away from Yngve. First, Hertha allowed herself to be swayed by an anonymous (and utterly inexplicable) letter that libeled Yngve as the father of an unfortunate girl's child. No slightest trait or behavior on Yngve's part lent this concoction the least credibility, yet Hertha could not resist believing it. Eventually, proof of his innocence emerged. Since this in turn seemed to testify to Yngve's sexual self-control Hertha agreed to a kind of lovers' truce. She repeated her fear of marriage: "I dread its consequences; dread the becoming a mother; dread, in particular, being the mother of a daughter!" She will not give up her "first love," her desire to "liberate my captive sisters," for Yngve.

I fear that it will be . . . long before our Swedish legislators will concede to woman the right of unrestricted human and social freedom and development; long before they will throw open to the daughters of Sweden . . . educational institutions . . . [long] before they will do for them that which they have done for the sons of our country.[10]

Yngve pledged himself to help. He had only one request: let boys "as well as young girls attend your classes, your lectures." Hertha was happy to oblige. Once Hertha felt sure she had been true to her sisters, the two might marry.

Had Bremer concluded her tale of Hertha and Yngve here, she might have won assent to the plea that time, rather than fantasy, would tell what the new-model marriages of a liberated future would be. But Bremer was writing under pressures too strong for such containment. She pursued the lovers' affair through a hundred more pages by means of the standard device of keeping them apart. First, Yngve's heroic firefighting in Kungsköping had left him injured. He had to be treated elsewhere. Then it took two more years for him to achieve "the certain prospect of a modest competency for the future" in his profession as railroad builder, which would enable him to provide for a family. Though Hertha's father had approved him as an eventual husband, when Yngve reappeared to ask for his bride, Director Falk insisted the time was not yet ripe. This impediment Hertha would not accept. "For the first time" she broke the "bonds of silence" that an "inherent reverence for the patriarchal guardianship" had imposed upon her. It was surprising to hear of such "inherent reverence" at this late date. It was more surprising that, despite breaking her silence, Hertha still did not defy her father and go to King Oscar at last for relief from her daughterly minority-hood. Yngve wanted her to. So did her most distinguished male feminist friend in town, Judge Carlson, who urged her not to carry filial duty too far. But Hertha held back: "I cannot do otherwise." She still had something to gain from daughterly subservience: protection from marriage. As though troubled by her heroine's decision, with its undertone of hypocrisy, Bremer, for one of the few times in the book, commented on her heroine "objectively":

... it was to [Yngve] unendurable to live near Hertha under the constraints which his half-engagement to her and her own wishes imposed. And he was right. Hertha did not love Yngve as he loved her. No woman can fully understand the passion which glows in the whole being of the enamored young man, nor can she participate [in] it. She loves equally as much, often more, or better than he, but in quite another manner.[11]

Better than Hertha, then, Bremer understood the reason for Hertha's feminism, not the patriarchal laws of Sweden, not the meanness or pettiness of her father, not the stinginess of "the legislators of Sweden," but her fear of a man she might have to marry. Bremer failed to notice that she had exempted herself from Hertha's disability: if no woman could "fully understand" a young man's glowing passion, then neither could Bremer. But she did, and she did not want her heroine succumbing to it.

Fleeing what was "unendurable," Hertha's lover took a job in Italy. Another year passed. In his senility, Hertha's father basked in various awards and honors. Hertha ran her school. The lovers wrote. Finally, after seven more years had gone by "and Hertha was no longer young," she called at last: "Yngve, come home! Come home, beloved friend! I cannot bear any longer to be separated from you." "Hertha's home was prepared as for a festival." But on the very morning—a Sunday morning—of the bridegroom's return, dreadful news was heard from Lake Vännern, just three miles away. There were screams, a steamer sinking, tragedies. There were also heroes, and one in particular, "the most energetic," swimming repeatedly between ship and shore, rescuing no fewer than fourteen persons, mostly women and children. Hertha soon had her Yngve home again, again exhausted from heroics, to be nursed again, as after the fire. "The bridegroom is in the house of the bride, but the wedding—that is a long way off!"[12] Yngve never did recover. Before his end, he and Hertha did marry, but a careful reading of the narrator's text forbids the hope that their union ever became "of earth." Bremer apparently tried to head off the temptation to ironize over this tale. To an impartial observer, her heroine might seem something less than a saint—a subtle hypocrite exploiting while pretending to filial piety, a sexual tease of remarkable endurance, and a heart anesthetized behind masks of service. Bremer certainly did not want her seen this way. Resourceful to the end, she made her heroine die of cancer. Who could ironize over that? More tellingly, she made her the recipient of another anonymous letter, this one declaring that all her troubles, together with those of her lover, she had brought on herself, by stubbornly refusing to take the freedom open to her. All she had had to do was avail herself "of the means which our Swedish laws provide to obtain their liberty," that is, going to King Oscar. The dying Hertha could not repel the charge: "Have I really been the cause? Is it I? I cannot see. I cannot clearly understand."[13] Nor can any reader.

The Individual (Male) versus Sex: August Strindberg

From the start of his career as playwright, storyteller, essayist, and critic, August Strindberg offered ideas to make Sweden better. His deepest impulse was as a realist, however, not as a reformer. Sweden provoked no utopian dreams in his head. His favorite Sweden lay in the past. He had registered his central outlook in the stories of *Married*, sketches like those of Almqvist's *Sara Videbeck*, but sketches that registered irony as often as sympathy, and a preference for complexity over simplicity, for struggle over harmony. Enraged at having been brought to trial, Strindberg left Sweden for self-imposed exile again, and soon released a new collection of stories under the title *Married II*. This time his preface indulged in plain hostility to feminism. The first volume of a psychological autobiography soon appeared, entitled *The Son of a Servant*.[14] The "servant" was his mother. When he got to the years of his courtship, he got out his wife's letters to him and his to her and published them. In 1887 he published a narrative, in French, of both courtship and marriage in which he revealed corrosive suspicions of his wife as an adultress, perhaps also a lesbian.[15] Although this volume was not translated into and published in Swedish for some years, Strindberg nonetheless quickly gained a reputation at home for scandalous exploitation of his own and his wife's private life. He had made himself notorious.

Strindberg met his wife-to-be, Sigrid Sofia Matilda Elisabeth von Essen Wrangel, in 1875, when he was twenty-six and she a year younger.[16] Siri Wrangel had grown up in Swedish Finland as the child of an aristocratic family. She married a man of her own class, a captain in the armed forces, a *friherre* or baron. In 1875 Strindberg was still an unknown. Although a play of his had won a stipend from the King some years before, he had had to get a job in the Royal Library, working in Chinese and other Far Eastern materials, in order to eke out his living as a newspaper writer. He remained a young man far more of uncertain prospects than of shining promise. So far as we know, Strindberg never read the classic text delineating the nexus between class and sex attraction, Stendhal's portrayal of commoner Julien Sorel's passion for the aristocratic Mathilde in *The Red and the Black*, but Strindberg may have found Siri's class attributes attractive. His own analysis, however, in *A Madman's Defense*, concentrated on psychological, not sociological, drives.

Little more than ex post facto conjecture can tell us why Baroness Wrangel left her husband for an unknown and still struggling artist. Presumably she found faults in her husband, but Strindberg's courtship must have been formidable. In the *Madman's Defense* he repeatedly linked Siri with his mother, as on their first meeting:

The girlish appearance and baby face of the Baroness, who must have been at least twenty-five . . . surprised me. She looked like a schoolgirl; her little face was framed by roguish curls, golden as a cornfield . . . the shoulders of a princess . . . a supple, willowy figure. . . . And this delicious, girlish mother had read my play without hurt or injury?

The house in which she was living with her husband was—lo and behold!—that in which Strindberg had grown up. She responded to his memories: " 'Can't we drive away those ghosts?' she asked, looking at me with a bewitching expression, full of motherly tenderness." Recalling his feelings, the autobiographer concealed no extremes:

The instinct of worship, latent in my heart, awoke . . . God was deposed, but His place was taken by a woman, woman who was both virgin and mother. . . . I could not understand how [her little girl] had been possible, for the relationship between her and her husband seemed to put all sexual intercourse out of the question; their union appeared essentially spiritual.[17]

His hopes were explicit: "What inexpressible happiness it is to be married!" he wrote. "To be always near the beloved one, safe from the prying eyes of the fatuous world. It is as if one had regained the home of one's childhood with its sheltering love, a safe port after the storm, a nest which awaits the little ones."[18]

Buried deep in Strindberg's story was the hint that Siri Wrangel saw some career advantages for herself in marrying him. He had connections with the court and the theater. Though born to high status, she was a provincial. She had hankerings for being an actress. She wanted to shine in the artistic world of Stockholm. After she married Strindberg, she did find some opportunities on the stage. She bore Strindberg two daughters in 1880 and 1881, but it was not until Strindberg took her away from Sweden in 1883 that she was cut off from any hope for a career. It would be easy to guess that the marriage began to fall apart then, reflecting a misunderstanding inhabiting it from the start. Yet the Strindbergs stayed together another eight years, until 1891. Perhaps it was too late for her, at forty-two, and with an eleven- and a twelve-year-old daughter to raise, to try to return to the stage, but in any case Siri Strindberg was never heard to offer ill report about her ex-husband. When her daughter Karin, in 1925, wrote a marvelously humane report on her parents' marriage as a kind of corrective to her father's infamous polemic, her primary source could only have been her mother.[19] While never finding real financial security, Strindberg kept up with child support for his daughters as best he could. Siri Strindberg did not marry again, dying in April 1912, just a month before the death of her famous ex-husband.

Most interesting of all the facts about the Strindbergs' marriage was that it lasted another four years after Strindberg had written and published his corrosive suspicions. While we do not know whether Siri Strindberg read what her husband wrote about her or, if she did, what she thought about it, it seems fair to infer that she understood his words to be a kind of exorcism or incantation.[20] Biographers were to write as though some application of psychoanalytic tools was necessary in order to penetrate into this marriage.

Gustav Uddgren, a friend who got to know Strindberg in 1890, judged that he "continually clung to the ideal of woman as wife and mother which he had formed in his youth." His first biographer, L. Lind-af-Hagaby, made a direct inference: "[The] future misogynist was fostered by the child's passionate and unrequited love for his mother." A later biographer, Elizabeth Sprigge, judged that "In [Siri] he had looked for his mother; in other women he had looked for her, in all women and their children he had sought his own childhood."[21] Yet obviously psychoanalysis was not needed to elicit such insights, for Strindberg had supplied them himself. "Is there anything abnormal about [my] instinct? Am I the product of some whim of nature? Are my real feelings perverse, since I find such pleasure in possessing my mother? Is this the unconscious incest of the heart?"[22] In Strindberg's case, the answer to his rhetorical question could only be "no," since he had transformed his unconscious instinct into something conscious. He had psychoanalyzed himself, using his marriage as the means. But his psychoanalysis of his marriage was not inspired by some breakdown in the marriage itself, for that did not occur until after he had analyzed it.

What was at stake at all times for Strindberg was his own creative power. In no doubt the most basic of his insights into himself, he wrote in 1885: "My brain has been on fire since I was a child."[23] He could not take this burning energy for granted. It was vulnerable. Threats to it had to be defined and repelled. In a chapter in *The Son of a Servant* entitled "Character and Destiny," he analyzed the deepest threat of all.

"A man's character is his destiny." That was then a common and favorable proverb. Now that John [obviously the young Strindberg] had to go into the world, he employed much time in attempting to cast his horoscope from his own character, which he thought was already fully formed.[24]

This was a mistake. Not only had the young man's character not been fully formed; it had been his great good fortune that it never should be. If character was destiny, then it was a petty destiny.

A man with a so-called character is often a simple piece of mechanism; he has often only one point of view of the extremely complicated relationships of life ... in order not to be accused of "lack of character," he never changes his opinion.... [A] man with a character is generally a very ordinary individual, and what may be called a little stupid. "Character" and automation seem often synonymous.

The matter involved the deepest of ethics and identity:

[All] acted parts.... It was a trait in human nature, a tendency to adapt oneself.... But when is one true, and when is one false? And where is to be found the central "ego,"—the core of character? The "ego" was a complex of impulses and desires, some of which were to be restrained, and others fettered.

John's individuality was a fairly rich but chaotic complex. . . . He had not yet determined which of his impulses must be restrained, and how much the "ego" must be sacrificed for the society into which he was preparing to enter.

In this passage, in the unstressed elision from "character" to "ego" we can discern the determination, both of Strindberg the mature auto-biographer and of his adolescent prefigurement, not to restrain his individuality, not to sacrifice his ego at all. Looking back, Strindberg thought he saw two "fundamental characteristics" in his youthful self that had helped maintain his freedom.

The first was Doubt. He did not receive ideas without criticism, but developed and combined them. Therefore he could not be an automaton, nor find a place in ordered society. The second was—Sensitiveness to pressure. He always tried to lessen this . . . by criticising what was above him, in order to observe that it was not so high after all, nor so much worth striving after.[25]

But of course, more than any man, Strindberg did not cease striving. He did not strive after the "higher" but sought to tell the truth about it. "John had learned to speak the truth. . . . [He] found brutal enjoy-ment . . . when people were trying to conceal the truth, to say exactly what all thought."

In effect, survival as a free man, escape from the routine and conven-tionality of "character," depended upon continuous access to the free-dom of boyhood. Some of Strindberg's most popular work showed this access in the directest possible way. Readers of *Hemsöborna* (The People of Hemsö) could not have guessed its author had also just written the bleakly realistic play of domestic tragedy, *The Father*. As Martin Lamm has pointed out, much of the popularity of Strindberg's early book on Stockholm, *The Red Room*, had followed not from the satirical barbs directed at various of the city's institutions and pomposities, but from the easy precision with which Strindberg had fixed the details of a life passing away.[26] The Stockholm he described in 1879 was really the city of the 1860s, being engulfed in "large-scale renovation and moderni-zation." For Swedish readers its colors conveyed a beloved yesteryear. Strindberg, too, obviously had loved it. In 1887, warned by his publisher of declining sales, he set about writing *The People of Hemsö*, offering a rich widow seduced and married by an unscrupulous servant, his phi-landering, her jealousy and eventual triumph, playing directly to the crowd. In later years the public enjoyed versions of *The People of Hemsö* as a play, a radio drama, a movie, and eventually as a version for television. But the book was no mere potboiler. Its tang inhered in its language and in the details it rendered of the unchanged life of the archipelago. "Reading it, one gets the feeling, similar to that generated by *The Odyssey*, *The Divine Comedy* or *Ulysses*, that a life which has lain concealed and anonymous for centuries is suddenly revealed and harvested by a skillful master of words." [27] Despite his intentions, Strindberg had written another masterpiece, and it derived from his unimpeded access to his own childhood when he had absorbed "anonymous life" freely. With the greed of easy creation, he plunged on to more archipelago stories, in *Men of the Skerries* of 1888. Though less popular than *The People of Hemsö*, probably because of its lack of a single plot, it too, nonetheless, in its rendition of detail in vivid, dancing language evinced a writer whose unfathomable resources were vested in a psyche still blessed with a boy's freedom from "character" and predictability.

Strindberg was fully aware of how precarious such freedom was. No relationship with a woman could help but inspire the hope that she would take up the role his mother had played, or at least that his ideal of a mother had played, that of letting him feel unbound. Intellectually, as he had shown in perfectly objective comments in the preface to *Married I*, he knew that that was an unreasonable expectation.

One partner develops in one direction, one in another, and their marriage breaks up. Or one of the two remains stationary, while the other develops, and they drift apart. Incompatibility . . . may arise when two strong spirits clash, and realize that no compromise is possible unless one partner gives way.[28]

But the rational response to such an objective insight took no account of its cost. During the years immediately after his divorce from Siri, Strindberg stopped writing, immersing himself in "science" and suffering several episodes of psychological fugue. He tried marriage again in 1894, his bride another would-be actress, twenty-one-year-old Frida Uhl of Austria. The next year they had a daughter, but by October had separated, and were divorced in 1897.[29] By then Strindberg was back in full creative flood. He found it nearly impossible to give up all hopes from marriage, however. At fifty-two, in 1901 he married for the third time, his bride, Harriet Bosse, still another young would-be actress. Again there was a daughter, then again, in 1904, a divorce, although the two sustained some kind of relationship until 1907, when Harriet Bosse Strindberg married someone else.[30] A recent Strindberg analyst, Gunnar Brandell, has cited passages in Strindberg's *Occult Diary*, written in the midst of his psychic stress, indicating both "outer signs of consistency in [Strindberg's] erotic choices" and "resemblances in Strindberg's own mind between all three of his wives." Yet subsequently Brandell cited Strindberg himself, as well as his second wife Frida in published letters, as evidence that "does not in any way suggest that Strindberg identified her with his mother, much less that such an identification was a decisive factor in their marriage." [31] Any obsessions preoccupying him with Siri had been burned away in the crisis of his creativity following his first divorce.

Strindberg had anticipated the central theme of his breakdown in a novel of 1890, *I havsbandet* (At the Edge of the Sea).[32] A scientist, refined and superior, serving an isolated island community as fishing commissioner, found himself becoming gradually psychically isolated as a consequence of his own penetrating "scientific" powers for analyzing everyone else. With every relationship eaten up by insight, he ended up alone and, in despair, sailed off over the edge of the sea.

Brandell has argued that what Strindberg won for himself out of his "psychotic episodes" of 1894–96 was "religion." If so, it was self-generated. Once, in his youth, Strindberg had shared the rationalism that had grown up at Uppsala and had attracted young men like Knut Wicksell and the incipient managers of Social Democratic Sweden. His own blasphemous alter ego, Theodore, had been something of a self-conscious, atheistic, rationalist materialist. Very briefly, Strindberg embraced the American Unitarian rationalist, Theodore Parker. But Strindberg lasted hardly beyond his youth as a "liberal," religiously. To say that Strindberg was innately religious, in some sense, or better, instinctively antiatheistic, would probably be fair, if not very helpful. "God's relation to Strindberg can be characterized in a single word— 'father'," Brandell concluded.[33] If so, this defined the progress—or at least movement—that Strindberg achieved during his crisis. If, as Erik Erikson's schema of "stages" on life's way suggests, the religious instinct is laid down in earliest infancy, with the newborn's first relationship with a mother, Strindberg had been burning away the mists and mystification that concealed that first worship, exposing it, and finally disposing of it. A free mind could not count on mother. No wife could be mother any more than the whole world could be mother. Strindberg had long ago got over a youthful infatuation with Rousseau's fantasy of a "mother nature." Now he was wrenching himself free of fixation on mother-wives. Whether this had to mean God as father was another question. Certainly in his postinferno period Strindberg showed fascination with Catholicism, empathy for the evangelicals' Jesus Christ, and interest in things occult, Easter, Nietzsche—all evidence of a ranging religiousness. Yet he never identified a father as his object of reverence. Whatever the essential powers of a good father might have been, he contained them within himself and did not project them outside. The powers for which he gave the most explicit thanksgiving confirmed his whole previous life:

. . . at my desk I really live . . . I live the many lives . . . I depict . . . I steal out of my own being, and speak through the mouths of children, of women, of old men . . . I confess all religions; I . . . have ceased to exist myself.[34]

With this inner power assured, Strindberg's second and third marriages did not provoke him to the same rage he had registered in *A Madman's Defense*. He visited no recriminations on Frida Uhl. He visited none on Harriet Bosse. By then he had written *Ensam* (Alone), his artistic reconciliation to personal solitude. In the religiousness following his psychic inferno crisis, personal grievance had been purged from his work. He had gained confidence in its source.

The years from 1897 to his death in 1912 were in many ways the most productive of Strindberg's life. He poured forth masterpieces defying standard classification. In *Inferno* and *Legends*, soon after his crisis, then above all in *A Dream Play* in 1901, he exploited his new access to an unintimidated inner life in fresh, liberating forms and language, subjective, expressionistic, yet at the same time perfectly explicit in speaking to ethical, psychological, and religious themes. Beginning in 1899, he began a huge cycle of Swedish historical plays and carried them through, undaunted by Shakespeare's precedent, without preciosity or imitation. He continued to avail himself of old forms, such as folktales and legends, for his new arguments. He did not stop writing of marriage as a kind of doomed power struggle, though now it loomed less large on his literary stage. Marriage in *The Dance of Death I* and *The Dance of Death II* fully deserved the appellation "nightmare" that was often applied to these plays of 1900. In *The Pelican*, a brief "chamber play" of 1907, he presented a husband and wife locked in lethal guilt, but also showed the two as lethal parents. Yet in these plays no longer was the onus placed only on the wife, as in *The Father* back in 1887. Strindberg had been dissolving that theme as early as 1890, for the forces impelling the superior hero of *At the Edge of the Sea* to self-destruction were not condensed into a wife but diffused into the community at large. In effect, wives had ceased to be vampires. Or rather, as in *The Dance of Death II*, the vampire could appear as husband and father as well as wife.[35]

The bargain implicit in his postinferno selflessness—"I have ceased to exist myself"—was that his creative powers would persist so long as he continued to tell the truth. He had already grasped that connection in defending the "brutality" of his earlier plays, *The Father*, *The Creditors*, *The Comrades*, and especially *Miss Julie* of 1888.

Not long ago they reproached my tragedy "The Father" with being too sad— just as if they wanted merry tragedies . . . I find the joy of life in its violent and cruel struggles. . . . And for this reason I have selected an unusual but instructive case—an exception, in a word—but a great exception, proving the rule, which, of course, will provoke all lovers of the commonplace. And what also will offend simple brains is that my action cannot be traced back to a single motive, that the view-point is not always the same. An event in real life—and this discovery is quite recent—springs generally from a whole series of more or less deep-lying motives, but of these the spectator chooses as a rule the one his reason can master most easily, or else the one reflecting most favorably on his power of reasoning.[36]

General ideas were inadequate to individual existences; general ideas fed "merry tragedies," tragedies pointing at a few social reforms or a little revolution as "answers." One such reform was of course feminism, and Strindberg continued to attack it. Pages of heavy debate on marriage and "woman's place" in *Götiska rummen* (The Gothic Rooms) echoed the polemic of *Married II*, while in *Svarta fanor* (Black Banners), written in 1904, Strindberg caricatured Ellen Key as Hannah Pie. Key had been an admirer of Strindberg as writer and truth-teller. Following Strindberg's final return to Sweden in 1899, the two had met as friends in the literary circles of the capital. Strindberg had sympathized with Key in her recoil from the antisexual righteousness of the Friends of Morality. Key's suspicions of the Bremer Society feminists as a kind of privileged clique, condescending to ordinary Swedish motherhood, had paralleled Strindberg's. Yet by 1900, presiding over her "dozens," which were attracting the young women of a new generation, Key was becoming a good-auntie figure, a Hertha of less obvious ambition. In presenting his Hannah Pie as, among other things, a lesbian, Strindberg was criticizing sisterhood as another case of wishful thinking. Key promised escape from, not engagement with, struggle.

It was not feminism as such, however, but a certain vision of Sweden that summoned Strindberg's most cutting assaults on positive thinking, and for these he singled out not women but two men, also erstwhile friends, for caricature. Hannah Pie was only a subordinate figure in *Black Banners*. In its central figure, Little Zachris, Strindberg pilloried a popular novelist and eager literary careerist, Gustaf àf Geijerstam.[37] Geijerstam's world was the magazines, journals, papers, and literary coteries. He aimed to be friends of all, ready to lend help to any, ready to be rewarded by any. Nine years younger than Strindberg, he had deplored the continuing hostility to Strindberg on the part of the Swedish Academy's secretary David àf Wirsen, although, typically, he tried to stay on good terms with both sides. Strindberg felt a kind of detached contempt for such types, and unerringly portrayed Geijerstam's essential opportunism. But he was not most interested in Little Zachris as a literary type. He was far more eager to pillory him as husband and father.[37]

By 1904 Geijerstam had been writing successfully for the market for more than twenty years. He had always met a popular taste, but in two books, *Mina pojkar* (My Boys) in 1896 and *Boken om lillebror* (The Book about Little Brother) of 1900, he had been particularly successful in speaking to and reviving an old Swedish sentimentality about home and family. Geijerstam seemed to be showing that urban Sweden, newly modernizing and potentially middle-class, could hope still to remain, as myth had it, the cozy, tucked-in Sweden of yore. Other writers of the 1890s too had been working the vein of nostalgia. Almost as a revivification of Erik Gustav Geijer, Verner von Heidenstam had recurred to the heroic icons of Viking and knightly pasts. Selma Lagerlöf was busy on yet another reworking of the immemorial country folk, this time carrying it all the way to a Nobel Prize. But if Heidenstam was a kind of Marion Crawford, and Lagerlöf Sweden's lesser Willa Cather, Geijerstam was a Booth Tarkington. He wrote not so much as though Freud had not yet been born (and he had not, yet, so far as respectable Sweden was concerned), but as though another kind of boy had not, that "son of a servant" whom Geijerstam had pretended to understand, even appreciate, but only patronized. Geijerstam had already been severely criticized by critics for his exploitation of himself, his wife, and his family in *Little Brother*. Hurt, he responded in the novel *Kvinnomakt* (Woman Power).

Whether in *Woman Power* Strindberg saw Geijerstam's most blatant pandering to sentimentality we do not know, but the book could only have invited his scorn. In method a kind of low-intensity imitation of some of his own confessional works, in substance *Woman Power* consisted of a middle-aged man's reminiscences, supposedly melancholy and philosophic, actually lingering and appetitive, over the details of his relationships with three women. One is a first, true love, lost out of youthful heedlessness; sadly, when they find each other again, she is married. The second is the wife, at first humble, then adulterous, finally fugitive. The third is the thirteen-year-old daughter; the father wins her from her mother, then arranges for her to live with his first true love and finally woos her back for himself: "It has been your little dream. . . . You and I, alone." [38] Inevitably, the little girl must die. The hero then goes to his first true love's husband and confesses his lifelong love for this man's wife, whereupon the three enter into a *ménage à trois* for years of "singular happiness." Too earnest to be taken as a parody, *Woman Power* apparently was Geijerstam's plea for the writer's right, and necessity, to draw upon the deepest materials of his most intimate life for his art. Unfortunately, the hero-narrator of *Woman Power* had neither artistic energy nor an independent inner life, only a passive intrigue with fantasies the real logic of which remained quite invisible to him. To compose what for Strindberg were the volcanoes of the inner life into trysts of wish-fulfillment defaced art.

The following year, 1908, Strindberg published his last book, *Ett blå bok* (A Blue Book), in one chapter of which he attacked still another friend, Carl Larsson, and his wife. Larsson was Sweden's most popular artist.[39] A cartoonist and illustrator in his youth, he had spent some years in France in the early 1880s as one of the *plein air* group of Impressionists. By 1908 he had painted mural canvases and frescoes for the National Museum, the Stockholm Opera House, the Dramatic Theater, and schools in Göteberg and elsewhere, and had illustrated novels and other works of Swedish writers. By far the most popular of his works were his watercolors of his home in rural Sundborn. Starting out in 1894 with the deliberate purpose, shared by many other Swedish artists, writers, and architects, of promoting a kind of reform in Swedish interior decoration from the darker, heavier old styles—or styleless-ness—to something lighter in color and line, in his art Larsson soon was lending greater emphasis to his personages, his children, seven in all, his wife and himself, than to his furnishings. Following *Ett hem in Dalarna* (A Home in Dalecarlia) in 1899, he titled his next simply *Larssons* (The Larssons). He was becoming "the good uncle of all Sweden," his family living in a "bucolic paradise" where one long summertime was interrupted by picturesque snow at Christmas. "Year after year, in drawing after drawing, the Swedish people were accustomed to hugging to themselves Carl Larsson's picture of family happiness."

There were parallels between Strindberg's and Larsson's lives. Both were born in Stockholm; Strindberg's mother was a servant, Larsson's took in wash. Both showed early artistic promise, and both found support from government funds. Both married girls from higher social stations. Strindberg had admired Larsson's youthful work; he had invited him to return to Sweden to illustrate a book he was writing on Swedish history. Larsson spent four months with the Strindbergs at Kymenndö in 1880: "It was a marvellous summer." Strindberg wrote an admiring notice of Larsson for a Swedish almanac. What attracted Strindberg, something of an amateur artist himself, was Larsson's evident readiness for fresh ways, a certain immediacy in the line of his drawings, his open-air approach to reality. Nor could Strindberg have been unimpressed by the very young Larsson's employment on one of Stockholm's satirical journals.

The Larsson that Strindberg attacked in 1908 was not necessarily a lesser artist than the one he had admired. He attacked Larsson's myth of domestic happiness, more specifically the myth of his marriage. The Larssons were not, Strindberg insisted, what they appeared to be in the perpetual theater of their home life as Larsson presented it. They were not the perpetually collaborative and sunny couple the illustrator exhibited. There was jealousy between them. Larsson's wife was a trained artist; Larsson impeded her efforts; she in turn constrained him to paint only her own involuntary realm, domestic life. They were, in short, another Strindbergian couple, frustrating each other's creativity, living out the logic of love-hate.

When Social Democratic working men marched in Strindberg's honor at his funeral, they were not misconstruing his hopes for Sweden. The year after his attack on Carl Larsson, at sixty, he wrote an essay on "The Origins of Our Mother Tongue" and another on "The Roots of World Language," in tacit Darwinian celebration of the tool of consciousness itself, language, in perpetual need of rescue from the drag of conventionality, certitude, orthodoxy. What he hoped was that, once social justice was achieved, people would not consume the sugar-sweet stories of Gustaf àf Geijerstam and the picture books of Carl Larsson. The political and economic improvement of society must not promote the delusion of "merry tragedies." The conflicts and struggles of the inner life would not be eased by social justice; bad art, cartoons of harmony and self-satisfaction, only concealed them. Strindberg's plays of personal disintegration—*Miss Julie, The Pelican, Queen Cristina*, and so on—testified that modernity demanded greater, not less, individuality. As external social and economic pressures on individuals declined, so also would the external walls holding up personality weaken. Marriage would implode, its whole substance the molten fires of inwardness. As social security succeeded family security, families would be the scenes of conflict, not cooperation. Strindberg saw clearly that domestic idylls such as those retailed by Carl Larsson constituted flights from self. This was no argument against social justice. But the whole point of social justice was to equip the individual for the joys of freedom, violent and cruel. Sweden enjoyed a special relationship with regard to this opportunity. In Italy, with its unending struggle for enough economic substance to afford some social justice in the first place, nostalgic fantasies of mass harmony such as Gramsci's could continue to exert sway. In the Soviet Union, with its officialization of harmony between culture and economy, between individual and society, Strindberg's insight was simply illegal. Ethnic, religious, and racial particularities in the United States could keep it cooped up, as in Eugene O'Neill's "Irish" despair, Richard Wright's "black" rage, Sam Shepherd's "Western" sensibilities. But in Sweden, in the good fortune of its isolation, its hardy folkish past, and its economic endowment, purgative tragedy could flourish. That Strindberg was so savage followed from his anxiety that so great an opportunity not be smothered.

The Individual Fulfilled through Sex: Ellen Key

Perhaps the finest writer who might have been a lifelong interlocutor for Strindberg had been cut off early. Victoria Benedictsson had died in 1888, at thirty-eight, just as Strindberg was coming into his full powers.[40] Born to a farmer father of forty-nine and his wife of forty-three, she was not an adored last of the litter but an unwanted accident. The Bruzeliuses were among the persisting poor in the modernizing countryside, their marriage and life that of drudges. The daughter's escape came through marriage, at twenty-one, to a small-town widower postmaster, nearly fifty, with five children. His new young wife bore him two more. She escaped from more drudgery, first through illnesses that put her on crutches, then by writing. Like Bremer and Anne-Marie Lenngren, Benedictsson wrote first of "folk," the people of the countryside she had known as a girl and young wife, in stories of remarkable precision, concision, and perception. She wrote her first novel, *Pengar* (Money), on the marriage problem, in 1884. *Money* met many of the wants of the new reading audience of the time. It told once again of a heroine marrying and suffering. Benedictsson included in her story a new solution: divorce. *Money* conveyed the qualities of modern young women as Bremer never had, and with no more salacity or biology than Strindberg ever used—that is, none—in rendering into art the truth excluded from the morality question and from much of the previous marriage literature, that love without physical passion was not much of an issue. It was an abstraction for casuists.

After two more stories, Benedictsson published her second marriage novel in 1887, her best book, *Fru Marianne*. This did not win the same applause from feminists or the younger generation. The young heroine, married to a solid, sober farmer, looked for excitement to a sophisticated artist friend, only to draw back and by the book's end become the wise and contented wife of her husband, aware of his virtues and interested in his world as well as her own. The happy ending no doubt guaranteed that Benedictsson's story would seem far slighter than the somber model, Flaubert's *Madame Bovary*, which had inspired it, but its treatment was not sentimental. Benedictsson was not reassessing her own irredeemable marriage. Her novel was an act of imagination; her art had not saved her from personal life. Two years before the publication of *Fru Marianne*, Benedictsson had fallen in love—"hopelessly," since the man she fell in love with, the Danish critic George Brandes, was a classic Don Juan. For all the help of friends such as Ellen Key, who had also survived a hopeless love, Benedictsson foundered. She committed suicide in 1888.

After her death, no woman of literary power came forth to engage feminists, whether those of the court, of socialism, or of the slowly emerging middle class. Just why not, Swedish literary history can hardly say. In terms of intellectual history, the question can be brought to a sharper focus, though perhaps no more answerable: why did Ellen Key not transmute her own private life into literature?

Marriage became an issue for Key in her twenties. When she was twenty-three, her mother discussed her daughter's future with the prominent Norwegian writer, Björnstierne Björnson. It was part of her mother's style of life to enjoy many distinguished acquaintances in the world of letters and art, and Björnson knew of Ellen Key's literary hopes. He knew that Sophie Adlersparre had invited her to submit pieces to the *Home Journal*, but he apparently judged that Key would not be a literary success. His recommendation was not offered lightly. He saw that Key was a special case. "Strong inner lives don't always help women understand men, and when love does come to a girl who has not yet known it at twenty-three, it is likely to be appallingly in earnest." But he made himself plain: "She ought to marry and make some man happy."[41]

Three years later, in 1875, when she was twenty-six, Key submitted a review of a book entitled *Protestantismens Mariakult* (Protestant Devotion to Mary) to the *Home Journal*. Steeped in high-church religious sensibility, the book warned feminists against forgetting values inherent in the differences between men and women. Adlersparre, believing the book backward if not reactionary, rejected Key's favorable review. Key placed it with a Stockholm paper. All this lent her praise of the book a special edge, which the pseudonymous author appreciated, and he said so in a pseudonymous letter to the reviewer. A year later an elderly friend informed Key that the author was his nephew, Urban von Feilitzen. Author and reviewer met at the uncle's estate outside Stockholm early in the summer of 1876. "Appallingly in earnest," Ellen Key at last fell in love. But Urban von Feilitzen was a married man. Their relationship, which was conducted mostly by letters—Feilitzen was writing her a hundred a year by 1879—lasted eleven years. At no time was Feilitzen close to divorcing his wife. Yet Key may, until near the very end, have nursed hopes for an eventual marriage.

It is hard not to locate one of the springs of Key's sex radicalism in her fifties and sixties in this love affair of her twenties and thirties. Whatever the reason for the delay of her awakening until twenty-six, the end of the affair when she was thirty-seven did not leave her destroyed. That she truly had been in love seems sure. The Feilitzens' marriage had left the way open. Some kind of conventionality, shallow and polite, had settled over it. By romantic standards it was not a "real" marriage. It was "no longer" a marriage. Feminists had been making these distinctions. Most likely Key had been ready to defy convention. With Feilitzen himself reluctant to break, however, she generated ethical restraints of her own: "I can't buy my happiness with another woman's tears." Years later one of her young admirers, Elin Wägner, already on the way to her own distinguished literary career, having met Feilitzen, by then in his sixties, described him as "a cool object for Ellen Key's warm maiden love." Considering that that maiden had been twenty-six when she met him, twenty-eight or twenty-nine when true intensity overtook their relationship, Wägner no doubt underestimated the degree to which Key, however "appalling" her earnestness, had been inhibited against heedlessness. Wägner's own far more youthful unhappiness in love, prompting her sympathy for Key, had misled her. But Key herself, in her last years, was ready to make her own explicit "impersonal" judgment about Feilitzen. "His fault was that he was weak." The Swedish word *vek* meant more than its English cognate "weak." It could mean "gentle" and "tender" and "yielding," along with "soft" and "pliant" and "indecisive." Key probably meant all of these. That her intention, by then, was at once forgiving of Feilitzen and still ambivalent, appeared in her explanation of his "weakness": "no wonder he had it. He did not have an easy time of it. He was caught between two strong women."[42]

That Ellen Key had become a strong woman by the time she said this, in her seventies, seems clear. (Whatever Fru Feilitzen had once been was another matter.) She never had written of her love for Feilitzen. Hardly anyone, even early biographers, knew of it to the end of her life. After Feilitzen died in 1913, and his wife the next year, Key could perhaps have written openly, but did not. In fact she had already written her spiritual autobiography, disguised, back in 1908, when she was fifty-nine, in the biography of another woman, Rahel Varnhagen. As autobiography, this biography was the story of a life never lived, yet perfectly real as an act of imaginative breakthrough. Her imagining it was remarkable at nearly sixty, when she had had so many opportunities to smother it. It was her own great act of mothering.

Rahel Levin Varnhagen had grown up in the Enlightenment Berlin of Frederick the Great and became famous in the age of Napoleon, as presiding spirit at one of the cosmopolitan salons common in the city. Although she was no means rich, Levin displayed a talent for empathy, intensity, and conversation that lent her salon substance. She corresponded with Schleiermacher, the von Humboldt brothers, the Tieck brothers, Jean Paul, Friedrich Gentz, and twice met no less than Johann Wolfgang von Goethe. In a second, later salon in post-Napoleonic Berlin after her marriage, she would come to know Heine, Hegel, the von Arnims, Grillparzer. Varnhagen wrote no books, novels, essays, stories, poetry. She wrote letters. After her death her husband, Karl August Varnhagen, compiled a three-volume set of these "for her friends." Forty years after her death a volume entitled *Aus Rahels Herzensleben* (From Rachel's Heart) could be published in the knowledge that all would know who "Rahel" was. Carlyle had written of her, as had many of her other acquaintances. A popular anthology, *Rahel, ein Buch des Andenkens* (Rachel, a Book of Memories) became a staple of romantic reading for educated young girls in Europe for years. When she came to write her book on Varnhagen, Key had full-scale recent studies to use as well, notably a biography of 1900 by Otto Berdrow. Writing of Varnhagen, then, was not to write just of private dreams but of European womanhood.

Key's book consisted of nine chapters. By far the longest was on "Love." Rahel Levin's first love arrived when she was twenty-five, a young count, two years younger, "blond as yellow brick," member of a Prussian landed family. "He was the first who wanted me to love him," Levin recollected years later. Since Levin herself was "remarkable neither for beauty, social position, nor wealth," Key found that his love for her proved Count von Finckenstein to be "a man who already belonged to the new age in spirit." But this love did not prosper. Soon Finckenstein felt "the oppression of [her] superior personality" and retreated to mother, sister, and estate. "Most women in Rahel's place would have used all the resources their love, their suffering, and their personality gave them" to keep their lovers. But Rahel Levin did not do so; "she gave up the struggle." In this withdrawal, Key discerned standards for a new age: "no human being has the right to retain another by any other power than that other person's inmost necessity."[43] Ultimately "a weak child," Finckenstein felt no such inmost necessity on his side; the four-year engagement was over.

Something had been missing not just in Finckenstein's but also in Rahel Levin's feelings during the first affair. The next love in Levin's life counted as a "great love," "that love which never comes twice in a human life." Don Raphael d'Urquijo was a secretary of the Spanish legation in Berlin. Now, at thirty, Rahel had "reached the dangerous age in a woman's life . . . when, as never before or after, [she] is ready for love in the full sense of the word." To "sympathetic exchange of ideas" and "sincere affection," that is, something was added, specifically, "erotic attraction." This affair too foundered. Exactly why, Key found puzzling. As she pursued the story to its end, she wondered if, after the breakup, Levin had perhaps regretted "some particular neglect of the call of passion." Yet once again she warmly approved her heroine's refusal to pursue her retreating lover:

Rahel was one of the ever-increasing class of women who no doubt have their share of sensuousness but do not try to win the man by means of this, desiring rather that sensuous unity shall be a result of the combined flame of two souls. Men, on the other hand, feel more attracted, and believe themselves more loved, by those women who by the power of their own sensuousness awake that of the man, and thus, if they themselves possess a soul, by degrees win his soul also.[44]

Clearly, if there were two kinds of women but only one kind of man, women like Levin were destined to loneliness. The only hope was that there might be, after all, two kinds of men. What was wanted was not the male virgin of the friends of Morality or Björnson's *The Glove*, for "sensuousness" and "erotic attraction" were not negotiable. But passion was to be result, not cause, "the surf in a sea of devotion and fidelity."

That this was for Key an issue of a felt psychological, not abstract, moral urgency, she had already displayed in discussing her heroine's attachment to a woman friend, Pauline Wiesel. Wiesel, first known to Levin as the wife of an acquaintance, had left her husband, with Levin's blessing, to become the mistress of Prince Louis Ferdinand of Prussia; after leaving the prince, she embarked upon a life of free love, eventually locating in Paris. Key's summary of the two women's friendship was accepting, even lyrical. Wiesel, Key wrote, was "pagan" and "Hellenic"—free, that is, of Christian Europe's perennial repression—and Levin had seen this:

Pauline Wiesel . . . was and remained Rahel's dearest woman friend on account of the complete and naive frankness with which she lived . . . When Pauline left her husband . . . Rahel gave her complete approval. . . . As the mistress of Prince Louis Ferdinand, and of many others, Pauline showed such inconstancy in her love, combined with such innocence, such ease of conscience, and such kindness, that she appeared like a Philene brought to life . . . Pauline's Greek, or childlike, or godlike, naiveté in the question of love's freedom . . . was as unlike Rahel's own conduct of life as possible. But Pauline, in Rahel's opinion, had thus led a more fully human existence than Rahel herself.[45]

In Levin's imagination, Pauline figured as "experimental" as well as "warlike," living according to a " 'light-hearted . . . nature.' " It would appear then that, while "purity and truth" had restrained Levin from pursuing d'Urquijo, her disappointed hopes had not been only spiritual.

With Karl August Varnhagen, engagement did finally lead to marriage. He was twenty-nine, Levin forty-three. They had known each other for six years. This marriage lasted the rest of her life. As Frau Varnhagen she accompanied her husband to a minor diplomatic post at the court of Baden in Karlsruhe; then, in 1819, after a change in government, they returned to Berlin, where she and her husband "formed the center of the Goethe cult" in another salon.

What was special about this marriage? As Key analyzed it, Levin got from Karl Varnhagen "the only love the modern woman wants"—love not for the fresh bloom of her beauty but for her "fully developed, gifted individuality." Not all—or many—men were capable of this, but Varnhagen was one, "rare then as now . . . to whom psychological interest is the greatest intellectual passion . . . in whom mental receptivity is greater than creative power . . . those who love the feminine *personality.*" So she was loved. But did she love him? "It is quite clear that Rahel was not in love with Varnhagen in the truest meaning of the term, that his *personality* did not fill her with the same transports as hers did him."[46] This was plausible, for as a young man lacking notable creative talents, Varnhagen could not have been as interesting a personality to her, either in prospect or in reality, as she to him. Then did some "erotic appeal," some "sensuousness" compensate? Apparently not. As Key had noted, her heroine's peak of sensuousness had been reached at thirty. At thirty-seven erotic appeal might still have exerted strong force, but the postponement of the marriage another six years suggests absence of utter urgency.

Key was aware of the puzzle. She noted that one of Rahel Varnhagen's salon friends, the writer Jean Paul, had once declared that, considering her real nature and calling, Rahel Levin ought not to have married at all. The ideological and spiritual point Key appreciated well enough. For truly free persons, the "true" marriage of true love did not require the binding of public, legal marriage. But she disputed Jean Paul's view on another ground: "if Jean Paul intended his words . . . absolutely, he was as much mistaken about her inmost nature as her most malevolent censurers, for thereby he denied her children." Key had not yet embraced the doctrine later prevalent in Sweden, that unmarried mothers were the equal of married mothers in law, rights, and official esteem. But her logic seemed clear; there was apparently no other reason than children for Levin to have married. Such logic fitted the views of the most formidable Swedish commentator on the marriage problem, Strindberg, who saw in children more than in anything else the only plausible basis for stable marriage. Then had Levin married Varnhagen in order to have children? The childlessness of the union hardly proves absence of intent, yet Key had no real evidence of even appealing lines of speculation to offer. That Frau Varnhagen found "compensation" for her childlessness in the small daughter of a niece was speculation that could as easily seem to prove the opposite. Key had to content herself with a perception accessible perhaps only to the intuitive biographer:

Rahel in her inmost soul was a motherly figure. Though herself deprived of true motherly affection, she says the most beautiful things of what motherhood ought to be. Motherliness forms an essential part of her love, and she sums up her nature in the words, "I am a mother without children."[47]

Nowhere more clearly had the biographer revealed why she was writing about this biographee.

Another biographer of Varnhagen, writing twenty-five years later, told a different story. When, in 1933, twenty-seven-year-old Hannah Arendt, student of Heidegger, Bultman, Husserl, and Jaspers, fled Hitler's Berlin, she carried in her luggage the nearly completed manuscript of her own study of her fellow Berliner and fellow Jew. Like Key, Arendt saw in Rahel Levin a person trying to be a "beautiful soul," the kind of vividly defined individuality that Goethe, having met her briefly once, had said she was. But, said Arendt, Levin found herself "in a situation . . . an unfortunate situation," specifically, "as a Jew" to whom the world attributed "what it considered to be Jewish qualities." But Levin had never had any particular Jewish training at all. "In those days Jews in Berlin could grow up like the children of savage tribes. Rahel was one of these. She learned nothing, neither her own history nor that of the country in which her family dwelt." Arendt argued that Levin's wish "to escape from Judaism" entailed a deadly cost. It was this wish that explained her marriage. Receiving baptism, becoming a Christian, from being Fräulein Levin becoming Frau Varnhagen von Ense, she was seeking "social existence," "security," and "established position in the bourgeois world," "a morsel of happiness." Even granting the possibility of assimilation, this could only entail the cost that an anti-Semitic society, an anti-Semitic "bourgeois world," would exact, that is, self-hatred. Arendt thought Rahel Varnhagen's marriage founded on quicksand, and Varnhagen herself emblematic of the kind of intellectual—like Goethe—who believed that intellectuals and artists could somehow make peace with society, power, and privilege. Arendt could hardly argue that Levin ought to have affirmed her Jewishness, for she had none to affirm. Instead, she should have "fit her private ill luck into a scheme of general social relationships . . . [should have ventured] into criticism of the society, or even into solidarity with those who for other reasons were likewise excluded from the ranks of the privileged." She should have joined "those who like herself had not arrived . . . who like herself were dependent upon some sort of future which would be more favorable to them." She should have identified herself with other "pariahs and schlemiels."[48]

With her access to the manuscript division of the Prussian State Archives, where she worked in the rich Varnhagen Collection, reading letters Key had known nothing about, to and from Varnhagen, Friedrich Gentz, Pauline Wiesel, and many others, Arendt can easily be judged the more credible biographer. In finding the Varnhagens' marriage pathetic rather than admirable, she could quote Varnhagen herself in evidence: "I should really like to present myself as just as old as I am; I cannot do that . . . because I have a young husband who loves me dearly. There is nothing more comical." As for Varnhagen himself, and his devotion after her death to the cult of his own wife: "No native dignity warned him against the preposterousness of making himself the prophet of a woman. No reticence restrained him from telling all."[49]

Yet Key had tried to do something Arendt simply finessed. She tried to describe marriage in terms of the ideal of personality, of being a beautiful soul, which Arendt agreed Levin had been guided by. Arendt could find no explanation different from Key's for Levin's failure to marry one of her earlier fiancés. Each would have served just as well as Karl Varnhagen to "escape Judaism," but Rahel Levin had not been willing to disguise her personality, dissimulate, and manipulate. It was on the basis of this ultimate integrity, which Arendt refused to credit, that Key proceeded to construct her idea of a "new European marriage."

In spite of Strindberg, Weininger, and other despisers of women, our time has witnessed rapid increase in man's appreciation of woman's personality. One among many signs of this is that marriages and love affairs between younger men and women who are a few or several years older than themselves, are becoming more and more numerous in our time.[50]

As evidence, not from "our time" but from earlier times, Key noted Mlle. Lespinasse's ardent Spanish lover, ten years younger; Mme. de Stael's young Italian, Rocca, twenty years younger; George Sand's younger lovers; Elizabeth Barrett Browning's Robert, years younger. Of all these, Rahel Varnhagen had been the real pioneer, most fully bringing out the spiritual logic of such a relationship.

Just why this new European love should be emerging, Key did not make clear. Why were there more young men like Karl Varnhagen to whom "young girls appear too undeveloped or indeterminate or insignificant," whereas, "in women of a maturer age" such young men found "the completed personal character, the complicated life of the soul, intensified by experience, the refinement of sensation, the many-sided culture, which to them form the greatest attraction in a feminine being"?

She did not say. But it was perhaps possible to comprehend the other side of the question: "[Owing] to the richer, freer life they are able to lead, [women in our time] preserve both their outward and inward youthfulness better than formerly." If this were true, women would be freed of perhaps the deepest of their anxieties, that, by waiting to marry until they were mature, and thus able to avoid transferring their dependency as daughters into dependency as wives, they were sacrificing their strongest card in the marriage market, their youthful physical promise.

That the issue of physical gratification remained at the heart of the "new European marriage" Key strongly implied in the most interesting example she cited, George Eliot. Eliot's "marriage of conscience" with her otherwise married lover, G. H. Lewes, had not, Key said, "according to my informant," been founded upon "true erotic feeling on *his* part." Eliot "had never herself been the object of a great emotion, an emotion capable of extravagant acts—in other words, the emotion every true woman desires to have met with before she dies." It was this emotion that underwrote Eliot's affair with a man "thirty years younger," John Walter Cross, whom she married for the last seven months of her life. (Actually, Cross was only twenty years younger.) Whether George Eliot, at sixty, really did quite illustrate Key's thesis about the growing youthfulness of older women mattered less than the registration of a hope. Whether the "masculine majority," admittedly still attracted to undeveloped, indeterminate, insignificant young girls, ever would decline to a minority was less important than the direction things were going: "[Love] affairs and marriages between men of [Varnhagen's] type, *but also of other types*, and women older than themselves are becoming more and more usual. No sign of the times is more significant of the evolution of man's love than this."

To this sentimental reading of Rahel Varnhagen's marriage, Arendt opposed a merely cautionary one. After all, as Arendt herself finally had to agree, Rahel Varnhagen did not finally surrender her personality to "social existence." At her salon, near the end of her life, with a new friend, Heinrich Heine, she took sardonic occasion to reidentify herself in her "unfortunate situation" as a Jew. But Arendt had uncovered far more compelling evidence of Varnhagen's integrity, in certain letters the purport of which Key had only been able to intuit. Practically on the day following her marriage, Varnhagen had resurrected her old friendship with Pauline Wiesel. She instructed husband Karl himself to locate Wiesel, which he did, in Paris, still indomitable, late in her forties, still free, though poor and isolated, "in a snarl of financial disasters, debts, and true or invented love affairs."[51] Soon, maliciously, Wiesel employed her matured wiles on Karl Varnhagen himself. He recoiled and complained to his wife. Delighted, Rahel Varnhagen only laughed. In effect Rahel Varnhagen had done exactly what Arendt wished she had done, identify with a "pariah." The Jewishness that she first appeared to want to escape but then reavowed may have been a kind of perennial misfortune in European history, but the misfortune of being a woman cut deeper than that of being a Jew, as Key saw, in recognizing Wiesel's—and Varnhagen's—"warlike" nature to be identical with her Hellenic freedom from European, that is, Christian history.

In reaffirming her sisterhood with Wiesel, Varnhagen affirmed not just "personality" and "beauty of soul" but female flesh. Wiesel's promiscuity—innocent, experimental, guiltless, and light-hearted as well as warlike—fulfilled not just her spirit but also her body, face, sex. A physical beauty in an immediate unmistakable sense, recognizable beyond mere taste, Wiesel possessed the female sexuality that had always been recognized as power. In her own insistent, uninflected approval of her, Varnhagen was thus affirming woman's sexual attractiveness as a power to be used by herself for herself in her own interests. Physical sexual beauty was a resource for women's freedom. Just as the slurs and slanders of anti-Semites showed that "free" Jews would not be accepted by conventional Christians, so did the scandal of Wiesel's life show that free women would not be accepted by conventional men. But to imagine that women might buy freedom by disavowing their sexual beauty was as misguided as imagining that Jews might do so by disavowing Jewishness. Levin had had no Jewishness to avow, but she did have her womanhood, her sex, her sexuality, and she avowed it.

Key knew this. Even though she did not know how dramatically Varnhagen had reasserted it after her marriage, she recognized her sexual self-affirmation. She could not locate this affirmation in terms of a specific historical tradition except in a diffuse hope for a "new European marriage." Nor could she decisively link this affirmation of sexuality to motherhood. But even so, she affirmed, in Varnhagen's affirmation of Wiesel, a kind of leverage on history, "outside" history, that offered women a point of reference for struggling for freedom within history, however hard-pressed they might be by the enemies of freedom. Varnhagen, she said, enlisted herself, alongside Wiesel, as the embodiment of "great, dark, bright Nature, who produces life after life." Because Pauline Wiesel—an "Ulla Winblad"—did this, Varnhagen said, "therefore she acts for me."[51]

By no means did this clarify links between sexuality and motherhood. It did not, for instance, declare that sexuality's fullest issue must be motherhood. Nor did it clarify the question, whether marriage was to be instituted as a middle term between sexuality and motherhood only to welcome children. But Key was on solid ground. No theory of history, of Geijer and heroic Sweden or of Bremer and maternal Sweden, had assimilated the presence in history of "great, dark, bright" Nature. Almqvist's individualistic utopia had evaded it. Only Strindberg had contemplated it, without resolution. To wait for nature to be wholly rationalized and reduced to history before granting freedom to women was to perpetuate their oppression. Nature's great, dark, bright opacity might be frightening, but men had ceased to have credibility in claiming to protect women against it. It was a pity that Strindberg himself had not taken up this banner.

Key died in 1924. During her last fifteen years she wrote little, published less. As the first generation of feminist leaders passed from the stage, younger figures moved forward, writers like her friend and follower, Elin Wägner, professionals founding the service and communal and welfare organizations that would begin to define a new social complex by the 1920s. They visited her at her summer home, for the counsel of a benign aunt, as a tie with an ancestral past, for good conscience in their battles for the future. As her vision of motherhood came gradually to seem simple social good sense, anticipating the day of the Social Democrats' Parliament of Mothers and Children, the radical edges of her sexual hopes at sixty tended to blur. The facts of her own long ordeal of love for Urban von Feilitzen remained unknown, and the tough-mindedness with which she continued to reflect upon her own experience muted. The mirror she had held up to herself in Rahel Varnhagen few looked into. But Key's very prestige testified to the witness she bore about Swedish history. In Sweden motherhood would not necessarily be a conservative status, serving the past. Swedish motherhood could be radical. But would it?

Modern Sexual Abundance versus the Individual

In the old villages of the immemorial Sweden of the common fields, cut up into private strips and scraps and slices, premodern Sweden was being rationalized away as late as the mid-nineteenth century. Here, as the poet Vilhelm Moberg pointed out, in his history intended to illuminate the "people" neglected in the traditional focus upon the heroics of kings, life could be oppressively close for the young. How much real sexual choice had young men and women had? Many of the young men wandered the roads, taking work in iron bogs or timber camps scores of miles away. This only heightened the anxieties surrounding the prospect of marriage. The solution had always been to let sex itself have its way. When a baby was started, time enough to marry.

But this marriage was contracted as much on the basis of impersonal drive as upon any discovery of abiding personal traits and affinities. Modern Swedes aspired to more than village values. The claustrophobia of the village was to be broken in favor of freer and wider association. At the same time the old permissiveness was not to be sacrificed. The temptation of Fredrika Bremer, to respond to the threats posed by the individualization of sexuality by repressing it, was not modern. On the other hand, merely perpetuating the old village ways would not suffice. That would be to let Sweden imitate only Iceland, homey and down-to-earth while exhibiting the world's highest rate of pregnant brides, fascinating to visiting social scientists until they grasped its essence as a kind of ancient cousinship engaged mostly in fishing. Iceland was about as liberated and paradisiacal as a provincial health spa.[53] Swedes could hope for more.

In 1933 a Riksförbundet för Sexuell Upplysning (National Association for Sex Education: RFSU) was founded with government approval. By 1938 the RFSU had begun introducing its voluntary sex education program in the schools. By 1946 it was selling contraceptives by vending machines as well as by mail and in clinics, and in another ten years had expanded its sex education to all grades and on a compulsory basis. Soon various Swedish writers were writing, more or less to order, a shelf-ful of stories that many would think pornographic, a kind of extension course for adults in sex education. These were published in volumes entitled *Love 1, Love 2, Love 3*. But they were about sex, not love.

Presumably the program of the RFSU represented the triumph, at last, of the outlook of Knut Wicksell over that of the Friends of Morality—the triumph of the Myrdals' determination that, whatever the population crisis might mean, it must be resolved only with full freedom of choice for the individual, man and woman. This view was affirmed by some foreign observers, the English visitor Roland Huntford for one:

The RFSU is a corporate organization closely related to the Labour movement. ... Almost single-handed, [it] has made Sweden contraceptive-conscious, and propagated a progressive, rational attitude toward sex. . . . [It] has done a great deal to eradicate the sexual obscurantism that once belonged to Sweden.[54]

But the idea of Swedes having been "obscurantist" about sex had difficulties, despite the Friends of Morality and *Hertha*. The practices of the ancient villages recalled by Moberg had been a kind of sexual straightforwardness. Swedish common life had been relatively free of the double standard haunting Anglo-Saxondom. The "thousand years of permissiveness" identified by Richard Tomassen had had nothing to do with some modern ideology of liberated enlightenment.[55] Ellen

Key had hoped that "modern," that is, urban, Swedish youth would find it possible to carry on the practices of their country cousins, obviously assuming that these country ways had been free of the obscurantism and Victorianism—named in Sweden after King Oscar—that she too deplored.

But in that case, had Strindberg been simply a bizarre exception in his sense of the impossibility of marriage, his sense of the war between the sexes, his sense that only irrationality supported love? As had nineteenth-century, so too did twentieth-century observers comment on some strain between the sexes in Sweden. An American psychiatrist, Herbert Hendin, studying Danes, Norwegians, and Swedes from suicide protocols, felt that Swedes were suffering from a kind of distance from their own feelings. Another English visitor, Sean Connery, found Hendin persuasive and offered views of his own: "[A] strange tension exists between male and female in Swedish life. Theirs is a nervous, not entirely happy, coexistence." The English poet and longtime resident in Sweden, Paul Britten Austin, married to a Swede, agreed: "No one can deny . . . the 'peculiar tension . . . ' All the evidence points to it." And Tomassen, even while favoring Swedish freedom from double-standard hypocrisy, concurred:

There is general agreement on the description of Swedes as stolid and stiff, shy or reserved, formal and conventional, inhibited—even dull, nonexpressive, more interested in things than people, and so forth . . . virtually polar opposites of the Italians as portrayed, for example, by Luigi Barzini and certain Italian film makers.[56]

Movies of Ingmar Bergman could, by the time of the great sex-role debate, have been cited to the same point.

But such observers were not only substantiating Strindberg's sense of marriage as, if not quite war, then a scene of cries and whispers, of chill, formality, distance, at the very least of "tension"; they also seemed to substantiate Strindberg's sense of where the advantage lay. That "the men proved to be in much poorer contact with their own feelings than were the women" was Hendin's clinically based assessment. Tomassen, after offering his comparison of Swedish with Italian characteristics, then added: "Yet what has impressed me and a number of other observers is that Swedish women approximate these labels appreciably less than do the men."[57] These paralleled the traveler Robert Colton's impression in the previous century that there was a kind of mismatch between Swedish boys and girls.[58] Paul Britten Austin too assigned the "peculiar tension" to the males, "empty . . . Vikings . . . [priding] themselves on their lack of insight into female psychology . . . [expecting women] erotically to rescue them . . . from the vacuum they live in."[59]

A kinder, more historical approach to this phenomenon was available. What if marriage was, as Strindberg had evidently discovered, more frustrating than fulfilling? Despite its poverty, despite its government by archaic elites, old village Sweden with wicked Stockholm as its capital had made it possible for the question to be asked. Axel Johan Uppvall had formulated the thesis in standard psychoanalytic terms in his effort to comprehend Strindberg's genius:

Through marriage man renounces his incestuous and polygamous instincts in favor of a single woman. Consciously man does this willingly, we are told, but unconsciously bitter feelings are born because of this sacrifice of personality, the shackling, smothering and partial stamping out of the ego.[60]

Should this be so, then Ellen Key's belief that women were erotically different from men had much to do with what the psychiatrists were finding. Women needed neither marriage nor the kind of civic status and power Alva Myrdal and Eva Moberg urged upon them. Like Hertha, like Rahel Varnhagen, like Key herself, women were motherly, and now the Social Democratic welfare state was supporting that motherliness with or without marriage, with or without power.

At least one visitor to modern Sweden, the Englishman Roland Huntford, was suspicious of the RFSU, the sex ed programs, the sex propaganda:

[It] has promoted a view of sex as the escape valve of society. . . . As social and political regimentation has progressed, so has sexual liberation. . . . The Swede is extraordinarily proud of this one freedom. . . . But it is not permissiveness; it is licensed release. The State, anxious to control the citizen absolutely, has taken sexuality in hand . . . [and] encouraged [Swedes] to release their political frustrations through the reproductive procedure . . . decently, hygienically and properly.[61]

But it was easier to see the Social Democrats' policy as simple realism: there was nothing it could do to suppress popular awakening to the costs of marriage. There was nothing it could do to promote ways and means for overcoming them. That would have to be the business of individuals, of art, of theater, of Strindbergs. No government had ever produced a Strindberg. It would be fatal politically to try to oppose what Swedes had already learned, freedom from thinking that marriage itself was the price for sex. That Swedes had not discovered an alternative to marriage, even Strindberg seemed to show. Nothing in the new welfare state seemed to render "un-Swedish" Ingmar Bergman's portrayal of distance, melancholy, despair, and silence.

That the new official permissiveness in sexuality was not itself a cure for despair and solitude, a much cruder, more commercial movie than Bergman ever made seemed to show. Its heroine was indeed erotically different from her boyfriend. Vilgot Sjöman's *I Am Curious (Yellow)* (1968) won a kind of notoriety neither of its two obvious constituents would seem to have earned, separately or together. Sjöman was already well known to Swedish audiences for his radical, anarchist, humanist outlook, contemptuous of bourgeois and Social Democratic hypocrisies alike. While not exactly standard fare, his movies' abundant nudity and representations of sexual intercourse were hardly unknown either. Even the mixture may not have been unduly provocative: in *I Am Curious (Yellow)* the lovers' copulation on the balustrade of the royal palace was no doubt intended as political, but not likely to provoke charges of blasphemy such as had been hurled at Strindberg. Moreover, the heroine, Lena Nyman, a girl reporter and drama student, was hardly unusual in behaving as an equal in sex. In her father, who had gone to fight in, but then abandoned, the Spanish Civil War, she saw a political coward. She certainly did not look for a hero in her boyfriend. She undertook political action on her own, throwing empty beer bottles at Francisco Franco's portrait, criticizing labor movement antifeminism, criticizing class society in Sweden. She was a kind of Hertha updated: "In every little village or town she passes through during her ride through Sweden Lena posts messages on trees and walls."[62] Most of all, she asserts an ultimate independence by moving out of the apartment of the director who was making the movie-within-the movie.

But Lena could hardly have pleased Alva Myrdal and Eva Moberg, for what Lena wanted most was love. She wanted not to despise but love her father, to love not mistrust her countrymen, to love and be loved by her boyfriend. But this did not work out. The route offered by the permissive new welfare state was sex suitably sanctified in a new "Ten Commandments," formulated by a real Swedish author, Lars Gyllensten, presumably for the instruction of real Swedish people. Lena studied them and tried to obey:

Third Commandment: Thou shalt reflect that comfort agrees as well with other people as it does with you.
Fourth Commandment: Thou shalt take care of those who cannot take care of themselves.
Sixth Commandment: Thou shalt not spread venereal disease, or bring unwanted children into the world, or expose other people to sexual violence. Also, you should play your part in keeping the birthrate as low as possible, because altogether too many children are born. For the rest, you may devote yourself freely to sexual intercourse, masturbation, pornography, and such other good things of this kind as your animal nature, in its grace, may cause you to desire.[63]

Lena could not really live up to this new free church. Her experiences with boys had not been exercises of grace:

> Lena (sighing): I slept with them because they want to sleep with me, so that they could have orgasms. I couldn't believe that anybody could like me the way I look: with drooping breasts, big belly, fat.[64]

The chief victim of Swedish uproar over the movie proved to be, not its maker, Sjöman, as one might expect, but one of its presumably innocent players, the actress Lena Nyman herself, who had played "Lena Nyman" in the film. Of course the actress Nyman's innocence was at least inflected by her willingness to play the role she did. But Swedes were hardly unused to actresses' naked bodies in their movies, usually displayed with the implication, and often simulation, of sexual use. Yet there was disapproval of Nyman's body, a disapproval separable from any question of what it had been used for. *Aftonbladet's* film critic called it an "unintelligent" body. What did this mean? Presumably, that a nude body was expected to have more than simple material reality, but also symbolic reality, symbolic meaning. It was supposed to mean and not just be. What was it about Nyman's body that denied this symbolic, spiritual meaning? It was fat. Obloquy was such that the actress Lena Nyman retired from the movies. She retreated to theater, where, in the course of the next few years, she clearly demonstrated what the movie itself could have told those willing to be told, that she was in fact a good actress, serious, gifted, attractive.[65]

Why should Swedes have cared whether Lena Nyman—or "Lena Nyman"—was fat or not? Swedes did care. "Obesity is almost nonexistent in Sweden" But its nonexistence was no accident of geography or genes: "*Fetma* (obesity) is a common and anxious newspaper topic." Swedes got their figures by running, skating, swimming, skiing, tennis, and of course by Swedish Dr. Ling's nineteenth-century invention, gymnastics. They worked for their figures. The movie itself had raised the issue with the heroine's mention of drooping breasts, big belly, fat.

It is impossible to be sure what director Sjöman's exact intentions were. If he had meant to plead the rights of an "erotic minority" (to use a new expression generated from the new sex religiousness), in this case the minority of the fat and unlovely, he presumably required a truly fat, unlovely actress. But to any open-eyed audience, actress Lena Nyman was not in fact fat and certainly not unlovely and unattractive. Nevertheless Nyman's body, copiously displayed so there was no mistake, certainly was sturdy, square, full, solid, stocky, not at all Ulla Winblad, lithe gymnast, fantasy partner for midsummer midnights. She was the unmistakable embodiment of old solid peasant Sweden, not the Sweden of modern design.

In Sjöman's movie the point was made at once in physical and class terms. Aware of her boyfriend Borge's sexual philanderings, Lena confronted him "as if conducting a public-opinion poll. " What color hair does her rival Madeleine have, "dark or blond?" "Dark." What social class? "Upper." "Fat or thin?" (Lena stuck her thumb in her mouth.) Borge: "Very thin." In short, Lena was quite incapable of rescuing "empty Vikings" from their "vacuum." For this, Madeleines were necessary. The Swedish audience, indifferent to the fixation of American and other darker peoples on blond beauty as normative, could see clearly that Lena's nudity rescued no man.

I Am Curious (Yellow) thus struck directly at the heart of modern Sweden's favorite social myth, egalitarianism, as no movie of Ingmar Bergman ever did. Bergman's movies, far more complex in their evocation of existential voids and inner vastnesses threatening all loves and marriages, nevertheless exuded a sensibility, if not that of aristocracies let alone of elites, then of realized individualities evolved beyond slavery to social myths. Sjöman explicitly declared his air of portraying a kind of girl who was "sort of unconscious of what is going on inside her," and a victim not of her body but of the modern Swedes' determination to have only a certain kind of body. In their prosperity, modern Swedes were rapidly gaining the reputation of being one of Europe's best-dressed people, a clear perpetuation of the old preoccupation with titles and formal manners. An "intelligent" body was what a well-dressed body looked like undressed.

Sjöman's movie thus renewed Strindberg's basic thesis that feminism, that is, the politics of egalitarian liberalism, had little to offer marriage and love. Whether Strindberg's sardonic hope, that in its irrationality love might still bind men and women together, was implied in the movie heroine's wrenching free from the movie itself, could only be debated. But in Swedish imagination there had once been a simple heroine, neither tall nor dark nor upper class, who had offered hope. A movie about Sara Videbeck in 1968 would no doubt have seemed but sentimentality. But so also, by 1980, did the hopes of the sex reformers. We had thought, said Hans Nestius, one of the RFSU leaders who had got the Law on Offending Decency and Morality repealed in 1971, that "serious artists, writers, photographers would produce warm, sensual depictions of the sexual act and drive out the shoddy, bad quality porn"; instead, pornography in Sweden had become worse, emphasizing sadism, exploiting children.[66] Sexual crimes against women had grown more numerous, prostitution had increased. Disappointed, horrified, disillusioned, Nestius now found himself trying to eliminate violent and child pornography and put the porn moguls out of business.

Then what about starting over at the beginning? In Marianne Fredricsson's novel of 1980, *Evas bok* (Eve's Book), the heroine, Adam's mate, appalled at the carnage around her of Cain murdering Abel, of brothers in conflict, of men at war, of manhood, turned herself square about and headed back for Eden, for the Garden from which only a terrible mistake had evicted her, the mistake of following Adam, the mistake of womankind's descent under the leadership of men. This time, paradise regained, Eve would not listen to false promises.[67]

Beyond the Folk

The linkages between Swedish political economy and literature were at once variable and loose. Swedish backwardness did not inhibit the most sophisticated sexual utopianism as in Almqvist, or the most sophisticated rendering of compensation and reconciliation as in Bellmann. The transformation of Sweden from political and economic backwardness into modernized affluence and stability did not generate optimism countering the pessimistic realism of Strindberg or the repressive utopianism of Bremer. As recorded in the movies of Ingmar Bergman, one might recur to the formula: the better things got, the worse they got, so far as satisfying harmony between the sexes was concerned. Whether Swedish literature, movies included, had been able, precisely through the achievements of social democracy, to more closely approach the individual, existential level of reality, a level of reality obscured by the political economy of less fortunate nations, is quite another question. Modern psychiatry, encouraged by Almqvist, Bremer, Strindberg, and Bergman alike, might argue that Swedish sexual melancholy derived from Swedish parental mores, with special attention to the mother. Vilhelm Moberg's notion that the greatest Swede of them all was St. Birgitta would confirm the case, for Birgitta stood forth as a particular kind of mother, anxious over the delinquencies of her folk, corrective, censorious, not capacious, not easeful, not forgiving. Surely, however, stretching such generalities to cover a whole culture is to deal in thin goods indeed.

It would be better, perhaps, to speculate that the record of Swedish culture suggests that the theme of child-rearing, of parents and children, of growing up, constitutes a kind of eternal substratum for any people to explore, more basic than that of marriage, love, and the engagements of adults of one sex with adults of another. Marriage and love were far more obviously "historical." Both could be dispensed with and life go on. Both could be linked tightly to economic and political manipulations. Parenthood and growing up too, of course, for all their roots in eternal nature, abided in history, but the direct contemplation of both far more surely challenged clear observation, for every observer brought to it the deepest kind of personal experience, much of it painful. Was Strindberg peculiarly Swedish? His plunge into the childhood depths of consciousness, his association of marriage and sexuality with the appetites of childhood, his refusal to tolerate the myths of Swedish togetherness and serenity, had required immense resources of individuality. Could such resources be assembled just anywhere? Italy's greatest analytic intellect, Gramsci, found himself tugged in the other direction, toward visions of Italian sexual serenity. If others—a Pirandello, a Svevo, a Moravia—might have become Italian Strindbergs, a sense of the hopelessness of politics drew them off. Fellini's Strindberg-like impulses persistently ended up transcended in myths of "eternal" creativity. In the Soviet Union, of course, politics ruled, and Soviet politics was anti-Strindbergian. Socialist realism practiced the art of sentimentality as to marriage, love, sex, parenthood, and growing up altogether. The Soviet educational system grasped each child firmly for the purpose of the "whole" development of the personality, by means of its total socialization into citizenship—Carl Larsson's Sweden wrought by Leviathan. In the United States, however, some of the autonomies of Swedish sexual imagination and the unimpeded realism of a Strindberg might be affordable, even on a mass basis, as well as by remarkable individuals.

13 Soviet Russia

Literature as Revolutionary Freedom:
Pilnyak, Gladkov, Kollontai

When revolution broke out in 1917, Russia had young poets of daz-zlingly self-conscious lyric force.[1] There was no way they could be put to the service of the revolution. They had one topic, the power of poetry itself, and they could sing only that. No one had harassed them before the revolution. Anna Akhmatova, twenty-eight in 1917, went on writing as she had, in shards and lancing lines of consciousness. By 1923 or so she had come under the ban of an emerging censorship. She had been married to a poet, Nikolai Gumilyov, and been shaken, although by then divorced, by his execution as a counterrevolutionary in 1921. She refused to consider exile, vowing to wait for the storm to pass. By then she had been matched by Marina Tsvetaeva, three years younger, as intense as Akhmatova in her considerations of poetry, of the life of a poet, and of poets' need for love. Tsvetaeva denounced the revolution and left in 1922 to join her exile husband. Vladimir Mayakovsky, twenty-four in 1917, did turn with eager energy to sing the revolution and its works; by 1930 he was ready for suicide. Boris Pasternak, twenty-seven in 1917, also tried, but his efforts to write on the sweeping epic scale prescribed by ideologues for the sweeping events of the epoch fell short, betraying lack of conviction. Although, as *Doctor Zhivago* would one day prove, Pasternak was not only a poet, in that vast novel too Paster-nak would show that the positive hero of right-thinking Soviet literature found no place in his soul. Like Akhmatova and Tsvetaeva, Osip Man-delstam, twenty-six in 1917, could not even try to write less than his shattering lyrics; he fell silent. The young Russian poets were offering the tools for individuality; they were not accepted. The link between liberating poetry and liberating revolution was missed; revolution grew less liberatory in consequence.

Yet Russian writers of force and resource continued to write through the 1920s and into the 1930s before the glaciation of socialist realism ground them down. In Boris Pilnyak's kaleidoscopic panorama of 1919, *The Naked Year*, published in 1922, place was found for private emotion. While still a student in Moscow, Natalia Ordynina, a young doctor, had undergone "a first, foolish love." She had vowed never to love again, but to devote herself solely to her work. Such vows would be taken by thousands in the next few years and were often hailed as typical of the new Russian girl, the new Bolshevik woman. Once the ambiguities and ambivalences of the NEP period were over, and Stalin's First Five Year Plan had begun, many government writers returned to the theme with even greater intensity: work first, everything for work, then maybe something for love.

This outlook left many problems unstated. Forsaking love was one thing, for the great emotions could indeed interfere with work. But did forsaking love mean sexual abstinence? Did it mean forsaking marriage? Perhaps there could be socialist marriage, marriage of two comrades, each of whom understood that both were committed first to duty, task, party, socialism.

Despite her vow, Natalia Ordynina succumbed again, not so much to love as such but to a feeling generated in the revolution itself, "these days in which life had to be snatched, or it was gone." With her new love for an archaeologist named Baudek, she "again felt sharply that for her the Revolution was bound up with happiness, a turbulent happiness, the happiness mingled with gnawing sorrow, wormwood sorrow." For Ordynina, no Bolshevik herself, no Marxist, no ideologist, the fusion of work and love in the revolution seized her with an existential grip. Theory, Leninist or otherwise, would not loosen it. "Each still uncertain touch of this new lover . . . burned her with the water of life." Then Baudek simply disappeared, swept away in the revolutionary winds.

A local Bolshevik, Arkhip Arkhipov, energetically reopening mines and shops and mills, now offered his hand. Should she marry the revolution?

"Yes, very well," she said, after a pause. "But I'm not a virgin. . . . Children, yes, that's the one thing. I don't love you like that—well, you know."

Arkhipov raised his head; looked into Natalia Eugraphovna's eyes—they were transparent and calm. Arkhipov clumsily brought Natalia Eugraphovna's hand to his lips and quietly kissed it. "Well, well. As for that—I'm not out for foolery—I want a partner." "It'll all be cold—no cosiness about it, Arkhipov." "What's that? Cosiness?" (He had never known the word. . . .)

But Arkhipov was no man of steel.

Moonlight in the study . . . moon rays on the linoleum. Arkhipov,—without intending to—touched Natalia Eugraphovna . . . and tenderly, womanly-softly she pressed up to Arkhipov, and whispered, "My dear, my own."

Arkhipov could not find words. . . .

Natalia, motionless, by her study window. . . .

"Without love—yet loving. Oh, but there will be cosiness, and children, and— we shall do our task! . . . My dear, my own one, mine." No hypocrisy; no pain

. . . Arkhipov . . . went . . . to his own room—in Galkin's little dictionary of foreign words used in Russian he tried, without succeeding, to find that word which, though it was a Russian word, he had never heard before: "cosiness."— "My dear, my own one, mine!"[2]

Pilnyak was no party writer, simply the latest in the great sequence of prose masters compelled by Russia itself, adapting his means to its transformation. Pilnyak sustained the investigation of psychological intimacy in the midst of mighty historical forces practiced by Tolstoy. Pilnyak's first commitment was to his writing, to his novel.

Fyodor Gladkov, on the other hand, wanted his writing to serve. As he composed his finest novel, the best-selling *Cement* of 1924, he imagined that he was, in accord with emerging new doctrines of the day, composing an epic. In fact, *Cement* offered a striking picture of the revolution transforming love, sex, and marriage in the depths of personality. Its hero, Gleb Ivanovich Chumalov, would have satisfied Lenin's sternest demands for self-denying commitment to the cause. Returning after three years in the civil wars to his hometown, Novorossiisk, he immediately threw himself into a new task, restoring, against skepticism and bureaucratic opposition within the party itself, the town's shattered cement factory. A hero in war, he proceeded to become a hero on the now far more crucial front of production. But he was by no means to be rewarded with marital mutuality and harmony. When he got back home, Gleb found his wife Dasha transformed. During his years away she too had suffered, brutally, she too had been caught up in the violence of the revolution, and it had changed her. His first night back, he found that his little daughter was living in the Children's Home. Dasha herself, after one incredulous embrace, had to rush off to a committee meeting. Things grew more, not less tense as the days went by:

Gleb . . . lying on the bed . . . watched Dasha through half-open eyes. No, it was not the same Dasha, not the old Dasha—that one had died. This was a different one, with a sun-burned face and a stubborn chin. The red kerchief made her head look big and fiery. She got undressed by the table . . . not looking at him. Her face was exhausted and dour. . . . He put his arms around her, picked her up, burning like fire. She hugged him, but kissed him warily, her eyes full of alarm, huge and stern. And when he lunged at her, completely out of control, she snapped in a practical, angry voice: "Now wait a bit, hold on! Stop right there!"

Dasha refused to be merely woman, merely wife. She wanted to be recognized as a comrade, as a person: " 'How can you love me . . . when you don't understand me? I just can't. . . . I won't live the way I used to, like a half-wit. Half-witted obedience, nice little girl, that's not me.' " Dasha Chumalova tested her husband for his respect and love, for his freedom from jealousy, and when he failed, she accused him of being a "bad Communist." Yet Gleb Chumalov's motive in struggling to win her back had nothing to do with Communism:

She laughed gently . . . then suddenly asked in a roguish tone: "Well now, Gleb, supposing I had slept with Badin that night? How would you feel about that?"
    Gleb was surprised; her cruel joke had not hurt him. She was testing him—at a time when it was impossible not to be straight with her, when he would have to show whether he was a human being or an animal. The one thing he felt then was that Dasha had become more to him than just a wife, that his heart was awash with tenderness for her, as if he had found a new friend.

But despite this melting moment—"She was silent for a little while, sighed a time or two, then stirred in her bed, jumped up and quietly came to his bedside"—Gleb and Dasha remained unreconciled. Gleb's sensitivity told him of the extremity of his wife's transformation, and he sensed his inability to "accept her as she is." "She's got something that's all her own, and it drives me mad." So Dasha in return "could not accept him as he was—there was too much of her old husband in him still: an excessive craving for overt affection, racking jealousy and an enduring desire to nail her to hearth and home."

    Gladkov had not fabricated a new positive heroine, however, incarnating some ideal of Soviet life. Dasha's relations with her child puzzled Gleb, her friends, herself.

I love your Dasha very much, Gleb Ivanovich—but why has she left Nurka to stew in the orphan's home? I mean, I had Nurka here—she could have stayed with me. How can a woman live without children and without a husband? It's not her fault, mind you.

Something hard and ideological had intervened. "Your Nurka's a lovely little girl," the children's home director said. Nurka's mother did not smile. "Nurka's nothing special. They're all the same here. They're all lovely, remember?" "Oh, indeed, indeed! We're doing it all for our proletarian children." Wasting away, Nurka prompted her mother to nightmares, but she died still forsaken in the Krupskaya Children's Home.
    Dasha's relations with the local Bolshevik chief were murky, too. One of the men in leather coats—black leather, heavy eyebrows, shaven head—Badin, with his drive, his energy, his ruthlessness, was a womanizer. He had virtually raped the head of the local Women's Department, Polya Mechova. Had Dasha let herself be taken by him? Again overcome by his helplessness, her husband railed at the Bolshevik chief openly: "Gleb was panting. His heart stood still, swelled to fill his whole chest. . . . he brandished his fist and roared aloud, with a sense of tremendous satisfaction: "'Skirt chaser! Filthy great tom-cat!'" At

the same time, when Dasha discovered Gleb, "swept with silent tenderness," embracing Polya, her reaction was suspiciously bright:

[There] was only a momentary flash of fear in her eyes and a whitish film leaped up behind her lashes. Perhaps Gleb imagined it, because he was afraid and hopelessly flustered himself.
  "You're not jealous, are you, Dasha? Your Gleb's just a big kid. He's a marvelous lad, really, but about as stupid as they make them. . . ."
  Dasha grinned and moved toward the table. . . she began to rummage busily through her briefcase. "Comrade Mekhova . . . we've got the women's conference right on our tails—you hadn't forgotten, I hope? There's a meeting of the trade union council at five. You'll be giving a report. . . . Turn off the waterworks, my pet. Crying's so easy. . . . So you just get your heart back under control and keep your eyes peeled." Then she stared mischievously at Gleb. "You can continue your conversation with Polya now, Gleb love—I'm going."

Perhaps Bolshevism was not going to produce "cosiness" after all.

Of Dasha Chumalova's ultimate wishes even she may not have known. As a worker in the Women's Department, she was a chauvinist:

Dasha gave them a really moving speech that night: she told them that they, not the men, were active champions of enlightenment. . . . The door would open—they would become officials, administrators. Knowledge was . . . power. . . . The women clapped, feeling themselves bigger and better than they were at home, cleverer and richer than they were when tied to children and housework.

Such triumphalism was easier in words than in the heart. At first, when Gleb had gone to the Women's Department head, Polya Mechova, to complain about his wife, Mechova had only laughed: "She's neglecting her wifely duties? My heart bleeds. The Revolution's ruined our women. Dasha laughed too." But Polya's share, "wildly exhilarated," in shooting Cossacks and looting the bourgeoisie apparently went together with her submissions, "laughing and crying," to Chairman Badin. She reached out:

"I'm not going to the women's department, Gleb. Come up to my room instead and sit with me for a bit. If you're there I won't feel so rotten. . . . I just want to have the feeling that I'm not alone. Maybe you'll say something that'll sober me up. . . ."

Polya's divided heart undermined her. She was purged from the party by a touring committee of investigation. Dasha moved in with her. Gleb dropped in to see how they were getting on:

"I have to leave, Gleb—take a rest, pull myself together. Men can be fearful things, Gleb. As I see it now, there's a Badin in every one of you. . . . Go away, Gleb, please. . . . another time, another place. . . . Why didn't you give me what I needed when I needed it? Then perhaps none of this would have happened. . . ."[3]

In *Cement*, with Dasha and Polya living together in hostility to all men, the feminist impulse toward separation was unmistakable. Had the revolution, in sweeping away old gender-linked roles, also swept away the illusion of romantic love? The ideology of Marx, Bebel, Lenin, and the male revolutionaries had always held that the revolution would open the epoch of harmony between the sexes, founded on the natural and uncorrupted impulses of the organism. What if the reverse should prove true? Many women activists appeared to think so. "Until its official dissolution the [Women's Department] continued to harp on woman's exploitation, to fan resentment of old prejudices, and to encourage rivalry between the sexes rather than to stress greater labor productivity." Indeed, it was precisely this un-Bolshevik, feminist outlook that was most likely the prime reason why the Women's Department was dissolved.

That the impulse had begun to run deep was shown by the most important of the Bolshevik women, though one of the lesser writers, Alexandra Kollontai herself. As though realizing that the time had come to give up theoretical and polemical writing for language more revealing of the heart, Kollontai began writing short stories.[4] In "Thirty Two Pages" the heroine, a scientist, decides she must choose her work over marriage. But her choice is easy. In reckoning her accounts, she stigmatizes her husband: he does not understand her, listen to her, value her work, comprehend what it costs her. In "Sisters," a woman betrayed by her husband—a Bolshevik—finds relief from her jealousy in communion with the girl who has prostituted herself to him. In "Great Love," presumably drawing on her relationship with Maslov, Kollontai portrayed still another emotionally incompetent, inept, unimaginative husband. In "Vasilisa Malygina" the heroine, a Bolshevik, rejects her husband, also a Bolshevik, because of his emotional crudity and materialism. In all these stories Kollontai abandoned any pretence at Marxist analysis. The reason for the sufferings of women was not class but sex, not capitalists but men. Bolshevik men were no better than capitalist men.

Kollontai completed her literary testament in the story that made her notorious, "The Love of Three Generations." This story was not quite what Lenin and the moralists made it out to be. It was true that its heroine, a young revolutionary named Zhenya, had been promiscuous. It was true that Kollontai refused to compose some Bolshevik disapproval of her behavior: her promiscuity had been but a function of the times, those hectic years of civil war and war communism. But Zhenya was far from constituting some ideal type Kollontai meant to urge upon socialism. She plainly was no embodiment of the "winged eros" Kollontai had celebrated in her essay of that name.[5] Zhenya, with her drink-of-water approach to sex—hardly distinguishable from August Bebel's—could only have been eros "wingless." Then where was winged eros, supposedly that highest and purest fruit of the revolution, the salvation of womankind? Zhenya's mother, Olga, was a revolutionary, too, but of a different type. Olga had taken up the banner from her own mother, Zhenya's grandmother. Zhenya's grandmother had been one of those girls who had "gone to the people" back in the 1870s, severe, ascetic, self-denying. Imbibing her mother's revolutionary idealism, Olga nevertheless rejected her ascetic, almost monastic self-denial in favor of the newer revolutionary ideal of monogamous free love with a comrade. So she still lived, after Bolshevism's triumph, in fidelity with a faithful comrade.

By Lenin's expedient canon, the ideal revolutionary woman would have been, presumably, the grandmother, preoccupied neither with sex nor with love, totally free for political seriousness. Then who was Olga? She could not have been "winged eros" by Kollontai's canon. It had been precisely to struggle free of monopolistic relationships that Kollontai had elaborated her utopian socialist social psychology. The thesis that once the temporary chaos of revolutionary breakdown and recovery was over, that once the inevitable and natural promiscuities of that epoch had ended, the new, higher love of winged eros would succeed, no longer seemed tenable.

The most shocking act in "The Love of Three Generations" had a surprising result. At home with her mother, on furlough from her party duties during the civil war, Zhenya more or less deliberately seduced her mother's faithful lover, slept with him, and did not conceal the deed from her mother. Mother and daughter confronted each other. But out of this confrontation, sisterhood followed. In a kind of awful resignation, mother and daughter joined in tacit dismissal of men as creatures incapable of meeting the challenges and needs of real women. Thus here, as in Kollontai's lesser stories, men, whether portrayed directly or through the consciousness of women, were shown as inferior to women. Reckless, drunk, lustful, greedy, emotionally shallow, obtuse, imminently and immanently violent, they were a different breed. Bolshevism had not improved them. Revolution had not softened them.

A New Heroine? Work over Heart

As Louise Luke showed more than thirty years ago, other novelists of the 1920s portrayed the relation between revolution and individual as one of danger and lethal tension. In Juri Olesha's *Envy* (1927) the hero called upon women to join him in a counterattack on industrial regimentation: "They are trying to rob you of your greatest posses-sion—your hearth and home . . . trying to turn you into wanderers in the wastes of history." In Sergei Semyenov's *Natalia Tarpova* (1929) the heroine defied party ideology in favor of the "great emotion" of personal love.[6] Still other novelists vividly portrayed the trivialization of person-ality among young women who had chosen the revolution against per-sonal life. How far such themes might have been explored, had the New Economic Policy been pursued together with a relaxation of Leninist political monopoly, can only be imagined. Even with the turn to collec-tivization and the First Five Year Plan for industry, however, free literary energy continued to be expounded on portraying the young women caught up in the drive to industrialize. In Luke's judgment, a kind of collective new heroine emerged. "[As] they gave the job priority and relegated their family functions to a secondary place, women were taking firm root in their occupations and losing the frustrations, the personal insecurity, and instability associated with the feminine role in modern industrial societies." It followed that such women would identify with the new order.

One measure of the mood of women workers is that they manifest none of the disaffection which produced widespread sabotage on the part of men. They stand apart or vigorously oppose conspiracy or wrecking. . . . Their freedom from the Soviet "terror" is a significant factor in the psychology of industrial women. "This fear . . . stalks behind those who wait for the return of the old order. . . ." According to the almost unvaried evidence of literature, among women not one was waiting for this; among men, many.[7]

The best evidence for the persistence of some degree of freedom for novelists into the early years of socialist realism inheres in exactly this portrayal of difference between man and woman, for what could have been a more devastating comment on the revolution and its new Five-Year Plans than that it had abolished class struggle only to incite a struggle between the sexes? The unstated premise of Luke's use of literature to read reality was that the literature did indeed mirror reality. One piece of reality the early Stalinist novels did not mirror was the fact that the new economy was not generating women writers. Of the novelists analyzed by Luke, all were men; there were no women to analyze.

The full preemption of free literature by socialist realism began with the new marriage decrees of 1936. From this time on, Soviet women were told they were to go on working while restoring their family functions to equal place in their lives. Sociology arose as the language of choice for mediating private lives. The revolutionary regime was not content with literary support. It had driven its most brilliant literary supporter, Mayakovsky, to destroy himself. As Ronald Hingley has noted, Nadezhda Mandelstam, widow of Osip Mandelstam, dead in the Gulag in 1938, cut to the heart of the revolution in her memoirs, remarking that loyalty to official ideology was not enough. Extermination was visited "above all [on] those who rejected its phraseology."[8] The essentially communal, antiromantic, anti-individualistic language of social science crowded into the vacuum. The means for thinking about self were removed. As the state imposed its edicts of 1936 and 1944 on marriage, family, and sex, individuals confronted with official social science were left to the shuttered privacy of isolated and fugitive selves for love. Personal life became choked, sour, intimidated, muffled.

The literary impulse would not be suffocated even under supreme pressures. In 1943 Mikhail Zoshchenko, a popular writer of humorous stories reasonably acceptable to the regime in the 1930s, published the first chapters of a kind of novel-autobiography, *Before Sunrise*. Catching infancy, boyhood, and youth in a kaleidoscope of memory bits and clots of analysis, Zoshchenko wrote as though epics and positive heroes had never existed. In a one-page segment he condensed the collapse of a love affair; in the next, the glitter of a new one. In each he professed extreme feelings—"I'm infuriated," "It strikes me as horrible—and even criminal"—feelings contradicted by the abruptness and swiftness of the sentences. The book set off wrath in the headquarters of wartime socialist realism. The most telling criticism was the truest: "The novella is full of the persona of Zoshchenko himself."[9]

After Stalin: Divided Lives

During the long quarter century of Stalin's dictatorship, Russians enjoyed one season of freedom from the contradiction between public and private, self and system. In 1941 an honest and exalted patriotism swept all classes into a supreme effort that in itself forced the relaxation of obsessive political surveillance. Perhaps the best novel to win approval during the regime of Stalin was Vera Panova's *The Train*, published in 1952, an affecting, serene portrayal of the staff of a hospital train during the war.[10] The nurses in particular were revealed as at once idiosyncratic and self-confident individuals. While the war divided husbands and wives and lovers from each other, the care with which Panova rendered hidden emotion strongly suggested that most of her cast brought with them a fund of personal disappointment rooted in more than the war itself, as well as new kinds of resources for assimilating that disappointment without personal breakdown. Even the stock figure of the train's flawless Communist political officer exuded a sense that personal happiness was indeed not a reasonable hope.

That identification with a collective effort like war offered escape from painful private lives was of course a truism of people everywhere and always, but the difference for Russians was that they had not been allowed, through their writers, to tell—and learn—just how painful those lives had been.

Once the war was over, Stalin and his apparatus returned to the task. In 1946 Akhmatova, who had begun to sing again, was singled out for pillorying; in 1949 her son was arrested and sent to concentration camp. For the first and only time, she wrung out of herself the prescribed phraseology in "Glory to Peace": "Where Stalin is, there too are Freedom, Peace, and Earth's Grandeur."[11] Zoshchenko was brought up for attack again, for of course it was not his indifference to the war effort in *Before Sunrise* that had earned him vilification, but his attempt to find speech for breaking out of the harmonies of Stalin's false peace.

In the brief thaw granted to writers after Stalin's death in 1953, they could begin to abandon the creed whereby men and women found harmony with each other through common dedication to their work. One such case of special bite was Vladimir Dudintsev's *Not by Bread Alone*, published in 1956. The central figure in the novel appeared in several other works published during the thaw: a high-level official in the Soviet elite guilty of profound corruption of original revolutionary ideals. These novels in effect anticipated the later historical and sociological analyses of the reemergence of class society in Russia. In Dudintsev's novel the heroine, Nadia, stimulated by Jack London's novels, had sought a "hero" and thought to find him in Drozdov, the high official. She soon realized her mistake, however, and discovered in another man, Lopatkin, the qualities she had hoped for. Dudintsev's novel was no searching psychological study. The heated debate set off by the book turned on Drozdov. Had Dudintsev intended him to be a representative figure or not? Had he libeled the Soviet bureaucracy? It was clear that Dudintsev had rendered Drozdov as a man of devastating cynicism. Deprecating Lopatkin as "genius," he identified himself as "a descendent of the common herd." Whereas Lopatkin embodied the fate of the individualist ignored because outside the collective, Drozdov identified himself as a "building ant": "As he pronounced this word, a cold monster of hatred stirred at the back of his ordinarily jolly eyes. 'Yes, we building ants are necessary . . .!' " Since the emotional focus of Dudintsev's novel fell on Drozdov, it offered a more mechanical than psychological challenge to the Stalinist myth of harmony. Dudintsev professed to be appalled at Western interpretations of the book. For an American edition, he wrote that he had meant to serve Soviet ideals. "We Soviet people jealously guard the basic principles of our life, that of the soul and that purity of new human relations which spring up in us from our early years."[12] As an effort to liberate private emotion, the considerable shortfall of the novel inhered in this conservatism. Neither Nadia nor Lopatkin, separately or together, radiated any defense of private rights. Nevertheless, Nadia's choice alone was an act of defiance.

The far more awesome fruit of the thaw, *Doctor Zhivago*, did affirm the private. Pasternak's special status with Stalin had won him survival but required his silence for more than a decade. In 1957 his voice spoke again. But his novel was published in Italy, not in Russia, although the thaw had made such a challenge at least imaginable. Ronald Hingley has formulated the highest case for the book: "Eloquently preaching the futility of preaching, *Doctor Zhivago* affirms the primacy of personal and private living over all the political and public considerations in the world." The superintendents of the Writers' Union got the message. "From the Soviet authorities' point of view *Doctor Zhivago* contains the most subversive of all possible political messages—that neither politics nor even antipolitical 'messages' matter at all in the last analysis, and that human beings should *live*, and not (as Soviet and other politicians would make them) *prepare for life*."[13] Yet, like Dudintsev's *Not by Bread Alone*, *Doctor Zhivago* did not assert the realm of relations between men and women as particularly critical for the defense of consciousness. The crucial action in the novel consisted of the hero's inexhaustible evasion of decisive self-possession and commitment. His stance toward the heroine, Lara, was that of a man toward a myth, a wood nymph, a screen idol, a mystic glow in the marsh at night. He was as averse to possession as he was drawn to contemplation. A principle of his own imagination, Lara was *die Ewigweibliche*. It was as though, in Dudintsev's assault on the hero-as-bureaucrat and Pasternak's reaffirmation of the hero-as-poet, preliminary ground had to be reclaimed before a further advance could be undertaken.

As the freeze revived after 1956, partly from political fears set off in Europe, partly from the debate impelled by *Doctor Zhivago* itself, literary energy fell back on itself for a few more years. Another thaw seemed to be signaled with the publication in 1962 of *One Day in the Life of Ivan Denisovich*, Alexander Solzhenitsyn's lacerating account of a northern work camp. While the novel served Nikita Khrushchev's de-Stalinization policy, it did not serve Solzhenitsyn much longer. All his later novels were rejected for publication in the Soviet Union. Still, as Deming Brown has shown, a growing number of writers began to write of "ordinary working-class Soviet citizens engaged in the business of daily living," the usual point being to show their utter indifference to ideology.[14] The system they took for granted might be shown to be cumbersome, corrupt, boring, petty, but their response, as in any ordinary nonrevolutionary society, was not protest but adaptation. In portraying such citizens, the new writers simply took the sexual scene as one for realistic presentation, rendering divorces, adulteries, quick affairs, and profane love, along with loneliness, seasoned marriages, and love young and sacred as though there never had been any socialist doctrine on these matters, as though Alexandra Kollontai had never written, as though bourgeois freedom was still struggling to be born.

In some of these stories an archetype familiar from the nineteenth century persisted—the strong woman prevailing over her men's weakness.[15] Now, however, the goal to which her strength was addressed no longer shone forth in radiant idealism but as immediate self-interest. In Yuri Trifonov's "The Exchange," published in 1969, the hero, Dmitriev, wallowed and wobbled as his wife, Lena, moved implacably toward her goal of capturing her dying mother-in-law's apartment. By narrating his story from within the mind of the husband, Trifonov avoided all allusions to some sentimental ideal by comparison with which the wife might appear to symbolize a society's failure. The hero's mistress, Tanya, "lived in constant fear and a kind of passionate bewilderment," and was finally boring. His wife saw through his mother, "doing good deeds to be always conscious of being a good person." As for Lena herself: embracing him, "she looked into his eyes with the dark blue caressing eyes of a witch. . . . she gnawed on her desires like a bulldog. Such a nice-looking lady bulldog. . . . She didn't let up until her wishes—right in her teeth—turned into flesh. A great trait! Wonderful, amazingly decisive in life. The trait of real men."[16] In this world of middle-class Moscow after Stalin, the primary preoccupation was money, money for doctors, for Scotch, for a tent for camping. Women were better than men about money. In some novels they made more of it than their husbands.

In Sergei Dovlatov's *The Compromise*, published outside Russia in 1983, two journalists were sent to report on the record-breaking achievements of one Linda Peips, an Estonian dairymaid. Their assignment became the occasion for drink, sex, and mockery. Modifying the interior perspective used by Trifonov in favor of narration as manic and unillusioned as the protagonists, Dovlatov used form as well as story for his satire. With every character, including an off-stage Leonid Brezhnev, sharing the tacit understanding of the fraudulence of all official language, the effect was acerbic rather than pathetic. The only figure of pathos was the party-hero dairymaid, as cowlike in her unawareness as the beasts she exploited. The defiance of society that had been implicit in Zoshchenko was here dissolved into a kind of absurdist play-acting. It was absurd even to wish for ideals: "And here I thought, if only there were no Party headquarters, no milk-crazed cow, if only I could live here without any serious assignments. The yacht, the river, the young ladies."[17]

Whether this kind of postromantic, often antipsychological, antisociological, expressionist perspective would prove best adapted to rendering the realities of modern urban Soviet life in literature remained to be seen, but obviously it took for granted that no compelling new possibilities for deeper relations between the sexes were clamoring to be expounded. Women's equalities in the marketplace had evidently underwritten neither finer marriages nor greater independence, neither richer love lives nor richer sex lives, for women or for men. The failure may not have inhered simply in the realities of modern Soviet politics and economics, however. Whereas telling of the Soviet present seemed to shrivel all stale old romanticisms, telling of the Soviet past seemed to revive them. In Solzhenitsyn's *One Day* women were absent altogether, but where the past comprehended some of the deeper roots of Soviet history, the old romantic images seemed to reemerge as though to occupy a vacuum.

In *The Old Man*, published in 1980, a far more complex novella than "The Exchange," Yuri Trifonov's hero recollected his days in the civil war of 1919–1921. By 1973 the old man had come to a clear understanding that the standard, official version of early Soviet history had little relationship to the reality. Official history lined everybody up in two camps, ours and theirs, the Reds and the Whites, Communists and enemies of the people. It had not been that way for the lost hero, a Cossack general named Migulin. The Cossacks themselves had been caught between and were horribly dealt with as a consequence. "That's what I don't understand: black and white, obscurantists and angels. And no one in heaven. Yet everyone is in between. There's something of the angel and something of the fallen angel in everyone. Who was I in August 1917?"[18] In ways that Trifonov was careful not to make clear and obvious, the old man found his revision of history intertwined with his lifelong love for the girl with whom he grew up. In a passion of adoration, she had married the heroic Migulin, whose heroism consisted eventually of his sheer inability to conspire in the brutal simplifications of heroic politics. In parallel to the elaborate recollections of the civil war, rendered basically through the mind of the old man, Trifonov presented the elaborate schemings of his children and grandchildren over the inheritance of a dacha, a rickety summer house on the outskirts of Moscow. These manipulations wearied the old man. Trifonov's point was not, however, to indict the pettiness of 1973 compared to the exalted days of 1920. On the contrary: the schemes of 1973, in all their complexity and deviousness, were to be read back into the past. A past simplified into glamour, heroics, and idealism suffocated the present. In the end, the old man could never quite penetrate to the mystery of Migulin's heroic individualism; he remained compelled instead by his feelings for the girl who had understood Migulin.

For Soviet historians, one of the most difficult issues was to decide how much Soviet history owed to pre-Soviet "Russian" history. In one of the most remarkable novels of the late 1970s, Valentin Rasputin's *Live and Remember*, peasant Russia provided the social matrix for a classic love story. Not only that. The time in which the story transpired was that of still another Soviet icon of glamour and glory, the Great Patriotic War for the Mother/Fatherland. The plot was simple. A young married couple living in a village on the banks of the Angara in central Siberia were divided by the war. Andrei was wounded, then he disappeared. Secretly he reappeared, making himself known only to his wife, Nastyona. He had deserted, the war was still on, he was a marked man. Soon, Nastyona became pregnant. She could not tell anyone by whom. The village turned on her with scorn. Finally, when Nastyona realized that even once the truth were known, her child would be stigmatized as the son (taken for granted) of a war deserter, she threw herself in the river. The cut of the book was not plot, however. Rather, both alone and during their secret trysts, both of the married pair generated themselves as individuals. Cut off from the village, they contemplated the meaning of love. With their future darkened, they confronted the immediate compulsions of sexuality. They had to distinguish between their responsibilities to themselves and to their father and mother. Andrei rehearsed the events of his desertion. Without pretending his status was other than deserter, he recovered the moment of exhaustion and apocalyptic violence at which he had broken. With no illusions about his fate, he plunged into deep identifications with the Siberian wilderness, in which he knew how to survive. In her pregnancy his wife cherished her deepest hopes despite the blackness ahead. She had come to realize life's deepest danger: the "soul could dry up before its time."

How many people, healthy and strong, do not distinguish their own, personal, God-given feelings from the common, dime-a-dozen feelings. Those people get into bed with the same unbridled pleasure, ready for anything that they sit at table with: just to be satisfied. And they cry and laugh looking around—to make sure that they are seen laughing and crying, so that their tears do not go to waste. . . . And all because they did not want or did not know how to be alone with themselves, they had forgotten and lost themselves, and now they couldn't remember or find themselves.[19]

In Rasputin's story, no blame was assigned for the lovers' fate. Unlike Shakespeare's *Romeo and Juliet*, in which the feud that destroyed the lovers stigmatized the Montagues and Capulets as foolish, vain, and coarse, in not a line did Rasputin imply that the Russians' war against

Hitler mattered less than any love. The peasant village proved itself cruel, but however cruel and purely social its response, it was hardly to blame. Rasputin's novel was not a commentary on the Great Patriotic War, however virtuous, or on peasant culture, however crabbed. It was a commentary on how to tell stories. The socialist realist way was to tell of the triumph of great causes that, in their turn, would bring triumph, happiness, and fulfillment to the individual. Individual happiness was harmonious with social unity. Such homogenization of individual with larger harmonies had not begun with Lenin. No greater expositor of such mystic onenesses could be found than Russia's own Leo Tolstoy, celebrating in the marriage of Kitty and Levin, in *War and Peace*, solidarity with the fields and harvests, hunting and the seasons, identification with nature itself. Rasputin's doomed lovers were forced beyond this ancient mysticism, too. To tell of individual spiritual growth, of sexual profundity, of true marriage was to tell nothing necessarily of either social order or nature's eternities. Pasternak's *Zhivago* had already affirmed that, if only in his solipsistic homelessness. Rasputin's married pair loved each other and understood each other. That was all. No oneness with any larger element was suggested.

It did not necessarily follow that Rasputin's somber and implacable story decreed that true love and individuality flourished only in extreme alienation and isolation. His novel did not seek universal discoveries. Like Almqvist's *Sara Videbeck*, it told of two people in specific circumstances. Yet its resonance might be felt anywhere. Even local cultures less rigid than Russian peasant culture and nations less haunted by wars of supreme desperation might understand: to be finally free for sexuality, for love, and for procreation, human beings needed less, not more, socialization; less, not more, moral superintendence; less, not more, community. If Dovlatov's disenchanted cynics and Rasputin's simple peasants could learn that, so might anyone.

The woman's point of view—if such there was—found few expositors in post-Stalin Russian writing. In succession to Akhmatova and Tsvetaeva came new poets, notably Bella Akhmadulina, described by Deming Brown as "an emotional, vulnerable, totally female poet who mistrusts rationality and longs to rely on her heart," and Novella Matveeva, a poet of nature and "little things," as indifferent as was Akhmadulina to politics and "affirmative" themes.[20] But such women hardly paralleled the male novelists in direct renditions of life in Soviet society past and present. In 1963 a surprising new author appeared, a fifty-six-year-old university professor of mathematics, Yelena Sergeyevna Ventsel, who wrote under the pseudonym "I. Grekova."

The heroine of the story "Ladies' Hairdresser" was herself the fiftyish head of a computer institute in Moscow, telling her story in a first-person style of brisk authority. She had two sons still at home, a sassy secretary, a temperamental deputy director, no husband, precious little time to "do something" about her hair. The tang of the story inhered in its quick, tart dialogues, its cameo scenes, and especially its revelation of a mature and observant consciousness, at once wry and eager, amused and self-mocking. Attending—for unexplained reasons—a "youth evening" at which a culture officer presided over "comic skits and group games"—"Don't interrupt, comrades. Comrades, make room for the group games. Be disciplined, comrades"—the heroine responded sympathetically, especially to the "high heels [dancing] with high heels, girls dancing with each other." "Oh you girls, you poor girls. The war's long been over, another generation has grown up, and there are still too many of you." Marya Vladimirova Kovaleva, busy as she was, availed herself of a young hairdresser who, for the sake of his own artistic freedom, worked independently of the official quotas of the Plan for hairdressing. In him she found a remarkable person. Brought up in an orphanage, in profound ignorance of life and learning, Vitaly nonetheless was vastly ambitious. He had embarked on a program of self-improvement, including reading through the complete works of Vissarion Belinsky. When Marya Vladimirovna mentioned *War and Peace*, he blinked, then added that title to his list. She introduced him to her attractive secretary, Galya, on whom he proceeded over the next few weeks to create hairdos of fabulous resource. While Galya fell in love with him, he proved interested in her only for her "lively hair." Once he had "exhausted all possibilities with her head," he had to move on. "I have to make progress." He fell victim of jealousy in the Hairdressing Sector of the Service Administration, but soon signed on as an apprentice metal worker, a first step toward the factory brigade, high school, college, the ladder of success. Marya Vladimirovna listened to all this, dazed. He will always do her hair, he said, "as an exception."

I put down the receiver and stood there looking at my palms. There's something here I missed. . . . "What happened? Good or bad?" asked Kostya. "Don't know myself. Probably good." Well, what next? Good luck to you, Vitaly![21]

Socialist realism demanded neat endings. This unusual story ended in a beginning.

A novella written by I. Grekova (the name being the equivalent of "Miss X") some years later, "The Hotel Manager," suggested that the self-confidence of the narrator of "Ladies Hairdresser" had indeed been highly contrived and somewhat vulnerable. Following its heroine—Vera, "Verochka"—from prerevolutionary girlhood through marriage, war, and widowhood to apotheosis at sixty as manager of a rest hotel on the Black Sea, the story registered an authorial presence hovering over its heroine's vicissitudes as often in a sentimental as in an analytic spirit, ever ready to blame men. However gay, and adoring of Verochka, her father had been, for his wife he had been just "a luxury item"; disabled in the war and doing little but play the balalaika. He died when Verochka was ten. A handsome military officer saw her at eighteen, rising from the sea like Aphrodite, but all he wanted from his young wife was service as his hostess on his constant tours of duty. Her happiest time was when her husband was away at war and she lived with a divorced friend, Masha, Masha's young son, and her own mother. "And how well they managed!" "How marvelously and happily they lived, despite difficulties, despite the war." "Masha and Vera lived like sisters, and they shared everything: bed, salary, rations, son, and mother." With her husband back, she settled down with him, "cheerful but firm," keeper of the pillows, cots, sheets, flowers, meals for guests and summer people. " 'You're really a hotel manager,' " her husband joked. Soon widowed, at forty-five Vera met another man, romantic, handsome, "no ring on his finger," but he vanished after a few weeks. Four years later he reappeared, now "fat, gray, bald." But it was he for all that. "My God, do I really love him?" Vera again gave herself to emotion. Quickly, though, the truth came out: Talya drank to excess. In despair, Vera cut off his vodka, but to no avail. He had to be sent off. "[Talya] was quiet and subdued, like a child who had misbehaved."[22]

For Vera, happiness was to be found only at work among women. As senior administrator of the rest hotel, "her greatest joy—and the greatest difficulty—came in working with people. . . . The staff . . . consisted almost entirely of nervous, middle-aged women ('menopausal,' she called them). They were morbidly vain, hypersensitive, poorly paid, but how those women worked! And out of true conscientiousness, too, not out of fear." Though Vera was their boss, she was much more. "The menopausal women loved her. . . . Each valued the opportunity to come to Vera Platonovna with her woes, to cry about things, to rail at fate, to 'share,' as it's called. They shared their jobs as well as griefs. Oh, how the Russian female heart likes sharing."[23]

A sense of Russian history divided in two suffused I. Grekova's "The Hotel Manager," a history of men on the one hand, of women on the other. Men were butterflies like Vera's father, or martinets like her husband, or sorry drunks like her lover. Men were not beings who shared. With its warm, deeply felt celebration of sharing, "The Hotel Manager" constituted a profound but bitterly ironic endorsement of socialism. That there was no true sharing to be had between the sexes in full adult maturity, the author implied by allotting her heroine one last man. At sixty, Vera and Sergei Pavlovich were like "tenth-graders in love." "They still just kissed, nothing more, didn't even think about anything more. There's a bond between early youth and early old age—in both there is something platonic." There was no question of marriage or even of living together. He had a sick wife whom he could not leave. He came down to see Vera three or four times a year, joining her little family, which consisted now—in addition to the menopausal workers—of an eccentric actress retired from the stage; a twenty-four-year-old daughter of her old friend Masha, retreating from the sexual wars and waxing sarcastic about "Looove"; and Kuzma the cat.[24] All was cozy, though not in the way Natalia Ordynina had had in mind back in that naked year of 1919. Vera realized she had at last found her first "real" love.

There were few women writers in postwar Soviet literature. If it was true, as Bernice Madison has said, that "Soviet . . . women are more grieved than men by the lack of satisfying personal life,"[25] would other women writers have found their way to sisterhood as did I. Grekova? If it was true that Russian women not only had brought a preference for the communal over the individual from their peasant heritage, but had had the heritage reinforced by Stalinism and a bureaucratic command economy, that would seem likely.

Russian women do have identities associated with their multiple roles—family, professional, and volunteer social activist—but the concept of a personal identity apart from the collective is one that so far belongs only to the Russian counterculture.[26]

Literature, with its premium upon consciousness of self as creative agent, would not flow easily from a communality that not only sheltered women from men but served the power that dominated the commune.

Thinking about the Unthinkable:
Sex in Modern Russia

In the late 1960s and 1970s sociology began to reach out to sex, marriage, and the family, not just as subjects for ideological and political manipulation but as objects for scientific study. Igor Kon's *The Sociology of Personality* (1967) urged a "resexualization" of Soviet sociology, by which he meant an end to the neglect of gender differentials in Soviet social science. Studies were launched of the division of responsibility within families. The steadily rising divorce rate was inspected for more subtle causations. Arguments critical of the sentimental post-1936 Stalinist views on family and marriage began to be heard. Love, it was said, was not the cement for marriage. Marital stability depended far more on pragmatic factors such as education, workplace, economics, and children. The general thrust of these studies was uncertain. On the one hand, they seemed postulated on a sense that marital stability was in trouble. On the other hand, some data suggested that a "drift to domesticity" was under way, a drift perhaps consciously followed as a refuge from the social controls of the state. Strengthening the family as a haven in a heartless world effectively commented on that world's heartlessness. But all this seemed contradicted by other studies finding that "many families now have been turned into real fields of battle in direct and indirect ways."[27] The shape of this battle was indicated in the title Vladimir Shlapentokh, a sociologist who emigrated to the United States in the late 1970s, chose for a chapter of his book on Soviet love and marriage, addressed to American readers: "Angry Soviet Women against Their Men." Gladkov's Dasha, Kollontai's Zhenya, Grekova's Vera might all have understood. Poignantly, in the census of 1970 no less than 1.3 million more women than men reported themselves married; evidently 1.3 million men whose women thought they were married did not agree.

In the late 1960s a few sociologists, including Shlapentokh, initiated discussion of dating services.[28] Unmarried women numbered over 28 million, compared to 5.5 million unmarried men. Although the greatest oversupply of women was in the age cohorts most affected by the terror of the 1930s and by World War II, the typical author of the letters to the sociologists proved to be "a divorced woman with one child, 25 to 40 years old, college-educated." Evidently older women had worked out their accommodations to singleness, perhaps in sisterhood. The younger divorcée-mother had not given up hope. Official quarters took alarm. Dating services were "alien to our Soviet moral outlook." After a few years, however, second thoughts occurred. Dating services were hardly likely to evolve into power centers competitive with the state, and just possibly might speak to the growing demographic crisis. By 1982 a few singles clubs, "for those who are older than thirty," had been approved in Moscow and a few other cities.

The reluctance of Communist authorities to give ground to popular feeling manifested the old Bolshevik conviction that socialism included everything, that to give way anywhere would be to give way everywhere. Perpetuating the outlook of the old Women's Department under Sophia Smidovich, publication chiefs into the 1970s deplored fashion and deprecated cosmetics. In print, on stage, and over electronic media, erotica continued to be proscribed and pornography despised as bourgeois decadence. Soviet schools offered no courses in sex education before 1965, the cautious introduction of books and curricula thereafter betraying at once a sense of an anomalous backwardness and anxiety that new candor not be construed as permissiveness. Whether a "pervasive hypocrisy and concealment" in "a 'hung up' generation of Soviet citizens"[29] would yield before popular wishes would depend in part on culture as well as on ideologies. By 1984 the largest circulation in the Soviet Union was enjoyed, not by *Pravda* or *Izvestia* but by *Zdorovie* (Health). For years after its start in 1955, *Zdorovie* ignored sexual matters, but by 1980 its editor, a woman gynecologist named Maria Dmitrievna Piradova, having noted innumerable queries about sex from readers, began giving space to psychiatrists, neuropathologists, "sexologists."[30] *Zdorovie* still refrained from discussing venereal diseases or prostitution or contraception. The party's Department of Agitation and Propaganda kept close watch. But movement had begun. Certainly social science and medicalized psychology could easily perpetuate the dominance of the collective and communal and harmonic. Rarely had either sociology or medicine been a medium for individualization. Yet in any effort they might make to break free of control by the center, they had resources to offer to the individual and private.

In the late 1970s what some Western critics would label a "new wave" in Soviet filmmaking had begun to become apparent. Evidently many Soviet filmgoers welcomed it, too. Gone was the addiction of Soviet filmmakers to epics, still resplendent in such 1960s products as *Ballad of a Soldier, My Name is Ivan,* and *The Cranes Are Flying,* movies still made to the pattern demanded by Lenin, who had been enthusiastic about film as a medium peculiarly suited to the mobilization of the masses, about film devoted to the symbolic, mythic, and heroic, to "the social idea." The new films began to portray *bytovye* (everyday life) to audiences unaccustomed to see themselves as they lived those lives. Sometimes, as in Eldar Riazonov's *Garage,* they were shown themselves quarreling over what had become precious in their real lives, a private parking space in their own apartment building. Sometimes, as in Pyotr Todorovsky's *Gavrilov,* they were shown succumbing to pathetic fantasies of escape from loneliness. In a two-character film of a middle-aged woman and her ex-husband, Nikita Mikhailov echoed Strindbergian intensities: "This film is my apology before women, because the lives of women are far more complex than those of men, however busy men may seem."[31] The most popular, Riazonov's *Moscow Doesn't Believe in Tears,* simply roamed over the wishes, fantasies, and desires of a new urban white-collar population for whom both peasant past and official ideology had become dim.

Modernization theorists might argue that with such films Russia was becoming, at last, middle-class, but these products of the last days of Leonid Brezhnev's creaking regime remained utterly vulnerable. The market to which they were responding remained itself vulnerable. Until all such new perspectives could condense into a cultural vitality feeding on experience rather than upon formulas, experience itself would remain fugitive. Surely Soviet women had no more at stake in such freedom than did Soviet men, but just as surely, their hopes for an equality that would also constitute a new freedom depended on poetry and novels and film produced by people whose only aim was poetry and novels and film.

14 The United States

"Unchained eager far and wild"—Together:
John Berryman and Anne Bradstreet

In 1953 John Berryman published his long poem—458 lines in 57 stanzas—*Homage to Mistress Bradstreet*. In his late thirties, Berryman was in crisis in his own life. An intense relationship with a woman not his wife had ended, his wife was leaving, and he faced life alone. One place to turn was psychoanalysis. Another was poetry. Many of his abundant sonnets of the time he would hold back from publication for many years, but *Homage* quickly took finished form in print.

Berryman felt guilty about women in general: "I suffered living like a stain:/ I trundle the bodies, on the iron bars,/ over that fire backward and forth; they burn;/ bits fall. I wonder if/ *I* killed them. Women serve my turn."[1] But Berryman would not flee to the desert, ascend to God, descend to hell. He would reach out one more time, this time to the First Woman, the first poet of America, Anne Bradstreet herself.

Berryman had prepared himself for writing his poem by a meticulous reading of all Bradstreet's own poetry as well as the scholarship about it, for example, Helen Campbell's biography. His homage was to be directed to a real person in a real history. But unlike historians seeking tradition and critics seeking a canon, Berryman did not want simply a Puritan poet, a Puritan Bradstreet. Berryman's Bradstreet was not at one with Puritan style: "Our chopping scores my ears,/ our costume bores my eyes/ . . . chop-logic's rife." Puritans "starch their minds./ Folkmoots, & blether, blether." Berryman's reading corresponded exactly with that greatest of all the attacks on Puritanism, William Carlos Williams' 1920s classic, *In the American Grain*, the kind of "anti-Puritanism" against which Morison, Morgan, and the literary expositors of an American canon had assembled themselves. Berryman embraced a feminist Bradstreet fully aware of the outrage perpetrated by the Fathers on Mrs. Hutchinson: "Factioning passion blinds/ all to all her good, all—can she be exiled?/ Bitter sister, victim! I miss you." But the case against the Fathers was not their political quarrel with a forward woman. Puritanism's affront to women had been its expropriation of what was womanly: "I see the cruel spread Wings black with saints!/ Silky my breasts not his, mine to withhold/ or tender, tender." Claiming themselves to be "nursing fathers," John Winthrop and his faction had provoked reaction: "I throw hostile glances towards God./ Crumpling plunge of a pestle, bray?/ sin cross and opposite, wherein I survive/ nightmares of Eden." "Father of lies,/ a male great pestle smashes/ small women swarming towards the mortar's rim in vain." Berryman's Bradstreet was America's first antinomian.

Berryman addressed her as one free. When she first hears him and asks "you who leaguer/ my image in the mist" to be kind, he replies: "Be kind you, to one unchained eager far and wild." But the Bradstreet the modern poet sought out was not in the first place Anne Bradstreet the poet, but Mistress Bradstreet, wife and mother. Her poetry "appalled" him: "all this bald/ abstract didactic rime I read appalled/ harassed for your fame/ mistress neither of fiery nor velvet verse." Had she written it "—To please your wintry father?" Bradstreet evidently felt the same way: "When by me in the dusk my child sits down/ I am myself. . . ./ How they loft, how their sizes delight and grate./ The proportioned, spiritless poems accumulate." It was obvious for whom Bradstreet must write, to replace wintry fathers as monitors of her art: "Prattle of children powers me home,/ my heart claps like the swan's/ under a frenzy of *who* love me & who shine." The modern poet devoted three and a half remarkable stanzas to empathy: "My world is strange/ and merciful, ingrown months, blessing a swelling trance./ . . . Below my waist/ he has me in Hell's vise./ Stalling. . . ./ I press with horrible joy down/ my back cracks like a wrist/ . . . Monster you are killing me. . . ./ Women do endure/ I can *can* no longer . . . drencht & powerful, I did it with my body!/ One proud tug greens heaven." In childbirth the poet had his model, his "paradigm" for poetry itself.

Mrs. Bradstreet realized something was wrong with her: "I sniff a fire burning without outlet,/ consuming acrid its own smoke. It's me." She realized she was in danger: "Once/ less I was anxious when more passioned to upset/   / the mansion & the garden & the beauty of God./ Insectile unreflective busyness/ blunts & does amend." She recognized in herself too a spirit "unchained eager far and wild" demanding more than unreflective busyness, she needed the terror and freedom of poetry/ childbirth. The modern poet, asserting himself, confronted her: "—I have earned the right to be alone with you." In her reply she wrought epiphany: "—What right can that be?/ Convulsing, if you love, enough, like a sweet lie./ Not that, I know, you can. This cratered skin,/" [Anne Bradstreet had caught smallpox in fresh America] "like the crabs & shells of my Palissy ewer, touch!/ Oh, you do, you do?/ Falls on me what I like a witch,/ for flawless holds, annihilations of law which Time and he and man abhor, foresaw." In this awakening from the insectile she understood the dangers and depths. "—Ravishing, ha, what crouches outside. . . ./ Often, now,/ I am afraid of you./ I am a sobersides; I know./ I *want* to take you for my lover." The poet responds: "Do." Bradstreet: "—I hear a madness. Harmless I to you/ am not, not/ I?" Modern poet: "No." Bradstreet: "—I cannot but be."

Not long after, in a critical essay on Walt Whitman, Berryman made still clearer his sense of himself as at one with the heroic tradition of American writing.[2] American writers had to make themselves. They could not expect to be made by tradition, by Puritanism (or even anti-Puritanism), or by schools or philosophies. Taking lawlessness and nihilism into their minds, they had to forge poems by themselves. This was in no way to embrace poetry as mere freedom, release from form, relief from repression. It was rather to accept poetry as an exhausting and painful task. The form-giving power was within the self. To embrace Mistress Bradstreet was to affirm the form-giving, life-giving power within the self. The self was not to be feared, by contrast with society, as some seething cauldron of criminal instinct. Generativity was the sign of God.

So far as we know, Berryman's embrace of Anne Bradstreet was not prompted by some notion, in concordance with Henry Adams, say, that American life was peculiarly lacking in the symbols and substance of generativity, maternity, femininity. But perhaps American literature was, and his act of petition thus suggested that it could be redeemed.

Classic American Lit Seeks a Heroine

Like farming, politics, and commerce, literature too, Alexis de Tocqueville said, would become an "industry" in democracy. "Democratic literature is always crawling with writers who look upon letters simply as a trade." He deduced logically which kind of literature would constitute what amounted to the first best-sellers:

Of all forms of literature it is generally the drama that is first affected by the [democratic] revolution. . . . The crowd can enjoy sights on the stage more easily than any other form of literature. . . . So the natural literary tastes and instincts of democracy are first seen in the theater, and one must expect them to break in vehemently there.

Tocqueville argued that democratic literature would not be interested in "literary rules," "perfect details," "externals." It would not be a literature of social observation at all. Democracy "turns man's imagination away from externals to concentrate on himself alone. . . . [It] is about themselves that [democratic peoples] are really excited."[3]

Once scholarship investigated, it found what Tocqueville had projected. Pouring over the evidences of popular Jacksonian theater, Constance Rourke found enthusiastic audiences patronizing troupes of players touring all over the East and into an expanding Midwest. This was a comic theater. "The legitimate theater came to a standstill. . . . [A] vigorous burlesque . . . usurped the stage, turning the serious drama upside down." This "serious" drama had hardly existed, anyway, and what there was had been non-American, English. That a new democratic American literature would be comic, Rourke explained with a perception of Henri Bergson: "The comic comes into being just when society and the individual, free from the worry of self-preservation, begin to regard themselves as works of art!"[4] So it was that, freed from the worry of self-preservation following Jackson's own great victory at New Orleans in 1815, American actors, playwrights, writers, monologuists, and producers began to ridicule English plays and English manners and offer their own creations. A comic theater would not call its audiences back to old covenants and identities. It would specifically mock New England and the Puritan mission. It would dismiss Puritan preachers' jeremiads bemoaning the apostasies of the day by comparison with the loyalties of the Fathers and Grandfathers. As Bergson implied, its qualifying mark would be exuberance. While offering the figure of the backwoodsman for popular delight, comic players took no pains in exact detail. Exaggeration, not description, mattered. No comment on slavery, no call for sympathy appeared in the tirelessly evoked black minstrel. Rather, he manifested sheer freedom: in song and dance, through body, voice, face, and costume, he obeyed no conventions. Always presented by white men in blackface, he promised that white men too could be spontaneous. Comic theater never troubled over the dark and sinister implications of the stage Yankee. Able, through exploiting sermonic devices, to open the tightest purses, he might have been thought the premonitor of "consumerism," inducing "artificial" wants in manipulable souls. But the comic stage Yankee emitted a far more powerful radiation: utterly self-conscious, he invited his audiences to appreciate how the trick worked. Everyone could come to know that the self was not homogeneous, that the self was a construct, an act, a performance. Everyone could learn acting.

As Rourke explicitly noted, this new theater was a masculine theater, a male literature, an elaboration of male freedom. "Women had played no essential part in the long sequence of the comic spirit in America."[5] Why? The essence of the comic theater was mobility, change, masks, disguises, transformations, transfigurations. Women embodied changelessness, roots, surety, persistence; woman's sphere registered the enclosed, the stable. There could be nothing comic about "true American womanhood." There could then, by inference, be nothing comic about relations between men and women.

Yet there was at the heart of this masculine culture an enterprise that could not forever exclude women. Of course the purely masculine persisted, sometimes refreshed, often routinized, through cowboy ballads, hobo lore, dime novels, sports journalism, on to the movie western. No less than one out of every five movies made in the 1920s was a western, directed not just at boys but at grown men, too. Veritably a kind of man's sphere was generated, parallel to woman's sphere, and increasingly also cut off from the great marketplace. And, coming to resemble woman's sphere, man's sphere tended to lose the note of comedy and buoyant self-inflation in favor of the expedient fellowship of Elks and Lions. Indeed, as it became often enough a boy's sphere more than a man's, it became stereotypic, solemnly iconic, condescended to by Booth Tarkington and Norman Rockwell. But another destiny pulsed within the comic spirit that would expand upon its creativity and open itself to women. The direction would not be obvious nor the way easy. Yet the "exultant 'I' at the very center of popular comedy" would affirm itself repeatedly. Not always would it reach out to sex and women. Emerson abstained. But when it did, it did so with remarkable originality.

No doubt the most compelling, "political" case was Walt Whitman, because Whitman unambiguously proffered his songs to democracy, or rather Democracy. The "body electric" that he installed as the central generator of democratic culture was woman's body as well as man's: "I am the poet of the woman the same as the man,/ And I say it is as great to be a woman as to be a man." As he went on to sing the body as the soul, head to toes, he of course named parts, both those common to the sexes and those specific to each: "Strong shoulders, manly beard. . . ./ . . . man-balls, man-root. . . ./The womb, the teats, nipples, breast-milk." And in the relation between these bodies/souls he specified what mattered most: "A woman waits for me, she contains all, nothing is lacking,/ Yet all were lacking if sex were lacking." Homosexual historians claiming Whitman as one of their own have rendered their trophy meaningless by doing so, since D. H. Lawrence was clearly right in arguing that Whitman's sexual poetry expressed not some unmediated "natural" drive but a highly self-conscious, contrived, political purpose. Lawrence was simply wrong in insisting that such "mentalized" sensual body was somehow illegitimate. Whitman's eagerness for "electric" body in any case connected with that of women as well as men.[6]

But the Whitman who preached body to some significant degree remained just that, a preacher, and thus prone to hector rather than to explore. Whitman's exploration of personal psychology followed the paths opened by the war and Abraham Lincoln more than any logic contained within sexualized body itself, so that after the Civil War he, like Puritan preachers before him, turned to lamentations over the nation's apostasy. Repeatedly, in *Democratic Vistas* (1870), Whitman bemoaned "fashionable life, flippancy, tepid amours, weak infidelism, small aims, or no aims at all." The problem was not the postwar pursuit of money. Like Tocqueville, like Bellows, like Emerson, Whitman approved of money and wealth. He hailed with "pride and joy" the "common and general worldly prosperity." Democracy itself, he insisted, "asks for men and women with occupations, well-off, owners of houses and acres, and with cash in the bank." "My theory includes riches," he declared. The fault lay elsewhere, and just where most pointedly he did not conceal. Everywhere he found a

pervading flippancy and vulgarity . . . everywhere the youth puny, impudent, foppish, prematurely ripe—everywhere an abnormal libidinousness, unhealthy forms, male, female, painted, padded, dyed, chignoned, muddy complexions, bad blood, the capacity for good motherhood decreasing or deceased, shallow notions of beauty.

Certainly, men too were guilty of this effete decadence, but the emotional heart of the matter rested with women. By no means was Whitman calling on women to get back into the cloister of sheltered domesticity. Rather he deplored "the fossil and unhealthy air which hangs about the word *lady*." Affirming equality for women, he called upon them to be the "robust" equals of men, and in calling upon them to give up "toys and fictions," he was directing them to "launch forth, as men do, amid real, independent stormy life." Nevertheless, however hard it might have been for those feminists also eager for stormy life to understand, for Whitman the apotheosis of American womanhood in all its robust independence was perfectly explicit. The "most precious" result of a "great democratic literature" would be to achieve

the entire redemption of woman out of these incredible holds and webs of silliness, millinery, and every kind of dyspeptic depletion—and thus insuring to the States a strong and sweet Female Race, a race of perfect Mothers.[7]

In short, Whitman was sucked back into conventionality, the conventionality represented exactly in the idea of a "Female Race," as contrasted to women who launched out as exultant "I's" on their own. Instead of berating paint and pads and chignons, fops and flirts and gallants, Whitman ought to have studied them, tried to understand them, tried to make a literature out of them. True, being the poet he was, Whitman was not likely to become the novelist he never tried to be, but the foreshortening of his "generic" and "inclusive" vision strongly suggested that a far more focused and psychological approach was required.

Melville tried that. The foundering of his efforts in the murky deeps of *Pierre* has been assigned to artistic errors, to a misguided abandonment of the setting of his six previous books, the sea, in favor of polite society, to a misguided abandonment of action for interior meditations, to a misguided turn from social, class, "Marxist" analysis to psychological, cultural, "Freudian" analysis, to a doomed—if tragic—struggle to combat rather than gratify the sentimental preconceptions of the American reading public. Melville being Melville, all arguments have merit. In *Pierre* a strong mother affected to believe her son was her brother; he affected to believe she was his sister. A dead father was discovered to be the progenitor of an illegitimate daughter. Inspired, son abandoned mother; mother died. Half-sister and half-brother dallied in powerful mutual sexual magnetism. The son, Pierre, was pursued by his mother-approved fiancée. When Pierre, despite his dalliance with half-sister Isabel, did not reject her, he had to kill her brother in a duel. Pierre then killed himself. Isabel, dying, toppled over Pierre.[8]

As Ann Douglas has brilliantly argued, Pierre was an insult to those readers who consumed the stories of ennobling family love and family relations being churned out by the new best-selling authors of the 1840s and 1850s, young women writing about young women for young women, the mainstay of their publishers and of editors who then bemoaned the failures of a Melville and a Hawthorne to win a paying audience.[9] But the simple truth was that Melville really had no wish—and possibly no craft—to write of other than the man's world of adventure, danger, and moral ambiguity. *Pierre* was not really an attempt to share a world with women, but a more or less choked and enraged rejection of woman's sphere and all the unadventurous, tucked-in warmth and moral conventionality it represented. Just possibly something might come one day of such rejection, to which women would respond, but not yet. Meanwhile, depressed at the evidence that American novel readers wanted only sentimentality, and angered that there seemed to be no audience for masculine realism, Melville, like many other men of his generation, took hope from the Civil War. Unlike many of the others, he, alone with Whitman, actually managed to forge fresh, masterful, profoundly disturbing poetry out of the carnage.

The act that did produce a masterpiece rather than a fiasco reversed Melville's attack completely. Hawthorne wrote a story in which a fully heroic, even triumphant, if not exactly exultant self came into being, except that in this case the hero was a heroine, Hester Prynne. In young Charles Brockden Brown's novels strong women had appeared, but these had been thesis novels, not psychological investigations.[10] Hester Prynne was no walking thesis. The first "full and living figure" of a woman in American literature, she registered Hawthorne's sense that such a figure must be presented, not as product of society but as product of self. Like Berryman's Anne Bradstreet, Hawthorne's Hester Prynne forged herself against her world.

In a characteristically oblique "Introductory," Hawthorne hinted at the revolutionary intentions he had for his tale. Poking about in the dusty archives of Salem's Custom House, he had, he said, found himself haunted by a "sort of home-feeling with the past," presumably the empathetic foundation for a story told by a nineteenth-century writer about seventeenth-century people. But this feeling was no happy thing. As "the dreary and unprosperous condition of the race" in Salem seemed to show, the past could be weight, burden, curse.

This long connection of a family with one spot . . . is not love, but instinct. . . . Human nature will not flourish, any more than a potato, if it is planted and replanted, for too long a series of generations, in the same wornout soil.

Afflicted "almost as a destiny" by his "strange, indolent, unjoyous attachment" to his native place, Hawthorne had decided that "the connection . . . should at last be severed." He wrote *The Scarlet Letter* to free the young: "My children have had other birthplaces, and, so far as their fortunes may be within my control, shall strike their roots into unaccustomed earth."[11]

Hester Prynne, comprehending that the resources supplied her by her society were inadequate for her salvation, learned to think her way beyond them, into a realm of intellectual honesty and individualistic acerbity. Focusing his own mind through his heroine's matured consciousness, Hawthorne then offered his awful prophesy for the future of populistic Puritanism's aspiration to total order:

As a first step, the whole system of society is to be torn down, and built up anew. Then, the very nature of the opposite sex, or its long hereditary habit, which has become like nature, is to be essentially modified, before women can assume what seems a fair and suitable position. Finally . . . woman cannot take advantage of these preliminary reforms, until she herself shall have undergone a still mightier change.[12]

No comfort here for defenders of woman's sphere. Certainly the opposite sex was to be "modified," but the "still mightier change" in women simply dismissed all notion of finding virtue in femininity in contrast to the male and the masculine.

For Hawthorne, the question was, what next? And Hawthorne's essential answer—"Nothing"—has often been described as a failure of nerve, a regression, a surrender to undertow dragging him back to conventionality. We can probably understand more by comparing Hawthorne with his peers and heirs. This first "full and living figure" of a woman had been possible for him, evidently, only by imagining her as existing 200 years in the past. Melville's effort at a contemporary story had come to disaster, and Whitman's was not a "full and living figure" of a woman at all, but an incantatory evocation of Woman. Henry James would not be able to imagine his full and living heroines except in the context of other countries. Henry Adams would conclude, at the end of the century, that the United States simply had no place for Woman— or women—at all. Hawthorne's feat, then, at once anticipated what some mid-twentieth-century feminists would declare, that change, basic change in the relations of the sexes, would mean revolution, and, at the same time, that such revolution was nearly unimaginable.

The American Girl Too Seeks Freedom:
H. B. Stowe and the End of Patriarchy

While Tocqueville hoped he had seen a self-possessed American woman, almost noble in her self-sacrificial rationality, in fact he had comprehended her deepest captivity. In America, he wrote, "the wife is still the same person that she was as a girl; her part in life has changed, and her ways are different, but the spirit is the same."[13] Harriet Beecher Stowe wanted to change that spirit. Daughter of one of the most formidable of surviving Puritan patriarchs, Lyman Beecher—husband of two prolific wives, father of multitudinous sons (all stamped into preacherhood), compulsive revivalist in both old Boston and new Cincinnati—Stowe, like her sisters, Catherine and Isabella, knew that life was struggle, but, more surely than either Catherine or Isabella, she realized that, for a woman, the struggle that mattered most was the struggle with father. In her own personal life, Stowe succeeded, more or less, by marrying a man, Calvin Stowe, who, although yet another clergyman, lacked all convicting, guilt-productive patriarchal powers in preference for solitary scholarship. Calvin and Harriet Stowe had a remarkably fashionable modern marriage: she earned, he stayed home. An imagination as constitutionally powerful as hers would not be appeased by the havens of private life. She first projected all her eagerness for freedom outward, on slavery, and committed her sentimental masterpiece. But it was not enough. Biographers have, shrewdly enough, located the triggering mechanism to Stowe's two major works, *Uncle Tom's Cabin* and *The Minister's Wooing*, in her response to the death of a beloved son.[14] But it was just that, a release of her deepest "material."

Had Stowe been free to ignore her father's heritage, she might have realized that, so far as her country was concerned, so far as an American national culture was concerned, her problem was already being resolved. Patriarchy was already vanishing. California and New York had been invented. The great archetypical figures of Yankee, backwoodsman, and black-faced white man posing as minstrel had been invented. Above all, the religious fortress itself had been taken from within: after Bushnell, religious patriarchy in America had no credit except in the hysterias and paranoias of abandoned flocks. But if democratic capitalism had enabled American men to begin to disencumber themselves of the responsibilities of Puritan fatherhood, Stowe understood clearly enough that this offered no equivalent freedom to women. Since the relegation of women to their own sphere had denied them any chance to manifest a California or a New York of their own, they still had to solve the problem confronting them in their own sphere: How, when they married, could they cease being a "girl"? How could they mature? become a woman? grow up? Stowe's answer, in *The Minister's Wooing*, was the simplest: Stop marrying patriarchal fathers.

In *The Minister's Wooing*, Mary, a Puritan girl of eighteenth-century Newport, Rhode Island, found herself confronted by two suitors. One was the town's minister, solid, a sage, utterly authentic in the deepest Puritan sense; the other was a young man her own age, poor but honest, stalwart and vigorous, but no observant Christian. Any popular appeal Stowe's novel might have had rooted here: she allotted her heroine to the young man. But *The Minister's Wooing* drew no widespread readership. It failed to count among the fabulous best-sellers being concocted by the young women writers whom a jealous Hawthorne had denigrated. Stowe tried. In Puritan reality, the men who became pastoral patriarchs ordinarily married at about the age of twenty-seven or twenty-eight. A young aspirant to the pulpit would not get married while he was still enrolled in college. Nor would he marry while still in his apprenticeship. He married when he was about to get his first church. The real-life model for Stowe's Doctor Hopkins, Samuel Hopkins of Newport, Rhode Island, had married at this normal age. (Later, as was not uncommon—though the fact has no bearing for Stowe's novel—as a widower, he had remarried.) But Stowe, obviously under a compulsion to render a psychological, as distinguished from a chronological reality, advanced her bachelor pastor from his late twenties to a man of forty. Old-fashioned New England Puritan girls had transferred their feelings for their fathers to their grooms. They married their fathers. This must end.

Almost certainly the reason Stowe's *The Minister's Wooing* failed to win not only best-sellerdom in its own day but critical respect since was its failure to provide a real young hero for its young heroine. While

James, Mary's final choice, was said to be a "gay, young, dashing sailor," nowhere in the long novel was he ever shown to be such. Nowhere were James and Mary shown together in intimate emotion. Having omitted any scene of emotional affinity before James left on a sea voyage (presumably in order to earn money sufficient to allow him to ask for Mary's hand), Stowe excused herself from any such scene after his return with an ellipsis: "But [his coming back] was no dream; for an hour later you might have seen . . ." As an improvement on a father-husband, James was bloodless indeed.

While the fault was hardly Stowe's alone, but that of a whole sociology, yet it is worth noting how strong a charge of emotion she still assigned to the father-pastor who was to lose out in her tale of a girl's conquest of sex and power. Stowe devoted page after page, not to the elucidation of young sailor James's attractions, but to those of the pastor-patriarch. Repeatedly showing the good Doctor at the center of a kind of worshipful feminine support-structure, Stowe converted all that had been awesome about the grandest Puritan pastors, not least her own father, into what was adorable:

[The] Doctor, apparelled in the most faultless style with white wrist ruffles, plaited short bosom, immaculate wig, and well-brushed coat, sat . . . serenely unconscious of how many feminine cares had gone to his getting-up. He did not know of the privy consultations, the sewings, stitchings, and starchings, the ironings, the brushings, the foldings and unfoldings and timely arrangements, that gave such dignity and respectability to his outer man.[15]

As though alerted by the urgency of her own feelings, Stowe broke through her tale in her own voice: "Will our little Mary really fall in love with the Doctor?" Though the question was rhetorical, there were still problems to be solved. Having previously presented the Doctor mythologically as a "grand old monster" and a "rugged elm," Stowe had to rescue him from the obvious question, so far as Mary was concerned. She invented easy interlocutors. " 'But he's too old!' says Aunt Maria." In her own authorial voice, Stowe replied: "Old? What do you mean? Forty is the very season of ripeness,—the very meridian of manly lustre and splendor." She insisted, "No; despite of all you may say and declare, we do insist that our Doctor is a very proper and probable subject for a young woman to fall in love with." Then, climactically, the one moment of immediate, spontaneous, unforced emotion in the book took place, not between Mary and James, but between Mary and the Doctor:

"Mary, my dear," the Doctor declared, "I will be to thee as a father, but I will not force thy heart." At this moment, Mary, by a sudden, impulsive movement, threw her arms around his neck and kissed him, and lay sobbing on his shoulder.[16]

No doubt this was admirable as a daughterly effusion, but the lack of any such warmth toward James prefigured a less than emotionally rich marriage. As though aware of its conventionality, Stowe only sketched it: getting James to stay home from the sea, Mary enlisted him for her own good work, shared with the Doctor—abolitionism. He was gay and dashing no longer.

Popular novels would try to do better. In the most famous advice book to American girls, Louisa May Alcott's *Little Women*, of 1860, father was dealt with by sweeping him off to war. (Other popular novelists disenabled fathers by death, crippling injury, and drink.) Life at home was a matter of mother and sisters. The sisters' leading friend among boys, Laurie, was house-bound, delicate, girlish. Jo, the heroine, consciously identified herself as "boyish." All the book's appeal inhered in the independence of the heroine growing up. But Alcott could not solve the critical problem. As though certain that sexual awakening meant a new captivity, yet clear that a young woman had few alternatives to woman's sphere, Alcott brought her heroine to marry, but the groom was another Doctor, a gentle, impractical patriarch, beside whom Jo took her own place, no longer as helpmeet but an equal matriarch, presiding over a household of boys. *Little Women's* long popularity attested to the widespread reluctance among middle-class American girls to risk themselves sexually.

Yet the potential for another kind of best seller was obvious, and it was realized by Augusta J. Evans's *St. Elmo*, of 1866, in which the heroine, Edna Earl, experienced passionate union in the end with a dark, Darcyish, even Heathcliffe-like hero, St. Elmo himself. But this climax was not quite what it seemed. Edna was revealed in early pages of the book as indeed a highly emotional being. She "trembled with pleasure." "Strange emotions" sent "her own heart throbbing." On occasion she could rage, on others find herself "dazzled." But none of these feelings had to do with St. Elmo. They were all linked to her own literary career.

The darling scheme of authorship had seized upon Edna's mind with a tenacity that conquered and expelled all other purposes, and though timidity and a haunting dread of the failure of the experiment prompted her to conceal the matter, even from her beloved pastor, she pondered it in secret, and bent every faculty to its successful accomplishment.[17]

Young women writing about young women writers were a staple among the mid-century best sellers, Mrs. Evans joining Alcott, Susan Warner,

Mrs. E. D. E. N. Southworth, and others. But the point of their writing was always hidden. Evans half revealed its underlying urgency in St. Elmo. The hero was not at all what he seemed. Apparently a ferocious misogynist, exploiting women cynically, in fact he was but another little boy. Once mistreated by a heartless flirt, who, professing to love him, had in fact betrayed him, he had bandaged his hurt in his own heartlessness. But Edna, who had known him since she had been adopted as an orphan of thirteen by his mother, realized the truth. All she had to do was offer herself to him as a little girl to elicit his true character. This was easy, because by then her literary exertions had induced migraines, anorexia, exhaustion. As assurance of her own intentions, she joined St. Elmo in his antifeminist harangues. Evans concluded the story in passages of invincible ambivalence. Upon being pronounced St. Elmo's wife, the heroine fainted—"two hours elapsed before she recovered." Whether this syncope followed from her pen-induced fatigue, from the relief of triumph, or from some further feeling, obviously neither Evans nor Edna knew. St. Elmo's therapy was kisses, repeated—for two hours?—on lips that at last refilled with blood. Clearly, *St. Elmo*, like many of the best sellers written for young women by young women through the mid-nineteenth century, was dealing with charged matter indeed. Just as clearly Mrs. Evans was catering, out of her own inner wishes, to wishes that the charge be drained away.

Stowe's problem was that she could not wrench free enough from reality to write on so elementary a level as mere wish fulfillment. As her later attack on Lord Byron showed, she harbored strong feelings about sexuality. In *The Minister's Wooing* she gave them voice in a contrivance quite irrelevant to her main plot but of central psychological significance. She brought Aaron Burr into her novel. Again, age distortion betrayed her deepest feelings. Born in 1756, the real Aaron Burr could only have been still a young man at the time of Stowe's novel, little older than James, but Stowe's purposes required him to appear in the full maturity of lurid popular myth of the nineteenth century:

Burr was practiced in every sort of gallantry; he had made womankind a study; he never saw a beautiful face and form without a sort of restless desire to experiment upon it. . . . Burr was one of those men willing to play with any charming woman the game of those navigators who give to simple natives glass beads and feathers in return for gold and diamonds.[18]

In short, for Stowe, sexuality was inextricable from domination, domination from male adulthood. The good Doctor's sexuality was locked up safely in his pastoral fatherhood, like her own father's and her husband's, but Burr's had become unleashed as a consequence of his rejection of fatherhood for predatory woman-hunting.

Burr had no function in the novel's story. Stowe could not thread him in as another of Mary's suitors. In one scene she did show him moved to tears by the heroine's plea for respect for women. But ultimately the story told of the heroine's powers, and up against Burr she could only experience defeat. Burr's prime service was to prompt an expatiation, rendered through the voice of a woman he had seduced, upon what was happening in America at large.

Poor Burr was the petted child of society; yesterday she doted on him, flattered him, smiled on his faults . . . today she flouts and scorns and scoffs him. . . . I know that man, Mary, and I know, that, sinful as he may be before Infinite Purity, he is not so much more sinful than all the other men of his time. Have I not been in America? I know Jefferson; I knew poor Hamilton,—peace be with the dead. Neither of them had a life that could bear the sort of trial to which Burr's is subjected.[19]

We need not think any of this registered some discriminating historical judgment about America in 1800 versus America in 1859. Stowe was commenting on her own America. Had she been in any way a novelist of manners, it is hard to see how she could possibly have imagined that the decline of Puritanism had meant the rise of great seducers, resourceful woman-hunters, libertines tireless in their machinations in America. While prostitution lurked on the edges of both California and New York, that was not the demoralization that preoccupied Stowe. As for those resignations from old patriarchy proceeding within the churches, validated by Horace Bushnell, they usually included a withdrawal from sexuality. If, in time, they could induce the prettified seductions of a Henry Ward Beecher (Stowe's little brother), that too was not part of her anxiety. As for broader, more popular stages, American men's embrace of boyish adventure in the archetypal figures of backwoodsman and cowboy, along with Yankee and minstrel, was conspicuously presexual. As Constance Rourke noted, all the new, post-patriarchal popular democratic culture was exclusively masculine.

Yet Stowe's view proceeded from a solid sociology. She gave it to Mary, attacking Burr, to enunciate: "You men can have everything, ambition, wealth, power; a thousand ways are open to you: women have nothing but their heart; and when that is gone, all is gone." [20] In short, while democracy had removed from women the strongest obstacle to their freedom and maturity, it had left them no way to express that freedom. A female cowboy? Or even a female Bushnell? But there was one opportunity, which explained finally why the Doctor was not the right choice for Mary, why a girl ought not marry a father. Stowe explained it in an explicit celebration of "Romance." Romance was not what sensible people rejected as delusion. It was not something *made* by poets and novelists. Rather, romance was the soul at its fullest, an "enkindling of the whole power of the soul's love." Stowe identified the relationship such love bore to its object: "In a refined and exalted nature, it is very seldom that the feeling of love, when once thoroughly aroused, bears any sort of relation to the reality of the object." What this meant in the specific case at hand followed:

What Mary loved so passionately . . . was not the gay, young, dashing sailor,—sudden in anger, imprudent of speech, and, though generous in heart, yet worldly in plans and schemings, but her own ideal of a grand and noble man, such a man as she thought he might become. He stood glorified before her.[21]

With this, the unsuitability of the Doctor, and James's suitability, stood plain. The Doctor offered Mary no task. He was already glorified. She could not improve him. Her services as a "soul priest" were not needed. James, on the other hand, could stand some remaking. Just why he would submit to it was another matter. In her efforts to lend some plausibility to this submission, Stowe further drained her novel of any popular appeal by draining James himself of vitality. Instead of a dashing young sailor—let alone a Burr to be tamed or a St. Elmo to be undone—James became a confused penitent.

I have been thinking that perhaps I gave you a wrong impression of myself this afternoon. . . . I do not confess to being what is commonly called a bad young man. . . . It is only in your presence, Mary, that I feel that I am bad and low and shallow and mean. . . . No, I have not been bad, Mary, as the world calls badness. . . . But do you remember you told me once, that, when the snow first fell and lay so dazzling and pure and soft, all about, you always felt as if the spreads and window-curtains that seemed white before were not clean? Well, it's just like that with me. Your presence makes me feel that I am not pure, that I am low and unworthy.[22]

Thus, setting out to identify the crucial mechanism by which American girls might win freedom and maturity, Stowe ended up not only de-masculinizing American men but propounding systematic fantasy as the proper course for women. Certainly in becoming wife-mother to James's husband-son, Mary was depriving him of his democratic American birthright to go back to sea, to wander the world, to gamble and to reinvent himself. But far more deeply disenabling was the commendation of "romance" as deliberate, welcomed evasion of "any sort of relation to the reality of the object." It would be in their cultivation of sisterhood, within their sphere, that American women, quite disencumbered of fathers and patriarchy, would go on being able to pursue lives unrelated to the reality of the object. It was one of the merits of

Stowe's novel that sisterhood never figured as an option for her new American girl. Her novel did not waver from the assumption that a girl's maturity and freedom would include some relation to the object. They required some assertion of a girl's heterosexuality. But it was not one that would attract a gay and dashing hero.[23]

The Hero Invents a More Honest Language: Mark Twain and the Emergence of Masculine Realism

Accompanying Bushnell's liberation of the self from biblical and evangelical authority had run his demand for the liberation of language. Most theological disputes were disputes over language. The liberation from repetitive orthodoxies lay in new flexible resourceful tongues. Bushnell never himself, however, experimented with fresh language. Certainly he never tried to find language for his own personal experience of lyric freedom as the boy he had not been allowed to be.

With the discovery of such a language, its expansion of the repertoire of masculine imagination proved remarkable. Yankee, minstrel, frontiersman had all practiced gifts of exaggeration, sly and purposeful double-talk, ironies at once self-referential and challenging. So had Whitman, Hawthorne, Melville. But in none of these had the new language seemed wrought from common popular speech. Theirs was language for mastery, as the frontiersman engaged himself with a wilderness he must subjugate more than enjoy, as the ecstasists in the California mines shot hydraulically intensified streams of water at nature, battered nature, dug it up, scoured it out, leveled it, pounded it down, surveyed it for long-term capture. With Mark Twain, though, a new language emerged facilitating mysticism rather than mastery, facilitating love, simple eagerness for the unchained, far and wild. Twain found it—or rather, generated it—in the psychology of a boy:

Here is the way we put in the time. It was a monstrous big river down there— sometimes a mile and a half wide; we run nights, and laid up and hid daytimes; soon as night was most gone we stopped navigating and tied up . . . and watched the daylight come. Not a sound anywheres . . . only sometimes the bullfrogs. . . . you see the mist curl up off the river, and the east reddens up, and the river . . . then the nice breeze springs up, and comes fanning you from over there, so cool and fresh and sweet to smell on account of the woods and the flowers; but sometimes not that way, because they've left dead fish. . . . A little smoke couldn't be noticed now, so we would take some fish off the lines and cook up a hot breakfast. . . . we would put in the day, lazying around, listening to the stillness. . . . Soon as it was night out we shoved; when we got her out to about the middle we let her alone, and let her float . . . we lit the pipes and dangled our legs in the water, and talked about all kinds of things—we was always naked, day and night, whenever the mosquitoes would let us—the new clothes Buck's folks made for me were too uncomfortable, and besides I didn't go much on clothes, nohow. Sometimes we'd have the whole river to ourselves for the longest time. . . . It's lovely to live on a raft.[24]

To what the homosociality of boyhood might yield as Huckleberry Finn grew up, Mark Twain never tried to say. Nor did he ever speculate about girls. Could girls possibly muster enough sensitivity, delicacy, grace to find a raft "lovely" ? Could there be a girl Huckleberry Finn? But Twain's language powerfully fortified the Tocquevillian psychology of American masculinity, and that language, as Twain's self-chosen heir, Ernest Hemingway, would show, would be capable of further, deeper applications. The great river served Twain as contrast to the constrictions of a society increasingly given over to tyrannies of greed and righteousness. But Hemingway, beginning to write at a time when society no longer shaded off into frontiers and territories into which to escape, could take up the fact that nature too could affront and destroy. Following Twain in rejecting the fine words of public, community-bonding discourse in favor of a boy's prosaic straightforwardness, Hemingway could go so far as to equate war and childbirth as killing times. But even more than Twain, Hemingway raised the question whether men and women ever could share. Just possibly a girl might join Huck and Jim dangling their legs in the thick water. But a woman along on the hunt? In "The Short Happy Life of Francis Macomber" that mixture exploded into murder. In *For Whom the Bell Tolls*, sexual sharing might come to blur into the mysticism of war and nature, but only as all three issued on to annihilation.[25]

The comic spirit would not simply rigidify into a "sphere," mingling sports, westerns, and fraternal lodges in a kind of encysted perpetual adolescence. Through language, it could deepen and expand its sway, still without any real opening for women.

The American Boy Protests the Absence of His Heroine: Henry Adams

The continuing absence of women—or Woman—from American national imagination prompted the greatest of all lamentations, surpassing Whitman's—Henry Adams's *Education* of 1907. Adams explained it as the fruit of a kind of intellectual maturation: "As he grew older, he found that Early Institutions lost their interest, but that Early Woman became a passion. Without understanding movement of sex, history seemed to him mere pedantry." Such maturation may have been impelled by personal catastrophe. In 1870, following an accident, his beloved older sister, Louisa Adams Kuhn, died in agony in Italy, forty years old: "God might be, as the Church said, a Substance, but He could not be a Person." [26] Fifteen years later Adams's wife, Marion Hooper Adams—"Clover"—following her father's death, killed herself. Adams finished up his work, the *History of the Jefferson and Madison Administrations*. Then, this rediscovery of the United States behind him, he set out to rediscover himself, and in the end discovered a different United States from the one about which he had just written.

First, escaping with his friend, the artist John LaFarge, Adams cast off on the Pacific to Hawaii, to the South Seas, to Tahiti. As embodiment of the state of nature, Tahiti had become a fixed point on the tour map of popular European—and American—liberalism. With LaFarge's artist's eye to cue him, Adams indeed found brightness and color there, but he also, perhaps despite himself, found history, the wrong kind of history, a history of politics, power-hunting, greed, conflict, wars, wars, and more wars. The most ironical development in "modern" Tahitian history had been the appearance, in 1828, of a fanatical anti-Western, antimissionary sect, the Mamaia, whose leader, announcing himself as Jesus Christ, promised his Tahitian followers a sensual paradise, that is, a Tahiti as fantasized by the West. Adams left his history of Tahiti unfinished, hardly even a first draft, full of undigested phonetic transcriptions, hazy geographical guesses, scraps of chronicle—a testimony to his historian's wish to offer Tahitians what philosophers, scientists, adventurers, poets, painters, and the self-interested generally could not, truth, but a testimony also to his sense that Tahiti was not the truth he himself needed.[27]

Adams's evocation of his research for *Mont-Saint-Michel and Chartres* (1904) evinced his real rebirth, in a return not after all to nature but to a particular moment in history. Traveling by car, a still exotic but by then exhilarating vehicle, through the Norman countryside, into the villages of Touraine, over into Champagne, back to the Île-de-France, Adams savored tourism at its most delicious, when his was the only car on the road, the true pleasure machine as no train or carriage could be, not yet its own nemesis, and the roads were good.

The hunt for the Virgin's glass opened rich preserves. . . . The ocean of religion . . . had left every remote village strewn with fragments that flashed like jewels . . . tossed into hidden clefts of peace and forgetfulness. . . . The student may still imagine himself three hundred years ago, kneeling . . . crying . . . beating his breast.

A scholar who "had set aside the summer for study," Adams explicitly equated his research with love, "wooing, happy in the thought that at last he had found a mistress who could see no difference in the age of her lovers." Now he went beyond LaFarge, who "felt the early glass rather as a document than as a historical emotion." [28] It was with the yardstick of such a rich historical emotion that he would measure the modern United States.

The Virgin that Adams found at Chartres was anarchistic:

In no well-regulated community, under a proper system of police, could the Virgin feel at home. . . . the Virgin cared [little] for criticism of her manners or acts. She was above criticism. She made manners. Her acts were laws. . . . She cared not a straw for conventional morality.

The Virgin encouraged hectic feelings:

Mary concentrated in herself the whole rebellion of man against fate; the whole protest against divine law; the whole contempt for human law as its outcome; the whole unutterable fury of human nature beating itself against the walls of its prison-house . . . in the Virgin man had found a door of escape. . . . she delighted in trampling on every social distinction in this world and the next.

Adams insisted upon the priority of the individual in Mariolatrous twelfth- and thirteenth-century France:

The instinct of individuality went down through all classes, from the count at the top, to the jogleors and menestreus at the bottom. The individual rebelled against restraint; society wanted to do what it pleased; all disliked the laws which Church and State were trying to fasten on them. They longed for a power above law. . . . like children, they yearned for protection, pardon, and love.[29]

When Adams then returned from this free, anarchic, individualistic, mother-blessed paradise in search of his own real past, he found a free, unrepressed little boy. "He first found himself sitting on a yellow kitchen floor in strong sunlight—he knew only the colour of yellow." This three-year-old, still unified by smell and touch, as well as sight, deserved to survive socialization into an abstract order. Adams evoked a sensual, not a Puritan world, a boy's, not a minister's order. Patriarchal, militarized, Indian-fighting old New England did not figure. Boys, not preachers and soldiers, knew New England best:

Boys are wild animals, rich in the treasures of sense, but the New England boy had a wider range of emotions than boys of more equable climates. He felt his nature crudely, as it was meant. . . . The bearing of the two seasons on the education of Henry Adams was no fancy; it was the most decisive force he ever knew; it ran through life.

In a New England where "light is glare, and the atmosphere harshens color," the senses spoke to the birth of self.[30]

Adams linked this earliest self to women. The fourth-born, hence of less account in family ambitions, he "was in a way given to his mother," but neither father nor mother really tried to control their "turbulent" child. School, which did try to control, he hated. The eldest child, Louisa, eight years his senior, was a sister, hence also of less account, thus left more free, sparkling, "the first young woman he was ever intimate with." A happy sister-mother was perhaps the best of all mothers: "he was delighted to give her the reins. . . . he was so much pleased with the results that he never wanted to take them back." [31]

The America Adams lamented in his *Education*, that of political decline, of corruption, of "bullet-headed" generals, was of course the America of the Dynamo, that awful principle of law and abstraction. An "immense force, doubling every few years" was at work, magnetizing men like iron filings around a magnet.[32] This was no place for a New England boy to flourish.

But Adams did not blame mere technology. Technology was less to blame than those who worshiped it. And for this Adams blamed those who had rejected the Virgin. "Why did the gentle and gracious Virgin Mother so exasperate the Pilgrim Father?" Presumably it was because of a vast pretension, the Puritans' confidence "of getting to heaven by the regular judgment, without expense." This pretension showed itself in a particular policy: "[The] Puritan reformers were not satisfied with abolishing [Mary], but sought to abolish the woman altogether as the cause of evil in heaven and on earth." In so doing, the Puritans forsook the most precious treasure of true faith:

The Mother alone was human, imperfect, and could love; she alone was Favour, Duality, Diversity. . . . the Mother alone could represent whatever was not Unity; whatever was irregular, exceptional, outlawed.

Here was where Tocqueville had misunderstood the real need of American men for women, not as cool and dutiful Puritan-style help-meets but as loving mothers. Recapitulating the popular religion of Chartres, Adams spelled out a theology as heterodox and feminist as any proposed by Mary Daly: "The Father seldom appears; the Holy Ghost still more rarely. . . . Chartres represents, not the Trinity, but the identity of Mother and Son. The Son represents the Trinity, which is thus absorbed in the Mother." [33] Here the modern feminist's accusation that men had stolen religion from women was anticipated by a boy-man's plea that good mothers, permissive mothers, ought indeed to replace God the Father. Unfortunately, despite Adams's own happy boyhood, things had not worked out this way in America. Adams never quite explained why, but the result was obvious: like Puritan America, modern America was sexless; it lacked Venus and Virgin both.

The problem was not that American men remained Puritan, for they did not. True, their new dynamo civilization did exhibit them some-times gripped as much in a vise as by divine law:

The typical American man had his hand on a lever. . . .his living depended on keeping up an average speed. . . . he could not admit emotions or anxieties or subconscious distractions, more than he could admit whiskey or drugs, without breaking his neck. He could not run his machine and a woman too.

But this was just as easily described as a commanding appetite as a fatality, an appetite comparable to the passion Tocqueville had described, and, in accord with Tocqueville, an appetite not so much for the possession of its object—"power" in Adams's terms, as it had been "money" in Tocqueville's—as for the sensation power gave, a sensation not unlike that rendered to the faithful at communion, as through the hand resting on the shell of the dynamo itself sensing the visionary rotors within. But Adams now, in the twentieth century, picking up on Bushnell, Twain, and the whole literature of lyric male freedom, perceived that this freedom was itself being contained. Though noting in *Mont-Saint-Michel* that the Virgin herself did not much like bankers and money, he himself did not expatiate upon either as the critical points of captivity. It was rather that the solid foundation on which men had enjoyed their freedom was being undermined. In a sense, men had only themselves to blame, for what they had done was to leave their women stranded, isolated, alone. They had abandoned their women. The American woman had then responded to her abandonment by trying to become manlike. "When closely watched, she seemed making a violent effort to follow the men. . . . all the world saw her trying to find her way by imitating him." Where all men were free, women could be free, too, "volatilized . . . almost brought to the point of explosion, like steam . . . myriads of new types."[34]

The result would be in fact to submit women as well as men to the desiccating abstractions of the dynamo. So long as women remained women, the dynamo would not wreak its worst effects.

Of all movements of inertia, maternity and reproduction are the most typical, and women's property of moving in a constant line forever is ultimate, uniting history in its only unbroken and unbreakable sequence.[35]

But the whole point Adams was making was that this "unbreakable" sequence was in fact being broken in the United States as women, desperately, imitated those who were not womanlike.

Thus what had changed in the lifetime of Henry Adams was not so much the rise of the dynamo and the decline of Adams family leadership, as the transformation in women. "All these new women . . . [had been] created since 1840." The new situation was not really women's fault. A modern woman knew what she was losing; she knew the substitute being offered her was no substitute. "She [sees] before her only the future reserved for machine-made, collectivist females." But she too was being overtaken by the "immense force." As usual, Adams professed a cool, scientific objectivity: "No honest historian can take part with—or against—the forces he has to study." "To him even the extinction of the human race should be merely a fact to be grouped with other vital statistics."[36] But it was not extinction of the species that defined the grief in *The Education of Henry Adams*, but the extinction of the little boy soaked in sunshine on the kitchen floor. Freedom depended on being able to bask in the warmth of that power above law, the power of protection, pardon, and love, of being able to recover oneself as a universe in oneself, known in the only mode that could know selves, known by love. Though insisting that American men did not want their women mixed into their lives of money and frontier and freedom, Tocqueville had seen that American men did need their women, without quite being able to say how or why. Henry Adams had no such difficulty. As if to undermine his pretension to calm objectivity, he announced that he had written *Mont-Saint-Michel*, that hymn to the lawless Virgin, not for historians or even for needful American men, but for his nieces. Nieces could grow up to become Louisas, loving Virgin-Venuses, delighted at the spectacle of their men at play.[37]

The Sentimental Heroine Transcends Herself: Henry James

But even as Henry Adams wrote, a far greater writer may have repaired the lack. Daisy Miller and Isabel Archer, then Milly Theale and Maggie Verver: these four alone might be thought a pantheon of American young womanhood, not just in supplement to the American male hero but, as Henry James arranged them, taking priority over the male, embodying the very meaning of American culture.

James had begun with a man. As Constance Rourke pointed out, Christopher Newman in *The American* (1877) derived directly from the legendary storytelling of the Jacksonian theater with its larger-than-life archetypes.[38] Newman fulfilled Tocqueville's description of the American male. He was vastly rich, having made his money in copper, oil, even washtubs, but: "I cared for moneymaking, but I have never cared so very terribly about money."[39] And the scene of his triumph was the West, San Francisco. In short, James had no interest whatever in some individualized psychological analysis of his hero. As his title told, he was presenting an ideal type, one utterly admirable—"long, lean, and muscular," a "liberal looseness," open, generous, wry. Among modern movie actors Gary Cooper would play his part.

Upon this "superlative American," the very "mould" of his race,

James proceeded to inflict defeat. At leisure—at the age of forty!—and fascinated by a daughter of old French nobility, Newman wooed and won her. But her family forced her to send him away. Neither his money nor his sterling manhood availed. Constance Rourke concluded: "Defeat had become at last an essential part of the national portraiture."[40] Yet nothing in James's novel explained why any of this had to be so. In the first place, what was Christopher Newman doing looking for a wife in France rather than back home? It was not a habit of American self-made men to go to Europe for their wives. The obvious but unstated implication was that there were no girls in America worthy of him. James betrayed his uneasiness with this implication. His hero had not really gone seeking a wife, he was simply idling around the Louvre and other standard resorts like any ordinary tourist, when he met his fate. In the second place, why must Newman's attractions fall short? In the preface he wrote years later for *The American*, James rather astonishingly agreed that, from the standpoint of real social history, his noble French family, far from turning away his "rich and easy American," would have snapped him up. Families like the Bellegardes needed the infusion of fresh money. In the novel itself, their materialism and their sense of identity had been made vividly clear.

In sum, then, *The American* told nothing of what was really happening in America or France. James had no interest in his hero's moneymaking. What his novel brought into focus was the problem effectively suppressed in Tocquevillian America, as in the Jacksonian theater. Was it really true that American men would be satisfied with an indefinitely extensible process? Newman loved the moneymaking more than the money, yes, but he had obviously had enough of moneymaking, too. What was this money to be used for? Effectively, he set out to buy the best piece of art he could find. This meant the best woman, the best wife. But if this meant that he had to go to Europe, it followed that American society did face a crisis. Of course, in Tocqueville's reckoning, an American man got married before he got rich. He certainly did not wait till he was forty. Part of the strength of American marriages was that money had nothing to do with them. But to assume, as Tocqueville apparently did, that money would forever remain sealed off from courtship was unjustified except by earnest hope. It was at least imaginable that some men—like Newman—would wait until they got rich just in order to see what they might get then. But such a linkage between money and sexuality was too obvious to engage the interest of a mind like James's. Although he contrived to preserve his hero's innocence, despite the essential corruption of what that hero was doing, it was only by letting him seem, in the end, näive if not faintly stupid. There was little more to be found in such a story. Men who set out to buy women would not attest to the corruption of innocence by money but would attest to some prior corruption. James eventually realized that the moral interest, the psychological interest, lay in seeing what women might do with money.

Where would he get his heroines? In effect, simply from woman's sphere. All sexuality being deferred until marriage, sexual innocence would distinguish them. Honesty, candor, and simplicity would characterize them, for the powers of calculation and the devious were not inculcated in woman's sphere. A tropism for art, taste, culture, the higher things figured in them, for these were theirs by right in the logic of the spheres. One thing he took away from them: mothers. Though Daisy Miller's mother did accompany her daughter to Europe, she had consciously retreated from active superintendence into spectatorial passivity, not so much in respect for her daughter's maturity, as in recognition of her evidently constitutional independence. After that James realized he wanted no mothers at all. Isabel Archer never knew her mother, hers having died when she was a baby. Part of Millie Theale's pathos inhered in her orphanhood. Maggie Verver's mother was dead. The reason is plain. What the heroine would do with her money must not be what her mother told her to do. Fathers, too, were not to be forces in control of their daughters. Daisy Miller's stayed back home working the moneymaking machine. The one clear case of a father raising his daughters was Isabel Archer's, but his main task, after providing them no permanent home and squandering their fortune, was to die in plenty of time to let Isabel's story proceed without him. Millie Theale had lost father with mother. But in his last investigation, James arrived at a final insight: perhaps what a girl would do with her money would have very much to do with her father, not as her educator and protector, but as her conspirator. From *The Golden Bowl* it was plain that the crucial absentee, then, was a girl's mother. In Harriet Beecher Stowe's *The Minister's Wooing*, Mary's mother had been a force for immaturity; she had wanted her daughter to marry the minister. James's heroines would be on their own.

Daisy Miller's money really made no difference in her story and fate, even though that story registered what was to seem James's irreducible conviction about what happened to independent rich girls: they got betrayed. Betrayal could hardly have seemed more painful than for Isabel Archer in *The Portrait of a Lady*. A husband who had married her purely for her money, without love, with contempt for her tastes, and, far worse, a child, and a mistress, the mother of that child, with whom he conspired: what could be worse? While James himself was fascinated with how his heroine coped with her betrayal, he could hardly fail to shed some light on an obvious question: How could she have got herself into such a situation? From all evidence, Gilbert Osmond, the man she picked for a husband, must have been recognizable for what he was, decadent, cold, and inert, from the start. Once, in her youth, Isabel had reflected on her future:

Few of the men she saw seemed worth a ruinous expenditure . . . it made her smile to think that one of them should present himself as an incentive to hope. . . . Deep in her soul—it was the deepest thing there—lay a belief that if a certain light should dawn she could give herself completely; but this image, on the whole, was too formidable to be attractive.[41]

Certainly Osmond, neither formidable nor attractive, had not begun to resemble such an image. Isabel had had a suitor who did, however. Caspar Goodwood was admirable, "tall, strong, lean and brown," another Christopher Newman or Gary Cooper. There could be no suspicion of his avarice for her money: he was a moneymaker himself, incarnate. Moreover, Goodwood was one of those gradually evolving men who not only accepted but welcomed greater freedom in the women they loved.

To his mind she always had wings. . . . He was not afraid of having a wife with a certain largeness of movement. . . . "Who would wish less to curtail your liberty than I . . . ? It is to make you independent that I want to marry you."

If he was not exactly a feminist, he was as close to being one as Isabel could have expected. From his standpoint there was no marriage crisis in America. He did not have to go to Europe to find a mate commensurate with his imagination. But Isabel rejected him, and the reasons suggested that if there was an American crisis, it came from certain new needs in women, not in men. For Isabel, it was precisely Goodwood's strength that counted against him.

[It] was part of the influence he had upon her that he seemed to take from her the sense of freedom. There was something too forcible, something oppressive and restrictive, in the manner in which he presented himself. . . . The difficulty was that more than any man she had ever known . . . Caspar Goodwood gave her an impression of energy.[42]

If there was one thing Gilbert Osmond lacked, it was energy. Was the American heroine then incapable of marrying vitality, strength, and energy? Did she want weakness over which to prevail? James almost seemed to say so. After their climactic confrontation, when Goodwood, having tried to win her, had left, in failure, Isabel, "by an irresistible impulse . . . dropped on her knees before her bed, and hid her face in her arms." Probably a hundred girls in a hundred popular sentimental novels had done the same. But in one of those exercises of craft showing that he intended deliberately to work against the grain of this standard fiction, James concluded the chapter there, then opened the next with an explicit statement of Isabel's real appetite:

She was not praying; she was trembling. . . . She was an excitable creature, and now she was much excited. . . . It was not for some ten minutes tht she rose . . . and when she came back to the sitting-room she was still trembling a little. Her agitation was to be accounted for by . . . the enjoyment she found in the exercise of her power . . . she had tasted of the delight, if not of battle, at least of victory.

The question was, victory over whom? or what? Over Goodwood, certainly, for he had been defeated, but since that victory was followed by marriage to the effete Osmond, it had been a hollow victory. Had not Isabel feared that?

Much later, after the full dimensions of her betrayal by husband and friend had become clear, Isabel found herself confronted by Caspar Goodwood once more. He urged her to free herself, join him. She would not.

He glared at her a moment through the dusk, and the next instant she felt his arms about her and his lips on her own lips. His kiss was like white lightning, a flash that spread, and spread again, and stayed; and it was extraordinarily as if, while she took it, she felt each thing in his hard manhood that had least pleased her, each aggressive fact of his face, his figure, his presence, justified of its intense identity and made one with this act of possession. So she had heard of those wrecked and under water following a train of images before they sink.[43]

It was in passages like these that James generated the eerily subliminal, almost otherworldly atmosphere of his supposedly social fictions. There was no drama of innocent America versus decadent Europe in *The Portrait of a Lady*. Caspar Goodwood was an American. So was Gilbert Osmond. Had James been interested in some study of international contrasts, he would have arranged crucial scenes for his heroine with her British suitor, Lord Warburton. The explicit message in Isabel's response to Goodwood's kiss was that she did not want his hard manhood, or any hard manhood, any good wood. Her girlhood apprehension that, were a "certain light" to dawn, she could "give herself completely," she had already short-circuited by finding that prospect too formidable to be attractive. The most sympathetic reading would not attribute this aversion to some neurotic deficiency, let alone sociologize it, as James himself did in his novel on feminists, *The Bostonians*, into some kind of pathology in modern women. Isabel could be thought to have discovered some perennial, ineradicable conflict between a woman's freedom and her sexuality. Alexandra Kollontai had wanted to revolutionize the world on the basis of that conflict. But James made it impossible to proceed to such an interpretation. In choosing to reject flight from her misery, the heroine might have been thought rising to the lofty moral freedom of living with the consequences of her mistake. In fact, it only freed her from having to face any more challenges from anyone. She left herself in solitude, but it was not that solitude of self to which Elizabeth Cady Stanton had referred in urging upon women greater responsibility for themselves. Isabel still seemed to be fleeing herself.

One of the problems that had lurked around the edges of *The Portrait of a Lady* as a sheer story came to haunt the very center of James's next portrait of a heroine, Millie Theale in *The Wings of the Dove*, twenty years later. Although Isabel Archer had been more often reactive than active in her own history, with her major act, her choice of Gilbert Osmond, left wholly offstage, she had been healthy, evidently up to various small initiatives, presumably capable of sexual feelings. In *The Wings of the Dove*, however, the heroine seemed often but a kind of hub, inert, an unmoving center around whom the other characters revolved. The heroine was in danger of being less interesting than peripheral figures. As a type, the ambitious Henrietta Stackpole in *The Portrait of a Lady*, a raw, eager journalist, crude yet sympathetic, a kind of grass-roots Margaret Fuller, had already been far more interesting than Isabel. In *The Wings of the Dove* the heroine would be much outclassed, in moral interest, by the young woman, Kate Croy, who engaged in the conspiracy directed at her. James flinched from carrying through on the conspiracy in its full ugliness as he first conceived it: Kate Croy was to collaborate with her lover in the pretense that he, Merton Densher, in fact loved Millie. He and Millie would marry. Then, one day—for Millie suffered from a fatal sickness—upon Millie's death he and Kate would enjoy Millie's inheritance. Since James first intended to let the tie binding Millie to Merton be fully and overtly sexual, the corruption of the tie between the conspiratorial lovers would have been far more complete. He in fact decided to allow Millie's sickness to bar real sexual union in favor of a dream with which Millie would be allowed to die happy. All this was the stuff of pure sentimental fiction. James got beyond it, however, in a way that anticipated the depths of his master-piece, *The Golden Bowl*. Presumably, the discovery of her supposed lover's duplicity left Millie certain options. One, of course, was to expire in despair. But she transcended this, instead, by signing over to Densher, in full knowledge of his betrayal, her full fortune. While this might be interpreted as further evidence of the invincible goodness of the hero-ine, James forebade such a judgment. While he did not explicitly credit her with foreknowledge of the results of her action, no reader could doubt it. Densher, presumably irradiated with the influence of his intended victim, refused to accept his ill-gotten booty and, in addition, abandoned his lover, Kate Croy, leaving her in writhing despair. If measured by its own canons, sentimental fiction had generated here its sadomasochistic classic. Once again, none of this had anything to do with transatlantic differences. Nothing required Kate Croy and Densher to be, as they were, English. James was instead continuing to make progress on his inquiry—what the impact of money was on these most intimate of relations. One conclusion had begun to emerge. While money did expose young girls to evil adventurers, it also offered them power, power to inflict things on others. Kate Croy no doubt had only herself to blame, but what had happened to her followed from what the rich heroine had done.

It was in *The Golden Bowl*, at last, that James finally found the way to impel his heroines into full self-possession. He hardly troubled to soften the blunt structure of his story. This time the rich American girl's father was very much in evidence. Adam Verver's plain purpose in coming to Europe with his daughter, Maggie, was to buy her a husband. This time the husband did have to be a European, though of no particular sort. No American man could be imagined being bought except another Gilbert Osmond, and Verver and his daughter were interested only in "the best." Goodwood could not be bought. The underlying reason for all of this was to set in motion once again James's investigation of how a heroine coped with betrayal. James was careful to layer the issue of why Prince Amerigo betrayed Maggie with alternative possibilities. One was simply the Prince's response to having had to let himself be bought. Another inhered in certain notions of the heroine.

[She] had been able to marry without breaking, as she liked to put it, with her past. She had surrendered to her husband without the shadow of a reserve or a condition, and yet she had not, all the while, given up her father by the least little inch.

A common view would have thought Maggie engaging in self-contradictory rationalization. A Prince who had contracted for a wife might have assumed at least a few inches less of father-in-law. But as Joel Porte has implied, perhaps the deepest reason was the fear and alarm provoked in the Prince upon his realization that Maggie—and her father—really were innocents, fully trusting in the future of a completely honest, open relationship.[44] The Prince tried to warn her of the opacities and frontiers in all inner life, her own included, but in her American optimism she seemed immune to such knowledge. By the end of the book she had learned about the "terrible," but by then it was clear the Prince himself had more to learn about just how terrible it could be.

Once again James turned to the device of a prior relationship as the machinery of betrayal. Maggie Verver's best friend, Charlotte Stant, had, it appeared, been Prince Amerigo's lover. Starved for greater depth than Maggie could offer, the Prince resumed his relationship with Charlotte. As the two pledged to protect the "innocents," Maggie and her father, from dangerous truth, the high point of explicit sexuality in the novel was reached—"lips sought . . . lips, their pressure their response and their response their pressure"—but James did not intend this to imply that the crack in the golden bowl of the Prince's marriage with Maggie was that—or only that—of some erotic deficiency in Maggie. His "story" consisted, rather, of the paper-flower-like exfoliation of awareness on the part of all parties. When and how did Maggie come to "know" about Charlotte's old liaison? When did she realize Charlotte and her husband had resumed it? When did the Prince realize she knew? When did Charlotte realize the Prince realized Maggie knew? When did Maggie know that the Prince knew she knew? Each stage of these discoveries was also made to resonate with moral issues: must not betrayal be concealed to save the victim from hurt? Must not one's own realization of betrayal be concealed so as to save the betrayer from humiliation? As this kind of consciousness chess progressed, it entered an end game that took on realities of power. With Adam Verver's preparation for return to America, it transpired that, for his role as inventor of his utopian venture, American City, somewhere "west of the Mississippi," he needed a hostess, a consort, a first lady. Charlotte would do. At first, in her determination not to have to surrender her father by the least little inch, Maggie had felt protective of him. She would take care of him as she once had cherished her doll. She would protect him from hurt by concealing her own hurt, inflicted by her husband and Charlotte. But perhaps her father, too, "knew." Perhaps her father knew and had devised the best possible resolution to her situation. By the end, James made clear, Maggie had no doubt what Charlotte's new condition had become. Her father held—"in a pocketed hand"!—a halter "looped around [Charlotte's] beautiful neck." As her father's young wife, Charlotte found herself in a golden cage, "richly gilt," no doubt, but firmly closed. Far from recoiling from the prospect of Charlotte in torment in exile forever, Maggie was fascinated by it as evidence of her father's psychological depth and cunning. He was "simply a great and deep and high little man."[45]

Maggie's father had not purposed to remove Charlotte to American City simply to allow Maggie to return to the Prince in some sentimental reconciliation. The elaborate game of layering awareness on awareness had strengthened new capacities in the heroine. Quite on her own, she asserted domination over the Prince. She refused to allow him to warn Charlotte, to let Charlotte know that Maggie "knew." Not only did she quite consciously let Charlotte be taken off to captivity, she inflicted on her husband the cruelty of his impotence to head off the harm he himself was responsible for bringing down on his lover. Father and daughter were left joined in triumph.

To say that incest lurked in this, James's greatest epic of American girlhood, is fair but in itself inadequate. James was not offering a clinical study. He certainly had no intention of commenting on incest as some American social malady. But he was preoccupied with the question of exploitation. Tocqueville had congratulated Americans for rigorously keeping money and sex apart. He had warned that disasters followed from mixing them. On the evidence of Isabel Archer and Millie Theale—with Daisy Miller a more ambiguous case—he had been right. But a rich girl was a rich girl; she had to find a way. On a simple reading, *The Golden Bowl* warned girls not to too quickly give up the help most obviously available to them, that of their fathers. But just as obviously, Maggie Verver had grown up. She was no longer daddy's girl, nor did she look for a father in her husband. She had learned how to conceal herself, sustain the most elaborate webs of deception, transcend the simplicity of innocence. She had discovered—or generated?—within herself talents for cruelty, which, in turn, fed her self-confidence. She had learned to dominate. What the sexual future was for Maggie and her husband James left deeply obscure. Presumably her discovery of her own strengths for psychological struggle also cleared the way for the heroine to sense connections between sexuality and aggression, hence the possibilities for her to take sexual initiatives, but James rigorously abstained from carrying his story into these darknesses. The darkest possibility was that, should the heroine prove newly capable of manipulating her prince sexually, this would be so only because her own deepest sexuality remained locked up, tabooed, with father.

Finally, James's new American Girl hardly constituted the answer to Henry Adams's prayer for an American Venus-Virgin. James's heroine was narcissistic, not permissive. Later literary explorations into wealth and courtship were more spectatorial and sociological. The risings into and fallings out of money inspired William Dean Howells to several social comedies. For Edith Wharton's Lily Bart, in *The House of Mirth*, lack of money, depriving the heroine of suitors she deserved, produced at least pathos if not tragedy. To the degree that this implied wealth would have been a good thing for Lily, Wharton was simply commenting on the emergence of new social hierarchies in America, a topic that had not interested James at all. Perhaps the next to find the demonic in money was F. Scott Fitzgerald, who reversed the perspective, to trace the fate of masculine innocence entangled with wealth.[46] That Daisy Buchanan's voice should "sound like money" proved her decisive attraction for Gatsby, but he then could not comprehend that if she lived for money she would not live for him. Mythic as it may be, *The Great Gatsby* showed Fitzgerald's empathies falling short for Daisy, a pity, since he put her in her impossible situation. His sympathy for his hero's innocence was less unguarded in *Tender Is the Night*. There, while only his wife's money could possibly have allowed Dr. Diver to succumb to the danger of trying to be therapist and husband at once, it was finally the hero's pretension, rather than the money, that mattered most, and Fitzgerald had no doubts about the fatality of that. The moral was twofold: just as marriage must not be a therapy, so, too, marriage must be only a part-time affair. But Fitzgerald's deeper interests, as *The Great Gatsby* had shown, were with the broad cultural myths that were sweeping democratic America. In the great fragment of *The Last Tycoon*, his hero was no longer victimized by innocent illusions; at the same time he realized his own self-consuming position, as a Hollywood producer, the manufacturer of myths and illusions. For this hero, Fitzgerald created an equally sophisticated heroine. For the first time in American literary history a man and a woman confronted each other as selves equally self-aware in their sexuality. We cannot know whether Fitzgerald would have completed his novel along the lines indicated in some notes. In the fragment, however, a hero had realized the crucial dimension of wealth as a kind of hallucinogenic agent, at once stimulating and distorting vision. That love alone was real which escaped such enchantments.

The Hero Invites the Heroine to Join Him on the Battlefield: Stephen Crane

How might the hero, immune to wealth and inoculated against power as well as money, find his way to a sexual heroine? No one more vividly defined the difficulty James would have had, had he tried to explore such a hero, than his fellow expatriate, who was for a few short seasons his neighbor in Old England's Kent. For whatever reasons deep in his origins, Stephen Crane realized that the extension of the comic tradition into further expositions of exaggerated mastery promised nothing but delusion. Though sometimes linked in some sort of literary naturalism with Jack London, Crane never dallied in stories about wolves and wolf-men or "calls" of the wild and primitive egos. Thomas Beer said the "mistress" of "this boy's mind" was fear.[47] Maybe so. But "this boy" had begun to forge art with words in a way no American had by the time he was nineteen.

Crane was born to Methodist parents in Newark, New Jersey.[48] Newark was then a middle-class town, in the Cranes' neighborhood at least, and there, and later in Bloomington, Paterson, and Port Jervis, New Jersey, Crane grew up in the air of late evangelical white mid-American Protestantism. Crane's father's forebears had run rather more to obscure soldiers, but he himself was a preacher; Crane was born in the parsonage. A success as both Methodist minister and Methodist journalist, Jonathan Crane died when his son was only six. Words were the medium of both parents, the evangelical words searching out the dark corners of inner spaces. Crane's Methodist heritage on his mother's side was formidable; her father was a clergyman and her great-uncle was one of the leading nineteenth-century Methodist bureaucrats, Bishop Jesse T. Peck. Forty-five when she bore Stephen (her husband was fifty-two), Mary Peck Crane was a dedicated Epworth worker; she wrote and reported for the Methodist press, and spoke frequently to religious circles across northern New Jersey. Though never far from home in miles, Mrs. Crane was often away in spirit during her last child's childhood; she assigned many of the tasks of homemaking, both before and after her widowhood, to her daughter Agnes, fifteen years older than Stephen. Crane's oldest brother, Jonathan T. Crane, Jr., gravitated to a word career, too, as a journalist for the *Newark Advertiser* and the *New York Tribune*. Another brother, Wilbur, before entering medicine, dabbled in journalism, and his sister Agnes, another little mother, planned to write. Before her sadly early death at twenty-eight, she admired and praised Stephen's earliest juvenile productions.

To many, Crane's life as a young man in New York City looked like that of a bohemian. He lived in poverty. He prowled New York City's more sinister neighborhoods. He consorted with prostitutes. He visited taverns and became knowledgeable about narcotics. But Crane never surrendered to mere environment. In no sense was he ever a drinker, let alone a drunk, and on the use of drugs he was if anything more scathing than standard moralists:

Opium holds out to them its lie, and they embrace it eagerly. . . . The influence of dope is . . . a fine languor, a complete mental rest. . . . The universe is readjusted. Wrong departs, injustice vanishes: . . . a quiet harmony of all things— until the next morning. . . . [The victim] has placed upon his shoulders an elephant which he may carry to the edge of forever.[49]

Nor was Crane a womanizer; at no time in New York did he live with a girl nor was he a patron of Manhattan's brothels.

His novel, *Maggie, a Girl of the Streets,* was written with astonishing precocity during a semester at Syracuse University when he was nineteen and before he had lived in the city of which he wrote. Crane had first learned the Bowery during many visits into the city from home in New Jersey. The Jersey shore towns too, such as Asbury Park, where his mother often evangelized, had offered much to see of low life. But "investigating" the infamous Bowery Five Points and other nefarious districts of New York City had been practically a standard exercise of professional Protestant moralists for decades. Two famous reports, Charles Loring Brace's *The Dangerous Classes of New York* and *The Abominations of Modern Society*, had appeared about the time of Crane's birth. In other volumes like Rev. T. Dewitt Talmadge's *The Night Side of City Life*, fallen women were stock characters.[50] In a sense, then, Crane simply rewrote these slum investigations. Those earlier investigators had not told the truth about the Bowery so much as exploited it. They had used it to affirm conventional sentiment. But Crane saw the Bowery as a test not of morality but of imagination.

Far from being an exercise in honest sociological realism, the Bowery of Crane's imagination seethed with theatricality. His famous color words—red, gold, yellow, orange, scarlet—attached to the horse-drawn vehicles of the crowded streets—cabs, trucks, wagons, carriages, above all the engines of the demonic fire brigades—were calculated for theatricality. With whip and reins, bawling oaths, threshing in the incessant wars of the chaotic intersections, their drivers presided as lords of the streets, embodiments of self-vaunting masculinity. That these lords of the traffic were in fact underpaid, self-deluded creatures of pathos, their fancy of themselves ludicrously at odds with their social, political, and economic situation, Crane's brilliant control of his deliberately inflated language exactly conveyed. But above all their pathos was sexual.

The greatest mockery, nearly contemptuous on Crane's part, of the men in the Bowery was mediated ironically through Maggie's own trusting vision of her boyfriend, Pete, seducer and betrayer. A victim, in nothing was Maggie more a victim than in taking her man at his own estimate of himself:

Here was the ideal man . . . his dignity, the attribute of a supreme warrior . . . nothing in space which could appall him . . . valour and contempt for circumstances . . . disdain for the inevitable and contempt for anything that fate might compel him to endure.

Maggie herself, as Crane could not help make clear, was an abstraction, in no way likely to elicit pity and tears. In a book carrying her name, she spoke hardly a hundred words, and those the simplest. No doubt the failure of the book to win popularity was rooted here. A few years later Edward W. Townsend's *Chimmie Fadden: A Daughter of the Tenements*, a slum romance, won the popularity denied to Crane's book precisely because it did cater to the conventions of sentimental sociology. Soon Israel Zangwill's *Abie's Irish Rose* would define the genre once for all, purged of the hostility many of the earlier investigators had felt for their subjects, and anticipating the new romantic sociology that would celebrate "pluralism," best expounded by Jane Addams. But Crane wrote in another spirit. Even at Maggie's moments of greatest pathos, her emotions forbade easy sympathy: "Maggie was pale. From her eyes had been plucked all look of self-reliance. She leaned with a dependent air toward her companion. She was timid, as if fearing his anger or displeasure. She seemed to beseech tenderness of him."[51] Such complicity in her own victimization invited diagnosis, not identification.

The ultimate judgment on Maggie's seducer, Pete, was registered less in his betrayal of Maggie than in his being betrayed by another woman. This was Nell or Nellie, a "woman of brilliance and audacity," who appeared with Maggie and Pete late in the book in a big music hall saloon. Crane carefully described her costume as a presentation of self:

[Her] black dress fitted her to perfection. Her linen collar and cuffs were spotless. Tan gloves were stretched over her well-shaped hands. A hat of prevailing fashion perched jauntily upon her dark hair. She wore no jewelry and was painted with no apparent paint. She looked clear-eyed through the stares of men.

This "brilliant and audacious" woman reduced Pete as Pete reduced Maggie. "Maggie was dazed. . . . She thought she noted an air of subservience about her leonine Pete. She was astounded." After Maggie's death, Pete made a sodden plea for himself to the women in the saloon. With "the trembling fingers of an offering priest," Pete gave the brilliant and audacious woman money; she took the bills and stuffed them "into a deep, irregularly shaped pocket," then stood up, looked down, said, "What a fool," and walked out.[52]

One of Crane's friends once showed him a sketch of a white cruiser anchored in the North River with Manhattan's towers, already skyscrapers, looming in the background. Instantly Crane titled it: "The Sense of a City Is War."[53] The whole genre of gangster movies stood anticipated; but Crane would not become the prophet of mass compensations. Instead, he pioneered a new vulnerability.

In 1895, with *The Red Badge of Courage* out in serial form, Crane underwent the most notorious of the sexual episodes that marked his reputation in his lifetime. The New York police just then were in a more than ordinarily sordid phase of the perennial symbiosis between law and prostitution, the standard system of bribes sagging into indulgence of individual officers' sadism. That summer Crane witnessed the behavior of one of these, Charles Becker, who was a more than ordinary rogue; he eventually went to the electric chair for murder. Crane saw

Becker arrest a girl, Dora Clarke, whom he knew Becker had seen do nothing illegal. Crane knew Clarke for what she was, a prostitute; he knew Becker; he knew Becker's act was not simply standard harassment but one aimed at personal gratifications. At the scene he protested the arrest, then appeared on Clarke's behalf in court. Then he sent the police commissioner—Theodore Roosevelt—a letter denouncing police harassments. Roosevelt summoned his captains, read the letter aloud, and exhorted them to police their men. When all this got into the papers, the police harassed Crane. A police notification to Crane miscarried, he was held in contempt, and more harassment followed.

Crane did not see all prostitutes as victims. He once wrote a friend that most streetwalkers would, "if they had the money," simply be "demi-mondaines." "Lots of women are just naturally unchaste," he went on, "and all you jays know it."[54] But prostitutes could be victimized by rogue police, and when they were, and a man knew it, it was incumbent upon him, if he was a true "aristocrat," that is, if he had courage and could "stand the strain whatever it may be," to do something about it.

Having thus tested himself with a dangerous gallantry in the war of the city, Crane set off for the war then going on in Cuba. But before departing, he exchanged several letters with Nellie Crouse, a young woman from Akron, Ohio, whom he had met at a tea on East Thirty-fourth Street early in the year. He was obviously interested in her. Crane tried hard to show himself honestly and to find out if they had real affinity. He spoke with irony over his new literary fame. He hoped the occasion of their meeting did not mean that tea parties and such meant anything to her. He thought she must know that he, "by inclination," was "a wild shaggy barbarian." When she replied, defending men of "social aspiration," he stiffened, shook off his act, announced that "I swear by the true aristocrat," and penned a corrosive dismissal of "society matrons." As for men of "very social habits," "there are a few . . . who can treat a woman tenderly not only when they feel amiable but when she most needs tender treatment. . . . There are an infinitesimal number who can keep from yapping in a personal way about women." Nellie Crouse did not understand him.[55]

Nine months later, in Jacksonville, Florida, Crane entered into the liaison with Cora Taylor that lasted the rest of his life. Like his sister Agnes, like Nellie Crouse, Cora Taylor knew and admired Crane's talent. When he went off to Cuba on the ship *Commodore*, he had, as an "Unnamed Sweetheart," signed one of his books to her. When the *Commodore* sank, Cora, at once frantic and resourceful, searched out Crane on the beach, insisted upon a special train to fetch him back to Jacksonville from Daytona, and nursed him back to life.

Cora Taylor's real name, when Crane met her, was still Cora Stewart, since her husband, an Englishman, Captain Donald William Stewart, was unwilling to accept a divorce.[56] The name Taylor she had adopted in Jacksonville apparently for legal reasons, as proprietress of a club called the Hotel de Dream. That the Hotel de Dream was a brothel seems unlikely. That Cora Taylor might on occasion have been referred to as a "madam" appears possible, although not necessarily with the usual implication. That various girls—"non-coms and privates"—who frequented the place did not live there appears certain; some were on occasion apparently sexually available for a price. Cora Taylor seems not to have been available herself. The Hotel de Dream itself was not on "the line," Jacksonville's redlight district, but that it could not, by any stretch of imagination, have been found suitable for any scenes of respectable fiction is certain.

How Cora Stewart had arrived there, at thirty-one, early in 1896, is uncertain. Born in Boston to a mother of old Quaker stock and a father who, though an artist, was respectable, she had lived six years in ordinary familyhood before her father died. Cora Crane's scrupulous biographer, Lillian Gilkes, cannot tell for sure why the girl soon was living, not with her mother and stepfather, but with an aunt in New York City, with whom she stayed until she was twenty. Then she moved out on her own. Within a year she had married Thomas V. Murphy, twenty-five, an aspiring dry-goods merchant. In another two years she divorced and at twenty-three married Stewart, the son of an ex-commander-in-chief of the British forces in India, a young man of twenty-eight of good English family. There was something deeply wrong with this marriage, too, though exactly what can only be imagined. How Cora Crane got to Jacksonville and the Hotel de Dream seven years later, is not known. Possibly a millionaire's yacht, Gilkes speculates. It is a nearly irresistible presumption that Crane came to know how, that Cora told him everything, but if so, he never told, nor did she, nor did anyone.

When Crane met her in 1896, Cora Taylor had come through whatever had befallen her, unbroken, unvictimized, unbowed, certainly unashamed, apparently utterly emancipated from the social norms that prescribed that she should have been ashamed. It is entirely possible that this was exactly what Crane had meant by "brilliance and audacity," when he had sketched his whore with such insistent precision in *Maggie* four years before. Brilliance and audacity were moral qualities, functions of self-consciousness, working to the same effect: seek truth and face it. Society, which pretends to be law and order, is really lies and war; there is only one source of honor, in yourself.

By early 1898 Crane had written his last great stories, "The Blue

Hotel" and "The Bride Comes to Yellow Sky." Using the West, a setting more powerfully mythologized in masculine culture than the slum or the sea or even war, Crane explicitly repudiated a certain normative masculinity. Why, asked the cowboy in "The Blue Hotel," did the paranoid newcomer in town, expecting and eager for violence, "act that way?" The answer: "it seems to me this man has been reading dime novels." The imitation of art by life was Crane's idea of how things ideally should be, and it intersected perfectly with his conviction that art was not for art's but for truth's sake, just as in the central evangelical tradition. Untruthful art drew men to act badly: "he thinks he's right out in the middle of it—the shootin' and stabbin' and all." " 'But,' said the cowboy, deeply scandalized, 'this ain't Wyoming, ner none of them places. This is Nebrasker.' " Perfect art might have stopped here. In evangelistic anxiety that his meaning not be mistaken, Crane went on: "The travelled Easterner laughed. 'It isn't different there even—not in these days. But he thinks he's right in the middle of hell.' Johnnie and the cowboy mused long. 'It's awful funny,' remarked Johnnie at last."[57] In "The Bride Comes to Yellow Sky" the sheriff returned to Yellow Sky as a married man, with his bride, and refused to play out any longer the stylized code of violence. To a foolish challenge, he turned the other cheek.

Holed up in Havana after reporting on the Spanish-American War, Crane wrote a novel about the war between Greece and Turkey, a scene that he and Cora had visited together the year before. In this novel, *Active Service*, a famous newspaperman, Rufus Coleman, arrived in Greece to report the war. A college class of archaeology students, headed by Professor Wainwright, also arrived in Greece; the professor's daughter, Marjorie, was in love with Coleman but unable to confess it even to herself. Completing the roster, a famous actress, Nora Black, onetime paramour of Coleman and on the hunt for him again, also arrived. In comic nightmare, all met on the battlefield. Rufus Coleman was comically heroic. He was attracted again by Nora, but also by Marjorie. Awakened, and transcending innocence, Marjorie pled her case. Rufus vacillated, then chose Marjorie. Nora went off in sarcastic dismissal. The plot was of the simplest, and when we note the hero's choice of the fair over the dark heroine, we can understand Crane's hope that, by satisfying canons of popular romance, he might make some money. But the book failed. The comic-ironic tone, unmistakably Crane's, lent pleasure to scene after scene, but it was not the tone of romance.

Some think Crane modeled Rufus Coleman on the most glamorous newspaperman of the day, Richard Harding Davis, whose by-line signified the romantic and heroic stance.[58] Davis had been the only one of Crane's friends and acquaintances to snub Cora. By this accounting,

Crane avenged himself on Davis by presenting Coleman as mock heroic on the battlefield and also as sentimental about women. Davis's famous "manliness" would be revealed for what it was in his preference for a "coldly beautiful goddess" over a real, sexual woman. But this argument does not hold up. Both Coleman's mock-heroism on the battlefield and his choice of Marjorie were justified in both tone and argument, not dismissed as contemptible.

For the readers of *The Red Badge of Courage*, the battlefield scene in *Active Service* might have seemed frivolous, but Crane was hardly interested in what he had already written about, the recovery from cowardice. With the sound of guns firing, Coleman and his Greek guide found themselves lost in pitch darkness. "The two men were equally blank with fear and each seemed to seek in the other some newly rampant manhood upon which he could lean." Any impression that this was preliminary to another exploration of how courage could grow from fear was quickly dispelled, as Crane brought Marjorie, her father and mother, and the eight college boys on the scene, all in bewilderment, all eager for Coleman to take charge, "almost their savior." Coleman "knew it was the most theatric moment of his life." By converting battlefield to theater, Crane made clear that what was at stake was not simply the hero's regard for himself, but his sense of the discrepancies between what others saw and what he knew of himself. Crane's light ironies over his hero's own awareness of the "mock" qualities of his heroism, rather than aimed to mock Richard Harding Davis, were meant to register the irony in the hero's own self-awareness. "It occurred to him that his position was ludicrously false, but, anyhow, he was glad. . . . His business was to be the cold, masterful, enigmatic man." Hailed as fair knight, when rescue was effected, "Coleman really began to ruminate upon his glory, but he found that he could not do this well without smoking." Though he knew that "on a basis of absolute manly endeavor," he had not earned any thanks from Marjorie, he "thought resentfully" that she ought to feel grateful anyway. Coleman was like the actor unable to reject all the adulations of those confusing him with his role. "[It] did penetrate his mind that it was indecent to accept all this wild gratitude," but at the same time "there was built within him no intention of positively declaring himself lacking in all credit."[59]

It was this ironizing appreciation of the illusions of heroism that prepared for the hero's rejection of Nora Black. In effect, she offered him victory on a sexual battlefield.

I like a man that a woman can't bend in a thousand different ways in five minutes. He must have some steel in him. He obliges me to admire him most when he remains stolid; stolid to me lures. . . . His stolidity is not real; no; it is mere art. But it is a highly finished art and often enough we can't cut through it. Really we can't. And then we may actually come to—er—care for the man. Really we may. Isn't it funny?[60]

Coleman found himself no longer interested in the charade of stolidity, of highly finished art. He felt no appeal in finding himself seen as a man of steel. This battle he rejected.

There were tensions in all this. By the end of the book the fair heroine, Marjorie, had changed. Whether she ever had been or not, she no longer was a coldly beautiful, basically asexual, sexually unchallenging icon. She herself had come to see that her own strongest feelings would not necessarily flow in safe channels and that she had to make choices. Following a meeting where she forced herself to pretend indifference to Coleman, she lamented, as her father put it, the "doom of woman's woe . . . this ancient woe of the silent tongue and the governed will."[61] It is easy to think that Crane was trying to imagine his way into the mind of Nellie Crouse, who, as he apparently wanted to think, had been attracted to him, had wanted to say so, but had not found the courage. Since Crane thus had never known a real-life liberated Marjorie, a courageous Nellie Crouse, the logical big scene for his novel, Marjorie's self-revelation to Coleman, he would have had to construct purely from his imagination. But there was no such scene in the book. Constructing war from imagination was one thing, for that required only logical manipulation of masculine principles. A liberated good girl, however, forced masculine imagination onto unmapped frontiers.

Some of the peculiar bind Crane was in could be seen in the fact that the rejected heroine much resembled Cora Crane. She galloped onto the scene as "Miss Nora Black, special correspondent of the New York Daylight, if you please." America's first woman war correspondent was in fact Cora Crane herself, who sent dispatches from Greece as an accredited reporter, however much or little written by Crane. Nora Black's qualities appeared most in focus in her stance toward men: like the brilliant and audacious woman in *Maggie*, she was challenging. We have no evidence that Cora Crane displayed the same high and challenging tone Crane gave Nora Black. But obviously Crane admired Cora's own independence, and Nora Black mediated his own challenging contempt for standard respectability. Yet the novel in no way disdained Marjorie's woes or affirmed, implicitly or explicitly, Nora's greater promise, for men in general or for Coleman. Whatever Cora meant for Crane personally, he could hardly help, even in a novel written deliberately for the market, pressing through barriers. Crane's interest in prostitutes derived from imaginative energy, not a fixation. The paradox of prostitution was that, while men got things from prostitutes they did not from good girls, it was with prostitutes rather than with good girls that they were safe. Like mothers, whores "had to" provide. The question of courage between the sexes was one of a readiness to run risks, to be endangered, to be harmed. In his tea with Nellie Crouse Crane had tried to get a good girl to be courageous, but he had not really taken any chance himself. In *Active Service* he was starting out. The popular failure of the book can be attributed to its tone, light and mocking, hardly suitable for popularity when it came to love. But mostly, the book failed to offer any assurances that some new formulas might work, to replace the old. For his happy ending, Crane contrived the device, of some psychological resonance, of having Marjorie's father, since she could not break her silence, speak for her. But finally the book took too great a chance. Giving up the devices of finished art, rejecting the poses of standard masculinity, the hero was not reassuring to good girls unaccustomed to pursuing what they wanted. The book's central void was here: Why did Marjorie want him? In effect, Crane had sketched out a book he was not yet ready to write but, someday, might have been.

Crane once said he expected to live to thirty-five. Had he been granted this—only six more years—American letters and American lovers might have benefited.

The Heroine as Culture Bearer: Willa Cather

In 1883 a nine-year-old girl picked up stakes with her family in northern Virginia and set out to join relatives on the plains of south-central Nebraska. Not only had the region of the Northern Neck been ruined by the Civil War. Many of Willa Cather's relatives had been Union people, hostile to the slavocracy that had dominated their native state. Nebraska was attractive for its Republicanism as well as for its promise of new fortunes.

As both Tocqueville and Fuller had seen, many—perhaps most—of the wives of the pioneers had hated going west. Anne Bradstreet had hated leaving England for America. But wives were women. Willa Cather was a little girl. Explanations for such genius of empathy and identification as the young Willa Cather exhibited can only grope among psychologies. In terms proposed by Erik Erikson, Cather must have enjoyed a girlhood in Virginia of the deepest possible early trust. Life was to be welcomed. In Nebraska, ten years old, she met people—Swedes, Norwegians, Germans, above all, Bohemians—quite unlike the Virginians with whom she grew up. Rather than recoiling from them, she was fascinated. She saw them as heroic. She identified with them. She was a girl; she identified with the women among them. It is not hard to see why the glamour of pioneering was enough to inspire a remarkable little girl to want never to lose it. Cather realized what the pioneer European farmers were doing: they asserted personality against the void. When her father, no farmer or true pioneer, took his family from the land into town, she felt diminished. Despite its splendid name—Red Cloud—the town was safe, complacent, vain, greedy, small. Cather was one of the witnesses against the small town in American history. She was fortunate, however. She found teachers—fellow dissidents—capable of recognizing talent. She had an attic at home into which to withdraw, and she had a mother who realized and affirmed what she was doing.

It took Cather years before she could summon her girlhood into art. At thirty she published some poems, at thirty-two some short stories, all competent, none in a special voice. At thirty-nine she published her first novel, *Alexander's Bridge*. It was a disaster. Not only was its hero a man, but his entire inner life was implanted from outside. Significantly enough, Cather made sure that that implanted inner life was as fractured as the bridge he built only to see it collapse into the mighty river it presumed to span. A woman writing a first novel about a man brought to ruin by pretension: here was unconsciousness and alienation in full measure. At no point was Cather's genius more apparent than in her quick recovery from this fiasco. Within weeks she was writing of her experiences on the Nebraska prairie as a ten-year-old; at forty she published her first independent work. The title itself, *O Pioneers*, in its unembarrassed cultural emotionality, registered her breakthrough. Her hero this time was a woman. As if to obliterate her mistake of the year before, Cather named her Alexandra—Alexandra Bergson, a Swedish immigrant farm woman in whose very life the perpetuation of culture and human strength under pressure seemed assured.

Five years later Cather published another version of *O Pioneers*, her paean to a friend of her girlhood, named Àntonia Shimerda in the novel. *My Àntonia* was a curious book. Its portrait of the evolution of a vital, vigorous, eager Bohemian girl into a solid, indomitable earth mother carried epic radiations. Yet Cather jeopardized its plausibility by consigning the telling of it to a narrator of uncertain character. As E. K. Brown has pointed out, to assign to a young man the task of telling about a young woman who, supposedly, "is the most important thing in his life," without letting him be in love with her, was to risk "an emptiness" at the center of the book.[62] The problem in Cather's imagination was to be seen elsewhere, too. In *My Àntonia* it was clear that, while Àntonia was many admirable things—high-spirited, loyal, even jovial, and certainly in time maternal, strong, everlasting—she was not particularly sexual. Another figure in the book, Lina Lingard, was so, in generous abundance, but the male narrator, Jim Burden, was not attracted to her either. It was as though Burden felt the feelings of an anthropologist intrigued by a fascinating but tabooed other race.

The impulse to return to the pioneer immigrant women she had known in her girlhood for a second try almost certainly had been prompted by the novel Cather had written immediately after *O Pioneers*, the longest novel she was ever to write, one of the most conventional so far as sheer form was concerned, but easily the most vibrant with autobiographical recollection. The heroine, Thea Kronborg, of *The Song of the Lark*, grew up, as had Cather, in a small town on the prairie. Like Cather she realized she was different from her siblings and friends. She had an understanding mother, as had Cather. She, too, found fellow feeling among settlers outside the town, as well as among a few older townsfolk able to recognize her special qualities. The first 200 pages of the 600-page book constituted a rich, spacious, probing and confident exploration of the girlhood of a great artist, as valuable for Cather's own biography as a diary or journal or oral reminiscence would have been. In a preface written eighteen years later, Cather regretted that she had not ended her book after these first 200 pages. "What I cared about, and still care about, was the girl's escape; the play of blind chance. . . .She seemed wholly at the mercy of accident; but to persons of her vitality and honesty, fortunate accidents will always happen."[63] Yet the latter parts of *The Song of the Lark*, if an artistic mistake, nonetheless powerfully registered where Cather, in her maturing imagination, was heading. Having conceived her heroine as a singer, Cather escorted her on to renown at the Met and in the opera houses of Europe in a career based on that of the real-life singer Olive Fremstad, with whom she had struck a friendship. Opera stars were mediators, conveying other people's words and music. Cather would see herself as such a mediator, a culture-bearer. But as though uneasy about the gender roles, indeed the traditional sexual charge, of opera, Cather had her heroine discover her deepest identifications with the cliff dwellers of Canyon de Chelly and the archaeological Southwest. It was as a genderless bearer of culture that Thea Kronborg best expressed Cather's own sense of herself as writer. Exalted simply as "Kronborg" by the end of the novel, the heroine was sheltered within a circle of more or less adoring males, wholly libidoless, just as Jim Burden would be toward Antonia.

Following the publication of *My Àntonia*, at forty-five, Cather wrote no more celebrations of the American epic. Her attempt, in *One of Ours*, to penetrate the experience of World War I failed, not so much because she had tried once again to put a male at the center of her stage but because she had no emotional curiosity about the contemporary United

States. It was no longer heroic. Indeed, Cather felt contempt for the successor generations. When she could exploit this contempt openly, she could again write a masterpiece. In *A Lost Lady* (1923) she again revealed her profound Tocquevillian identification with the age of pioneering, here most emphatically including the men who had built the railroads, sent through the first locomotives, established the first banks of new and hopeful communities. *A Lost Lady*—Cather's *Gatsby*—recorded the apparently irreversible decline of that heroic age into petty greed. Determinedly, Cather stuck to modern stories for a few more years. In one, a Northwestern University professor watched his own life disintegrating around him while realizing that his student, Tom Outland, had, like Thea Kronborg before him, discovered the secret of life in the cliff dweller's eternal Southwest. Next, in *My Mortal Enemy*, a quasi-Strindbergian exercise in minimalist surrealism, Cather presented, for the first and only time, a modern marriage: it drove the wife, Myra Henshawe, to a death-to-self in vast impersonal identifications. Taken in conjunction with *A Lost Lady*, Myra Henshawe's escape from marriage liberated Cather for her own final transcendencies.

In *Death Comes for the Archbishop*, Cather became the first woman in American literature to construct a book wholly around convincing men. Not only the Archbishop himself, but especially his friend and coadjutor Father Vaillant, a figure of near-picaresque vividness, fully occupied the spacious realm of time and place Cather constructed for them from copious reading of mid-nineteenth-century New Mexican history. Yet in truth neither the Archbishop nor Father Vaillant were themselves creators, builders, pioneers. Profoundly moved by both the physical and the cultural landscape to which they had been sent as shepherds, they tended their flock, again with the respect and fascination of anthropologists. Though outsiders, yet their most powerful emotions attached to Santa Fe in all its original colors still undisturbed by commerce and modernity and the United States. Once again Cather returned with a sequel. Once again she evoked the life of a mediator of culture, another priest, Bishop Laval, shepherd over the still more distant, austere, and premodern scene of late-seventeenth-century Quebec. Her sheer powers of economy as an artist carried her through *Shadows on the Rock*, but Quebec had no resonance in her personal life as the Southwest had; it did not invite her deeper into her own origins. At sixty Cather began writing another Nebraska novel, *Lucy Gayheart*, but this time, instead of conducting her young heroine on to power and fame as an artist, she drew her to an early death. It was as though Cather realized that, were she to preserve artistic vitality, she had to break her way through her identifications, based on her own Nebraska girlhood, with essentially genderless culture-bearers, the two earth mothers Alexandra and Àntonia, and the Archbishop and the Bishop. So far as personal life was concerned, Cather had lived forty years in tranquil companionship with Helen Lewis. She had thought of herself from her girlhood as different, "boyish." In her last novel she returned for the first time to Virginia. Her parents in their retirement had stayed in Red Cloud, her father dying in 1928, her mother in 1931. The house in Red Cloud, where she had continued to visit them every summer, was sold. A beloved brother died in 1937. On a visit to Virginia in 1938, Cather found her old hometown, Winchester, practically unchanged. But for *Sapphira and the Slave Girl* she went back, not to her own girlhood, but to a generation earlier, the generation of her own parents' childhood. Sex pulsed at the heart of *Sapphira and the Slave Girl*. A husband was suspected of lusting after the slave girl; to forestall the husband she was offered to another man; the girl's mother could only remain passive in the face of her daughter's danger; her owner could find nothing in his Bible or his conscience instructing him to save her. But above all, in this novel, utterly chaste and pure in its language, utterly lurid at its heart, true evil appeared in the person of the jealous wife, Sapphira, a lady of the tidal-plantation aristocracy. It was Sapphira who indulged in the most uncontrolled fantasies, conspired to expose the slave girl to ruin, most deliberately calculated the weakness of her male accomplice, and goaded him to indulge it. The fusion of slavery, sex, and degradation was complete. Sapphira Dodderidge Colbert was hardly Willa Cather's mother, but like Sapphira, Virginia Boak Cather had been a stronger figure than her husband, more eager for society, more incessant in activity, commanding and quick. It was as though Cather, at the end of her life, had at last realized what it was her mother—and she herself—had been saved from by moving to the frontier. There, their remarkable talents and energies had not been tempted.

Although at the time of Cather's death in 1947 her fame had been somewhat dimmed by seven years of silence, her works had been republished in an edition of thirteen volumes and she had been admitted into the canon of respectable writers, sometimes categorized, absurdly, because of her Nebraska, Southwest, and Canadian scenes, as a local colorist in the line of her admired mentor, Sarah Orne Jewett. But Cather's career from first to last was autobiographical, borne on a powerful quest to unlock the deepest springs of personal freedom. Evidently she herself was unacquainted with the novelist who had analyzed, to far more devastating effect than anything she ever composed, the ultimate slavery of the self to sexuality. Kate Chopin's *The Awakening* had been published back in 1899, before Cather herself had written a book. It had drawn Chopin into silence, and the disappearance of the book from critical as well as public attention itself testified to the explosive potentials from which Cather had so brilliantly defended herself through her career.

The Heroine Awakens to the Void: Kate Chopin

Widowed in Louisiana at thirty-one, in 1883 Kate Chopin had taken her children back to St. Louis, where she was born and where her mother still lived. When her mother died within little more than a year, the old family doctor urged her to consider writing stories for a living. Her first, "Wiser Than a God," told of a young woman with a choice. Should she go to Europe to pursue a career as a pianist, or marry the young man who loved her and whom she presumably loved in return? Love was not enough; it threatened her freedom. Therefore she chose Europe, not the lover.

Biographies concur that Chopin and her husband had been happily married. Oscar Chopin, a New Orleans businessman who had lived in France during the Civil War, apparently appreciated his young wife's talents as a pianist and her literary sophistication as well as her vivid manners and Egyptian cigarettes. When Chopin's business collapsed in the depression of the late 1870s, and the family had to forsake New Orleans, husband and wife seemed to keep their spirits in the raw circumstances of rural upstate Louisiana. But Oscar Chopin's death only four years later may have registered hidden stresses.[64]

By far the majority of Chopin's stories dealt with marriage and getting—or not getting—married. Like Strindberg, Chopin recorded varieties of marriage. In "The Kiss," a girl determined to marry for money strove to devalue the kiss—that has excited her—of a poor boy. An egalitarian couple leading a modern marriage in "A Point at Issue" found their sophisticated arrangements undercut by old-fashioned jealous suspicions. In "Her Letters," a woman incited jealousy in her husband after her death by leaving him a packet of letters with instructions to destroy them unopened; he did, by hurling them into the river, but then, unable to shake the suspicions they had aroused, followed them some months later. Sometimes Chopin is thought of as a feminist, but these stories passed no judgments. The pianist heroine of "Wiser Than a God" drew no special approval from her creator. In "The Kiss" the gold-digger was not portrayed as bad or sad, simply as a "chess player" who won what she wanted.

Chopin was born Katherine O'Flaherty, but the literary culture that she gained from her Creole mother's grandmother after Thomas

O'Flaherty's death when she was four, and from Catholic sisters in St. Louis, was French. Writing meant form. Writing meant language exactly adapted to its purposes, it meant economy, precision, calculated effects. Like Stephen Crane, Chopin, from a powerful religious inheritance, drew on the drive of high religion toward objectivity, clear sight, and impersonal truth rather than wish-fulfillment.

Her early stories lacked place and often had only the vague time of nineteenth-century modernity. Soon, however, she began to draw more heavily on a specific place, Creole Louisiana, and its premodern folk time. Some of these stories won her her first wide reputation and popularity. In "Desiré's Baby," two lovers were destroyed by the man's ruthless reaction to discovering the woman's black origins; then he discovered the same of himself. In "Madame Celestin's Divorce," an Anglo lawyer was disappointed in his hopes of marrying the sexual Creole heroine when she, after weeks of denigrating her worthless absent husband, nevertheless took him back on his return. Here the use of Creole dialect effectively held tragedy and suffering at a distance. Themes already evident in Chopin's earlier stories grew plainer. The wife in "The Story of an Hour" was filled with joy at the news of her husband's death in a railroad disaster, then fell dead when he returned. This story was reversed by the "Lady of Bayou St. John," where the heroine, on the verge of abandoning her husband for her lover, embraced her husband's memory when he died, and sent her lover away. Like the French short stories she knew, these stories were unsentimental, ironical, highly crafted, and detached. But Creole folk culture allowed Chopin the opportunity to deal with more than social pathos. It allowed her to become more explicit about sex.

By no means did Chopin indulge herself in some notion of simple, natural, unrepressed sexuality among the Creoles in contrast to, say, repressed Protestant Anglos. In the most important of these stories, "A No-Account Creole," rewritten in 1891 from an earlier effort, the passion-based illicit love affair was between a Creole girl and a young Protestant Anglo New Orleans businessman, "both scintillant with feeling." For her licit Creole fiancé, the girl could summon only forced loyalty. The fiancé then decided that his love required him to surrender her to her true lover, the Anglo. Unlike Harriet Beecher Stowe, who could not finally show any urgent attachment between Mary and James, Chopin was explicit about the thrill, the blood, the passion, the sheer physical affinity that drew true lovers together. The point was made in reverse in a three-page non-Creole sketch: a girl whose absent lover fell victim to tuberculosis found herself physically repelled by him; ruthlessly, she fled any further relation. The sense of sex and sexuality as having a source different from love, friendship, or ethics suffused these stories. In "Athenaïse" the Creole heroine abandoned her husband by no means for any fault of his but simply out of a gathering sense that she had become averse to being a wife to anyone. " 'No, I don't hate him. . . . It's jus' being married that I detes' an' despise. . . . I can't stan' to live with a man.' " But then, on her own in New Orleans, she discovered herself pregnant. "Her whole being was steeped in a wave of ecstasy." She thought of her husband: "The first purely sensuous tremor of her life swept over her."[65] She went back. Life was not led by ideology. Unlike Margaret Fuller, Katherine O'Flaherty Chopin had her chance to write out her deepest personal discoveries.

The Awakening still challenges categorization in both literary and social history. Grouped with Whitman and with Dreiser's *Sister Carrie* as a casualty of censoriousness, it can be used to illuminate the repressive shape of Victorianism as late as the early twentieth century. On the other hand, as "pioneering," it can be said to reveal the roots of radical liberation in Victorian times. While neither approach is wrong, both may leave in shadow the most vital question: just exactly what does *The Awakening* say?[66]

In its last paragraph—fewer than seventy words—a mature woman was shown being drawn back into her childhood:

Edna heard her father's voice and her sister Margaret's. She heard the barking of an old dog that was chained to the sycamore tree. The spurs of the cavalry officer clanged as he walked across the porch. There was the hum of bees, and the musky odor of pinks filled the air.[67]

These were of course experiences not only lived but relived by a woman who, unclothed, was drowning by choice in the Gulf of Mexico off Louisiana's Grand Isle, a location already realized in several of Chopin's previous stories. Just before her recall of father, sister, old dog, spurs, and humming bees, the heroine wondered if her doctor might have helped. She had said good-bye to her absent lover, and before that had thought, without emotion, of her husband and children and, with defiance, of her teacher of art, who had doubted her courage. As these last attachments at the end of her life fell away, she returned to the start of her life when, a very little girl, she had "traversed the ocean of waving grass" in Kentucky, "beating the tall grass as one strikes out in the water." In death, is there rebirth? In dying, is there affirmation?

Edna Pontellier's "awakening" in *The Awakening* was to her individuality. As this "light" began to "dawn dimly within her," so consciousness began to replace unconsciousness, will to replace role. For the first time in her life she defied her husband. Leonce Pontellier did not mistreat her. The WCTU could have made no case against him. Margaret Fuller could not have placed him among the wild beasts, nor could C. P. Gilman have put him among the sexuo-economic oppressors. Nor did Edna Pontellier's husband not love her. Yet something was wrong.

Her marriage [had been] purely an accident. . . . He fell in love . . . and pressed his suit. . . . He pleased her; his absolute devotion flattered her. She fancied there was a sympathy of thought and taste. . . . As the devoted wife of a man who worshiped her, she felt she could take her place . . . in the world. . . . She grew fond of her husband, realizing with some unaccountable satisfaction that no trace of passion or excessive and fictitious warmth colored her affection.[68]

But now after six years, at twenty-eight, a "vague anguish" seemed to have overtaken her, an "indescribable oppression." Out on Grand Isle to escape the heat of New Orleans in summer, she seemed unusually sensitive to stimuli—the Gulf air, music, a certain novel, the water itself, the "candor" and "excessive physical charm" of Adele Ratignolle, another of the summer wives. Like Strindberg, Chopin knew that causation was a many-splendored thing. Back on the island after his week in the city, her husband grew exasperated with her. She stayed out in the night air, refusing to come in till just before dawn, and then to a sleep that was "troubled" and "feverish."

In Chopin's portrayal of the stages of her heroine's awakening, all sociological and ideological elements were purged away, dissolved wholly into psychology, so that at the end the heroine's achievement of self-consciousness carried complete conviction. She recognized that individuality did not consist of satisfying the claims of anyone else, whether husband, father, friends. Her most explicit insistence concerned her children. "Edna . . . once told Madame Ratignolle that she would never sacrifice herself for her children, or for anyone." A "mother-woman," and one of the very best, Adele Ratignolle was shocked. Edna tried to explain: "I would give up the unessential; I would give my money, I would give my life for my children; but I wouldn't give myself."[69] In another character, dried-up, embittered Mlle. Reisz, Edna saw the claims of art—or, in Charlotte Perkins Gilman's terms, work—but just as clearly she saw the awful price that art—and work—exacted. Individuality, existence as an individual, as a self, required expression, not repression. All the elemental resources available to every individual had to be expressed, if life was to be free. Her awakening was not simply to her sexuality but to the meaning of her sexuality.

Like Gilman, Kate Chopin saw her heroine as strong, fit, vital. Compared to the body of the marvelously rounded, maternal Madame Ratignolle, her own was "long, clean and symmetrical." In the surf her body was "splendid." Awakening to herself, she herself observed the "fine, firm quality and texture of her flesh." As she began to enjoy the satisfaction of hunger, she tore brown bread with "her strong, white teeth." To her doctor, anxious for her, her voice seemed "warm and energetic." "There was no repression in her glance or gesture. She reminded him of some beautiful, sleek animal waking up in the sun." Watching her busy at setting up her new house, a new acquaintance and would-be seducer found her "splendid and robust."[70]

That the fullest expression of this strength and vitality and splendor might not be sexual did not occur to Mrs. Pontellier. With Robert, the attentive young man, two years her junior, with (but not by) whom her awakening had been incited, she did not "surrender" to the sexual energies awakened in her as to some irresistible force of nature, but on the contrary asserted them as identical with her self. To be a self at all was to be a unity—"my character." Various persons, usually Creole, in Chopin's earlier stories had "surrendered" to passion, but not Mrs. Pontellier. She affirmed it.

Edna Pontellier was the one woman in the book explicitly identified as an old-stock, Anglo-Saxon, Puritan-derived Protestant American. It was as though Chopin meant to make her point against American myths of womanhood and sexuality, quite separated from local color portraits of exotic Creole folk. Her heroine's fundamental freedom was from all passivity, whether sensual or cold, and from all socialization, whether Puritan or Creole:

When she came back . . . Robert sat off in the shadow, leaning his head back on the chair. . . . Edna lingered a moment. . . . Then she went across . . . to where he sat. She bent over the arm of his chair. . . . "Robert," . . . "are you asleep?" "No," he answered, looking up at her. She leaned over and kissed him—a soft, cool, delicate kiss, whose voluptuous sting penetrated his whole being.

When Robert confessed having hoped she would become his wife, Edna made clear that that was not in her thoughts. "I am no longer one of Mr. Pontellier's possessions to dispose of or not. I give myself where I choose."[71] Being more than irresistible force or imperious appetite, her sexuality fed her strength, her splendor, her freedom. In her artful kisses she showed the power of art, no longer based on sublimation and repression.

Unlike Tolstoy, who sent his awakened heroine, Anna Karenina, off to live in unsanctified love with her lover, to show her that passion could not survive when cut off from society, Chopin inflicted no such testing on hers. Unlike Count Vronsky, Robert simply fled from more splendor than he was prepared for. Edna then found her way to the meadowy sea. Chopin's exact intentions in this conclusion are not clear. Almost as though anxious to make a point her novel may have obscured, she wrote a new story, "The Storm," as a kind of postscript to an earlier story, "At the 'Cadian Ball." In "At the 'Cadian Ball" a young planter, Alcee Laballiere, in despair at the loss of his rice harvest, rushed off to the ball, where he found hot-blooded Calixta, betrothed to plodding Bobinot. In their mutual heat, Calixta and Alcee nearly fuse. But the girl whom Alcee had already been wooing, "slim, tall, graceful Clarisse," "cold and kind and cruel by turn," overcame her pride, came after Alcee, and got him back. Now, years later, in the second story, comes a violent thunderstorm. While Calixta's husband, Bobinot, waited in town for it to pass, out at their farm Calixta herself gave shelter to a passing rider. This turned out to be no other than Alcee Laballiere himself, by now Clarisse's husband. Their old passion from the ball reignited. This time they did flare, fuse, commit adultery. The thunderstorm passed. Alcee left, Bobinot returned home. Wife Calixta greeted him warmly. Alcee wrote his wife a letter telling her he loved her. She read it happily. "So the storm passed and everyone was happy."

Nothing whatsoever in this story had anything remotely approaching the precision of psychological analysis of *The Awakening*. Yet its treatment of sexuality was far more explicit, even quasi-pornographic, compared to the far more compelling reserve of the novel:

"Calixta," he said, "don't be frightened. . . ." He pushed her hair back from her face that was warm and steaming. . . . As she glanced up at him the fear in her liquid blue eyes had given place to a drowsy gleam. . . . Her firm, elastic flesh . . . knowing for the first time its birthright. . . . The generous abundance of her passion, without guile or trickery . . . found response in depths of his own sensuous nature. . . . When he touched her breasts they gave themselves up in quivering ecstasy, inviting his lips. . . . He stayed cushioned upon her, breathless, dazed, enervated. . . . With one hand she clasped his head. . . . The other hand stroked with a soothing rhythm his muscular shoulders. . . . He turned and smiled at her with a beaming face; and she lifted her pretty chin in the air and laughed aloud.[72]

It was as though Chopin feared that somehow a radical truth about sexuality had got lost in her novel: sexual passion could be detached from marriage, detached from morality, embraced, pursued, enjoyed for its own sake, without fatal results. Sexual passion could be separated from guilt.

But then why had Edna too not been allowed happiness rather than death following her awakening? Surely not because she was not Creole, not a Calixta. Had she perhaps misunderstood the nature of sheer sexual passion? Before Robert's flight, when she still was glorying in their love, she had spoken words that a Tolstoy and other realists might have imagined cause for retribution:

"I love you," she whispered, "only you, no one but you. It was you who awoke me last summer out of a life-long, stupid dream. . . . Oh! I have suffered, suffered!

Now you are here we shall love each other, my Robert. We shall be everything to each other. Nothing else in the world is of any consequence."

To be everything for another—was this not Anna's fatal mistake with regard to Vronsky? For nothing else in the world to matter—was this not hubris, a fatal misunderstanding of love's real vector toward connections, not separation? Once Edna had tried to explain to Mlle. Reisz why she loved Robert and no one else:

"Why? Because his hair is brown and grows away from his temples; because he opens and shuts his eyes, and his nose is a little out of drawing, because he has two lips and a square chin, and a little finger which he can't straighten from having played baseball. . . ." "Because you do, in short," laughed Mademoiselle.

Yet it was not with Robert that Edna had experienced her first truly compelling sensuality, but rather with a practiced man of the world, Alcee Arobin, whose kiss was "the first kiss of her life to which her nature had really responded. . . . a flaming torch that kindled desire." Was there some desperation in her insistence upon Robert and only Robert, some defense against the impersonality of sex, against the prospect of a gathering promiscuity and its coarsening? As she lay awake all night after finding Robert's note of farewell, an even more chilling thought arrived:

Despondency had come upon her. . . . There was no one thing in the world that she desired. There was no human being whom she wanted near her except Robert; and she even realized that the day would come when he, too, and the thought of him would melt out of her existence, leaving her alone.[73]

Absolutely nothing in *The Awakening* suggested that if "the whole system of society" was "torn down" and then "built up anew," Edna's tragedy would no longer be necessary. No extirpation of the "long hereditary habit" of the masculine sex, nor any "mighty change" in women, was suggested in a single line. Any idea that an Edna might find solace and compensation in sisterhood was explicitly dismissed. *The Awakening* was not a feminist novel in any sense. It was not about any version of a war between the sexes. Edna was unprepared for what her awakening had brought her—solitude, separateness, isolation, loneliness. Those with special talents, such as the old-maid pianist Mlle. Reisz, could sublimate their individuality into art, or into Romance, as Stowe's Mary did, or in real life, as Margaret Fuller did, into marriage itself with an Ossoli. But Edna's talent was precisely her individuality itself, focused in that unrepressed animality, "splendid and robust." No de-eroticizing of that strong, fine, clean body into piano-playing fingers, let alone into spiritual projects, would escape desolation; no little Ossoli, let alone a succession of affairs, would avail. Was there out there in the democratic universe some perfect match, an Edward for such an Edna? Chopin offered no comfort to those of her readers who brought that familiar wish to her book.

In treatments of Chopin it is common to note the hostility with which her novel was received in various quarters; its rejection as crude if not immoral; and the advice, sometimes well-intentioned, that she return to her local-color Creole stories, as though these reactions might explain her diminished productivity in the five years remaining to her of life. No doubt, the failure of some important sector of the American critical establishment and reading public to recognize the book for what it was—the most exacting portrayal of the growth of individual consciousness yet written in the country—constitutes a major fact in American social as well as literary history, and in the history of American women. But the sources of Chopin's final silence are to be sought in Chopin herself, as revealed in her book. It would be incorrect to say that she had frightened herself with darkness. But it would not be condescending to say that she was ready to leave to others further investigation of the horrors in that darkness.

The Hero Transformed into Dancing God: Movie Masculinity in the 1930s

Visions of manhood undone by sex uncoiled in early twentieth-century imaginations. Theodore Dreiser, Frank Norris, Sherwood Anderson, Eugene O'Neill, as well as Hemingway and Fitzgerald, wrote of men undone, undermined, overcome. As though to combat just these specters of impotence, confusion, decline, and disintegration, a dramatic new kind of hero emerged, first in the theater and then, quickly and with sweeping force, in the movies. What had been conspicuously foresworn in Bushnell, Twain, Adams, and Hemingway, the new hero manifested in open candor—aggression toward women. Men willing to pay for their freedom by sticking to boys' things had every reason to avoid confrontation. But the embrace of boyhood was postulated on purely negative reasons: Bushnell was in protest against the ministry; Huck Finn lit out for the territories in flight, not in search; Adams was in protest against a whole society, Hemingway against nature itself. If turning back from escape threatened defeat, however, the obvious response was to sharpen the attack.

As Carlos Clarens has pointed out, both Clark Gable and Spencer Tracy won their first renown in gangster dramas on the New York stage, in *Killer Mears* and *The Last Mile*. These plays, as Clarens has noted, emerged out of a Chicago school of writers, of course including Theodore Dreiser, but also Whit Burnett (*Little Caesar*) and Ben Hecht (*The Front Page*), drawing on that city's real-life gangster dramas.[74] As Hollywood negotiated its transition from silence to sound, it drew on these actors and, quickly, on others like them in what amounted to the creation not only of a genre in the movies, but of a generation of new and emphatically masculine stars: Gable and Tracy, along with another stage actor, Humphrey Bogart, plus Edward G. Robinson and James Cagney, gangsters all. Ironically, perhaps, the finest of the new gangster films in purely cinematic terms, Howard Hawks's *Scarface*, did not establish its lead, Paul Muni, as one of the dominating stars of the decade, even though, drawing on Hawks's *The Dawn Patrol*, the finest war movie of the 1920s, it more plainly revealed than the others a key motif in the new masculinity, "teamwork, male bonding, group loyalty, and most important . . . a certain deadly skill." Reinforcing this theme, the gangster hero's death in *Scarface*, as in others, followed from his "one careless, unprofessional crime," that is, revenge impelled by sexual jealousy. Far better than such vulnerability to women was the contempt registered in the most famous of all scenes in the new genre, Cagney's pulping a grapefruit in the face of the heroine, Mae Clarke. And it was the dance critic Lincoln Kirstein, analyzing Cagney's performance in *The Public Enemy*, who brilliantly identified the "certain deadly skill" that was to matter most for male stars from the first gangster epics to, say, *Gone With the Wind*:

Cagney has an inspired sense of timing, an arrogant style, a pride in the control of his body. . . . No one expresses more clearly in terms of pictorial action the delights of violence, the overtones of a semiconscious sadism, the tendency toward destruction, toward anarchy, which is the base of American sex appeal.[75]

This "regeneration through violence," to use Richard Slotkin's telling term, effectively smothered the sentimental view of women, but at a cost. The troupe of young women writing scripts in the 1920s broke up and disappeared. The new scripts did not resurrect Mary Pickford, however—except in the vastly inflected and far more sexually ambiguous form of Shirley Temple. Instead, as though conceding the achievement of the Twenties, they offered embodiments of womanhood in powerful female stars such as Bette Davis, Rosalind Russell, Katharine Hepburn, and quintessentially, carrying over from the late Twenties, Joan Crawford. These then were shown repeatedly in surrender, after suitable combat, to their male counterparts. In the most popular such story of all, Margaret Mitchell's best-selling novel made into the overwhelming hit, *Gone With the Wind*, the hero, after winning his combat, disdained even taking possession of his prize. From the standpoint of Hollywood myth logic, it was a remarkable moment. By the late 1930s Clark Gable had become the masculine star par excellence, and all his victories were assumed to issue in possession. By spurning Scarlett O'Hara—assigned, it is true, to the British actress Vivien Leigh, who, though fully up to her role, could not bring to it the extrinsic charge of established star—Gable's Rhett Butler reevoked the original gangster hero's vesting of his freedom in contempt. This did solve a problem. Obviously, when the hero confirmed his victory by embracing and marrying the heroine, he lost much of what had defined him, his heedlessness, his guiltless play with his bonded male friends, his sexual opportunities themselves. But reversion to the origins of the myth in open violence was dangerous. On occasion Hollywood rose to visions of pure equality, as in the series starring William Powell and Myrna Loy, neither one a star in the basic sense of radiating some elemental force independent of story, plot, or circumstance, but both equipped with a high level of wit, emotional sophistication, and capacity for martinis, a drink long established as the lubricatory agency of choice for consenting heterosocial adults. Appropriately, these two were portrayed as already married, and their joint endeavor as being itself sophisticated, that of illuminating darkness, dispelling subterfuge, enhancing understanding: Nick and Nora Charles were private detectives.

Yet, although private detection would prove a pliable medium for elaborating new styles and codes of heterosocial relations right into the 1980s, it would remain a kind of subgenre, like westerns, ever waiting for its Poe to raise it out of its conventions. Another purification of the gangster's menacing grace achieved far more powerful expression in the movies of the 1930s, with Fred Astaire transfiguring Cagney's exquisite tensions into a hail of release. Consistently performing with a partner, Astaire's art resonated with the promise of reconciliation, yet, as his partners changed over his career, the symbolization of equality in any given dance or movie was compromised. The preemption of popular dance by men saw still more emphatic affirmation in Gene Kelly, whose most celebrated routines might not include a woman or a partner at all. The consolidation in popular culture—still on the impetus of the democratic logic Rourke had analyzed at its source—of the American male as dancing hero would proceed from the movies of the 1930s into the commercial culture of rock after World War II. His origins in aggression would sometimes be flaunted in vibratory hips, sometimes swaddled in infantile boyish romps, parodied in transvestite menace, then sweetly lamented in androgynous innocence. But it would never be denied.

Feminism Confronts the Hero Imprisoned by Sex

In 1970 the sculptor and feminist critic Kate Millett, in her manifesto *Sexual Politics*, a major early expression of feminist imagination, attacked the novelists Henry Miller and Norman Mailer. Commencing with a long quotation from Miller's *Sexus* (1965), Millett proceeded to assimilate Miller's description of sexual interaction to "deliberate sensuality," to "classic masculine fantasy," to a "genre of sexual narrative." Turning next to Mailer, introduced by a long quotation from *An American Dream* (1964), Millett proceeded to higher conclusions:

Sexual congress in a Mailer novel is always a matter of strenuous endeavor, rather like mountain climbing—a straining ever upward after achievement. In this, as in so many ways, Mailer is authentically American.[76]

Though careful to stop just short of charging either Miller or Mailer with "obscenity" or "pornography," Millet found "misogynist" attitudes in both of them. The fact that these attitudes were manifest not in tracts or polemics but in novels, she dismissed. Both writers so evidently identified with their protagonists, she felt, that their fictions could be read as direct renditions of their own attitudes. Both wrote autobiographical novels.

In characterizing Mailer—and by implication Miller as well—as "authentically American," Millett implied what she then apparently proceeded to contradict in her book. Evidently, both Miller and Mailer registered, not some long tradition in American culture, but a "counterrevolution" occupying the years 1930–60. This was an epoch countering a general trans-Atlantic "revolution" of 1830–1930. There were peculiarities in this scheme, so far as American history was concerned. In sketching her century of revolution, Millett divided it into sectors, and for the "political" sector she did draw on American as much as on English events. At the center of her section on "polemics," however, she set a debate between John Stuart Mill and John Ruskin, followed by an excursus on Friedrich Engels, and for her "literary" section she drew on Thomas Hardy, George Meredith, and Charlotte Brontë, followed by brief notice of Alfred Tennyson, Algernon Swinburne, and Oscar Wilde. The "authentically American" had disappeared. When it came to "counterrevolution," she also offered two parts. The first dealt with sexual reaction in Nazi Germany and Soviet Russia, the second with Sigmund Freud, then with "some Post-Freudians" and with postwar "functionalist" social science generally. Only in this second section did Millett explicate American figures. With Ferdinand Lundberg and Marynia Farnham's *Modern Woman: The Lost Sex* (1947) as her prime text, she echoed Betty Friedan in excoriating postwar psychology for its prescription of motherhood, domesticity, and "sexual surrender" as nature's prescription for fulfilled womanhood. But obviously, Henry Miller at least was no prophet of motherhood and suburban domesticity. Expounding on "Womanhood and the Inner Space," the psychoanalyst Erik Erikson had the womb in mind. Miller's organ of choice was the "cunt." In Mailer's novel, the organ cathected was the "butt," plus the anus. Both Henry Miller and Norman Mailer might well have been as shocking to the antifeminist prophets of inner space as to Kate Millett.

As her inclusion of D. H. Lawrence with the two Americans showed, Millett's real aim was to strip Miller and Mailer—above all Miller—of their reputation as liberators. Had not Henry Miller defied the censorship that had long imposed a kind of genteel smog over American letters? Censorship had kept his own books confined to underground channels in the United States until 1961: he therefore could figure as a hero in the struggle for honesty, candor, forthrightness, indeed, as a hero in the fight to carry American democracy where that democracy had long been reluctant to explore, into the realm of sex itself. As for Mailer, had he not, in his first book, his best-selling war novel of 1947, *The Naked and the Dead*, portrayed American soldiers as they really were, talking as they really did, using the word they did use, endlessly (even if in 1947 he still had to veil it as "fuggin")? And had not Mailer then gone on to unprecedentedly direct fictional analysis of sexuality stripped of genteel and psychologistic mystifications?

Millett ignored these issues. Instead, she pointed at what apparently went on in Miller's and Mailer's novels: the degradation of women. The reader picking up Miller's first novel in Paris in 1934, *Tropic of Cancer*, after being told by the author on page 2 that "it is to you, Tania, that I am singing," found the following by page 5:

At night when I look at Boris' goatee lying on the pillow I get hysterical. O Tania, where now is that warm cunt of yours, those fat, heavy garters, those soft, bulging thighs? There is a bone in my prick six inches long. I will ream out every wrinkle in your cunt, Tania, big with seed. I will send you home to your Sylvester with an ache in your belly and your womb turned inside out. Your Sylvester! Yes, he knows how to build a fire, but I know how to inflame a cunt. I shoot hot bolts into you, Tania, I make your ovaries incandescent. Your Sylvester is a little jealous now? He feels something, does he? He feels the remnant of my big prick. I have set the shores a little wider, I have ironed out the wrinkles. After me you can take on stallions, bulls, rams, drakes, St. Bernards. You can stuff toads, bats, lizards up your rectum. You can shit arpeggios if you like, or string a zither across your navel. I am fucking you, Tania, so that you'll stay fucked. And if you are afraid of being fucked privately, I will tear off a few hairs from your cunt and paste them on Boris' chin. I will bite into your clitoris and spit out two franc pieces.[77]

Any reader might well sense that this was a different kind of love song from those of Hardy, Meredith, and Brontë.

For feminists fired with their own impatience at the mystification of sex, such language arrived as a kind of surprise attack, an onslaught from their blind side. Surely there could be no hope for equality, if such came to be accepted as literature. A female Henry Miller? Yet Miller's book had arrived with a preface written by a woman writer of the epoch, Anaïs Nin. While agreeing first that the "predominant note" in Miller's novel was "bitterness," Nin moved quickly to hail "a wild extravagance" also, "a mad gaiety, a verve, a gusto, at times almost a delirium."[78] Her language matched that of Constance Rourke describing the rapture of the gold-rush Californians. Miller was highly self-conscious about his own literary antecedents: he saw himself as the heir of Emerson and Whitman, carrying further the peculiarly American development of Self by means of freely exaggerated self-expression. Like Whitman, Miller saw that his task included prophetic denunciation of America for its perversion of its democratic destiny: "The whole country is lawless, violent, explosive, demoniacal." "Outwardly they seem like a fine, upstanding people—healthy, optimistic, courageous. Inwardly they are filled with worms."[79]

Millett could hardly fail to recognize this later dimension in Miller. She agreed: Miller had articulated "the disgust, the contempt, the hostility, the violence, and the sense of filth with which our culture, or more specifically, its masculine sensibility, surrounds sexuality." This miasma extended to women themselves, "for somehow it is women upon whom this onerous burden of sexuality falls." Just so far, then, and no further, as critic of a sexual culture that feminists too criticized, Miller belonged with them. But Millett refused to take Miller's attack on sexual hypocrisy as a key to reading his books. Conceding only that he was "fleetingly conscious" of the hostility and violence surrounding sexuality, she proceeded to insist again upon his "arrested adolescence," the confinement of his humor to "the men's house, more specifically, the men's room," his "parasitic" dependence upon the conventional morality he pretended to attack. Noting "orgies" in his books, presented "as lessons in a free and happy sensuality," Millett declared them really exercises of male will given "absolute license."[80]

In fact, at no point did Millett offer analysis of any single book Miller ever wrote, and it was evidence of her need to read him in only one way that the passage on which she based her first long introductory discussion was drawn not from either of his first epochal works written in

Paris, the two *Tropics* of 1934 and 1939, but from *Sexus*, part of a trilogy, *The Rosy Crucifixion*, written after his move to Big Sur, California. The passage just quoted from *Tropic of Cancer* by no means represented the book. At one point, for instance, the author ruminated over eighteen pages about Hindus he had known in New York and Paris. At another he commented on Matisse. He dilated upon the comedies and absurdities of spreading the gospel of Franco-American amity by lecturing on American literature. The sex passages hunted out by the American tourists on shipboard hoping to smuggle copies past customs in New York were never orgies, but, rather, functions of portraits of people—of Van Norden endeavoring to recall every detail of every experience he had ever had with all his "cunts," of Irene, of Carl. Prostitutes appeared frequently in both Miller's famous novels, vividly portrayed, not according to the canons of sentimental psychology but as persons with as much autonomy as any other persons in the books. They were not called "prostitutes," however, but "whores," "broads," "cunts." People who called prostitutes "prostitutes" were not the people who patronized prostitutes. As well as prostitutes, Miller was writing about—and in the voice of—people who patronized prostitutes. Almost invariably, they "knew" the prostitutes they patronized as persons.

As for the autobiographical hero-narrator himself, the reader of *Tropic of Cancer* gradually learned that, so far as women were concerned, he had, not a happily sensual orgiastic life, but a complex, difficult, painful, and obsessed inner life: "For seven years I went about, day and night, with only one thing on my mind—*her*."[81] And again:

Whenever I try to explain to myself the peculiar pattern which my life has taken, when I reach back to the first cause, as it were, I think inevitably of the girl I first loved. It seems to me that everything dates from that aborted affair. A strange, masochistic affair it was, ridiculous and tragic at the same time.[82]

Millett had her own prescription for literature. She implied it in her discussion of Charlotte Brontë's *Villette*, "a book too subversive to be popular," then confirmed it in her analysis of the last of her quartet of modern writers, the only one in whom she found hope, Jean Genet. As if to prove that it was not the sheer brutality of Miller's language, his iteration of the "iconographic four-letter words," that offended her, Millett noted that Genet too disdained euphemism; he too wrote of "pricks" and "cunts." But Genet, forging meaning out of his own criminality and homosexuality, had transcended the original primitive drives that had driven him to them. Specifically, he had transcended the prison in which Miller and Mailer—and D. H. Lawrence, too—still found themselves: "Alone of our contemporary writers, Genet has taken thought of women as an oppressed group and revolutionary force, and has chosen to identify with them." "It's perfectly natural," she quoted Genet as saying in his *Thief's Journal*, of a "virile" bandit whom he had serviced, "He's a prick and I'm a cunt." Millett glossed the passage:

When a biological male is described as a "cunt," one gets a better notion of the meaning of the word. By revealing its primarily status or power definition, Genet has demonstrated the utterly arbitrary and invidious nature of sex roles.

Having found a French homosexual the only modern counter-counter-revolutionary writer around, Millett could offer little more than a hope that in "the emergence of a new feminist movement" "progressive forces" would reassert themselves. How far these might show themselves through a "truly feminine" literary sensibility she had only implied in her pages on Brontë's *Villette*:

Lucy is free. Free is alone; given a choice between "love" in its most agreeable contemporary manifestation, and freedom, Lucy chose to retain the individualist humanity she had shored up, even at the expense of sexuality. . . . Charlotte Brontë is hard-minded enough to know that there was no man in Lucy's society with whom she could have lived and still been free.[83]

Another program for a new literature was soon spelled out in a literary speculation by the feminist academic critic Caroline Heilbrun, *Toward a Recognition of Androgyny* (1973). In contrast to gay and lesbian homosexuality, with their closed, in-group, separatist tendencies, androgyny offered new opportunities. It affirmed community between the sexes, a new style, a new psychology and morality between the sexes, possibly even a new politics. Androgyny could be seen in movies and manners, in fashion and rock, and all of these could be read as evidences of some deep evolution, registering itself most fundamentally perhaps in generational terms, with youth in its most recent embodiment showing itself at last averse to confinement in gender-linked roles and stereotyped masculinity and femininity. Barbara Ehrenreich, alarmed at the narcissistic hedonism in "male revolt," found hope in an "androgynous drift" that the sexes might come back together in mutual respect after all.[84]

Yet why should androgyny, whether as ideal or as avant-garde social evolution, generate literature? Heilbrun professed herself "confident that great androgynous works will soon be written." What might they be like? Aside from Nathaniel Hawthorne's *The Scarlet Letter*, Heilbrun had none to point to in American history. What would the new androgynes make of Emerson and Melville and Whitman? Of James and Crane and Chopin? Would they dismiss them as Millett had dismissed Henry Miller? Heilbrun did have examples of androgyny to discuss: Charlotte Brontë again, and also Virginia Woolf, but what was in fact the historical connection between Brontë and Woolf and American literary history? Were sensitive Americans once again provincials learning from their sophisticated cousins? With some irony, the novelist Joyce Carol Oates responded to Heilbrun's hope: "How unfortunate that certain misogynous works by Faulkner are masterpieces, and certain gentle, intelligent reasonable works by androgynous writers are inferior?"[85]

Whether Henry Miller and Norman Mailer had or had not written masterpieces might have been argued systematically, but to dismiss them for misogyny was to betray that the mere ideology of feminism guaranteed no breakthrough into new language and new vision with which to render even feminist values. At the very least, Miller and Mailer had shown, in unprecedented candor, what feminists had to cope with. The tradition of writing they exemplified was hardly dying at their hands. The nonandrogynous hero kept announcing himself: "I was and have always been ready to venture as far as possible."[86] All the protagonists of Saul Bellow and Philip Roth "used" women in their quest to live lives unchained, eager, far, and wild. The women of Bellow's Herzog, of Roth's Zuckerman, were neither Virgins nor Venuses, resembled the Heiress of All the Ages in no way, were autonomous, yet fitted into no new model of marriage, androgyny, or equality at all.

Women Writers: As Feminists and as Writers

Whether out of the twenty, fifty, or one hundred fresh women writers who had established themselves by 1985 a new literature of androgyny would emerge, nothing yet indicated. Judith Rossner's *Looking for Mr. Goodbar* (1975) linked the new permissiveness with disintegration both personal and social, a new chapter in the history of the heroine as victim. After curing her heroine of a *Fear of Flying*, Erica Jong consciously claimed the tradition of a picaresque hero-hood for heroine-izing. A score, a hundred hard-edged studies of marital discord and divorce dispelled any last lingering *Life* magazine rosedust from the suburbs. Husbands, lovers, and even fathers were portrayed in their shallows, their adolescence, their narcissism. Often these investigations took on a kind of anthropological glow, illuminating obscure precincts and parishes. Mary Gordon's heroines extricated themselves painfully from an immigrant Catholic puritanism as airless and stale as any old Protestant Winesburg, emerging less eager and wild than crippled and numb. In contrast to Philip Roth, whose excoriations of tribal culture prompted accusations of anti-Semitism, Cynthia Ozick explicitly sought a "new Yiddish," implicitly hoping to cope with Jewish and Judaic patriarchy by acrobatic finesse.

Perhaps most striking, strong heroines appeared just where critics of the "white woman's movement" might have predicted. Black women writers indulged in no picaresque fantasies, nor did they trace a route to freedom in escape from repression or church. They did not write parallels to male writers' chronicles of disintegration. Instead of reviving the behavioristic naturalism Richard Wright had used to present his doomed hero Bigger Thomas, Alice Walker worked in more expressionistic modes, with more interior lightings, for the women tied to her tragically violent father-antihero, Grange Copeland, then traced the emergence of a full-fledged heroine in *The Color Purple*, drawing richly on the symbols and resources of a specific historic culture in a way no ideologically feminist novel, whether utopian or realist, could. In *Tar Baby*, Toni Morrison offered quick sketch of the surreal gender contrast among black lives in Manhattan:

[If] ever there was a black woman's town, New York was it. No, no, not . . . making decisions. But . . . kicking ass at Con Edison offices, barking orders in the record companies. . . . They refused loans at Household Finance, withheld unemployment checks . . . issued parking tickets. . . . gave enemas, blood transfusions and please lady don't make me mad . . . turned an entire telephone company into such a diamondhead of hostility the company paid you for not talking to their operators. The manifesto was simple: "Talk shit. Take none."

The counterparts of these lean, taut, loud young women were the ghetto's "great underclass of undocumented men, gamblers, part-time mercenaries, full-time gigolos. . . . Calibans, Staggerlees . . . John Henrys." Between these young women and these men the question was not so much that of a revolutionized new egalitarian marriage but of any marriage at all. Morrison formulated the brutal question that pointed at once to cause and dilemma: "Mama-spoiled black man, will you mature with me?"[87]

Of course so far as sheer literary equality was concerned, success equaled freedom from liberatory ideology itself. Flannery O'Connor, Eudora Welty, and Shirley Ann Grau all three testified to treasures still unexhausted in the unemancipated South available to imaginations unchained enough. From the standpoint of precocity and fecundity, the most remarkable case was Joyce Carol Oates. Oates did library research, she herself reading through the files of *Hotrod* magazine to get the details right for her picture of auto racing in her first novel, *With Shuddering Fall*, written in 1964 when she was still a college student.[88] But Oates was not interested in sociological realism. As her later novels would make progressively clearer, the reality of riots in Detroit, the reality of suburban affluence, of rural upstate New York, was never stable and solid, "out there," independent of the minds of the people coterminous with it. It was more often phantasmagoria than environment. Oates renewed that vision Rourke had identified, taking reality as occasion for comedy, the comedy of self-invention, of dreaming the world over again. Whether or not it was because of the novel itself, with its built-in tendency to generate self-reflective skepticism, Oates, like her predecessors, rendered comedy into pathos, desperation, disaster, defeat. Like Strindberg analyzing the destruction of Miss Julie, Oates had a powerful sense of the vulnerability of self and ego. Her sense of modern America as a particularly kaleidoscopic reality was reciprocal with her sense of American selves as engaged in a particularly desperate struggle not to sink, drown, dissolve in that reality. Sex, passion, the erotic, sexual violence, sexual obsession, romance all flared and burned through Oates's novels like the automobile races, the riots and flaming streets, the obsessions with money, with politics, with machines, arsons committed by frozen souls. In *With Shuddering Fall* Oates had no moral counsel to offer in detailing the terrible struggle of a husband, driven mad by his wife's dependency, passivity, and objectlike inertia. His act of doing away with himself followed from intolerable inner conflict: he could not give up his passion for her but he could not accept the violence his passion impelled. There were no lessons: had she been a stronger person, had he had more self-control, and so on.

Consistently, through her later work Oates registered the compulsion, grandeur, and transformative power as well as the violence of passion and passionate love, and, just as consistently, the terrors and nightmares they brought upon their bearers. To try to escape the anguish and torments of passion by means of purging passion itself, by means of rationality, by means of orderly work-contained comradeship, was the death of self, but to imagine there were "causes" for the failures and desperations of passion, causes susceptible to "reform," to "revolution," to "overthrowing patriarchy," to winning "equality," was to misread human psychology. If Oates finally saw literature as Whitman, Blake, and D. H. Lawrence did, it was as fuel for the passionate self, critically needed in a nation like the United States of America, where the forces of externality bombarded selves ceaselessly, ceaselessly inviting the passivities of mere consumption. More could be learned about modern America from Oates than from ordinary realist writers, but only through responding to her prophetic sight of that hidden America still—as ever—about to be revealed.

Not that more accessible novels could not reveal remarkable autonomies in more familiar heroines. In Diane Johnson's *Lying Low* (1978) the heroine, Marybeth, had been involved in illegal antiwar protests, had committed violent acts. On the wanted list, she was lying low under a false name in a California boarding house. She was befriended by other women. One of these was an older person, Theo, the companion of Anton. Theo was neither a traditional woman nor a new woman, neither awakened nor unawakened, simply active and empathetic in mind and imagination:

Theo thought of men as blind baby birds, chirping "That is the way the world works" with every gape of their hungry beaks. . . .

Men like going to war—I really think they do—because it gives them secrets. No woman can imagine war. Well, I suppose those Israeli girls can, and nurses, nurses see the things. Still, do you really want to see them? Aren't you grateful not to have to see them? Theo could not decide. . . .

"Don't you find men touching," Theo said, turning to the eggs and stove, trying to raise the level of the conversation. "So bravely, so uncomplainingly do they do things—for instance, go to war or sea."

She could not go away like that, she thought, to sea. . . . To say nothing of going to war. How could men? And the way they try to do things for themselves, brushing their own shoes and coats. What do men think of? It's hard to imagine the mind of a man; she thought, minds lacking the rich fullness of a woman's mind, all kinds of ideas cut off from them, no ideas about sewing or the colors of things. . . .

"All that trying men have to do," she said, "How often they must be cold and afraid. Think of being a soldier of Napoleon, a common soldier, with frozen feet. How horrible." It was true she didn't find Anton particularly touching. He was more of a woman to her. A great artist, it was said. Well.[89]

The heroine, wary, skittish, fearful of every tie, nevertheless found space beyond her fears. Somehow emotion reawoke, sex revived. She wondered about a newcomer to the boarding house: "His hands are so huge and strong, Marybeth thinks. I wonder if he has a big cock? No matter what they say, big ones are better." Lying beside him later, she marveled:

It is working, getting large and hard and ready. Is Chuck awake, too, or just *it*? He seems asleep. She snuggles close in upon him and bites his earlobe. His eyelids stir. "Chuck, Chuck," she whispers, "*you* have to wake up, too." Chuck so wonderful he can do it in his sleep.[90]

Conclusion

Strindberg's misogyny; D'Annunzio's sensuality; Gladkov's abandonment of the epic for psychological realism; Adams's yearning for a little boy's elementary bliss: can all these be given a "social" reading? Can we combine Marx and Freud into a "social construction of sexuality," then locate works of literature within it? Powders, oils, perfumes, unguents; silks and satins; the nuances of coiffure, ensemble, toilette: it is hard to imagine these seething into novels and poetry on the shores of Mälaren. Ulla Windblad's iconic perfection repelled the accoutrements of artifice: her beauty inhered in pure line, best revealed nude, in the fashion to which Swedes remained attached in the modern movies; line was spoiled by fat. For D'Annunzio flesh concealed/revealed behind lace and lattice would be enjoyed by hand, nose, mouth, not just the distant critical alienated eyeball. When Strindberg proceeded to penetrate sleek blond, blue-eyed beauty for its psychological inwardness, his prose turned pungent, acid, cleanly. He never rendered his women sensuously, for their flesh. For D'Annunzio to experience Woman without inhalation, savor, tactility was sterile; in Strindberg's engagements the fate of mind, heart, soul, not senses, was at stake.

Classic moralizing Freudianism would want to classify each of these orientations: obsessive, narcissistic, certainly not healthy and normal. But the social construction of sexuality is unwilling to agree that the healthy and normal were defined for good by Freud in Vienna, by, say, 1920. Marxist specialists in social construction, however, could agree that in principle sexuality would be "freed" one day, the day that the "contradictions" in sexuality were overcome, that on that day we would at last know what "healthy" and "normal" sexuality was like, and that, finally, both Strindberg's and D'Annunzio's could certainly safely be categorized as deformations traceable to the deformities and contradictions in their societies. The reasons for their particular deformations would not be hard to identify: in Italy, the desperate search in a foundering economy of a dying aristocracy for new sources of self-esteem, a flush of vitality, Woman as cocaine; in Sweden, the desperate fear of an emergent middle class that its freedom and individualism had no real long-term basis, Woman as scapegoat.

Instead of these deconstructions, feminist history might prefer to emphasize simply how both sensuality and misogyny demonstrated—once again—the oppression of women, the projection onto women by men of the fantasies useful to them, the monopolization of literature as much as of politics for masculine self-interest. Prudence might warn feminist criticism against classifying D'Annunzio and Strindberg in the same box: it would then become necessary to identify what was in common to both Italy and Sweden, but calling this, say, "patriarchy," let alone "capitalism," would be once again to reject the individualities of Strindberg and D'Annunzio (as well as of Italy and Sweden) and, of course, to lose hold of real history. Cautious, sophisticated history would entertain the possibility that the first task of the historian was not to deconstruct Strindberg or D'Annunzio or to classify them as the enemy, but to understand them.

In any case, analyzing and classifying D'Annunzio's sensuality and Strindberg's misogyny was not to cope with their art. Misogynists might multiply, sensualists swarm, with never a Strindberg or D'Annunzio among them. Strindberg swept down, not only on Swedish, but on Western European literature like a wolf on the fold, not because of his misogyny, but because of the arrangement of his words, his voice, his language. The social roots, the historical context for this unprecedented voice are unquestionable: it did not come down from the clouds, from God, from heaven. But from the standpoint of the history of society as the history of the resources for culture, the most important single fact in turn-of-the-century Swedish history could not be otherwise than, quite simply, Strindberg. Swedish history, in its roots, its "structures," its "contradictions" and continuities, had proved capable of generating an unprecedented new resource for consciousness. It was the way Strindberg wrote, more than *what* he wrote, that most mattered.

That, in European perspectives, D'Annunzio counted as a lesser figure than Strindberg—by far—does not, however, truly let us reduce D'Annunzio to less than an innovative, creative writer, for *what* he wrote, no doubt deriving from dilemmas, desperations, anxieties, and agonies peculiar to Italy, did not compromise the power of the *way* he wrote it. What other European country needed relief from failure in theatricality, illusionism, defiance of reality in *una bella figura*? It was Italy, not Sweden; Italy, not France, Germany, or Britain, that fell to Mussolini. Yet in Italy, too, a history seeking to identify the emergence of structures or contradictions as well as powers and resources ought to be tempted to conclude that the most important single feature of turn-of-the-century Italian history was, if not perhaps D'Annunzio, then that new language emerging through Luigi Pirandello, too, and soon in Italo Svevo. If the leading question in Italian literary history was whether literary life would continue to be dominated by the traditional intellectuals, neither national nor popular, as Gramsci had lamented, the answer had become clear. But the new language would not be what Gramsci had hoped, emerging in organic association with the vital life of the workers. The new writers, while no longer as serenely confident as Croce in cultural leadership "from above," remained as distant from mass life as ever. For all his desperate need for immersion, Pier Paolo Pasolini remained as isolated as the cultivators of the elegances of Tuscan. The route to a major evolution in Italian literary imagination was shown at base by D'Annunzio and Aleramo: the chance for the "populistic" literature Gramsci believed he wanted hardly compared with the chance for the individualistic, romantic-heroic literature both D'Annunzio and Aleramo produced. The blighting of this, first by Fascism, then by Italy's continuing failure to shake free of its premodernity, led only to the gathering pessimism, however brilliant, of the postwar moviemakers. It seems reasonable to conclude, then, that in Italy feminism never came to enjoy the contribution of a robust literary confrontation with the immensely multifarious lives of modern Italian women. Investigation of real-life dramas suffered. The abstractions of political rage and desperate utopian nostalgia continued to dominate.

In Sweden, the potential for dialectic vibrating tautly between the poles of warm homelikeness and awful isolation persisted from Bellman to Ingmar Bergman, but the very incomprehension with which Vilgot Sjöman's translation of this more or less esoteric tradition into popular terms was greeted testified again to why Strindberg had assailed with such vehemence the national readiness to succumb to the little home and its passions for abstract equalities. The exploration of solitude would continue in Swedish lyric poetry, practically all by men, but their isolation, too, registered the resistance to plunging still more deeply into stories of relationship. By the 1970s Swedish writers were again engaged in social democratic thesis novels, righteous and anti-individual.

By comparison with both Sweden and Italy, the single most important fact in Soviet history was the absence of a Strindberg, of a D'Annunzio, indeed of a Henry Adams or Stephen Crane. This absence escorts the historian to the very heart of Soviet history. Indeed, it may well be argued—I for one urge it—that the peculiarity of Soviet history consists precisely in the fact that at its heart the historian—Marxist, "liberal," or whatever—must try to explain an absence, a void, a voicelessness, rather than a presence, an ideology. We have seen that the Soviet Communist Party imposed voicelessness upon Soviet feminism (assuming, to repeat, that "feminism" can rightly be imputed to the

Soviet Union as a kind of suppressed social consciousness). Far more important, as measured by the record of Italy and Sweden (and the United States) was the suppression of fresh language. Soviet history itself has helped us measure this suppression. The painters, sculptors, theater and movie directors, poets, and novelists of the Soviet 1920s rivaled Weimar Berlin and New York City for daring, audacity, analytic power, productive sweep, all starved, betrayed, mangled, crushed by the rise of "Socialism in One Country."

This in itself does not declare that the central void in Soviet history has been the absence of a Strindberg, a D'Annunzio, an Adams, for the annihilated Maleviches and Zemyatins and Eisensteins in Soviet history were not preoccupied with women. Many of them were eager celebrants of the Revolution, anti-individualist practitioners of "epic" as shackled to triumphalism as Dante and Michelangelo. The first great suppression was not that of such revolutionary, but of pre-Revolutionary, literature. From the standpoint of the history of consciousness, the single most important fact of pre-Revolutionary Russia was Count Leo Tolstoy, and as Ruth Crego Benson has shown, Tolstoy's conception of women was not only conflicted and obsessive but also central to his whole sense of life. Thus, the first great suppression of Bolshevik history suppressed woman-centered consciousness. Nevertheless, the new revolutionary literature did include a Fyodor Gladkov, at least tolerated an Akhmatova, might have nurtured a Kollontai, as well as others a historian may wish to include in some melancholy record of those who "might have" written freely, not of "Soviet women," but of women in Soviet Russia. Boris Pilnyak alone may be enough to show the potential that was lost. While catching the epic, panoramic elements of the Russian drama at its most intense, in *The Naked Year—1919*, Pilnyak's cinematic literary devices also drew him on into acute psychological dissection, which, left free, ought to have borne him on to novels as liberating in their way as Tatlin's architectural ideas or Akhmatova's poetry. Had literary freedom remained in 1935 what it had been in 1925, even Gladkov's blocky realism in *Cement* could have generated the kind of power another blocky, once-censored writer, Theodore Dreiser, was to manifest in the United States. Speculation can only guess at further possibilities. Men had totally dominated the nineteenth-century novel: might women have found their voice under a "free" Communism? The pre-Revolutionary painter Olga Rosanova continued to display force after the Revolution, as did the painter Vera Kozintseva. Vera Mukhina helped define Soviet sculpture, Asja Lacis stage design. And, above all, were the women poets: Akhmatova, Zinaida Gippius, Marina Tsveyaeva. Women had been part of the revolutionary agon for fifty years: Breshkovskaya and Figner, Spridonova and Krupskaya, Kollontai herself. True, Russian revolutionary logic had never invited a literature by women about women for women, that work of "woman's sphere" conspicuous in the United States. But women had always been a vital presence, and as Kollontai's own last stories hinted, Soviet women novelists might well have had interesting things to say, said in interesting ways, quite apart from what the Pilnyaks and Zamyatins and Gladkovs might have said had they, too, been free.

Nevertheless, the commanding comparison remains that between a Sweden with Strindberg and a Soviet Union without, an Italy with a D'Annunzio and a Soviet Union without, for of course the issue of "woman's voice" remained yet to be resolved in Sweden and Italy too. From this perspective we can go back and revise our estimate of Strindberg. Though the way Strindberg said what he had to say was more decisive for his significance than what he said, there were intimate, indeed ineradicable connections between how and what. Most succinctly: there is no modern literature that is not about women. What was most critically wrong with Soviet literature and art was not that it was "socialist realism," or that it was "propaganda," or that it was "political," but that it was not about women. Naturally so, for, to have been about women, Soviet literature would have had to defy Soviet politics, ideology, and myths of identity. What was the reason, after all, that modern literature had to be about women? As modern societies, industrialized, organized, managed, drawn under the controls of politics and science, evolved farther and farther from tradition and the natural, it was in the deepest relations between people, in private life, in love, marriage, sex, family that the dialectic intensified between seeking resource against depersonalization on the one hand, and, on the other, succumbing to the introduction of politics, disguised as science, in these very most intimate spheres. The struggle of consciousness to escape capture by organization, politics and science, had no more crucial an arena than where it was tempted at once to yield to regressive nostalgia for mythical "natural" havens and to welcome the promises of those new sciences addressed to body, heart, and mind. It was up to literature—that is, to literature aiming to be modern, not nostalgic— to find the languages by which to resist both temptations, to steadily forge new instruments to dispel the encapsulations of psychology and sociology alike. Nowhere could these instruments be more powerful, and their lack more devastating, than at that peculiar intersection of sociology and psychology, sex. Thus, in Strindberg's recognition of the linkage between creativity and childhood, the "marriage" he excoriated was not only the symbol of larger forms of captivity, but it was also itself the iron cage. Thus, in D'Annunzio's deliberate exaltation and exaggeration of the senses, he attested to realization that freedom in the modern world had an enemy, not an aide, in harmony, that modern freedom required the individual to open himself to the dangers of addiction.

Brilliant critics of American literature have found it "innocent," "almost juvenile," for failing to treat "the passionate encounter" of a man and a woman, a view evidently confirmed by the record of Emerson, Whitman, Twain, Henry Adams, Henry James, and so on, a literature, not so much for, but of, boys—*Huckleberry Finn* its greatest achievement, as hailed by Ernest Hemingway, its greatest modern. This view has been rejected as unduly, unfairly selective: what about *The Scarlet Letter*? Emily Dickinson (correctly read)? What about *The House of Mirth* and *Sister Carrie*? Indeed, what about the long-neglected *The Awakening*? And was this view really fair to the James of, say, *The Ambassadors* and *The Golden Bowl*? Yet preeminent exponents of the first view, such as Leslie Fiedler, were not likely to be defeated by a battle of lists. As criticism gave itself over more and more to the pursuit of "myths" and to "semiological" excavation of "structures" and "discourses," Fiedler's discovery of such stereotypes as "the Dark Lady," the "Good Good" and the "Good Bad" girl, the "Good Bad" boy, and so on, could only seem legitimate. Far more telling was the objection that Fiedler and his peers had not identified peculiarly American, but more broadly Western, literary traits. Fiedler himself had found the roots of American literature in the eighteenth-century English novel, sentimental and double-dealing. But had there been some discourse of more "mature" sexuality prior to this, and to its new audience, the emerging Protestant middle classes? If American novels were to be judged according to some measure of mature sexuality, where was that measure to be seen? To claim that it might be found in, say, Shakespeare and/or Chaucer, would be to enter upon historical incoherence, for it was not necessary for feminist criticism to make out Shakespeare's conventional views of women; it was necessary only to see that Shakespeare's views on sex, marriage, family, and women were those of another, premodern, "medieval" world. Or was the critic to believe that some standard of mature sexuality had been manifest through long ages only to fall victim to modernity? As for candidates for maturity elsewhere, Ruth Benson's analysis of Tolstoy did not suggest that it had been maturity, but, rather, preoccupation, that the Bolshevik censorship liquidated. Had French literature embodied sexual maturity? It did not take only Simone de Beauvoir to undermine any such idea as that. German? Italian? Once the modern "scientific" language of sexual maturity and immaturity was applied, every literature deserved to be found ungrown-up.

Yet, however cogent the criticism of views such as Fiedler's might have been, his central insight remained intact: American literature was different, just as Tocqueville had predicted and Constance Rourke had confirmed. It celebrated masculine freedom. It has evolved from the crude lyricism of the Jacksonian comic theater to the supremely American prose of *Huckleberry Finn*. Stigmatizing this literature for its "adolescence," its "sexual immaturity," its lack of full-bodied women obscured the main point: it had been a great modern literature, in all its versions, that of Emerson, Whitman, and Melville as well as that of Twain and Hemingway. It had drawn directly on American economic and political history and, with its unprecedented new resources of language, had equipped Americans to defend themselves against being made hostage to their own successes.

It is in this context, not that of an abstracted sexual maturity, that the growing attention of men like Henry James, Henry Adams, and Stephen Crane to women had its resonance. It was not going to be enough simply to celebrate masculine individuality endlessly. Tocqueville's idea, that the proper arrangement of the sexes would persist in America simply because it was sociologically right and fitting, would not suffice. Anticipating the modern social science of Mead and Erikson, men like Horace Bushnell and Walt Whitman grew anxious that modernity might change women. Women might cease to exhibit that almost mystical sense of what men needed to remain free in a capitalistic democratic society. Women must remain good mothers, as Mead and Erikson were to repeat. Henry Adams, witness to the full force of the new economy, as Bushnell and Whitman were not, felt that the fatal transformation in women had perhaps already gone too far. At the same time, however, he went beyond simply a reactionary call for the revival of Mother. Diagnosing the lack of both Virgin and Venus, of both Mother and Lover, he began to get beyond celebration of old freedoms and anxiety at their loss. It had been Hawthorne's genius to sense early that abandonment of sentimental and merely sociological ordering of sexuality exposed both individuals and society to shattering transformations. It was hardly surprising that he could not proceed further. Stephen Crane's own deepest personal wishes obviously were heading into this new revolutionary territory, and before his early death he, too, had generated, in *Maggie*, an antisentimental language for claiming sexuality for consciousness. There seems no reason not to continue exploring Henry James for the same. That this "awakening" was not more euphoric and optimistic and positive-thinking than Kate Chopin's novel was, again, hardly cause for surprise. Its context remained that heritage of masculine freedom and individualism. It would be easy, and still "American," for heroes, no longer boys, fully aroused to the glamour of sex, to be victims, logical for Theodore Dreiser to entitle his masterpiece of sexual catastrophe *An American Tragedy*. In reaching out for sexuality, whether in its glamour or in its companionability, there was something to be lost, that old freedom itself. This was what remained far clearer in American literature than in Italian or even Swedish, let alone Soviet, and what was to permeate the new medium of the movies as it won its mass audiences. Even as the movies supplemented literature in rendering sexuality as itself a realm of refreshment, invigoration, and self-elaboration for the individual, the clear sense of a specific heritage at risk persisted. The fact that in literature, in Hemingway, Fitzgerald, and Faulkner, the dark anxieties continued to dominate, in contrast to the deliberately stimulative modes of the movies, simply attested to the danger in all notions of images replacing words. As the art of words, literature remained in far more reliable touch with history.

In sum, if American history had underwritten a literature that had not been about women, the most important fact about modern American history was not that some new genius, a Strindberg or a D'Annunzio, who did write about women had not burst forth, but, rather, that American writers had become aware of the problematic, contingent, vulnerable tradition of literature by men about men for men, and that that literature was in flux. Whether it would hunker down into last-ditch resistance, give itself over to melancholy, embrace revolutionary indeterminacies, decades might be required to know. So long as the answer was in the form of literature, it seemed likely that no new ideologies of feminism, equality, and androgyny would matter. No less than in Sweden and Italy, literature in America had flourished in the freedom of individuals to lead lives no one could possibly have imagined until they were led, lives beyond roles and status, beyond duty and responsibility, the kinds of lives that were themselves the source of fresh language.

When women began to write, they would be compromised by feminism. If, as Alexandra Kollontai believed, socialism served women by protecting them from being victimized by their own sexuality, what could a feminist woman write about? As victims, women induced tracts, polemics, protest novels, not literature. As heroines of the revolution, women induced propaganda, portraits of women serving the cause, not explorations of the individual. It hardly follows that, had Kollontai been less of a revolutionary she would have been a better writer, but neither does it follow that the fresh writing that might have followed upon revolution would be done by revolutionaries. In the United States, women writers would be threatened by both aspects of feminism. Those seeking to strengthen, expand, and enforce woman's sphere would quite naturally stress the evils opposing such an expansion, and, thus, invite a complacent triumphalism in woman's sphere itself. On the other hand, those seeking escape from woman's sphere, quite naturally anxious to put the old life behind them, would have only fantasies to write about, life as it had not yet been lived. Of course these two modes could be mingled, as in Fredrika Bremer's vision of a mother-dominated public life or Gilman's vision of a community of equal professionals devoid of private life. In both cases modern literature could be dispensed with: there would be no sexual dramas to write about.

Where woman's sphere failed to organize sexuality, the dominant force in women's writing would be sheer wish, the wish that sex could be welcomed without disturbing social order, the wish for sex without price, the wish to have one's cake yet eat it too. At its worst this produced *St. Elmo*, at its best what never appeared in America, a *Pride and Prejudice* or a *Wuthering Heights*. Far more powerful were those startlingly unprecedented voices whose analyses of sexually liberated individual women partook of defeat, bleak isolation, tragedy, rather than of wish fulfillment: Kate Chopin, Sibilla Aleramo. It would be hard for feminism to embrace these sisters. Marketplace equality offered no obvious solution to the stories of Edna Pontellier and *una donna*, nor did some postulation of an androgynous equivalence do more than change the shape of sentimental wish fulfillment, in the direction of Mrs. Stowe's *Minister's Wooing*, say. Yet it was likely that as women, too, wrote modern literature they, too, would discover the dangers of optimism, share Strindberg's horror of "little homes," agree to the necessity of risking self and language in D'Annunzian excess, prefer Californian "rapture" to common vigilantism.

Before their rise into such a literature, however, before, say, writing about rape, not simply as a victimization of all women by all men, but as a constituent in love, women might well devote an epoch of consciousness-raising to the theme, not of perfecting relations with men, but of again withdrawing from them. In woman's sphere, women had led separate lives, but this separateness had been strongly qualified and limited. Women had hardly begun to live all their lives in woman's sphere. In the United States far more than in Italy, Sweden, or the Soviet Union, the twentieth-century economy itself seemed to be at once inviting and enforcing larger and deeper separations between the sexes. Feminism would have to choose its course: should it combat this tendency or exploit it? Nowhere was the opportunity greater to explore the question whether such a thing existed as "woman's consciousness,"

linked irreducibly to women's physical existence, than in a language
generated to illuminate and irradiate the new separateness. Berryman's remarkable poem was an instance: language inspired by the
most intense effort at overcoming separateness, by the most intense
eagerness for intercourse. What further resources might be required
to speak of his failure?

General Conclusion

In a big book one animus of which has been to depreciate premature formulas, question transnational generalization, discourage overarching universalities, I recognize the irony of summation.

It has been the argument of this book that the history of modern women is best told as parts of the histories of separate nations. No doubt there is a history of modernization, but modernization has not fought wars, generated political parties, promulgated ideologies. The women of Soviet Russia were not put to work by modernization, but by Joseph Stalin. Patriarchy may or may not have a history, but patriarchy has not pursued industrialization, induced mass emigration, debated population policies. Italian women endured their perpetuation of backwardness, not because of the patriarchy vested in Italian life, but because of the inability of Italian leaders to get a powerful Italian economic machine running. There is a history of capitalism, no doubt, but the leaders of Great Britain, the United States, Germany, Japan, and so on pursued their interests as British, Americans, Germans, Japanese far more vigorously than as capitalists. Nineteenth-century American women were assigned their separate sphere not out of some logic inherent in capitalism but due to the democratic marketplace specific to American history. Socialism no doubt has an international history, if only in the hopes of many socialists, but socialism's international embodiments in such institutions as the Internationales were only phantasms compared to the powerful organs of nations. Swedish women came to enjoy social benefits, not because Sweden belonged to some category of nations labeled socialist or social democratic, but as a consequence of the Swedish Social Democrats' commitment to the perpetuation of specifically Swedish values.

Telling the history of women as part of national histories means telling different stories, not one big story, and getting what was specific and particular to each story into sharp focus. Women remained subordinate to men in Italy, Sweden, Russia, and the United States despite all the changes in their lives, but this fact was not an invitation to try to figure out some element in common to explain this common fact. Such a search did run the risk, of course, of nourishing antifeminist impulses; for instance "women remained subordinate through modernization, democracy, capitalism, socialism, through thick and thin, because that subordination expressed the natural relationship of the sexes." But this danger was not the reason for refusing to look for a big story that incorporated the little stories. The reason was that the big story resulted in bad history.

The story of Russian women in Soviet history was not summed up in their continuing political subordination. For many Russian women, Soviet history meant escape from old subordinations. It meant a rise from economic and social backwardness, greater equality with their own men. For many men, that same history, impelling a rise for women, impelled a decline for them. The traditions and powers of craft work were shattered in Stalin's industrialization; the powers of unions were destroyed by Stalinist politics. Russian women had, in short, made a major advance toward equality with most Russian men, but that equality was with men who themselves had lost power. Russian history thus clarified a crucial question: What was the significance of greater gender equality if it followed from decline in the power of one gender? Feminist history had little to gain in seeking some factor in common between Soviet and other history. It would instead take the point Soviet history had to offer: the issue underlying the feminist quest for equality was that of power. In seeking equality with men, women wanted to share in the powers men enjoyed. If equality meant sharing, not power, but powerlessness, then feminism was called upon to adjust its own agendas.

In Sweden the relative absence of women from the directorates of the unions, the parties, the corporations, and the state did not provide an illuminating perspective on women in modern Swedish history. Certainly Swedish women's political shortfall could not be explained in the same way as was Russian women's. There was no monolithic unitary party-state in Sweden. There was no ban on feminism in Sweden. There was no prohibition on voluntary association for every sort of purpose in Sweden. Sweden was, in fact, one of the most fully liberalized societies in the West. Not only did its state church press upon almost no consciences; its "free" religious culture had, by the twentieth century, ceased to generate tribal coercions. Thus, feminist history would be hard-pressed to tell the story of Swedish women in terms primarily of subordinations, inequalities, repressions, and failures. Swedish men and women had shared a great fear, that of the collapse of an old culture into class division and widespread degradation. They had responded together in forging the labor and party institutions that would issue in their high-tech, high-tax welfare social democracy. The national economic success story had not divided the sexes. It had not invited Swedish men onto a kind of American-style adventure while reserving Swedish women for a purely domestic culture. If this seemed only to make the continuing political inequality of Swedish women more mysterious, the route for feminist history was not to go outside Swedish history in search of some transnational, underlying, overarching factor for explanation. It was to persist in enriching the Swedish story. The rapid decline in Swedish fertility, the beginnings of state support for mothers, the tax treatment of marriage, the legal treatment of contraception, sex education, pornography, the debates over part-time work and parental leave, all manifested a people increasingly self-conscious in trying to clarify what they wanted and how they might combine and compromise their wishes. Swedes had gone far to disentangle themselves from old restraints and inhibitions upon free consideration of their own interests. It would be dangerous for feminist history to ascribe much—or any—of the way Swedish women lived to standard subordinations and inequalities. No doubt subordinations and inequalities still persisted, but that story of Swedish women in Swedish history would be thin, flavorless, and distorted that did not stress the spread of choices, options, and freedom among Swedish women. The story of women in Swedish history thus helps clarify the feminist goal of equality further: not only must equality mean power; it must mean freedom. If the two might be taken to be identical, so be it. Since Swedish history has displayed a more or less continuous quest to bring political power ever more into the service of intimate human wishes, the history of women in Sweden especially is drawn to reach out for the data of such wishes in all realms, in literature and movies, among other places, and not only in data of workplace and politics. A history of women in Sweden that omitted Strindberg would distort the history of the Swedish welfare state. Sexuality in Swedish movies pointed directly to political policy as well as at elusive, ancient mores. That seeming apathy or indifference to organized feminism among Swedish women could not safely be assigned to mere co-optation without reckoning with the subtlest expressions of art and culture.

In Italy, by contrast, the continuing subordination of women might indeed plausibly be ascribed to large transnational systemic forces such as capitalism and patriarchalism. Yet this would be to distort the Italian story irredeemably. The failure of capitalism in Italy was the failure of Italian capitalism. The strength of patriarchy in Italy was the strength of Italian patriarchy. Patriarchy construed as a kind of protean demon with a thousand faces, found now in classical Greek homosexuality, now in modern imperious heterosexuality, here in feudalism, there in monarchy, first in competitive capitalism, then in monopoly capitalism, provided opportunity for anthropological field chases. But what mattered about patriarchy in Italy was its persistence as Italian patriarchy. For all their dedication to an Italy freed for modern political debate, the men of the Risorgimento could not shake Italy free of the

Vatican and the Catholic church; Giolitti had to deal with it; Mussolini did; so did De Gasperi and the Americanized Italy of post-World War II. Nor could Italian intellectual culture shake itself free of its traditional intellectuals, from Croce through Gramsci. Nor, despite Giolitti's democratization of male suffrage, woman suffrage after 1945, and Togliatti's espousal of a "mass" party, was Italian politics ever able to shake off the tradition of parties managed by self-perpetuating elites. No surges of populist feeling washed periodically through Italian public life; there was no guarantee that had Italian economic production flourished more mightily all these would have changed. On the contrary, as Mussolini's Fascism provisionally suggested and the postwar Communist Party's program outlined, higher levels of economic production in Italy might well have deepened the hold of the old pre- and antidemocratic forms of Italian life, just as it did in the Soviet Union. But in reality, as well as in these might-have-beens, the context for Italian women's condition was an emphatically Italian one, saturated with the Italian past and riven with all the tensions and dilemmas of Italy's painful course in modern times. Perhaps more in Italy than elsewhere in the West, feminism found itself in a painful vise. Since Italy's backwardness appeared so deeply rooted in peculiarly Italian circumstances, should Italy then de-Italianize itself? de-Catholicize itself? Americanization was more another definition of its problems than a star for guidance. Bolshevization? Sovietization? As Gramsci, Palmiro Togliatti—the "Italian way to Communism"—and Enrico Berlinguer—"Eurocommunism"—all showed, even the leadership on the Left shrank from this. Italy's escape into power, freedom, and prosperity somehow had to fulfill Italy's history, not abstract dreams of utopia. Italian feminists were hardly likely to dispute this deep, almost physically felt nationalism. Despite the occasional impatience of a Mozzoni or ideological obeisance of a Ravera, feminists in Italy could find practically no ground of their own. They had constantly to associate themselves with parties and movements often not only condescending and even indifferent to them but sometimes actually hostile, parties and movements, moreover, which persistently showed themselves unable to break through Italy's perennial difficulties. For feminist history, the story of women in Italy is certainly not one chapter in a big story of global womanhood, nor is it a chapter in the frustration of women everywhere by vast systemic forces. The story of women in Italy offers another useful lesson: measuring women's history by various yardsticks of failure and success, progress or regress, may often interfere with the main task, of getting the story right. Italy's modern history in general, as well as of its women, is one—of many—calling for maximum empathy and sympathy, and one source of such sympathy may very well be found in historians' recognition that in many stories the only victories to be recorded are not in political, economic, or even cultural data but those that are their own reward, in consciousness, awareness, self-consciousness that affirms itself even though it may have no other fruits. Feminist history that forgoes triumphalism does not thereby undermine feminism.

In the United States, where women would seem to have had the most freedom and power, and feminists the best opportunity to exploit that freedom and power in a struggle for equality, the problem for historians of coping with women's subordination would seem most urgent. Some feminist historians have been inclined to press the problem toward paradox. Why, in the richest and politically freest of modernized nations, should the United States rank last in guaranteeing parental leave time, last in providing day-care centers, worst in numbers of impoverished single mothers, in extramarital teen-age pregnancies? Why has American women's pay continued to stall at around 65 percent of men's while women's pay has started to climb in other countries? Why are American mothers far more often left economically devastated by divorce than in most other Western nations? Why has wife abuse, child abuse, marketplace sex harassment evidently swelled in the United States more than in other countries? Apart from inquiring into the reliability of some of these comparisons, historians will want to accept them as challenges. But it would be to compound paradox to invoke for the United States systemic forces that in the United States have been far less obviously lethal than elsewhere. Capitalism? However "general" capitalism's failures may or may not have been, two features special to capitalism in the United States compared to its story elsewhere have been the democratization of its marketplace and the abundance it has supplied to that marketplace. The task for feminist history of women in America is not to dilate upon capitalism's failures but to connect women's lives—and feminism—with the abundant democratic marketplace. Have democracy and abundance contributed to the subordination and inequality of American women? Whether the answer turns out to be yes, no, both, or neither, the question derives from a story that is peculiar to the United States. As David Potter's analysis in *People of Plenty* suggested, such linkage immediately brought other institutions than politics and the economy into focus: family, childrearing, marriage, sexuality. In the most emphatic shorthand, it was in the United States that both men and women found themselves with the power and freedom to invest time and money in these institutions, tinker with them, experiment with them, improve them. Often while still proclaiming their loyalty to what was "natural" and "God-given" in these relations, Americans were in fact historicizing them, and, indeed, thereby proving they were historically created and thus proper topics for historians. American history itself thus offered in its particularity a particularly rich opportunity, both to feminist historians and to all historians, to expand history's scope to its proper dimensions. How American capitalism did and did not function to contain American women in one form of subordination and inequality or another certainly remained a part of the story to be told. Yet, to miss what was particular to American history was to miss the historian's greatest chance.

And patriarchy? Quite apart from the evident eagerness of American men, as analyzed by Constance Rourke, long before Hugh Hefner's *Playboy* revolt, to leave household and children to women for their own "games," patriarchy was being leached from institutional embodiments too. On the one hand, the competitive pluralism of American enterprise checked the pretensions of any one hierarchy. On the other hand, the very expediency on which most organization was founded deprived it of the stability inherent to patriarchy. In the United States democratic capitalism underwrote a new kind of manhood. No doubt, as an ideal this kind of manhood had been formulated in Europe during the century before. No doubt, if Tocqueville was right and what democracy released was basic human nature, all Europeans, and all mankind, would want to be like what Americans were becoming. As Henry Bellows argued, Americans were different, not in having their own national character, to be added, Mazzini-style, to the roster of all national characters, but in having the character all men would one day have once they too were rich and free.

That deep anxieties were released in all this disintegration of traditional authority was certain, and the response could take the form of such superpatriarchies as Mormonism and Oneida's socialism, in which the resubordination of women was emphatic. But the very extremity of such responses suggested the contrary story. As men embraced the "wonderland" Tocqueville understood them to have realized, most women became freer to project themselves in their own spheres. They were free to render family life, child-rearing, marriage, and sexuality far more complex, difficult, and potentially both more damaging and more gratifying, both to themselves and, eventually, to men. At the same time, they were free to project the basic qualities of their own sphere outward, in expansion, first against palpable vices consequent upon men's freedom, then in hopes of sharing perhaps some of the experiences men had. Again, it was American history itself, in its particularity that provided perspective on the theme of women's inequality. For the historian of women, little was fruitful in reiteration of the injustice and inequality imposed on women by their exclusion from men's realm of enterprise. Search for evidence of women's own sense of injustice and exclusion would be difficult. The realm of enterprise was new. Women were not being pushed out of it. They were being denied acquaintance with its possibilities. A powerful imaginative intellect such as Margaret Fuller's could negotiate a breakthrough, but even Fuller's lament over women's estate more nearly defended women against men than demanded that women be allowed to share in men's enterprises.

Aside from the rich history of women engaged in exercising the freedoms and powers they did have in their allotted spheres, the theme of inordinate interest offered by American history to the historian of women was that of how women imagined what men were like, and men women, across the chasm dividing experience. Gender differences were not so much maintained in nineteenth-century America as steadily submitted to comprehensive imaginative reworking. Once again, American history offered a special opportunity for feminist history's electrolytic task: as the changes in gender differences proceeded, gender differences themselves could more clearly be shown to derive not from nature but from history.

In the crumbling of nineteenth-century feminism following its historic suffrage victory in 1920, American history offered another special opportunity to both feminist history and the history of women. It would be more than paradoxical to argue that feminism in America crumbled in the 1920s because of transnational systemic forces such as capitalism—even, now, "monopoly capitalism"—and patriarchy. The most obvious theme was that of feminism's goals themselves. Feminism's transformation from powerful movement into ineffectual competitive fringe groups clearly suggested that the central theme in the history of feminism was not so much its successes and failures, its struggles with enemies and its alliances with friends, but, rather, its own inner history of self-transformation. This history of self-reflection, of the reflection of women upon themselves as women, not only encouraged, but required, historians to trace the fortunes of women's consciousness playing upon all the institutions and relationships of women's lives. No inference from the post-1920 disintegration of feminism had to be drawn that women's consciousness had suffered regression or even that nineteenth-century feminism had failed. It was as plausible to hypothesize that women in the 1920s, in their own powers of self-creation, were discovering nineteenth-century feminism inadequate for their purposes and evolving ideas about themselves and their prospects unknown to Susan B. Anthony, Carrie Chapman Catt, and their cohorts. The bifurcated, if not multiple and conflicted, qualities of the newly explicit feminism after 1965 strongly suggested a continuing exfoliation of such inwardness. The victories and defeats of the feminist struggle were surely of

vital interest to feminists themselves. But for feminist history the advantage lay in continuing so search out the new powers and freedoms
being generated in specific circumstances.

Focusing the history of modern women within national histories
helps feminist history fulfill its task of gathering not just all women's
lives, but all of women's lives, into mainstream history. The argument
from justice that all persons deserve to be included in history cannot
be refuted, but history generated by justice cannot be adequate for
feminist history. As a form of struggle, feminist history is focused not
on women as such but on women's relationships to power. Left unlo-
cated in the realms of power, the history of women lacked accumulative
power of its own. From the standpoint of justice, domestic workers were
indeed as deserving of history as politicians, as Birgitta Wistrand con-
tended, but telling their story from an impulse of justice alone by no
means fulfilled feminist history. Why should historians choose to write
of domestic workers rather than, say, shopgirls? Both had been neglected. The feminist historian's choice would be directed by her—and
his—sense of how well prepared she—or he—was to tell the story of the
domestics or the shopgirls as an illumination of the story of power.

Claiming all realms of women's lives for the history of power and
politics must be persuasive within stories of real political power and
conflict. National stories narrate such power and conflict at its most
comprehensible in modern times. But as I have tried to suggest in the
last part of this book, national histories can be of immense service
without coming to constitute straightjackets. It is not so much that in,
say, Strindberg, Aleramo and D'Annunzio, Pilnyak, "I. Grekova," and
Trifonov, Chopin and Cather, Crane and Mailer, we have a kind of
international roundtable from whose exchanges we can elicit discourses larger than national. It is, rather, that such writers—and their
counterparts in all the other arts—compel us to carry still further our
understanding of power. It is perfectly true that the kind of transnational
consciousness generated by a Strindberg, say, can be seized upon by the
American historian, say, in order to ask questions of American history.
And it is true that such themes as family, courtship, gender, sexuality
find forms of expression in one art and another closed to ordinary public
political discourse. But for historians, novels, movies, the arts matter
most in the opportunity they offer for far more realistic conceptions of
power and politics. The private must be understood politically. The very
sharpness of Strindberg's art, the temper of its steel, would be dulled
if its origins in a specific, historically real history, in the "little story"
of Sweden were ignored. The story of Bolshevism and Communism in
the Soviet Union loses much of its cut if the history of poetry in the
Soviet Union is left out: in the Soviet Union certain things are not

possible in poetry. The unsuccessful struggle of Italian moviemakers to induce a certain new populism in their art derived from Italy's whole modern history. The powerful pessimisms of a Kate Chopin or a Willa Cather were lightning bursts in certain very American darknesses. Feminist history was fulfilled not only as it succeeded in converting all aspects of women's lives into historical terms, but also as it demonstrated that the materials of culture were the materials of mainstream history, the history of power.

Of course all this meant that feminist history's subjects were not women but men-and-women. It is not so much that men, too, are implicated in all those institutions to which women have often been confined, those founded directly on relationships between the sexes. Stalin's private life is not really at issue. Rather, the equality sought by feminism was always equality in certain situations with certain men. Just who these men were had to be clarified in every feminist history. Karl Staaff and the Swedish Liberals were probably more nearly feminists than the leaders of the Swedish Social Democrats, yet few Swedish women were ready to cast their lot with a policy opening Sweden to the rigors of free trade. Alexandra Kollontai discovered that antifeminists were to be found flourishing in Bolshevism, yet never thought of disavowing her own Bolshevism for the less certain promises of the NEP men. Both modern Italian and modern American feminists found themselves outraged by young men of the New Left; in both Italy and the United States feminists found it hard to decide just which sorts of men were the worst. But in the United States some feminists could organize for a purpose incomprehensible to Italian feminists: the National Organization of Women at least professed to be ready for equality with men within the marketplace as it was. Such evaluations of men derived not from psychological manuals measuring degrees of patriarchalism but from the specifics of national histories. If it was true, as Arthur Schlesinger, Sr., had said in 1922, that women's contributions to American history had been unjustly ignored, it was also true that their contributions could not be narrated without specifying to just what kinds of men they had contributed.

Feminist history aspired, not to the feminization of history, but to the politicalization of women's lives so that they joined men in mainstream history. One day, history itself might become feminist history. As the study of the consciousness generated by the conflicts of mankind, history offered hope that in telling the true story of conflicts it might help in bringing conflicts to an end. No longer would nations need to war with each other, races dominate other races, cultures engage in subordination. But rarely had visions of androgyny been preferred for resolution of the tensions and conflicts of the sexes. The hopes each sex invested in the other were as everlasting as the species, and there would be no end to their conflicts, hence to the need for their history.

The business of feminism is to politicalize all of women's lives. The business of feminist history, however, is to claim feminism for the history of culture. The history of culture includes politics, economies, and societies, but it resists lending any of these determinative priorities. It finds culture focused in imaginative activity, activity that is in fact the ultimate source of politics, economies, and societies themselves. The liberated brain "infinitely varies and continually increases its delights." Habit, conventions, mere persistence, inertia are penetrated and shaken. Stereotypes crumble. The most fundamental activity of the liberated brain is to imagine new sources of its own vitality. Since feminism, as an imaginative activity, has challenged the most inertial forms of habit, convention, and mere duplication, those of gender, its contribution to new vitality for the liberation of the brain has been fundamental. But at the same time, as a politics feminism has found itself repeatedly drawn into sacrifices of its own central vitality for the sake of hoped-for political and economic gains. That is why feminist history must not limit the history of feminism to its pursuit of equality, but broaden its perspective so that feminism is understood as creative imagination, which is to say, as culture. It is then the cultures of Italy, Sweden, Soviet Russia, and the United States that finally matter most for the feminist history of each. Getting their politics and economies straight is preliminary to comprehending the imaginative energy at work in each. It is then from this perspective that we can appreciate how yardsticks for measuring one kind of progress or another achieved— or not achieved—by feminism can become themselves sources of mystification. Thus, while we cannot really say that Strindberg appeared in Sweden rather than in Italy, Russia, the United States (or elsewhere) just because of certain equities and equabilities and folkish unities in Swedish life, his case can remind us that one point of political and economic progress may well be to liberate brains, both female and male, to engage in the ever-deepening conflicts that are inherent in the ever-increasing visions of new delights.

Notes

Introduction

1. Smith-Rosenberg, Carroll, "The Female World of Love and Ritual: Relations Between Women in 19th-century America," *Signs: A Journal of Women in Culture and Society*, Autumn, 1975, pp. 1–29, reprinted in Smith-Rosenberg, *Disorderly Conduct: Visions of Gender in Victorian America* (New York, 1985).

2. Morgan, Robin, ed., *Sisterhood Is Powerful: An Anthology of Writings from the Women's Liberation Movement* (New York, 1970), p. xvii.

3. Morgan, Robin, ed., *Sisterhood Is Global* (New York, 1984).

4. Schlesinger, Arthur M., Sr., *New Viewpoints in American History* (New York, 1922), "unthinkable," p. 158; "full part," p. 126; "heart and soul," p. 130; war machine, p. 142; "indispensable part," p. 156; democracy, p. 126.

5. Beard, Mary Ritter, *Woman as Force in History* (New York, 1946); Carroll, Berenice A., "Mary Beard's Woman As Force in History: A Critique," in Carroll, ed., *Liberating Women's History: Theoretical and Critical Essays* (Urbana, 1976), is an acute analysis of the Beard's book.

6. Wistrand, Birgitta, *Swedish Women on the Move* (Stockholm, 1981), p. 49; such histories of servants were already appearing in American scholarship: for example, Katzman, David A., *Seven Days a Week: Women and Domestic Service in Industrializing America* (Urbana, 1981) and Dudden, Faye, *Serving Women: Household Service in Nineteenth-Century America* (Middletown, 1983).

7. Brinton Crane, *The Anatomy of Revolution* (New York, 1952).

8. Marx, Karl, Letter to J. Weydemeyer, March 5, 1852, in Marx, Karl, and Engels, Friedrich, *Correspondence 1846–1895* (New York, 1934), pp. 55–58; Engels, Friedrich, Letter to Florence Kelley Wischnewetsky, June 3, 1886, in *ibid.*, pp. 448–49.

9. 'America is a mistake; a gigantic mistake, it is true, but none the less a mistake;' quoted in Jones, Ernest, *The Life and Works of Sigmund Freud: Years of Maturity 1901–1919* (New York, 1955) II, 60; a light, or perhaps sour-hearted remark, but yet 'symptomatic.' See Berger, Peter, "Towards a Sociological Understanding of Psychoanalysis," *Social Research*, v. 32, 1965, 26–41, on the deformation of Freud's ideas by America's cultural optimism.

10. Tocqueville, Alexis de, *Democracy in America*, tr. by George Lawrence, ed. by J. P. Mayer (Garden City, 1969), pp. 493–96.

1. Italy. An Epic of Pathos

1. The notes to follow will show my reliance on monographs for detail, but for general guidance to the history of Italy since 1848, I have drawn on the essays of Valerio Castronovo, Alberto Asor Rosa, and Ernesto Ragionieri in the magisterial *Storia d'Italia* (Turin, 1974), IV, "Dall' unità a Oggi," in three parts.

2. Bortone, Sandro, "Prefazione," in Belgiojoso, Cristina di, *Il 1848 a Milano e Venezia* (Milan, 1977). Ossoli, Margaret Fuller, quoted in Griffith, Gwilyn O., *Mazzini: Prophet of Modern Europe* (New York, 1972), p. 213.

3. Salvemini, Gaetano, *Mazzini*, tr. by I. M. Rawson (Stanford, 1957). Griffith, op cit. Myers, F.W.H., "Giuseppe Mazzini," in *Essays—Modern* (London, 1883). Richards, E.F., ed., *Mazzini's Letters to an English Family* (London, 1920).

4. Mazzini, Giuseppe, *Life and Writings of Joseph Mazzini* (London, 1891), IV, 284.

5. In addition to Castronovo, in *Storia d'Italia*, IV, pt. i, I have drawn on Cafagna, Luciano, "Italy 1830–1914," in Cipolla, Carlo M., ed., *The Fontana Economic History of Europe* (Glasgow, 1975); Clough, Shepard B., *The Economic History of Italy* (New York, 1964); Greenfield, Kent Roberts, *Economics and Liberalism in the Risorgimento* (Baltimore, 1964; 1st ed., 1934); Neufeld, Maurice, *Italy: School for Awakening Countries* (Ithaca, 1961), ch. 2.

6. Ravera, Camilla, "La donna nella produzione," in *La Donna Italiana dal primo al secondo Risorgimento* (Rome, 1959), offers data on women at work in both industry and agriculture. See also, Gallavresi, E., *Il lavoro delle donne e dei fanciulli* (Bergamo, 1900), and most of the economic histories cited in n. 5, passim; Invernizio, Carolina, "Le Operaie Italiane," in *La Donna Italiana* (Florence, 1890), pp. 187–201.

7. Gramsci, Antonio, *Sul Risorgimento* (Rome, 1975). Gramsci, "The Problem of Political Leadership in the Formation and Development of the Nation and the Modern State in Italy," in Gramsci, *Selections from the Prison Notebooks of Antonio Gramsci*, tr. by Quintin Hoare and G. N. Smith (New York, 1971), esp. pp. 77–79. Sereni, Emilio, "Introduzione," to *Il capitalismo nelle campagne 1860–1900* (Turin, 1968), discusses Gramsci's approach sympathetically in response to critics of the first edition of his—Sereni's—book in 1947.

8. Romeo, Rosario, *Risorgimento e capitalismo* (Bari, 1959). For a less sympathetic view: Sereni, Emilio, "L'emigrazione," in *Il Capitalismo nelle campagne*, pp. 351–69. A classic study of the emigration itself is Foerster, Robert F., *The Italian Emigration of Our Times* (Cambridge, Mass., 1919).

9. Jemolo, Arturo Carlo, *Chiesa e Stato in Italia dalla unificazione a Giovanni XXIII* (Turin, 1974), ch. 1, "Il Risorgimento (Cavour e gli avversari)."

10. Rota, Ettore, and Spellanzon, Silvia, *Maternità illustri* (Milan, 1948), discuss Maria Drago and Risorgimento mother myths generally. See also, Luzio, A., *La madre di Mazzini* (Turin, 1919); Vittori, Giovanna, "Le Eroine e le patriotte," *La Donna Italiana*, pp. 153–83.

11. On Crispi, see Ragionieri, Ernesto, "La storia politica e sociale," *Storia d'Italia*, IV, pt. iii, pp. 1808–21.

12. Gershenkron, Alexander, "Notes on the Rate of Economic Growth in Italy, 1881–1913," in Gershenkron, ed., *Economic Backwardness in Historical Perspective* (Cambridge, 1961). On women workers: Neufeld, op. cit., p. 141.

13. Quoted in *Storia d'Italia*, IV, pt. ii, p. 824.

14. Asor Rosa, Alberto, "La cultura," in ibid., pt. ii.

15. Pirandello, Luigi, "I vecchi e i giovani," quoted in ibid., p. 834.

16. On Manzoni, see Gramsci, Antonio, "Del carattere non popolare-nazionale della letteratura italiana," in Gramsci, *Letteratura e vita nazionale*" (Turin, 1975).

17. Villari, Pasquale, *Le lettere meridionale*, quoted in *Storia d'Italia*, IV, pt. ii, p. 899.
18. Lombroso, Cesare, *Gli anarchici*, quoted in ibid.
19. Candeloro, G., *Il movimento sindicale in Italia* (Rome, 1950), estimates the white unions to have been 115,000 strong in 1914. Canuti, G., *Cinquant'anni di vita del' Unione di ACI* (Rome, 1959), treats of Catholic Action and the activities of Catholic women.
20. See, in addition to Ragionieri, Ernesto, "Il movimento cattolico," in *Storia d'Italia*, IV, pt. iii, 1786–95, De Rosa, Gabriele, *Il Movimento cattolico in Italia Dalla Restaurazione all'eta giolittiano* (Rome-Bari, 1974), and Rossi, Mario G., *Le origini del partito cattolico* (Rome, 1977).
21. *Il Popolo Italiano*, Dec. 24, 1897, quoted in ibid., p. 41.
22. On Lazzaretti and standard history, see Gramsci, Antonio, *Il Risorgimento* (Turin, 1974), pp. 198–204; Nesti, A., *"Gesu Socialiste," Una tradizione popolare italiana 1880–1920* (Turin, 1974); Prezzolini, G., *Il cattolicismo rosso* (Naples, 1980). "I believe": quoted in Rossi, op cit., pp. 50–51.
23. De Rosa, op. cit., passim; Rossi, op. cit.; Zoppi, Sergio, *Romolo Murri e la prima democrazia cristiana* (Florence, 1968).
24. In addition to De Rosa and Rossi, see Scoppola, Pietro, *Dal neoguelfismo alla democrazia cristiana* (Rome, 1963), ch. 4, "Il decennio di Pio X e Giolitti."
25. De Rosa, op. cit., ch. 13, "Luigi Sturzo e la questione meridionale," provides background for the story of the PPI. De Rosa, G., *L'utopia politica di Luigi Sturzo* (Brescia, 1972), and Malgeri, F., *Vita di Luigi Sturzo* (Rome, 1972), provide different lights on the PPI's founder and leader, the mentor of Alcide De Gasperi.
26. Quoted in Asor Rosa, Alberto, *Storia d'Italia*, III, pt. ii, p. 836, n. 1.
27. Croce, Benedetto, *A History of Italy, 1871–1915*, tr. by Cecilia M. Ady (Oxford, 1929), pp. 149, 152. Croce, B., *Materialismo storico ed economia marxista* (Milan, 1900), is his full case for—and against—Marxism and socialism. Jacobitti, Edmund E., *Revolutionary Humanism and Historicism in Modern Italy* (New Haven, 1981), in which Croce dominates, discusses Croce and Marxism passim.
28. Cortesi, Luigi, ed., *Turati giovane: Scapigliatura, positivismo, marxismo* (Milan, 1962), offers interesting essays on both Turati's youth and his times. Catalano, F. *Filippo Turati* (Milan, 1957), covers the life. DiScala, Spencer, *Dilemmas of Italian Socialism: The Politics of Filippo Turati* (Amherst, 1980), fulfills its title. Ragionieri, Ernesto, "La nascita del partito socialista," in *Storia d'Italia*, IV, pt. iii, pp. 1774–86, is a characteristically subtle analysis of both socialism and the new Socialist Party.
29. Damiani, Franco, and Rodriguez, Fabio, *Anna Kulioscioff: Immagini, scritti, testimonianza* (Milan, 1978). See *Critica Sociale*, May 27, 1977, for seven brief commemorative articles on A.K. For debates over woman suffrage within the PSI, see Bortolotti, Franca Pieroni, *Socialismo e questione feminile in Italia, 1892–1922* (Milan, 1974), especially chs. 4–7 passim.
30. Coppa, Frank J., *Economics and Politics in the Giolittian Era* (Washington, D.C., 1971), p. 254, offers the explicit similitude between Giolitti and FDR as "conservatives" of the best type, the kind Croce admired. Carocci, G., *Giolitti e l'eta giolittiana* (Turin, 1961), ranks well among the numerous studies of the statesman. Salvatorelli, L., "L'opera e la personalità di Giovanni Giolitti," in *Miti e storia* (Turin, 1964), is stimulating. For the most

famous attack on Giolitti, see Salvemini, Gaetano, *Il ministro della mala vita e altri scritti* (Milan, 1962).

31. Gramsci, *Il risorgimento*, pp. 112–13, classifies the election of 1913 as the first wth a "popular" character, one of those moments of "intense collectivity" in the development of true unity. Galli, Giorgio, and Prandi, Alfonso, *Patterns of Political Participation in Italy* (New Haven, 1970), Appendix B, Table B-1, offer statistical series showing the dramatic jump in suffrage and participation in 1913.

32. Although Parca, Gabrielle, *L'avventurosa storia del femminismo* (Milan, 1976), entitles her section on the suffrage extension "Giolitti, nemico delle donne," she does not show that Giolitti was in any way an "enemy" of women, but rather that he had been given no reason for going beyond manhood suffrage. For feminist efforts, see Bortolotti, op. cit., ch. 6, "L'eta giolittiana."

33. Ragionieri, Ernesto, "La 'grande guerra' e l'agonia dello stato liberale," in *Storia d'Italia*, IV, pt. iii, pp. 1961–2072.

34. Ibid., p. 2021.

35. Ragionieri, Ernesto, "L'acesa dei partiti de massa," in ibid., IV, pt. iii, pp. 2072–85. On Federterra, see Zangheri, R., ed., *Lotte agrarie in Italia. La Federazione nazionale dei lavoratori della terra* (Milan, 1960), a collection of documents. The secretary of Federterra from 1905 to its collapse in 1924 was a woman, a PSI member and a feminist, Argentina Altobelli. For a brief sketch of Altobelli, see *Problemi del Socialismo*, Oct.–Dec. 1976, pp. 232–33.

36. Chabod, F., *L'Italia contemporanea (1918–1948)* (Turin, 1961), p. 39.

37. Spriano, Paolo, *The Occupation of the Factories* (London, 1979), p. 69.

38. Quoted in ibid., p. 66.

39. See Ragionieri, Ernesto, "L'ora di Mussolini," *Storia d'Italia*, IV, pt. iii, p. 2106, for labor statistics.

40. Gramsci, Antonio, "Cocaina," in *Sotto la mole, 1916–1920* (Turin, 1971), p. 399.

41. Gramsci, Antonio, "Interpretazioni del Risorgimento," in *Sul Risorgimento*, pp. 55–57; Femia, Joseph, *Gramsci's Political Thought* (Oxford, 1981), esp. chs. 5–6.

42. Gramsci, Antonio, *Scritti politici* (Rome, 1973), pp. 122, 141. Mancini, Federico, "The Theoretical Roots of Italian Communism: Worker Democracy and Political Party in Gramsci's Thinking," in Serraty, Simon, and Gray, Lawrence, *The Italian Communist Party: Yesterday, Today and Tomorrow* (Westport, Conn., 1980), finds Gramsci a populist and Italian nationalist, not a Marxist.

43. Gramsci, *Prison Notebooks*. "The New Type": p. 304; "In reality": p. 292.

44. Ibid., p. 304.

45. Ragionieri, Ernesto, *Storia d'Italia*, IV, pt. iii, "Lo Stato Autoritario," pp. 2163–99, is a subtle discussion of the alternatives open to the Fascist leaders. De Felice, Renzo, *Interpretations of Fascism*, tr. by Brenda H. Everett (Cambridge, 1977), is the most notable historiographical discussion, to be supplemented with De Felice, Renzo, *Fascism: An Informal Introduction to Its Theory and Practice* (New Brunswick, 1976), an interview by Michael Deleen. I have followed Castronovo, Valerio, "Dall'unità a oggi," *Storia d'Italia*, IV, pt. i, pp. 276–84, on reclamation and the "battle for wheat."

46. Meldini, Piero, *Sposa e madre esemplare: Ideologia e politica della donna e*

della famiglia durante il fascismo (Rimini, Florence, 1975), "We live": p. 138; "Maybe you believe": ibid.

47. See the discussion by Meldini, ibid., pp. 60ff. See also Santarelli, Enzo, "Il fascismo e le ideologie antifemministe," in *Problemi del Socialismo*, Oct.–Dec. 1976, which on p. 83 dates the onset of antifeminist fascist "demagogy" from 1926.

48. Meldini, op. cit., "I have here": p. 137; "Gentlemen" and "Are we maybe": p. 138; "This is the century": ibid.

49. Ibid., p. 143.

50. Ragionieri, Ernesto, "Il conciliazione," in *Storia d'Italia*, IV, pt. iii, pp. 2199–2205; Jemolo, Arturo Carlo, *Chiesa e stato in Italia dalla unificazione a Giovanni XXIII* (Turin, 1974), chs. 5 and 6; Guizzardi, Gustavo, "La 'civiltà contadina', Struttura di una ideologia per il consenso," in Carbonaro, A., et al., *Religione e politica: Il caso italiano* (Rome, 1976).

51. Meldini, op cit., pp. 142, 143, 150.

52. Ibid., pp. 140, 144.

53. See Livi-Bacci, Massismo, *A History of Italian Fertility during the Last Two Centuries* (Princeton, 1977), the basic demographic study, pp. 52–53 and 267–76, on the Fascist period.

54. Macciocchi, Maria Antonietta, *La donna "nera": "Consenso" femminile e fascismo* (Milan, 1976), pp. 179ff. For a Marxist feminist review accusing Macciocchi of postulating "masochism" to Mussolini's women followers, see Pelaja, Margherita, *Problemi del Socialismo*, Oct.–Dec. 1976, pp. 280–84.

55. Meldini, op. cit., p. 161.

56. Ibid., p. 257, in "Restaurazione della sudditanza della donna all'uomo," 1938. Barbagli, Marzio, *Educating for Unemployment: Politics, Labor Markets and the School System—Italy, 1859–1973* (New York, 1982), pp. 158–63, notes that as unemployment among women rose after 1930, their enrollment in secondary schools rose too.

57. Ragionieri, Ernesto, "L'Italia divisa," *Storia d'Italia*, IV, pt. iii. p. 2364.

58. Banfield, Edward C., *The Moral Basis of a Backward Society* (Glencoe, Ill., 1958), pp. 163–66 and passim.

59. Mammarella, Giuseppe, *Italy after Fascism: A Political History, 1943–1965* (Notre Dame, 1966), pt. ii, ch. 1.

60. Parca, Gabriella, op. cit., p. 94: "After so many battles and so many polemics, the right to vote arrived almost unexpectedly, as fighting continued in the North. The press gave it little notice."

61. Mammarella, op. cit., p. 104.

62. In addition to Mammarella, op. cit., Galli, Giorgio, and Prandi, Alfonso, *Patterns of Political Participation in Italy*, provide rich information on the internal life and structures of the DC and PCI. Some of the peculiarities of the postwar Italian political scene are brought out in Barnes, Samuel H., "Italy: Oppositions on Left, Right, and Center," in Dahl, Robert A., ed., *Political Oppositions in Western Democracies* (New Haven, 1966).

63. See n. 62 above.

64. Mammarella, op. cit., p. 144.

65. Ibid., pt. ii, chs. 2 and 8.

66. Macciocchi, Anna Maria, *La donna "nera,"* p. 137. The comrades may have been right: Galli and Prandi, op. cit., p. 57, cite studies showing more than

60% of DC votes to be women's. But to infer from this that, had women not had the suffrage, the two Marxist parties together—PCI and PSI—would have become "the principal political force in Italy," would be hazardous: the very presence—as once the absence—of women voters could have mattered to men voters.

67. Mammarella, Giuseppe, op. cit., pt. v, ch. 4, "The Economic Miracle," offers a brief overview. La Malfa, Ugo, *La politica economica in Italia, 1946–1962*, is the moderately hopeful view of a distinguished "liberal." Pesenti, A., and Vitello, V., *Tendenze del capitalismo italiano* (Rome, 1962), offers a skeptical view from the left.

68. See Pezzuoli, Giovanna, *La stampa femminile come ideologia* (Milan, 1975) on these magazines. See also, Parca, Gabrielle, "La stampa femminile," in *L'avventurosa storia del femminismo*.

69. See Mammarella, op cit., pt. v, on the opening to the left.

70. Castronovo, "La storia economica," in *Storia d'Italia*, IV, pt. i, carries his story to the end of the miracle.

71. Vergati, Stefania, "Il lavoro femminile: emancipazione o doppia schiavitù?" in Statera, Gianna, ed., *Il privato come politica: temi attuali del femminismo* (Cosenza, 1977), pp. 211–34; Balbo, Laura, "Famiglia e condizione femminile dell'Italia del dopoguerra," in *Stato di famiglia* (Milan, 1976); Frey, L., ed., *Occupazione e sottoccupazione femminile in Italia* (Milan, 1976). The quote appears in Vergati, loc. cit., p. 230.

72. Parca, Gabriella, *Plusvalore femminile* (Milan, 1978), ch. 6, discusses *lavoro nero*, with special attention to Naples.

73. For an example of economic turnaround in the swollen state sector, see Ingrassia, Lawrence, "Italtel's Iron Lady Is Aiming for Bigger Markets . . .," *Wall Street Journal*, June 24, 1985, the "iron lady" being Marisa Bellisario, Italian business's highest-ranking woman executive. For two examples in the private sector, see Cohen, Roger, "Italy's Family-Led Derruzzi Group Drives toward Status . . .," ibid., Oct. 8, 1985, and Mulassano, Adriana, et al., "Italian Fashion," *International Herald Tribune*, October 1982.

74. Mammarella, op. cit., p. 286. Writing only four years later, Galli and Prandi, op. cit., p. 305, assigned the PCI only a basic 25%. Elections since 1970 have shown it winning over 30%, but as n. 75 suggests, on a changing basis.

75. See Barkan, Joanne, "Italian Communism at the Crossroads," in Boggs, Carl, ed., *The Politics of Eurocommunism: Socialism in Transition* (Boston, 1980), for the change in the PCI. For one later result, see Dionne, E.J., Jr., "Italy's Communists Have Lost Their Grip on City Halls," *New York Times*, Oct. 6, 1985. On the dilemmas in economic policy posed to the PCI by its new constituency, see Dionne, "Italy's Communists Often Speak a Strange Dialect," ibid., March 24, 1985.

2. Sweden. Family Tale

1. Brorson, Kestin, *Singing the Cows Home: The Remarkable Herdswomen of Sweden* (Seattle, 1985).

2. See Moberg, Vilhelm, *A History of the Swedish People from Renaissance to Revolution*, tr. by Paul Britten Auston (New York, 1973), for a discussion of the old village marriage market. Tomassen, Richard R., "A Millennium of Sexual Permissiveness in the North," *American Scandinavia Review*, 1974,

pp. 370–78, locates the source of "modern" Swedish sexual mores long before modernization.

3. Roberts, Michael, ed., *Sweden's Age of Greatness* (New York, 1973), and *Sweden as a Great Power, 1611–1697* (New York, 1968), offer good background to the seventeenth century; Roberts, Michael, *Swedish and English Parliamentarianism in the 18th Century* (Belfast, 1973), offers the same for its epoch.
4. Chydenius, Anders, *The National Gain*, tr. by Georg Schaumann (London, 1931). In the Introduction, Schaumann sketches Chydenius's career. Eli Heckscher discusses Chydenius in his *An Economic History of Sweden* (Cambridge, Mass., 1954), pp. 204–05; quote from Heckscher, p. 25.
5. Hennings, Beth, *Gustav III: En biografi* (Stockholm, 1957), has not been translated. Bain, Robert N., *Gustavus III and His Contemporaries: An Overlooked Chapter of 18th Century History* (London, 1894), 2 v., remains the most extensive study in English.
6. Malthus, Thomas, *An Essay on the Principle of Population*, 3rd ed. (London, 1806). Boys fatter: p. 315; Norway: p. 324; "strange to say"; p. 335.
7. The preeminent authority on Geijer is the Swedish scholar Johan Landquist, whose two biographies of 1924 and 1954 remain untranslated. Landquist, Johan, "Erik Gustav Geijer: Swedish Poet and Historian," *American-Scandinavian Review*, VI, 1928, pp. 589–601, is a sketch in English. Kjellen, Alf, *Sociale idéer och motiv hos svenska förfaterl* (Stockholm, 1937), pp. 90–132, is a valuable discussion in Swedish. Gustafson, Alrik, *A History of Swedish Literature* (Minneapolis, 1961), pp. 168–77 and 590–91, offers discussion and bibliography.
8. For a good brief discussion of the rising economic liberalism, see Hovde, Bryn J., *The Scandinavian Countries, 1720–1865* (Boston, 1943), I, ch. 7. Scott, Franklin D., *Sweden: The Nation's History* (Minneapolis, 1977), easily the best one-volume history of the nation in English, discusses political liberalism in ch. 14. Nilsson, Göran B., "Swedish Liberalism at Mid-20th Century," in Koblik, Stephen, ed., *Sweden's Development from Poverty to Affluence, 1750–1970* (Minneapolis, 1975), discusses the precariousness of the very concept of "liberalism," as applied to the mid-nineteenth century Swedish scene.
9. See Janson, Florence D., *The Background of Swedish Immigration, 1840–1930* (Chicago, 1931), a book far broader than its title indicates, for a thorough discussion of the Swedish agricultural revolution.
10. Baird, Robert, *Visit to Northern Europe* (New York, 1841), II, 193–94.
11. Thomas, Dortohy Swaine, *Social and Economic Aspects of Swedish Population Movements, 1750–1933* (New York, 1941), tables 16 and 17, pp. 95–96. See also, Janson, op. cit.
12. Marryat, Horace, *One Year in Sweden* (London, 1860), II, 106–7.
13. Brace, Charles Loring, *The Norse-Folk: or, a Visit to See the Homes of Norway and Sweden* (New York, 1857), "He directed us": p. 215; "Here dwell": p. 244; train: p. 209.
14. Laing, Samuel, *A Tour in Sweden in 1838* (London, 1839), p. 215. Hovde, Bryn J., *The Scandinavian Countries*, II, ch. 9, discusses the popular revival. Lundqvist, Sven, "Popular Movements and Reforms," in Koblik, Stephen, ed., *Sweden's Development*, pp. 180–93, links the revival to politics. Stephenson, George, *The Religious Aspects of Swedish Immigration* (Minneapolis, 1935), offers rich information, as does Janson, op. cit.

15. Quoted in Scott, op. cit., p. 306. Hovde, op. cit., II, XVIII, offers a good brief discussion of the earlier temperance movement. Lundqvist, loc. cit., links temperance to turn-of-century politics. Paulson, Ross Evand, *Women's Suffrage and Prohibition: A Comparative Study of Equality and Social Control* (Glenview, Ill., 1973), ch. 5, "The Alliance of Temperance and Women's Suffrage," discusses Scandinavia in 1879–90, but a careful reading shows no "alliance," only at most some possible parallelism between the two movements, but little even of that. See Thompson, Walter, *The Control of Liquor in Sweden* (New York, 1935), for a straightforward review.

16. "The great majority": Carlsson, Sten, "Sweden and America after 1860: A Research Project," in Barton, H. Arnold, ed., *Clipper Ship and Covered Wagon: Essays from the Swedish Pioneer Historical Quarterly* (New York, 1979), p. 208. See also the commission's reports: *Emigrationsutredningen* (Stockholm, 1908–14). Many anthologies and distillations have appeared in English: Barton, H. Arnold, ed., *Letters from the Promised Land* (Minneapolis, 1975); Dahlof, Tell G., "Three Americans Look at Sweden," in Arnold, ed., *Clipper Ship and Covered Wagon.*

17. The classic economic history of Sweden is Heckscher, Eli F., *An Economic History of Sweden*, tr. by Giran Ohlin (Cambridge, Mass., 1954). Koblik, Stephen, ed., *Sweden's Development*, includes several analytic essays on Swedish economic growth, particularly Jorberg, Lennart, "Structural Change and Economic Growth in 19th Century Sweden." Scott, Franklin, *Sweden: The Nation's History*, the admirable standard modern history in English, discusses "The Industrial Breakthrough" in ch. 16. Montgomery, Arthur, *The Rise of Modern Industry in Sweden* (Stockholm, 1939), orients the Swedish economic breakthrough with a deep look at social history. See also, Samuelsson, Kurt, *From Great Power to Welfare State* (London, 1968).

18. Marrryat, op. cit., I, 159.

19. Heckscher, op. cit., p. 262.

20. "O Blessed Land," the last chapter in Samuelsson, op. cit., is a brilliant five-page reflection on the themes of "luck" and "continuity."

21. Thomas, op. cit., pp. 114–15.

22. Ibid.

23. Montgomery, Arthur, *How Sweden Overcame the Depression* (Stockholm, 1938), is a stimulating book for all Americans.

24. See Thomas, op. cit., passim, for figures on towns and cities.

25. The standard history of the rise of the unions is Lindblom, Tage, *Den svenska fackföreningsrörelsens uppkomst* (Stockholm, 1938). Of course it is possible to underemphasize the "class struggle" in Swedish history, but while Scott in *Sweden: The Nation's History* does stress conflict in early trade-union history, he places his discussion of the rise of the unions in a section entitled "Folk Movements and Democracy," in consistency with a practice common among Swedish historians, too, who link the rise of a "free church" and of temperance movements with the rise of the unions as all together constituting symptoms of a general democratic populism. See also Galenson, Walter, "Scandinavia," in Galenson, Walter, ed., *Comparative Labor Movements* (New York, 1952).

26. Marriage statistics in Thomas, op. cit., table 89, p. 363 and passim. An official assessment of 1952 indicated that the urban-rural gender skew still persisted even then: *Social Sweden* (Stockholm, 1952), p. 119.

27. The preeminent authority in English on Swedish parties and politics for the

period is Verney, Douglas V., *Parliamentary Reform in Sweden, 1866–1921* (Oxford, 1957). In addition, Scott, Franklin D., *Sweden: The Nation's History;* Scobbie, Irene, *Sweden* (New York, 1972); and Andersson, Ingvar, *History of Sweden* (Westport, Conn., 1975), provide good guidance to nineteenth-century Swedish politics. Rustow, Dankwart, *The Politics of Compromise: A Study of Parties and Cabinet Government in Sweden* (Princeton, 1955), illuminates the twentieth century. Herlitz, Nils, *Sweden: A Modern Democracy on Ancient Foundations* (Minneapolis, 1939), offers a long view stressing continuity. Hancock, M. Donald, *Sweden: A Multiparty System in Transition?* (Denver, 1968), and Hancock, M. Donald, *Sweden: The Politics of Postindustrial Change* (New York, 1972), approach Swedish politics with the modernization theory, to which I have preferred a more historical approach. Stjernquist, Nils, "Sweden: Stability or Deadlock?" in Dahl, Robert A., *Political Oppositions in Western Democracies* (New Haven, 1966), after a brief historical overview, discusses the operation of the four-party system since the rise of the SSD.

28. Verney, op. cit., ch. 7, illuminates the Liberal Party in its season of incipient triumph and basic weakness, 1900–1906. See also, Verney, Douglas, "The Foundations of Modern Sweden: The Swift Rise and Fall of Swedish Liberalism," *Political Studies,* XX, 1972. Rössel, James, *Kvinnorna och kvinnorörelsen i Sverige, 1850–1950* (Stockholm, 1950), ch. 4, discusses the suffrage movement.

29. The Liberal women ran an ill-fated slate of their own in 1928: Torbacke, Jarl, "Kvinnolistan 1927–38—ett kvinnopolitiskt fiasko," *Historisk tidskrift,* v. 89, no. 2, 1969, pp. 145–84; Rössel, op. cit., ch. 8; Rustow, op. cit., pp. 86–87, 241.

30. Tingsten, Herbert, *The Swedish Social Democrats: Their Ideological Development,* tr. by Greta Frankel and Patricia Howard-Rosen, (Totowa, N.J., 1973), is the basic treatment in English of the "de-Marxification" of the SSD. For a discussion of other views critical of Tingsten, see Stephens, John D., "The Ideological Development of the Swedish Social Democrats," in Denitch, Bogdan, ed., *Democratic Socialism: The Mass Left in Advanced Industrial Societies* (Montclair, N.J., 1981). See also, Blake, Donald, "Swedish Trade Unions and the Social Democratic Party: The Formative Years," *The Scandinavian Economic History Review,* VIII, 1960, 19–44. Björk, Kai, "Individualism and Collectivism," in Hancock, M. Donald, and Sjöberg, Gideon, eds., *Politics in the Post-Welfare State: Responses to the New Individualism* (New York, 1972), after declaring Tingsten's "end of ideology" thesis discredited, proceeds to demonstrate its cogency in showing a Swedish consensus against any "new individualism."

31. Tingsten, op. cit., p. 265.

32. Ibid., pp. 465–66. See Scott's discussion, op. cit., p. 486.

33. Flood, Hulda, *Den socialdemokratiska kvinnorörelsen i Sverige* (Stockholm, 1939), follows women in SSD history.

34. Moberg, Eva, *Kvinnor och manniskor* (Stockholm, 1962), passim.

35. Lindbeck, Assar, *Swedish Economic Policy* (Berkeley, 1975), treats of postwar strategies.

36. Social Welfare Board, *Social Sweden* (Stockholm, 1952), p. 47. The most famous discussion of the cooperatives remains Childs, Marquis, *Sweden, the Middle Way* (New Haven, 1936), particularly chs. 1 and 2.

37. Myrdal, Gunnar, and Myrdal, Alva, *Kris i befolkningsfrågan* (Stockholm,

1934). The data had been gathered earlier for a report on the pension system: Wicksell, Sven, *Ur befolkningslären* (Stockholm, 1931). Myrdal, Alva, *Nation and Family: The Swedish Experiment in Democratic Family and Population Policy* (New York, 1941), is a revision and translation of the 1934 report.

38. Myrdal, Gunnar, *Population: A Problem for Democracy* (Cambridge, Mass., 1940), "Pictures": p. 118; "Swedish culture": p. 219; "I assume": pp. 222, 225, 223.

39. The Swedish Social Welfare Board began publishing reports in English on the Swedish social programs as early as 1928: *Social Work and Legislation in Sweden* (Stockholm, 1928). A second report in 1938 was succeeded by the revised, expanded, and updated report of 1952, *Social Sweden*, which included chapters on social insurance, family welfare, and child welfare. Rosenthal, Albert H., *The Social Programs of Sweden: A Search for Security in a Free Society* (Minneapolis, 1967), surveys the programs from a later date. The political architect of the welfare program was the Social Democrat economist Gustav Möller, long-time head of the Ministry of Social Affairs, fully committed to *jämlikhet*, fully committed against social "revolution": Tingsten, "The Disintegration of the Theory of Socialisation and the Victory of the Welfare Ideology," in op. cit.

40. See *Social Sweden*, pp. 115–19, on the birth rate of the 1940s.

41. Wistrand, Birgitta, *Swedish Women on the Move* (Stockholm, 1981), pp. 50–51.

42. McIntosh, C. Alison, *Population Policy in Western Europe: Responses to Low Fertility in France, Sweden, and West Germany* (Armonk, N.Y., 1983), p. 144.

43. Wistrand, op. cit., p. 26.

44. McIntosh, op. cit., pp. 141–43.

45. Ibid., p. 142.

46. Ibid., p. 144.

47. Ibid., pp. 147–50, for the Aberg/Nordin book and subsequent debate.

48. Himmelstrand, Ulf, "Sweden: Paradise in Trouble," in Denitch, Bogdan, ed., *Democratic Socialism*, an analysis from the perspective of the SD defeat in 1976.

49. For a view that the SSD was returning to "true" socialism in the 1980s as a consequence of the steady rise of both blue- and white-collar workers in the unions, see Stephens, John D., "The Ideological Development of the Swedish Social Democrats," in Denitch, op. cit. From this perspective the "partnership" with business had only been a prolonged tactic; whether Stephens was right or not did not undercut the equivalence of SSD programs with a *volkshem*. See also, for similar views, Hancock, M. Donald, "Sweden's Emerging Labor Socialism, in Brown, Bernard E., *Eurocommunism and Eurosocialism: The Left Confronts Modernity* (New York, 1979), and Otter, Casten van, "Sweden: Labor Reformism Reshapes the System," in Barkin, S., *Worker Militancy and Its Consequences, 1965–1975* (New York, 1975).

50. Wistrand, op. cit., politics: p. 84; unions: pp. 91–93.

51. Ibid., nuclear energy: p. 99; defense, p. 102.

3. Soviet Russia. Morality Play

1. Gershenkron, Alexander, "The Rate of Industrial Growth in Russia since 1865," *Tasks of Economic History, Journal of Economic History* (1947), Supp.

VII. Of course Russian industrialization had its more distant roots: see Blackwell, William L., *The Beginnings of Russian Industrialization, 1800–1860* (Princeton, 1968).

2. On Witte, see Witte, Sergei Y., *Memoirs* (London, 1921), and von Laue, Theodore H., *Sergei Witte and the Industrialization of Russia* (New York, 1963).

3. See Robinson, G. T., *Rural Russia under the Old Regime* (New York, 1932), and Shanin, Teodor, *The Awkward Class: Political Sociology of Peasantry in a Developing Society, Russia, 1910–1925* (1972). Both deal with the Stolypin policy.

4. Monkhouse, Allan, *Moscow, 1911–1933* (Boston, 1934), pp. 33–34.

5. Quoted in Charques, Richard, *The Twilight of Imperial Russia* (London, 1965), pp. 177–78.

6. Shanin, Teodor, op. cit., in a wide-ranging analysis of the old peasant extended household, agreed that the revolution and civil war of 1917–21 "swept away" the Stolypin reforms, leaving the old household dominant until it too was swept away after 1929. For a view that the peasant economy was *sui generis*, neither capitalist nor socialist, see Kerblay, Basile, "Chayanov and the Theory of Peasantry as a Specific Type of Economy," in Shanin, Teodor, ed., *Peasants and Peasant Societies* (Harmondsworth, 1971), pp. 150–60. Chayanov was arrested in 1930 as a defender of peasants; he died in 1939.

7. Stone, Norman, *The Eastern Front: 1914–1917* (London, 1975), ch. 9, "The Political War-Economy, 1916–1917" and ch. 13, "War and Revolution, 1917," has shown the surge in the Russian war economy and explained how this led to its paradoxical result.

8. Florinsky, Michael, *The End of the Russian Empire* (New York, 1961), p. 238: "The aggressive nature of the peasant movement became more evident as time went on. . . . They gradually realized that the moment for the fulfillment of their age-long dream had at last arrived . . . by the autumn of 1917 Russia found herself in the grasp of a violent agrarian revolution." I have been instructed by, among others, Thompson, John M., *Revolutionary Russia, 1917* (New York, 1981); Shapiro, Leonard, *The Russian Revolutions of 1917: The Origins of Modern Communism* (New York, 1984); and Rabinowitch, Alexander, *The Bolsheviks Come to Power: The Revolution of 1917 in Petrograd* (New York, 1976). Chamberlain, William Henry, *The Russian Revolution, 1917–1921* (New York, 1935), 2 v., of course remains classic.

9. Meyer, Alfred G., *Leninism* (New York, 1965), ch. 8, "Eight Months of Revolution," follows the "extreme flexibility" with which Lenin responded to events between March and November 1917. Medvedev, Roy, *The October Revolution* (New York, 1979), focuses on Lenin's role and argues that the Bolshevik coup was not inevitable.

10. Stites, Richard, *The Women's Liberation Movement in Russia: Feminism, Nihilism and Bolshevism, 1860–1930* (Princeton, 1978), pt. ii on the nineteenth-century scene.

11. On the German Social Democrats generally as well as Zetkin, see Thönnessen, Werner, *The Emancipation of Women: The Rise and Decline of the Women's Movement in German Social Democracy, 1863–1933*, tr. by Joris de Bres (London, 1973), and Evans, Richard, *The Feminist Movement in Germany, 1894–1933* (London, 1976).

12. For an illuminating brief discussion of Lily Braun, see Meyer, Alfred, "Marxism and the Women's Movement," in Atkinson, Dorothy, Dallin, Alexander, and Lapidus, Gail W., eds., *Women in Russia* (Stanford, 1977), pp. 107–10.

See also, Meyer, Alfred, *The Feminism and Socialism of Lily Braun* (Bloomington, 1985).

13. Krupskaya, Nadezhda, "Preface," in *The Emancipation of Women: From the Writings of V. I. Lenin* (New York, 1972), dates his attention to women back to 1899.

14. On Kollontai, in addition to Stites, op cit., ch. 9, see the biographies cited below, n. 12, ch. 6.

15. Stites, op. cit., ch. 9.

16. John Reed interpreted Lenin less concisely—"We shall now proceed to construct the Socialist order!"—in *Ten Days that Shook the World* (New York, 1919), p. 126. Radkey, Oliver H., *The Sickle under the Hammer: The Russian Social Revolutionaries in the Early Months of Soviet Rule* (New York, 1962), follows the peasant party, whose Left and largest faction was headed by a woman, Maria Spiridonova, who in 1920 was shut up for good in a Bolshevik prison. In ch. 9, "The True Face of the SR's," Radkey concludes that the Socialist Revolutionaries never constituted a coherent majority and could never have constituted a government; the way was left open for Lenin.

17. Shapiro, Leonard B., *The Origin of the Communist Autocracy: Political Opposition in the Soviet State, First Phase, 1917–1922* (Cambridge, 1955). For a Menshevik's retrospect, see Dan, Theodore, *The Origins of Bolshevism* (New York, 1964). See also, Daniels, Robert V., *The Conscience of the Revolution: Opposition in the Soviet Union, 1917–1929* (Cambridge, 1961).

18. Lenin, V.I., *Collected Works*, XXIX, 442–43.

19. As Lenin himself agreed, in a speech of July 4, 1919: ibid., pp. 456–69.

20. Pilnyak, Boris, *The Naked Year* (New York, 1928), pp. 58–59.

21. Quoted in Yugoff, op. cit., p. 42; from Lenin, V.I., *Collected Works*, XVIII, 369–73.

22. Serge, Victor, *Year One of the Russian Revolution* (New York, 1972), argued in 1930 that Communist totalitarianism came not from within but from extrinsic forces such as the civil war. Bettelheim, Charles, *Class Struggles in the U.S.S.R.* (New York, 1976), v. 1; Daniels, Robert V., *The Conscience of the Revolution*; Cohen, Stephen, *Nicolai Bukharin and the Bolshevik Revolution* (New York, 1974); and Meyer, Alfred, *Leninism*, ch. 5, "Democratic Centralism," are illuminating on the early years of the party in power.

23. Carr, E. H., *The Interregnum, 1923–24* (New York, 1954), is indispensable. Nove, Alex, *An Economic History of the U.S.S.R.* (Harmondsworth, 1984), chs. 4–6, is a useful brief discussion. Cohen, op cit., reanimates a familiar story by seeking to restore credibility to a historic alternative.

24. Monkhouse, op. cit., p. 134.

25. Jasny, Naum, *Soviet Economists of the Twenties* (New York, 1972), shows just how flexible supposedly ideological minds could be in the critical decade.

26. Monkhouse, op. cit., p. 136.

27. Dewar, Margaret, *Labour Policy in the U.S.S.R., 1917–1928* (London, 1956), passim, touches on women's position in the labor market. Dodge, Norton, *Women in the Soviet Economy* (Baltimore, 1962), ch. 2, "Demographic Factors Affecting Employment," is a convenient distillation.

28. Carr, E. H., *Socialism in One Country* (London, 1958–64), I, 297, is incisive on the grain crisis.

29. Cohen, op. cit., pp. 322–23: "The Right was an opposition with potential mass support in the country. . . . Bukharin's tragedy . . . lay in his unwill-

ingness to appeal to this popular sentiment. . . . It derived from the Bolshevik dogma that politics outside the party was illegitimate."

30. Quoted in Carr, *Socialism*, I, 215–16.

31. "Notwithstanding all the laws emancipating woman, she continues to be a domestic slave, because petty housework crushes, strangles, stultifies and degrades her, chains her to the kitchen and the nursery, and . . . wastes her labour on barbarously unproductive, petty, nerve-racking, stultifying and crushing drudgery": Lenin, *Collected Works*, XXIX, 429. Lenin never explained which women had provided him this information.

32. Grey, Ian, *Stalin, Man of History* (London, 1979), p. 222.

33. Quoted in Schwartz, Harry, *The Soviet Economy since Stalin* (New York, 1965), p. 14. Bettelheim, *Class Struggles*, pp. 565–66, sees a prerevolutionary "Great Russian chauvinism" rising among Bolsheviks well before Stalin's rationalizations.

34. Hingley, Ronald, *Joseph Stalin, Man and Legend* (New York, 1974), pp. 379, discussing the February 9 speech, notes that its truculence registered Stalin's division of the postwar world into two.

35. Nove, Alex, *Economic Rationality and Politics: Or, Was Stalin Really Necessary?* (New York, 1964), is a refreshing discussion of basic historiographical issues. In addition to Edward Hallett Carr's monumental multivolume *A History of Soviet Russia* (New York, 1950–65), I have pondered Dobb, Maurice, *Russian Economic Development since the Revolution* (London, 1928), and his more recent *Soviet Economic Development since 1917* (New York, 1966), both determinedly sympathetic to Bolshevik managers, as well as the more thoroughly historical Jasny, Naum, *Soviet Industrialization: 1928–1952* (Chicago, 1961). Yugoff, Aron, *Economic Trends in Soviet Russia* (New York, 1950), is a detailed early (1930) study by a Russian economic historian.

36. Quoted in Monkhouse, op. cit., p. 246.

37. Pilnyak, Boris, "Mahogany," in *Mother Earth and Other Stories* (Garden City, 1968), p. 111.

38. Quoted in *The Woman Question: Selections from the Writings of Marx, Engels, Lenin, Stalin* (New York, 1951), pp. 86–87.

39. Ibid., p. 87. The American visitor Anna Louise Strong got this point: "The emancipation of peasant women came more slowly. Scores of women presidents of villages have told me of their difficulties with the peasant men who sneered at 'petticoat rule.' 'They laughed at the first women we elected . . . at the next election we put in six women and now it is we who laugh' ": *This Soviet World* (New York, 1936), p. 198.

40. Quoted in Dodge, op. cit., p. 168.

41. Dallin, David J., *The Real Soviet Russia* (New Haven, 1944), p. 152.

42. Ibid., p. 156. Gordon, Manya, *Workers before and after Lenin* (New York, 1941), and Hubbard, Leonard E., *Soviet Labor and Industry* (London, 1942), ch. 16, evince an unsympathetic view of the use of women in crash industrialization. See also Schwarz, Solomon, "Activation of Urban Labor Resources: Female Labor," *Labor in the Soviet Union* (New York, 1951), pp. 64–75. For a highly favorable view based on visits to the Soviet Union in 1929–30 and 1932 by two American women professors of "social economy," see Kingsbury, Susan M., and Fairchild, Mildred, *Factory Family and Woman in the Soviet Union* (New York, 1935). Kingsbury and Fairchild were delighted in particular that "the family in Soviet Russia today . . . seems stronger, not weaker, than it was in pre-revolutionary years" (p. xxv). Filtzer,

Donald, *Soviet Workers and Stalinist Industrialization* (London, 1986), "Appendix: The Growth of Female Employment," pp. 63–67, provides statistics on the growing proportions of women in selected industries and discusses their rapid channeling into "the lowest-skilled and worst-paid jobs."

43. Nutter, Gilbert W., *Growth of Industrial Production in the Soviet Union* (Princeton, 1962), goes into the problems of flexible statistics. So does Nove, *Economic History of the U.S.S.R.*, "Appendix: A Note on Growth Rates."

44. Luke, Louise E., "Marxian Women: Soviet Variants," in Simmons, Ernest J., ed., *Through the Glass of Soviet Literature: Views of Russian Society* (New York, 1953), p. 63: "[That] women as a whole were more amenable to the new collective methods is borne out statistically: a higher percentage of women workers than of men participated in socialist competition and shock-brigading during the First Plan." See also, Serebrennikov, G.N., *The Position of Women in the U.S.S.R.* (London, 1937), a favorable view, and Hubbard, Leonard, *Soviet Labor and Industry*, refreshingly judicious even if finally negative.

45. On Masha Scott, see Buck, Pearl, *Talks about Russia with Masha Scott* (New York, 1945), and Scott, John, *Behind the Urals* (Cambridge, 1942), passim.

46. Dan, Theodore, *Origins of Bolshevism*, p. 422.

47. Buck, op. cit., p. 92.

48. Ibid., p. 46.

49. The first and still classic study is Dallin, David, and Nikolaevsky, Boris, *Forced Labor in Soviet Russia* (London, 1948). Swianiewicz, Stanislaw, *Forced Labour and Economic Development* (London, 1965), links forced labor to Stalinism as inherent.

50. Scott, op. cit., pp. 135, 130–31.

51. Dodge, "Trends in the Birth Rate," op. cit.

52. Lapidus, Gail W., ed., *Women, Work, and Family in the Soviet Union*, "Introduction," summarizes the data. See Dodge, Norton, "Women in the Professions," in Atkinson, Dallin, and Lapidus, eds., *Women in Russia*, for a special section on women at work.

53. Petrova, L., and Gilevskayan, S., compilers, *Equality of Women in the U.S.S.R.* (Moscow, 1957), p. 10.

54. Stites, op. cit., pp. 396, 393.

55. Shulman, Colette, "The Individual and the Collective," in Atkinson, Dallin, Lapidus, eds., *Women in Russia*, p. 382.

56. See Shabad, Theodore, "Bureaucracy Is the Target of a Siberian," *New York Times*, Aug. 14, 1983, on Volgin's book. Also interesting is Granick, David, *The Red Executive: A Study of the Organization Man in Russian Industry* (London, 1960).

57. Moses, Joel C., "Women in Political Roles," in Atkinson, Dallin, Lapidus, eds., op. cit., p. 349.

58. Ibid., pp. 342–43. For the persistence of this pattern, see Austin, Anthony, "Kiev Woman Rises in Party Job but Not All the Way," *New York Times*, March 6, 1981.

59. Schwartz, Harry, *Russia's Postwar Economy* (Syracuse, 1947), and Schwartz, *The Soviet Economy since Stalin* (Philadelphia, 1965), offer rich detail on the period since the war.

60. Pietromarchi, Luca, *The Soviet World* (New York, 1965), pp. 373–75.

61. Campbell, Robert, "The Economy," in Byrnes, Robert F., ed., *After Brezhnev:*

Sources of Soviet Conduct in the 1980s (Bloomington, 1983), discusses the labor crisis.

62. Lapidus, Gail W., "Social Trends," in Byrnes, ed., op cit., discussing the rates, suggests that infant mortality was in fact rising (p. 127).

63. Quoted by Campbell, Robert, "The Economy," in ibid., p. 74. Studies in Moscow and two other cities showed that men constituted 85 percent of alcoholics. *Izvestia* declared: "Drunkenness and alcoholism have reached such magnitude in our country that, to put it briefly, it can be called a disaster": Schmemann, Serge, "Soviet, Once Again, Proclaims Measures against Alcoholism," *New York Times*, May 17, 1985.

64. Silk, Leonard, "Andropov's Economic Dilemma," *New York Times*, October 9, 1983.

65. Sacks, Michael Paul, *Women's Work in Soviet Russia: Continuity in the Midst of Change* (New York, 1976), pp. 173, 177. Sacks drew on the well-known article of Tilly, Louise A., and Scott, Joan W., "Women's Work and Family in 19th Century Europe," *Comparative Studies in Society and History*, XVII (Jan. 1975), pp. 36–64.

66. See Wright, Arthur W., "Soviet Economic Planning and Performance," in Cohen, Stephen F., Rabinowitch, Alexander, and Sharlet, Robert, *The Soviet Union since Stalin* (Bloomington, 1980), for a discussion drawing on Soviet data.

67. And intensified in the 1983 paper of economist Tatyana Zaslavskaya, widely noted in the West: Silk,, Leonard, op. cit.

68. Rizzi's book has been published in an English edition recently: Rizzi, Bruno, *The Bureaucratization of the World*, tr. and with an introduction by Adam Westoby (New York, 1985).

69. Meyer, *Leninism*, p. 181, quoting from a letter from Engels to Joseph Weydemeyer, April 12, 1853.

70. Pilnyak, Boris, *The Naked Year*, p. 119.

71. Thompson, Dorothy, *The New Russia* (New York, 1928), p. 263.

4. Italy. Frustration

1. On the Democrats generally, see Lovett, Clara, *The Democratic Movement in Italy, 1830–1876* (Cambridge, Mass., 1982). On p. 206 Lovett notes the supporters of rights for women, including Agostino Bertani, Oreste Regnoli, and Mauro Macchi as well as Morelli.

2. Quoted in Parca, Gabriella, *L'avventurosa storia del femminismo* (Milan, 1976), p. 50.

3. Quoted in Bortolotti, Franca Pieroni, *Alle origini del movimento femminile in Italia, 1848–1892* (Turin, 1963), p. 150.

4. With Giuseppe Garibaldi as their greatest figure, Italian Masons in the 1860s were eager for a "Masonic Rome," yet, influenced by the example of British Masonry, contemplated moves toward equality for women within the lodges and affirmed the value of various social reforms. But these early gestures were not followed up. Masonry ended up at once suppressed by Mussolini and categorized by Gramsci as representative of "bourgeois capitalism." See: Mola, Aldo Alessandro, *Storia della Massoneria italiana dall' Unità alla Repubblica* (Milan, 1976), pp. 98, 101, 115, 117, 230–31, 480–84.

5. Quoted in Bortolotti, op. cit., p. 14.
6. Mozzoni, Anna Maria, *La liberazione della donna* (Milan, 1975), ed. by Franca Pieroni Bortolotti, includes a biographical introduction by the editor (pp. 7–32) as well as numerous writings by Mozzoni. In two books by Bortolotti, Franca Pieroni, the leading historian of Italian feminism, *Alle origini del movimento femminile in Italia* and *Socialismo e questione femminile in Italia, 1892–1922* (n.p. [Milan], 1974), Mozzoni appears far more frequently than any other individual.
7. In Mozzoni, *La Liberazione*, pp. 14, 55, 58.
8. Loc. cit., criticism of Mazzini: pp. 52–53; high view of U.S.A.: p. 127: can't Italy lead: p. 97.
9. On *La Donna*, see Bortolotti, *Alle origini*, pp. 118ff., and Serao, quote ibid., p. 126.
10. Asor Rosa, Alberto, "La questione della scuola," in *Storia d'Italia* (Turin, 1975), IV, pt. ii, 1224–34; Ulivieri, Simonetta, "La donna nella scuola dall' Unità a oggi; leggi, pregiudizi, lotte e prospettive," in *dwf: donnawomanfemme*, Jan.–Mar. 1977, pp. 20–74. Bertoni, Jovine D., *La scuola italiana dal 1870 ai nostri giorni* (Rome, 1958) is a standard work.
11. See Bortolotti, *Socialismo e questione femminile*, passim and especially pp. 74–81, for the Mozzoni-Kulioscioff debate.
12. In addition to Bortolotti, op. cit., ch. 6, Discala, Spencer, *Dilemmas of Italian Socialism: The Politics of Filippo Turaii* (Amherst, 1980), ch. 7, discusses the tensions between the PSI and the Confederazione Generale del Lavoro (CGL), the labor organization that Socialists themselves founded in 1906. See also *Anna Kulioscioff: Immagini, scritti, testimonianze* (Milan, 1978), ed. by Damiani, Franco, and Rodriguez, Fabio.
13. Quoted in Bortolotti, *Socialismo*, pp. 93–94.
14. Quoted in Bortolotti, *Alle origini*, pp. 132–33.
15. Canuti, G., *Cinquant'anni di vita del'Unione di ACI* (Rome, 1959), treats of Catholic Action and the activities of Catholic women.
16. Cecchini, Francesco, M., *Il femminismo cristiano* (Rome, 1979), pp. 79ff.
17. Ibid., Murri reluctant: p. 209; American experience: pp. 217–18; Murri 1906: p. 210; family absolute: pp. 55–56.
18. The most extensive analysis of the ideas of this early Catholic feminism is in De Biase, P. Gaiotti, *Le origini del movimento cattolico femminile* (Brescia, 1963).
19. De Biase, op cit., "two feminisms": p. 22; "prudent and conservative": p. 28; "for one brief moment": p. 97; "our readers will notice": p. 100.
20. Canuti, op cit., pp. 14ff., and De Biase, op cit., pp. 146–71, treat of the 1908 meeting, as do Parca, op cit., pp. 74–77, and Bortolotti, *Socialismo*, pp. 112–13.
21. Parca, op cit., p. 80, for the leap in the dark; Bortolotti, *Socialismo*, p. 133.
22. On the Unione Femminile Nazionale, see ibid., pp. 96–97.
23. Parca, op cit., pp. 82–84; Bortolotti, *Socialismo*, pp. 139–40; and, for a more extensive discussion, Bortolotti, Franca Pieroni, *Femminismo e partiti politici in Italia, 1919–1926* (Rome, 1978). In 1920 the deputies again voted for woman suffrage, but now only for local elections. Protesting, the head of one suffrage group indicated that the political impasse was to be found among women as much as among politicians: "Clerical and socialist women fear the liberal women; socialist and liberal women fear the clericals; liberals and clericals fear the socialists": Parca, op cit., pp. 83–84.

24. Bortolotti, *Socialismo*, ch. 8, and *Femminismo*, pp. 39ff.
25. On Salerno, see Cecchini, op cit., passim; De Biase, op cit., passim; *Problemi del Socialismo*, Oct.–Dec. 1976, pp. 258–59.
26. Coari receives major attention as editor of *Pensiero e Azione* in De Biase, op. cit., chs. 2 and 3 and passim; *Problemi del Socialismo*, pp. 237–38.
27. See ibid., pp. 246–47, for Guidi.
28. See Bortolotti, *Femminismo*, p. 193, for an assertion that both Mussolini and a key woman aide, Margherita Sarfatti, understood the appeal of woman suffrage among workers and did not want to be cut off from it.
29. On Labriola, see Bortolotti, *Socialismo*, passim; *Problemi del Socialismo*, pp. 248–49. See Cecchini, op cit., for an interview with Labriola by Ugo Marchetti.
30. On Terruzzi, see Bortolotti, *Socialismo*, p. 37n and passim and *Femminismo*, passim. On Mariani, see *Problemi del Socialismo*, pp. 251–52.
31. Meldini, Piero, *Sposa e madre esemplare: Ideologia e politica della donna e della famiglia durante il fascismo* (Rimini, Florence, 1975), pp. 19–20 and photograph #1.
32. Sarfatti, Margherita G., *Dux* (Milan, 1926). Sketches of Sarfatti and six other women in Mussolini's personal life are found in Fusco, Gian Carlo, "Mussolini e le donne," *Storia*, Feb. 1977, pp. 20–27. Rafanelli, Leda, *Una donna e Mussolini* (Milan, 1946) is an autobiography by one of Mussolini's early women friends, depicting him as a womanizer.
33. Meldini, op. cit., pp. 82–83. Castellani, Maria, *Donne italiane di ieri e di oggi* (Florence, 1937), displays this "Fascist feminism" in a wider frame.
34. Bordiga quoted, Bortolotti, *Socialismo*, p. 138; Bortolotti, "La questione femminile nel partito communista," in *Femminismo*. Ravera, Camilla, *La donna italiana dal primo al secondo Risorgimento* (Rome, 1951), discusses the early and underground period of the party briefly.
35. Quoted in Ascoli, Giulietta, "L'UDI tra emancipazione e liberazione (1943–1964)," in *Problemi del Socialismo*, Oct.–Dec. 1976, pp. 112, 111.
36. Ibid., p. 112. But Gobetti herself, somewhat later, emphasized the "anonymous and collective" character of the women's resistance—an approach useful to Ravera, op. cit., offering orthodox Communist Party history: see pp. 141ff.: "Le donne nel secondo Risorgimento nazionale (1943–1945)."
37. Ascoli, op. cit., is a systematic and critical analysis. Ravera, op. cit., by the PCI's leading woman activist, offers in chs. 7–9, an early celebration. Spano, N., and Camarlinghi, F., *La questione femminile della politica del PCI* (Rome, 1972), is a systematic survey. See also, Tiso, Aida, *I communisti e la questione femminile* (Rome, 1965), and later editions; and Censi, Antonietta, "Appunti per una storia del movimento femminista in Italia," in Statera, Gianni, ed., *Il privato come politica: Temi attuali del femminismo* (Cosenza, 1977). Buttafuoco, Annarita, "Italy: The Feminist Challenge," in Boggs, Carl, and Plotke, David, eds., *The Politics of Eurocommunism: Socialism in Transition* (Boston, 1980), follows the PCI's view of feminism from 1960.
38. On Steno, see *Problemi del Socialismo*, pp. 259–60.
39. Rossi, Degiarde, Verlicchi, *Obiettivo donna* (Milan, 1977), "Un nuovo impegno politico: Movimento Femminile DC e Centro Italiano Femminile," pp. 59ff., offers a brief sketch of the origins of both MF and CIF. Galli, Giorgio, and Prandi, Alfonso, *Patterns of Political Participation in Italy* (New Haven, 1970), pp. 192–95, discuss CIF-DC relationships. See also, Canuti, G., *Cinquant'anni di vita dell'Unione Donne di ACI* for the postwar activities

of Catholic Action, and Galli and Prandi, op. cit., pp. 188–92, for the relationship of Catholic Action and DC.

40. Tiso, op. cit., pp. 63–64.
41. Spriano, Paolo, *Storia del partito communista italiana* (Turin, 1967), I, 170.
42. Bortolotti, *Femminismo e partiti politici*, pp. 290ff.
43. See n. 44, ch. 1 above.
44. Ravera, Camilla, *La donna italiana dal primo al secondo Risorgimento* (Rome, 1951).
45. On Ravera's help holding the party together in the early years of Fascism: Bortolotti, *Femminismo*, pp. 301ff. Also on Ravera, see *Problemi del Socialismo*, pp. 256–57.
46. On Noce: ibid., pp. 254–55; Bortolotti, *Femminismo*, pp. 304ff.
47. Both quotes: Tiso, op. cit., pp. 67–68, 68.
48. Quoted in Ascoli, loc. cit., p. 121.
49. Quoted in ibid., p. 119.
50. Quoted in Tiso, op. cit., p. 69.
51. Quoted in Ascoli, op. cit., p. 127.
52. Ibid., p. 123.
53. Quoted in ibid., p. 143.
54. Ibid., p. 151.
55. Tiso, op. cit., p. 133ff.
56. Ibid., p. 100.
57. Macciocchi, Maria Antonietta, *Letters from Inside the Italian Communist Party to Louis Althusser*, tr. by Stephen Hellman (London, 1973), pp. 43–44.
58. Ibid., p. 282.
59. Ibid., "The comrades": p. 260; "pride": p. 208; "They almost never came": p. 139; "Birth control": p. 43; "To myself, I think": p. 43; "Family allowances": p. 64; "The proletariat": p. 66; "I learned": p. 66
60. Spagnoletti, Rosalba, ed., *I movimenti femministi in Italia* (Rome, 1976), offers statements from the most prominent of the new groups. Menapace, Lidia, "Le cause strutturali del nuovo femminismo," in *Problemi del socialismo*, Oct.-Dec. 1976, and Gramaglia, Mariella, "1968: il venir dopo e l'andar del movimento femminista," in ibid., are analyses of the new feminism. See Censi, Antonietta, "Appunti per una storia del movimento femminista in Italia," in *Il privato come politica: Temi attuali del femminismo*, for much interesting information, arranged topically, and interviews.
61. Vergati, Stefania, "Il lavoro femminile: emancipazione e doppia schiavitu?" in Statera, Gianni, ed., *Il privato come politica*, pp. 214–17.
62. Parca, Gabrielle, ed., *Le italiana si confessano* (Milan, 1964). The UDI sponsored a later inquiry: Cecchini, Fausta, et al., eds., *Sesso amaro: Trentamila donne respondono su maternità sessualità aborto* (Rome, 1977). See Venuti, Maria, "Resultati di un'indagine svolta a Palermo e provincia sulla condizione della donna," in Mafai, Simone, et al., *Essere donna in Sicilia* (Rome, 1976), for a survey on that island.
63. Marzani, Carl, *The Promise of Eurocommunism* (Westport, Conn., 1980), ch. 6, "When Women Counted," attributes the 1976 surge in the PCI vote in the parliamentary elections directly to the 1974 divorce referendum and the votes of women. Nonetheless, the referendum probably turned on a shift in view among Catholics: Colombo, Arrigo, *Proposte di un cattolico per il divorzio in Italia* (Manduria, 1970), and *Per una scelta di liberta cattolici e referendum* (Rome, 1974). For the broadest spectrum of prodivorce views,

see Tannozzoni, Franco, ed., *25 donne parlano di divorzio e altre cose* (Rome, 1966).

64. Caravaggi, G., et al., *La donna e il diritto dell'incapacità giuridica al nuova diritto famiglia* (Rome, 1976), offers eight useful essays on the history and 1976 status of laws affecting women in different regards.

65. See Buttafuoco, Annarita, "Italy: The Feminist Challenge," in Boggs and Plotke, eds., op. cit., on the abortion reform, as well as on divorce and the posture of the PCI toward both. See Censi, Antonietta, "Appunti," loc. cit., pp. 75–79, on the new feminists' demand for abortion. On PCI attitudes toward sexuality generally, see Tarizzo, Domenico, *Socialismo e sessualità* (Milan, 1976).

66. Lonzi, Carla, *Sputiamo su Hegel: La donna clitoridea e la donna vaginale* (Milan, 1974), p. 22.

67. Ibid., p. 33.

68. Ibid., pp. 33–34.

69. See Censi, "Appunti," sect. 3, "Autonomia e separatismo," loc. cit., pp. 69–73.

70. Ballardin, Gianfranco, "Le femministe a convegno in tutta segretezza," *Corriere della Sera*, Dec. 12, 1976.

71. Quoted in Ballardin, Gianfranco, "Critiche delle nuove generazioni alle sacerdotesse del femminismo," *Corriere della Sera*, Dec. 7, 1976.

72. Ballardin, Gianfranco, "Divise le femministe sui ruoli da assumere," *Corriere della Sera*, Dec. 9, 1976.

73. Lonzi, op. cit., p. 118.

74. Seroni, Adriana, *La questione femminile in Italia, 1970–77* (Rome, 1977), pp. 21–22.

75. See Barkan, Joanne, "Italian Communism at the Crossroads," in Boggs, Carl, ed., *The Politics of Eurocommunism*, for the change in PCI membership. Thus the Communists of the 1970s came to most resemble the Fascists of 1922 in being the socially "most diversified" party in Italian history.

76. Rossanda, Rossana, *Le altre: Conversazione a radiotre sui rapporti tra donne e politica, libertà, fraternità, uguaglianza, democrazia, fascismo, stato, partito, revoluzione, femminismo* (Milan, 1979), p. 155.

77. Menapace, ibid., pp. 176ff. Fossati, Roberta, *E Dio creo la donna: Chiesa, religione e condizione femminile* (Milan, 1977). Fossati was aware of American counterparts, specifically Mary Daly and Rosemary Reuther. Amyot, Grant, *The Italian Communist Party: The Crisis of the Popular Front Strategy* (London, 1981), argues that Enrico Berlinguer's policy of "historic compromise" directly repudiated the classic "lay" positions of the PCI Right, in favor of the "Catholic Communists" with their exaltation of "social" and "collective" ideals as against "individualism" and "anarchy." He thus suggests that the rebellion of the new feminists against the old PCI will meet a new PCI waiting to gather them in again after all.

5. Sweden. Co-optation

1. See Gustafson, Alrik, *A History of Swedish Literature* (Minneapolis, 1961), pp. 126–27, on Nordenflycht.

2. Blanck, Anton, *Anna Maria Lenngren* (Stockholm, 1948), is a brief biography. Gustafson, op. cit., pp. 142–45, offers a brief sketch.

3. Gustafson, op. cit., pp. 59–595, discusses Almqvist and provides a bibliography of works in Swedish on Almqvist, pp. 595–96. I have relied heavily on Kjellen, *Sociala idéer och motiv, hos svenska författarl* (Stockholm, 1937), ch. 4, "C. J. L. Almqvist," and Westman Berg, Karin, *Studier i C. J. L. Almqvist's kvinnouppfattning* (Göteborg, 1962), for his social and utopian ideas.

4. Westman Berg, op. cit., ch. 4, discusses *Marjam*.

5. Moberg, Vilhelm, *A History of the Swedish People*, tr. by Paul Britten Austin (New York, 1972), p. 152. The best biography of St. Bridget in English is probably Jorgensen, Johannes, *Saint Bridget of Sweden*, tr. by Ingeborg Lund (New York, 1954). But Moberg's few pages on her, loc. cit., pp. 152–58, are worth volumes.

6. Bremer, Charlotte, ed., *Life, Letters and Posthumous Works of Fredrika Bremer* (New York, 1869), includes an unusually revealing "biography" of 100 pages by Bremer's sister. Kjellen, *Sociala idéer och motiv* . . ., ch. 3, pt. ii, and Kjellen, *Sociala idéer frön patriarkalism till Marxism* (Stockholm, 1950), ch. 8, pt. ii, discuss Bremer in the context of Swedish liberalism. Axberger, Gunnar, *Jaget och skuggorna: Fredrika Bremer studier* (Stockholm, 1951), presents, as its title—"Ego and Alteregos—suggests, a psychoanalytic analysis of Bremer through her novels.

7. Bremer, Fredrika, *Hertha*, tr. by Mary Howitt (New York, 1856) (an edition given the American title *Three Sisters*), p. xxi.

8. Qvist, Gunnar, *Fredrika Bremer och kvinnans emancipation: Opinionshistoriska studier* (Göteborg, 1969), carefully shows that Bremer was not a direct, only an indirect, influence on legal reform.

9. Bremer, *Hertha*, p. xxi.

10. Bremer, Fredrika, *The President's Daughters—Nina* (New York, 1843), p. 74.

11. Bremer, *Hertha*, "Faithful as a mother": p. 123; "from the hour": p. 372; "The youths": p. 323; "Call her mother": p. 347; "Egeria-like": p. 393.

12. Qvist, Gunnar, *Kvinnofrågan i Sverige, 1809–1846* (Göteborg, 1960), is a meticulous scholarly study of the earlier period by Sweden's leading authority on Swedish feminism; Qvist is director of a series of monographs on Swedish women's history. Rössel, James, *Kvinnorna och kvinnorörelsen i Sverige, 1850–1950* (Stockholm, 1950), is the first scholarly study. Wahlstrom, Lydia, *Den svenska kvinnorörelsen* (Stockholm, 1933), is an earlier popular history of Swedish feminism.

13. See Rössel, op. cit., chs. 1 and 2, on attitudes toward women.

14. See Hovde, Bryn J., *The Scandinavian Countries, 1720–1865* (Boston, 1943), II, ch. 15, for a good brief discussion of educational reforms.

15. Boëthius, Ulf, *Strindberg och kvinnofrågan till och med-Giftas I* (Stockholm, 1969), pt. i, "Kvinnofrågan i Sverige, 1856–1884," is the liveliest treatment of the woman question for that period; see pp. 46–63 on the marriage question.

16. Ibid., pp. 63–70.

17. Baird, Robert, *Visit to Northern Europe* (New York, 1841), II. 188.

18. Thomas, Dorothy Swaine, *Social and Economic Aspects of Swedish Population Movements: 1750–1933* (New York, 1941), Table 3, pp. 34–38.

19. Brace, Charles Loring, *The Norse-Folk: or, A Visit to See the Homes of Norway and Sweden* (New York, 1857), pp. 260–61.

20. Ibid., "Mothers": p. 244; "*grisettes*": p. 243.

21. Boëthius, loc. cit., is the best scholarly discussion of the Wicksell contro-

versy. See also, Gorland, T., *Knut Wicksell* (Stockholm, 1956). Myrdal, Gunnar and Alva, *Kris i Befolkningsfrågan* (Stockholm, 1934), ch. 1, discuss the "neo-Malthusianism" issuing in the anticontraception measures. Kock, Karin, *Nymalthusianismens genombrott i Sverige* (Uppsala, 1944), is a basic scholarly history of the birth control debate.

22. See Rössel, op. cit., ch. 3, on the Bremer Society and Aldersparre. There is also a biography: Leijonhufvud, S., *Sophie Adlersparre (Esselde)* (Stockholm, 1923).
23. Strindberg, August, *Getting Married* (New York, 1972), tr. by Mary Sandbach, pp. 45–50.
24. Ibid., pp. 32–33.
25. Ibid., p. 41.
26. Ibid., p. 42.
27. Ibid., p. 43.
28. Lamm, Martin, *August Strindberg* (New York, 1971), tr. by Harry Carlson, is organized more by the works than the life; see pp. 167–69.
29. Strindberg, August, *The Birth of a Soul* (London, 1913), tr. by Claud Field, p. 139.
30. Ibid.
31. Sandbach, Mary, "Introduction," in Strindberg, *Getting Married*, provides a helpful sketch of events.
32. Ibid., p. 71.
33. Quoted in Lamm, op. cit., p. 139.
34. The Queen has her biographies: Nyström, V., *Drottning Sophia* (Stockholm, 1944), and Huber, A.M., *Drottning Sophia* (Stockholm, 1958). An American diplomat's estimate: "Queen Sophia is a lovely woman, a mother in Israel, famous for her beauty, her piety, her charity and her amiable disposition. . . . She speaks English freely, is particularly fond of Americans, and subscribed for religious newspapers published in the United States. Several of Moody's sermons have been translated into Swedish by her Majesty. . . . She is never without a volume of his sermons by her side, while his biography occupies a conspicuous place upon the book shelves in her little boudoir": Curtis, William E., *Denmark, Norway and Sweden* (Akron, 1903), p. 289.
35. Rössel, op. cit., ch. 3.
36. Nor could a woman get a man's drink. *Social Sweden* (Stockholm, 1952), p. 271, under the heading "Great Accuracy Is Essential," depicted a Rube Goldbergish "mechanical contraption . . . devised . . . to obtain an accurate dispensing." "In the licensed restaurants a glass must not contain more liquor than prescribed. But the guest may . . . demand that the liquid content of his glass be checked. . . . There is a difference, however, in the size of the drink served men and women. In a first-class restaurant, a man can obtain 15 cl., . . . whereas a woman is entitled to only half the volume. Checkers employed by the liquor authorities will report on any infractions of the rules, whether, for example, a drink is consumed by some other person than the one ordering it."
37. Leche-Löfregen, Mia, *Ellen Key: Hennes liv och werk* (Stockholm, 1930), is an intellectual biography. Nystrom-Hamilton, Louise, *Ellen Key: Her Life and Her Work*, tr. by A. E. B. Fries (New York, 1913), is a panegyric, not very helpful. Rössel, op. cit., p. 45, notes Key's influence within feminism.
38. On communal child-rearing: Key, Ellen, *The Renaissance of Motherhood*, tr. by Anna Friess (New York, 1914), p. 147. On Gilman: Key, Ellen, *The*

Woman Movement, tr. by Mamah B. Borthwick (New York, 1912), n. 1, p. 176. On destruction of homes: Key, *Renaissance,* p. 150.

39. Key, Ellen, *Love and Marriage,* tr. by Arthur G. Chase (New York, 1911), "personal characteristics": p. 158; "The book world": p. 90; "We seldom hear": p. 96.

40. Ibid., "If no baseness": p. 92; "when sensuousness": pp. 81, 80; meeting: p. 246; "The modern woman's": pp. 89–90.

41. Flood, Hulda, *Den socialdemokratiska kvinnorörelsen i Sverige* (Stockholm, 1939), follows women in SSD party history from 1888. Rössel, op. cit., ch. 3, discusses Socialist women.

42. Flood, op. cit., p. 31

43. Rössel, op. cit., chs. 5 and 8 on labor; Qvist, Gunnar, "Landsorganisationen en Suède et les femmes sur le marché du travail (1878–1973)," in Dofny, Jacques, ed., *Sociologie et Sociétés,* VI, no. 1, 1974 (Montreal).

44. Rössel, op. cit., ch. 4, discusses the suffrage movement.

45. Wägner, Elin, *Väckerklocka* (Stockholm, 1942), p. 145.

46. Swedish Social Welfare Board, *Social Sweden,* pp. 129–30, notes the ten organizations under the C.S.A. umbrella. Rössel, op. cit., chs. 4 and 8.

47. See Rössel, op. cit., ch. 7, for voting figures.

48. Martinson, Harry, *Elin Wägner* (Stockholm, 1949), is a brief biography. Gustafson, *A History of Swedish Literature,* pp. 376–79, characterizes her novels. Linder, Erik Hjalmar, "Introduction," in Wägner, *Väckerklocka,* sketches Wägner's career.

49. Wägner, *Väckerklocka,* sex laws: pp. 142ff.; Addams: p. 54; population crisis: pp. 160ff.; Balkan mothers: p. 158; Bachofen, Briffault, Halle: pp. 33ff.

50. Ibid., Wahlstrom: p. 114; Key: pp. 118–19; SSD: p. 122; population debate: p. 164.

51. Klein, Viola, and Myrdal, Alva, *Women's Two Roles* (London, 1956), exempt from work: pp. 185. 189; futility: p. 6; "Those who oppose,": p. 27; "Revolutionary,": p. 188.

52 Ibid., p. 192.

53. Moberg, Eva, *Kvinnor och människor* (Stockholm, 1962). On the sex-role debate more widely, see Dahlstrom, Edmund, ed., *Kvinnors liv och arbete* (Stockholm, 1962), revised and translated as Dahlstrom, Edmund, ed., *Changing roles of Men and Women* (Boston, 1967). See also, Liljeström, Rita, "The Swedish Model," in Seward, Georgene H., and Williamson, Robert C., eds., *Sex Roles in Changing Society* (New York, 1970).

54. *The Status of Women in Sweden: Report to the United Nations* (Stockholm, 1968), p. 23.

55. Moberg, Eva, quoted in Lejon, Anna-Greta, *Swedish Women—Swedish Men,* tr. by Paul Britten Austin (Stockholm, 1968), p. 149.

56. Quoted in Linner, Birgitta, *Sex and Society in Sweden* (New York, 1972), pp. 129–30.

57. It was not really hard to tell where they were coming from. In Lorwin, Val R., "Trade Unions and Women: The Most Difficult Revolution," in Brown, Bernard E., *Eurocommunism and Eurosocialism: The Left Confronts Modernity* (New York, 1979), Lorwin, after noting the preponderance of "proper masculine types" in all Western European labor movements, including the Swedish, nevertheless lists factors explaining why "Sweden is the only country to have made something like a serious commitment to women's equality" (p. 359), only then to list the multiple evidences of the shortfall

of the egalitarian program, and to end with the words of a public relations officer of SACO, the union of professionals: "We can achieve greater equality between the sexes far more quickly and effectively if we concentrate our energies on changing the male role. The only correct answer to the question, 'What shall we do about women?' is 'We must do something about men.' " Lorwin has no evidence that such a task was generated within the ranks of Swedish blue- or white-collar workers; in fact, one of the factors he cites as explanation for Sweden's greater commitment to sex equality—Swedish labor's "less distrustful" attitude toward intellectuals—shows these intellectuals remaining what they had always been, the bureaucratic administrators of yore.

58. Barrett, Nancy S., "Have Swedish Women Achieved Equality?" in Glazer, Nona, and Waehrer, Helen Y., eds., *Women in a Man-Made World* (Chicago, 1977), pp. 398–99. Barrett is a professional economist.
59. Wistrand, Birgitta, *Swedish Women on the Move* (Stockholm, 1981), words: p. 7; "Sweden, despite," p. 15.
60. Ibid., p. 90
61. Ibid., pp. 89–90.
62. Ibid., own growth: p. 101; women must allow: p. 25; "More and more men": p. 24.
63. See ch. 10, below.
64. Wistrand, op. cit., justice: p. 89; "We must urge": pp. 102, 103; "is it possible": p. 103.
65. Ibid., p. 73.
66. Ibid., pp. 103–05.

6. Soviet Russia. Suppression

1. Stites, Richard, *The Women's Liberation Movement in Russia: Feminism, Nihilism, and Bolshevism, 1860–1930* (Princeton, 1978), ch. 7. See also, Edmondson, Linda H., *Feminism in Russia, 1900–1917* (Stanford, 1984).
2. Stites, op. cit., pp. 289–95.
3. In addition to Stites, op. cit., chs. 9 and 10, the biographies of Alexandra Kollontai cited in n. 12 below are full of detail about Bolshevik policies and personnel during 1917–18.
4. For a contemporary view of the Women's Department, see Smith, Jessica, "Woman's Entrance into Public Life," in *Woman in Soviet Russia* (New York, 1928). Stites, op. cit., pp. 329–45, presents the Women's Department. For a much less enthusiastic treatment, see Lapidus, Gail, *Women in Soviet Society: Equality, Development and Social Change* (Berkeley, 1978), pp. 63–73.
5. Kollontai, Alexandra, "Prostitution and Ways of Fighting It," in Holt, Alix, ed., *Selected Writings of Alexandra Kollontai* (Westport, Conn., 1978), pp. 261–75.
6. Leonid Leonov's *Skutaresky*, quoted in Luke, Louise, "Marxian Women: Social Variants," in Simmons, Ernest J., ed., *Through the Glass of Soviet Literature: Views of Russian Society* (New York, 1953), p. 71.
7. Lenin, V.I., *The Emancipation of Women: From the Writings of V.I. Lenin, with an Appendix, "Lenin on the Woman Question,"* by Clara Zetkin, preface by Nadezhda Krupskaya (New York, 1972), p. 100.
8. Bebel, August, *Woman under Socialism* (New York, 1971), p. 344.

9. Lenin, loc. cit., "The revolution": p. 107; "I consider": p. 106; "Healthy sports": p. 107; *Mens Sana*: p. 107.

10. Ibid.

11. Massell, Gregory, *The Surrogate Proletariat: Moslem Women and Revolutionary Strategies in Soviet Central Asia: 1919–1929* (Princeton, 1974).

12. The mythologizing of Kollontai was reflected in such early biographies as Palencia, Isabella, *Alexandra Kollontai* (New York, 1947). With the revival of feminism since the 1960s, feminist scholarship inevitably revived Kollontai. No less than three biographies appearing in 1980, not always free of the temptation to revive the myth. Porter, Cathy, *Alexandra Kollontai: The Lonely Struggle of the Woman Who Defied Lenin* (New York, 1980), is an English writer's wholly uncritical portrait, undermined by its inference that, since Kollontai did indeed "defy" Lenin, she must therefore have been a true feminist and even a democrat. Farnsworth, Beatrice, *Alexandra Kollontai: Socialism, Feminism and the Bolshevik Revolution* (Stanford, 1980), pursues the paradoxical course of using Kollontai to try to show that early Bolshevism was betrayed by Stalin, thus leaving the fact that Kollontai defied not Stalin but Lenin unresolved. Clements, Barbara Evans, *Bolshevik Feminist: The Life of Alexandra Kollontai* (Bloomington, 1980), agrees, as her title indicates, that Kollontai does not fit easily into any niche, whether of heroine, martyr, "early" or "late" Bolshevik. That she was a Bolshevik seems true only in part. That she was *also* a feminist—despite Bolshevism— seems true, too, with the contradiction constituting the chief point of interest in her life. My own emphasis upon her search for escape from captivity by sex seeks to explain why she strove to be both. For a study of Kollontai as an example of "political socialization," see Kelly, Rita Mae, and Boutilier, Mary A., *The Making of Political Women: A Study of Socialization and Role Conflict* (Chicago, 1978), which treats of thirty-six women all told.

13. Sorokin, Pitirim, *Leaves from a Russian Diary* (New York, 1924), p. 59.

14. Kollontai, Alexandra, *The Autobiography of a Sexually Emancipated Woman*, ed. by Irving Fetcher (New York, 1971), p. 40.

15. Quoted in Clements, op. cit., p. 167.

16. Kollontai, *Autobiography*, p. 11.

17. Holt, op. cit., p. 241.

18. Ibid., p. 240.

19. Kollontai, *Autobiography*, p. 22.

20. Quoted in Clements, op. cit., p. 70.

21. Kollontai, "The New Woman," in Holt, op. cit., p. 86.

22. Both Clements, op. cit., and Farnsworth, op. cit., discuss Kollontai's relations with Schliapnikov and Dybenko.

23. Holt, op. cit., pp. 270–71.

24. Ibid., p. 277.

25. Ibid.

26. Ibid., pp. 278–79.

27. Ibid., p. 289.

28. Ibid., pp. 289ff.

29. Ibid., p. 290.

30. Kollontai, *Autobiography*, "to work": p. 11; "the greater the demands": p. 22.

31. Lenin, V.I., *Collected Works*, XXIX, 428: "Take the position of women. In this field, not a single democratic party in the world, not even in the most

advanced bourgeois republic, has done in decades so much as a hundredth part of what we did in our very first year in power."

32. Beattie, Bessie, *The Red Heart of Russia* (New York, 1919); Hindus, Maurice, *Humanity Uprooted* (New York, 1929); Thompson, Dorothy, *The New Russia* (New York, 1928); Halle, Fanina, *Woman in Soviet Russia* (New York, 1933).

33. Smith, Jessica, *Woman in Soviet Russia* (New York, 1928), p. 143.

34. Ibid., pp. 139, 143.

35. Hindus, op. cit., pp. 86–87, 138.

36. Smith, Jessica, "Making a Marriage Law," in *Woman in Soviet Russia*, portrays the 1925–26 debate over marriage law revision. Schlesinger, Rudolph, ed., *The Family in the U.S.S.R.: Documents and Readings* (London, 1949), pp. 81–153, offers many excerpts from the published public debate and, on pp. 154–68, the new laws themselves. Farnsworth, Barbara B., "Bolshevik Alternatives and the Soviet Family: the 1926 Marriage Law Debate," in Atkinson, Dorothy, Dallin, Alexander, and Lapidus, Gail, eds., *Women in Russia* (Stanford, 1977), offers a modern analysis.

37. Schlesinger, op. cit., p. 145.

38. On Krupskaya, and Smidovich, see Halle, op. cit., p. 133.

39. Schlesinger, op. cit., presents Kollontai in the marriage law debates.

40. Stites, op. cit., p. 344.

41. Schlesinger, op. cit., pp. 251–347, provides extensive documentation on the new decrees. See Lapidus, op. cit., pp. 110–15, for a modern discussion of the changes. See also Stites, op. cit., pp. 384–88.

42. Schlesinger, op. cit., pp. 255, 257, 259.

43. Volfson, Samuel, *Society and the Family*, excerpted in Schlesinger, op. cit., pp. 280–315.

44. Ibid., p. 252.

45. Quoted in Stites, op. cit., p. 386.

46. Schlesinger, op. cit., pp. 296, 310.

47. Trotsky, Leon, *Women and the Family* (New York, 1979), pp. 62, 64, 67.

48. Ibid., pp. 68, 70, 71.

49. Ibid., p. 71.

50. See Schlesinger, op. cit., pp. 235–50, on the wives of Krivoi Rog.

51. Scott, John, *Behind the Urals* (Cambridge, 1942), pp. 132–33.

52. Schlesinger, op. cit., pp. 367–406, provides documents on the 1944 decrees. Stites, op. cit., pp. 388–90.

53. Schlesinger, op. cit., pp. 397–98.

54. No postwar baby boom: Dodge, "Trends in the Birth Rate," in *Women in the Soviet Economy* (Baltimore, 1966), pp. 19–25; Lapidus, *Women in Soviet Society*, pp. 92–94. Relegalization of abortion: Lapidus, pp. 298–99. On the new 1968 codes, Lane, David, ed., *Politics and Society in the USSR* (New York, 1978), appendix H, pp. 595–607, provides the texts; Lapidus, op. cit., pp. 255–65, discusses the new family law of 1968. See also, David, Henry P., *Family Planning and Abortion in the Socialist Countries of Eastern Europe* (New York, 1970); Brackett, J.W., and DePauw, J.W., *Population Policy and Demographic Trends in the Soviet Union* (Washington, D.C., 1966); Field, M.H., "The Relegalization of Abortion in Soviet Russia," *New England Journal of Medicine*, v. 30, August 1956.

55. Lapidus, Gail W., ed., *Women, Work, and Family in the Soviet Union* (Armonk, 1982), is an exceptionally valuable collection of translations from Soviet, usually women, sociologists, economists, and demographers. Jancar, Bar-

bara Wolfe, *Women under Communism* (Baltimore, 1978), draws on extensive interviews with professional women in the Soviet Union and under five other East European Communist regimes.

56. Danilova, Y.Z., et al., *Soviet Women (Some Aspects of the Status of Women in the USSR)* (Moscow, 1975), Yankova: p. 143; Yazykova: pp. 130, 140; Yemelyanova: p. 68; Danilova: pp. 176, 181; Yankova: pp. 133, 143.

57. Baranskaia, Natalia, *Une Semaine Comme Une Autre* (Paris, 1976). In Atkinson, Dallin, Lapidus, eds., *Women in Russia*, three of the contributors, Hough, Rosenhan, and Shulman, draw on the story as evidence, as does Lapidus, *Women in Soviet Society*.

58. Dallin, Alexander, "Conclusions," in Atkinson, Dallin, Lapidus, eds., op. cit., pp. 391–92.

59. Shulman, Colette, "The Individual and the Collective," ibid., p. 378.

60. Ibid., p. 377.

61. Dallin, loc. cit., p. 395.

62. Dodge, Norton, "Women in the Professions," ibid., p. 395; Stites, Richard, *The Women's Liberation Movement*, p. 414.

63. Yankova, Z.A., in *Soviet Women*, p. 135.

64. Chapin, Janet, "Equal Pay for Equal Work," in Atkinson, Dallin, Lapidus, eds., op. cit., p. 235.

65. Madison, Bernice, "Social Services for Women: Problems and Priorities," ibid., p. 309.

66. Hough, Jerry F., "Women and Women's Issues in Soviet Policy Debates," ibid., pp. 371–72.

67. Shulman, ibid., p. 378.

68. Moses, Joel C., "Women in Political Roles," ibid., p. 349.

69. I have used Mamanova, Tatyana, ed., *Femmes et Russie* (Paris, 1980) and *Des femmes russes* (Paris, 1980). Mamanova, Tatyana, ed., *Women and Russia: Feminist Writings from the Soviet Union* (Boston, 1984), does not include Oulianova, Natalieva, Nobatova, or Sororeva, while including essays not found in the French translations. Sariban, Alla, "The Soviet Woman: Support and Mainstay of the Regime," ibid., pp. 205ff., argues that women sustain the system: "Soviet women, in some inner part of their beings, frequently without being aware of it, have a distinct tendency to make common cause with the Soviet system and to identify with it. . . . All Soviet people are dissatisfied with the status quo and curse it. Women curse it no less actively than men. In fact, women even exceed men in this, since women have more reason to curse. Yet . . . you find that rarely do any of their complaints turn into an outright rejection of the system itself. . . . The average Soviet woman's consciousness, and even to a significant degree her unconscious, are rigidly confined to the everyday world. . . . [The] practical life of Soviet women, and for that matter of all Soviet people, is limited to everyday concerns much more so than is that of people in democratic countries. For nothing in Soviet society depends on the individual."

70. Hindus, op. cit., p. 114.

71. Lapidus, *Women in Soviet Society*, p. 334; Madison, "Social Services for Women," loc. cit.

72. *Des femmes russes*, p. 93.

73. Mamanova, ed., *Women and Russia*, pp. 215ff.

74. Abramov, Fyodor, *One Day in the "New Life"* (New York, 1963), p. 50.

7. Early Wonderland

1. Adams, Henry, *The United States in 1800* (Ithaca, 1955), "in spite of": p. 15; "If Americans agreed": p. 45.
2. Hamilton, Alexander, "Report on Manufactures," in Folsom, Michael B., and Lubar, Steven D., eds., *The Philosophy of Manufactures: Early Debates over Industrialization in the United States* (Cambridge, 1982), pp. 81–94.
3. Ibid. For an interesting discussion of a later prophet of technology, see Kasson, John F., *Civilizing the Machine: Technology and Republican Values in America, 1776–1900* (New York, 1976), ch. 3, "Technology and Imaginative Freedom: R. W. Emerson," in which Kasson has not quite decided whether to emphasize Emerson as stimulated by machines (and "riches") or as simply determined not to be intimidated into nostalgia by them.
4. Adams, Henry, op. cit., institutions: p. 114; "Reversing": p. 115; moral atmosphere; p. 125.
5. Tocqueville, Alexis de, *Democracy in America*, tr. by George Lawrence, ed. by J. P. Mayer (Garden City, 1969), land of wonders: p. 404; man vs. animals: p. 546; "The universal movement": p. 404.
6. Ibid., any American: p. 404; on the South: p. 361; "chance is" and gamble: p. 553; "For an American": p. 404. See also, Hirschman, Albert O., *The Passions and the Interests: Political Arguments for Capitalism before Its Triumph* (Princeton, 1977), for views nurturant of what Tocqueville saw. The "passionate" root of capitalism contrasts of course with that postulated by Max Weber in *The Protestant Ethic and the Spirit of Capitalism*, which is discussed in American context by Bruchey, Stuart, *The Roots of American Economic Growth, 1607–1861* (New York, 1965), pp. 42–48. Essentially, Tocqueville saw American men as individualists no longer in need of Puritan, Protestant shells. See Crowley, J. F., *This Sheba, Self: The Conceptualization of Economic Life in 18th Century America* (Baltimore, 1974), for the eighteenth century, the epoch of last religious resistance.
7. Ibid., trade: pp. 400–07; little undertakings: p. 554; "I cannot help": p. 407.
8. For American economic development generally, I have benefited from the "pioneering work" of the New Economic History, North, Douglass C., *The Economic Growth of the United States, 1790 to 1860* (Englewood Cliffs, 1961). See also, Sutch, Richard, "Douglass North and the New Economic History," in Ransom, Roger L., et al., eds., *Explorations in the New Economic History: Essays in Honor of Douglass C. North* (New York, 1982). Habakkuk, H.J., *American and British Technology in the 19th Century* (Cambridge, 1962), provides acute analysis of the logic of labor-saving machinery. Bruchey, Stuart, *Roots*, speaks to the "success" of the American story. I have much benefited from Cochran, Thomas, *The Age of Enterprise: A Social History of Industrial America* (New York, 1942), and other of Cochran's writings. Siracusa, Carl, *A Mechanical People: Perceptions of the Industrial Order in Massachusetts, 1815–1860* (Middletown, Conn., 1979), avoids the convention that "industrialization" automatically meant fear and anxiety. For larger background, see Rosenberg, Nathan, and Birdzell, L.E., Jr., *How the West Grew Rich: The Economic Transformation of the Industrial World* (New York, 1985), persuasive analysis.
9. Tocqueville, op. cit., pp. 535–38.
10. Ibid., love of money, cooperation, keeping score, multiplies the purposes:

pp. 614–15; no limit: p. 404. On the Jacksonian politics presiding over this scene, there is no end to debate, much of it still stimulated by Schlesinger, Arthur M., Jr., *The Age of Jackson* (Boston, 1945). For guidance to party history generally, I am indebted to Kelley, Robert, *The Cultural Pattern in American Politics: The First Century* (New York, 1979).

11. Schumpeter, Joseph, *Capitalism, Socialism and Democracy*, (New York, 1975), pp. 73–74.
12. Tocqueville, op. cit., p. 283.
13. Smith, Henry Nash, *Virgin Land* (New York, 1951); Peterson, Merrill, *The Jeffersonian Image in the American Mind* (New York, 1962).
14. Rourke, Constance, *American Humor* (Garden CIty, 1953). For the Jacksonian epoch as culture, Fish, Carl Russell, *The Rise of the Common Man, 1830–1850* (New York, 1927), remains classic. Bode, Carl, *The Anatomy of American Popular Culture, 1840–1861* (Berkeley, 1960); Riegel, Robert E., *Young America, 1830–1840* (Norman, 1949); and Miller, Douglass T., *The Birth of Modern America, 1820–1850* (New York, 1970), continue in this essentially Tocquevillian line of setting what is "democratic" at the center of American history. See also, Saum, Lewis O., *The Popular Mood of Pre-Civil War America* (Westport, Conn., 1980). In all these books it would be proper to say the emphasis in Fish's title is maintained: this was a culture of men, not feminized at all.
15. Tocqueville, op. cit., p. 489.
16. Rourke, op. cit., p. 164.
17. Taylor, Bayard, *Eldorado, or, Adventures in the Path of Empire* (New York, 1850): "A better idea": I, 114; "The most immediate": II, 64; "Perhaps there was": II, 64–65; "The appearance": I, 117; "Towards the close": II, 59–60; "Think of a city": II, 59; "Several tents": II, 51–52; "If every married man": II, 59; "I was constantly reminded": II, 60.
18. Russell, George, in Hunt, Freeman, *Lives of American Merchants* (New York, 1858), p. xxxix.
19. Ibid., p. 355.
20. Bellows, Henry, *The Leger and the Lexicon: or, Business and Literature in Account with American Education* (Cambridge, 1853); "Might you penetrate": p. 46; "Our people are": p. 49; "Men everywhere seek": p. 45.
21. Ibid., "The savage and the saint": p. 25.
22. Ibid., "Nationality has done": p. 45; "We are working": pp. 43, 48.
23. Lipsky, George A., *John Quincy Adams: His Theory and Ideas* (New York, 1950), treats JQA as the visionary intellectual he was.
24. Dorfman, Joseph, *The Economic Mind in American Civilization* (New York, 1946), I, pt. ii,
25. Conkin, Paul K., *Prophets of Prosperity: America's First Political Economists* (Bloomington, 1980), pt. v, offers meticulous discussion of Carey.
26. Carey, Henry C., *The Past, the Present, and the Future* (Philadelphia, 1869), natural tendency: p. 430; Carey, Henry C., *The Harmony of Interests: Agricultural, Manufacturing, and Commercial* (Philadelphia, 1868), not good to live alone: p. 87; disposed to home: p. 204.
27. Carey, *Harmony*, tavern: p. 203; gambling: p. 206; *Past, Present, Future*, "No set of men,": p. 444; millions of men: ibid.
28. Tocqueville, op. cit., "In Europe," "That is far," "In America," "You will never": pp. 600, 601. The original student of woman's sphere was of course Tocqueville himself; a host of modern studies have deepened his portrait.

Taylor, William R., and Lasch, Christopher, " 'Two Kindred Spirits': Sorority and Family in New England, 1839–1846," *New England Quarterly*, 1963, pp. 25–41, anticipated later studies emphasizing the "homosocial" extensions of woman's sphere far beyond the home. In a thesis, Melder, Keith E., "The Beginnings of the Women's Rights Movement in the United States: 1800–1840," Yale, 1963, eventually revised and published as *Beginnings of Sisterhood: The American Woman's Rights Movement, 1800–1850* (New York, 1977), presented woman's sphere as basically a captivity against which women protested. In her seminal article, Welter, Barbara, "The Cult of True Womanhood, 1820–1860," *American Quarterly*, Summer 1966, pp. 151–74, as her title implies, treated the sphere ironically throughout, then, on the last page, noted the dialectical opportunity:" "if woman was so very little less than the angels, she should surely take a more active part in running the world, especially since men were making such a hash of things." Lerner, Gerda, "The Lady and the Mill Girl: Changes in the Status of Women in the Age of Jackson," *Midcontinent American Studies Journal*, Spring 1969, pp. 5–14, saw only "deterioration" in the period. A sharp turn from this approach was offered in Smith-Rosenberg, Carroll, "The Female World of Love and Ritual: Relations between Women in 19th Century America," *Signs: A Journal of Women in Culture and Society*, Autumn 1975, pp. 1–29. Cott, Nancy, *The Bonds of Womanhood: "Woman's Sphere" in New England* (New Haven, 1977), as both the pun and the quote marks in her title imply, developed the dialectical approach and included a brief historiography on the issue. By the late 1970s scholars were commonly presenting woman's sphere dialectically as a kind of screen or camouflage behind which, and in the name of which, women were winning larger powers; the question of whether this was a deliberate, "conscious" or an intuitive, "unconscious" process was often left unresolved. See Freedman, Estelle, "Separatism as a Strategy: Female Institution Building and American Feminism, 1870–1930," *Feminist Studies*, 1979 and Bordin, Ruth, *Women and Temperance: The Quest for Power and Liberty, 1873–1900* (Philadelphia, 1981). From another perspective, Kessler-Harris, Alice, *Out to Work: A History of Wage-Earning Women in the United States* (New York, 1982), and Matthaei, Julie A., *An Economic History of Women in America: Women's Work, the Division of Labor and the Development of Capitalism* (New York, 1982), offer diametrically opposed assessments of the impact of confinement to woman's sphere upon women, Kessler-Harris judging it wholly limiting, frustrating, and demeaning, Matthaei viewing it dialectically as an offer of space and freedom for generating identity. The need for construing these issues in a more thoroughly "materialist" mode was being urged in numerous quarters, such as the journal *Feminist Studies* and an issue of *Radical History Review*, "Sexuality in History," Spring/Summer 1979. See also, Norton, Mary Beth, "The Paradox of 'Woman's Sphere,' " in Berkin, Carol Ruth, and Norton, Mary Beth, *Women of America: A History* (Boston, 1979).

29. Tocqueville, op. cit., p. 592.
30. Ibid., deep affection: p. 598; chaste and cold: p. 592.
31. Pierson, George, *Tocqueville and Beaumont in America* (New York, 1938).
32. Beaumont, Gustave de, *Marie, or Slavery in the United States* (Stanford, 1958), p. 18.
33. Tocqueville, op. cit., p. 598.

34. Barker-Benfield, G. J., *The Horrors of the Half-Known Life: Male Attitudes toward Women and Sexuality in 19th Century America* (New York, 1976), pt. iii, is a brilliant discussion of the affinity of this sexual ideology with mainstream American Calvinist Puritanism.

35. Beaumont, op. cit., p. 7.

36. Tocqueville, op. cit., evil: p. 592; courtesans: p. 598.

37. Potter, David, *People of Plenty* (Chicago, 1955), ch. 20; Aries, Philippe, *Centuries of Childhood: A Social History of Family Life* (New York, 1962), pt. iii.

38. Ryan, Mary P., *Cradle of the Middle Class: The Family in Oneida County, New York, 1790–1865* (Cambridge, 1981). See also, Farber, Bernard, *Guardians of Virtue: Salem Families in 1800* (New York, 1972), for an earlier study of the "post-Puritan" family.

39. Tocqueville, op. cit., p. 601. Carey, *Past, Present, Future*, p. 271. Carey was emphatic on the benefit to American housewives of growing prosperity: "With each step in the progress of wealth and population, we may see an improvement in the condition of woman," ibid., p. 268; "That . . . woman everywhere may acquire power over her own actions, determining for herself who she will marry and who she will not; that she may everywhere obtain a home . . . becoming the mother of children: it is essential that wealth should be permitted to increase," ibid., p. 272. The major occupation of most of these fortunate women can be deduced from Carey's prediction that, "properly cultivated," the United States east of the Mississippi alone could support 640 million in affluence; to repeat, he insisted that such affluence was possible only by industry and agriculture concentrated together, with the elimination of unproductive trade and transport.

40. Chevalier, Michael, *Society, Manners, and Politics in the United States* (Garden City, 1961), dress: p. 413; "What a contrast" and "Since the man": p. 330.

41. Martineau, Harriet, *Society in America* (Garden City, 1962), p. 295. Bremer, Fredrika, *The Homes of the New World* (New York, 1853).

42. Tocqueville, op. cit., p. 594; Fuller, Margaret, *Summer on the Lakes*, in Wade, Mason, ed., *The Writings of Margaret Fuller* (New York, 1941), p. 44; Kolodny, Annette, *The Land Before Her: Fantasy and Experience of the American Frontiers, 1630–1860* (Chapel Hill, 1984). It is interesting to note that Smith, Henry Nash, *Virgin Land* (New York, 1950), did not inquire whether the hope for a "garden" in the West was perhaps more commonly linked to women.

43. Ryan, op. cit., p. 157; in addition to Gordon, Linda, *Woman's Body, Woman's Right: A Social History of Birth Control in America* (New York, 1976), and Smith, Daniel Scott, "Family Limitation, Sexual Control, and Domestic Feminism in Victorian America," *Feminist Studies*, I, 1973, pp. 40–57. See also, Cott, Nancy F., "Passionlessness: An Interpretation of Victorian Sexual Ideology, 1790–1850," *Signs: A Journal of Women in Culture and Society*, IV, 1978, pp. 219–36. Smith-Rosenberg, Carroll, "The Female World of Love and Ritual: Relations between Women in Nineteenth-Century America," loc. cit.

44. Tocqueville, op. cit., pp. 587–89, 590. See Wishy, Bernard, *The Child and the Republic: The Dawn of Modern American Child Nurture* (Philadelphia, 1968), and Kuhn, Annie, *The Mother's Role in Childhood Education: New England Concepts, 1830–1860* (New Haven, 1947), on ideology surrounding this crucial nexus. For a classic discussion of American mothering, see Erikson,

Erik, "Reflections on the American Identity," in *Childhood and Society* (New York, 1950). For a modern discussion with attention to feminism, see Klein, Carole, *Mothers and Sons* (New York, 1984).

45. Martineau, op. cit., clergy: p. 347; "I cannot enlarge": p. 354.

46. Epstein, Barbara Leslie, *The Politics of Domesticity: Women, Evangelism, and Temperance in 19th Century America* (Middletown, Conn., 1981).

47. Bagwell, Philip S., and Mingay, G. E., *Britain and America: A Study of Economic Change, 1850–1939* (New York, 1970), links industrial growth in 1850–1914 to agriculture as well as capital markets, trade, and labor. North, Douglass C., *Growth and Welfare in the American Past: A New Economic History* (Englewood Cliffs, 1966), carries his earlier story of growth into the twentieth century. See also, Vatter, Harold G., *The Drive to Industrial Maturity: The U.S. Economy, 1860–1914* (Westport, Conn., 1975). Campbell, Helen, *Women Wage Earners* (Boston, 1893), throws a concerned light on its theme. See also, Erickson, Charlotte, *American Industry and European Immigrants, 1860–1885* (Cambridge, 1957).

48. Fredrickson, George, *The Inner Civil War* (New York, 1965), ch. 11.

49. Massey, Mary Elizabeth, *Bonnet Brigades* (New York, 1966).

50. Again, from an extensive literature, I note as having been particularly stimulating, Rayback, Joseph G., *A History of American Labor* (New York, 1959). I have drawn on Taft, Philip, *Organized Labor in American History* (New York, 1964).

51. On Moody, see Findlay, James F., Jr., *Dwight L. Moody: An American Evangelist 1837–1899* (Chicago, 1969).

52. Josephson, Matthew, *The Politicos, 1865–1896* (New York, 1938), remains unrivaled as an evocation of the atmosphere peculiar to post-Civil War politics. Another perspective is found in Waite, Leonard, *The Republican Era, 1869–1901: A Study in Administrative History* (New York, 1958). Hays, Samuel P., *The Response to Industrialism, 1885–1914* (New York, 1957); Summers, Mark W., *Radical Reconstruction and the Gospel of Prosperity: Railroad Aid under the Republicans, 1865–1877* (Princeton, 1984); Marcus, Robert D., *Grand Old Party: Political Structure in the Gilded Age, 1880–1896* (Oxford, 1971); Montgomery, David, *Beyond Equality: Labor and the Radical Republicans, 1862–1872* (New York, 1967); and De Santis, Vincent P., *Republicans Face the Southern Question: The New Departure Years, 1877–1897* (Baltimore, 1959), all touch on tactics in the party.

53. Kelley, Robert, *The Cultural Pattern in American Politics*, and Josephson, Matthew, *The Politicos*, both illuminate the postwar Democrats' problems.

54. Marx, Karl, and Engels, Friedrich, *Correspondence, 1846–1895* (New York, 1934), pp. 448–49 for Engels's letter to Florence Kelley Wischnewetsky, June 3, 1886.

55. In Stearn, Gerald Emanuel, ed., *Gompers* (Englewood Cliffs, 1971), the mutual cross-examination between Gompers and the longtime Socialist Morris Hillquit nicely brings out Gompers's pragmatism: pp. 47–58.

56. Foerster, Robert F., *The Italian Emigration of Our Time* (Cambridge, Mass., 1924), traces the Italian emigrants from Italy to North Africa and South America as well as to the United States. McLaughlin, Virginia Gans, "Patterns of Work and Family Organization: Buffalo's Italians," *Journal of Interdisciplinary History*, II (Autumn 1971), pp. 307–13; Parenti, Michael J., *Ethnic and Political Attitudes: A Depth Study of Italian Americans* (New York, 1975), and Kesson, Thomas, *The Golden Door: Italian and Jewish Immigrant*

Mobility in New York City, 1880–1915 (New York, 1977), are part of a large literature illustrating the assimilation of the immigrants to the middle class: the ultimate such study may be Herberg, Will, *Protestant, Catholic, Jew* (Garden City, 1955).

57. Notable studies of Swedish and German acculturation include: Babcock, Kendric, *The Scandinavian Element in the United States* (Urbana, 1914); Stephenson, George M., *The Religious Aspects of Swedish Immigration* (Minneapolis, 1932); and Faust, Albert B., *The German Element in the United States* (New York, 1927).

58. Shannon, Fred A., *The Farmer's Last Frontier* (New York, 1961), remains classic. Gates, Paul W., *The Farmer's Age* (New York, 1960), and Robbins, Roy M., *Our Larger Heritage: The Public Domain, 1776–1936* (Princeton, 1941), provide basic guidance. Fite, Gilbert C., *American Farmers: The New Minority* (Bloomington, 1981), tells the twentieth-century story.

59. Carey, *Past, Present, Future*, chs. 1, 4, and 10, present his views on agriculture.

60. Buck, Solon, *The Granger Movement* (Cambridge, Mass., 1913), remains classic. Destler, Chester, *American Radicalism, 1865–1901* (Menasha, Wis., 1946), contains essays on farm radicalism still fresh. Pollack, Norman, *The Populist Response to Industrial America* (Cambridge, Mass., 1962), is written in full awareness of the historians' debates, to which Saloutos, Theodore, ed., *Populist: Reaction or Reform* (New York, 1968), offers helpful guidance.

61. For immigrant eagerness and optimism, see Kesson, Thomas, *The Golden Door*, among many other studies. For reasons possibly inherent in historiographical logic, the traumas of immigrant experience have been stressed at the expense of the exhilarations.

62. Wiebe, Robert, *The Search for Order, 1877–1920* (New York, 1967), most fully corrected the idea that "progressivism" referred only to the defense of local small-town culture against corporate Big Business, although all sensitive students of Theodore Roosevelt, together with Herbert Croly, had never thought otherwise: Chandler, Alfred, *The Visible Hand: The Management Revolution in American Business* (Cambridge, 1977), offers sharp focus for the broader canvas sketched by Wiebe, wherein the origins of the "search," whether in wish, fear, desire, nostalgia, or innovation, are less clearly located.

63. For a sophisticated study of resistance to the new epoch of industrial capitalism, see Lears, Jackson, *No Place for Grace* (New York, 1981), a book nicely revealing the essentially "anti-democratic" nature of the rising lament over "consumerism."

64. On cars, see the essays in Lewis, David L., and Goldstein, Lawrence, eds., *The Automobile and American Culture* (Ann Arbor, 1983), particularly Sanborn, Charles, " 'Woman's Place' in American Car Culture," pp. 137–52.

65. Lynd, Robert, and Lynd, Helen Merrill, *Middletown: A Study in Contemporary American Culture* (New York, 1929), p. 251 on cars.

66. The best way to enter TR's presidency remains the skeptical and ironic Pringle, Henry, *Theodore Roosevelt: A Biography* (New York, 1930), followed by Mowry, George E., *The Era of Theodore Roosevelt and the Birth of Modern America* (New York, 1958).

67. On TR as a self-dramatizing personality, no one rivals his friend and tireless admirer, Hagedorn, Hermann, *Roosevelt in the Badlands* (Boston, 1921).

68. Hagedorn, Hermann, *The Roosevelt Family of Sagamore Hill* (New York, 1954). See also, Bishop, Joseph Bucklin, ed., *Theodore Roosevelt's Letters to His Children* (New York, 1926).

69. For Roosevelt's attitudes toward women, I am indebted to Silverman, Eliane Leslau, "Theodore Roosevelt and Women: The Inner Conflict of a President and Its Impact on His Ideology," Ph.D. diss., UCLA, 1973, in particular, ch. 5, "Accommodating the Conflict: Woman Suffrage."
70. Roosevelt, Theodore, *An Autobiography* (New York, 1924), p. 162.
71. Ibid., pp. 161–62.
72. Ibid., p. 162.
73. TR to Will Hays, in Morison, Elting, E., ed., *The Letters of Theodore Roosevelt* (Cambridge, Mass., 1951), VIII, 1305, cited in Silverman, loc. cit., p. 195.

8. The First Feminism

1. Richardson, Robert, "The Puritan Poetry of Anne Bradstreet," in Bercovitch, Sacvan, ed., *The American Puritan Imagination: Essays in Revaluation* (Cambridge, 1974), pp. 105–22; Waggoner, Hyatt, *American Poets from the Puritans to the Present* (Boston, 1968), p. xvii; Bercovitch, op. cit., p. 3; Campbell, Helen, *Anne Bradstreet and Her Time* (Boston, 1890), p. iii; Morison, Samuel Eliot, *Builders of the Bay Colony* (Boston, 1930), p. 32; Morgan, Edmund, *The Puritan Family* (New York, 1966), pp. 167–68.
2. Watts, Emily Stipes, *The Poetry of American Women from 1632 to 1945* (Austin, 1977), p. 5. Martin, Wendy, *An American Triptych: Anne Bradstreet, Emily Dickinson, Adrienne Rich* (Chapel Hill, 1984), on the other hand, does argue that there is a real "gynecocratic" literary tradition to be found, beginning with Bradstreet (though with heavy appeal to Anne Hutchinson, no poet).
3. Barker-Benfield, Graham, "Anne Hutchinson and the Puritan Attitude toward Women," *Feminist Studies*, Fall 1972, pp. 65–96.
4. Kerber, Linda, *Women of the Republic: Intellect and Ideology in Revolutionary America* (Chapel Hill, 1980); Norton, Mary Beth, *Liberty's Daughters: The Revolutionary Experience of American Women, 1750–1800* (Boston, 1980).
5. Adams, Charles Francis, ed., *Familiar Letters of John Adams and His Wife Abigail during the Revolution* (New York, 1976), "I admire": p. 330; "I regret": p. 339; Akers, Charles, *Abigail Adams: An American Woman* (Boston, 1980), p. 100 for beautiful country; men of sense, letter to Mercy Otis Warren, May 1777.
6. On Brown, see Friedman, Lawrence *Inventors of the Promised Land* (New York, 1975), ch. 3, "Dissidence: The Case of Charles Brockden Brown." Hendrickson, Robert A., *The Rise and Fall of Alexander Hamilton* (New York, 1981), discusses Hamilton and Angelica Church as well as others; although Jefferson's "heart" is usually discussed with regard to Maria Cosway and Sally Hemings, far more remains to be understood with regard to his daughters, the raw material for which is in Randolph, Sarah N., *The Domestic Life of Thomas Jefferson* (New York, 1972).
7. Albanese, Catherine, *Sons of the Fathers: The Civil Religion of the American Revolution* (Philadelphia, 1976).
8. Friedman, Lawrence, *Inventors of the Promised Land*, ch. 4, "True American Womanhood."
9. See n. 115 below for references on the organized women's movement.
10. Fuller, Margaret, *Summer on the Lakes*, in Wade, Mason, ed., *The Writings of Margaret Fuller* (New York, 1941), p. 22.

11. Ibid., "In Milwaukie": p. 69; "I liked very much": p. 87; "I have not wished": p. 91.

12. Ibid., the ladies: p. 44; the girls: p. 41; the guitar: p. 46.

13. Quoted in Blanchard, Paula, *Margaret Fuller: From Transcendentalism to Revolution* (New York, 1978), p. 199.

14. Higginson, Thomas Wentworth, *Margaret Fuller Ossoli* (Boston, 1884), while judging that Margaret Fuller as a child had had too little of her mother and too much of her father, warned that the "fragment of autobiographical romance in which she vividly describes the horrors of [her father's] method must not . . . be taken too literally": pp. 28, 27, 22. Miller, Perry, "Introduction," in *Margaret Fuller, American Romantic* (Gloucester, 1969), p. x, characterizes Timothy Fuller's education of his daughter as "persecution" or even "sadism," presumably on the basis of his educational regimen for her rather than any independent evidence. Blanchard, Paula, *Margaret Fuller*, p. 3, complains that Mason Wade, in his biography of 1940, failed to appreciate the "contradiction" into which Fuller was thrown when her father began encouraging her in feminine ways; this "contradiction," according to Blanchard, "became an internal one, siphoning off energy which a man could have used in a direct, uncomplicated way to reach his life goals"—a curious argument since, by any ordinary reckoning, Fuller had far more energy at her disposal than most men. Blanchard, op. cit., p. 40, also observes of Timothy Fuller that, for him, women "were the charming ornaments of an otherwise austere and frequently dull society," thus rendering it hard to see why he should have educated his daughter to be a bluestocking in the first place. Allen, Margaret Vandehaar, *The Achievement of Margaret Fuller* (University Park, 1979), likens Fuller's father to Mme. de Stael's mother as having provided an education with more discipline than love. Douglas, Ann, in *The Feminization of American Culture* (New York, 1977), pp. 263–66, "The Legacy of Timothy Fuller: The Will to Action," judges that Margaret Fuller benefited far more than she suffered from her father, a judgment with which I agree.

15. Rusk, Ralph L., ed., *The Letters of Ralph Waldo Emerson* (New York, 1939), II: "I once": p. 336; "an extraordinary person": p. 332; "You have your own methods": p. 336.

16. Ibid., "taxed him": pp. 325–26; "So, dear child": p. 327.

17. Ibid., "Write to me": pp. 327–28; "How often have I left" and "my soul": pp. 340, 341.

18. Ibid., "You have a right": p. 342; "I have your letter," "A robust understanding," and "tell me that I am cold": p. 352.

19. Ibid., pp. 352–53.

20. Emerson, Ralph Waldo, "Friendship," in *Essays—First Series* (Boston, 1903), pp. 214–15.

21. Quoted in Gregg, Edith W., ed., *One First Love: The Letters of Ellen Louisa Tucker to Ralph Waldo Emerson* (Cambridge, 1962). See also, Pommer, Henry F., *Emerson's First Marriage* (Carbondale, 1967), p. 111.

22. Gregg, op. cit., "Here I sit": p. 134; "She led": p. 134.

23. Emerson, Ralph Waldo, in Emerson, E. W., and Forbes, W. E., eds., *Journals of Ralph Waldo Emerson* (Boston, 1909), II, 257–58.

24. Gregg., op. cit., "I am resolved": p. 28; "Waldo says": p. 98; "Riding at the circus": p. 165.

25. Ibid., p. 34.
26. Rusk, ed., *Letters*, II, 141.
27. Gregg, op. cit., pp. 119–20.
28. Ibid., pp. 123–24.
29. Ibid., pp. 66–67.
30. Rusk, ed., *Letters*, IV, 33.
31. Wade, ed., *The Writings of Margaret Fuller*, p. 567.
32. Higginson, *Margaret Fuller Ossoli*, p. 200.
33. Fuller, Margaret, *Woman in the Nineteenth Century*, in Wade, ed., *The Writings of Margaret Fuller*, "Knowing that there exists": p. 122; "Men have been": p. 199.
34. Ibid., p. 201.
35. Ibid.: "wild beasts": p. 175; early marriages: p. 197; old maids: p. 187; cold water: p. 208.
36. Allen, *The Achievement of Margaret Fuller*, pp. 143–44. Hawthorne, in Hawthorne, Julian, *Hawthorne and His Wife* (Cambridge, 1887), II, 261. Hawthorne added: "I do not know but I like her better for it; because she proved herself a woman after all, and fell as the weakest of her sisters might" (p. 318).
37. Miller, Perry, ed., *Margaret Fuller*, pp. 297, 299.
38. Ibid., p. 305.
39. Ibid., "I presume that": p. 304; "About him": p. 313.
40. Ibid., p. 313.
41. Fuller, *Woman in the Nineteenth Century*, in Wade, ed., *The Writings of Margaret Fuller*, p. 176.
42. Miller, ed., *Margaret Fuller*, "Ossoli sends his love": p. 312; "Ossoli has always": p. 313.
43. Ibid., "As was Eve": p. 298; "I do not know": pp. 307–8.
44. Fuller, *Woman in the Nineteenth Century*, in Wade, ed., op. cit., p. 213.
45. Miller., ed., *Margaret Fuller*, p. 314.
46. Douglas, Ann, op. cit., pp. 279–86.
47. Tocqueville, Alexis de, *Democracy in America*, ed. by J. P. Mayer, tr. by George Lawrence (Garden City, 1969), alliance: p. 298; "If the Americans": p. 298; "It may be that": p. 448; "a world apart": p. 448.
48. Ibid., p. 291.
49. Berg, Barbara, *The Remembered Gate: Origins of American Feminism* (New York, 1978), unity: p. 176; consciousness: p. 267.
50. Douglas, op. cit., ch. 3.
51. My remarks on Beecher draw on her *Treatise on Domestic Economy for the Use of Young Ladies at Home and at School* (Boston, 1841), where she affirms her Tocquevillian views. Sklar, Kathryn Kish, *Catherine Beecher: A Study in American Domesticity* (New Haven, 1973), the modern biography, discusses Beecher's adherence to Tocqueville on pp. 156–61.
52. Quoted in Melder, Keith, *Beginnings of Sisterhood: The American Woman's Rights Movement, 1800–1850* (New York, 1977), p. 80. On Grimke, see Lerner, Gerda, *The Grimke Sisters of South Carolina: Pioneers for Women's Rights and Abolition* (New York, 1967).
53. Thayer, James Bradley, *A Western Journey with Mr. Emerson* (Boston, 1884), pp. 39–40. Emerson went on: "But one would think that after this Father Abraham could go no further."

54. Kern, Louis J., *An Ordered Love* (Chapel Hill, 1981), "Mormons were obsessed": p. 148; monopoly of women: p. 152.

55. Ibid., pt. 4, offers a sophisticated discussion of sexuality and sex roles at Oneida.

56. Bushnell, Horace, *Life and Letters of Horace Bushnell*, ed. by Mary B. Chaney (New York, 1880), p. 73.

57. Ibid., p. 61.

58. Ibid., "His life": p. 53; "I saw at a glance": p. 33.

59. Cross, Barbara M., *Horace Bushnell: Minister to a Changing America* (New York, 1958), complements Munger, Theodore T., *Horace Bushnell, Preacher and Theologian* (Boston, 1899). On Bushnell's thought, see Smith, David L., *Symposium and Growth: The Religious Thought of Horace Bushnell*, (Chico, Calif., 1983).

60. Bushnell, Horace, *Views of Christian Nurture and of Subjects Adjacent Thereto* (Delmar, N.Y., 1975), p. 178.

61. Ibid., p. 185.

62. Bushnell, *Life and Letters*, "The surf roars": p. 86; wretched place: p. 112.

63. Ibid., "I have had": p. 111; wife's power: p. 429; "Though an invalid": pp. 497–98. For Bushnell's personal psychology, I am indebted to Hogeland, Ronald W., "Femininity and the Nineteenth Century Post-Puritan Mind," diss., UCLA, 1968, ch. 6, "Horace Bushnell and Feminine Providence."

64. Bushnell, Horace, *The Fathers of New England* (New York, 1850): "They are not": p. 11; "Here was, in fact": p. 27.

65. Ibid., "The very greatness": p. 7; "All kinds of progress": pp. 43–44.

66. Mead, Margaret, *And Keep Your Powder Dry* (New York, 1942), p. 148. For a contemporaneous British anthropologist's view that Americans were indeed mother-created, see Gorer, Geoffrey, *The American People: A Study in National Character* (New York, 1948), esp. ch. 2, "Mother-Land."

67. Erikson, Erik, "Reflections on the American Identity," in Erikson, Erik, *Childhood and Society* (New York, 1950), p. 292. On early and mid-nineteenth-century ideologies as to Mother, see, in addition to Kuhn and Wishy, n. 41, ch. 7, Ryan, Mary P., *The Empire of Mother: American Writing about Domesticity, 1830–1860* (New York, 1982). See also Smith, Page, *Daughters of the Promised Land: Women in American History* (Boston, 1970), ch. 14, "Home and Mother."

68. Bushnell, *Life and Letters*, p. 449. His words opening the autobiographical sketch he wrote in his old age, at once lamentation and exultation: "I have filled no place at all" (ibid., p. 2).

69. Brereton, Virginia L., and Klein, Christa R., "American Women in Ministry," in James, Janet, ed., *Women in American Religion* (Philadelphia, 1984), p. 177; Smith, Page, *Daughters*, ch. 13, "Raising Up the Heathen"; Hill, Patricia, *The World Their Household: The American Woman's Foreign Mission Movement and Culture Transformation, 1870–1920* (Ann Arbor, 1985).

70. Bennett, Katherine, and Hodge, Margaret, quoted in ibid., p. 182. Welter, Barbara, "Women's Missionary Careers," in ibid., p. 125.

71. Tocqueville, op. cit., p. 451.

72. Meyer, Donald B., *The Positive Thinkers* (New York, 1980), p. 47.

73. Ibid., p. 120.

74. Bordin, Ruth, *Woman and Temperance: The Quest for Power and Liberty,*

1873–1900 (Philadelphia, 1981), p. xvi; this is the finest recent work on both the organization and Willard. Willard's autobiography, *Glimpses of Fifty Years* (Boston, 1889), like any other autobiography, is to be read for its art of image-making as well as for information. Earhart, Mary, *Frances Willard: From Prayers to Politics* (Chicago, 1944), draws deeply on Willard's writing. Hill, Patricia, *The World Their Household*, p. 195, n. 1, citing various sources, argues that the largest women's organization was the women's foreign missionary movement, swelling to its numerical peak in the years 1910–15. But it is not at all clear that the WCTU of the late 1880s and early 1890s was not in fact the first true mass women's organization, no doubt later surpassed not only by mission groups but by the General Federation of Women's Clubs.

75. Bordin, op. cit., p. 46.
76. Ibid., p. 262.
77. See Paulson, Ross Evans, *Women's Suffrage and Prohibition: A Comparative Study of Equality and Social Control* (Glenview, Ill., 1973), for an approach arguing that temperance—and the suffrage movement— was essentially an exercise in social control. For a similar view, without the explicit linkages to women, see Gusfield, Joseph, *Symbolic Crusade* (Urbana, 1963).
78. Royce, Josiah, *California: From the Conquest in 1846 to the Second Vigilance Committee in San Francisco (1856); A Study of American Character* (Boston, 1886), p. viii.
79. Tocqueville, op. cit., pp. 495–96.
80. Royce, *California*, "Any chance number": p. 396; "Even in so early a book": p. 393; "Everybody used to gamble": pp. 394–95.
81. Clendenning, John, ed., *The Letters of Josiah Royce* (Chicago, 1970), pp. 11–14. See also, Clendenning. *The Life and Thought of Josiah Royce* (Madison, 1985), ch. 1.
82. Royce, *California*; "ought to be": p. viii; "whatever its faults": p. 394, n.1.
83. Leach, William, *True Love and Perfect Union: The Feminist Reform of Sex and Society* (New York, 1980), p. 324 and elsewhere.
84. Melder, Keith, *Beginnings of Sisterhood*, chs. 5–8. Kelley and Stone quoted in Friedman, Lawrence, *Gregarious Saints: Self and Community in American Abolitionism* (Cambridge, 1982), p. 137.
85. Friedman, Lawrence, *Gregarious Saints*, p. 159.
86. The literature on Gilman is vast. Degler, Carl, "Charlotte Perkins Gilman on the Theory and Practice of Feminism," *American Quarterly*, Spring 1956, for both date and insight, occupies pride of place as an analysis of Gilman's ideas. The fine modern biography is Hill, Mary A., *Charlotte Perkins Gilman: The Making of a Radical Feminist, 1860–1896* (Philadelphia, 1980), which despite its egregious adjective, is acute on its heroine's formative years. See also, Berkin, Carol Ruth, "Private Woman, Public Woman: The Contradictions of Charlotte Perkins Gilman," in Berkin, Carol Ruth, and Norton, Mary Beth, *Women of America: A History* (Boston, 1979).
87. Hill, op. cit., p. 45.
88. Gilman, C.P., *The Living of Charlotte Perkins Gilman* (New York, 1935), p. 71.
89. Hill, op. cit., p. 77.
90. Ibid., p. 185.
91. Gilman, op. cit., pp. 119, 121, 96.

92. Gilman, op. cit., p. 235.
93. Gilman, Charlotte Perkins, *Women and Economics* (New York, 1966), pp. 30, 31.
94. Ibid., pp. 43–44.
95. Ibid., p. 132.
96. Ibid., pp. 134, 316.
97. Gilman, *The Living of Charlotte Perkins Gilman*, pp. 341, 281.
98. Gilman, *Women and Economics*, pp. 341, 281.
99. Ibid., "The selection": p. 235; "Our general notion": p. 237; "The limitless personal taste": p. 249; "As cooking becomes": p. 251; "This is forever impossible": p. 141.
100. Ibid., pp. 298, 299, 300.
101. Ibid., pp. 139–40.
102. Gilman, C.P., *The Man-Made World, or, Our Androcentric Culture* (New York, 1971), pp. 115–16.
103. Ibid., pp. 120, 254, 135.
104. Gilman, Charlotte Perkins, *Herland* (New York, 1979), p. 128.
105. Ibid., no dirt: p. 19; everything beautiful: p. 19; no adventures: p. 49; Dutch kitchen: p. 53; roads like Europe: p. 18.
106. Erenberg, Lewis, *Steppin' Out* (Greenwich, Conn., 1981).
107. Gilman, *The Living of Charlotte Perkins Gilman*, pp. 318–19.
108. Milford, Nancy, *Zelda: A Biography* (New York, 1976), p. 176.
109. Rosenberg, Rosalind, *Beyond Separate Spheres: Intellectual Roots of Modern Feminism* (New Haven, 1982).
110. In Stanton, Elizabeth Cady, *Eighty Years and More: Reminiscences, 1815–1897* (New York, 1971), she tended to neglect her good fortune; she also forgot about the Woodhull imbroglio and a few other bad moments along the way.
111. Dubois, Ellen Carol, ed., *Elizabeth Cady Stanton, Susan B. Anthony: Correspondence, Writings, Speeches* (New York, 1981), "The solitude of self": p. 251.
112. Ibid., "Whatever the theories": p. 251; "An uneducated woman": p. 250; "To appreciate the importance": p. 248.
113. Ibid., p. 245.
114. Ibid., "Each soul": p. 251; "Seeing, then": p. 248.
115. Stanton, Elizabeth C., Anthony, Susan B., and Gage, Matilda J., *History of Woman Suffrage* (New York, 1881–1922), 6v., in addition to offering a wide range of fascinating basic material, in many ways set the course for "triumphalistic" scholarship thereafter, nicely criticized by Mary Beard (see Introduction above); the six volumes have been distilled in Buhle, Mari Jo, and Buhle, Paul, *A Concise History of Woman Suffrage: Selections from the Classic Work of Stanton, Anthony, Gage and Harper* (Urbana, 1978). Irwin, Inez, *Angels and Amazons* (Garden City, 1933) exemplified the heroic tradition in good popular form. The heroic tradition was continued by Flexner, Eleanor, *Century of Struggle: The Woman's Rights Movement in the United States* (Cambridge, 1959), though it is focused more on organizations than individuals. An exemplary exercise in demystification, Grimes, Alan P., *The Puritan Ethic and Women Suffrage* (New York, 1967), showed how suffrage could serve social control rather than women's liberation. The women who sit for a kind of group biography in Riegel, Robert E., *American Feminists* (Lawrence, 1963), were mostly suffragists. Arguing

that suffragists were but a minority among a much larger number of "social feminists" interested primarily in moral reform, O'Neill, William L., *Everyone Was Brave: The Rise and Fall of Feminism in America* (Chicago, 1969), nonetheless turned the heroic story upside down in inquiring why the postsuffrage era proved sterile. Dubois, Ellen, *Feminism and Suffrage: The Emergence of an Independent Women's Movement in America, 1848– 1869* (Ithaca, 1978), reprises the heroic view of the founders.

116. Degler, Carl, *At Odds: Women and the Family from the Revolution to the Present* (New York, 1980), pp. 249–50.

117. See Gusfield, Joseph, *Symbolic Crusade: Status Politics and the American Temperance Movement* (Urbana, 1963); Timberlake, James, *Prohibition and the Progressive Movement, 1900–1920* (Cambridge, Mass., 1963), for cultural and social perspectives on the prohibition movement.

118. See Dye, Nancy Schrom, *As Equals and As Sisters: Feminism, Unionism, and the Women's Trade Union League of New York* (Columbia, Mo., 1980).

119. Kraditor, Aileen, *Ideas of the Woman Suffrage Movement, 1890–1920* (New York, 1965).

120. Gordon, Linda, *Woman's Body, Woman's Right: A Social History of Birth Control in America* (New York, 1976). Gordon, who saw the period 1910– 1918 as the peak of potential for combining sexual and social revolution, criticizes the Socialist Party itself for its silence on birth control and its conventional views on women's sphere, thus revealing that her idea of socialism was that of some culture rather than of a politics, but why that culture was not more obviously "middle-class" than otherwise she failed to explain. Reed, James, *From Private Vice to Public Virtue: The Birth Control Movement and American Society Since 1830* (New York, 1978), treated the first eighty or so years of his story in perfunctory fashion, in favor of emphasis upon birth control "technology" since 1920, thus finessing rather than confronting Gordon's approach. The crucial role of doctors in delegitimizing abortions in the nineteenth century has been traced by Mohr, James C., *Abortion in America: The Origins and Evolution of a National Policy, 1800–1900* (New York, 1978). For a materialist review comparing Gordon (favorably) with Reed (unfavorably), see Fee, Elizabeth, and Wallace, Michael, *Feminist Studies*, Spring, 1979.

121. Ditzion, Sidney, *Marriage, Morals and Sex in America* (New York, 1953). Ditzion made clear that all the reformers victimized by the Comstock laws were typical "middle-class" utopians, far from socialists.

9. Wonderland as Old Faith and New Reality

1. On the new plenitude as mere "consumerism," that is, customers manipulated by advertising of "false" needs, see Ewen, Stuart, *Captains of Consciousness: Advertising and the Roots of the Consumer Culture* (New York, 1976). An earlier study, Potter, David, *People of Plenty* (Chicago, 1954), argued that advertising was the "institutional" expression of "plenty," that is, the prime force in American culture. See also Paxson, Fred L., "The Highway Movement, 1916–1935," *American Historical Review*, January 1946, pp. 236– 253.

2. Liebs, Chester H., *Main Street to Miracle Mile: American Roadside Architec-*

678   NOTES TO PAGES 357–368

ture (Boston, 1986), offers vivid entrée into the new world created by Americans in cars.

3. Meyer, Donald, *The Positive Thinkers: Religion as Pop Psychology from Mary Baker Eddy to Oral Roberts* (New York, 1980), pp. 277–80, on Barton.

4. The best study of college students in the Twenties is Fass, Paula, *The Damned and the Beautiful* (Oxford, 1977).

5. From a considerable literature, see Soule, George, *Prosperity Decade* (New York, 1962); Mills, Frederic C., *Economic Tendencies in the United States* (Washington, 1932).

6. O'Hara, John, *Appointment in Samarra* (New York, 1945), p. 244.

7. Callahan, John F., *The Illusions of a Nation: Myth and History in the Novels of F. Scott Fitzgerald* (Urbana, 1972); O'Hara, op. cit., p. 230.

8. Carter, Paul, *The Twenties in America* (New York, 1968), p. 21; Mowry, George, *The Twenties: Fords, Flappers, and Fanatics* (Englewood Cliffs, 1963), p. 1.

9. Allen, Frederick Lewis, *Only Yesterday* (New York, 1964), p. 1.

10. Gilman, Charlotte Perkins, *Herland* (New York, 1979), pp. 15, 26.

11. Steele, Valerie, *Fashion and Eroticism: Ideals of Feminine Beauty from the Victorian Era to the Jazz Age* (New York, 1985), ch. 5, "Victorian Sexuality."

12. Fass, *The Damned and the Beautiful*. chs. 6, 7.

13. Romasco, Albert, *The Poverty of Abundance: Hoover, the Nation, the Depression* (New York, 1965), is somewhat harsher on Hoover than I have been.

14. Cochran, Thomas C., *The Great Depression and World War II* (Glenview, Ill., 1968), remains a lucid survey. The best brief discussion of the New Deal remains Conkin, Paul, *The New Deal* (New York, 1967). Bernstein, Irving, *The New Deal Collective Bargaining Policy* (Berkeley, 1950), is acute. See also, Mitchell, Broadus, *Depression Decade* (New York, 1962); Shannon, David A., *The Great Depression* (Englewood Cliffs, 1969); Allen, Frederick Lewis, *Since Yesterday, 1929–39* (New York, 1940).

15. Black, John D., *Parity, Parity, Parity* (Cambridge, Mass., 1942), offers a unique perspective. Kirby, John B., *Black Americans in the Roosevelt Era: Liberals and Race* (Knoxville, 1980), is thorough.

16. Ware, Susan, *Beyond Suffrage* (Cambridge, Mass., 1982), traces these women.

17. Scharf, Lois, " 'The Forgotten Woman,' Working Women, the New Deal, and Women's Organizations," in Scharf, Lois, and Jensen, Joan, eds., *Decades of Discontent: The Women's Movement, 1920–1940* (Westport, Conn., 1983), pp. 243–60.

18. Wandersee, Winifred D., "The Economics of Middle-Income Family Life: Working Women during the Great Depression," in ibid., pp. 45–58.

19. Lynd, Robert, and Lynd, Helen Merrill, *Middletown in Transition*, (New York, 1937), pp. 178ff.

20. Mead, Margaret, *And Keep Your Powder Dry* (New York, 1942), p. 199.

21. Ibid., government for the people: p. 166; "She looks": pp. 148–49.

22. For some reason, women during the years 1930–40 have drawn less focused attention than women during the 1920s and World War II. Like Scharf and Jensen, op. cit., Chafe, William, *The American Woman* (New York, 1972), devotes Part I to 1920–40, presumably in the interests of his thesis that World War II "marked a turning point in the history of American women" (p. 195). One of the best studies from the time is Angell, Robert, *The Family Encounters the Depression* (New York, 1936). Scharf and Jensen, op. cit., pp. 299–304, offer a helpful list of readings.

23. Mead, op. cit., children, people of town, local brains: pp. 167–68.
24. Blum, John, *V Was for Victory* (New York, 1976), discusses the turn to the establishment.
25. See Chafe, op. cit., Part II, on women in wartime.
26. Hartman, Susan, *The Home Front and Beyond: American Women in the 1940s* (Boston, 1982), p. 164.
27. Mead, op. cit., p. 215.
28. Chafe, op. cit., p. 172, in British anthropologist Geoffrey Gorer's best-selling book of 1946, *The American People: A Study in National Character* (New York, 1946); see ch. 2, "Motherland."
29. See Blum, op. cit., ch. iv, on the rejection of planning and the anxiety over slump.
30. Gilbert, James, *Another Chance: Postwar America, 1945–1985* (Chicago, 1986), pp. 57–58.
31. Easterlin, Richard A., *The American Baby Boom in Historical Perspective* (New York, 1962), a popular study, full of interest. See also, Jones, Landon Y., *Great Expectations: America and the Baby Boom Generation* (New York, 1980); and Easterlin, Richard, *Birth and Fortune: The Impact of Numbers on Personal Welfare* (New York, 1980).
32. Vatter, Harold G., *The U.S Economy in the 1950's* (New York, 1963), is at once lucid and meticulous. Jackson, Kenneth T., *Crabgrass Frontier: The Suburbanization of the United States* (New York, 1986), offers a long view culminating in the climactic postwar suburbanizing. I believe Jackson has underestimated the degree to which suburbs fulfilled rather than frustrated cultural aspirations: Americans did not want to be apartment dwellers; Americans wanted houses of their own. See Gans, Herbert, *The Levittowners: Ways of Life and Politics in a New Suburban Community* (New York, 1967), for a sympathetic view. However slow the decade, it did not lack utopian projections: Burns, Arthur F., *Prosperity without Inflation* (New York, 1957); Chase, Stuart, *For This We Fought: Guidelines to America's Future as Reported to the 20th Century Fund* (New York, 1946); Jacoby, Neil, *Can Prosperity Be Sustained? Policies for Full Employment and Full Production without Price Inflation in a Free Economy* (New York, 1956); U.S. Chamber of Commerce, "The American Competitive Enterprise Economy," Washington, D.C., 1953: 17 pamphlets. For an interesting echo, see Richard Hofstadter's 1955 "Introduction" to his book of 1944, *Social Darwinism* (Philadelphia, 1964).
33. Vatter, op. cit., pp. 240–48, sketches the transformation of the unions into special-interest groups. Although written before the Great Depression, Perlman, Selig, *A Theory of the Labor Movement* (New York, 1928), remains an acute explanation for American labor's concentration on bread-and-butter issues—jobs—rather than politics. Aronowitz, Stanley, *Working Class Hero: A New Strategy for Labor* (New York, 1983), discusses the alienation between labor and left-wing intellectuals, not without hope that that alienation might yet be overcome.
34. For politics, I have followed the outlook offered by Lubell, Samuel, *The Future of American Politics* (New York, 1952), chs. 10–12, in which he discusses the Democratic New Deal coalition as the "sun" around which all politics will continue to circle until it finally disintegrates; I believe his thesis still holds in 1987.
35. Harris, Seymour, *The Economics of the Kennedy Years* (New York, 1964),

and Heller, Walter, *New Dimensions in Political Economy* (Cambridge, Mass., 1966), tell stories of insiders.

36. Discussions of the destabilization of the economy form a small library. Those that anticipated rather than simply glossed events may well prove of some enduring value: see Bazelon, David T., *The Paper Economy* (New York, 1965); Lekachman, Robert, *Inflation: The Permanent Problem of Boom and Bust* (New York, 1973); Rothschild, Emma, *Paradise Lost: The Decline of the Auto-Industrial Age* (New York, 1973).

37. Apart from the mystifications of supply-side economics, the following offers a broader basis for the economic optimism of the new administration: Kahn, Herman, *The Coming Boom* (New York, 1982). Piore, Michael J., and Sabel, Charles F., *The Second Industrial Divide: Possibilities for Prosperity* (New York, 1985), after declaring the epoch of mass-production industry at an end with the saturation of its markets, foretell an advance/return to decentralized, local, even domestic craft production based upon the new computer capacities, in effect, a revival of the workplace Henry Carey had praised. Though Piore and Sabel did not emphasize it, it was clear that such a new workplace would resemble what many of the new women workers were already experiencing.

38. On women in medicine: Morantz-Sanchez, Regina Markell, *Sympathy and Science: Women Physicians in American Medicine* (New York, 1985); in law: Abramson, Jill, and Franklin, Barbara, *Where They Are Now: The Story of the Women of Harvard Law 1974* (New York, 1985). See also, Klemesrud, Judy, "Women in the Law: Many Are Getting Out," *New York Times*, August 9, 1985. For the first time, women were entering engineering in growing numbers: 744 bachelor degrees in 1974 grew to 4,716 in 1979, to 10,761 in 1984; see Teltsch, Kathleen, "Today's Engineer Is Often a Woman," *New York Times*, September 19, 1985, a story based on data generated by the Engineering Manpower Commission. But the implications of this report were soon shaded by a congressional survey: "Panel Reports Sex Disparity in Engineering," ibid., December 26, 1985: "Not only are women who are scientists and engineers paid less and receive fewer promotions than their male counterparts, but they are also discouraged from taking such jobs in the first place." The same pattern could be found on a broader scale. Greer, William R., "In Professions Women Now the Majority," ibid., March 19, 1986, followed by Shapiro, Charlotte, and McCormick, Lillian, "Women in Professions: The Bad News," ibid., April 5, 1986, pointed out that women's professional preponderance still reflected heavy enrollment in the traditional "women's work" professions, still saw women's median weekly income as 39 percent less than men professionals, and found male administrators even in the traditional female professions; moreover, only 15 percent of all women workers were in the fifty professions. Even so, women had surpassed men in once male professions, as psychologists, statisticians, editors, and reporters. See also, McBroom, Patricia A., *The Third Sex: The New Professional Woman* (New York, 1986).

39. Women moved up a bit, from 32 percent to 36 percent of executives, managers, and administrators, but there were dark sides to the rosy shadings where the stakes were highest: Loden, Marilyn, "A Machismo That Drives Women Out," *New York Times*, February 9, 1986, discusses a "mass exodus" of "some of the best and brightest" women from the corporate world owing to the persistence of its "paramilitary" leadership style. Such women pre-

ferred to start businesses of their own; see Parrish, John B., "Why Many Women Opt to Go It Alone," ibid. See also Hennig, Margaret, and Jardim, Anne, *The Managerial Woman* (Garden City, 1977).

40. Studies of the low quality of new jobs were frequent: Serrin, William, "Growth in Jobs since '80 Is Sharp, but Pay and Quality Are Debated," *New York Times*, June 8, 1986, reporting a federal Bureau of Labor Statistics survey. Women took 84 percent of the 9,160,000 new jobs created since January 1980. A private economist estimated that one-third of all U.S. workers were "contingent" workers—part time, temporary, sub-contracted, self-employed; 80 percent of part-time work was in retail and services, and adult women made up 57 percent of part-time workers. "Some experts conclude that many of the jobs being created, particularly clerical jobs, are being deliberately aimed at suburban white women who will, in some employers' views, be malleable, not interested in unionization and not demanding about wages," ibid. Previously, Krebs, Juanita, *Sex in the Marketplace: American Women at Work* (Baltimore, 1971), had offered statistics by fields and projections for the future; Krebs, Juanita, ed., *Women and the American Economy: A Look to the 1980s* (Englewood Cliffs, 1976), offered essays by a variety of authorities, some illustrating the difficulty of relying on projections from the past to discern the future—or even comprehend the present; Foner, Philip S., *Women and the American Labor Movement: From World War I to the Present* (New York, 1980), is massive and attuned to feminist issues.

41. Congressional Budget Office, *Children in Poverty* (Washington, D.C., 1984), shows how the poorest U.S. families got poorer between 1968 and 1983 while the richest got richer. Sidel, Ruth, *Women and Children Last: The Plight of Poor Women in Affluent America* (New York, 1986), argues that the social-welfare policies installed in the 1960s have failed. See also, Moynihan, Daniel Patrick, *Family and Nation* (San Diego, 1986).

42. Oreskes, Michael, "Panel Sees Change in U.S. Family but Not in Jobs," *New York Times*, January 17, 1986, quotes a panel of labor, corporate, and academic leaders: "The majority of Americans are finding that their work and family lives increasingly come into conflict." Hewlett, Sylvia Ann, *A Lesser Life: The Myth of Women's Liberation in America* (New York, 1986), is addressed explicitly to the "conflict" between home and marketplace. See also, Weitzman, Lenore J., *The Divorce Revolution: The Unexpected Social and Economic Consequences for Women and Children in America* (New York, 1985).

43. Howard, Robert, *Brave New Workplace* (New York, 1986), after predicting the worst for the new computerized workplace, argues that organized labor could redeem it by taking over from management. As the ranks of organized labor steadily dwindled, such hopes were rendered empty.

44. See Zelman, Patricia G., *Women, Work and National Policy: The Kennedy-Johnson Years* (Ann Arbor, 1980), for a discussion of the politics of affirmative action.

45. See Morris, Charles R., *A Time of Passion: America 1960–1980* (New York, 1984), pp. 134–37 on the Democrats in 1972.

46. Among many discussions of women in politics: Abzug, Bella, with Melber, Kim, *Gender Gap: Bella Abzug's Guide to Political Power for American Women* (Boston, 1983); Smeal, Eleanor, *Why and How Women Will Elect the Next President* (New York, 1984). See also, Klein, Ethel, *Gender Politics* (Cam-

bridge, Mass., 1984). Baker, Paula, "The Domestication of Politics: Women and American Political Society, 1780–1986," *American Historical Review*, June 1984, pp. 620–47, makes the case for broadening the definition of "politics" to include many more women's public activities.

10. The Second Feminism

1. Freedman, Estelle B., "The New Woman: Changing Views of Women in the 1920s," in Jensen, Joan M., and Scharf, Lois, eds., *Decades of Discontent: The Women's Movement, 1920–1940* (Westport, Conn., 1983). Beard, Charles A., and Beard, Mary R., *The Rise of American Civilization* (New York, 1939), "Already potent": II, 754; freed from working: II, 752; lord of creation: II, 758.
2. Freedman, loc. cit., p. 27.
3. Ibid., pp. 30–31.
4. Sinclair, Andrew, *The Emancipation of the American Woman* (New York, 1965), "too much, too soon": p. 344; suburbs: p. 353; leisure, Victorianism, fear: pp. 364–67.
5. Ibid., magazines: p. 361; "Some wives": p. 367.
6. O'Neill, William L., *Everyone Was Brave: The Rise and Fall of Feminism in America* (Chicago, 1969), "the heart": p. 21; Gilman: p. 133; odds against: p. 137. The most elaborate exposition of the thesis that women's equality has been at odds with the family is Degler, Carl N., *At Odds: Women and the Family in America from the Revolution to the Present* (New York, 1980).
7. O'Neill, "For all their problems": p. 46; "What she could not": pp. 45–46.
8. Ibid., "Women are not": p. 144; "In retrospect": pp. 143–44; odds: pp. 137, 145.
9. Chafe, William H., *The American Woman: Her Changing Social, Economic, and Political Roles, 1920–1970,* (New York, 1972). In his introduction, "A Narrowing of Vision," devoted to the last years of the suffrage movement, Chafe accepted O'Neill's view that the battle was lost before 1920; ch. 10, "The Revival of Feminism," discusses where the new feminism was coming from.
10. Ryan, Mary P., *Womanhood in America from Colonial Times to the Present* (New York, 1975), p. 181.
11. Freedman, Estelle B., "Separatism as Strategy: Female Institution-Building and American Feminism, 1870–1930," *Feminist Studies*, V (1979), 512–29.
12. Beard, C.A. and M.R., op. cit., II, 752–53.
13. Discussions of the Depression era include Scharf, Lois, and Jensen, Joan, eds., *Decades of Discontent: The Women's Movement, 1920–1940*, and Milkman, Ruth, "Women's Work and the Economic Crisis: Some Lessons from the Great Depression," in Cott, Nancy F., and Bleck, Elizabeth, eds., *A Heritage of Her Own: Toward a New Social History of American Women* (New York 1979).
14. Hartmann, Susan M., *The Home Front and Beyond: American Women in the 1940s* (Boston, 1982), ch. 8, "Women in the Political Arena," notes the parties' actions.
15. Myrdal, Gunnar, *An American Dilemma* (New York, 1944), II, appendix 5, "A Parallel to the Negro Problem."

16. Gans, Herbert, *The Levittowners: Ways of Life and Politics in a New Suburban Community* (New York, 1967), criticizes the myth of 1950s conformity. See also, Donaldson, Scott, *The Suburban Myth* (New York, 1969), and Rapson, Richard L., ed. *Individualism and Conformity in the American Character* (Boston, 1967).

17. Robinson, Paul, *The Modernization of Sex* (New York, 1976), ch. 2, is a devastating discussion of Kinsey and his reports.

18. On Hefner and his magazine, see Miller, Russell, *Bunny: The Real Story of Playboy* (New York, 1985).

19. Zelman, Patricia G., *Women, Work, and National Policy: The Kennedy-Johnson Years* (Ann Arbor, 1980), traces the internal politics of affirmative action from Esther Peterson's first initiatives for a President's commission in 1960 to the organization of NOW in 1966.

20. Freeman, Jo, *The Politics of Women's Liberation* (New York, 1975), sets NOW at the center of discussion of women's liberation as a "social movement" aiming to affect "public policy."

21. Because based in part on interviews, notably with Atkinson, Firestone, and Friedan, as well as on "participant-observation" of the meetings, brochures, letters, and polemics of the time, a most interesting discussion of the ferment of 1968–71 is Ballorain, Rolande, *Le nouveau féminisme américain* (Paris, 1972); Friedan's comments: p. 80; Goodman: p. 81. See also, Atkinson, Ti-Grace, "Resignation from N.O.W.," in Atkinson, *Amazon Odyssey* (New York, 1974), pp. 9–11.

22. Atkinson. The "Equality Issue," *loc. cit.*, pp. 65–75.

23. Morgan, Robin, ed., *Sisterhood Is Powerful* (New York, 1970), pp. xvi–xvii. Perhaps the best personal testimony to disillusionment with New Left male chauvinism is Evans, Sara, *Personal Politics: The Roots of Women's Liberation in the Civil Rights Movement and the New Left* (New York, 1979). See also, Evans, Sara, "Tomorrow's Yesterday: Feminist Consciousness and the Future of Women," in Berkin, Carol Ruth, and Norton, Mary Beth, eds., *Women of America: A History* (Boston, 1979), pp. 389–414. Freeman, Jo, op. cit., pp. 57–62, discusses some of the alienating episodes at SNCC, SDS, and others. See also, Fritz, Leah, *Dreamers and Dealers* (Boston, 1979), ch. 5, "Feminism and the Left."

24. In addition to Freeman, op. cit., Hole, Judith, and Levine, Ellen, *Rebirth of Feminism* (New York, 1971), was a more or less instant history of the new movement. Numerous anthologies quickly appeared, eclectically venting voices across a variety of spectrums: Morgan, Robin, ed., *Sisterhood Is Powerful*, a vast collection confined to the "women's liberation" sectors; Thompson, Mary Lou, ed., *Voices of the New Feminism* (Boston, 1970), with fewer readings stretched over a wider span, from Friedan to Roxanne Dunbar; Gornick, Vivian, and Moran, Barbara K., *Women in Sexist Society: Studies in Power and Powerlessness* (New York, 1971), ranging widely with more academic studies. Problems in nomenclature arose immediately: e.g., Firestone, Shulamith, "On American Feminism," in Firestone, *The Dialectic of Sex: The Case for Feminist Revolution* (New York, 1970), p. 32, rejected the "Women's Liberation Movement" in favor of "Radical Feminism." On the other hand, Freeman, op. cit., p. 50, criticizing Hole and Levine, op. cit., as well as Lockwood, Maren Carden, *The New Feminist Movement* (New York, 1974), wrote: "It is a common mistake to try to place the various feminist organizations on the traditional left/right spectrum and concomitantly to

describe the two branches as 'women's rights' and 'women's liberation.' The terms 'reformist' and 'radical' . . . are convenient and fit into our preconceived notions . . . but they tell us little of relevance." My own view is that "women's liberation" serves well enough to distinguish all those distinct from the early NOW.

25. Dunbar, Roxanne, "Asexuality," untitled, undated pamphlet (v. 1 of *No More Fun and Games*, Cambridge, Mass., 1969), n.p.

26. Dunbar, Roxanne, "Female Liberation as the Basis for Social Revolution," in Thompson, Mary Lou, ed., *Voices of the New Feminism*, p. 56.

27. Beal, Frances M. "Double Jeopardy: To Be Black and Female," in *Liberation Now! Writings from the Women's Liberation Movement* (New York, 1971), p. 188.

28. Moraga, Cherrie, "Interviews: This Bridge Moves Feminists," *off our backs*, XII, no. 4, April 1982, both quotes, p. 4.

29. Smith, ibid.

30. Rich, Adrienne, *Of Woman Born: Motherhood as Experience and Institution* (New York, 1977), p. 259.

31. Ware, Celestine, *Women Power: The Movement for Women's Liberation* (New York, 1970), frontier: p. 8; "There had been": p. 9; "A generation": p. 12.

32. Firestone, Shulamith, *The Dialectic of Sex: The Case for Feminist Revolution*, women: p. 8; basic mother: p. 9; half the race: p. 205.

33. Ibid., "Now, in 1970": p. 180; childbearing: p. 238.

34. Harding, Sandra, *The Science Question in Feminism* (Ithaca, 1986).

35. Jaggar, Alison, *Feminist Politics and Human Nature* (Totowa, N.J., 1983), p. 93.

36. Quoted in Firestone, op. cit., p. 73.

37. Rich, op. cit., p. 21.

38. Daly, Mary, *Beyond God the Father* (Boston, 1973), p. 92.

39. Brownmiller, Susan, *Against Our Will: Men, Women and Rape*, (New York, 1975), p. 15.

40. Ibid., typical rapist: p. 174; typical perpetrator: p. 176; no getting around: p. 181; kick him: p. 404.

41. In Dworkin, Andrea, *Right Wing Women* (New York, 1983); Dworkin had commenced her assault on pornography in *Woman Hating* (New York, 1974), pt ii, "Pornography," and continued it in *Pornography: Men Possessing Women* (New York, 1981).

42. Brownmiller, Susan, *Femininity* (New York, 1984), my face: pp. 159–60; feminine insecurity: p. 159; inevitable: p. 160.

43. For the "National Association to Aid Fat Americans," see Manfred, Erica, "Is Thin Still In? Not at the Big Beautiful Woman Beauty Pageant," *Village Voice*, July 31, 1984. On the "deconstruction" of images of women's sexuality generally, without regard to weight, see Schjeldahl, Peter, "Introduction," *Cindy Sherman* (New York, 1984).

44. Rich, op. cit., "I know no woman": p. 290; "I have come to believe": p. 21; "Physical motherhood": pp. 290–91; "Some of the most": p. 291. See also, Belenky, Mary Field, Clinchy, Blythe McVicker, Goldberger, Nancy Rule, and Tarule, Jill Mattuck, *Women's Ways of Knowing: The Development of Self, Voice and Mind* (New York, 1986).

45. Stanton's suspicion of Christianity led her to blame it for deflecting women's sexuality. See Dubois, Ellen Carol, ed., *Elizabeth Cady Stanton, Susan B. Anthony: Correspondence, Writings, Speeches* (New York, 1981), p. 184.

46. Quoted in Hageman, Alice L., *Sexist Religion and Women in the Church: No More Silence!* (New York, 1974), p. 117.

47. Phipps, William E., *Influential Theologians on Woman* (Washington, D.C., 1980), p. 101.

48. *Woman and Roman Catholic: Is It Possible?* (North Easton, Mass., 1981), p. 107.

49. Greenberg, Blu, "Judaism and Feminism," in Koltun, Elizabeth, ed., *The Jewish Woman: New Perspectives* (New York, 1976), p. 190. See also, Plaskow, Judith, "The Jewish Feminist: Conflict in Identities," in ibid., pp. 3–10.

50. See Schlesinger, Benjamin, ed., *The Jewish Family: A Survey and Annotated Bibliography* (Toronto, 1971).

51. Daly, Mary, *The Church and the Second Sex* (New York, 1968), p. 31.

52. Maitland, Sara, *A Map of the New Country: Women and Christianity* (London, 1983), pp. 141–42.

53. Daly, Mary, *Beyond God the Father: Toward a Philosophy of Women's Liberation* (Boston, 1973), "web of inauthenticity": p. 75; on Mary: pp. 82ff.; on second coming: pp. 95ff.; Jesus feminist: pp. 73ff. In a paper delivered one year before the book, Daly used language still harsher: "Theology after the Demise of God the Father: a Call for the Castration of Sexist Religion," in Hageman, Alice, ed., op. cit.

54. Weidman, Judith L., ed., *Christian Feminism: Visions of a New Humanity* (San Francisco, 1984), pp. 2, 3.

55. Fiorenza, Elizabeth Schüssler, "Emerging Issues in Feminist Biblical Interpretation," in ibid., p. 46.

56. Way, Peggy Ann, "An Authority of Possibility for Women in the Church," in Bentley, Sarah, ed., *Women's Liberation and the Church* (New York, 1970), p. 82.

57. Brock, Rita Nakashima, "The Feminist Redemption of Christ," in Weidman, ed., op. cit., p. 69.

58. Russell, Letty M., *Human Liberation in a Feminist Perspective—a Theology* (Philadelphia, 1974), pp. 157–63.

59. Collins, Sheila D., *A Different Heaven and Earth: A Feminist Perspective on Religion* (Valley Forge, Penn., 1974), pp. 134, 115, 116, 53.

60. Ibid., p. 115. Her reference was to an "unpublished paper," "The Scope of Women's Liberation," delivered by Ruether on March 4, 1970, to a conference, "Manhood and Womanhood in the Church," at Yale.

61. Smith-Rosenberg, Carroll, *Disorderly Conduct: Visions of Gender in Victorian America* (New York, 1985), p. 256.

62. Smith-Rosenberg, Carroll, "The New Woman as Androgyne: Social Disorder and Gender Crisis, 1870–1936," in ibid.

63. Gordon, Linda, in Eisenstein, Zillah, ed., *Capitalist Patriarchy and the Case for a Socialist Feminism* (New York, 1979), p. 123.

64. Faderman, Lillian, *Surpassing the Love of Men: Romantic Friendship and Love Between Women from the Renaissance to the Present* (New York, 1981), is a broad survey. See also, Smith-Rosenberg, *Disorderly Conduct*.

65. Radicalesbians, "The Woman-Identified Woman," in *Writings from the Women's Liberation Movement: Liberation now!*, pp. 289, 290.

66. Abbott, Sidney, and Love, Barbara, "Is Women's Liberation a Lesbian Plot?" in Gornick, Vivian, and Moran, Barbara K., *Women in Sexist Society: Studies in Power and Powerlessness* (New York, 1971), p. 617.

67. Radicalesbians, "The Woman-Identified Woman," loc. cit., p. 287.

68. Abbott, Sidney, and Love, Barbara, loc. cit., p. 609.
69. Medvec, Emily, "Money, Fame and Power," *Quest: A Feminist Quarterly*, I, no. 2, pp. 3–4.
70. French, Marilyn, *The Woman's Room* (New York, 1977), "We hate": p. 586; "And I thought": p. 630; "I belong": p. 632.
71. Farrell, Warren, *The Liberated Man: Beyond Masculinity: Freeing Men and Their Relationships with Women* (New York, 1974), pp. 151–52.
72. For examples of the polarizing approach: Farrell, op. cit., pp. 16–17; Fasteau, Marc Feigen, *The Male Machine* (New York, 1974), pp. 212–13, drawing on Broverman, Inge, et al., "Sex-Role Stereotypes: A Current Appraisal," *Journal of Social Issues* (1972); David, Deborah S., and Brannon, Robert, eds., *The Forty-Nine Percent Majority: The Male Sex Role* (Reading, Mass., 1976), in the very chapter headings.
73. Clark, Don, "Homosexual Encounter in All-Male Groups," in Pleck, Joseph H., and Sawyer, Jack, eds., *Men and Masculinity* (Englewood Cliffs, 1974), p. 93.
74. Brenton, Myron, *The American Male* (New York, 1966), esp. ch. 5, "The Paradox of the Contemporary American Father"; Ruitenbeek, Hendrik M., *The Male Myth* (New York, 1967).
75. Mead, Margaret, *And Keep Your Powder Dry* (New York, 1942), chs. 8–10; Wylie, Philip, *Generation of Vipers* (New York, 1941), ch. 11; Strecker, Edward A., *Their Mothers' Sons* (New York, 1946).
76. Mailer, Norman, "The White Negro; Superficial Reflections on the Hipster," *Dissent*, Summer 1957, pp. 276–93.
77. Sexton, Patricia, *The Feminized Male: Classrooms, White Collars and the Decline of Manliness* (New York, 1970), p. 190.
78. Ehrenreich, Barbara, *The Hearts of Men* (Garden City, 1983), pp. 180ff.
79. Chafe, William, *Women and Equality: Changing Patterns in American Culture* (New York, 1977), underlying trends: p. 117; no longer irrelevant: p. 123.
80. Freeman, Jo, op. cit., pp. 238, 240.
81. Quoted in Ehrenreich, *Hearts of Men*, pp. 146ff.
82. For analyses of the defeat of ERA, see Katzenstein, Mary Fainsod, "Feminism and the Meaning of the Vote," *Signs*, Autumn 1984, pp. 4–26; Berry, Mary Frances, *Why ERA Failed: Politics, Women's Rights and the Amending Process of the Constitution* (Bloomington, 1986); Mansbridge, Jane J., *Why We Lost the ERA* (Chicago, 1986). All three authors—though in varying degree and ways—suggest that certain changes in political and rhetorical tactics might have yielded a happier result.
83. Kinder, Melvyn, and Cowan, Connell, *Smart Women/Foolish Choices* (New York, 1985); Norwood, Robin, *Women Who Love Too Much* (New York, 1985); Forward, Susan, *Men Who Hate Women and the Women Who Love Them* (New York, 1986); Russianoff, Penelope, *Why Do I Think I Am Nothing without a Man?* (New York, 1982).

11. Italy

1. Gramsci, Antonio, "Del carattere non popolare-nazionale della letteratura italiana," in Gramsci, *Letterature e vita nazionale* (Turin, 1975), p. 87.
2. Bortolotti, Franca Pieroni, "Introduzione," in Mozzoni, Anna Maria, *La*

liberazione della donna (Milan, 1975). Bortone, Sandro, "Prefazione," in Belgiojoso, Cristina di, *Il 1848 a Milano e a Venezia* (Milan, 1977), offers a brief sketch of her life, drawing from recent scholarship. See Albonetti, Pietro, ed., *Lettere d'amore a Andrea Costa, 1880–1909* (Milan, 1976), for Kulioscioff.

3. Croce, Benedetto, *Letterature della nuova Italia* (Bari, 1929–30) V, 79–86, on "Emma" and the "Marchesa Colombi"; II, 335–56, on Ada Negri; III, 119–38, on "Neera." See also Pacifici, Sergio, *The Modern Italian Novel from Capuana to Tozzi* (Carbondale, Ill., 1974), ch. 4, "Women Writers: Neera and Aleramo."

4. Croce, *Letteratura*, III, 122–23.

5. Ibid., pp. 121–22.

6. Ibid., III, 33–72; Cattaneo, Giulio, "Matilde Serao," in *Storia della letteratura italiana* (Milan, 1969), VIII, 372–86; Pacifici, loc. cit.

7. James, Henry, *Notes on Novelists, with Some Other Notes* (New York, 1914), p. 300 and passim.

8. Aleramo, Sibilla, *Una donna* (Milan, 1977), includes prefaces by Maria Antonietta Macciocchi and Emilio Cecchi. Contin, Bruna, "Introduzione," in Aleramo, Sibilla, *La donna, il femminismo* (Rome, 1978), a collection of Aleramo's journalism of 1897–1910, is a helpful biographical sketch; an Appendix reprints three Italian reviews of *Una donna*, 1906–7. Aleramo, Sibilla, *A Woman*, tr. by Rosalind Delmar (Berkeley and Los Angeles, 1980), has a helpful sketch by Richard Drake. The first translation into English was Mary Lansdale's in 1908. *Problemi del Socialismo*, Oct.–Dec. 1976, pp. 231–32, lists Italian writings on Aleramo. Strangely, not only did Croce snub Aleramo, but the editors of the great nine-volume *Storia della letteratura italiana* left her out, in one of the few obvious failures of modern Italian historical scholarship, in general a remarkably open and syncretic activity.

9. Aleramo, *Una donna*, pp. 41–42; I have used my own translations.

10. Ibid., p. 48.

11. Ibid., pp. 176–77 and 182.

12. Ibid., p. 114.

13. Ibid., "I was the oldest": pp. 19–20; "I was twelve": pp. 28–29.

14. Ibid., "A good mother": pp. 114–15; "how could she": p. 115.

15. Raimondo, Ezio, "Gabriele D'Annunzio," *Storia della letteratura italiana*, IX, 3–86: For the approach that does proceed from Verga through Pirandello and Svevo to Silone—and Pasolini!—(omitting D'Annunzio), see Pacifici, Sergio, ed., *From Verismo to Experimentalism: Essays on the Modern Italian Novel* (Bloomington, 1969). In addition to the study of D'Annunzio by Raimondo, loc. cit., I have found the biography by Jullian, Phillipe, *D'Annunzio*, tr. by Stephen Hardman (New York, 1973), stimulating. Although I do not find "nostalgia" suited to bring out D'Annunzio's significance, Drake, Richard, *Byzantium for Rome: The Politics of Nostalgia in Umbertian Italy, 1878–1900* (Chapel Hill, 1980), is interesting. James, Henry, op. cit., discusses D'Annunzio. Marinetti, Filippo, *Gabriele D'Annunzio in Time* (Milan, [ca. 1905]), is a brief celebration by a fellow artist.

16. Quoted in Jullian, op. cit., p. 38.

17. Croce, Benedetto, *A History of Italy, 1871–1915* (Oxford, 1929), "With him": p. 104; "uneasy state of mind": p. 240; "Even in . . . Italy": p. 240; "The aim of his art": p. 157.

18. Gatti, G., *Le donne nella vita e nell'arte di Gabriele d'Annunzio* (Modena, 1951), and Germain, A., *Vie amoureuse de d'Annunzio* (Paris, 1954), are examples of inquiry into D'Annunzio's interest in women.

19. Duncan, Isadora, *My Life* (New York, 1968), pp. 228–31.

20. Valera, Paolo, *Milano Sconosciuta* (Milan, 1976), p. 185. Ghidetti, Enrico, "Introduzione," provides a brief sketch of Valera and his book.

21. Ibid., "They work": p. 185; "The parents?": p. 186.

22. Ibid., pp. 201–2.

23. Gramsci, Antonio, "Scritti sul teatro," in *Marxismo e letteratura* (Rome, 1975), on Ibsen: p. 406; "The only form": p. 408.

24. Ibid., p. 409.

25. Gramsci, *Letterature e vita*, p. 477.

26. On Gramsci's own life, see Cambria, Adele, *Amore come rivoluzione* (Milan, n.d. [1976]), consisting of letters from Gramsci's wife and sisters-in-law, edited by Cambria, and Cambria's play based on the letters, *Nonostanta Gramsci*. Gramsci married the daughter of a Russian revolutionary, Appolo Schucht, a personal friend of Lenin.

27. *Marxismo e letteratura*, "In the beginning": p. 335; "The Borelli case": p. 337.

28. Ibid., pp. 416–17.

29. Gramsci, Antonio, "Il problema di Milano," *Scritti politici* (Rome, 1973), pp. 56–59.

30. Gramsci, Antonio, "Americanism and Fordism," in *Selections from the Prison Notebooks of Antonio Gramsci*, ed. and tr. by Quentin Hoare and G. N. Smith (New York, 1971), "The attempts made by Ford": p. 304; "Abuse": pp. 296–97, 304; "The truth": pp. 297, 304–5.

31. Ibid., p. 305.

32. Ibid., "It would be interesting": p. 305; "The male industrialist": p. 306.

33. Gramsci, Antonio, "Consulta araldica," in *Sotto la mole, 1916–1920* (Turin, 1975), p. 431.

34. Gramsci, "Americanism and Fordism," loc. cit., "What is today": p. 317; "But it is not": p. 317.

35. Ibid., p. 304.

36. Ibid., p. 296. "Until women": p. 296.

37. Ibid.

38. Maraini, Dacia, *Donna in guerra* (Turin, 1975), may be the exception proving the rule.

39. Paris, Robert, "Il cinema," in *Storia d'Italia*, IV, pt. 1, pp. 792–806, discusses Rossellini as well as Fellini and Antonioni, among others, though for rather different purposes than mine.

40. Betti, Liliana, *Fellini*, tr. by Joachim Neugroschel (Boston, 1979), and Fellini, Federico, *Fellini on Fellini*, tr. by Isabel Quigley (New York, 1967), are among a host of writings on Fellini. Kauffmann, Stanley, "Fellini's 8½," *Horizon*, Spring, 1976, pp. 4–46, is stimulating.

41. Cameron, Ian, and Wood, Robin, *Antonioni* (New York, 1971), offers guidance.

42. Stack, Oswald, *Pasolini on Pasolini: Interviews with Oswald Stack* (Bloomington, 1970), "While the peasant": p. 21; "In the immediate": p. 19.

43. Ibid., p. 23.

44. Ibid., "Objectively": p. 25; "My hatred": p. 26.

45. Ibid., "Gradually": p. 29; "The avant-garde": p. 148; "I had instinctively": p. 29; "At first": p. 29.

46. Ibid., p. 49.
47. Ibid., p. 67.
48. Grazzini, Giovani, *Gli anni settanto in cento film* (Bari, 1976), pp. 307–12, discusses *Salo*.
49. See ibid., pp. 244–46, on *Il portiere di notte*.
50. Ravera, Lidia, and Lombardo-Radice, Marco, *Porci con le ali: Diario sessuo-politico di due adolescenti* (Rome, 1976), p. 13. A translation, *Pigs Have Wings*, tr. by Jane Sebastian (New York, 1977), makes the serious mistake of trans-lating the opening dirty words into a silly limerick: "A prick, a proc, a cock/ Coming in bravely to dock,/So the little new whore/Gets laid on the floor/ and now fucks the jocks round the clock," presumably on the pretext that the heroine then says that once she could "come" by just thinking of a limerick. Happily, while off to a wrong start, the translation does not portend general bowdlerization, so that the "pornographic" dimension of the orig-inal is saved: Ascoli, Giuletta, "Scritto da maschi," *Noi Donne*, Sept. 12, 1976, pp. 44–45, dismisses the book as nothing but (male) pornography: I have used my own translations.
51. *Porci con le ali*, "I felt like a dog": pp. 61–62; "Listen": p. 67; "No": p. 67.
52. Ibid., "Dear Rocco": pp. 181–82; "Dear Antonia": pp. 183–85.
53. Ibid., p. 40.
54. Ibid., Marcello shifted: p. 40; "Come in": p. 45; "Now, you": p. 46.

12. Sweden

1. The lack of access to Bellman through scholarship in English was remedied by Austin, Paul Britten, *The Life and Songs of Carl Michael Bellman, Genius of the Swedish Rococo* (Malmö, 1967), a brilliant piece of cultural history. Van Loon, Hendrik Willem, *The Last of the Troubadours* (New York, 1939), offers not only many Bellman songs translated into English but also the music.
2. Austin, *Bellman*, p. 74.
3. Almqvist, Carl J.L., *Sara Videbeck* (New York, 1972), pp. 107–8.
4. Ibid., pp. 116–17.
5. Ibid., p. 21.
6. Ibid., pp. 29–30.
7. Bremer, Fredrika, *The Neighbors: A Story of Every-Day Life* (New York, 1943), p. 9.
8. In an earlier novel Bremer had, however, postulated a general cooling effect exerted upon passion by Sweden: "In the south . . . passion . . . speedily . . . burst out into a flame . . . snapped asunder all bonds . . . surmounted all impediments . . . kindled the marriage-torch or the funeral pyre. In the quiet, serious north . . . it took, however, another shape"; Bremer, Frederika, *The President's Daughters, Part II—Nina* (New York, 1843), p. 87.
9. Bremer, Fredrika, *Hertha* (Three Sisters) (New York, 1856), pp. 210, 227, 237.
10. Ibid., p. 292.
11. Ibid., p. 311.
12. Ibid., pp. 328, 366.
13. Ibid., p. 389.
14. Among all those responding to the temptation to psychoanalyze Strindberg, no doubt the most eminent was Jaspers, Karl, *Strindberg und van Gogh*

(Bremen, 1929). Less inspired but more orthodox is Uppvall, Alex Johan, *August Strindberg: A Psychoanalytic Study with Special Reference to the Oedipus Complex* (Boston, 1920). Sprigge, Elizabeth, *The Strange Life of August Strindberg* (London, 1940), remains one of the best of all the "strange life" studies written in English. Brandell, Gunnar, *Strindbergs Infernokris* (Stockholm, 1950), most successfully analyzes Strindberg psychologically through his works while avoiding psychological reductionism. Certain friends and acquaintances sought to provide keys to their hero: Lind-af-Hagaby, L., *August Strindberg: The Spirit of Revolt* (New York, 1913); Uddgren, Gustav, *Strindberg the Man* (Boston, 1920).

15. Strindberg, August, *The Confessions of a Fool*, tr. by Elie Schleussner (London, 1912), was replaced by Strindberg, August, *A Madman's Defense*, tr. by Evert Sprinchorn (New York, 1967), a more accurate and complete translation.

16. While all biographies necessarily dwell upon the marriage, Norman, David, *Strindbergs skilsmässa fron Siri von Essen* (Strindberg's Divorce from Siri von Essen) (Stockholm, 1953) is devoted to that topic alone, as is a Danish study, Jacobsen, Harry, *Strindberg og hans förste hustru* (Copenhagen, 1946), which I have not been able to use.

17. Strindberg, *A Madman's Defense*, "The girlish appearance": p. 35; "Can't we drive away": p. 39; "The instinct of worship": p. 42.

18. Ibid., p. 195.

19. Smirnoff, Karin, *Strindbergs förste hustru* (Stockholm, 1925). When Normann, op. cit., published his study of 1953, Fru Smirnoff protested his views: Smirnoff, Karin, *So vär det i verkligheten* (The Way It Really Was) (Stockholm, 1956).

20. In an excellent study of Strindberg's novels, Johannesson, Eric O., *The Novels of August Strindberg* (Berkeley, 1958), follows Jacobson, op. cit., in classifying *A Madman's Defense* as a work of fiction. Nothing forbids us to guess that Siri Strindberg understood this, too.

21. Uddgren, op. cit., p. 28; Lind-af-Hagaby, op. cit., pp. 22–23; Sprigge, op. cit., p. 219.

22. The passage was partially suppressed in the first English translation by Schleussner, op. cit., p. 144, but restored by Sprinchorn, op. cit., p. 156.

23. Quoted in Lamm, Martin, *August Stringberg*, tr. by Harry Carlson (New York, 1971), p. 6. The magisterial Swedish biography, Lamm's is organized almost wholly by the works.

24. Strindberg, August, *The Son of a Servant*, tr. by Claud Field (New York, 1913), p. 253.

25. Ibid., "A man": p. 253; "All acted parts": p. 260; "The first": p. 261.

26. Lamm, op. cit., pp. 76ff.

27. Lagercrantz, Olof, *August Strindberg* (New York, 1984), p. 178; the most psychological of Strindberg's biographers, Lagercrantz offered a devastating corrective to standard views: "There is ample material proving that Strindberg was insane, at least when . . . compared to the 'ordinary' person. But his works suffer from incurable health."

28. Strindberg, August, *Getting Married*, tr. by Mary Sandbach (New York, 1972), p. 38.

29. Strindberg, Frida Uhl, *Marriage with Genius* (London, 1940), offers its author's special perspective.

30. See Paulson, Arvid, *Letters of Strindberg to Harriet Bosse* (New York, 1959), for light on what in some ways was Strindberg's most revealing marriage.
31. Brandell, op. cit., p. 284, n. 28 and p. 67.
32. Johannessen, op. cit., ch. 10, on *At the Edge of the Sea.*
33. Brandell, op. cit., p. 158.
34. Lamm, op. cit., p. 383.
35. Johnson, Walter, *August Strindberg* (Boston, 1976), is a compact study successfully dividing Strindberg's work into its diverse modes and phases.
36. Strindberg, August, "Preface to Miss Julie," in Strindberg, August, *Eight Famous Plays,* tr. by Edwin Björkman and N. Erichsen (London, 1949), pp. 105–6.
37. Johnsson, Melker, *En ottilatist: Gustaf af Geierstam 1858–1890* (Göteborg, 1934), stops before reaching the Geierstam of interest here. A brief discussion in English, Gustafson, Alrik, *A History of Swedish Literature* (Minneapolis, 1961), observes on p. 609: "Swedish critics look upon Geierstam's later novels as sentimental."
38. Geierstam, Gustav, *Woman Power* (New York, 1927), p. 170.
39. Lindwall, Bo, *Le Grand Livre de Carl Larsson* (Paris, 1982), sketches in Larsson's career and comments on Strindberg's attacks.
40. *Gustafson,* op. cit., pp. 284–87, discusses Benedictsson and, on p. 610, the considerable scholarship on her. No major study is available in English. Maury, Lucien, *L'Amour et la mort d'Ernest Ahlgren* (Paris, 1945) is valuable (Ernest Ahlgren was Benedictsson's pseudonym).
41. Forsström, Axel, *On Ellen Key* (Malmö, 1949), p. 76. Forsström devotes most of his attention to Key's theretofore unknown relationship with Urban von Feilitzen.
42. Ibid., another's tears: p. 97; Wägner: p. 109; weak/strong women: pp. 108–9, 109.
43. Key, Ellen, *Rahel Varnhagen: A Portrait* (New York, 1913), "He was the first": p. 92; "no human being": p. 98.
44. Ibid., "that love": p. 109; dangerous age: p. 108; neglect: p. 120; "Rahel was one": pp. 120–21.
45. Ibid., pp. 57–58.
46. Ibid., p. 136.
47. Ibid., Jean Paul: p. 121; "Rahel": pp. 172–73.
48. Arendt, Hannah, *Rahel Varnhagen: The Story of a Jewess* (London, 1957), pp. 219, 5, and passim.
49. Ibid., "I should": p. 213; "No native dignity": p. 150.
50. Key, *Rahel Varnhagen,* p. 83.
51. Ibid., richer life: p. 138; Eliot: p. 85. "Love affairs": p. 138.
52. Ibid., p. 130.
53. See Connery, Sean, *The Scandinavians* (New York, 1966), for an interesting discussion of Iceland.
54. Huntford, Roland, *The New Totalitarians* (New York, 1972), pp. 334–37.
55. Tomassen, Richard R., "A Millennium of Sexual Permissiveness in the North," *American Scandinavian Review* (1974), pp. 370–78.
56. Hendin, Herbert, *Suicide and Scandinavia* (New York, 1964), p. 43; Connery, op. cit.; Austin, Paul Britten, *On Being Swedish* (Coral Gables, 1968), p. 146; Tomassen, Richard F., *Sweden: Prototype of Modern Society* (New York, 1970), p. 173. For one suggestion of a deep historical root of the "peculiar tension,"

see Moberg, Vilhelm, *A History of the Swedish People from Renaissance to Revolution*, tr. by Paul Britten Austin (New York, 1973), p. 210: "[The] women of the people, the soldiers' wives who stayed at home on the smallholding after their men had been conscripted for the wars . . . are to be counted in their hundreds upon hundreds of thousands, a nameless mass, a vast unknown segment of the Swedish nation"; another form of separation in old Sweden was the *fäbod*, young women spending the summer apart in the mountains tending the cows: Brorson, Kerstin, *Sing the Cows Home: The remarkable Herdswomen of Sweden* (Seattle, 1985).

57. Hendin, loc. cit.; Tomassen, *Prototype*, loc. cit.

58. Colton, Robert, *Rambles in Sweden and Gotland* (London, 1847), pp. 277–79. The girls of Stockholm would have been "the very nicest creatures in the universe, if well treated, and allowed 'fair play,' " but this "they are not." "The males . . . were the most brusque, yet solemn specimens of revellers it was ever my misfortune to behold. . . . There are no impromptu or unguarded likes or dislikes in Scandinavian dovetailing, nothing like spontaneous combustion or involuntary mistakes . . . the many tidy 'flickas' . . . are singing "Oh dear, what can the matter be?" See also pp. 319–22.

59. Austin, *On Being Swedish*, loc. cit.

60. Uppvall, op. cit., p. 82.

61. Huntford, loc. cit. Huntford explicitly compared Swedish with Soviet policies of state surveillance and supervision. Connery, op. cit., noted the low birthrate Sweden shared with East European countries, but attributed it not to oppressive state supervision but to the "peculiar tension" between the sexes.

62. Sjöman, Vilgot, *I Am Curious (Yellow)*, tr. by Martin Minor and Jenny Bohman (New York, 1968), p. 112.

63. Ullerstam, Lars, *A Sexual Bill of Rights for the Erotic Minorities* (New York, 1966).

64. Sjöman, op. cit, p. 143.

65. Eder, Richard, " 'I Am Curious' Star Recalls Struggle," *New York Times*, Dec. 26, 1974.

66. Mosey, Chris, "Sex Isn't All It Should Be," *Sweden Now* (1981), n. 2, pp. 28–29.

67. Fredrikson, Marianne, *Evas Bok* (Stockholm, 1981).

13. Soviet Russia

1. Hingley, Ronald, *Nightingale Fever* (New York, 1981), is not only a remarkable study of the poets Anna Akhmatova, Marina Tsvetyeva, Osip Mandelstam, and Boris Pasternak, but of the supremely stressful conditions under which they wrote. See also Poggioli, Renato, *The Poets of Russia, 1890–1930* (Cambridge, 1960), on Akhmatova, Tsvetyeva, and others.

2. Pilnyak, Boris, *The Naked Year* (New York, 1928), "these days": p. 158; each touch: p. 160; "Yes, very well": p. 172; "Moonlight": pp. 267–70.

3. Gladkov, Fyodor, *Cement* (Moscow, 1981), "Gleb" and "How can you": pp. 56–57; "she laughed": p. 195; "she was silent: p. 196; "she's got something": p. 283; "she could not accept": p. 380; "I love": p. 112; "Your Nurk's": p. 72; "Gleb was panting": p. 390; "There was": pp. 284–85; "Dasha gave":

p., 317; "She's neglecting": p. 89; "I'm not going": p. 281; "I have to leave": p. 401.

4. Clements, Barbara, *Bolshevik Feminist: The Life of Aleksandra Kollontai* (Bloomington, 1979), pp. 228–32, discusses the six stories; she agrees they were badly written.

5. Kollontai, Alexandra, "Make Way for Winged Eros," in Holt, Alix, ed., *Selected Writings of Alexandra Kollontai* (Westport, 1978).

6. Luke, Louise, "Marxian Woman: Soviet Variants," in Simmons, Ernest J., ed., *Through the Glass of Soviet Literature: Views of Russian Society* (New York, 1933), Olesha: pp. 41–42; Semyenov: pp. 42–45.

7. Ibid., p. 88, for both quotes.

8. Mandelstam, quoted by Hingley, op. cit., p. 171.

9. Zoshchenko, Mikhail, *Before Sunrise* (Ann Arbor, 1974), pp. 49–50, v.

10. Panova, Vera, *The Train*, in Panova, *Selected Works* (Moscow, 1976).

11. Akhmatova, quoted by Hingley, op. cit., pp. 238–39.

12. Dudintsev, Vladimir, *Not by Bread Alone* (New York, 1957), "herd": p. 83; "monster": p. 173; "We Soviet people": p. 9. Author and novel are discussed at length in Gibian, George, *Interval of Freedom: Soviet Literature during the Thaw, 1954–1957* (Minneapolis, 1960).

13. Hingley, op. cit., preaching: p. 242; authorities: ibid.

14. Brown, Deming, *Soviet Russian Literature since Stalin* (Cambridge, 1978), p. 291.

15. Dunham, Vera S., "The Strong-Woman Motif in Russian Literature," in Black, Cyril E., ed., *The Transformation of Russian Society: Aspects of Social Change since 1861* (Cambridge, 1960).

16. Trifonov, Yuri, "The Exchange," in Trifonov, *The Long Goodbye* (New York, 1978), Tanya: pp. 49–50; mother: p. 58; wife: p. 79.

17. Dovlatov, Sergei, *The Compromise* (New York, 1983), p. 123.

18. Trifonov, Juri, *The Old Man* (New York, 1980), p. 52.

19. Rasputin, Valentin, *Live and Remember* (New York, 1978), p. 78.

20. Brown, op. cit., p. 116.

21. Grekova, I., "Ladies Hairdresser," in Grekova, *Russian Women: Two Stories* (San Diego, 1983), youth evening: p. 41; girls: p. 39; progress: p. 51; something missing: pp. 60–61.

22. Grekova, I., "The Hotel Manager," ibid., luxury item: p. 81; hotel manager: p. 193; "hotel well they managed," pp. 144–45; fat: p. 225; Talva: p. 238.

23. Ibid., greatest joy: p. 252; sharing: p. 253.

24. Ibid., tenth-graders: pp. 279, 277; "looove": p. 264.

25. Madison, Bernice, "Social Service for Women: Problems and Priorities," in Atkinson, Dorothy, Dallin, Alexander, and Lapidus, Gail W., eds., *Women in Russia* (Stanford, 1977), p. 309.

26. Shulman, Colette, "The Individual and the Collective," in ibid., pp. 383, 379.

27. Shlapentokh, Vladimir, *Love, Marriage and Friendship in the Soviet Union: Ideals and Practices* (New York, 1984), Kon: p. 49; "drift to domesticity": p. 69; "fields of battle": p. 202.

28. Ibid., ch. 9 on the dating services.

29. Dallin, Alexander, "Conclusions," in Atkinson, Dallin, Lapidus, eds., op. cit., p. 396; Burns, John F., "Demurely the Russians Launch Sex Education," *New York Times*, Aug. 17, 1982. See Stern, Mikhail, *Sex in the Soviet Union* (New York, 1980), for an extended review of Soviet sex mores and ideologies.

694   NOTES TO PAGES 554–562

30. Pollack, Jack Harrison, "Russian Readers Line Up for a Partial Dose of Bland Medicine," *Wall Street Journal*, March 15, 1984. Issues of health elided of course into issues of sex appeal: "The Russian word for thin, *khudaya*, is a derivative of the superlative of the word 'bad,' and it can have negative connotations when applied to women. Many husbands are still frowned upon if their wives are not *polniye*, or 'full.' The men are sometimes thought to be bad providers in such cases. This is quite liberating for Soviet women, who feel free to go to the beach in scanty bikinis (or just underwear) even at 250 pounds. Nobody even stares. The slimness of liberated women in the West is increasingly accepted as a standard for young women in the Soviet Union, however, and diminutive variations of the word *khudaya*, such as *khudinkaya*, are taking on positive overtones. It can be expected that once they are thoroughly 'liberated' by Western values, the fat women will be ashamed to appear on the beach." Shipler, David K., "In Soviet, Too, Quest for Beauty Leads to the Plastic Surgeon," *New York Times*, Jan. 8, 1979.

31. Mikhalkov quoted in Schmemann, Serge, "Ordinary Life Stars in Soviet Films," *New York Times*, Aug. 14, 1983.

14. The United States

1. For Berryman's poem I have used Berryman, John, *Homage to Mistress Bradstreet and Other Poems* (New York, 1970); I forgo specific page or stanza references. For a "memoir" on Berryman by his first wife, from whom he was separated in 1953 and whom he divorced in 1956, see Simpson, Eileen, *Poets in Their Youth: A Memoir* (New York, 1982).

2. Berryman, John, " 'Song of Myself': Intention and Substance," in Berryman, *The Freedom of the Poet* (New York, 1976).

3. Tocqueville, Alexis de, *Democracy in America*, ed. by J. P. Mayer, tr. by George Lawrence (Garden City, 1969), democratic literature: p. 475; the drama: pp. 489–90; themselves: p. 484.

4. Rourke, Constance, *American Humor* (Garden City, 1953), legitimate theater: p. 101; Bergson: p. .22.

5. Ibid., p. 118.

6. Whitman, Walt, *Leaves of Grass and Democratic Vistas* (New York, 1912), "I Sing the Body Electric," pp. 41, 86–87, 87, 83. Allen, Gay Wilson, *Walt Whitman as Man, Poet, Legend* (Carbondale, 1961), discusses the sexually various Whitmans in critical literature. In Martin, Robert K., *The Homosexual Tradition in American Poetry* (Austin, 1979), ch. 1 is devoted to Whitman. Lawrence, D.H., *Studies in Classic American Literature* (New York, 1951), p. xii.

7. Whitman, *Leaves of Grass and Democratic Vistas*, fashionable life: p. 310; riches: p. 321; "pervading flippancy": p. 310; lady: p. 325; stormy life: p. 325; entire redemption: p. 311.

8. On Melville in general and *Pierre* in particular, I have benefited from Mumford, Lewis, *Herman Melville: A Study of His Life and Vision* (New York, 1956), and Berthoff, Werner, *The Example of Melville* (New York, 1962), as well as Howard, Leon, *Herman Melville* (Berkeley and Los Angeles, 1951).

9. Douglas, Ann, *The Feminization of American Culture* (New York, 1977), p. 309 and ch. 9 generally.

10. On Brown, I have profited from Friedman, Lawrence J., *Inventors of the Promised Land* (New York, 1975), ch. 23.
11. Hawthorne, Nathaniel, *The Scarlet Letter* (New York, n.d.) (The Modern Library), "This long connection: p. 10; "My children": p. 11.
12. Ibid., p. 189, ch. 13.
13. Tocqueville, op. cit., p. 594.
14. Both the popular biography of Wilson, Forrest, *Crusader in Crinoline: The Life of Harriet Beecher Stowe* (Philadelphia, 1941), and the analytic one of Foster, Charles, *The Rungless Ladder: Harriet Beecher Stowe and New England Puritanism* (Durham, 1954), emphasize the death of a son as a kind of trigger for *The Minister's Wooing* (as indeed for *Uncle Tom's Cabin* also). Obviously, I believe the trigger released issues long prepared in her mind.
15. Stowe, Harriet Beecher, *The Minister's Wooing* (Ridgewood, N.J., 1868), the Doctor: p. 122; despite all you say: p. 151.
16. Ibid., "despite all you say": p. 151; "Mary my Dear": p. 402.
17. Evans, Augusta J., *St. Elmo* (New York, 1921), p. 140. Evans has been discussed in all the many treatments of popular nineteenth-century fiction. Baym, Nina, *Woman's Fiction: A Guide to Novels by and about Women in America, 1820–1870* (Ithaca, 1978), ch. 10, "Augusta Evans and the Waning of Women's Fiction," is interesting. Baym's approach extends that of Papashvily, Helen, *All the Happy Endings* (New York, 1956), a popular literary history arguing that the sentimental novels often concealed protest. Kelley, Mary, *Private Woman, Public Stage: Literary Domesticity in 19th Century America* (New York, 1984), on the other hand, stresses the service of her twelve writers—including Stowe but not Evans—to the Cult of True Womanhood.
18. Stowe, *Minister's Wooing*, pp. 156, 168.
19. Ibid., p. 416.
20. Ibid., p. 346.
21. Ibid., p. 95.
22. Ibid., "I have been thinking": p. 98' "Mary rose": p. 377.
23. Not that Stowe herself followed any simple path; returning to the Old New England villages for what some regard as her best writing—*Oldtown Folks, Poganuc People*—she simply forgot about new-model maidens in favor of tangy old maids. Yet she also tried to carry her concern for modern marriage into a more modern setting, New York City, in *My Wife and I* and *Pink and White Tyranny*. Plunging into psychological depths in her attack on Byron—*Lady Byron Vindicated*—she also sublimated all modern dilemmas in *Agnes of Sorrento*, ending up, not unlike Bushnell and Henry Adams, a devotee of Mary Eternal. While no doubt the most interesting recent discussion of Stowe, Douglas, Ann, *The Feminization of American Culture*, pp. 244–56, imposes rather than demonstrates her conclusion: "Stowe's late novels hint painfully at the tragic dead end of Victorian American culture." Rather, the evidence of Stowe's immense productivity would seem to suggest that Stowe could not fulfill all the potentials brewing in that perhaps underestimated, overly maligned culture.
24. Twain, Mark, *The Adventures of Huckleberry Finn* (New York, 1912), pp. 161–63 (ch. 19).
25. Sokoloff, Alice Hunt, *Hadley, the First Mrs. Hemingway* (New York, 1973), specifically notes Hemingway's attitude toward women: "He was always very touched and reacted tenderly if sombody loved him whether he himself

was in love or not," p. 90. See also, Kert, Bernice, *The Hemingway Women: Those Who Loved Him—the Wives and Others* (New York, 1983).

26. Adams, Henry, *The Education of Henry Adams* (Boston, 1961), "As he grew older": p. 442; "God might be": p. 289.

27. Adams, Henry, *Tahiti* (New York, 1947). Samuels, Ernest, *Henry Adams: The Mature Years* (New York, 1964), discusses the South Seas trip.

28. Adams, *Education*, "The hunt," wooing, Lafarge: pp. 470–71.

29. Adams, Henry, *Mont.-Saint-Michel and Chartres* (Garden City, 1959), in no community: pp. 286–87, 308; "Mary concentrated": p. 307; "The instinct": pp. 289–90.

30. Adams, *Education*, p. 8.

31. Ibid., p. 85.

32. Ibid., p. 447.

33. Adams, *Chartres*, "Why did the gentle": p. 289; "The Puritan reformers": p. 308; "The Mother alone": p. 290; "The Father seldom": p. 109.

34. Adams, *Education*, typical man: p. 445; "When closely watched": p. 445; "volatilized": p. 444.

35. Ibid., p. 441.

36. Ibid., "All these new women": p. 445; "She sees before her": p. 446; "No honest historian": p. 447.

37. Adams, *Chartres*, pp. xv–xvi.

38. Rourke, op. cit., pp. 194–201.

39. James, Henry, *The American* (New York, 1907).

40. Rourke, op. cit., p. 201.

41. James, Henry, *The Portrait of a Lady* (London, 1960), p. 55.

42. Ibid., "To his mind": p. 172; "It was part of the influence": pp. 121–22.

43. Ibid, "She was not praying": p. 175; "He glared": p. 644.

44. James, Henry, *The Golden Bowl*, (New York, 1909), II, 5; Porte, Joel, *The Romance in America: Studies in Cooper, Poe, Hawthorne, Melville and James* (Middletown, Conn., 1969), pp. 215–17.

45. James, *The Golden Bowl*, lips: I, 312; halter, II, 287; great little man: II. 274.

46. I have benefited from Callahan, John F., *The Illusions of a Nation: Myth and History in the Novels of F. Scott Fitzgerald* (Urbana, 1972).

47. Beer, Thomas, *Stephen Crane: A Study in American Literature* (New York, 1924), p. 117.

48. Stallman, Lawrence, *Stephen Crane: A Biography* (New York, 1967), is the most thorough biography; Berryman, John, *Stephen Crane* (New York, 1950), is the most inspired.

49. Quoted in Berryman, op. cit., p. 138.

50. See Cunliffe, Marcus, "Stephen Crane and the American Background of Maggie," *American Quarterly*, Spring 1955, pp. 31–45, for "slum exposé" writings.

51. Crane, *Maggie, A Girl of the Streets*, in Crane, *Stories and Tales*, ed. by Stallman, Robert (New York, 1955): "Here was the ideal man": p. 57; "Maggie was pale": p. 80.

52. Ibid., "Her black dress": p. 86; "Maggie was dazed": p. 88; pocket: p. 102.

53. Linson, Corwin, *My Stephen Crane* (Syracuse, 1958), p. 37.

54. Berryman, op. cit., p. 139.

55. Cady, Edwin H., and Wells, Lester G., *Stephen Crane's Love Letters to Nellie Crouse* (Syracuse, 1954).

56. Gilkes, Lillian, *Cora Crane* (Bloomington, 1960), a remarkable book, devotes its first twenty-eight pages to Cora Crane's life before she met Stephen Crane. Berryman, op. cit., pp. 298ff., using Freud, analyzes Crane's attraction to Cora as a "damaged" woman.

57. Crane, Stephen, "The Blue Hotel," in Stallman, R.W., ed., *Stephen Crane: Stories and Tales* (New York, 1955), p. 297.

58. Stallman, op cit., p.; 291. Berryman on the other hand—op. cit., p. 229— sees Coleman as Crane's "coarsening" of himself; aware that Crane threw away the first ending of the book, Berryman speculates: "Did Coleman first succumb to Nora Black, and did Crane rewrite away from autobiography?" (p. 230).

59. Ibid., "Coleman and the dragoman": p. 128; "He knew it was": p. 131; "It occurred to him": p. 135; "It did penetrate his mind": p. 144.

60. Ibid., p. 72.

61. Crane, Stephen, *Active Service* (New York, 1899), pp. 42, 43.

62. Brown, E.K., *Willa Cather* (New York, 1953), p. 154. A recent biography is Robinson, Phyllis C., *Willa: The Life of Willa Cather* (New York, 1983).

63. Cather, Willa, *The Song of the Lark* (Cambridge, Mass., 1937), p. vii.

64. Seyerstad, Per E., *Kate Chopin: A Critical Biography* (Baton Rouge, 1969), superseded Rankin, Daniel S., *Kate Chopin and Her Creole Stories* (Philadelphia, 1932), as the most useful biographical study.

65. Chopin, Kate, "A No-Account Creole," in Chopin, *The Storm and Other Stories: With The Awakening* (Old Westbury, N.Y., 1974), p. 66; "Athenaise," in *ibid.*, don't hate: p. 203; her whole being; p. 223.

66. Whether *The Awakening* can be appropriated to "feminist literature" and Chopin be seen as a "feminist writer" has engaged the attention of numerous critics of the 1970s. On the whole, book and and author have withstood efforts at capture; critics variously describe the work as "irony," "tragedy," and ambiguity." For a convenient bibliography of some thirty-odd critical discussions, see Chopin, Kate, *The Awakening and Selected Short Stories* (New York, 1981).

67. Chopin, Kate, *The Awakening* (New York, 1972), p. 190.

68. Ibid., pp. 32–33.

69. Ibid., pp. 79, 80.

70. Ibid., pp. 27, 62, 63, 116, 141.

71. Ibid., "When she came back": p. 177; "I am no longer": p. 178.

72. Chopin, Kate, "The Storm," in Chopin, *The Storm and Other Stories* (Old Westbury, Conn., 1974), pp. 251, 252.

73. Chopin, *The Awakening:* "I love you": p. 179; "Why? Because" p. 135; first kiss, p. 139; "Despondency": pp. 188–89.

74. Clarens, Carlos, *Crime Movies: An Illustrated History* (New York, 1980), ch. 5, "The Nights of Chicago."

75. Quoted in Clarens, op. cit., p. 65.

76. Millett, Kate, *Sexual Politics* (New York, 1970), p. 14.

77. Miller, Henry, *Tropic of Cancer* (New York, 1961), p. 5.

78. Ibid., p. xxix.

79. Miller, Henry, *Tropic of Capricorn* (New York, 1961), pp. 41, 42.

80. Millett, op. cit., "the disgust" and women: p. 295; adolescence, men's house: p. 303; orgies: p. 305.

81. Miller, *Tropic of Cancer*, p. 160.

82. Miller, *Tropic of Capricorn*, p. 335.

83. Millett, op. cit., Genet alone: p. 356; "When a biological male": p. 343; "Lucy is free": p. 71.

84. Heilbrun, Caroline, *Toward a Recognition of Androgyny* (New York, 1973); Ehrenreich, Barbara, *The Hearts of Men* (Garden City, 1983).

85. Oates, Joyce Carol, *New York Times Book Review,* April 15, 1973.

86. Bellow, Saul, *The Adventures of Augie March* (New York, 1953).

87. Morrison, Toni, *Tar Baby* (New York, 1981), "If ever there was": p. 222; Caliban, p. 166; "Mama-spoiled black man": p. 269.

88. See Waller, G.F., *Dreaming America: Obsession and Transcendence in the Fiction of Joyce Carol Oates* (Baton Rouge, 1979), ch. 4.

89. Johnson, Diane, *Lying Low* (New York, 1978), "Theo thought": p. 160; "Men like": p. 201; "Don't you find": p. 229; "*She* could not": p. 229; "All that trying": p. 229.

90. Ibid., "His hands": p. 205; "It is working": p. 221.

INDEX

About the Author

Donald Meyer's interest in women's history began thirty years ago in his classes at UCLA, where he educated himself as well as his students. He taught at UCLA from 1955 to 1967. He is now professor of history and American studies and Walter Crowell Professor of the Social Sciences at Wesleyan University. Meyer attended Deep Springs College, received his B.A. from the University of Chicago in 1947, and his Ph.D. from Harvard University in 1953. He is the author also of *The Protestant Search for Political Realism* and *The Positive Thinkers*. His home is in East Haddam, Connecticut.

About the Book

Sex and Power was typeset in Aster by Monotype Composition Company of Baltimore; it was printed on 60-pound Miami Book paper and bound by Arcata Graphics/Kingsport of Kingsport, Tennessee. The design is by Joyce Kachergis Book Design and Production, Bynum, North Carolina.

Wesleyan University Press, 1987